STRINDBERG

To Graham Greene
for forty years of friendship

CONTENTS

LIST OF ILLUSTRATIONS

PREFACE

The principal source for any life of Strindberg must, or should, be the monumental edition of his letters edited by the late Torsten Eklund, fifteen volumes of which appeared between 1948 and 1976. These cover Strindberg's life up to April, 1907. His unpublished letters from that date until his death in 1912 number some three thousand; photo-copies of these have been assembled at Kungliga Biblioteket in Stockholm. I am grateful to Albert Bonniers Förlag AB for allowing me to quote from the published letters, and to Redaktionskommittén för Strindbergs *Samlade Verk* for permission to quote from those not yet published.

From 1896 to 1908, Strindberg kept a diary, which he called his "Occult Diary" because he started it mainly to record what he regarded as occult, or supernatural, experiences. In the event it contained a good deal else, including intimate details of his third marriage to Harriet Bosse. To date, the complete version of this diary has appeared only in a limited facsimile edition, though extracts from it, together with some of the letters exchanged between Strindberg and Harriet, were published under the title *Ur ockulta dagboken* (*From the Occult Diary*) in 1963, after Harriet's death. I am again grateful to Messrs. Bonnier for allowing me to quote from both these books.

Strindberg also, as is well known, wrote a series of "autobiographical" volumes under the overall title of *The Son of a Servant* (which was also the title of the first volume). Some of these, such as *Time of Ferment*, about his years at Uppsala University and his first steps in the theatre, seem, as far as can be ascertained, to be close to the facts; others, notably the scurrilous account of his first marriage, *A Madman's Defence*, are largely fictionalised. Even the famous *Inferno*, which purports to be a straight account of the time in Paris in the 1890s when he came very close to madness, is shown by comparison with his diary for the period to be part fact, part fiction. This is not because Strindberg was a compulsive liar, though he has often been called one; it is simply that, in his latter years especially, he did not distinguish between what most people call reality, and fantasy. He was also notoriously inaccurate and slipshod regarding facts and dates, even to the extent of misremembering when he had written his plays. He did not like to read through what he had written, believing that criticism was a kind of blasphemy against the act of creation, and he wrote very fast, tossing each page on the floor as he finished it. Nor, normally, did he bother to read proofs. One result is that his plays contain inconsistencies, not least between the cast list as written by Strindberg and the characters who actually appear in the play.

Strindberg's punctuation presents a problem. In his plays, diary and letters especially, he uses exclamation marks the way other writers use full stops. These, nowadays, give an impossibly melodramatic effect, as well as making things very difficult for actors, and, as in my translations of the plays, I have felt free to end most of his sentences with full stops. Swedish spelling was officially changed at the beginning of this century; Gustaf became Gustav, Carl became Karl, and so forth. This creates a problem concerning the Christian names of those active before that time. I have followed the convention whereby the old spelling is kept except in the case of monarchs; thus, Gustaf Fröding remains Gustaf, but all kings of that name are spelled Gustav.

Strindberg made enemies all his life, and some reminiscences of him were written with the same hatred and malice of which he himself was so often guilty. To name only three, Stanislaw Przybyszewski, Adolf Paul and Ola Hansson were all at one time very close to Strindberg but had become hostile to him by the time they wrote about him. Yet the evidence of enemies is as important to a biography as that of friends. Love can distort the truth as much as hostility.

The literature about Strindberg is immense, and my bibliography lists only those works which I have found useful, though this is not to disparage some of the rest. When quoting from Strindberg's own writings, other than his letters and diary, I have used what has hitherto been accepted as the standard edition of his works, the fifty-five volumes of

Samlade skrifter, edited by John Landquist and published between 1912 and 1919. A new edition, which it is estimated will run to seventy-five volumes, including his correspondence and diary, is currently in preparation, but to date only a few volumes have appeared.

All translations used in this book are my own except where otherwise specified. In addition to the debts already expressed, I am grateful to the following for permission to use copyright material: Mrs. Mary Sandbach and Hutchinson & Co., Ltd., for her translation of *Inferno*; Mrs. Sandbach, Victor Gollancz, Ltd., and Viking Penguin Inc., for her translation of *Getting Married*; Jonathan Cape, Ltd., for Frida Strindberg's *Marriage with Genius*; Albert Bonniers Förlag AB, for Karin Smirnoff's *Strindbergs första hustru* and *Så var det i verkligheten,* and for Harriet Bosse's commentary on Strindberg's letters to her in *Strindbergs brev till Harriet Bosse*; Wahlström & Widstrand for *Ögonvittnen,* edited by Stellan Ahlström; Rabén and Sjögren for Stella Falkner-Söderberg's *Fanny Falkner och August Strindberg*; and Mr. John Mortimer for his essay, "The New Drama ?" published in the *Spectator* on 3 January 1976.

I owe a particular debt to Docent Gunnar Ollén for reading my typescript, guiding my research, correcting my errors and generously placing his wide knowledge of Strindberg at my disposal. His admirable *Strindbergs dramatik* is the source of most of my factual details concerning both the writing and the stage history of Strindberg's sixty plays. I am also much indebted to Dr. Stellan Ahlström's *Ögonvittnen,* a two-volume collection of reminiscences about Strindberg by those who knew him, and to Professor Gunnar Brandell's four-volume selection of contemporary press comments, *Strindberg i offentligheten.* My debt to the late Docent Torsten Eklund for his edition of Strindberg's letters and commentary on them has already been expressed. Other works that I have found especially valuable have been Professor Brandell's *Strindbergs Infernokris* and the late Professor Martin Lamm's *August Strindberg*; when quoting from these, I have used the excellent translations by Barry Jacobs and Harry G. Carlson, respectively. Dr. Stellan Ahlström's *Strindbergs erövring av Paris* is an invaluable guide to Strindberg's Paris years, as are Dr. Allan Hagsten's *Den unge Strindberg* to his youth and Docent Ulf Boethius's *Strindberg och kvinnofrågan* to the development of his attitude towards women. Karin Smirnoff's *Strindbergs första hustru* and *Så var det i verkligheten* present a balanced picture of the relationship of her parents, Strindberg and Siri von Essen, as do Stella Falkner-Söderberg of another relationship in *Fanny Falkner och August Strindberg,* and Harriet Bosse of Strindberg's marriage to her in her commentary to *Strindbergs brev till Harriet Bosse*. Frida Strindberg's *Marriage with Genius* gives a vivid if selective impression of Strindberg's second marriage. Other debts are acknowledged in my bibliography and notes.

Finally, I must thank Mr. and Mrs. Jan Molander, Mrs. Mary Sandbach, Mr. Gordon Hølmebakk, Mr. Casper Wrede, Mr. Edwin Mullins, Dr. Michael Yudkin, Mr. Peter Meyer, my editors Mrs. Anne Freedgood and Ms. Barbara Willson in New York and Mr. Tom Rosenthal in London, Fru Anita Persson and Fru Gunilla Norming of Strindbergssällskapet, Stockholm, the staff of Kungliga biblioteket, Stockholm, especially Docent Lars Dahlbäck and Fru Margareta Brundin, and the staffs of Örebro stadsbibliotek, the British Library, the Library of University College, London, and the London Library. For the illustrations, I am indebted to Kungliga biblioteket, Strindbergsmuséet, Nordiska muséet, Stockholms stadsmuseum, Drottningholms teatermuseum, Stockholms nationalmuseum, Albert Bonniers Förlag AB, Sveriges Radio AB, Harvard University Theatre Collection, Munchmuséet, Oslo, Örebro stadsbibliotek and Universitetsbiblioteket, Göteborg.

Michael Meyer
London, 1984

Part One

THE EARLY YEARS
(1849–1883)

Chapter One

~~~~~~

ANCESTRY AND CHILDHOOD

Johan August Strindberg was born on 22 January 1849 at Riddarholms-hamnen 14, on the tiny islet of Riddarholmen in the centre of Stockholm. It lies just north of the mediaeval old town, separated from it by only a few yards of water. Carl Oscar Strindberg, the dramatist's father, was a shipping agent, and his son, his third surviving child but the first since his belated marriage, entered the world in an already crowded family apartment above the office, overlooking the frozen harbour.

Strindberg's ancestors came from Ångermanland province in northern Sweden. The earliest to adopt the surname was August's great-grandfather Henrik, a farmer's son from Strinne, born in 1708; previously, each child had simply had "*son*" or "*dotter*" added to his or her father's Christian name, as is still done in Iceland. Henrik took his new surname from his birthplace, spelling it Strinnberg. He became a clergyman and married Maria Elisabeth, daughter of Zacharias Åkerfelt, a soldier who had fought under Charles XII and risen to the rank of major. They had eight children, the second of whom, born in 1758, they christened Zacharias.

This Zacharias, the dramatist's grandfather, left home young and made the long journey south to Stockholm, where he became a successful spice-merchant. He also wrote plays and poems, which gained him

membership of a short-lived but respected literary society called the
Aurora Order. In 1793 he married Anna Johanna Neijber, the daughter
of German immigrants. They had three children, Johan Ludvig (1794),
Elisabet (1797) and, fourteen years later in 1811, Carl Oscar.[1]

In 1837, at the age of twenty-six, Carl Oscar Strindberg reluctantly took
over his father's spice business; in old age, his daughters remembered, he
would recall with distaste "the dreadful stickiness of syrup on my
fingers."[2] He spent nine miserable years there until a family connection
offered him the chance of a more congenial job.

In 1822 his sister Elisabet had become the third wife of an English
industrialist and inventor, Samuel Owen, twenty-three years her senior.
This remarkable man, the uncle of the dramatist, was in the grand
tradition of Victorian industrialists. Humbly born at Northon in Shrop-
shire in 1774, he had no formal education, was a farmer's boy, drove canal
horses, and at eighteen became a carpenter's apprentice. He worked in
factories in Birmingham and Leeds, but his real career began at the age of
thirty when he visited Stockholm to install steam engines. Two years
later, in 1806, he settled permanently in Sweden, which thanks to him
became the first country in Europe after Britain to have its own steamship
industry. In 1817–18 he built his first paddle-steamer, which made a
sensational trip up Lake Mälaren to Uppsala and Västerås. A keen
temperance advocate, he did much to introduce Methodist evangelism
into Sweden. Sadly, his business acumen did not match his inventive
genius; he went bankrupt and ended his career as a factory foreman, dying
in Stockholm in 1854 at the age of eighty.

Because of the family connection, Samuel Owen's shipping operations
became combined with the Strindberg spice business. In 1846 the
shipping company moved to Riddarholmen; Carl Oscar was put in charge
and moved in to live above the office. By this time, though not yet
married, he was the father of a son.

The mother of this child, and in due course of the dramatist, was
Eleonora Ulrika Norling, born in Södertälje, just south of Stockholm, on
18 January 1823. Her father, Johan Olof Norling, had been an unsuccessful tailor who later became a manservant and an office caretaker. He
died in 1834, the year of a cholera outbreak, when Nora, as Carl Oscar
was to call her, was eleven. Her mother remarried, and her stepfather sent
her out early to fend for herself. By the age of fourteen she was a
nursemaid; then, briefly, she became servant to a prison officer at
Långholmen gaol in Stockholm; and from 1838 she was a serving-maid at
the Liljeholmen Inn in south Stockholm, where Carl Oscar met her. We
do not know the exact date or circumstances of this, but on 7 October

1842 they became betrothed, though it was to be nearly five years before they married.[3]

In September 1843 Nora moved in to live with Carl Oscar, who had just taken a new apartment at Klara Västra Kyrkogata 15, near where Stockholm Central Station now stands. On 28 February 1844 their first child was born, but he died on 4 July. (Nora was to have eleven pregnancies, and four of these children were to die in infancy, three of them before August was born.) The following month their home was sold at auction, and they ceased living together. Carl Oscar arranged for Nora to live with a Fru Frödelius on the island of Lidingö, just outside Stockholm; according to his diary, he visited her two or three times that winter, but never alone. Was he perhaps easing himself out of the relationship? If so, he had a change of heart, for eight months later, on 1 April 1845, he set her up in a flat by herself with two servants in Ladugårdslandet, now the fashionable suburb of Östermalm, but then a semi-rustic area just inside the city boundaries. There, on 17 June 1845, their first surviving child, Carl Axel, was born.

To occupy herself and help their finances, Nora made candles; and in the autumn of 1846 Carl Oscar moved to Bryggargränden 7 and took her with him. On 9 June 1847 another son, named Oscar after the then king, was born, and on 24 September they married. On 1 October they moved back to their former apartment at Klara Västra Kyrkogata, but they stayed there only six months and then, in April 1848, moved yet again, to Carl Oscar's old flat above the shipping office at Riddarholmen where, nine months later, a third son, the subject of this biography, was born.

Stockholm at that time was a small city of about 90,000 inhabitants, roughly the size and population of modern Cambridge. Although new stone and brick buildings were beginning to rise, it was still essentially a rustic town, more so than most European capitals. Even in the heart of the city unpaved country lanes were common; until 1855, two pillories still stood at Roslagstorg, on the present site of Birger Jarlsgatan. More attractively, there were large houses with orchards, and as late as 1870 twenty-four windmills; standing on high ground, they formed a characteristic feature of the city skyline. In Ladugårdslandet, hundreds of cows grazed on the meagre and trampled grass. Tobacco patches abounded. Until the late 1840s, the city boasted no pavements at all, and even then they were slow to spread. Such roads as were paved were usually surfaced with cobblestones, hard on the feet and ruinous to shoes, a fact frequently commented on by foreign visitors. A water system was not started until 1858; until then, everyone had to go to public pumps. There was only one bathhouse for the entire city, and that contained but twelve baths. Open sewers full of nightsoil ran down the sides and sometimes the centre of the streets, and were cleansed only by rain; things became especially unpleasant when spring unfroze the three-month detritus of winter. Gas lamps were not seen until 1853, nearly forty years after they had reached London.[4]

The first twenty years of Strindberg's life were a period of great economic and industrial growth for Stockholm. Sweden had been a poor and backward country, half a century behind its time; now it began to enter the modern world. Cafés, hotels and museums sprang up; a contemporary of Strindberg recalled that in his youth the city contained eighty-five restaurants and over five hundred pubs. In 1860 it acquired its first daily morning paper, *Dagens Nyheter*, and its first railway connection, to Södertälje; other lines followed, to Gothenburg in 1862, Malmö in 1864, Uppsala in 1866. That same year a Great Exhibition of Industry and Art was held; and in 1880 came the first telephones. Nevertheless, writes a Swedish historian, "even as late as the 1870s Stockholm was still one of the most squalid capitals in Europe . . . a town of dreadfully overcrowded, cold and damp wooden hovels in narrow, dirty streets which were often nothing but muddy country lanes . . . for most western Europeans an exotic and primitive place almost Siberian in character, a byword for poverty, epidemics and underdevelopment."[5]

The Strindberg shipping company owned ten small paddle-steamers, which carried passengers and freight along Lake Mälaren to the neighbouring towns of Uppsala, Nyköping and Örebro. In the absence of rail connections, this was the quickest and most convenient method of travel. Stage coaches existed but, since they also delivered mail, they took eight to twelve hours to cover the forty miles between Stockholm and Uppsala. By 1854 Carl Oscar's fleet had doubled and was serving ports as far distant as Gothenburg and Malmö; a third of the steamships plying from Stockholm sailed under the Strindberg flag (and Stockholm was reckoned at this time to have more steamships than any other city in the world).[6] A contemporary photograph shows them and their rivals crowded in the harbour at Riddarholmen—long, low ships, with a mast and a high funnel and a flat sailcloth roof stretched over the deck to protect passengers from the sun and rain. In a story entitled "Short Cuts," which he wrote in 1887, August Strindberg recalled the scene of a summer morning:

> Steam whistles shrieked, cables clanked, captains roared, ships' bells clanged . . . There was a suffocating stench of tallow, machine-oil, coal-smoke, sweat, and an intoxicating odour of lilac over the swirling mass

of people as they streamed from their dark factories, damp shops, smoky kitchens and fusty nurseries to breathe the sea air, and thronged aboard the flag-decked, green-dressed ships. Finest of all is the great *Aurora*, painted blue with red waterline and flagged rope-ladders and standard at the mast, and its after-deck transformed into an arbour by great birch-boughs . . . As the gang-plank is drawn up, the band starts up on the bridge; the steamer moves out with ten others, and each set of musicians strives to drown its rivals.

But this apparently prosperous façade concealed financial uncertainty. The company had been in grave trouble even before Carl Oscar's marriage. In 1843 when Samuel Owen went bankrupt, Carl Oscar lost almost everything (this no doubt was why he had had to sell his house and send Nora to live on Lidingö). His brother Ludvig helped him out, and at first it seemed he would survive this crisis. But in 1851 Ludvig went bankrupt too. Carl Oscar's debts to him, amounting to 24,500 riksdaler, * were included in Ludvig's assets, with the result that on 24 January 1853, two days after August's fourth birthday, Carl Oscar suffered the same fate as his brother. August Strindberg was not, as he sometimes declared, born into the house of a bankrupt, but he had early memories of the bailiffs removing the furniture. (Even in that, he exaggerated. He wrote that they were left with only "beds, tables and a few chairs," whereas in fact Carl Oscar was permitted to keep a good deal of his furniture, including a piano; and barely a year after his bankruptcy, on Samuel Owen's death, he was able to lend Owen's widow several hundred riksdaler.)[7]

Strindberg once observed that "the wanderlust lay in our blood." He himself was to be an Ishmael, not merely as the son of a handmaid but also as a restless wanderer, and his father, though not an international vagabond as his son was to be, was forever moving home. Between 1848 and 1869, according to a list in his own hand,[8] he lived in ten different dwellings in or around Stockholm. In the following ten years, he moved five more times. With the four homes he had between his betrothal to Nora and August's birth, this makes a total of nineteen homes in twenty-seven years.

Nora Strindberg bore her husband five more children in the nine years following August's birth: Olle (1853), Anna (1855), Elisabeth (1857), Nora (1858), and a fifth which did not survive. August recalled his crowded childhood home:

*The Swedish riksdaler was worth 12 to the pound in 1850. In 1873 the unit of currency was changed and the riksdaler became the crown. From then until Strindberg's death the crown hovered around 18 to the pound, or 4 to the dollar.

In three rooms lived Father with his wife, seven children and two
servants. The furniture consisted mainly of cradles and beds. Children lay
on the ironing boards and chairs . . . Another room was occupied by an
uncle and a cousin . . . And in the nursery there was Eleonora's [his
mother's] mother, a sharp old woman who patched trousers and shirts, read
us the alphabet, rocked us and pulled our hair. She was religious and turned
up at eight each morning after first having attended matins. In winter she
carried a lantern, since there were no gas lamps in the streets . . . Father had
no room of his own, but he was always at home [in the evenings]. He never
accepted an invitation from his many business friends because he could not
invite them back. He never went to a restaurant or a theatre. His pride and
joy was a piano. A niece came in every second evening and they would play
Haydn's symphonies together (never anything else, though later they
progressed to Mozart).[9]

Carl Oscar loved flowers, too, and grew them in his windows, but only
pelargoniums.

Why pelargoniums? When Johan [i.e., August] was older and his mother
dead, he always seemed to see his mother beside a pelargonium. His mother
was pale, she had undergone twelve [sic] pregnancies and become con-
sumptive. Her face resembled the pelargonium's transparent white leaf shot
with blood . . . Father was seen only at mealtimes. Sad, tired, strict, grave,
but not hard . . . Mother had a nervous temperament. Flared up, but soon
became calm . . . She drank coffee in bed in the mornings; she had nurses,
two servants and her mother to help her. She probably didn't overstrain
herself . . . She could be unjust, violent, punish us unfairly on the casual
accusation of a servant, but it was she who fed and consoled us, and so we
loved her, while Father always remained a stranger.[10]

Considering how badly he and Carl Oscar got on in later years,
Strindberg's portrait of his father in *The Son of a Servant* is surprisingly
sympathetic:*

Father was a reserved man . . . an aristocrat by birth and upbringing . . .
clean-shaven, delicate-complexioned . . . always dressed elegantly and

---

*As Torsten Eklund has observed, when Strindberg wrote *The Son of a Servant* in 1886
he was bitterly antagonistic towards the women's liberation movement and, viewing
himself as a wronged husband and father, and as a man approaching middle age who felt
threatened by the young, painted his father much more sympathetically and his mother
much less so than he might otherwise have done. He identified himself with the role of
breadwinner. Later, in a speech on his sixtieth birthday, Strindberg said: "I always
regarded my father as a hostile power, nor could he endure me." But Eklund rightly
comments that this is not the whole truth; Strindberg respected and even admired his
father's power, authority and aristocratic bearing, and hoped in at least these respects to
become like him. His definitive break with his father did not happen until 1876. (Torsten
Eklund, *Tjänstekvinnans son*, Stockholm, 1948, pp. 18 ff.)

loved clean linen. The servant who brushed his boots was enjoined to wear mittens since his hands were thought too dirty to be permitted inside his master's boots . . .[11]

Strindberg's sisters Anna and Nora, in reminiscences written in old age, confirm this picture. "Meticulously dressed, he demanded meticulous order around him in everything that concerned the children and the home. In a word, he was a typical paterfamilias of the time." They add that this concentration of omnipotence in one person "we often found oppressive and inhibiting. But beneath his demand for absolute obedience there beat a warm heart." He was a good pianist and cellist, was unconventional in employing female clerks in his office (including, eventually, his own daughters), and loved to hear news of the theatre world from his nephew Ludvig, an actor. Anna and Nora characterised their mother more briefly as "a mild, God-fearing woman, sensitive and generous to the poor."[12]

Strindberg's stern image of his father was modified when as a child he visited him one day in his office:

> There Johan was surprised to find his father a brisk and cheerful man who joked with sun-tanned steamship captains and had a beautiful warm smile . . . He had never seen his father in his working environment before; he had only seen him at home as the tired and hungry breadwinner and judge who preferred living with nine persons in three rooms to being alone in two . . . He admired him but felt that he feared him less now that he had seen him thus, and thought he might some time be able to like him.[13]

Carl Oscar gradually regained and even improved his position. By the late 1850s or early sixties, when August was around ten, his income is estimated to have been around 5,500 riksdaler, the same as a judge of appeals and 1,000 riksdaler more than a university professor; and by 1870 he was probably earning around 7,000 riksdaler. By then his fleet had expanded to forty-one ships and once again represented roughly one-third of all the steamships plying out of Stockholm.[14] But in the early years of Strindberg's childhood, conditions remained hard for the family. "There was no real poverty," Strindberg admitted, "but food was rationed and was scarcely ample; meat was seen only on Sundays."[15]

Nevertheless, August grew well enough and was tall for his age. He remembered the first gas lamps being lit in the street when he was four, and the cholera outbreak the following year.[16] Soon after his seventh birthday, in April 1856, the family moved from the centre of town to Norrtullsgatan on the northern edge of the city. It lay only twenty minutes' walk from the centre, but so small was Stockholm then that this new home stood in the country, on an unpaved tree-lined avenue with as yet few houses. Cattle grazed in the fields; such traffic as there was consisted mainly of farmers and dairymen on their way to and from market, and hearses driving to the nearby cemetery.[17] The house, number 14, had been built at the beginning of the century, probably as a summer residence. It was two-storeyed, with additional rooms under the gable, built of wood with a thin covering of brick. The family occupied only part of it. Strindberg remembered their apartment as consisting of six rooms and a kitchen; his sisters, probably more accurately, say it had seven, and a big loft where they kept fruit during the winter.[18] There was a large dining-room and a study for Carl Oscar, lined with books from floor to ceiling. More importantly for the children, there was an extensive garden. "Long avenues containing at least a hundred apple trees and numberless berry bushes crossed each other; there were thick bowers of lilac and jasmine, and a mighty old oak still stood in one corner. . . . East of the garden rose a gravel hill, overgrown with maples, birches and rowans; on the summit stood a temple from the previous century. My first spring there was a time of marvellous surprises."[19]

Carl Oscar at once started to plant and sow, and the children helped. They went bird-nesting in nearby Haga Park, caught bats and, sad to relate, shot small birds.[20] But that same spring brought a less pleasant change. August went to his first school, Klara. "It was a rich school for superior people's children, for it was a rich neighbourhood. I wore moleskin trousers and cheap boots which smelt of whale-oil and blacking, so that other children in velvet blouses shrank from sitting by me." Klara was a puritanical establishment, and August hated it. "It was preparation not for life but for hell . . . My worst dreams as an adult, when I had eaten something heavy in the evening or had had an unusually taxing day, were of finding myself back at Klara."[21]

Strindberg spent four years at Klara, and his account of conditions there are confirmed by one of his fellow pupils. "The very name of Klara," wrote Robert Geete, "sends a chill down the spines of its old pupils." There was much beating, and none of the boys dared venture out of doors even when at home in the afternoons, for fear of meeting one of the teachers, who expected them to devote all their out-of-school time to homework. Speaking from hindsight, Geete wondered whether this atmosphere of terror might not have been partly responsible for Strindberg's later nervousness. Of Strindberg's remark that his worst adult dreams took the form of finding himself again at Klara, Geete comments: "This experience has certainly been shared by many." He remembered

Strindberg as "a quiet, shy, almost insignificant lad who as yet aroused not the slightest attention" and never took part in the fights with other schools. [22]

After only a year at Norrtullsgatan, the Strindbergs moved a mile or so farther out into the country north of Stockholm to a larger house named Loviseberg near what was then the village, and is now the suburb, of Sabbatsberg. A drawing by August's brother Axel shows it as a handsome, broad, low two-storeyed house, with rooms under the gable as at Norrtullsgatan. [23] "It stood in a tree-lined courtyard," Strindberg recalled, "and resembled a country parsonage. It was surrounded by gardens and large tobacco patches; broad meadows with ponds stretched away from it." [24] In January 1860 Strindberg was removed by his father from his hated Klara School to Jakob School, not far away on the corner of Regeringsgatan and Brunnsgatan. This was humbler, but Strindberg found it much more congenial:

> Jakob was a school for poor children. Here he came into contact with the working-class. His schoolmates were worse dressed than he, with sores on their noses, and smelt. His moleskin breeches and cheap boots created no bad impression here. He felt happier in these surroundings, which suited him; he was more at home with these children than with the snobbish boys at Klara . . . Johan felt that he had "come down" in the world, but he had wanted this . . . Here there was no pressure from above. He did not want to be up there, for he felt that there should not be anyone up there. But it vexed him that his old schoolmates regarded him as having come down. [25]

To Strindberg's embarrassment, when the pupils from Jakob went to the Central Institute for Gymnastics they would sometimes meet pupils from Klara who mocked their poor appearance. His new companions were a rough bunch; some of them fought with sweeps and tobacco-binders, and frequented pubs to drink aquavit in their lunch break. There was a big difference between the appearance of the parents on examination day and those at Klara. Instead of bland speeches by an archbishop, the occasion was presided over by the school inspector, who read out the names of the lazy or ignorant and publicly rebuked the parents. [26]

In April 1860, after three years at Sabbatsberg, the Strindbergs returned to their old house on Norrtullgatan. It was less rustic and isolated than when they had left; there had been much building in the neighbourhood as the city spread northwards, with property speculators erecting apartment houses of four and five storeys. August had inherited his father's passion for flowers, and had his own flower and vegetable bed where he sowed stock and mignonette, radishes, lettuce and parsley, and developed an impressive herbarium. "He had no peace until he had learned to recognise all the flora of Stockholm."[27] He also began to collect insects and minerals. "He was preternaturally shy," recalled his brother Axel, "so shy of us brothers that when he changed his underclothes he went into the cupboard. Nor can I remember that he showed the least sign of artistic interests. We played music, but he never took part . . . I drew a little, but that didn't interest him either . . . His chief interests at that time were natural science—the latest discoveries—and religion . . . He was strong and muscular, wrestled and fenced."[28]

Axel gave more details about Strindberg's early preoccupation with science, which was to remain with him all his life:

> Among the natural sciences, he was . . . most interested in galvanic electricity and galvanoplasty. He both silvered and gilded. I remember for example that he once gilded a watch, and through this interest he came close to his father, who was also much fascinated by science. In that area, at least, they were happily agreed. In general, his character most resembled that of his father, who was enclosed and brooding, taciturn and reserved. In appearance, though, he took after his mother. In those days no ships sailed in winter, so that Father . . . was often at home then. He and August worked together a lot at these experiments.[29]

Axel added that Strindberg was also keen on photography as a child, another interest that was to be lifelong. "Strangely enough, I cannot recall that as a boy he was even interested in the theatre, unlike myself . . . In a summer-house in the orchard at Norrtullsgatan . . . we once acted a one-act squib about women's emancipation—but I cannot remember that August made any great impression, though he was certainly in it." But he recalled that August took part in performances which they gave in the loft; and kept canaries.[30] His sisters Anna and Nora remembered him as "very difficult to get on with . . . He had a deeply rooted distrust of everyone and everything."[31]

Strindberg's mother was deeply religious, but she did not follow the state Lutheran Church. She was a Pietist, a sect founded in the seventeenth century which had much in common with Methodism, and indeed had profoundly influenced John Wesley. Pietists believed, among other things, that the laity should share in the government of the church, and that all worldly amusements such as dancing and the theatre should be banned (though according to his daughters Carl Oscar liked to hear about the theatre when his actor nephew Ludvig visited them).[32] Pietism, which appealed particularly to the poor and the downtrodden and emphasised the simple puritanical virtues, was opposed by the state church but flourished in Scandinavia at this time; only ten years previously, Ibsen's family, though not Ibsen himself, had been similarly converted, which had caused Ibsen, a free-thinking disciple of Voltaire, to break with his mother and brothers in early manhood.

But Strindberg, on the threshold of adolescence, was not yet a free thinker, and he embraced Pietism as fervently as his mother—indeed, more so, for he once refused to accompany his family on a Sunday excursion on the ground that it was sinful to enjoy oneself on the sabbath. Instead he stayed in town "and attended both matins and evensong."[33] He read, indigestible as it sounds for one not yet in his teens, the German theologian Friedrich Wilhelm Krummacher, and also Thomas à Kempis, who nearly forty years later was to become a favourite author of his after his Inferno crisis.

In the autumn of 1861, after only a year at Jakob School, Strindberg was removed to a private school, Stockholm Lyceum, principally it seems because his elder brother Oscar, an attractive extrovert who was his parents' favourite, was also at Jakob, and August, being the cleverer, seemed likely to outshine him. The Lyceum was nearer the centre of town, on Regeringsgatan, where it had been founded in 1839. Conditions there were almost as primitive as at Jakob; there was no washbasin, no playroom or playground, nor even a room in which to hang overcoats and galoshes, which the pupils had to take into the classrooms.[34] But it had a remarkably high proportion of teachers to pupils (twenty-three to two hundred) and a liberal atmosphere. "Here for the first time," Strindberg was to declare, "I felt that I enjoyed human rights."[35] Discipline was lax, but the teaching good; the boys started Latin at the age of seven. The headmasters were Otto von Feilitzen and Karl Johan Bohman, the latter a splendid eccentric who taught in a fur coat and galoshes, "however hot the weather."[36]

During his six years at the Lyceum, Strindberg made much better progress than he had at Klara or Jakob. But his mother, he bitterly recalled, resented his cleverness. "He should beware of pride and always remain simple . . . Johan sensed in her the uneducated person's distrust of education."[37]

She was not to remain with them long. One Sunday, as Carl Oscar was reading prayers to the family, she had a violent haemorrhage:

> Mother had been weak for a long time, after her twelve [*sic*] pregnancies. Now she had to take to her bed, and rose from it only occasionally. Her temper sharpened and, when contradicted, red flared in her cheeks. On her last Christmas she had become embroiled in a violent dispute with her brother about lay preachers . . . She collapsed in hysterics. This was merely

a symptom . . . She then began, before she became bedridden, to put the children's clothes in order and tidy the drawers. She often talked to Johan about religion and other important questions. One day she showed him some gold rings. "You children shall have these when Mamma dies," she said. "Which is mine?" asked Johan, not dwelling on the thought of death. She showed him a twisted ring with a heart on it. It made a big impression on the boy, who had never owned anything of gold, and he often thought about that ring.

A *mademoiselle* came to live in and take care of the children. She was young, pretty, said little and sometimes wore a critical smile. She had been with the family of a Count and probably thought it demeaning to work in as humble a house as ours. . . .

One night Johan is wakened from his sleep by his father's voice. He jumps up. It is dark in the room. In the darkness he hears a voice, deep and trembling: "Come in, children. Mamma is dying." . . . So they stood at the deathbed. They wept for an hour, wept for two hours, three. After three hours, their tears ceased. Their thoughts ran hither and thither. The dying was over.[38]

Two days later August wrote to the brother who was away from home:*

Stockholm, 22 March [1862]

My dear brother Oscar,

Now we have no mother any more. She died on the night between Wednesday and Thursday, we were all there with her, but she was unconscious so didn't recognize us. Sophie [a servant] has laid her out, and she is much changed . . . We are very sad but Father has calmed us by telling us that it was God's will. The mother of Herr Carlsson, father's former book-keeper, died a short while ago very suddenly. Falk the butcher died last night next door. It is almost spring now, Drottninggatan is quite clear of snow and we have fine weather, but this morning it is minus eleven degrees . . . Don't cry too much or doubt that it was God's will but calm yourself and take comfort in the word of God, as we have done.

Your affectionate and grieving brother
August

"Since your mother's death," their father wrote to Oscar on 5 April, "August has become quite a different child. He shows me real friendship and has been of much help to me during these sad days."[39] Strindberg put it somewhat differently. "Enmity was laid aside," he recalled, "but friendship was impossible."[40] He was surprised, and ashamed, to find that

---

*Oscar had been at school in France since the previous September, and Axel had, for the same length of time, been working in the daytime to pay for his music studies, so that for the last six months of his mother's life August had been closer to her than before.

his real grief for his mother lasted barely three months. Yet he could never free himself of her:

> A desolate longing for his mother stayed with him all his life. Had he come too early into the world, was he an aborted foetus? He never found an answer to this question in books or in life, but the situation remained; he never became himself, he was never liberated, never a complete individual. He remained a mistletoe that could not grow without being supported by a tree . . . He came frightened into the world and lived in perpetual fear of life and of people.[41]

Did Strindberg exaggerate his love of his mother? Was it perhaps an abstraction and an ideal that haunted him rather than the woman herself and his memories of her? A Swedish critic, Martin Lamm, has written:

> She had favoured the older children, betrayed him to his father and, as he grew older, seemed to him to be uneducated. With the passage of time, however, he came to create what he called a purified and glorified image of her. Throughout his life he felt a sense of loss and longed for an ideal maternal figure, an ideal maternal embrace, in which his stormy emotions could be cradled to rest. He worshipped his mother in all the women with whom he fell in love during his lifetime. To him, sexual desire, once it had been satisfied, was a profanation. His programme for sexual reform as stated in the preface to the story collection *Getting Married* culminates in a glorification of woman as mother.[42]

Carl Oscar Strindberg did not remain a widower for long. Within a year of his wife's death he married "Mademoiselle," his children's governess. Emilia Charlotte Petersson (christened with the good Swedish names of Emma Charlotta, she had changed these at her confirmation to more pretentious and exotic forms) was the daughter of a caretaker. At twenty-two, she was thirty years younger than Carl Oscar, who announced his betrothal to the children in a speech in which he explained that "the time of passions was, for him, past, and that only his concern for the children had dictated his decision to make Mademoiselle his wife."[43] This was evidently not the whole truth, for the following year she presented him with a son, Emil. Her sister, known to the children as Aunt Ida, also came to live in the house.

Emilia Charlotte was not popular with any of the children. Anna and Nora recalled that her coming markedly worsened their relationship with their father. "We children instinctively felt that the path to Father's heart was as good as cut off. Over-parsimonious and deeply religious, she had difficulty in winning our confidence." They add that August got on particularly badly with her and came to regard her as his worst enemy.[44]

At fifteen, Strindberg (by his own account) fell in love for the first time, with their landlord's thirty-year-old daughter, Edla Hejkorn. It was a harmless, platonic affair; they attended a French conversation circle and took long walks home, talking French together. "It was easier to say delicate things in a foreign language." He wrote French compositions for her, and was rebuked by his father for speaking French to her in the presence of the family, who could not understand. When in October 1864 the Strindbergs moved to the next house, no. 12, which lay some distance away, August and Edla corresponded for a year, using Aunt Ida as postwoman. "What were the letters about? Everything—Jesus, the fight against sin, life, death, love, friendship, despair."[45]

"There was something dark and depressing about this new house. We children sensed ghosts."[46] Perhaps they were ghosts from the future, for eleven years later, after the family had left, a fateful meeting was to take place there between Strindberg and the house's new occupants.

Whether because of Edla's influence or because of the rising sap within him, Strindberg now moved away from Pietism. He developed a taste for the pleasures of life; he went to restaurants, drank and flirted with waitresses. To pay for these pleasures, he managed to get work as a private tutor and as usher in a girls' school, where he taught history, geography, nature study and, at his own request, physics; also, ironically, considering his unorthodox views on the subject, religion. His sister Anna was one of his pupils there. He recalled that he taught the smallest girls while "the big ones wandered around and showed their stockings . . . which attracted him, though he dared make no approaches."[47]

At his own school, he gave up Greek and mathematics, which he found were not necessary for his matriculation if he took Latin (interestingly, they were the two subjects in which Ibsen had failed in his preliminary examination at Christiania University in Norway). Surprisingly for one who was later to become a useful linguist, he disliked Greek and had for some time begged his father to be allowed to drop it; he now did so without his father's knowledge. He also disliked Latin and "during lessons read French, German and English novels . . . The living languages and natural sciences now became his strength . . . During all this time, Jesus was suspended . . . He still prayed from habit, but without hope of his prayers being heard . . . and, to tell the truth, he was not over-eager to be heard. If the door had been opened and Jesus had told him to step in, he would not have been happy. His flesh was too young and healthy to want to be crucified."[48]

A great relief was afforded him, and thousands of other Swedish children, when a Board of Education enquiry into school morality revealed that most girls and boys indulged in masturbation. These findings were, surprisingly for that time, published in the newspapers, and "the subject was now discussed openly in school as being a necessary part of normal human experience,"[49] instead of being regarded as an unmentionable crime committed only by the few.

Strindberg read the usual internationally admired authors; disliked Byron's *Don Juan*, found Scott's novels "too long, especially the descriptive passages," and dismissed the elder Dumas as an author of "Indian romances." But he loved Dickens (later he was to name him as his favourite English writer) and devoured the whole of Shakespeare in Hagberg's recently published translations. "But I always found it difficult to read plays, where the eye had to jump down from the name of the character to the text. My exaggerated expectations of *Hamlet* were not fulfilled, and I found the comedies just plain rubbish."[50] Rather unexpectedly, he enlisted (on 17 February 1866) as a volunteer in the militia, donned uniform, exercised and learned to shoot. "The company was a motley mixture of all social classes," wrote a fellow-volunteer, Edvard Selander. "There was no great discipline, but my brother Nils had a good aide in one of the corporals, our second cousin August Strindberg, who took the business very seriously and performed his subordinate duties with great zeal. Strindberg long remembered this responsible office, and up to his last years [when Colonel Nils Selander was treasurer of the Dramatic Theatre] would announce himself at the theatre offices by clicking his heels and exclaiming, 'Colonel! Corporal Strindberg reporting!' "[51]

In the summer of 1866, at the age of seventeen, he got a vacation job as private tutor to the three children of a palace secretary named Carl Otto Trotz at his country estate in the Stockholm skerries. It was Strindberg's first visit to the skerries, and he fell in love with them, a love which he was to retain all his life. "This was his landscape, his true milieu," he declared of himself. "Harsh, rugged stone islets with pine forests scattered over great stormy bays backed in the distance by the boundless ocean. He remained faithful to this love, not merely because it was his first; neither the Swiss Alps, the olive groves of the Mediterranean nor the cliffs of Normandy could displace this rival."[52]

An additional pleasure was that of living with an aristocratic family, or anyway one in which the lady of the house was the daughter of a baron. Looking back twenty years later, Strindberg recalled his boyhood admiration for the upper crust, an admiration that despite his political beliefs he was never to lose. As a small boy he had been taken to Drottningholm Palace, where the Crown Prince, later King Charles XV, had addressed a few words to him from his horse.

> He had distantly glimpsed the splendour of the aristocracy, and he longed
> for it as for a homeland, but his mother's slave blood rose against it . . . He
> felt he didn't belong there. But he didn't belong to the slaves either. This was
> to be one of the discords in his life. [53]

It was a bitter disappointment to Strindberg, when he joined the
Trotzes, to find himself treated not as one of them but as a servant.
Nevertheless, merely to be away from home was itself a freedom. Religion
and scepticism continued to battle within him, as within so many at that
time throughout the West. On a visit to the local curate he dropped a hint
that he might himself take the cloth, and was invited to preach a sermon
in the church, which—with much trepidation, for he was never a good
public speaker—he did. It was a boldly Unitarian sermon, against dogma
and Pietism; the congregation remained unshocked. When autumn
came, he returned with the Trotzes to Stockholm and continued to live
with them and tutor the children outside his own school hours. Ironically, they were pupils at his first, hated school, Klara, suffering under
the same headmaster who had tormented him. [54]

During the January term of 1867, Strindberg led a classroom rebellion
against school religion. He not only refused to attend school prayers, but
persuaded several of his classmates to do the same. It says much for the
liberalism of the Lyceum that he was not disciplined for this. His family,
after a few attempts to redeem him, gave him up as lost; and the Pietists,
seeing him dressed in militia uniform one Sunday morning, offered a
prayer for him in the Bethlehem Church. [55]

In April, Carl Oscar moved the family back to Norrtullsgatan 14, for
the third time. In May, Strindberg passed his matriculation, the
studentexamen, albeit with undistinguished marks, * and proudly bought
the white-velvet peaked cap to which this entitled him. His father
refunded him the cost of it but, according to Strindberg, did not
congratulate him. He was now qualified to enter university. Sweden then
boasted two universities, both ancient foundations: Uppsala, forty miles
north of Stockholm, and Lund, three hundred miles to the south.
Uppsala was his natural choice. He had dreamed of it as Hardy's Jude
Fawley was to dream of Christminster; it was, as universities have been to
every aspirant, the symbol of freedom. "There one might walk in shabby
clothes, be poor, and yet be a student, in other words a member of the
privileged class. There one might sing and drink, come home drunk, fight
with the police, without losing one's good name." [56]

*His only A was for diligence (*flitbetyg*). He got AB for Swedish composition, religion,
French, natural history and history-with-geography; B for "maturity," Latin, German and
philosophy, and C for written mathematics. [57]

That summer of 1867 he stayed at home, did some private tutoring, and slept with a girl for the first time. "He felt disappointed, like so many others. So that was all it was! The joke was that it happened exactly opposite the Bethlehem Church. But why hadn't it happened before? It would have saved him so many years of anguish. But he felt quite peaceful afterwards, healthy and happy as though he had fulfilled a duty."[58] When autumn came, the old servant Margret packed his bag and made him accept a loan of 15 riksdaler from her. His father gave him a box of cigars. He had saved 80 riksdaler from his tutoring and, thus equipped, on 13 September 1867, he set off to begin his university career.[59]

Chapter Two

FIRST STEPS IN THE THEATRE

Uppsala is, after Lund, the oldest university in Scandinavia. Founded in 1477, it stands on a hill by the river Fyris, with a famous castle and cathedral. Two of the most dramatic scenes in Swedish history took place in the castle, the murder by the mad King Erik XIV of five of his barons in 1567 and the abdication of Queen Christina in 1654. Strindberg was to portray both monarchs memorably in his plays. The castle, together with most of the town, had been largely destroyed by a fire in 1702, but the cathedral, completed in 1435, had survived, and the university boasted several fine eighteenth- and early nineteenth-century buildings, as well as the botanic garden where the great Linnaeus had worked. Photographs and engravings of Uppsala from the 1860s show a still largely rural town with cows grazing beside the river and a huddle of small red wooden houses among gardens and orchards; from the castle hill, the effect was said to be that of a plate of tiny crabs in spinach.[1]

As befitted his father's son, Strindberg travelled there not by the new railway but free on one of the family steamships up Lake Mälaren. With a friend from the Lyceum, August Strömbäck, he took a single room, which they shared at a cost of 15 riksdaler each for the term. For a further 6 riksdaler they got a midday meal; breakfast and supper comprised a glass of milk and a sandwich. "He had a demijohn of paraffin as a present from home, and was allowed to send his washing to Stockholm."[2]

Living thus modestly, he hoped to survive the three months on his savings of 80 riksdaler. Writing to his father on 21 September 1867, eight days after his arrival, he said that he was living "quite well" on 40 öre a day.

His euphoria did not last long. A broad gulf lay between the professors and their pupils, whom the former seemed to regard as an intrusion on their research. Strindberg studied humanities and attended lectures on, among other subjects, Aristotle's *Ethics* and Shakespeare's *Henry VIII*. He found them all dreadfully dull. "Uppsala University in 1867 had not a single outstanding teacher . . . Almost everything that was taught was borrowed from abroad, mainly Germany. The text books were mostly written in German or French—very few in English, because nobody knew it. Even the Professor of Literary History couldn't pronounce English and began his lectures by apologising for this . . . Most of the doctoral theses were just bad borrowings from German." He joined a student fraternity, but found little joy there, though he played the B-cornet in their sextet. He read Swedenborg but thought him "daft";[3] thirty years later, Swedenborg was to save his sanity.

Nor did the flat countryside around Uppsala help. "The dreadful landscape with its endless clayey fields depressed him. He was not a plainsman, but had his roots in the Stockholm countryside with its hills and watercourses."[4] He despaired at the thought of returning for another term, let alone for several years. "He had heard from a friend that one could become an elementary schoolteacher at a country school without a university degree."[5]

Such teaching vacancies were advertised in the newspapers, offering salaries of 300 to 600 riksdaler a year, with accommodation including a garden and pasture for raising livestock. Strindberg applied for several of these but received no answer, and had to settle for a job at an elementary school in Stockholm. The salary was 900 riksdaler a year, a big improvement on that at a country school. Carl Oscar did not approve of his son's becoming an elementary schoolteacher, which he likened to "being a sergeant," and granted permission only on condition that August live at home, where his father could see that he continued with his university studies (his teaching ended each day at 1 p.m.).[6] So, after only a term, his new-found freedom was lost.

The *folkskola* was in the Klara quarter where his first school had been, so that he found himself treading the same path each morning at seven-thirty that he had walked as an eight-year-old. "As afraid, even more afraid, of coming late, he entered the big class where . . . he would teach over a hundred children. There they sat, the same children as from the Jakob School, but younger. Ugly, stunted, pale, starved, sickly and with downcast eyes, coarse clothes and heavy shoes."[7]

At least, now that he was earning a salary, he could afford to buy books. Throughout his life Strindberg was, unlike many authors, a great book-buyer; he disliked borrowing from libraries even when he was hard up. He also indulged for the first time what was to be another of his lifelong extravagances, clothes.

He read his Italian grammar in the school yard during breaks and so discovered Boccaccio's *Decameron*. This, by his own account, encouraged him to "sow his wild oats in all directions. He usually had three affairs going on at the same time; a great, holy and (he called it) pure love-at-a-distance, with marriage plans in the background—i.e., a marriage bed, but a pure one. Then a little flirtation with a waitress, and then the whole free company, blonde, brown, red, black." For a year he went out with a waitress at Stallmästaregården, a fashionable restaurant in Haga Park; she "granted him all favours but the ultimate one."[8] How many of the other girls granted him the ultimate favour is not clear.

With some other young teachers he took part in a playreading of Schiller's *The Robbers*. Strindberg was allotted the principal part of Karl Moor, the respectable young man who becomes a rebel against society, and was greatly excited. "Here were his hazy dreams set down in words; his revolutionary criticisms in print. So someone else, and that a great and famous author, had felt the same loathing for the whole system of school and university education . . . Here was the anarchist programme a hundred years before its time . . . But there was a preface in which the author apologises and withdraws, and rejects all identification . . . Schiller had to creep in under the skirt of the state and accept sinecures to live; even lick the hands of Dukes. Thus his writing steadily declined. What had begun as a condemnation of society as a whole became merely a condemnation of monarchs."[9]

Through the recommendation of a friend, Strindberg was offered extra work as private tutor to the daughters of a professor of medicine, Oscar Sandahl, who lived at Klara Strandgata 2, "a rich and cultivated home, at that time the grandest private house in Stockholm."[10] This was in the afternoons after his work at the school. Thus he taught each morning from eight to one, read till four, taught the Sandahl girls in the late afternoon and evening, and read again in the evening for his degree "after having taught for altogether ten hours." Byron's poetry attracted him. "*Don Juan*, which he had read before, he found simply frivolous, but in *Manfred* he met Karl Moor again in another guise . . . He started to translate *Manfred*, but had not got far before he discovered afresh that he could not write verse."[11]

That summer of 1868 he accompanied the Sandahls to their summer house at Blockhusudden in Djurgården, the great park on the southern outskirts of Stockholm. There he met another doctor, Axel Lamm, who took a liking to the shy and saturnine young man and suggested that he should start reading medicine, give up his work at the *folkskola* and come and live with him and tutor his sons while he, Dr. Lamm, directed his medical studies. Strindberg accepted this offer and lived with the Lamms in their villa at Stora Trädgårdsgatan 19, opposite where the huge NK department store now stands, for over a year.

He attended chemistry classes at the Technological Institute, and under Dr. Lamm's guidance read zoology, anatomy, botany, physics and Latin. But the location of the Lamms' villa offered a serious distraction. Less than a hundred yards away, on the far side of Kungsträdgården, stood the Royal Theatre, and Strindberg soon found himself going there two or three times a week. "Standing in the gallery he saw unfolded the gay and elegant world of French comedy . . . The light Gallic temperament, which the sombre Swede admires because he lacks it, enchanted him."

In other respects too, life with the Lamms broadened his outlook. The doctor's wife owned "a beautiful library containing books in every language" and the doctor himself had a fine collection of paintings and engravings. Conversation was mainly about paintings, plays, actors, books and writers. "Associating with artists opened his eyes to a new world, a free society within society."[12]

Yet another world was revealed to him when he accompanied Dr. Lamm on the latter's rounds:

> He is awakened at 7 a.m., enters the doctor's back room and manually assists at the cauterising of a sore resulting from a venereal disease. The room smelt of human flesh and was repellent to an empty stomach. Or he holds back a patient's head while the doctor removes the tonsils with a fork. "You soon get used to it," said the doctor, and it was true, but reality with its burns and blood-clots was unlovely.[13]

In May 1869 he went to Uppsala to take his oral exam in chemistry. The interview did not go well. "Johan presented himself, was eyed suspiciously, and told to return in a week. He explained that . . . he was too poor to keep himself in Uppsala for a week and was graciously granted leave to return the next day." When he did, he was rejected. On complaining that he had worked for a year in a laboratory he was told, "The Institute is for artisans. We here are scientists."[14]

Depressed, he walked out into the Caroline Park and sat down on a bench outside the university library.

> As he sits there, a group of happy people comes and stands laughing outside the library. They look up at the windows where the long lines of books are visible, shelf upon shelf. They laugh! . . . It is Levasseur's company of French actors whom he has seen in Stockholm and who are now visiting Uppsala. They were laughing at the books. Happy people, who could dispense with books and yet be emissaries of culture and genius! . . . The thought occurred again to him that he might enter this privileged elite which stood outside and above the petty conventions of society, which by-passed all questions of rank, and in which one need never feel oneself to be an inferior human being . . . He walked down into the town, resolved to return home and seek a place as an actor in the Royal Theatre. [15]

Strindberg made an appointment with Frans Hedberg, dramaturge of the Royal Theatre and head of its acting school, and asked if he might take private lessons in acting and in time be auditioned for a place in the company. Hedberg explained that the term was ended and told him to return in three months, on 1 September, when the theatre would have reopened. Strindberg gave up his job of tutoring the Lamm girls in order to spend the whole summer preparing for his audition. He borrowed a volume of Shakespeare's plays from the City Library, but his English was (and was to remain) poor, his German good, and most of his reading that summer was in the latter language.

> He had laughed at books, but the first thing to which he now turned was books . . . He had heard that in the palace there was a library belonging to the state where one could get permission to borrow books . . . The small rooms were solemn and full of books, with grey-haired, silent old men reading . . . From Schiller he learned about the deep significance of the theatre; from Goethe . . . how one should walk and stand, move, sit down, enter and exit; in Lessing's *Hamburgische Dramaturgie* he read a whole volume of theatre reviews full of the finest perceptions. Lessing it was who gave him most hope of success, for he went so far as to declare that the art of the actor had brought the theatre into decline, and demanded that actors should be replaced by dilettantes of the educated classes who would be better able to understand the roles . . . Moreover, he underwent practical exercises. At home at the doctor's he went through scenes when his pupils were away. He practised entries and exits . . . costumed and made himself up as Karl Moor and acted him. He went to the National Museum and studied the poses of the antique sculptures; laid aside his walking stick when going out in order to practise walking without it . . . He did gymnastics every day at home and fenced with his pupils; studied the movement of every muscle; practised walking with his head high and his chest out, his arms hanging free and his hands loosely clenched, as prescribed by Goethe,

his fingers falling beautifully in a rhythmic pattern. His main problem was in voice training, for when he declaimed he could be heard throughout the house. Then he hit on the notion of going outside the town. The only place where he could be undisturbed was Ladugårdsgärde [the open fields to the northeast]. There he could see across the flat plain if anyone was coming, and there the sound died away so that he had to strain to hear himself. This gave him a strong speaking voice. He went there every day and raged against heaven and earth.[16]

That July, Henrik Ibsen visited Stockholm for two months. Ibsen was then forty-one, and although the great prose plays still lay in the future and he was virtually unknown outside Scandinavia, the publication of *Brand* in 1866 and *Peer Gynt* in 1867—both written only to be read, not acted, and as yet unperformed—had spread his fame to Sweden. Strindberg did not meet him, then or ever, but eight years later he was to recall the impression Ibsen made, though whether he actually saw Ibsen or took the description from hearsay we do not know. "Who does not remember the famous poet's appearance? . . . Dressed in a velvet jacket, a white waistcoat with black buttons, and a cape of the latest fashion, with an elegant cane in his hand, and a protective self-mocking curl to his lip, he went his way, avoiding all deep subjects of conversation."[17]

Brand particularly excited Strindberg, who at once identified himself with the title character, "a fanatic who dared to think that he was right and the rest of the world wrong . . . No half-measures, just press on, break and wrench everything down that stands in your way, because you alone are right. Johan's so-sensitive conscience, which winced at every step he took because it would pain his father or his friends, was anaesthetised by *Brand*. All bonds of scruple, of love, must be rent asunder for the sake of the 'cause' . . . *Brand* gave him belief in a conscience purer than the conscience which his upbringing had instilled in him, and a right which was above justice." Ibsen's other plays disappointed him. *Peer Gynt* he thought "obscure rather than deep, its main virtue being as a counter to chauvinism," and *Love's Comedy*, with its cynical attitude towards marriage, he found "disgusting."[18] This divided attitude towards Ibsen was to remain with Strindberg all his life. But the effect of *Brand* on him was immediate and overwhelming; he described it as "the voice of a Savonarola . . . Bjørnson charmed me; Ibsen awoke me."[19]

But it was not as a writer, but as an actor that Strindberg thought of himself that summer of 1869, and in September he presented himself at the Royal Theatre and offered himself as a member of the company. The procedure for entry seems scarcely credible: candidates were expected to name the role in which they would like not to be auditioned, but to appear. Strindberg suggested Karl Moor in *The Robbers*. He was informed that that play was not in the repertory and that he might attempt the small part of Härved Boson in *The Wedding at Ulfåsa*, a historical drama by Frans Hedberg, who had interviewed him in May. In his autobiography, Strindberg dismissed this as "no part,"[20] but it was in fact a good little role in which several young actors had previously made their mark.

While waiting for rehearsals to begin, he had a couple of lessons; then his teacher said he had no further time to devote to him and advised him to attend the theatre school, which one might have thought would have been the obvious course in the first place. Strindberg, however, was unwilling "as one who had himself been a teacher" to attend a school which "he had heard described as a kind of kindergarten or Sunday school which accepted everyone whether they had had a school education or not."[21] His arrogance and ignorance of the theatre world strike one as astonishing. A single visit to a class convinced him that this was no place for him, whereupon his teacher suggested that he seek a place in the theatre as a non-speaking extra. He did so and was allotted the tiny part of a Nobleman in Bjørnson's *Mary Stuart in Scotland*. He had a single line: "The lords have sent an envoy with a challenge to the Earl Bothwell."

So, at the opening rehearsal of this play, Strindberg trod a stage for the first time.

> He stood in the wings and listened to the play. He didn't like Mary Stuart, she was cruel and coquettish; Bothwell was too coarse and strong; Darnley, the weak Hamlet-like figure, who could never stop loving this woman and burned with love for her despite her infidelity, he liked him. And Knox: hard as stone, with his moral demands and his dreadful Norwegian-style Christianity. Yet this was something, to be able to step forward and live out a piece of history . . . Once he had gone on and said his line, he left, determined to endure everything for the sacred art.[22]

Strindberg also appeared as a non-speaking extra "in one opera after the other." He found little joy in the work. "After a couple of months he was bored with the whole thing. It was mechanical work. The leading actors were weary and indifferent, they never discussed art, only engagements and money. Never a hint of that happy life behind the scenes of which so much had been written."[23]

At last the rehearsals for *The Wedding at Ulfåsa* began. But Strindberg was never to appear in it before an audience. After a run-through on 16 November the head of the theatre, Erik af Edholm, noted in his diary: "I had to sack young Strindberg as Härved Boson."[24] Strindberg "wept with fury, went home and ate an opium tablet which he had long kept hidden, but without effect. Then a friend dragged him out and he got drunk."[25]

By his own account, this reverse was the stimulus that provoked him to write his first play. As he lay miserably in bed next morning, he recalled a story he had recently read in Zacharias Topelius's *Tales of a Military Surgeon* which dealt with the problems and eventual reconciliation of a stepmother and her stepson. His conflict with his father troubled him, and in four days he wrote a two-act comedy entitled A *Nameday Gift* in which just such a conflict is resolved by a stepmother—an unlikely thing to have happened in the Strindberg home, Carl Oscar's second wife being the woman she was. Strindberg read it in his attic at Dr. Lamm's to two friends, who approved it, and he offered it anonymously to the Royal Theatre, continuing meanwhile with his non-speaking appearances in order to keep the news of his failure from his father "or until it could be balanced by the acceptance of his play, for of course it would be accepted."[26] But it was refused. The manuscript has never been discovered, and Strindberg evidently did not think it worth offering elsewhere or rewriting.

Such is Strindberg's account; unhappily, it illustrates his unreliability as a witness. It may well be that he wrote A *Nameday Gift* in the circumstances he describes, but if so it was not, as he claims, his first play. A friend of his, Axel Berg, in a letter dated 6 November,[27] ten days before Strindberg got the sack, wrote that he had just read another play by Strindberg, *The Freethinker*, which has survived; and there is reason to think that he may also at least have planned a third play, *Greece in Decline* (later retitled *Hermione*), which he was to complete before the end of the year. There seems no special reason why he should have altered the sequence of events in his autobiography; he was simply not interested in recording things as they had really happened. It is the same with his claim that he was born into the house of a bankrupt. Yet no biography of Strindberg can be written without reference to and quotation from his autobiographical books; one can only repeat the caveat that he may or may not be telling the truth.

Strindberg continued as a humble member of the Royal Theatre company for the rest of the autumn season. One of his non-speaking roles was as a country lad in *William Tell*; another as a gladiator in a dull patriotic play, *The Swordsman from Ravenna*, by a contemporary Viennese dramatist, Friedrich Halm; a third as one Theobald in a play by Charlotte Birch-Pfeiffer entitled *The Lady of Worsley Hall*. His final humiliation came when the drama school, of which he still counted himself a member, gave its end-of-term performance and he found himself with no role save that of prompter. "So there in the prompter's box his career as an actor ended; a sad decline from his dream of playing

Karl Moor on the stage of the Royal Theatre." On the evening following this performance, there was a party for the pupils. "Johan was invited and declaimed a toast in verse so as to make his departure as unridiculous as possible. He got drunk as usual, made a fool of himself and so bade farewell to the acting profession."[28]

But at least he had written three plays, and the second and third of these, though they read poorly today, were in due course to meet with a more encouraging reception than A *Nameday Gift.*

The Freethinker, a half-length prose play in three scenes, deals with the problems of religious belief which had obsessed Strindberg during his last years at school. Karl, the play's young hero, rejects the conventional idea of God as an Old Testament Jehovah, nor does he accept that Christ is divine, but rather an ideal human being sent by a loving deity to preach peace and enlightenment on earth. In particular, he pours scorn on the idea that Christ should atone for men's sins: "Those souls must be weak that need a scapegoat on whom they need only throw all their crimes and sins so that they may fold their arms and await salvation." His profession of these heresies shocks his fellow-students, and especially a priest, Gustaf, to whose sister, Agda, Karl is engaged. When he returns home he finds that his parents, and Agda too, reject him; he is sacked from his post as teacher; and the play ends with him refusing to recant and emigrating to America.

The Freethinker contains most of the usual faults perpetrated by young playwrights. The characters, especially Karl, hold forth at enormous length; and none of them except Karl has any real life. What raises the play above mediocrity is the vitality of the language and the evidence it provides that Strindberg, even this early in his career, knew how to write dialogue.

Neither *The Freethinker* nor its successor, *Hermione*, seems ever to have been staged, and it is scarcely thinkable that they should be. The heroine of the latter play, at first called Antigone, is the daughter of a Greek high priest who is sent to murder Philip of Macedon when the latter threatens Athens, but instead falls in love with him, and is killed by her father Kriton, who then kills himself. Written in ponderous blank verse, it has few virtues, though Strindberg apparently preferred it to *The Freethinker*, since he allowed it, but not the earlier play, to be reprinted twelve years later in his collection of early work entitled I *vårbrytningen* (*Spring Harvest*). He described it as his "first real creative work," meaning that it was the first not to be drawn from his own experience, and summed it up fairly enough as "fully and clearly composed, with somewhat hackneyed situations and a good deal of declamation."[29]

Strindberg claims that he completed these two plays within the space of two months "with some minor verse besides."[30] He also, before the end of the year, started to write a comedy set in Rome earlier in the nineteenth century, and a tragedy about Christ "intended to destroy for all time the myth of his being the Son of God, and to deal a death-blow to Christianity." But after writing a few scenes of the latter play he "realised that the subject was too big and needed lengthy study," and, fortunately, abandoned it; as he did, temporarily, the comedy.

Despite the unactability of these first three plays, Strindberg's mentor at the Royal Theatre, Frans Hedberg, himself a dramatist, perceptively sensed the talent struggling to emerge. He told Strindberg that his true bent was for writing rather than acting, and advised him to give up the latter career, return to Uppsala, take his degree and then apply himself to authorship.

Chapter Three

"A RESTLESS SEEKER"

In January 1870, two years after having, as he had hoped, left it for ever, Strindberg found himself again a student at Uppsala. On the 22nd of that month he came of age and took possession of a tiny inheritance due to him under his mother's will: only 180 riksdader (£10), but this was more than twice the sum on which he had survived his first term in 1867.[1]* He found an attic room at Odinslund 2 and settled down again to the study of aesthetics and modern languages; and, more importantly, to write further plays.

At first he was depressed at being back in a student's attic, where the rain came in through the roof. As a result of his prolonged sojourn with the Lamms, "he was now used to luxury, large rooms, good food, service and company. Accustomed to being treated as an adult, and to associating with mature and cultivated people, he found himself a mere student again."[2] But now, as he had not done earlier, he went out to look for company, and soon had three separate circles of acquaintances. "First, the students he messed with—medicos, atheists and scientists, from whom for the first time he heard the name of Darwin . . . Then, his evening companions, a priest and a law student, with whom he played

---

*An English visitor to Sweden five years previously had noted that: "A young student told me that at Lund about £3 and at Uppsala about £4 per month would cover all expenses." (*Ten Years in Sweden*, by "An Old Bushman" [H. W. Wheelwright], London, 1865, p. 81.)

cards late into the night . . . And later in the term he came into contact with a group which was to become his circle for the whole of his time at Uppsala and beyond."[3]

As was to be the case throughout his life, his moods varied from elation to the blackest depression. On 2 March he wrote in high euphoria to his cousin Johan Oscar Strindberg:

> One leads a godlike existence here. Uninhibited freedom! Great ideas! . . . Pleasures as good as free . . . a healthy life of comradeship—that's the main thing. If one needs, say, tobacco, one borrows—if hungry, I go to a friend who has food and his larder is open to me—wallets—everything is shared. It's enough that I feel happy—today—the devil knows how it may be tomorrow! One's mood changes.
>
> The work's progressing—writing—but not to neglect one's studies! that's the problem I've undertaken to solve—and I will. "Erik" is doing pretty well—Act 1 complete (600 lines of verse)—to encourage my muse I have acquired companions for her—a society, founded by yours truly—called R (Rune = song) which this morning is to have its second meeting—when I am to make the opening speech—only 6 members yet . . . No word yet of the play, which is now called *Hermione*.

Strindberg was not being quite truthful in claiming to have founded the Rune Society himself; but at least he co-founded it, with two fellow students, Joseph Josephson and Axel Jäderin, leaders of his third circle of acquaintances. The membership, it was decided, should not exceed nine, and each member chose a rune, or character of the ancient Teutonic alphabet, as pseudonym—Strindberg's was Frö (Seed)—and wore a steel ring with his rune engraved on it. In the tradition of literary societies, they read their works to each other and were criticised, the first casualty resulting from this process, as far as Strindberg was concerned, being the "Erik" mentioned in his letter. This was to have been a five-act historical drama in verse about Erik XIV, that king who, after unsuccessfully proposing marriage to Queen Elizabeth I of England, murdered his barons in Uppsala Castle and was deposed and murdered himself. By the time his fellow-Runists condemned it, Strindberg had reached the middle of the third act, and it needed some courage to abandon it.[4*] Twenty-nine years later he was to return to the subject and to make of it one of his finest plays.

*In his autobiography, Strindberg claims sole credit for deciding that the play was unworthy of continuance and says he destroyed it before joining the Rune Society; "he found it bad and burned it, for self-criticism had now awoken in him and his demands on himself were greater" (SS, XVIII, p. 39). But see Carl Reinhold Smedmark's introduction to In Rome (*August Strindbergs dramer*, I, ed. Carl Reinhold Smedmark, Stockholm, 1962, p. 139).

Axel Jäderin recalled Strindberg at this period of his life as "so adolescent . . . gay and agreeable . . . but . . . easily became depressed and doubted his own ability . . . a restless seeker groping after self-knowledge and feeling his revolutionary strength stirring within him."[5] The following year he differed from the rest of them in sympathising with the Paris Commune. Jäderin describes Strindberg's verse attempts at Uppsala as "laboured," a description borne out by the specimens which have survived. He adds some interesting details on the young Strindberg's attitude towards women. "Strindberg was a favourite with the ladies at this time. His figure was stylish, his head interesting, and he had a certain elegance in his bearing which helped. But his chief attraction was his attitude towards them. He was always respectful, attentive and warm, without ever fawning. He did not flirt, but was certainly no misogynist, and respected women . . . Strindberg's way of life was very simple . . . I remember one term he limited his drinking to a toddy once a week on Saturday evenings. The other evenings he ate bread and milk and played backgammon . . . At 4 or 5 in the morning he would charge in and shake me awake, crying: 'Up, lazybones, let's get to work!' . . . He wore old clothes with such elegance that one didn't notice they were old . . . He had a guitar which he sang to . . . Fragilely sensitive . . . He won sympathy by his capacity for sympathy."[6]

An old classmate from the Lyceum named Gustaf Eisen was studying science at Uppsala, and Strindberg was in the habit of visiting him to peer through his microscope and learn about Darwin. Eisen proposed that Strindberg should fill the gap left by the abandonment of "Erik" by returning to the one-act verse comedy *In Rome* which he had begun in Stockholm the preceding autumn. Strindberg followed his advice and completed *In Rome* within a fortnight on 30 March,[7] a fact that he conveyed to his cousin Oscar two days later in a letter of over a thousand words written in breathlessly exhilarated snatches punctuated only by dashes. He asked Oscar to submit the play under a pseudonym to the Royal Theatre.

In June the Royal Theatre rejected *Hermione*. Undeterred, Strindberg rewrote it over the next couple of months, expanding it from three to five acts. The month of August brought two excitements. Thanks to the generosity of his cousin Oscar, who paid for the printing, *The Freethinker* was published under the pseudonym of Härved Ulf; even better, the Royal Theatre accepted *In Rome*. It was put into rehearsal at once, with a distinguished cast, and received its premiere on 13 September 1870 as part of a triple bill. Thus, for the first time Strindberg saw a play of his performed, and he found it a traumatic experience. "He crept up to the back of the gallery to stand and watch his play. The audience applauded now and then, but Johan knew that this came mostly from his family and friends and was not fooled by it." He was so embarrassed by the play's shortcomings that he left before the end. "The actors were good, the staging more atmospheric than he had dreamed it could be. Everything was good except the play. He ran down to the water and wanted to drown himself."[8]

Strindberg had arranged to meet his family and friends after the performance in the Hotel du Nord, next to the theatre. He saw them outside looking for him, but kept away. They went back to see the rest of the programme, which lasted for two hours. When this was over and the audience had disappeared, he saw a little group looking for him and calling his name.

> They congratulated him on his success . . . The verdict of the spectators who had sat near them was repeated. Eventually they calmed him, led him by the collar into the restaurant and forced him to eat and drink. Then they took him off to some girls . . . The next morning he went to the grocer's and bought a paper. He tore it open and read that the language of the play had been beautiful and that it was believed, for the author's name had not been revealed, to have been written by a well-known art critic . . . That cheered him somewhat. Around noon he returned to Uppsala.[9]

Strindberg was not always a good critic of his own work, but his assessment of *In Rome* was not far from the mark. It is a thin little piece that has never been professionally revived and does not deserve to be: the Danish sculptor Bertil Thorvaldsen, then young and unrecognised, has just completed what was to be accepted as his first masterpiece, a statue of Jason. His money has run out, and his father has ordered him to return home and take an honest job. His friend Pedersen tries to persuade him not to abandon his calling, but Thorvaldsen's belief in himself is uncertain. A French art lover enters and admires the statue, but when he opens his wallet it is only to offer Thorvaldsen his card and invite him to visit him in Paris. The Italian landlord demands his rent, is struck by Pedersen and summons the police. But at this crisis a rich Englishman enters, buys the statue, and that is that. It is the slightest of pieces, agreeably turned in rhymed couplets, lively and humorous enough in its dialogue but desperately short on plot. One's chief reaction on reading it today is amazement that any theatre could have thought it worth staging. But there was so little of any quality being written in the theatre then, not merely in Sweden but anywhere else outside Russia and Norway, that the directors of the Royal Theatre doubtless felt that even so faint a glimmer of promise as this was worthy of encouragement.

Nor were the reviews unsympathetic, though several commented on the "somewhat hasty ending." *Dagens Nyheter, Stockholms Dagblad, Aftonbladet* and *Ny Illustrerad Tidning* all, while noting the faults of the play, acclaimed its promise. It was performed eleven times, a fair number then, was printed in a "Library for Friends of the Theatre," which published plays for amateur performance, and brought Strindberg 258 riksdaler in royalties, enough to pay his living expenses at Uppsala for more than a term.

As it happened, he was less hard up than usual that term. For some unknown reason his father had agreed to pay his lodging expenses in Uppsala—probably not because of his success as a writer, since we know that Carl Oscar disapproved of this distraction from his studies. Strindberg had indeed promised his father that he would not write anything more before he had taken his exam. It may simply have been that Carl Oscar's situation had improved sufficiently for him to be able to afford this. His two elder sons were now employed, Axel in an insurance company and Oscar in the family shipping office, and were off his hands.

Carl Oscar arranged lodgings for August with a clergyman's widow conveniently near the university library. This proved unexpectedly rewarding, for students of all ages and every field of study lived there —theologians, medical students, lawyers and even women. But despite his promise to his father, Strindberg remained more interested in his play-writing than his studies. By the end of September he was working on a fifth play (his seventh if we include the abandoned efforts about Erik XIV and Jesus), a study of an eleventh-century usurper-king named Blot-Sven (Sven the Sacrificer), who sacrificed the future St. Eskil and was finally himself murdered. In setting his play in that remote period, Strindberg was following a recent trend in Scandinavian drama; Ibsen (*The Warrior's Barrow* and *The Vikings at Helgeland*) and Bjørnson (*Between the Battles*) had both written plays about the Viking age, and Strindberg, thanks to his Icelandic studies, was now able to read the great sagas in the original. Meanwhile, on 1 October he submitted his new five-act version of *Hermione* to the Swedish Academy's competition for new plays (it is not known whether he re-submitted it to the Royal Theatre). A reversal came on 9 November, when the Stockholm newspaper *Nya Dagligt Allehanda* published a mocking review of *The Freethinker* by one J. R. Spilhammar, who dismissed the play as "so remarkable for its inferiority in every respect that it scarcely merits any close attention."

During this autumn term Strindberg read for the first time Søren Kierkegaard, the Danish philosopher who had died in 1855 and whose

effect on Scandinavian thought in the sixties and seventies was considerable and widespread. Strindberg was especially interested in Kierkegaard's
denunciation of state religion on the ground that this was a matter for the
individual soul. Strindberg borrowed *Either/Or* from a friend and read it
"with fear and trembling." His reactions were mixed, "sometimes carried
away, yet always ill at ease, as though at a sickbed"; he found A *Seducer's
Diary* "the fantasies of an impotent or of a born onanist who had never in
his life seduced a girl." Strindberg continues:

> But Kierkegaard would not have affected him so deeply but for various
> coincidental circumstances. In *Letters of the Aesthete*, Kierkegaard
> preached the pleasure of suffering. Johan suffered from public mockery; he
> suffered from the hardness of his academic studies; he suffered from
> unrequited love; he suffered from unsatisfied sexual hunger, it being
> difficult in Uppsala to find girls; he suffered from alcohol, since he was
> drunk almost every second night; he suffered from spiritual conflicts and
> from doubt regarding his artistic vocation; he suffered from Uppsala and its
> ugly landscape; from his unpleasant lodgings; from his examination books;
> and from a bad conscience that he was not reading but writing. But beneath
> all this lay something else. He had been brought up to believe in hard
> work and duty. Now he was living well, without worries, and was in fact en-
> joying himself. His lower-class conscience stirred and told him it was not
> right to enjoy life while others were working, and he enjoyed his work
> because it brought him honour and perhaps gold. Hence his perpetually
> bad conscience nagged him.[10]

Another Danish writer excited Strindberg in 1870. The twenty-eight-
year-old Georg Brandes published his *Criticisms and Portraits*, and
Strindberg was especially struck by Brandes' demand that a writer, as
Strindberg put it, "should no longer be a mere buffoon indifferent to the
problems of his time. He should abandon dreams and enter the reality of
his age, thereby opening the way for what now goes under the name of
realism and naturalism."[11] Brandes was to repeat this demand even more
forcefully the following year, in a book that was powerfully to influence
both Ibsen and Strindberg.

Another considerable influence at this time, Strindberg claims, was
Victor Hugo, whose novels, with their message of rebellion against
society and against conventional religion, and their love of nature, closely
reflected Strindberg's own principal concerns.[12]

"I am damned happy—reading like a horse!" he wrote to his cousin
Oscar in September,[13] and a few days later in another letter he expressed
ill-punctuated puritanical disgust at the laziness of some of his fellows.
"Opposite live five students towards 10 a.m. they raise the blinds—toilet

and breakfast till 11 then they sit or lie on sofas till 2 when they go out and eat dinner what they do all morning I don't know they just sit and talk and smoke pipes—never a book seen in the day and never a light in the evening."[14] But his own reading was not as prescribed by the authorities. "Books are my only solace! I don't mean exam books but such as will give me inspiration for future work in the field which I intend to plough. Just now I'm so full of a plan for a Swedish historical tragedy in the romantic e.g. Hedberg's style that I shall have no peace till it's finished—but please no word of this—my conscience is eased by the conviction that I'm using my time to the best advantage!"[15]

This "historical tragedy" was *Sven the Sacrificer,* and on 13 October, Strindberg wrote excitedly to Frans Hedberg about its progress. "My background reading includes Icelandic . . . I work behind closed doors and rolled blinds—for I hate this city of pedantry and cramming, where strangely no life of the spirit can be traced."

But *Sven the Sacrificer* was destined never to be completed. That term a thirty-year-old student named Josef Linck joined the Rune brotherhood, "a little thin man . . . with a beer-stained filthy hat such as one saw on organ-grinders, a face like a Mediterranean rat-trap salesman, and black hair hanging down to his shoulders."[16] The others were amazed at his learning, although they never saw a book in his room; he became, in modern parlance, their guru. Strindberg gave him his new play to read; Linck said nothing about it directly, instead making suggestions for a new play reflecting his, Linck's, temperament. The result was that one evening Strindberg burned *Sven the Sacrificer,* of which he had written three acts out of a proposed five.

One morning Strindberg learned that a student friend of his had committed suicide by cutting his throat. A few days earlier, while Strindberg was writing in Caroline Park, this student had asked if he might speak to him. Strindberg had replied that he did not wish to be disturbed, and the youth had walked sadly away.

"Now the dead youth haunted Johan, and he did not dare to be alone in his room at night but slept with friends."[17] He contemplated suicide himself, how seriously we do not know. He got hold of some prussic acid; a friend who surprised him pretended to sympathise with the plan, but suggested that they drink a farewell glass together first, got Strindberg drunk and left him in a snowdrift. This seems to have cooled his desire for self-annihilation. When, at the end of term, his train steamed out of Uppsala "he breathed again. It was as though he had left behind him something ugly and hateful, like a Scandinavian night thirty degrees below zero, and he swore that he would never return to live in this town where souls exiled from life and from society seemed to rot from cerebral excess . . . to catch fire like millstones grinding emptiness."[18]

On returning home, he confessed to his father that he had wasted his time in Uppsala and begged permission to stay at home for the next three months to prepare for his spring examination. "This was granted, and he planned his campaign for the forthcoming term. First he would write Latin for a good teacher in Stockholm, then in the spring he would go back and pass his examination in that. And he would write a thesis for a *laudatur* in aesthetics and prepare for the examination in that subject."[19]

Five days before Christmas 1870 he learned that *Hermione* had won—not, alas, the prize, but an honourable mention in the Swedish Academy's play competition. The citation described it as "a study of the ancient world, containing good individual portraits and a vivid appreciation of the conditions then prevailing."[20] With a humility that he seldom manifested later in life, least of all in his relations with the Swedish Academy, he went along to ask for a detailed criticism of the play. The secretary of the Academy, Count Ludvig Manderström, who as foreign minister had first advocated, then deprecated Swedish intervention in the matter of Prussia's invasion of Denmark in 1864 (thus incurring the wrath of Ibsen, who drew a halter round the count's neck in an illustrated magazine in the Scandinavian Club in Rome as a protest) gave his impressions of the young author in a letter to Carl Wilhelm Böttiger:

> The author of *Hermione* has presented himself . . . The guilty party's name is Strindberg, a student of the Stockholm fraternity at Uppsala, 21 years old, son of Strindberg the steamship commissioner. He looks pleasant and modest and says he wants to be criticised so as to become aware of his shortcomings. He is apparently the author of a little verse play which has been performed here, *In Rome*—an episode from Thorvaldsen's youth which won some approval, but struck me as rather weak and undramatic, though not without a certain facility of dialogue.[21]

Encouraged by this success, Strindberg decided to take a couple of weeks off from his studies (after all, it was Christmas) and rewrite *Sven the Sacrificer* as a one-act play in prose. This he completed in two weeks.[22] He called it *The Outlaw*, probably basing it on Bjørnson's short play *Between the Battles* (later he was to say he had written it "in the Norwegian manner").[23] On 2 February he visited Uppsala for a meeting of the Rune Society, read it to them and won their approval; he also offered it to Frans Hedberg at the Royal Theatre, who "liked it very much and suggested only one alteration."[24] He was reading a good deal more Kierkegaard; that February he borrowed no less than twelve volumes of his work from the Royal Library in Stockholm.[25]

An unexpected relief of his financial situation now occurred, and from an unexpected source. Two of his old classmates from Stockholm Lyceum, Gustaf Eisen and Georg Törnqvist (the latter a young actor with whom Strindberg had often watched plays from the gallery of the Royal Theatre in the spring of 1869 when he was tutoring at the Lamms'), decided to offer Strindberg enough money for him either to finish his studies or to devote himself to authorship. Even more generously, they planned to do this anonymously. "Decide soon how we can best send him the first instalment without anyone betraying our secret," wrote Törnqvist to Eisen on 15 February 1871.[26] They offered it to him by letter over a joint pseudonym, Alessandro Florelli. Nine days later Törnqvist wrote again to Eisen:

> He has for some time now been less cheerful, gave up the idea of having the Royal Theatre stage his last play and even thought of burning it, but luckily did not. These perpetually recurring paroxysms of depression and despair will not leave him. His sombre and melancholy temper makes it impossible for him to bear a reversal of fortune with calm and self-control, he takes everything more deeply than is needful . . . He mentioned that he had now found a patron who had anonymously offered him support . . . [but] the money had been offered as help for him to complete his exam, something which he did not wish to commit himself to do in the shortest possible time. This would mean his living in Uppsala, where he cannot be happy . . . He wanted freedom to go on trying to write plays or read for an exam as seemed best to him but would feel grateful if support could be offered to him on such conditions or unconditionally . . . I leave it to you to reply to his letter as you think best. Personally I regard it as unimportant whether his knowledge receives official recognition or not.[27]

In the event, Strindberg compromised by deciding to read for his exam but to do so in Stockholm. "Unknown benefactor!" he wrote to "Alessandro Florelli" around 1 March. ". . . Three terms in Uppsala have revealed to me Uppsala life in all its helpless misery—its dissipation of time and energy—I am not of a weak nature, but I fear Uppsala."[28]

So he stayed in the capital, returning briefly to Uppsala in April to take his written examination in Latin which, despite a disagreement with his professor, he passed. In June he presented his aesthetics thesis, choosing as his subject the Danish playwright Adam Oehlenschläger's tragedy *Earl Haakon*, which Oehlenschläger, a friend and disciple of Goethe and Schiller, had written in 1805 at the age of twenty-five. It is a curious choice for Strindberg to have made, for *Earl Haakon* is a static, old-fashioned play of exactly the kind that Ibsen had tried to get away from when he wrote *Brand* and *Peer Gynt*, and Strindberg's thesis reads as though it had been written by someone with no practical knowledge of the theatre at all. "Why is the greatest singer in Scandinavia no longer read? Why are his tragedies no longer played here? Of the twenty-six, only five are even in print here in Sweden." He goes on to describe *Earl Haakon* as "the most interesting, the most moving, the most effective tragedy I have ever read. Even, dare I say it, Shakespeare seems to me dry in comparison with Oehlenschläger." One especial advantage of Oehlenschläger, Strindberg continues, is that "his plays leave one with a feeling of peace, whereas Shakespeare leaves one in a state of deep disturbance when the curtain has fallen on the final act,"[29] an extraordinary judgement from the future author of *The Father* and *Miss Julie*. Even thus early in his career it is surprising to find Strindberg taking so conventional a view of tragedy. This very argument was later to be used as a stick by critics to belabour both him and Ibsen.

It is not a very good thesis, rather an enthusiastic eulogy, and his interview with his Professor, C. R. Nyblom, was not a success. Nyblom, who, Strindberg admits, was regarded as a liberal and humane man, "handed back the thesis with a near-contemptuous expression, remarking that it was more suitable reading for the lady subscribers to *Ny Illustrerad Tidning* [an illustrated cultural magazine], and that Danish literature was not of sufficient interest to serve as a subject for specialised study . . . Johan was offended and retorted that he thought Danish literature was of more interest to Sweden than such writers as Malherbe and Boileau. The result was that he received a lesser mark than he had hoped for."[30]

During this time, Strindberg's relationship with his father had taken a turn for the better. He says (and it seems unlikely that he would have lied on this matter) that, living at home this spring, he "spent many hours in the evenings discussing all life's questions with him."[31] He even persuaded the old man to read Thomas Parker, the American Unitarian evangelist whose teachings still influenced Strindberg, and heard through one of his brothers that Carl Oscar had been impressed, though he was too proud to admit it. But they had a row, and as a result Strindberg left home in June to spend three months in the skerries preparing for his modern-languages examination in the autumn. Before leaving, he wrote to his cousin Oscar:

> I have arranged board and lodging with a farmer on Ornö, outside Dalarö, for 30 riksdaler a month, for the situation here at home grows daily worse and I have boldly decided to go straight back in August to Uppsala, whence I shall not return until I have taken my degree . . . If I can't stick it out in Uppsala . . . then—I'll take a room in Stockholm, any damn where, except at home—where the old man refuses to think of me as anything but a

child. But it's strange that I shall miss that home when I leave it, perhaps for ever—it pains me to think of leaving it just for two months—blood is thicker than water after all, and family bonds do exist—at least between us brothers and sisters. *The Outlaw* has been accepted, on condition that I rework it a bit—Hedberg wanted them to do it at once, but the other board members . . . decided not . . . Anyway I'm going to work on the play enough at least so that people won't have to sit and yawn and when the final curtain comes down ask if that's the end—for it's pretty short![32]

As things turned out, he stayed, not on Ornö but outside, on Kymmendö, an island which was to play an important part in his life. He lodged at a fisherman's together with three friends from the Rune Society, Eugène Fahlstedt, Joseph Josephson and Arvid Wikström. His decision to continue his studies at Uppsala instead of at home meant that the modest support of "Alessandro Florelli" would not suffice, and in July he wrote two pathetic begging letters to Oscar Seippel and John Fredrik Rossander, both wholesale dealers, the former a childhood friend, the latter a former employer of his cousin Oscar, asking for help to see him through the next two terms. "Will you invest 300 riksdaler in a young man's future?" he asked Seippel,[33] which seems a lot considering that he had managed to survive his first term on barely a quarter of that sum, and had the Florelli money besides. In August he posted his revised version of *The Outlaw* to Hedberg at the Royal Theatre.

His begging letters were evidently unsuccessful, for his poverty when he returned to Uppsala at the beginning of September was extreme even by undergraduate standards. After camping out with five different friends, plus three nights at a cheap hotel, he eventually managed to acquire a room—"a pigeon-hole with a camp-bed, lacking sheets or pillow-cases. No candlestick, nothing. But he lay in bed in his underclothes and read with a candle in a bottle. Now and then friends brought him food." There was no heating apart from a chimney-pipe "which was warm every Thursday, when they did the washing."[34] "These two and a half weeks have been the bloodiest I've known," he wrote to his cousin Oscar in mid-September (he had a maddening habit at this time of heading his letters with the month but not the date), "as regards all the troubles and tribulations,"

but the pleasantest in that I've never in my life felt such energy and high spirits united with a mental excitement which hasn't relaxed for a moment —yes, I haven't had one attack from the evil spirit—although I have six (6) times removed my luggage—consisting of my toothbrush and a tallow candle—from one place to the next . . . I congratulate myself on having outgrown such childishnesses as not being able to read or be happy without having my own desk my inkwell and my pipe—I've been reading like mad and had tutorials from two crones and a half-crazy old college hack—who must now be paid—so I haven't had time to think and still enjoy an extraordinarily fresh sense of calm—   Have scrounged a shilling here and a shilling there, so I haven't starved—   At length weary of sleeping half-dressed on sofas I acquired a room—or rather a hole—which exudes a magnifique smell of suicide, so my friends assert. I hadn't seen how awful it was, but am damned happy although (see illustration) the window looks on to a wall twenty feet away—   The room has two great advantages 1 the chimney-pipe which admittedly makes the hole a bit misshapen—but keeps it warm all day—a great advantage since otherwise it's only 5 or 6 above zero—God it's cold here—2 the view over the rooftops to the cathedral tower—which last as you can imagine I especially rejoice in. [35]

On 19 September he sat his examination in modern languages, comprising German, English, French and Italian, and passed with *approbatur*. Next day Georg Törnqvist wrote to Gustaf Eisen: "Yesterday we had a rehearsal of August's piece [*The Outlaw*]. I think it a notably beautiful play in which the author gives great hope for the future of our drama . . . I am convinced that our mutual friend has a great future. His rich talent combined with his huge capacity for work could achieve this."[36]

Somehow Strindberg now discovered the true identity of Alessandro Florelli. By the end of September a black mood had replaced his earlier euphoria, possibly because he had done less well than expected in his examination, possibly due to that natural cycle of moods which was to torment him throughout his life. "Visit him often and try to soothe this ill-omened melancholy which now seems to rule him," wrote Törnqvist to Eisen on 2 October.[37] At least Strindberg did not turn on his benefactors as he was sometimes later to do. He wrote and thanked them individually and warmly.

On 16 October *The Outlaw* received its premiere at the Royal Theatre. Unlike *In Rome*, it was poorly received; *Aftonbladet* noted that not a hand was raised in applause, and *Post- och Inrikes Tidningar* observed that "the chill which permeates the play transmitted itself to the audience." Although some critics praised individual scenes, the general objection was that the characters were "unsympathetic," a complaint that was to be levelled at Strindberg's best plays throughout his life (as against many of Ibsen's plays when they first appeared, notably *The Wild Duck* and *Hedda Gabler*).

The Outlaw is set in Iceland in the twelfth century. A heathen and fiercely anti-Christian chieftain, Thorfinn, despises reliance on God and trusts in his own strength. On a voyage to Norway to raise men to help him become master of Iceland, his fleet is destroyed in a storm. When he returns, his daughter Gunlöd tells him that she has become a Christian; he also hears that he has been proclaimed an outlaw for his misdeeds, so that any man may kill him with impunity. As his enemies surround his house to burn it, he realises that no man can be self-sufficient and accepts the Christian faith before he goes out to be killed.

The Outlaw does not really work as a play for the same reason that Ibsen's early play set in the same period, *The Vikings at Helgeland*, does not work. Both dramatists attempted to write dialogue that was a pastiche of the simple yet highly formalised style of the Icelandic sagas, and the result in both cases was impossibly unnatural. Ibsen's play was successful in his lifetime because audiences then did not seek nor wish to identify with characters onstage, but rather to admire them as superhuman beings like the characters in Wagner. But *The Vikings in Helgeland* was Ibsen's eighth play; he was twenty-nine when he wrote it, had spent six years directing plays in the theatre and was approaching maturity as a dramatist. *The Outlaw* is very much an apprentice work, and Strindberg's modernism of outlook and his natural style, which he had described in a letter to his cousin Oscar the previous year as "telegraphese,"[38] clashed with the Homeric simplicity of his characters and the saga style. These ancients keep breaking into modern speech and modern thought. This makes it fascinating study for a reader who knows what Strindberg was to write in the future, but despite its moments of power and insight it remains a broken-backed and operatic play, the more so because of Strindberg's inability to avoid melodramatic phrases and situations, a fault he was never totally to overcome even in his best work.

The Outlaw managed only six performances, but it acquired one important admirer. "The King is the only person who likes this tragedy," noted the head of the theatre, Erik af Edholm, in his diary;[39] and a week after the premiere Strindberg was astonished to receive a letter in Uppsala from the Royal Chamberlain informing him that the King wished to see him and requesting him to travel forthwith to Stockholm. At first he supposed this to be a hoax; he took the letter to a friend who telegraphed to an actor he knew at the Royal Theatre asking him to check with the Chamberlain. The reply came that the letter was genuine; so Strindberg took the train to Stockholm and was received by King Charles XV, a merry monarch who was much loved, had loved much and was now, in his forty-sixth year, dying of tuberculosis (and, some said, syphilis). Strindberg described the audience:

> The King was by now very sick, looked emaciated and shrunken, so that
> he made a painful impression. He stood mildly with his long tobacco pipe

and, smiling, watched the young beardless author enter through the rows of equerries and chamberlains. He expressed his gratitude for the pleasure the play had given him. He himself in his youth had competed for the Academy with a Viking poem and liked the olden times. Now he wished to help the young student to get his degree, and he ended the audience by showing Johan down to the court chancellery, where he had arranged for the first payment [of 200 riksdaler] to take place. There would be more later; he assumed that Johan had a couple more years before taking his degree.[40]

At the end of that autumn term of 1871, Strindberg took his examinations in philology, astronomy and political science, but in each subject got a class lower than he had hoped. Thus discouraged, he would have liked to leave Uppsala, to concentrate on his writing and, hopefully, earn a living by it; but his acceptance of the royal stipend made this impossible. He began to read philosophy, but could work up no enthusiasm for it. He took up painting, and made another attempt to get on the stage; seeing that a travelling theatrical company was visiting Uppsala, he wrote asking for an audition but received no answer. He moved from the dismal room on Järnbrogatan across the river to Svartbäcksgatan 4, where he shared with a student named Hugo Philp who was later to become his brother-in-law and one of his kindest benefactors.

On 27 October, a few days after his audience with the King, Strindberg borrowed from the Caroline Library at Uppsala a biography of Olaus Petri, the sixteenth-century Swedish disciple of Martin Luther. Some time before the end of the year he completed the first draft of a play about this character. In due course it was to become his first great play, *Master Olof*.

In *Time of Ferment*, his account of his student years, Strindberg implies that this autumn term of 1871 was his last at Uppsala and that after the encouragement of the royal stipend nothing good happened to him before he left. On 8 December, however, the Stockholm evening paper *Aftonbladet* published a most sympathetic review of *The Outlaw*, condemning the general dullness of the repertory at the Royal Theatre but naming this, "an original Swedish play by a young Herr Strindberg, student," as a promising exception, declaring that the author deserved every encouragement. The following day *Hermione* was published, thanks to the generosity of Strindberg's cousin Oscar, who paid the cost, just as twenty-one years earlier a student friend of the young Ibsen, Ole Schulerud, had paid for the publication of Ibsen's first play, *Catiline*. The publisher of *Hermione* was a former classmate of Strindberg's at the Lyceum, Isidor Bonnier, who in 1867 at the age of nineteen had taken over his father Adolf Bonnier's publishing house; Adolf's more famous brother, Albert, was to figure prominently in Strindberg's life. *Hermione* appeared anonymously, as *In Rome* had, and was not widely reviewed, but *Aftonbladet*, while admitting that as a play it was suited only for reading, found it one of the most interesting items in the flood of Christmas publications and prophesied that the author "will be heard of again." How many writers could claim, before their twenty-third birthday, to have had two plays performed at their country's leading theatre, one of them honoured by praise and a stipend from the King, and a third play published and praised by the national literary academy and a leading newspaper?

To give a further lie to Strindberg's account: he returned to Uppsala in January 1872 for the spring term. Around the beginning of February, three months having elapsed since the first payment of the royal stipend, he wrote to the palace asking if the second payment might be expedited. He received a reply that "there had never been any question of regular payments, His Majesty having merely intended to make the one gracious gesture; however, in view of Herr Strindberg's needy circumstances, an additional *ex gratia* sum of 200 riksdaler would be sent to him."[41]

Strindberg's feelings on receiving this news must have been mixed. No doubt he reflected bitterly on the whimsicality of kings. But at least this meant that he need no longer stay at Uppsala. On 2 March his friends gave a farewell party for him, and the following day he left the hated city for ever to seek his living in Stockholm as a writer.

Chapter Four

ᷡᷡᷡᷡᷡᷡᷡᷡᷡᷡᷡᷡᷡᷡᷡᷡᷡᷡᷡᷡᷡᷡᷡᷡᷡᷡᷡ

MASTER OLOF

By 14 March 1872, within twelve days of leaving Uppsala, Strindberg had settled at Grev Magnigatan 7, on the southwest corner of Stockholm near the park of Djurgården. His room, as he later described it, was "very poor, with no outlook. It smelt of poverty, like the whole house."[1]

Journalism was the first field to which he turned; not, characteristically, to one of the established newspapers but to "a new little evening paper which claimed to be radical," *Stockholms Aftonpost*. On 14 March he had an article published in its columns entitled "Why Has Our Capital Still No Free University?" using the opportunity to attack the outdated methods of teaching and general somnolence of Uppsala. He also tried his hand at art criticism; in the same newspaper, on 21 and 27 March, he discussed two recent and controversial paintings by Swedish artists, M. E. Winge's "Thor's Battle with the Titans" and Georg von Rosen's "Erik XIV and Karin Månsdotter," the sixteenth-century king and his working-class mistress about whom Strindberg had begun but abandoned a play two years earlier.

Strindberg was still receiving financial support from Törnqvist and Eisen; on 14 March, Törnqvist wrote to Eisen underlining the importance of letting "our friend see that Florelli, although not a king, has not yet forgotten him; recent events show that kings have bad memories. It is deeply distressing that August should, for lack of means, have been unable to complete his examinations when so near his goal."[2] In an undated letter to Eisen later that month describing his journalistic activity, Strindberg informed him that he had completed another article, about the novelist Wilhelmina Ståhlberg, for a magazine, *Svalan,* "and am working on two short stories as well as reading for my journeyman-play [*Master Olof*]."[3] He did not set much store by this journalism. "Don't say anything about it," he begged Eisen in the same letter, "for I don't want these rough scribblings to be thought of as successors to *The Outlaw*—I only throw off this rubbish to earn bread so as to be able to write plays." His journalism was, he said, earning him 10 riksdaler a column, "which is good money." He planned further articles for *Stockholms Aftonpost*, but unluckily it ran into financial difficulties and ceased publication on 15 May.

He was also painting vigorously, though as a relaxation rather than as a serious means of self-expression. "He had no thought of *becoming* a painter, exhibiting and selling," he wrote of himself. "To go to the easel was like sitting down and singing."[4] He made friends with several painters. "They wore long hair, slouch hats, gaudy scarves and lived like birds in the sky. They read and quoted Byron, and dreamed of canvases with subjects so huge that no studio had yet been built which could house them . . . The thing was to paint one's inner self and not draw sticks and stones . . . So they didn't study out of doors but painted at home, from memory and imagination." He himself "always painted the sea, with the coast in the foreground: gnarled pines, a few naked rocks in the distance, a white beacon, a sea-mark, a buoy. The sky was usually overcast, with a faint or a strong light on the horizon; sunsets or moonlight; never clear day."[5]

He was happier among these painters than among his fellow journalists. "Among them he felt a stranger. They didn't think as he did, seemed uneducated, which they were; gossiped more than they talked about serious things. Oh, they were concerned with reality, but with the day's trivia rather than big questions . . . He was, despite himself, too much of a university elitist to be able to sympathise with these democrats, who had not chosen their profession but, like most people, had been thrown into it."[6] Seven years later he was to paint a vivid description of these contrasting circles in his novel *The Red Room*.

That spring he read two books which greatly excited him, Thomas Henry Buckle's *History of Civilization* and the opening volume of Georg Brandes' *Main Currents of Nineteenth-Century Literature*. Buckle, an Englishman, had died ten years previously at the age of forty, leaving his huge project unfinished, but the two volumes which he completed had a widespread international impact. What particularly interested Strindberg was Buckle's left-wing bias and his insistence on the power of ordinary human beings, as opposed to that of kings and warriors, in shaping history. Brandes' book had appeared that February; its theme, as stated in the introduction, was "the revolution waged by the first decades of the nineteenth century against the literature of the eighteenth, and the victory of that revolution," as reflected in French, English and German literature up to 1848; in other words, the gradual victory of liberal ideas through such writers as Byron, Hugo, Lamartine and Heine. Among other things, Brandes demanded that writers should live in the present and future instead of in the past, and should deal with contemporary social problems. The book greatly excited Ibsen, who was then midway through *Emperor and Galilean*, and influenced him to treat of just such contemporary problems in his next four plays, *The Pillars of Society*, *A Doll's House*, *Ghosts* and *An Enemy of the People*. "A more dangerous book could never fall into the hands of a pregnant writer," Ibsen assured Brandes from Dresden on 4 April. "It is one of those books which set a yawning gulf between yesterday and today . . . Is our spiritual constitution in the North strong enough to survive this shock? I don't know; but it doesn't matter. Whatever cannot sustain these new ideas must fall."[7]

Strindberg had tried to deal with contemporary social problems in *The Freethinker* three years earlier, but not in any play since. Brandes' book was as much a revelation to him as it was to Ibsen; he wrote to Eugène Fahlstedt that May that Brandes "must have ascended Mount Everest . . . because only thence could a man see as far as he does."[8] But what theatre would accept a play with a modern setting that attempted to deal with contemporary problems? Not only Ibsen's modern dramas, but Bjørnson's too (which anticipated Ibsen's) lay in the future; Bjørnson was not to write *The Editor* and *A Bankrupt* until 1874, nor Ibsen *The Pillars of Society* until 1877. (Strindberg in a later essay was to describe Bjørnson's two plays as "signal rockets."[9]) The fashion in Sweden as elsewhere in Scandinavia was for historical plays, and it was through this medium, Strindberg felt, that he must deal with the problems that bothered him. Had he not, in his preliminary notes for *Master Olof* the previous December, written of the need to "arouse God's kingdom" and to combat "the spiritually dead"?[10]

In June he went to Kymmendö, the island in the Stockholm skerries where he had spent the preceding summer. Eugène Fahlstedt again accompanied him, as did two other Uppsala friends, Hugo Philp and Algot Lange. He stayed there two months and, between 8 June and 8

August, completed *Master Olof*, using, in his own words, "simple, everyday speech such as people use off the stage."[11] Into the character of the troubled young priest he poured his own problems: the dilemma of the young who wish to revolutionise society and pull down what is old and dead, yet who shrink from violence and from a violent death. "You were born to make men angry," says one of the characters to Olof in the opening scene. "You were born to fight." Olof defies the might of the established church. The young king, Gustav Vasa, recruits him as a weapon against that establishment. But in his new official position, Olof finds the King an establishment figure against whom he feels compelled to rebel, as against the Church, and when Gert, a seasoned old revolutionary who is Olof's father-figure, plans to assassinate the King, Olof joins the conspiracy. They are discovered and condemned to death; Gert welcomes martyrdom as the best way to advance the cause of radicalism, but Olof allows himself to be persuaded that he can achieve more as a living new Luther (which, historically, he indeed did). In a magnificent final scene a young follower, ignorant that Olof has recanted, kneels to him in the pillory and blesses him for choosing martyrdom while Gert, on his way to the block, cries the final word of the play: "Apostate!"

Master Olof is arguably as astounding a play as was ever written by a dramatist of twenty-three, except Büchner's *Woyzeck* and *Danton's Death*; vividly characterised, sharply written, and told in a series of swift and powerful scenes rising to a superb climax. It has the usual young playwright's defect of verbosity; played uncut, it would run for four hours or more; and for non-Swedish audiences it presents a problem that was to recur in all Strindberg's historical plays, the presupposition of a basic background knowledge that few non-Swedes possess. To work in any other country it needs a good deal of adaptation. But it is full of fire and eloquence, and in one respect, it surpasses Strindberg's more mature plays: the minor characters are all sharply drawn and worth playing, which cannot be said for many of the minor characters in *The Father*, *The Dance of Death* and *To Damascus*. And, to repeat what is often forgotten, it anticipated Ibsen's "contemporary" plays; it was written five years before *The Pillars of Society* and seven years before *A Doll's House*. If it had been accepted and adequately performed, what plays might Strindberg not have written in the next decade and a half? As things turned out, its rejection turned him away from the theatre towards the novel and the short story, and it was to be fifteen years before he wrote another play that mattered.

Strindberg was so short of money when he finished *Master Olof* that, although his share of the rent of the cottage was no more than 1.75

riksdaler a day, he had to borrow from his friends to pay it. It was not the only writing he did at Kymmendö. A few months earlier he had met another member of the Bonnier family, Isidor's uncle Albert, who had his own publishing house. Strindberg asked Albert Bonnier if he could give him any work, and Bonnier sent three short English children's books for him to translate—"to be kept in a childish style and language," Bonnier instructed him. "You may adapt them as freely as you like."[12] His three sisters visited him on the island, with their stepmother as duenna, and it proved an important visit for one of them, for Anna Strindberg and Hugo Philp fell in love and in due course married.

On his return to Stockholm in the autumn, Strindberg wrote an article on "Life in the Stockholm Skerries" which appeared in *Dagens Nyheter* on 4 September and for which he was paid 20 riksdaler. Lorentz Dietrichson, a Norwegian art critic then living in Stockholm, did him a good turn by persuading Albert Bonnier to let him translate several of his magazine articles on art history. But Strindberg was gloomy about the prospects for his latest play. On 30 September he wrote a long and depressed letter to Eugène Fahlstedt:

> I am already fed up with *Master Olof*! It's no good. I've only read it to four people and they all fell asleep . . . I have some commissions: an Icelandic novel for *Handelstidningen* [the leading Gothenburg paper] and a short story for Bonnier about Charles XV, but I can't do either, for I don't want to! . . . I'm tired, that's all I know . . . Today I read [Byron's] *Manfred*; it was great and somewhat reconciled me with the past . . . I can't afford to write and if I could afford it I'm convinced it would meet the same fate as *Master Olof*. *Master Olof* is being fair-copied but I can't collect it till I have the cash. Anyway I'm certain the theatre will refuse it, though Hedberg said it was a "powerful" work, which for a moment flattered me.

Strindberg's fears proved right; the Royal Theatre did refuse *Master Olof*. Their decision is not surprising; the qualities that make it admired today, the sharp modernity of its dialogue and characterisation, were regarded as unsuitable for a play about ancient heroes. Admittedly, Ibsen had demonstrated precisely these qualities in *The Pretenders* nine years earlier, but *The Pretenders* was not to be performed in Sweden until 1879. Poetry was still regarded as the only possible medium for stage tragedy, not only in Sweden but throughout the Western world. The play lacked the declamatory monologues which audiences, and actors, expected, and the humanness, the five-feet-six quality of the famous historical figures, bothered them; they wanted to see, and act, giants. The subtle relationships, too, needed the kind of acting which would emerge later in the century with Stanislavsky and Duse. Although Strindberg was to rewrite *Master Olof* twice in an effort to compromise with popular taste, the play had to wait nine years before it was staged, and then, ironically enough, in the original version. It was an experience with which Strindberg was to become increasingly familiar; several of his finest plays were to meet a similar, or worse, fate.

In his dejection Strindberg sought to try his luck again as an actor. He went to Gothenburg, where his cousin Ludvig worked at the Grand Theatre as both actor and translator, and applied for a position in the company there. Strindberg disliked Gothenburg, "dark, correct, expensive, pompous, withdrawn."[13] For his audition, he chose the role of the Scottish railway pioneer George Stephenson in Lorentz Dietrichson's currently successful play *A Worker*.

> He had found a certain resemblance between Stephenson's locomotive and his own rejected play, and hoped to be able to give true expression to the engineer's contempt for the mockery of the mob, the apprehension of intellectuals and his family's grief at a wasted existence . . . He auditioned one afternoon by gaslight in an empty room. Naturally, he could achieve no stature. He felt it himself and asked to be allowed to rehearse in costume. No, it was not necessary. The director had heard enough. There was talent but it needed development. He was offered an engagement from 1 January at a salary of 1,200 crowns. Johan considered: to kick his heels in Gothenburg for two months and then act servants or peasants at a provincial theatre? But what alternative was there? To borrow money and return home. Which he did.[14]

So the year ended and things looked black.

The new year, 1873, began with Strindberg accepting a most improbable job: the editorship of an insurance periodical, *Svensk försäkringstidning*. One Otto Samson had founded an insurance company called Pole Star; he asked Albert Bonnier to arrange some form of publicity, and Strindberg accepted the commission. He wrote a naïve little story in which a girl is persuaded of the benefits of life insurance, as un-Strindbergian a piece as he was ever to pen, and it so delighted Samson that he invited Strindberg to edit the new magazine. He was to devote most of the next seven months to this work. "The paper appeared twice a month, expensively printed and carefully edited. It was a somewhat arduous task to study the subject, write the entire magazine, arrange the printing, correct the proofs and see to the distribution . . . He had to live as befitted his new station, be correctly dressed, and pay for the printing, paper and advertisements, leaving himself 1,000 crowns a year for his work as editor, editorial staff, proofcorrector and distributor."[15] The first issue of the magazine appeared on 15 February 1873.

Strindberg found the subject of insurance interesting. He had to meet and interview the directors of the various insurance companies, thus obtaining his first real glimpse into the world of commerce. For a time the magazine went well enough. But that spring Strindberg read a pamphlet published the previous year by an English Member of Parliament, Samuel Plimsoll, against "coffinships," the practice by unscrupulous shipowners of overloading unseaworthy vessels and heavily insuring them. Plimsoll's famous denunciation in Parliament of such shipowners as murderers and of the politicians who supported them as scoundrels lay two years in the future, but Strindberg was sufficiently impressed by the pamphlet to write in the May issue of his magazine a hostile article about these practices, being careful to limit his targets to English and German shipowners. One might suppose that such views would have coincided with those of his sponsors, since it was the insurers, after the unfortunate crews and their families, who suffered most from this policy. But whether they felt that their young editor was of too independent a temper to edit a journal the main purpose of which was advertisement, or whether it was not paying its way, *Svensk försäkringstidning* ceased publication on 31 July after eleven issues.

Strindberg spent that summer, like the previous two, on Kymmendö, but seems to have done no writing there apart from translating an unidentified English book for Bonnier and writing captions to illustrations for a magazine called *Svea*. On 12 October he took a job as apprentice at the telegraph office in Sandhamn, also in the skerries. This was to have a surprising result. A week after his arrival a ship was wrecked offshore, and Strindberg wrote a vivid piece about the incident which was printed in *Dagens Nyheter* on 3 and 4 December. As a result, he was taken onto the permanent staff of the paper.

He worked there for five months, writing artistic, dramatic and literary criticism, reporting parliamentary debates, translating snippets of news from foreign newspapers, and much besides. He found himself a mistress, a waitress named Ida Charlotta Olsson. We know almost nothing about her; according to Strindberg "she called herself Mrs., claimed to be married but childless; one never saw her husband."[16] Their relationship continued for over a year and was to end, like most of Strindberg's relationships with women, in hysteria and recrimination.

In May 1874 Strindberg's employment with *Dagens Nyheter* ended. The editor, Rudolf Wall, criticised his style of writing as being too literary for the requirements of a daily newspaper, especially in his translation work. For a while he worked for a rival newspaper, *Svenska Medborgaren*, the organ of the Farmers' Party, which appeared twice weekly; but he was not happy there and wrote to Wall asking if he might write again for *Dagens Nyheter*. Wall wrote him a kindly letter saying that he had never wanted Strindberg to leave, but "as regards whether you could translate the C-pieces I could not truthfully answer anything but No, since you had just insisted that you did not *want* to translate them like other people. Now, firstly, translation is nothing to be ashamed of, and secondly it is not easy to translate these C-pieces because it requires pretty well the whole gamut of human knowledge. Write!"[17] Strindberg replied, accepting the rebuke and adding: "It was my curious way of writing that bothered me and it has convinced me that I do not write like ordinary people."[18] He recommenced writing for *Dagens Nyheter* as a free-lance; this association was to continue for many years.

He had spent the winter living with his brother Axel on Djurgården, but during the spring he found a room in an eighteenth-century house at Kaptensgatan 18 (now 5) near the centre of the city. It was an attic, but commanded a fine view over the harbour, beyond which he could see a new theatre rising. It was, in fact, called the New Theatre, and was to play an important role in his life.

In July, Iceland celebrated the thousandth anniversary of the first landings there, and Strindberg, with his by now considerable interest in that country and its ancient literature, asked *Dagens Nyheter* and *Handels-tidningen i Göteborg* for an assignment to cover the celebrations. But nothing came of this; a pity, for with his keen eye for landscape he would surely have found that remarkable country inspiring. He offered his play *The Outlaw* to the Grand Theatre in Gothenburg; they accepted it, but for some reason never staged it, a chain of events with which he was to become increasingly familiar.

His main creative occupation during 1874 was to complete his rewrite of *Master Olof*, which he managed to do on 3 December after over two years' work. Seldom can any rewrite have been so inferior to the original. If the Royal Theatre, to whom he now sent it, had handed the original to one of their hack dramatists such as Frans Hedberg and asked him to remodel it to suit their audiences, the result would have approximated to what Strindberg had now produced. The passion and originality are gone, replaced by heavy platitudinous moralising; the sharp outlines of the characters have become blurred. Although it is still in prose, it is a much less exciting prose. The whole effect is as though Strindberg had deliber-ately set out to show the debilitating result of abandoning one's beliefs. The Royal Theatre rejected it, and Strindberg sent it to Edvard Stjern-ström at the New Theatre.

Meanwhile, he took another job, as assistant librarian in the Royal Library, which he had used a good deal as a reader. The library was then situated in the northeast wing of the palace. Normally, a university degree would have been an obligatory qualification for a post there, and Strindberg had none. But in March he had published two articles in *Svenska Medborgaren* praising the library and appealing for it to be granted greater economic support. The articles especially extolled the efforts of the chief librarian, Gustaf Klemming, and this no doubt helped to get him accepted.

Strindberg was to spend eight years in this post; from all accounts he liked the work and was conscientious in performing it. To those who know him only through such works as *The Father* and *Miss Julie*, this may seem surprising, but there was another side to Strindberg, that of an insatiable reader and researcher into varied fields of knowledge, and to this aspect of him, working in a library must have been meat and drink. The conditions under which the staff worked before the library moved to its present home in Humlegården were, however, appalling. The rooms were lofty, cramped, dirty and overcrowded, containing six kilometres of books. A contemporary engraving shows a scene of extraordinary chaos, with staff and readers seated, standing and leaning shoulder to shoulder as they read, catalogued or made notes. There was no heating, and in winter the temperature indoors would drop to minus twelve degrees. It was open only five days a week, and then from eleven to two. Young men often worked at several such institutions simultaneously for tiny part-time salaries.[19] Robert Geete, who worked there with Strindberg, recalled that the floors and galleries were piled with books waiting to be reshelved "which because of the cold and the lack of manpower sometimes took weeks or even months."[20]

Strindberg's salary was pathetically small; in 1875 he earned 180 crowns, in 1876 140 crowns, in 1877 150 crowns.[21]* His work, to begin with, consisted of handing out books to borrowers, writing to publishers who had failed to send copies of new books, and cataloguing and arranging a large bequest that had been donated by Count Lars von Engeström. In time he was also given control of printing assignments. Johan Mortensen, who knew Strindberg at this time, writes that he had a "respect bordering on fear" for his boss, Klemming, who "with his tall figure and powerful features surrounded by bushy grizzled hair and a beard almost to his waist could have been taken for an ancient god. Strindberg used to liken him to Zeus."[22] A bust of him, which confirms

---

*The crown had now replaced the riksdaler.

this description, still stands in the entrance to the Royal Library. Klemming was a spiritualist with a fondness for Swedenborg. He liked the awkward young newcomer; and Strindberg painted two watercolours of him, which have survived.

In general, Strindberg found his other colleagues congenial too. One of them, Elof Tegnér, recalled the impression Strindberg made on his arrival:

> No one knew who he was . . . Gradually we learned that the young man was a student from Uppsala who had not completed his degree . . . It was also rumoured that he had tried to become an actor, a painter and an elementary school teacher, had written plays and was now [sic] with *Dagens Nyheter*. In brief, he was a young hack. He looked off-putting with his gloomy and suspicious eyes, his unruly combed-up hair and his brow which always looked as though swathed in cloud. But his face was neither ugly nor ignoble . . . To most of us he was unapproachable, partly because of his patent lack of the most elementary social graces. When he attended parties which we librarians sometimes held, he didn't say much until he got drunk, when he would grow noisy and disagreeable.[23]

Naturally, he had to eke out his tiny salary with other work. He translated *feuilletons* for *Dagens Nyheter* for 40 crowns a month (his limitations as a translator of news items evidently did not apply to serialised fiction and the like), and wrote art criticisms for the same paper, praising the new artists and attacking the Academy and the National Museum. On 28 October the paper printed a long anonymous article, probably by Lorentz Dietrichson, expressing appreciation of the new critic.[24] He wrote captions to illustrations of famous paintings and sculptures for an illustrated magazine, *Förr och Nu*, and taught at a private girls' school run by a Miss Hilda Widell. One of his pupils was Gurli Linder, later to become a writer herself; she remembered that he taught her history, geography and nature study, was very fierce about their remembering dates, and was a marvellous raconteur:

> How he could tell stories! I still recall his accounts of Gustav Vasa, the Greek civil wars, the Persian wars and Alexander the Great. I had several good history teachers later, but never one whose teaching left such a vivid impression, as well as giving a solid foundation of knowledge. The school possessed no visual material to assist in the teaching of nature study, but Strindberg borrowed stuffed animals, probably from the state museum. He also asked Miss Widell if he might teach us physics. He especially excited our interest in electricity . . . If he came among us during a rest period when we were playing and romping, he was as though one of us . . . Strindberg was one of the teachers we adored . . . I can see him still, slim and elegant,

in a dark-grey suit . . . I remember his well-manicured hands, his dense, bushy hair, his beautiful friendly smile and his soft and melodious voice . . . When I had to change to another school, my chief regret was that I would lose Strindberg as a teacher.[25]

A photograph of Strindberg from this year shows a handsome face with an incipient fair moustache, abundant hair brushed roughly back, an unusually broad forehead, high cheekbones, penetrating eyes and a small pursed mouth.

The first months of 1875 were a bad time for Strindberg. In February the New Theatre rejected his rewrite of *Master Olof*. "It begins with a very interesting dialogue which arouses expectations," wrote Edvard Stjern-ström, the director of the theatre, "but these are not fulfilled; the great and famous characters seem to me not really brought out; the threads of the action are not clear, nor its causes. While fully appreciating the fine intent of the play, I feel unable, for the above reasons, to accept it."[26] Two days later Strindberg wrote to Frans Hedberg at the Royal Theatre:

> If I were rich I would, as I should, destroy the MS and rewrite the thing from scratch. This is impossible. I can't do anything else, and yet I must, because the art of writing plays is so difficult and requires practice. I am 26 and have not had much practice. My play has degenerated into an *idée fixe*, for which I gave up everything else for two years and ruined myself economically. To repair this I am now a private teacher, work at the library, translate and write *feuilletons* for a daily paper. My free moments are devoted to correcting school exercises and preparing lessons. In such circumstances I cannot undertake any new enterprise and have no wish to. I surrender unconditionally and will rewrite my play if I have any prospect of getting it performed. Of course I don't think it worse than the worst beginner's stuff. But if I am to work with no hope of success I must weary and if I weary then my career as an author is finished. This perhaps would be regarded by many as a blessing . . .[27]

He wrote to the literary critic Karl Warburg, asking to be considered as a translator of a projected Swedish edition of Georg Brandes' essays, but was turned down. In March his mistress, Ida Charlotta, became pregnant. Strindberg denied paternity of the child, born that December, but could never escape the suspicion that he might have been the father. Later, in his Inferno period, he was to refer to Ida as a whore, but he used that term freely concerning women, not least his three wives.

In his novel *The Red Room*, Strindberg was to describe his life at this time, mixing with writers, painters, fellow journalists and the younger among his fellow librarians, borrowing from each other, sharing humble meals at each other's lodgings, visiting girls of easy virtue and, surprisingly often considering their poverty, meeting for food and drink in the salon of Berns' restaurant, a large, baroque, crowded place with an orchestra on a dais and a gallery with dining tables, not unlike the old Café Royal in London. The combination of overwork, poverty and literary failure became almost insupportable. "To work all day so as to be able to eat, and then to eat so as to be able to work all the next day, is a horrible circle," he wrote to Eugène Fahlstedt on 18 April. "Poverty makes a man . . . petty and mean—there's no broad view of the world from a rubbish heap." With what must have seemed foolhardy determination, he sat down that spring to make a third version of *Master Olof*, this time in verse in obedience to the prevailing dogma concerning stage tragedies. But although this was to bring him no more joy than his earlier efforts, in another respect that summer of 1875 was radically to change his life.

Chapter Five

∿∿∿∿∿∿∿∿∿∿∿∿∿∿∿∿∿∿∿∿∿∿∿∿∿∿∿∿∿∿∿∿∿∿∿

SIRI

None of Strindberg's three wives was Swedish. Siri von Essen, the first of them, was a Finn, born on 17 August 1850. Her father, Carl Reinhold von Essen, was an army officer who had abandoned his military career to live the life of a scholar, "happiest in his dressing-gown among his books, buried in Rousseau, Plato or Homer."[1] His Swedish wife Betty, born Elisabeth In de Betou, was of an opposite temperament; lively and gregarious, she painted, wrote poetry and played the violin. Siri (baptised Sigrid) was their only child. She was born and brought up at Jackarby, an old country house near the little town of Borgå, a pretty, fair-haired girl with dark eyes, a firm chin and a boyish face. She loved open-air pursuits, especially riding, and acquired the nickname of *slarvan*, the tomboy.

Her parents sent her to complete her education at a convent school in Paris, where she became fluent in French. Her main interest, however, was the theatre; she wanted to become an actress, but on her return to Finland her parents, regarding the stage as an unsuitable profession for a girl of aristocratic birth, sent her to the Music Academy in Stockholm to train as a singer. Inflammation of the vocal chords forced her to leave after a year; she consoled herself with amateur theatricals, and thus, at the age of twenty-one, she met Baron Carl Gustaf Wrangel, an officer in the Swedish Life Guards seven years her senior, who had started an amateur theatre group within his regiment. He was a handsome and charming man of an ancient and famous family, a most suitable match; they fell in love, and married in 1872 on Siri's twenty-second birthday. Ten months later they had a daughter, Sigrid.

In May 1875 a young Finnish pianist, Ina Forstén, came to perform in Stockholm. She had introductions to both Siri and Strindberg, the latter from her fiancé, Strindberg's old Uppsala friend Algot Lange. The Wrangels had read and admired *Hermione,* and one day Ina brought them the manuscript of *Master Olof,* which Strindberg had lent her, and read it to them. They asked her to bring him to visit them, but (according to Siri's and Strindberg's daughter Karin, who had it from her mother) the prospect of meeting members of the nobility daunted him and he refused.[2] (Siri had in fact seen him onstage in his tiny role in *Mary Stuart in Scotland,* but had not realised who he was as his name was not on the programme.) In *A Madman's Defence,* written twelve years later, Strindberg says that Siri sent him a letter arranging a rendezvous outside a laboratory on Drottninggatan; he would recognise her by a roll of music which she would be carrying.[3] In one of his better poems, he nostalgically recalled the meeting:

> A crowded street in Stockholm,
> A burning summer's day.
> A face beneath a blue veil—
> You glanced and turned away
>
> Into the shop's doorway.
> Your skirt's silk rustle died.
> Your small heel tapped to silence—
> I followed you inside—

The account in *A Madman's Defence,* as malignant a book as can ever have been written by one partner in a marriage about another (and they were still married when he wrote it), describes his first impression of Siri as "extremely blurred. Age uncertain, between twenty-nine and forty; dress adventurous. Artist or bluestocking? . . . Emancipated or a flirt? . . . She was like a little bird, twittering ceaselessly. Within half an hour I knew everything about her, what she felt, what she thought."[4] But Strindberg wrote this when his love for Siri had become twisted into jealousy and hatred. It seems much more probable, in view of what was to happen over the next few weeks, that he was immediately infatuated with her, a state of mind to which the fact of her being a baroness no doubt contributed. All his life Strindberg, while affecting to despise aristocrats, was unwillingly attracted by them. And her physical attractions he could not deny, even in *A Madman's Defence.* "Shoulders like a princess . . . slim as an osier . . .

a way of dropping her head towards you which was at the same time aristocratic and seductive."[5]

That first meeting was in late May or June (Strindberg in different works names both months). The Wrangels then invited him to visit them. By the kind of macabre coincidence which was to haunt Strindberg throughout his life, they lived at Norrtullsgatan 12, the house where he himself had lived from October 1864 to April 1867. As he stood before the gate, "I was seized by a sudden sickness. I nearly turned and fled . . . When I rang the bell, I couldn't avoid the thought that my father himself might open the door."

Although within the past year Siri had discovered that her husband was in love with her young cousin Sophia In de Betou, she did not immediately think of Strindberg as a prospective lover, nor he of her as a mistress.[6] Both the Wrangels were charmed by the young playwright, as others, even those who disapproved of his political and social attitudes, were to be charmed. Strindberg found Wrangel sensitive, courteous and civilised, * and was delighted to find himself accepted in this superior circle. It was to be nine months before he declared his love. During that time he and Siri conducted an enormous correspondence, of a tediousness (to all but themselves) scarcely to be endured by even the most passionate Strindberg admirer. (For anyone who wishes to test this assertion, their letters are to be found in Strindberg's fourth autobiographical volume, *He and She*.)

On 25 June 1875 Strindberg addressed the first (apart from a brief note of thanks for the introductory party) of these dreadful epistles jointly to Siri and Carl Gustaf. It runs to nearly four thousand words, divided into chapters each with its own heading. One of the few rewarding passages tells how in November 1869, as a minor actor at the Royal Theatre, he had appeared in the minor role of Theobald in Charlotte Birch-Pfeiffer's *The Lady of Worsley Hall*, as "a drunken barber returning from a masquerade with a red cock's feather in a clown's cap, and bells on my coatsleeves, and exhorted some other hired wretches to strike down a nobleman; then when the woman throws herself between us and saves him I stood ashamed while she heaped curses on me and my comrades, and I let myself be crushed by her words, which I naturally admired and was most ready to acknowledge. And then I had to slink sheepishly out while the audience applauded the noble lady and hissed me!" He went on to urge Siri, since her husband did not wish her to become a professional

---

*Strindberg's sister Anna later described Siri and Carl Gustaf as "the most sympathetic people one could imagine" (Philp and Hartzell, p. 63).

actress, to write. The advice in itself may not have been good, but his tips on how to go about writing were excellent:

> Write everything that you don't say as you sit over your knitting, say everything you would like to say when you are angry but must stay silent, write write [*sic*] everything that your husband confides in you and in you alone . . . Instead of playing dumb sonatas on the piano, take some paper and a pen. (Don't write poetry, for God's sake! There's no room in those short lines—least of all when one is rich in ideas and everything floods over one.) To write for you is simply to remember. Think of some small significant event in your life. First, isolate it. See that it has a beginning and an end—above all, an end. One has to know where it's leading! . . . When your story is finished, let me read it—not before! Not before! But then you'll be cured of your acting sickness and then you'll be happy and calm!

The next day he visited them. Siri evidently raised objections to his suggestion that she take up authorship, for on the following day, 27 June, he sent her further advice.

> If you get angry, your style acquires colour, for anger is the strongest of all spiritual emotions. You say you lack education! God preserve us from writers who retail what they have read in books. It's people's secrets that we want to know.

He urged her to write about her experiences in the Paris convent school when she was thirteen, preferably as a magazine article rather than as a book to avoid hostile criticism.

> If you have succeeded, you'll hear, if you don't hear, there'll be silence and that'll be good! . . . If you succeed . . . then you can write a one-act play . . . If you see it staged—well, then you'll thank God that you didn't become what you wanted to [i.e., an actress].

Returning to the idea of the convent story, he continues revealingly:

> First go through in your mind everything that you experienced during that period in your life—before you sit down to write. At first you'll think there's nothing interesting—but then you'll think of something—the blood will rush to your head—think of an injustice—get angry . . . Bring forth invisible enemies, create adversaries . . . be "mad"—it isn't everyone who can be that, and not many of those lucky enough to be able to, have the courage. . . . There was something called the sin against the Holy Ghost! I think they meant by that: resisting one's calling. That was said to be the only unforgivable sin. Remember that!

Anyone who supposes from the above extracts that Strindberg's letters to Siri and her husband were not tedious should read them in their entirety. He was busy that summer rewriting *Master Olof* in verse and translating Lorentz Dietrichson's essays in art criticism, one of which, "Florentine Studies," must especially have interested him, since it dealt at length with that Strindbergian character Savonarola.

In July, Siri went to Finland for three weeks, and Strindberg wrote her (30 July) a mercifully short letter in French, including a doggerel poem:

> Revenez
> Et vous serez
> La bienvenue
> Longtemps attendue
> Et maintenant
> En avant!
> Le bâteau
> S'en va.
> Ah et Oh!
> Il n'y a
> Plus de quoi—
> M. le Baron
> Me prend le papier
> Mon Dieu!
> Adieu!*

He had, he told her, been seeing a good deal of her husband during her absence. "*Ah! Nous sommes comme de vieux garçons! Il n'y a guère quelque restaurant que nous n'avons pas visité pour chercher de quoi paître nos âmes dévastées.*"† The friendship with Wrangel was, somewhat to Strindberg's embarrassment, to survive Siri's transfer of her affection from one to the other.

On her return to Sweden, Strindberg continued to write to her and Carl Gustaf jointly. In a letter dated 3 August and headed with a poem by Heine, he made one of those references to the possibility of suicide which were to recur so frequently and unconvincingly in his correspondence over the next forty years. "It is possible that I shall no longer trouble God or man with my unblest presence. Why should I intrude my griefs into your friendly and peaceful life? . . . Stay in your peaceful valley." Enormous letter followed enormous letter, self-pitying, eccentrically punctuated and couched in hideous purple prose. "That young man with the ravaged appearance who sits in there by the candle, he is made to be sacrificed—he is born to be unhappy—that is his pride! Let him be what

---

*"Come back, and you will be the welcomed one, long awaited. And now, on! The boat is leaving. Ah and Oh! There is no more—the Baron takes the paper from me. My God! Goodbye!"

†"Ah! We are like grown-up children. There is hardly a restaurant which we have not visited to look for something to revive our shattered spirits."

he is—he cannot be helped—let him go to hell—he will be most at home there." Thus on 5 August; and on 17 August, the anniversary of her wedding day: "You found me in the desert, warmed me at your own hearth . . . I have sunned myself in your happiness, your love."

That August or September (the letter is undated), Strindberg asked Rudolf Wall, the editor of *Dagens Nyheter,* to send him to Paris for a month. "If I haven't by the end of that time sent you several <u>excellent</u> pieces for the paper, then forget me. Otherwise I could stay another month and study art and theatre so that you could use me on the paper when I return . . . I think the French view of life will completely liberate me from that melancholy which breeds unhealthy thoughts about living, that is, dying, starving for one's ideas which is a pretty name for obstinate attitudes."[7] One imagines that his main reason for wanting to go away was that he feared his feelings for Siri were becoming uncontrollable.

Wall agreed to this. On 5 October, Strindberg's sister Anna, now a teacher, married Hugo Philp. The two were to be most generous to him in future years, and he was to reward them cruelly. Two days later he set off for Le Havre (on a ship that belonged to his father), pretending to the Wrangels that he was leaving to forget Ina Forstén, who was about to marry Algot Lange. But a few hours out from Stockholm he saw the little peninsula of Dalarö, where he had spent several holidays in his boyhood and (as he wrote in *A Madman's Defence*) "had been last spring with her and him and spent the night with them after a day of boat trips and walks in the forest . . . It was just there, on that rock, beneath the ash-trees, on the verandah, that I gazed at her pretty face illumined by her blonde hair as though by the sun, her little Japanese hat with the sky-blue veil, and her kid-gloved hand waved down to me that lunch was ready."[8] As the memory flooded over him, a pilot boat approached, the ship slowed, and acting on impulse, he boarded the pilot boat and went ashore. "I took a room at the hotel, ordered an absinthe, lit a cigar and sat down to think." He walked out, retracing the path which he and Siri had trodden together, then in a frenzy stripped and plunged into the water "which in October cannot have been much above zero." When he returned to land "the moment had come for the great deed . . . I sat on the most exposed part of the rock and let the October north wind whip my naked back."[9] Back at the hotel, he sent Carl Gustaf a telegram and then wrote him (not, be it noted, to Siri or to them jointly) a long and distraught letter pouring out his feelings for Siri under the pretence that they were his feelings for Ina ("My whole soul had become one with hers . . .") and concluding, in his worst style: "Forget me! Do not let your little home be infected by an unclean spirit—close your doors on my sorrows . . . Sometimes I think I am worthy of a night in Gethsemane!"[10]

He asked at the hotel for a doctor and, on being told there was none in the vicinity, settled for a minister. One came, and turned out to be the kind of narrow puritan that Strindberg most hated. On attempting to repeat his visit, the minister was refused entry and subsequently received a note from Strindberg "informing me that our acquaintance should be regarded as closed. . . . From that day," he recalled on Strindberg's death, "August Strindberg was one of my chief objects of prayer."[11]

Strindberg survived both his physical and his emotional crisis, as he was to survive others of both kinds until the cancer which killed him. Carl Gustaf and Siri came to Dalarö and, improbable as it seems, the baron suggested that Strindberg should come and live with them. "To my honour, I must say it, I answered him with a categorical 'No;' I sensed the imminent danger." After they had left, the hotel proprietress said to Strindberg, "That was your sister, wasn't it?" and on being told that she was not, remarked, "Well, you look astonishingly alike," provoking him to speculate, as he was often to, whether love, or infatuation, could cause people to adopt each other's facial expressions and mannerisms as it causes them to borrow each other's verbal phrases.[12]

He returned to his attic, and in the New Year had a tremendous row with his father, causing a break between the two which was never to be healed. Carl Oscar's diary records that on 8 January 1876 he was "attacked in my room by my son-in-law H.v. Philp and my son August with the grossest abuse. Shall have no more to do with these fellows," and the following day: "Visited again by Philp and August; they physically assaulted my wife."[13] The immediate cause of this seems to have been Carl Oscar's decision to leave his shipping agency solely to his son Oscar with no share in it to either August or Philp's wife, Anna. Although Carl Oscar was reconciled with Anna two years later, he never saw August again during the seven remaining years of his life. Strindberg did not even attend his father's funeral, although he was in Stockholm at the time. He does not refer to this row in his autobiography except for a single sentence about a "family drama" in which he had partaken, though a sense of guilt at not attending the funeral remained with him (a reference to it occurs over twenty years later in his play To Damascus).

That January, Strindberg and Siri began to meet secretly at cafés, in museums and at the Philps'. On 12 March he told her for the first time, at any rate on paper, that he loved her, in a monstrous epistle of three thousand words in his most erratically punctuated and florid prose.

O when shall I be able to say all this to you?—when can I cast off the iron mask—but one hour to show you and tell you with trembling lips and flashing glances that I love you! I must or I shall die—I must fall on my knees, lay my head in your bosom and kiss your hands a thousand million times . . . Rise up, young lioness, shake your golden mane and shoot lightnings from your regal eyes so that the fools tremble, tear yourself loose from this loathsome menagerie—out to the forests to the fresh free countryside where a heart a head and a bosom await you and love which can never die . . . Our love cannot die, for we both grow, we have both acquired wings, we can never weary of each other because each day we are new . . . Beloved little princess born to sit on the throne in the world of genius . . . You shall be an actress—I shall create for you your own theatre . . . I shall play opposite you and write and—love you . . . Fulfil your calling become the greatest actress or authoress in this land . . . If you lack the courage to live with me, then die with me and let our love continue pure and sacred on the other side of death when we are freed from these wretched bodies which would drag all down! Die with me—O with my hand in yours I shall gladly go forth into the infinite unknown where our souls may embrace with no need to be ashamed or to ask leave of anyone save God!

He also suggested that she move to where he was, not to live with him but to lease a couple of rooms in the same apartment. "My old ladies have two rooms on the other side of the hall—they would love to have a woman whom they could cosset." Not surprisingly, Siri did not accept this invitation. He did not in fact give the letter to Siri until 15 March, whether through diffidence or because it took him three days to finish it we do not know. Siri for her part had expressed similarly passionate feelings towards Strindberg in several letters which she wrote to him between 6 and 16 March but (according to him) had not sent and did not give him until now.

I long for you . . . I love you with a sisterly intensity, without coquetry . . . There have indeed been moments when it would have been a joy to me—a longing to take your beautiful little head between my hands, look into your wise, true eyes and I would without doubt have pressed a kiss on that clear brow which I love so much—but that kiss would have been the purest you had ever known . . . Were you a woman I would love you equally much, could I respect a woman as I do you.[14]

After Strindberg had visited them, so she told him, Carl Gustaf had asked her permission to go and make love to Sophia, who was now staying with them.

My first reaction was vexation, my second amusement, and my third, satisfaction . . . He is head over heels in love with her and tells me so . . .

After he had seen you to the door he came back, took my hands, looked me in the eyes . . . and said pleadingly: "Let me go to her tonight, I am too dreadfully in love with her." . . . And he asks this of me, who am tormented by pangs of conscience, who am forced to love you from a distance . . . Mark the contradiction, the duality of my feelings . . . I love you both, and I could not live without him, my true, loyal friend . . . nor without you![15]

On 16 March, having received his declaration of love, she replied in similar style:

Thank you, my dearest, for what I received from you yesterday . . . Many, many times have I read it . . . So there does exist on earth a love which stands above all else—so free from sensuality, so holy and pure. O my fairest, my dearest dream! . . . Thank you for this happiness! I cannot think it is a crime—no—I cannot![16]

Siri visited Strindberg at his sister Anna's. He read part of Longfellow's *Excelsior* to her, and was "truly moved by this captivating poetry."[17] (Strindberg's taste in literature was always unpredictable; later he was to admire the novels of Marie Corelli.) They kissed, and for the first time she addressed him by the familiar *du*, though he declined to reciprocate "because it would cheapen her." In *A Madman's Defence* he wrote: "She wishes to seduce me. It was she who gave the first kiss, made the first approach. But from now on it is I who shall choose the role of seducer, for I am no Joseph."[18] He was of course referring to Joseph's chaste rejection of the advances of Potiphar's wife. But apart from the general unreliability of *A Madman's Defence*, this was the kind of self-excusing remark that Strindberg was constantly to make; whenever he got involved and the affair soured, it was always the woman who had originally been to blame.

He does seem to have urged her to tell her husband the truth so that they might become lovers. On 23 March she did this. Carl Gustaf's reaction was unexpected and somewhat embarrassing. "He is not angry with us," noted Strindberg, "and has no objection to our continuing our intimacy provided we are *chaste*! This is a final insult to my manhood, and I am replying with a positive and final adieu!"[19] A hectic correspondence ensued; on 24 March the baron wrote twice to Strindberg begging him to remain his friend and come and see them, and Strindberg, the same day, refused twice and then accepted.[20]

The combination of her husband's infidelity, her passion for Strindberg and her desire to become an actress determined Siri to seek a divorce that spring. The last of these reasons was perhaps not the least. "I was not born for a quiet home with peace and the smell of roses," she wrote to her mother on 13 April. "I need strife to find my happiness . . . I was not born just to be a woman. God intended me for an artist . . . As Gustaf's wife I could never become an actress."[21] But to lay blame at her husband's door would have necessitated his resigning his commission. She therefore decided to leave him and let him sue her for desertion.

Several times during April she shrank from the idea, wondering whether it might not be preferable for them to stay married and continue with their separate affairs (though as late as that summer she was still asserting that Strindberg and she were not in love). But at length she took the step. She had originally planned to go to Paris but in the end decided on Copenhagen, where she could stay with her mother's sister Augusta Möller. Wrangel and Strindberg agreed to see her off at the station together, and also to meet in public during her absence to dispel any suggestion that she and Strindberg might have been lovers. (Strindberg also asked Rudolf Wall to publish pieces by him in *Dagens Nyheter* with a Stockholm dateline during her absence as evidence that he was still there and not with her in Copenhagen.)

In the event, Carl Gustaf failed to turn up at the station for her departure, so that Siri and Strindberg found themselves in exactly the kind of situation they had wanted to avoid. She begged him to accompany her for at least part of the journey, and he agreed. They went together as far as Katrineholm, an hour or so outside Stockholm; there, since there was a long halt, they supped together in the station restaurant. Within a few days the story was around Stockholm. Strindberg's fellow librarian Elof Tegnér tells how, hearing that a colleague had eloped with a baroness, he entered the library crying "Have you heard—?" to be greeted with silence and warning gestures in the direction of Strindberg.[22]

The day after her departure, Carl Gustaf filed his application for divorce on the ground of desertion. In Copenhagen, Siri was subjected to much pressure from her aunt to return to him. She resisted, and poured out her feelings in frequent letters to Strindberg. "My God! How I am suffering!" she wrote to him on 5 May. "Is the step I have taken wrong? Is it a sin? . . . O why, why did he not love me, he who was my husband, he whose duty it was? . . . Is it God's will that you and I, only we, should love each other? I think I love him still—yes, I do, but I love you too—O why cannot I love you both?" On 8 May and again the following day she begged him to come to her: "I must see you if I am to survive this hell. Bring your *Master Olof* with you and go on writing it here."[23]

Meanwhile, the news was spreading. On 10 May the Stockholm newspaper *Fäderneslandet* reported, without naming names, that the wife of a captain in the Guards was planning to divorce her husband and become an actress. In a place as small as Stockholm was then, many people must have known to whom this referred. On 11 May Strindberg wrote to Carl Gustaf asking whether the required document had been sent to Copenhagen and threatening to go there the next day unless he received a satisfactory answer. Carl Gustaf replied that it had been sent and warned Strindberg that for the latter to visit her now would ruin her good name. Siri's mother complicated things by writing to Carl Gustaf begging him to go to Denmark and bring her back ("Besides, she will surely never succeed in the wanton world of the theatre with her Finnish accent, poor health and helplessness"), and also to Strindberg asking him to drop the affair. Both requests were predictably ignored; instead, Gustaf, as anxious as anyone for the divorce to go through, wrote comforting letters to Siri.[24]

On 19 May, Siri returned to Stockholm and moved into her mother's apartment at Drottninggatan 44. Strindberg's letters to her during the next few days included one in French, addressing her as Thérèse and signing himself Léon,* and one in eccentric English:

> Darling, my Love, Ophelia!
> You are sorrow and I have been very cruel to You. Forgive me! My head is sick and I cannot tame my wild thoughts when I think you would less me!
>
> I love You by all my heart and therefore You must not be angry with me!
>
> Love me but for a little and I am not unhappy as I have been't for long, long years! Peace to You!
>   Your
>   Hamlet

Soon after he wrote this affectionate letter, they evidently had a row. "I wanted to free you from these warders and what do you do?" he asked her in an undated letter later that month. "Now you are free and you crawl into prison. And you want to bind me too. Remember that I never allow myself to be bound by anyone! Why must everything be sacrificed to your love for your child? What has that to do with me?" The writing was on the wall if only Siri had seen it. But she had told her mother that she needed strife to find happiness. On 16 May Carl Gustaf's suit for divorce came to court, and on 20 June the divorce was made absolute. The way lay open for the first of Strindberg's three ill-fated marriages.

He had not been creatively idle during these hectic weeks. By 19 May he had finished the verse rewrite of *Master Olof*, his third version, and

---

*As Torsten Eklund has pointed out (*Brev*, I, 357n), Thérèse and Laurent are the chief characters in George Sand's *Elle et Lui*. Eklund suggests that Strindberg either mis-remembered the lover's name or was referring to, or confusing him with, Emma Bovary's lover, Léon.

sent it off to the Royal Theatre. He also, in his capacity as art critic of
Dagens Nyheter, wrote five articles under the general heading of "Art,
Artifice and Naturalism" which appeared between 23 May and 15 June,
pleasantly chatty pieces of no great interest, dealing mainly with Swedish
artists and sculptors now forgotten. He even planned to edit a weekly
cultural magazine of his own. "It is to be called *Stockholm Gazette,*" he
told Rudolf Wall on 23 August. "Art I shall write myself . . . Foreign
contributions (will perhaps be our *pièce de résistance*). I have got into
contact with Sw. artists in Paris, Rome, Munich, Düsseldorf . . . As
regards *feuilletons* I already have a particularly fine little sketch by S v.E.
describing her convent lodging house in Paris, and when she has more
experience I shall always be able to rely on her pen. She has much to say
. . . I had also thought of winning women readers by dealing with their
activities such as the Friends of Handicraft . . . Editorial expenses will be
cheap, since the Editor will write most things himself." To leave himself
free for this, Strindberg resigned his post as Stockholm correspondent of
Handelstidningen i Göteborg. The *Gazette* duly appeared but alas! like so
many of Strindberg's enterprises, it failed, and folded after a single issue.

Siri spent the second half of July and part of August in the country near
Upplands-Väsby, "so that she is free from her wardresses [wrote Strindberg in A *Madman's Defence*] and can meet me each Saturday and
Sunday without witnesses."[25] On her return to Stockholm she again lived
for a while with her mother, then moved to an apartment of her own. She
and Strindberg had a row, and for a while he spent his evenings in cafés
with friends. Their life seems already to have taken the pattern which it
was to follow throughout their marriage: ecstatic days and nights, followed by rows and partings, reconciliation and more rows.

On finishing the verse *Master Olof,* Strindberg turned to writing short
stories and sketches about his student days, and on 13 October he offered
these to Albert Bonnier. "Yesterday I got some Uppsala sketches from
Strindberg," Bonnier wrote next day to his wife and son. ". . . They're
not exactly rounded masterpieces—but there are good things in them
—the girls think them very amusing—so perhaps I shall take them."[26] In
the same letter Bonnier expressed sadness that there were no Swedish
writers alive whom he could pay as handsomely as Frederik Hegel in
Copenhagen was paying Bjørnson, little guessing how profitable, if
fraught, his association with Strindberg was ultimately to prove.

The Royal Theatre rejected the verse *Master Olof* and, perhaps to
counter the depression thus caused, perhaps also to relieve the strain of his
situation with Siri, Strindberg left that October on a trip to Paris, where he
stayed for three weeks in a pension on the rue de Douai. His ostensible

reason was, as befitted an art critic, to look at the new school of French painting and find out where the Swedish painters in France were heading. So, for the first time, he saw the works of the Impressionists.

Strindberg himself was to develop into an interesting painter, very much in the Impressionistic manner (unlike Ibsen, whose earliest ambition was to become a painter, but whose efforts were naturalistic and pedestrian). One would therefore have expected that his first contact with French Impressionism would greatly have excited him, but in fact his reaction was mixed—so much so, indeed, that several commentators have described it as wholly condemnatory. That is not true. On his return to Sweden that winter, he wrote three articles which appeared in *Dagens Nyheter* describing, often vividly, what this new school was trying to do. Thus, on a painting by Sisley:

> The whole canvas is painted in a colourless white, light red and light blue, matte and bloodless—the effect is as it were albino. It is meant to be a summer landscape, but it looks as though snow or frost lay over it. In the foreground is a railway line; a train has passed. How do we know? Because in the right-hand corner we see the steam from the engine at the moment of condensation. Another train runs across the centre of the painting—yes, runs, because that is how it is painted, the speed, the motion of the wheels, the vibration and the passengers looking out of the windows; and the landscape is painted just as it looks from a carriage window as one traverses a cutting or glimpses it through trees. In a word—it was simply a moment's *impression*; like a photograph when the subject has moved, or like trees photographed in a high wind.

Eighteen years later, in his introduction to the catalogue of his friend Paul Gauguin's exhibition, written in the form of a letter to the artist, he was to reveal the same uncertainty. "I do not understand your art and I do not like it," he declared. ". . . But I know that this avowal will not surprise or hurt you, for you seem fortified by scorn." Recalling his first contact with Impressionism in 1876, he continued: "I surveyed these modern paintings with a cool indifference. But the next day I returned, without knowing why, and discovered 'something' in these bizarre manifestations. I saw a throng of people on a quay, but no actual people; I saw an express train rushing through a Normandy landscape, the movement of the wheels on the line, horrible portraits all of ugly old men who had not been able to pose motionless. I conveyed the effect of these remarkable canvases in an article in one of my country's newspapers, in which I sought to reflect the impressions which these Impressionists were trying to portray, and my article, if not fully comprehended, achieved a certain success."

Strindberg's confusion mirrored that of Swedish artists in Paris. He was more at home describing the works of the forerunners of Impressionism —Delacroix, Courbet, Corot and, especially, Turner and Constable. They, rather than their French followers, were to be the direct inspiration for his own painting. On his way back to Sweden he saw in Hamburg an exhibition by the Munich painter Gabriel Max, which impressed him; when Strindberg died, a quantity of photographs of Max's paintings were found among his papers. [27]

He also, while in Paris, paid at least one visit to the theatre. "I saw," he later recalled, "a dreadful tragedy called *Rome vaincue,* in which the writing and acting touched the extremes of unnaturalness, bordering on the grotesque. But there was one actress who stood out against all the others and, amid all this wretchedness, offered a faint hope of something better. It was Sarah Bernhardt. She played a blind mother, and she performed with a truthfulness that was overwhelming."[28] Later, he was to try to persuade her to appear in at least one play of his, but without success. *

By early December Strindberg was back in Sweden. On 4 December Siri had an audition with Frans Hedberg at the Royal Theatre, which proved successful. On 16 December Strindberg's elder brother Oscar married. "You must forgive me if I correct your oversight and regard myself as invited to your wedding!" Strindberg wrote to him.[29] The letter contains just that one sentence; according to his father's diary, the list of guests included neither August nor Hugo and Anna Philp, but we do not know whether he, or they, attended.[30]

Strindberg's Uppsala stories, *Town and Gown* (*Från Fjärdingen och Svartbäcken*), were published that month. They make lively reading still, with their sharp characterisations of students and dons, and their account of the debilitating effect that university life can have. The prevailing theme is the whittling away of youthful idealism. Strindberg's attitude towards idealism was at this time divided: ideals are necessary, he seems to imply, but naïve idealism is as futile as Philistinism. As Ibsen was to suggest eight years later in *The Wild Duck,* idealism is for the few and most of us have to compromise on our ideals if we are to go on living, a viewpoint which Strindberg had already adumbrated in his epilogue to the verse version of *Master Olof.* Although *Town and Gown* lacks the power and sweep of *Master Olof* in its original version, the stories have an immediacy which the play lacks in its printed form, simply because the

---

*See page 111 below. *Rome vaincue,* set at the time of the battle of Cannae, was by a dramatist with the unfortunate name of Alexandre Parodi.

play contains so much that is superfluous; it is ironical that the economy which playwriting, above all other literary forms, demands is lacking there but present in the stories. No wonder it was to be with a novel rather than a play that Strindberg made his first real breakthrough three years later.

His early play *The Outlaw* was also published that month, in the Christmas issue of a magazine, *Nu*, and was well received. The breach with his father remained unhealed. On Christmas Eve, Carl Oscar sadly noted in his diary: "All the children at home except the two lost ones, August and Anna."[31] He insisted that his two other daughters, Elisabeth and Nora, should cease contact with the renegades; and they complied.

Chapter Six

〜〜〜〜〜〜〜〜〜〜〜〜〜〜〜〜〜〜〜〜〜〜〜〜〜〜

MARRIAGE AND FAME

The year 1877 began tragically for Siri. On 13 January her daughter by Carl Gustaf, Sigrid, died of tuberculosis at the age of four. The death seems not to have been unexpected, for only two weeks later Siri made her debut as an actress at the Royal Theatre in a French play, *A Theatre Piece*, by L. Leroy. Among the audience was a rising dramatist and short-story writer, Anne-Charlotte Leffler, who noted in her diary: "I liked her very much and expect much of her. Cultivated, intelligent, pleasing, distinguished, unpretentious, uncommonly simple and reposed, but with warmth and true feeling. She has beautiful eyes with a real madonna look, and a pleasing voice. Poor little thing, I feel so sorry for her, she has already suffered much in her few years."[1]

To add to Siri's troubles, her mother died that spring. But professionally, at least, the omens were encouraging. In April she acted Jane Eyre, in an adaptation by Charlotte Birch-Pfeiffer, and made sufficient impression for the Royal Theatre to give her a year's contract at a salary of 2,100 crowns, plus 3 crowns for each appearance. She stayed in the company for four years, and might have remained longer had Strindberg not forced her to leave. Once they were married, his enthusiasm for his wife's career began to wane. But according to their daughter Karin, who presumably had it from her mother, their first four years of marriage were "really happy" for both Strindberg and Siri, each respecting and encouraging the artist in the other. They were also agreed, ironically in view of what was to come, on the importance of women's freedom.

Librarians often have to learn the rudiments of exotic foreign languages for their work of cataloguing; thus, five years earlier, Ibsen had found his first English admirer in a junior assistant at the British Museum, Edmund Gosse, who was studying Norwegian. Strindberg now began to study Chinese, and we find him proudly drawing Chinese characters in some of his letters and writing to the Swedish vice-consul in Shanghai, and other Sinologues in Europe, asking them to help improve the library's Chinese collection. It has been said that he never learned more of the language than could be found in encyclopaedia handbooks, but he was hugely proud of his knowledge, such as it was, in this field. Three years later he was to take three months' leave to learn enough Japanese to be able to catalogue in that language too.

It was probably around this time that he wrote another play, *Anno 48.* * It is a political comedy set in Stockholm in 1848, the year of revolutions. Even Stockholm had its riots that year. *Anno 48* is a naïve little piece, which has never been performed. Feeble in plot, it contains some lively characters, such as a reactionary member of Parliament who, fearful lest the revolutionary spirit abroad might spread to Sweden, proposes in Parliament that all servants should be dressed in grey so that the army will know at whom to shoot; his nephew Arvid, a liberal poet; an old actor; a stagestruck bookkeeper; and a painter who loses his revolutionary ideals and ends up as a member of the establishment. In many ways it anticipates the novel he was about to write, *The Red Room*. Several of the characters who appear in the novel may be traced in the play under different names. *Anno 48* was probably influenced by the contemporary French school of political stage comedy; Strindberg had praised such writers as Ponsard and Augier in his drama reviews, and perhaps he felt that, with the continued rejection of *Master Olof*, he stood a better chance of getting a play performed if he tried his hand at this genre. He may also have been influenced by Ibsen's political comedy, *The League of Youth* (1869), which had enjoyed considerable success throughout Scandinavia. But although Strindberg was later to succeed in black comedy, the kind of jolly romp attempted in *Anno 48* was foreign to him. Its

*On the title page of this play when it was first published in 1881 in his collection of early work, *I vårbrytningen*, Strindberg gives its date as 1875, but his dating in that volume is often inaccurate (he states that *The Outlaw* was staged in 1872, when in fact it was staged in 1871). He told Isidor Bonnier (15 July 1878) that he had written it in 1876 before *Town and Gown* (Smedmark, I, 221). Gunnar Ollén, on the other hand, thinks he may have written it as late as 1877.

failure, coupled with the success of *The Red Room*, must have made it seem to his contemporaries, and possibly to him too, that the novel, not the drama, was to prove his true medium.

About now, he made an important literary discovery of a writer whom he was always henceforth to admire and whom he claimed as a considerable influence: Charles Dickens. He had, so he tells, read *David Copperfield* when he was younger but had "found it boring," and had failed to finish *Our Mutual Friend*. Now a friend persuaded him to reread *David Copperfield*; he did so, and "was bewitched." Previously, he had found little but sentimentality in the book; now he found that "Dickens could be venomous when he attacked what he regarded as social anomalies, sparing no one nor any revered institution," and this aroused in him "the desire to launch a similar and concerted attack on the whole of this society with which he had never been able to reconcile himself. At first he thought of inventing a Swedish Pick-wick-Club [*sic*], but then his [Johan's] personal memories returned and he sought to group and frame them until, after a long incubation, they became ready to be delivered,"[2] in *The Red Room*.

A colleague at the library, Nathan Hellberg, describes Strindberg at this time. "He divided his day between his work at the library, writing, and mixing in, by choice, journalistic and artistic circles . . . One moment he was weak, the next defiant; now timid, now ready to challenge the world . . . He seldom smiled, but when he did, it was with either a child's innocence or a weak, sad pursing of the lips. Sometimes the fire in his spirit would flare up, and then his bitterness would vent itself against anyone or anything." Hellberg remembered that once they were walking in violent rain sharing an umbrella. "Suddenly Strindberg stopped, shut his umbrella and banged it against a tree, smashing both the shaft and the fabric. 'Damnation!'—the only profanity he permitted himself. 'If our Lord allows it to rain, he must mean it to fall on us mortals too!' "[3] A young journalist of his circle adds: "Strindberg usually sat silent and withdrawn. He sometimes took part in the arguments, of course; but he liked to listen."[4]

The continued rejection of *Master Olof* weighed heavily on him. His frustration found expression in a letter to Karl Warburg on 26 October. "For five years the Royal Theatre has put me off with talk and five times [*sic*] I have rewritten the enclosed play, till last year I got it back again with the excuse that it contained nihilism and blasphemies, was too pessimistic, etc. Stjernström [at the New Theatre] explained that he couldn't afford to provide new sets. So my five best years have been wiped out of my life!" He asked Warburg to offer it to the Grand Theatre in Gothenburg, but they were to reject it too. The only slight consolation was that the magazine *Nu* published a single scene from it (Act IV, scene 5) in its November–December issue.

In November the Royal Library moved from the Palace to its new quarters at Humlegården, where it stands today. With six thousand metres of books to be shifted, the operation took two months. All those involved got extra pay, and Strindberg received 500 crowns. The library's prize possession was an illuminated mediaeval bible, and on New Year's Day 1878 Klemming, unwilling to entrust so valuable an object to other hands, rode from the Palace to Humlegården clutching it to his chest, Zeus-like in an open sleigh despite the bitter weather, "which unusual sight," recalled one of his staff, Robert Geete, "aroused considerable attention from the passers-by."[5]

Geete noted that once they had moved into the new premises, Strindberg withdrew into himself and isolated himself more and more from his colleagues. For a while he surprised them by working with a glove on his left hand; then his engagement to Siri was announced, and the concealment was no longer necessary. Geete once accompanied him and Siri on a carriage ride and "at once received a strong impression of warmth, not to say heat, in their feelings." In Djurgården a large Saint Bernard playfully approached them, at which Strindberg ran away in terror. "On my asking him what had come over him, he nervously replied that he knew of nothing worse than mad dogs."[6] Strindberg admitted this cowardice in *Time of Ferment*: ". . . still afraid of the dark, afraid of dogs, horses, strangers." After work at the library, Geete says, Strindberg liked to relax in cafés, especially Gropen (The Pit) in the basement of the Grand Hotel, where, having a poor head for liquor, he would become noisy.

On 30 December 1877 Strindberg and Siri married. They could hardly have postponed it longer, for she was heavily pregnant.* The ceremony took place in an apartment they had just leased at Norrmalmsgatan 17 (now Biblioteksgatan), conveniently situated near the new library at what is now the corner of Kungsgatan and Stureplan. The area then consisted of a huddle of humble wooden houses, some idyllically rustic, some slum shanties; Strindberg's sister Anna remembered the occasion as "very festive."[7] Carl Gustaf Wrangel was among the guests. The wedding had been preceded a few days earlier by a stag party in the old library at which Strindberg "suddenly went berserk and broke some chairs." When asked

---

*As late as mid-November, when she was over six months gone, she was appearing in the small role of Fru Lynge in the Swedish premiere of Ibsen's new play, *The Pillars of Society*.

what pleasure he could find in this, Strindberg "meekly replied that he didn't understand it himself. It had suddenly come over him like a frenzy."[8]

On 21 January 1878 their first child, a girl, was prematurely born. It was evident that she could not live; writing to his cousin Oscar ten years later (11 April 1888), Strindberg says she "was taken home by the midwife and died there two days after her birth. The midwife gave her emergency baptism, and the child at our request was named Kerstin." She was described in the parish register as being of "unknown parents"; this, Strindberg explains, was "to safeguard the delicate position of the mother and father as employees of the Crown."[9]

Thus within a year and a week Siri had lost two children and her mother. Nor was the remainder of 1878 to give her and Strindberg much joy. She got only a few small parts at the theatre, and he seems to have written little, apart from three pieces on art for *Posttidningen* which appeared in February. He spent the summer translating with Siri some pieces by American humorous writers, including Mark Twain and Bret Harte, which appeared in three volumes during 1878 and 1879.* He was reduced to reading proofs for Isidor Bonnier, who also advanced him 500 crowns against unspecified future writings. He attempted some articles for a Finnish magazine, *Finsk Tidskrift*, but the editor complained that they were too pessimistic. Strindberg's reply to him on 29 June shows his depressed state of mind:

> I spend my whole day among books, am never out among people . . . never go to the theatre or other public places, except occasionally to the Art Society; so I don't know what is happening in the world . . . I never go to exhibitions any more because the artists are as nervous as I! If one praises them, they despise one, if one doesn't praise them they still despise one. Besides, I am now a pessimist, or worse, a nihilist; I can have no eye for excellence, because I regard everything as bad . . . Were I a professional man of letters, there would be no problem because then my pen would flow of its own accord . . . But that isn't the case, so I regard myself as highly unsuited to this vocation.

*The series consisted of four volumes, the first of which was translated by Strindberg's old professor at Uppsala, C. R. Nyblom. In addition to Twain and Harte, the humorists included Artemus Ward, Charles Dudley Warner, T. B. Aldrich and "The Danbury Newsman," J. Bailey. An anonymous handwritten note in the Royal Library of Stockholm copy of Vol. 2 states that several of the Bailey translations were plagiarised from a Swedish-American newspaper, that Strindberg's Uppsala friend Algot Lange assisted with the other translations, and that "despite Strindberg's strict order to the contrary, it was announced in all the papers that Strindberg was the translator" (he appeared only as "A.S." on the title pages). His English being poor, he probably contributed the least of the four credited translators.

An old Uppsala friend, Anton Stuxberg, a zoologist, offered to pay for the verse rewrite of *Master Olof* to be printed. But that summer Stuxberg went with Nordenskiöld's expedition to discover the long-sought North-East Passage (a voyage they were to complete successfully after being frozen in near the Bering Strait) and, finding himself unable to meet the printer's bill, asked their mutual friend Isidor Bonnier if he would pay the 558 crowns needed to release the six hundred copies which had been lying at the printer's for two months. "You know as well as I do," Stuxberg wrote to Isidor from Tromsø in north Norway in July, "that Strindberg is a young writer of uncommon talent (perhaps a bit wilful sometimes, one must admit), and he surely needs a little encouragement if he is to succeed."[10] Strindberg did not lack friends who believed in him. Bonnier, who had already stood surety for a loan that Strindberg had taken out that year, refused; but somehow the money was found, for the play appeared under another imprint in September. It attracted little notice, and such reviews as did appear were lukewarm or hostile. *Aftonbladet* thought it interesting only as a curiosity, and *Nya Dagligt Allehanda* complained of "the pessimistic viewpoint borrowed from abroad," though admitting "traces of a genuine if in some respects misguided originality."

On 1 October, Strindberg and Siri moved to a flat in another house in the same street, no. 6, which he described to a friend as "the old brothel."[11] They had stayed only ten months in their first married home, and were to change house four more times in the next five years.

Strindberg's salary at the library had brought him only 915 crowns during 1878, and his writing, such as it was, had been so unprofitable that he was unable to repay the money he had borrowed that year. On 9 January 1879 he went bankrupt, twenty-six years to the month after his father had suffered the same fate. He had debts of 9,252 crowns and assets of only 5,591 crowns.[12] Undeterred, on 20 January he wrote a desperate letter to a journalist he had known on *Dagens Nyheter*, Gustaf Christiernsson, suggesting the formation of a new magazine. "Could we find some people who will not—to start with—write *just* for money, but out of interest, pure or impure, revenge, personal or objective, anger, hatred, envy, especially the last? I shall take charge of the art section . . . You and Ohlsson can trail your coats in theatre and literature (in which fields I may shoot an arrow now and then, anonymously of course, so they won't take it out on my wife)." On 20 March he wrote to August Lindberg, a young actor-director who four years later was to present the first European performance of Ibsen's *Ghosts*, asking if he could help to find Siri work in Malmö (where Lindberg had just enjoyed a notable success as Hamlet), "to appear as guest artiste during Easter week, when she is free, in the following roles: Jane Eyre, Ophelia, Blanche in *The Sphinx*, Geneviève in *Les Inutiles.*"* Neither suggestion brought any result.

Between writing these letters, Strindberg had broken new ground by embarking on a novel. On 29 March he wrote to Rudolf Wall at *Dagens Nyheter* offering him the first three chapters for serialisation. His intent, he explained, was "to portray a society which I do not love and which has never loved me . . . It is not malicious, it does not recognisably portray living persons, it speaks for the oppressed, it seeks to expose the injustices which society perpetrates against the man of letters and, in certain justified instances, his revenge on society . . . I have not attempted any strict constructive pattern, but offer the reader a panorama of society by describing what the hero happens to see in his capacity as a newspaper correspondent." A week later, on 5 April, he wrote again to Wall: "On closer consideration of the manuscript of my novel I think it unsuccessful as a novel, and feel the effect would be better if isolated scenes and individual portraits were extracted and presented simply as such."

The offer was rejected. Strindberg did not take his usual holiday in the skerries that summer, presumably because he could not afford it. He took a few days off, likewise no doubt for financial reasons, to translate three English children's books, *Hush-a-bye-baby*, *Tottie's Nursery Rhymes* and *Childhood's Delight*,† and to help Siri with the translation of a French novel, André Theuriet's *Le Filleul d'un Marquis*, a commission he had received from Albert Bonnier as long ago as 1877. But by 15 August he had finished his novel and sent it to Joseph Seligmann, for whom he had translated the American humorists. He did not offer it to Albert or Isidor Bonnier because of the ugly caricature of a Jewish publisher which the book contains and which was clearly based on Albert Bonnier. [13]

Strindberg's oriental studies brought him some reward this year, albeit prestigious rather than financial. "I am now a member of several learned societies abroad," he wrote on 24 September to his explorer friend Anton Stuxberg. He had been elected to La Société des Études Japonaises, Chinoises, Tartares et Indo-chinoises in April, an essay "Relations de la Suède avec la Chine et les Pays Tartares" had been read at the Académie des Inscriptions et Belles-Lettres in Paris in June; and for discovering in his library a map of Central Asia which a Swedish sergeant-major, Johan Renat, had made during his seventeen years of captivity in Siberia from 1716 to 1733, and offering it to the Imperial Geographical Society in St.

*Plays by, respectively, Octave Feuillet and V. E. Cadol.
†Only the last two were published, that December, both anonymously.

Petersburg, he had received that Society's silver medal. Telling Stuxberg of these consolations, and of his bankruptcy, he concluded stoically: "These have been bitter times, but with a wife like mine even death holds no terrors."

On 1 October he moved house yet again, a few hundred yards to Stora Humlegårdsgatan 16. On 1 November he read the final proofs of his novel, and thirteen days later, the way things happened then, it appeared.

The Red Room has often been described as the first modern Swedish novel. Strindberg was right when he told Rudolf Wall it was unsuccessful as a novel; it is rather a series of sketches, some of them brilliant, but loosely strung together and of uneven quality. It tells how an ingenuously idealistic young civil servant named Arvid Falk abandons his career for that of author and journalist. But everywhere he finds corruption and hypocrisy, and for relief he turns to a Bohemian circle of writers and artists. Strindberg subtitled the book *Portraits of Artistic and Literary Life*, and its picaresque form owes much to Dickens, as does the savagery of the social satire. The American humorists whom he had recently translated also left their mark; their jesting, he later observed, "foreshadowed the anarchy of thought that would later explode; it was the beginning of the demolition."[14] At the end of the book, Falk is back in his government office, having sold out on his ideals, reflecting no doubt (as Martin Lamm has noted) the guilt Strindberg must have felt at continuing his own civil-service career at the Royal Library while denouncing the social system that supported him.

As usual in Strindberg's novels, including his quasi-autobiographical works such as *The Son of a Servant* and *A Madman's Defence*, what is good and what is bad in *The Red Room* corresponds almost precisely to the dialogue scenes on the one hand and the non-dialogue social commentary on the other.* The best scenes in *The Red Room*, such as the visit by the Bohemians to the brothel, and the episode in the studio when they burn the floorboards to keep warm and try to appease their hunger by reading aloud recipes from a cookery book, are equal to the best scenes in his plays. The direct social commentary, by contrast, is both ponderous and shrill. The only field in which the narrative prose equals the dialogue is the descriptive passages, in which Strindberg evokes the Stockholm of the seventies as vividly as, later, he was to evoke the landscape of the skerries.

Predictably, *The Red Room* had a mixed reception. "For young people

---

*By general consent his finest novel, *The People of Hemsö*, contains little or no direct, but merely implied, social commentary, and is immensely the better for it. The same applies to the best of his short stories.

in their ferment," a contemporary recalled, "it was a symbol of liberation; for those more balanced and conservative it was the quintessence of all that was immodest and disruptive."[15] Some of the favourable reviewers were shocked by the "realism"; some of the hostile ones grudgingly admitted the book's power. Thus, *Stockholms Dagblad*, while welcoming it as "the most notable event in Swedish fiction for many years," thought it "in many respects an ugly and repellent book, but the product of an honest mind and of a very talented writer." *Folkets Tidning* found "nothing in the book that is not gloomy, disagreeable and depressing," and the whole analytically cold and lacking in excitement. *Nya Dagligt Allehanda*, though disliking the "pessimism, caricatures and lack of a solidly drawn central character," praised its "originality both of conception and of execution," and concluded that it demonstrated "indisputable evidence of genius." *Aftonbladet*, despite "brilliant descriptions and sharp characterisation," could find "no development, no warmth," and subsequently printed a violent attack on the book by Professor F. A. Cederschiöld: "The public would surely be grateful if the critics spoke out more strongly against such works before they overstep the narrow frontier which distinguishes them from the kind of wretched product that lies within the province of the police." A leader in the same issue praised Cederschiöld's article as "a ringing protest against an unwholesome development in our literature."[16]

In Denmark, where the critics in general were much more receptive to Strindberg than those in Sweden, *The Red Room* was acclaimed. Virtually the entire Copenhagen press adjudged him a writer of genius; even the conservative papers, while disapproving of his moral and social attitudes, admitted his quality. The brothers Georg and Edvard Brandes, the two most influential Danish critics, praised it highly, and lost no time in conveying their enthusiasm to other Danish and Norwegian authors. "You should read August Strindberg's *The Red Room*," Georg wrote to the Norwegian novelist Alexander Kielland. "It is a remarkably clever book, witty and gifted. Untidily composed, and the hero is split into three characters, it has a hundred beginner's faults, but is good . . . only that he caricatures in an excessively coarse and English manner."[17] Edvard told the Danish novelist J. P. Jacobsen: "You must read him. He is the only talent in Sweden . . . He will become something big . . . He stands quite alone in his battle against the most lunatic and repellent hypocrisy."[18] Kielland found the book "gripping, salubrious, truthful and positive, if not quite deft enough for my taste . . . I think he paints life in too stark primary colours, but that makes his writing glow in the reader's mind long after one has closed the book."[19] Bjørnson and Jonas Lie both admired it, and Henrik Ibsen, holidaying in Berchtesgaden, praised it to his young admirer John Paulsen, his first recorded comment on Strindberg.[20] *The Red Room* contains a scene in which Falk is struck dumb with admiration on meeting a publisher who has been permitted to address Ibsen as *du*; Strindberg's famous hostility to Ibsen had not yet begun.

The book sold well. The first edition of 1,550 copies sold out immediately, and three further editions appeared before the summer. (Over the next seven years it was to sell 7,500 copies, making it, as *Dagens Nyheter* noted on 28 February 1887, the second-bestselling of all Swedish books during that period.) It did not bring Strindberg much money: 500 crowns per edition. But it was his breakthrough; it not only made him the most discussed writer in Sweden, but also established him throughout Scandinavia. As a result, Isidor Bonnier, despite the portrait of his uncle in the book, offered to publish a collected edition, in four volumes, of everything that Strindberg had written prior to *The Red Room* under the overall title of *I vårbrytningen* [*Spring Harvest*], and this duly appeared towards the end of the following year.

So 1879, which had begun so disastrously for Strindberg, ended in triumph. It was an important year for another Scandinavian dramatist; on 4 December, less than three weeks after *The Red Room*, *A Doll's House* was published. Ibsen had already made his breakthrough, as far as the Scandinavian public was concerned, in the previous decade with *Brand* and *Peer Gynt*; and *The Pillars of Society*, in 1877, had spread his fame to Germany. But *A Doll's House*, over the next decade, was to make his name a household word throughout the Western world. Later Strindberg was to attack the play vehemently and often for what he regarded as its championship of feminism (a claim which Ibsen repeatedly denied). But although Strindberg must surely have read it, or at least heard it discussed—it was performed at the Royal Theatre in Stockholm within five weeks of its appearance—there is, surprisingly, no mention of it in his letters over the next year, nor any hostile reference until his preface to the first volume of *Getting Married* in 1884 (though *Sir Bengt's Wife* in 1882 was intended as a reply to it). He was to claim in his autobiography[21] that he did not read it until two years after its publication, though this, as Martin Lamm has pointed out, seems unlikely.[22] The reason for Strindberg's lack of immediate hostility to the play was simple. He was still happily married, and his hatred of feminism lay in the future.

The reception of *The Red Room* so exhilarated Strindberg that within nine weeks of its appearance he had completed a new play, *The Secret of the Guild*. Set in Uppsala in 1401–2, it deals with the conflict between two master masons for the right of completing the city's cathedral, still unfinished after a hundred and fifty years. Both, in their way, are idealists; but where Sten is virtuous, Jacques is ruthless. Jacques wins the right to build the tower, but it is destroyed in a thunderstorm and Sten ends as the victor. The first act is as good as anything Strindberg had yet written, but the play fades badly. However, by now he was a celebrated author, and within a week the Royal Theatre accepted it. To compound his happiness, on 26 February Siri gave birth to a daughter, Karin.

The Secret of the Guild received its first performance on 3 May 1880, with Siri in the role of Margaretha, Jacques's loving and long-suffering wife. It was Strindberg's first theatre premiere for nearly nine years. The audience was sympathetic, the author being called for twice, and it was favourably reviewed in two leading dailies, *Stockholms Dagblad* and *Aftonbladet*; but it managed no more than six performances and has seldom been revived (the last recorded occasion was in 1916). It evoked, however, a letter of congratulation from Strindberg's old professor and enemy C. R. Nyblom; and, as every writer knows, there is no surer sign that one has arrived than a laudatory letter from a previously hostile teacher. The curious thing is that after so big a success with a contemporary novel, Strindberg should have written another historical play; presumably he believed that a historical play had a better chance of acceptance.

That spring Strindberg made the acquaintance of the painter Carl Larsson, who by a coincidence had lived as a child in another apartment in the house on Grev Magnigatan where Strindberg had settled eight years earlier after leaving Uppsala. They were to become close friends and, later, as so often happened with Strindberg's friends, enemies. Larsson had written an enthusiastic letter to Strindberg on reading the poetic version of *Master Olof*; Strindberg called on him and, Larsson recalled: ". . . we met often. We dug around in the rubbish heaps in the Roslag marshes, where we found bits of old porcelain stoves and layers of glued wallpaper . . . We would go into the Old Town, and run up and down the staircases, borrowing keys to attics and studying all the evidence we could find of seventeenth-century architecture and domestic life. Then we would go to his home or mine and sit over a glass of wine and a pipe of tobacco, usually some humble brand, and discuss the matters of the day . . . I worshipped him."[23]

Another future friend and enemy saw him for the first time now, though they did not meet until four years later. Verner von Heidenstam, ten years Strindberg's junior, relates how "I stood at one of [my grandmother's] windows and watched a slim and elegant gentleman struggling against a snowstorm sweeping round the corner. He held the brim of his top hat with both hands and found great difficulty in at the same time keeping his portfolio under one arm. 'That young gentleman,' exclaimed my grandmother, 'is from the library and often walks past. He is apparently called Strindberg, and writes.' Little did I guess then that I should one day become friends with this elegant gentleman and that we should then turn our backs on, and attack, each other, as often happens among well-known writers and musicians."[24]

Now that his inhibitions about writing had evaporated, Strindberg was full of projects. In May he offered Albert Bonnier, who had asked if he had anything new in mind, a miscellany of essays which was to appear a year later as *Cultural-Historical Studies*. During the summer, which he spent at Dalarö and Kymmendö, taking three months' unpaid leave from the library,[25] he told both Seligmann and Isidor Bonnier that he was planning a play ("a five-act comedy which I first planned in 1871") and a book of stories, though in neither case can we be sure to what he was referring[26] (eighteen months were to elapse before his next play, *Sir Bengt's Wife*, and four years before the story collection, *Getting Married*.)* "I am afraid the stories will come before the play," he wrote to Joseph Seligmann on 13 June. "They will be a bit immoral—but some of them very beautiful—above all, new! I have discovered quite virgin soil which I have ploughed up! . . . If only I could escape my money troubles for two months, I would flourish like a rose in Sharon and enrich the whore literature of Sweden with several notable contributions." He was also working on *Old Stockholm*, a nostalgic book about the past of his native city on which he was collaborating with a scholar named Claes Lundin, and before the year was out he was to open negotiations with yet another publisher, Fritzes, for a history of Sweden based, like Buckle's, on sociological principles, to be entitled *The Swedish People*.

The diversity of these plans is significant and regrettable. The greatest novelists and dramatists have concentrated on one medium at a time, and it is difficult to think of an exception to this rule. Drama seldom goes hand in hand with narrative prose. There have been writers who have succeeded in both, but not at the same time. Chekhov, like Shaw and Synge and Beckett, did not become a great playwright until he put narrative fiction aside; Turgenev left only one major play, *A Month in the Country* (which he never intended for the stage); and Pirandello only started writing plays in his fifties and abandoned narrative fiction almost at once. A playwright may write short stories between his plays, as he may write

---

*It is possible that *Anno 48* was written later than is usually supposed, and that he was referring to this.

poems, but although occasionally a novelist, such as Graham Greene, may turn out an isolated good play or two, the careers do not go together. This was a lesson that, sadly, Strindberg was never to learn. For the remainder of his life he was to diffuse his genius, not merely between plays and novels, but over numerous fields, and was to pay the price.

Towards the end of July, he received a letter from Edvard Brandes, who, with his brother Georg, had six years previously founded a magazine, the *Nineteenth Century*, a brilliant and stimulating publication. Repeating his enthusiasm for *The Red Room*, Brandes wrote: ". . . it makes the reader want to join the fight against hypocrisy and reaction . . . Norwegian and Danish writers are currently hatching plans for cooperation, e.g., Bjørnson, Kielland, my brother G. Brandes and myself. I wonder if you might possibly join us, and I know we should greatly like to have you." This was a reference to a projected Dano-Norwegian magazine, which unfortunately did not materialise. Strindberg was greatly excited both by the praise of so distinguished a man of letters and by the contact with a spirit akin to his own. He replied to Brandes on 29 July from Dalarö:

Most honoured Herr Doctor!

Your kind communication has given me much encouragement, both because you are a prominent and progressive figure, and because I stand quite alone, virtually isolated in the battle which I flatter myself I have begun. Your recognition and still more your sympathy have given me courage, since in this country people live like the dead and rend each other from sheer envy (a fault of all small nations!), so that no faction can ever be formed. This indeed became apparent after the publication of *The Red Room*, when I became the target for a mean and sordid attack [in *Afton-bladet*], and not a single voice was raised in protest.

You can therefore understand the strength and pride I feel at the recognition you have accorded me, not as a writer or as a talent . . . but as a fighter. What use I should be to any party I dare not predict! I fear it would be small, for I am still picking up the pieces of my own broken vessel, what they are I'm not sure, I think just a handful of smashed convictions. I have fought till I am exhausted and . . . have become so sceptical that, after seeing almost everything that I believed in unmasked as vanity, I scarcely have anything left but my great and beautiful hatred of all oppression and all gilded measures!

Besides, I am quick to attack, but then my humanity intervenes and I grieve at having struck my fellow mortals, even if they have deserved it! So I cannot be a trusty friend nor a constant enemy. I have withdrawn to my home (I am married) and shun worldly matters, I bury myself in the 200,000 volumes of the Royal Library (I am an amanuensis there!), study Sinology, geography, archaeology—for a while. But beneath all this I ferment and smoulder till another blister like *The Red Room* will swell and burst. Then I shall feel happy and liberated!

As you see, I am a bad person to know! A Gaul who is swift and ruthless in attack, but who leaves defence to others!

As regards my career as an author. I began as a playwright: in 1870 I had a one-act play in rhymed verse called *In Rome* performed at the Royal Theatre. It dealt with an actual episode in Thorvaldsen's life. I was then 21 and a young student at Uppsala. Two years later [*sic*] they staged *The Outlaw*, a one-act play based on the Icelandic sagas. At the same time I had a tragedy published, *Hermione*, in five acts, dealing with Greece's last war against Macedonia, and her fall. Then followed a sea of newspaper articles. In 1877 appeared *Town and Gown*, studies of university life, which I rate highly. In 1878 *Master Olof* was published, a play. I began this in 1871, intending it for the stage, but it was rejected time and again! I would ask you to read this play, ragged though it is through much rewriting, for it is the story of my life and contains quite deep things. The critics greeted it in silence! One solitary paper elected to demolish me! Then came *The Red Room*. This was in autumn 1879. In spring 1880 *The Secret of the Guild* was staged at the Royal Theatre. People had expected something iconoclastic and instead saw something "beautiful," the gossip magazines abused it and the conservatives joyfully reclaimed the prodigal son. Next time I shall pull no punches—and I think they'll be fierce ones!

A few words about my political beliefs in case you want to enlist me. I am a socialist, a nihilist, a republican, anything that is anti-reactionary! . . . I want to turn everything upside down to see what lies beneath; I believe we are so webbed, so horribly regimented, that no spring-cleaning is possible, everything must be burned, blown to bits, and then we can start afresh . . .

Your brother once excited me, but now I find him too aesthetic and reactionary.* You Danes still suffer from that unfortunate "aestheticism." You worship form, beauty, but that's just the surface—and yet—and yet you have your Kierkegaard! Ah, that man!

Strindberg's conviction that "no spring-cleaning is possible, everything must be burned, blown to bits" precisely reflects Ibsen's feelings ten years earlier. In a poem written in 1870, "To my Friend who Talks of Revolutions," Ibsen had declared:

> I've never been one for shifting pawns.
> Blow the board to glory—*then* I'm your man! . . .
>
> You unleash the waters to make your mark.
> I set a torpedo under the Ark.

"How the ideas tumble about us now!" Ibsen had written that same year (20 December) to Georg Brandes. "All that we have been living on until

*Torsten Eklund (*Brev*, II, 168n) thinks this is a reference to Georg Brandes' book two years earlier on the Swedish poet Esaias Tegnér (1782–1846) which Strindberg in a later letter to Edvard Brandes (26 July 1882) condemned as a canonisation of a writer "reactionary and useless to our future."

now is but scraps from the table of the last century's revolution, and that gristle has been chewed and re-chewed for long enough. The ideas need to be scoured and re-interpreted. Liberty, equality and fraternity are no longer the same as they were in the days of the lamented guillotine. That is what the politicians refuse to understand, and that is why I hate them. These fellows only want individual revolutions, external revolutions, political, etc. But all that is just small change. What matters is the revolution of the spirit."[27] Ibsen, though a left-winger all his life, believed that politicians, once they had achieved power, invariably compromised with their ideals, and that the only way to avoid doing the same was to keep oneself free from all party loyalties. He shared with Strindberg an instinct to stand outside the political struggle, unlike such activists as Bjørnson and Edvard Brandes (who was to become finance minister in Denmark's first radical government).

Strindberg retained, however, one sadly illiberal streak. Anti-Semitism was common in Sweden then, as in most if not all European countries, but it was not a vice of which Swedish liberals were often guilty. But on 10 September we find Strindberg writing to Willehad Lindström, a merchant friend of his brother Axel, and a violent anti-Semite: "The pamphlet is absolutely first-rate . . . But I'd like to make one amendment. Page 8, line 15 onwards, it says (about Axel Lamm), that by crooked property dealing he acquired a respectable fortune. For this read: 'by abortions and crooked property dealing.' " The background to this unpleasant sentence is even nastier. A list of unpublished writings which Strindberg drew up in the mid-eighties includes "A Jew Pamphlet," and another friend of his, Klas Ryberg, recalled seeing around this time a manuscript of this with a note on it by another friend, a well-known scientist: "Print this."[28] What makes Strindberg's letter to Lindström particularly odious is the fact that Axel Lamm was the doctor who had befriended Strindberg when the latter was a student of nineteen, given him a room in his house, treated him as a member of the family and directed his medical studies.

The first parts of *Old Stockholm* began to appear in September, and were well received. *Aftonbladet, Dagens Nyheter* and *Nordisk Tidskrift* all gave it excellent reviews. The book still reads agreeably today, especially the chapter entitled "A Walk through Stockholm in 1730." In November and December, there followed the first two volumes of his collected early works, *Spring Harvest;* several critics condemned the contents, including *Master Olof,* for their "modern" approach to historical subjects.[29]

On 23 November, Strindberg founded a club, called simply The Club, with Siri and himself as secretaries. They met at least twice a year, at Easter and Christmas, and numbered about thirty members, including at least two other actresses and one opera singer. They had their own marionette theatre, with six puppets; the Club's other possessions, as appears from an inventory dated Easter 1881, included "two elm clubs, a guitar, a tin pipe with six holes, a toy ocarina, ten masks and a packet of wormwood buds" (these last presumably for the flavouring of a particular type of schnapps). The plays, written by the members, were mostly topical; one such entertainment was *"The Complicated Adventures of Ulspiegel with the Priest's Housekeeper and His Horse.* Freely translated by Aug. Strindberg . . . Herr Strindberg will make his debut in the role of the Horse."* Members had to wear white tie and tails (except, presumably, when performing), and Strindberg "was a stern secretary who thought that everyone should work if they were to enjoy themselves in the Club." The last publication of the Club, on 6 April 1882, announced: "(1) The Club is eternal and lustrous and can never be dissolved, even if no meetings are held, until the last member dies. (2) The Purpose of the Club is Pleasure." But the following year Strindberg and Siri left Sweden for six years, and the members seem to have met no more.[30]

Chapter Seven

DISTRACTIONS

The publication of *The Red Room* made Strindberg the logical standard-bearer for radical opinion in Sweden, but he had a difficult time adapting himself to the role. It is a lonely business to be the scourge of society; Ibsen revelled in the loneliness and the attacks upon him, Strindberg hated them. As Martin Lamm has observed, he was "by inner inclination a romantic, by social conscience a realist."[1] "I am so lonely that I am dying," he wrote to Edvard Brandes on 19 January 1881. "Those who share my views are so cowardly that they keep silent." Quoting this remark in a letter to Alexander Kielland (1 February), Edvard Brandes commented: "Is that not a common situation for us all? But Strindberg has better reason to feel oppressed by it, since the Swedes are far more contemptible than your countrymen or mine."[2] Brandes invited Strindberg to contribute to the Copenhagen daily *Morgenbladet*, of which he was co-editor, and Strindberg agreed. He was to find it a useful outlet for his opinions over the next few years.

One might have supposed that Ibsen's success with *The Pillars of Society* and *A Doll's House* would have shown Strindberg what a powerful medium the drama could be in drawing attention to social problems; but the continued rejection of *Master Olof*, and his conviction that the theatres were the servants of the establishment, discouraged him from further attempts in this field. Now, however, a new and powerful ally appeared.

Ludvig Josephson had built a considerable reputation during the 1860s as manager and stage director at the Royal Theatre, as well as writing several successful plays; but he had had to leave because the Swedish actors disliked being ordered about by a Jew. He was then appointed head of the Christiania Theatre, the leading theatre in Norway. This appointment was not popular, for Josephson, in addition to being a Jew, was a Swede; the premiere of his first production there in 1873 had been repeatedly interrupted by boos, hisses and cries of "Out with the foreigner!"[3] But he stuck to his post and, during his four years there, raised the artistic standard of the theatre to a height it had never previously attained. Among other things, he presented the first stage production of *Peer Gynt*, seven years after Ibsen had written it. But eventually he was forced to resign and returned to Stockholm, where in due course he took over the New Theatre, the previous director of which, Edvard Stjernström, had recently died.

Strindberg had offered Josephson the verse rewrite of *Master Olof*. Josephson rejected it, but he evidently did so sympathetically, for on 28 January 1881 Strindberg sent him the original prose version, which was shortly to be printed as Volume 6 of *Spring Harvest*. He suggested to Josephson that an actable text might be made from a combination of the two versions. "I can, naturally enough," Strindberg explained, "not share the opinions of those who regard the play as fit only for reading. It is written for the stage, and with cuts and additions could, I think, act well." Josephson reacted enthusiastically. Only three days later he replied: "On rereading *Master Olof* in its original form, I hasten to say that I have not for many years read a play which has made such an overwhelming impression on me. I say plainly that there can never have been a more short-sighted, insensitive, lazy and un-Swedish theatre board than that which refused to accept this piece for production."[4] He scheduled it for production later that year.

Josephson also suggested that Strindberg might translate Ibsen's *Love's Comedy*, the premiere of which he had staged in Christiania seven years earlier. Strindberg was tempted. "I have looked at Ibsen's comedy," he replied on 14 March. "It will be a long and expensive job. If you want me to translate it, make me a formal offer and name a deadline, for I daren't risk attempting so big a task for nothing." Whether because Josephson could not offer enough or whether Strindberg cooled on the idea, the project lapsed. One wonders what Strindberg would have made of this play, with its message that love and marriage are incompatible; his own marriage, as far as one can tell, was still happy. The fact that he should even have considered translating an Ibsen play a year after the publication of *A Doll's House* is further evidence that his hostility towards Ibsen did not develop until his own marriage began to fail.

One might have thought that the acceptance of *Master Olof* would have encouraged Strindberg to settle down to writing another play. But that seemingly perverse wish to do almost anything else persisted. He came up with an extraordinary project. "While planning a saga-play," he wrote to Josephson on 26 March, "I happened to read Atterbom's* *The Island of Happiness*, and was astounded that a play as beautiful, deep and simple (or difficult) as *Faust* has not been performed on the Swedish stage, and I lost all desire to attempt a genre in which such a masterpiece already exists . . . I therefore offer to adapt for the stage the five hundred and eleven pages which the play contains." Not surprisingly, and fortunately for Strindberg, Josephson refused.

But an even greater distraction now offered itself. In April, Strindberg signed an agreement with Fritzes, a bookshop "by Appointment to the Court" and also a prosperous publisher, to write a "Swedish cultural history" in the form of essays depicting the lives of ordinary Swedes from the ninth century to his own time. He had put this idea to Joseph Seligmann, who had published *The Red Room*, *The Secret of the Guild* and *Old Stockholm*, but Seligmann rejected the idea, as did Isidor Bonnier.[5] Defending his decision, as a nihilist and critic of the establishment, to publish with a bookshop patronised by the royal family, Strindberg declared that the book "was commissioned by Fritzes, not offered to them by me,"[6] which may or may not be true. His main reason for writing it was financial; Fritzes offered him an advance of over 10,000 crowns. If he had only had a private income, how much second-rate Strindberg we might have been spared! Yet Dickens, Ibsen, Melville, Chekhov and Shaw had no private income; it is simply that their judgement was better than Strindberg's.

He was to work furiously for the next twelve months on *The Swedish People*; in its original edition of four parts, it fills more than a thousand pages, a dreadful waste of a year, especially at this stage of his career, though the research was to prove useful eighteen years later in the writing of his historical plays.

In April he appeared as a horse in a puppet play staged by the Club for its members. Siri was now pregnant again; at his insistence, she resigned from the Royal Theatre that spring. In May they went to Kymmendö. The painter Carl Larsson visited them there to work with Strindberg on the illustrations to *The Swedish People*:

---

*Per Daniel Amadeus Atterbom (1790–1855), a minor and now almost forgotten poet.

> Strindberg was sweet and lovable, as he could be. His time for real work
> was from 6 a.m. . . . We used to jump into the water from a rock. Once
> when Strindberg, naked and ready to jump, looked down into the clear
> green water through which one could see the bottom many metres down as
> distinctly as through a glass, he hesitated and said: "You lack the moral
> courage to show your fear and get dressed and go home," which he then did.
> . . . Gradually I began to discover the brutal and unpleasant side of
> Strindberg's nature . . . Small meannesses, unworthy and sordid assump-
> tions, and plain ridiculous lies made me cautious and fearful of this
> demonic creature.[7]

Larsson appreciatively noted Strindberg's affection for his daughter.
"He would eat breakfast with her on his knee while Siri slept on well into
the day." Strindberg's zoologist-explorer friend Anton Stuxberg was
staying with them; he was known as Stux and Strindberg as Strix. On 9
June, Strindberg's second child, Greta, was born, and he arranged a
baptismal party, to which several of the other inhabitants of the little
island were invited. This party turned out, to Larsson's surprise, to be a
highly formal affair.

> We were commanded to attire ourselves in tail-coats. We did so. But now
> a storm broke. In the midst of the party, in front of the priest and everyone
> else, Strix shouted at Stux: "Where are your medals? When I invite people
> to a baptismal party they must wear *everything!*" Stux could not believe that
> a radical like Strix, especially out there among these simple people, could
> demand such things . . . Soon he returned and you could hardly see his
> black coat for all the medals he had received following his North-East
> Passage.[8]

"We miss you here," Edvard Brandes wrote to Strindberg from
Copenhagen on 19 June. "All we 'new' people long to know you."[9] That
month Albert Bonnier published *Cultural Historical Studies*, a miscellany of essays which Strindberg had written over the past decade,
including his first encounter with Impressionism, his excursions into
Sinology, and a survey of the early history of aquavit in Sweden. It was
well received.[10] On 26 June, Strindberg sent Edvard Brandes a copy of the
book, together with an enthusiastic preview of *The Swedish People*:

> I am living on an island in the skerries, have had a daughter, cultivate the
> soil and am writing my great work: A Swedish Cultural History . . . When I
> have finished this book, which will unmask the whole Swedish nation, I
> shall go into exile in Geneva or Paris and become a writer in earnest. Not
> one of these *littérateurs* but someone who writes to *say* what he cannot
> *speak!* ruthlessly! I don't believe any political half-measures can lead to any
> result—I believe only in the stupidity and scourge of education and in

rebirth through a return to nature—abolishing cities—breaking up the state
into village communities without a sovereign leader . . . The nihilists are
my men! I must speak with them!*

He named Geneva and Paris because they were the centres of nihilistic
thought, thanks to the exiles gathered there. One wonders what the Royal
Bookshop would have made of this letter.

Strindberg was not alone among international writers and thinkers in
believing that anarchy was the pathway to political reform. Ten years
earlier, Ibsen had come to a similar conclusion. "The state must be
abolished!" he had written to Georg Brandes on 17 February 1871.
"There's a revolution to which I will gladly lend my shoulder. Abolish the
conception of the state, establish the principle of free will and all that is
spiritually akin to it as the one prerequisite for universal brotherhood
—*there* is the beginning of a freedom that is worth something!"[11] Ibsen
was to retain this attitude for some time, for as late as 1883 Ingvald
Undset, father of the novelist Sigrid Undset, was to write of him: "Ibsen
refuses to acknowledge nationalism or anything anymore; he is a complete anarchist, wants to wipe everything out—put a torpedo under the
ark—mankind must start from the foundations to rebuild the world . . .
The great task of our age is to blow the existing fabric into the air—to
destroy."[12]

In order to concentrate fully on *The Swedish People* and *Old Stockholm,* Strindberg had taken six months' unpaid leave from the library
from 8 February to 8 August, and he was to take another four months'
leave from 1 September to 31 December. His advance from Fritzes
enabled him to do this. His work at the library was in fact almost finished;
he took a further eight months' unpaid leave the following year and finally
gave up his post there on 31 August 1882.[13]

In September, the first volume of *The Swedish People* appeared. It was
violently attacked in some newspapers and magazines, notably the three
influential dailies, *Stockholms Dagblad, Aftonbladet* and *Nya Dagligt
Allehanda,* which were especially incensed at Strindberg's denigration of
the classic poet-historian Erik Gustaf Geijer (1783–1847) as one who had
told only of his country's kings and not of the common people. But the
hostility was not unanimous; other papers rallied to the book's defence,
and *Handelstidningen i Göteborg* praised it for its "brisk and lively way of

*Daniel Fallström tells how Strindberg spoke to him enthusiastically around this time
of the Russian nihilists, and quoted Herzen: "We do not build, we tear down. We writers
do not proclaim new revelations, we kill the old lies," adding: "We need a revolution here
in Sweden too."[14]

presenting even heavy material . . . even if it sometimes slides into chattiness."[15]

As always, Strindberg reacted paranoiacally to the attacks. "I stand so hellishly alone in this conflagration I have started," he wrote untruthfully to Alexander Kielland on 3 October. "There is no one who does not want to burn me in the stove! I think I have got my fellow countrymen wrong—they are so damned stupid and conservative that no one supports me and those who should are envious and leave me in the lurch." The many expressions of support and friendship were forgotten; he remembered only the enemies.

On 1 October Strindberg and Siri moved from Stora Humlegårdsgatan 14–16, where they had been for two years, a few hundred yards to Östermalmsgatan 23 (now 63). Volumes 2 and 3 of *The Swedish People* appeared in late October and mid-November and were attacked, and praised, as the first volume had been. The idea of voluntary exile tempted Strindberg more than ever. "It is so strange up here," he wrote to Kielland on 6 November. "No enthusiasm, just either servility and stupidity or whining, most often indifference. People laugh when others fight, because it is funny to see someone get beaten, never mind who." Kielland had apparently (his letter to Strindberg has not survived) warned him of the danger of a writer uprooting himself, for Strindberg continued: "Your observations about exile confirm my most secret suspicions. I believe that man is a flower that does not tolerate replanting once one has reached a certain age; besides, every individual flight looks bad and damages the cause. But don't you find it difficult to live in the place where you have portrayed people, and a small place at that?"

Occasionally his manic mood enabled him to regard the situation more humorously. On 16 November he sent Carl Larsson a list of suggestions for further illustrations:

> How are you? I have been abused greatly, but have just lifted a hind leg and pissed on the leash! Don't worry about this, everything's going fine . . . Now to the 16th century, you've got the manuscript, The City and the Country. Go on Sir!* You are enjoined for all our sakes to draw no more of the following:
>
> > Shit-houses
> > whoring (fornicating, screwing)
> > drunkenness (with vomiting!)
> > beheadings (with naked women)
> > venereal diseases

*Strindberg wrote these three words in English.

—since the demand for such delights is apparently small and the supply must be measured accordingly.

On the other hand, the Royal Bookshop strongly urges:

> Kings with crowns on their heads
> Angels bearing palm leaves
> Young smartly dressed women . . . etc.

But such cheerfulness was infrequent. In history, as in so many other fields that he entered (Sinology, science), he was an enthusiastic but unskilled amateur, and laid himself open to attack. "I was condemned to write in a popular manner, i.e., never be able to say all I wanted to, and exhaust the subject," he complained to Hans Hildebrand; but Hildebrand rightly commented: "Your approach was aggressive from the start and you cannot therefore be surprised that you got the kind of criticisms you did."[16]

On 20 November he wrote a battle-weary letter to Edvard Brandes:

> I have fought a fight which was worth it; but I'm so tired and want to rest in the cool groves of creativity . . . No anger, no revenge; peace and humanity; small human problems seen big . . . You once said you were beginning to distrust politics as being of secondary importance. Yes, they are! A question which can be decided by a vote is not a big question and does not carry the seeds of immortality; and men of talent should not rack themselves with small passing questions. Their field is literature, where they can speak for as long as they please without being interrupted or distracted by wrangling.

Alexander Kielland, whose new novel, *Elsa*, had been coolly received by his radical friends, including Edvard Brandes, wrote to Strindberg that month in words which must have echoed Strindberg's state of mind. "My soul is full of revulsion against 'my own party'—dreadful word! fancy belonging to a party! Well, I haven't descended that far. I still hold aloof; but under great pressure. Innumerable little opportunities pop up and lure one into the outskirts of the maelstrom called 'we,' 'the party'—from which one cannot remove oneself without being branded a traitor and the like. I sense that you too stand alone—well, you complain as much yourself. Be happy, brave friend! and never envy him who lives among those who think as he does! It is comforting, but horribly depraving."[17]

Kielland's rejection of politics for the field of human passions and relationships was exactly the encouragement that Strindberg needed. On 2 December he replied:

Dearest friend!
    Many thanks for *Elsa*. It portrays reality in all its cruel nakedness, but tinged with poetry. Such matters as these seem to me so much bigger than any political ones that it amazes me how any writer of talent can waste his time on the latter. (My little daughter is sitting in my lap and won't let me write in peace.) . . . I feel happy, encouraged and fortified when I see that there are others who dare to think as I do. The symptoms of a younger generation awakening are beginning to manifest themselves, and you will see how before long we shall each stand at the head of his army. And that can't happen without encouragement. Alone, one withers. Is it not so? My daughter won't let me write any more!

Further encouragement to abandon polemical for creative writing came that month. On 30 December, Strindberg's fourth wedding anniversary, Ludvig Josephson presented the stage premiere of *Master Olof* at the New Theatre, in the original prose version. The production was directed, not by Josephson, but by the young actor August Lindberg who, two years earlier, under Josephson's direction, had been an exciting Hamlet. The performance lasted for over five hours, from seven until after midnight. The audience showed signs of restiveness, but the reviews were favourable. "With its faults and its many qualities," wrote *Ny Illustrerad Tidning*, "it is one of the finest Swedish plays to have appeared"; and Carl David af Wirsén, a very conservative critic who was to be one of Strindberg's (and Ibsen's) chief enemies—and who, as Secretary of the Swedish Academy, was to be responsible for many of that body's worst errors of judgement in allotting the Nobel Prize for Literature during its early years—praised it in *Post- och Inrikes Tidningar* as being "constructed with great assurance and full of genuine dramatic life." Even *Aftonbladet*, which had attacked *The Red Room*, *Spring Harvest* and *The Swedish People*, grudgingly admitted that the play made "a somewhat more favourable impression when performed."[18]
    Strindberg, who suffered what sounds like a psychosomatic illness at the time of the performance, wrote to Josephson the next day: "After a dreadful evening and night of rheumatic agony I have gradually returned to life and begin to understand from various signs that the play last night achieved a certain success." The play achieved twelve performances, a fair run for so long and demanding a work.
    Evidence of Strindberg's increasing reputation in the other Scandinavian countries appeared that month in the shape of a laudatory piece about him in the Danish conservative paper *Morgenbladet*, describing him as "an indisputable talent and one of the best writers in Scandinavia." In January 1882 another Danish paper, *Illustreret Tidende*, published a

long eulogy of him, praising especially *Master Olof, The Red Room* and *The Secret of the Guild*, which the writer wished might "find its way onto every Scandinavian Christmas table with its message of reconciliation."[19] And on 11 January *The Secret of the Guild* was staged in Helsinki, the first performance of any of his plays outside Sweden. All this stimulated Strindberg, once he had put *The Swedish People* behind him, to complete two new plays in the new year, both in the same optimistic, "reconciliatory" vein as *The Secret of the Guild*. On 18 February he wrote to thank Georg Brandes for defending Ibsen's *Ghosts* against accusations of immorality (Strindberg admired it for its courageous outspokenness). After reporting that "Master Olof has had a brilliant success," he added a postscript: "Yesterday I handed in a five-act saga-play to the New Theatre." This was *Lucky Peter's Journey*. Although Strindberg dismissed it as a pot-boiler, it was to provide him with his first real popular success in the theatre.

Strindberg's divided feelings about which way to go, his desire to enter the political arena, and his hatred of all the strife and abuse that this involved, emerge in a long letter which he wrote on 24 January to his old professor at Uppsala, C. R. Nyblom, and his wife, Helena, who had together sent him a letter of praise and encouragement about *Master Olof*.

> I feel that in the not too distant future I shall be used by a rising younger generation as a sort of chess piece. You know the sort? To them I am an idealist, a deist, an old-fashioned conservative . . . they will not hesitate to tear me to pieces when I don't go with them, and I don't want to go with anybody; I want to be angry when I have cause, to go mad when my heart bids me, to climb over barricades and tread forbidden territory when the desire takes me and I feel young, I want music, I want the right to walk in the countryside, to love my wife and children, to keep my naïve belief in God, I want to be free! . . . I shall come forth when duty calls me, but I do not want to be hustled forth and tied hand and foot to a programme; but that is the way things are shaping. And it's the young whom I fear, I am informed enough to be able to understand and respect the old when they are right. So my future position will not be comfortable, halfway between two camps, and that is why I am seriously thinking of going into exile, especially since I have sensed a new spring resulting from the sunshine which *Master Olof* has brought me.

Restless as ever, he wrote to Albert Bonnier on 12 February asking him to back an "absolutely radical" magazine which he was planning with Knut Wicksell. This came to nothing. His distrust of the theatre appears in a letter he wrote to Ludvig Josephson (22 March) asking him to give Siri an engagement. "My interest in the theatre, I must frankly state, has but

one focus and one goal—my wife's career as an actress . . . Perhaps you
have not seen her on the stage. Well, she is no miracle, but she is more
talented than all these petty celebrities. The reason she didn't succeed at
the . . . Royal Theatre was that after a fine debut she committed the folly
of marrying me, who was persona non grata and didn't express open
approval of the brothel situation prevailing there . . . That is the extent of
my theatre interest. What I have to say I can say better in a novel than in a
play, but I will write plays for her sake. Let her make her debut as Lisa in
Lucky Peter and you will see that she will succeed."

Josephson yielded to Strindberg's plea, and gave her two parts in his
1882–83 season, though when *Lucky Peter's Journey* was at length
presented she could not appear in it, for the same reason that Strindberg
could not attend the premiere. Again it seems surprising that, with the
examples of Ibsen and Bjørnson, and with Josephson in charge at the New
Theatre, Strindberg should still regard the novel rather than the drama as
his natural medium. Ibsen had described his mission in life as "to wake
the people up and make them think big," which is precisely what
Strindberg was attempting, and Ibsen had shown how powerful a medium
the theatre was for such a purpose. But if one studies *The Red Room* and
the story collection he was to write later this year, *The New Kingdom*, one
senses that Strindberg was not yet ready, or willing, to concentrate his
fire-power as one must in a play. He wanted to bash around at everything
and everyone, and this was perhaps the chief reason why he shrank from
the theatre and took so long to develop as a playwright.

Meanwhile, he slaved away at his ill-fated cultural history. "Strindberg
keeps indoors the whole time," reported old Klemming to Carl Snoilsky,
"working on his famous and unfortunate big book, *The Swedish People*.
Thin before, he has now dwindled into a skeleton, and has aged
incredibly."[20] Strindberg confirmed this description in a letter to his
cousin Oscar on 10 April: "Overstrained by work and many worries, still
suffering from the consequences of a party on Maundy Thursday, my
brain is so battered that I dare not show myself in public . . . I can't bear to
see or talk with a lot of people, for then my brain becomes like a spinning
wheel." But three days later he finished *The Swedish People*; a thousand
pages written in a year.

Chapter Eight

"THE THEATRE IS OMEGA"

Siri, unable to find theatre work in Sweden, left that spring for her native Finland, to play Jane Eyre for two weeks in Helsinki. Strindberg found even so brief a parting insupportable. He wrote her four letters in little over a week, full of affectionate information about the children, and with the good news that "I have managed to borrow money so that we are free of debt."[1] "Don't take any more work in Finland," he begged her; and finally sent her a telegram saying that he had fallen ill, causing her to cancel the remainder of her engagement and hasten home, where she found him in excellent health.

They had now been married for four and a half years, and there is evidence that, happy as he may have been, the strain was beginning to tell on her. Dr. Edvard Selander, a cousin of Strindberg who saw a good deal of them around this time, recalled: "Siri von Essen, when I first came to know her, was an uncommonly charming and delightful woman, and evidently very affectionate towards her husband. Though not exactly beautiful, she was, with her tall, slim figure, light blonde hair and beautiful eyes, of very pleasing appearance . . . in conversation lively, agreeable and entertaining, without revealing any outstanding talent. She got on well with her husband's friends, one might say too well, for as time passed she gradually adopted their bad habits, which more rapidly affected her sensitive and weaker nature than the more resistant male nervous system." He says she got used to spending whole nights drinking, and became "immoderate" in this respect. He cites an occasion at Östermalmsgatan when she spent a whole morning drinking with guests. "To interrupt the bacchanal was impossible because of Fru Strindberg's obstinate opposition, and towards the end of the morning the party was more than merry, with the young lady and Frithiof Kjellberg completely drunk. When I mentioned this unfortunate situation to Strindberg, he said it didn't help to cause a scene and that he couldn't absolutely forbid her or she would drink in secret and that would be worse."[2]

This impression of Siri is confirmed by Strindberg's friend Daniel Fallström, who, on the publication of Selander's book containing the above passage, wrote to another mutual friend: "What Edvard Selander writes about Siri Strindberg is unfortunately correct." But he added: "I always get annoyed at the way whenever anyone writes about Strindberg they paint too black a picture of him. From the time I knew him, in the early eighteen-eighties, I retain only a bright and happy memory of him, sleigh-rides and skittles and endless drinking of punch."[3] But to be a drinking companion of Strindberg's was very different from being married to him.

Yet to those who did not arouse his enmity, he could be enchanting. August Lindberg tells how he came to Strindberg this spring of 1882 to ask for the touring rights of *Master Olof*. He explained he could not offer much.

> "Can you manage a hundred crowns?" Strindberg asked.
> "Just about." I laid them on the table in gold.
> "Wait a minute," he said . . . "We must knock off two crowns for the medicine you got me twelve years ago."
> Twelve years ago! That was when he was lying sick with the first draft of *Master Olof* under his pillow.
> When we had seated ourselves in Berns' restaurant we began to talk about *Master Olof*. "Why didn't you cut it?" he asked. "The play was much too long." "We didn't dare." "You theatre people are always such cowards . . . You must be rude to people. Then they will be polite to you." . . .
> A joy to his friends, a terror to his enemies; that was the Strindberg I knew. He could be as weak as a child and as fastidious as a woman, but also proud and stubborn. Had it not been for that stubbornness, he could never have waited all those years.[4]

In mid-May, Strindberg and Siri went to Kymmendö, where he spent the summer writing feverishly. By the beginning of July he had completed *The New Kingdom*, a volume of short stories attacking the Swedish establishment.

Kymmendö, as usual, engendered a mood of euphoria in Strindberg. "I have been out and greeted all my old friends among the trees and stones," he wrote to Pehr Staaff on 16 May. "I have picked mushrooms, carried horse-shit to the cucumber bed, dug, sowed spinach, radishes, etc. Drunk evening toddy with the fishermen and nattered about sea-birds and fish, not neglecting the opportunity to spark their hatred of the royal family and other institutions, which small seeds fall in well-manured soil." He accompanied this letter with a caricature of himself, portly with a pipe; but ten days later he told Staaff: "Sitting on my rump on the rocks has brought back my bladder catarrh to such an extent that I have become a total abstainer; I drink herbal tea, Vichy water and milk. A gentle attempt at beer turned out most unfortunately." He illustrated his plight with another delightful caricature, showing himself very thin and leaning on a stick, subtitled: "The results of abstinence."

"This autumn I am leaving Sweden for sure," he informed Edvard Brandes on 26 June, "for I can't stand it here alone. You have a party in Denmark, but here I am quite alone and they tie one leash after another on me. But now I think I will flay the pack with my new book [*The New Kingdom*], which is due out in the autumn and which between you and me is savage. But I haven't the stomach to hear their howls, so I shall go with the family to Paris." Brandes replied expressing disappointment with *Lucky Peter's Journey*, which Strindberg had sent him ("The whole thing is too Hans Andersen—spiced of course with authentic Strindbergian nihilism"),* but promised to do his best to get it staged in Copenhagen. He suggested, however, that Strindberg was overdoing the self-pity. "Aren't you being a little hyper-sensitive? Aren't things going pretty well for you? Even if you have to endure untruthful and insulting criticism, surely you have also received much recognition. Your books sell well, don't they? . . . So don't complain too much about standing alone; there are those who would envy you."[5]

Strindberg explained his position in a long letter (26 July) to Brandes which reflects the paranoia which now increasingly gripped him:

> Dear Brother!
> . . . I am leaving Sweden not out of fear for myself or discontent with criticism, I am going so as to be in peace from—my friends, and so that my wife and children may be freed from outright persecutions which they could not endure. My literary adversaries (the idealists!) have so many strange ways of replying to my attacks. They insult my small daughters when they

---

*In private, Edvard Brandes was even less kind about *Lucky Peter's Journey*. "Pretty mediocre," he wrote to his brother Georg on 6 July. "So intemperate and bitter. And he moralises too much"—a verdict on the play with which one would agree.[6]

are out walking, they send foul postcards, the best of them send anonymous letters, the worst intrigue against my wife in her professional career (she is, alas, an actress), the best of all buy up my old IOUs (I was born to financial disaster) and slander me behind my back, the most cowardly smear filth on my visiting cards and scrawl on my doors. That disturbs my work and depresses me, so I am leaving—to return, once a party has managed to form!

It may amuse you to know of my financial situation . . .

The Red Room, which enjoyed unprecedented sales, brought me from all four editions (6,000 copies) 2,200 crowns. It took me nine months to write. One can't nowadays keep a wife and children on less than 6,000! How much did I borrow that year? *Master Olof* which enjoyed a great success (even Wirsén praised it!) brought me 750 crowns. Ten years' work! *The Secret of the Guild* at the Royal (!) Dramatic Theatre 260 crowns. *Spring Harvest* was partly sold 7 years ago for 10 (ten) crowns per ark [of 16 pages]. Hasn't sold more than 1,000 copies. *The Swedish People*, which was to have been a cultural history but turned out a party political brochure, brought 10,000 crowns, of which I had to pay out around 10,000 crowns in debts.

Are you satisfied?

Now I have completed a new work, a sequel to *The Red Room*; crazy satires in pure prose. It will appear in the autumn. Keep this secret.

I pretty well share your opinion of *Lucky Peter*. But love has been for me as it was for Peter. When life was shit and I wouldn't have given two rotten berries to go on living, I found a woman (I had found many before!) and life became worth while . . .

One thing I would like to explain to you in advance.

I am regarded as an anti-Semite and have satirised the Jews in my new book. I do not hate the Jews, only *our* servile, medal-greedy, despotic, oppressive Jews who with all the power of wealth (they have found it easy to cheat the stupid Swedes of their money!) work, in their ruthless way, to support the reaction against us. Thus they are your enemies as well as mine.

Uppsala University has three docents in Swedish literature, for example, and they are all small-minded, stupid, conservative Jews who carp at everything new. All (virtually all) our publishers are Jews who sell Luther's writings and the New Testament to show themselves liberal, but if one wants to be liberal in politics or literature, oh no! It is a coincidental misfortune for them that they are Jews and I should like them as little were they Swedes. They are foreigners and behave in a hostile foreign manner towards us; they are in their right, fair enough, as I am in my right when I defend myself.

So this is not a question of Jewry, nor even of Jews, but of *our* Jews in Sweden! . . .

Let us stick together and not break for the sake of a detail. You are not a Jew because you have publicly forsworn Jewry,* while our Jews cling to

*Brandes' father had been born Cohen, but the family name had been changed to Brandes when Georg and Edvard's grandmother was remarried to a man of that name. Georg and Edvard were freethinkers, hence Strindberg's remark about forswearing Jewry. Edvard had been elected to the Danish Parliament in 1880 and there had been much controversy about whether as a Jew he could take the oath.

their old superstitions to arouse interest, but they don't believe in them a bit. That is why I have felt able to speak to you about this and I am surely above the suspicion of being so narrow-minded as to be an intolerant religionist or racist.

Brandes found it difficult to accept Strindberg's attitude in this matter, and although they exchanged letters in August and September, there ensued a three-year break in their correspondence.

The intensity with which Strindberg composed *The New Kingdom* had not exhausted his compulsion to write that summer on Kymmendö. No sooner had he finished it in early July than he started work on a new play. His main reason for returning to drama, despite his feelings against it, seems to have been domestic rather than artistic: Siri was restless to advance her career as an actress, and he wanted to provide her with a part that would keep her in Sweden. (Although Ludvig Josephson had accepted *Lucky Peter's Journey*, he did not intend to stage it that year, and was in any case doubtful whether she would be right for the role of Lisa.)[7] So now, for the first time, Strindberg wrote a play in which the main role was a woman's, *Sir Bengt's Wife*.

He was to complete this by the beginning of September. Meanwhile, Fritzes rejected *The New Kingdom*. This was not surprising, considering that *The New Kingdom* attacked practically every aspect of the Swedish establishment, on whose patronage Fritzes prided itself. So Strindberg, whose *Lucky Peter's Journey* was already being printed by Isidor Bonnier, switched publishers yet again. Replying on 3 August to an inquiry from a young publisher, Claes Looström, he wrote: "You ask if you can have my next book? You can have all my next books (except one), if you pay Isidor the 3,000 crowns that bind me to him . . . I would dearly love to escape the clutches of the Jews, I can't deny, and would rather see an original native of this country earn a few pence than an Asian. If you take me you will have all young Sweden, which is beginning to blossom forth beneath my caring hands."

Looström was tempted by this offer but uncertain whether he could afford to buy Isidor out, and on 14 August, Strindberg wrote him a letter of such hideousness as to make a modern admirer of his work despair. He dug out that unprinted anti-Semitic pamphlet which he had compiled two years earlier and sent it to Looström suggesting that he should show it, together with the story in *The New Kingdom* entitled "Moses," which portrays a grasping Jewish publisher, to a wealthy industrialist and banker named A. O. Wallenberg, the head of a bank who was reputed, rightly or wrongly, to be anti-Semitic, in the hope that he might be willing to advance the 3,000 crowns needed to release Strindberg from his contract with Isidor:

> Since the most urgent thing for us both is that the Bonnier business be settled with all speed, never mind how, I suggest this as the simplest and surest method.
>
> You (as a respected citizen with the reputation of being an honourable man) should forward, or personally hand, the attached manuscript [of the pamphlet], together with the "Moses" chapter, to A.O.W.; tell him that Sg plans to publish this shortly, but tell him too with what risk to myself, my wife and my children. If A.O.W. says no, that would be no affront to you. It would be to me; but this would not embarrass me if we achieve our object. But A.O.W. will probably be so mistrustful of so ruthless a writer as Sg that he will want nothing to do with him and then we shall be stuck with nothing achieved. If you don't want to ask A.O.W. for the whole amount, then get some names of genuine Jew-haters who, if they haven't the money themselves, might be willing to ask others who are better-heeled to raise it. [He then names four.] I'm not going to go around cap in hand, but should others be willing to free me from the Jews, I shall accept it with no particular feeling of obligation and none of shame.

Wallenberg did grant the loan, but not for publishing the pamphlet, which, luckily for Strindberg's reputation, was to remain unprinted.

On 31 August, Strindberg formally terminated his employment with the Royal Library, where he had spent only six months in the past two years. Henceforth, for the rest of his life, he was to depend entirely on his pen. A few days later he handed the completed manuscript of *Sir Bengt's Wife* to Josephson (how dependent he was on Jews!), who at once accepted it for production that autumn, and forthwith started work on a new collection of stories, *Swedish Destinies and Adventures*. Apart from completing *The Swedish People*, this was his fourth new work that year, and he was to have eleven stories ready to appear by Christmas. Did any author of comparable stature, anywhere, ever, write so much, so fast? This, sadly, was to be the pattern for the remainder of Strindberg's life.

On 8 September he left Kymmendö for Stockholm; on 13 September he signed a contract with Looström for the publication of *Sir Bengt's Wife*; and on 25 September Looström, having, thanks to Wallenberg, paid off Strindberg's debts to Isidor Bonnier and Fritzes, published *The New Kingdom*. It carried on the title page a quotation from *Pickwick*: "You are a humbug. I will speak more plainly if you wish. A traitor, sir!"

In these ten stories Strindberg attacked the Royal Theatre, the Swedish

Academy, the civil service, the army, the universities, such sacred cows of Swedish literature as Bellman and Geijer, the historians and archaeologists who had condemned *The Swedish People* as unscholarly, and, of course, the Jews. Individual targets were thinly disguised and easily recognisable. Most of their names are forgotten or mean little today, but the stories still make lively reading; anger tended to bring out the best in Strindberg, though it sometimes brought out the worst. What mars the book most is the illiberalism which so often disfigures his writings, and which was particularly regrettable in one who regarded himself as a spearhead of reform.

Considering the nature of the book, *The New Kingdom* received a better press than might have been expected. *Dagens Nyheter* praised it, finding that the justifiable attacks on general targets outweighed the personal sniping. Both the Gothenburg dailies, though likewise regretting the exposure of private vendettas, came down on the side of the book. Karl Warburg in *Handelstidningen* liked the style and some of the satire, but complained that Strindberg suffered from fixed ideas and reacted sourly to criticism; *Göteborgsposten* deplored the wildness of some of the attacks but praised Strindberg's earnest desire "to flay what is wrong in our society, to scrape away the varnish and the rouge and show everything as it really is." *Nya Dagligt Allehanda*, by contrast, found the book "depressing and repellent . . . It is deeply to be regretted that a writer of Herr Strindberg's otherwise manifest talent should sink to enrich himself by turning to this genre."[8] More damaging than such hostile reviews was the fact that several influential papers, notably *Stockholms Dagblad* and *Aftonbladet*, ignored it completely.

Nevertheless, *The New Kingdom* sold well, and a second edition appeared within a month. It led, predictably, to a number of violent attacks on Strindberg, which increased his resolve to leave Sweden. Although vigorous in dishing out abuse, Strindberg was not good at taking it. He received some letters of support. Bjørnson wrote to him: "I am sure that a new and brave poetry will bloom in your footprints in Sweden, even though we may have to wait a while for it,"[9] and Carl Snoilsky, then the leading poet in Sweden and an aristocrat who might have been expected to take offence at the book, told Gustav Klemming that he regarded Strindberg as "the most important figure in contemporary Swedish literature" and praised his "hatred of all false pretences."[10] But such support, like that which he was later to receive in connection with his trial for blasphemy, seemed small compared with the attacks.

Among those who disliked the book was Edvard Brandes. After sympathising with Strindberg for the attacks that had been launched on him ("Literature hardly excites such hatred here. But the fact is that you do stand alone. Here there are many of us to share the pricks") and for the poor payment he was getting, he continued: "Albeit reluctantly, I have to tell you that I expect no good from your new book, no good for our friendship or for our mutual aims. I fear that you will involuntarily aid our enemies, or anyway mine. The war you want to wage against the Swedish Jews will harm me and every Jew, whether a believer or not . . . You rightly complain of the insults to which your little daughters are subjected. That is exactly what every little Jewish boy or girl has to suffer, year in, year out, as my own two little girls will find. You speak of the hatred under which you shrink; that is just what every Jew who is not willing to abase himself before the Cross meets every day of his life . . . No article is ever written against my brother or me in which anti-Semitism is not manifest."[11] He returned his copy of *The New Kingdom*. Strindberg did not reply to this letter.

Despite the commotion aroused by *The New Kingdom*, Strindberg proceeded busily with his new story collection, *Swedish Destinies and Adventures*. On 1 October, Siri and he had moved to yet another apartment, at Storgatan 11, their fifth in less than five years of marriage. To find peace from the children he leased a work-room in the park of Djurgården "with a view over the sea," he told Looström (13 October). Before the month was out he had completed the first two volumes, containing the long story "Cultivated Fruit" and ten others. They appeared towards the end of November, with a third in mid-December.

Strindberg originally intended to call this collection *A Swedish Decameron*,[12] and it is a pity he did not, or at least choose some less clumsy title than *Swedish Destinies and Adventures*, which has deterred many people in Sweden as elsewhere from reading these vivid tales. They have well been described as a fictional and far superior counterpart to *The Swedish People*.[13] The recurrent theme is of ordinary men and women oppressed by kings, masters and bureaucrats. A young monk is wrongly accused of heresy and burned; two neighbours on different sides of the Danish-Swedish border (in the days when Denmark ruled the southern part of Sweden) who have always been friends are commanded by their kings to destroy each other; soldiers gathered around the coffin of the warrior Charles XII reflect on the price of his glory. Other stories tell of a young man of noble lineage but no inheritance who is compelled to work, finds himself useless and commits suicide, a kind of preliminary sketch for *Miss Julie*, and of an unwanted child in a large family who goes out into the world, returns famous and is fawned upon by his former detractors, but wearies of it all and returns to exile.

These tales are marred by the defects which were so often to flaw his plays as well as his narrative fiction. Brilliant scenes alternate with dull passages which, had he read them through with any sense of self-criticism, he would surely have cut; he was never a man to carry his scholarship lightly; and his characters stray into banalities and his plots into melodrama. But there are passages unlike anything else that was being written anywhere then, such as the closing sentences of "New Weapons":

> Then he leaned down and saw a small pile of sand on the floor. The longer he looked at it, the bigger it grew. He looked up at the roof. There was a hole there through which something was pouring. Then he fell asleep. He dreamed he was lying in a huge hour-glass watching the sand run; and he knew he must die when the sand was finished. He wanted to save himself; but there was glass on every side, such hard glass that he could not break it. Then he dreamed that he dreamed that he lay in an hour-glass that ran, but he could not wake. He dreamed that he dreamed that his mouth was full of sand and that he heard a voice which said: "Eat now." And he wanted to wake to escape from the bad dream. Then he dreamed that he woke; but he did not wake.

Swedish Destinies and Adventures, though criticised for historical inaccuracy, received higher and more general praise than anything else that Strindberg had written; indeed, the reviews were the most favourable that he was to receive for many years. Edvard Brandes wrote a particularly glowing notice in *Politiken*, and Karl Warburg in *Handelstidningen i Göteborg* perceptively observed that what had been a fault in *The Swedish People*, Strindberg's tendency to make his portrayals as much a satire on modern society as a depiction of the old, here became a strength. But, to Strindberg's annoyance, the stories were praised everywhere as fiction. The lessons that he sought to teach were ignored.

In the same week in which *Swedish Destinies* appeared (25 November), *Sir Bengt's Wife* had its premiere at the New Theatre with Siri in the title role. Set in Sweden in the sixteenth century, it tells of a knight who rescues a girl from a convent and marries her. She is nearly seduced by another man, is saved by a father confessor, tries unsuccessfully to commit suicide, and in the end is reunited with the knight. It is a terrible play, yet it contains the seeds of the great dramas which Strindberg was to write later that decade. *Sir Bengt's Wife* is really a study of any nineteenth-century marriage and its petty irritations. Here, for the first time, Strindberg was writing not about political, religious or social problems, but about sexual relationships and, in particular, the problems that married couples face when love and hatred ride hand in hand. This was

Strindberg's main obsession, and it is scarcely an exaggeration to say that, though he sometimes wrote well on other subjects, such as life in the skerries, he was, by the severest international standards, only a great writer when he was writing about this obsession. *Sir Bengt's Wife*, feeble melodrama though it is, was the forerunner of *The Father, Creditors, The Dance of Death* and *To Damascus*.

Margit, the title character, bears, as Gunnar Ollén has noted,[14] certain marked resemblances to Miss Julie: she is of noble birth, haughty, passionate and attracted by masculine brutality. "I weep like a romantic, with the father confessor," wrote Strindberg to Karl Warburg (5 January 1883), "at the erosion of a beautiful image," which he could equally have written of Miss Julie, and he described Sir Bengt as "a romantic with one leg in the Middle Ages and the other in the Age of Reformation—just like, *inter alia*, the author of *The Red Room*." Sir Bengt is not a flattering self-portrait—"pedantic, materialistic, fond of food . . . veering abruptly between weakness and brutality, bad at money matters, industrious, but runs away when things go badly";[15] but, as in his mature plays, it is a mercilessly truthful one. The characterisation in *Sir Bengt's Wife* is penetrative, but the plotting, and above all the final act, are feeble in the extreme.

Strindberg intended *Sir Bengt's Wife* as a reply to Ibsen's *A Doll's House*. Like Torvald Helmer in the latter play, Sir Bengt treats his wife like a doll; like Nora, Margit rebels and tries to escape. But unlike Nora, she fails; love proves stronger. When the play was printed in November, Strindberg asked his publisher to send a copy to Ibsen in Rome. We do not know Ibsen's reaction; but it is difficult to believe that he could have thought much of it. Bjørnson, to whom he likewise sent a copy, did not like it but discerned the talent. He wrote to Strindberg (27 November) assuring him that he would write splendid plays and urging him to attempt a modern, not a historical one.[16] Unfortunately, it was to be four years before Strindberg followed his advice.

Strindberg's radical friends applauded loudly at the premiere, but the critics expressed surprise at such sentimentality from the author of *The Red Room* and *Master Olof*. "With this play," wrote *Nya Dagligt Allehanda*, "the author has by no means sustained the reputation which he rightly won through both [*sic*] his earlier plays, a reputation which is seriously threatened by the mass of writings which he has lately poured out." The magazine *Kasper* thought it "rather an argument about the rights and wrongs of marriage than a play," and *Ny Svensk Tidskrift* felt that he had forced a subject into historical dress which did not properly belong there.[17] Siri, by contrast, got good reviews, and her performance was seen by many as the only redeeming feature of the evening. Strindberg, as always, took the criticisms harshly. To quote Ollén again, it wounded him on two of his most vulnerable points: his dependence on his wife and his tendency to sentimentality.[18] Henceforth he was to shun romanticism, through both a markedly naturalistic approach and a chauvinistically scornful and superior attitude towards women. He felt that Siri, succeeding where he had failed, had humiliated him.

The play ran for only seven performances and brought him no more than 166 crowns. He tried to blame the actors and the production ("Herr Svedberg spoke four times as slowly as I had intended").[19] The experience reawoke his distaste for the theatre, and four years were to elapse before he wrote another play.

The final volumes of his history, *The Swedish People*, appeared that month and were largely ignored by the press. On 11 December, Strindberg wrote to Rudolf Wall: "My hopes of getting away from here and breathing an air free from poison where I could write my stories collapsed with *Sir Bengt's Wife* . . . So I feel condemned to stay, in the centre of the tumult into which I am gradually drawn deeper, until the creative writer dies and only the lampooner remains. And I have no right to complain, since I myself started the battle, but I deserve the right to rest and tend my wounds, to muster the strength to continue . . . All I need is the price of our tickets to Paris and the cost of clearing up my affairs here, which I reckon cannot cost less than 2,000 francs." The same day he wrote to his publisher Looström asking for help. But two days later he told Wall that Siri felt it was impossible for them to leave so soon. "Nothing arranged, one of the children ill, we dare not move her during the winter, etc." Perhaps, having succeeded in *Sir Bengt's Wife*, she was unwilling to abandon her career, for although she had a good knowledge of French, it would have been very difficult for her to find theatre work in France. So they stayed. This clash of their careers may have been, though we have no firm evidence for it, the first serious crack in their marriage.

On New Year's Eve he wrote to Pehr Staaff: "A headful of ideas and economic worries (New Theatre isn't paying yet) has caused me seriously to consider New Year resolutions, so that I'm not in the mood for getting pissed. I shall begin 1883 by avowing moderation, forswearing punch, cognac and schnapps, since every minute demands the full use of my mind and a calm and equilibrium without which nothing great can be achieved." However: "This will not prevent my going to parties, for I use the milder forms of malt and wine."

So 1882 ended, unpropitiously. It had been a year of great fertility; he had finished *The Swedish People* and written two plays (*Lucky Peter's*

Journey and *Sir Bengt's Wife*) and two collections of short stories (*The New Kingdom* and *Swedish Destinies and Adventures*). But of these only the last had been really well received. *Lucky Peter* had not yet been staged or published. Most woundingly, *The New Kingdom* had been repudiated by the young radicals, of whom he regarded himself as the spokesman; and Siri had succeeded where he had failed.

On 26 January 1883 the prose version of *Master Olof* opened at the Grand Theatre in Gothenburg, where his old mentor Frans Hedberg was now in charge. It was the first performance of any of his plays in Sweden outside Stockholm. Next day he received a telegram from Hedberg: "*Master Olof* has achieved a great and deserved success." Strindberg immediately sent a letter by hand to Staaff quoting the telegram and adding: "I want to get pissed tonight. Meet me in the Crypt [the café of the Grand Hotel] at 8.30." Karl Warburg in *Handelstidningen i Göteborg* reported that there were no less than twenty curtain calls, and praised the play for something that others had criticised as a fault: its relevance to contemporary life as well as to the Middle Ages. Gert, he wrote, would have been "in the eighteenth century a Jacobin, today a nihilist or anarchist . . . It cannot fail to stimulate debate." It achieved eleven performances, most of them to full houses. But even this success was to bring Strindberg no financial reward. Hedberg went bankrupt and could pay him nothing.

On 3 February, Strindberg's father died. They had not met since their quarrel six years previously. "Since I don't think my presence is called for at the reading of the will," he wrote to his brother Oscar, "I prefer to stay away."[20] As expected, his father left him nothing, but he seems to have got something, probably as a good-will gesture from Oscar, who now took over the family firm.[21] He kept busily at *Swedish Destinies*; by 9 April he was able to hand Looström the ninth part of that work. He also suggested to Looström that he might edit a selection of "Authors of the French Revolution," to include *Candide* ("one of the wittiest stories ever written"), Rousseau's *Origine de l'inégalité des hommes* and Bernardin de Saint-Pierre's *La chaumière indienne*. "Naturally," he explained, "I shall not do the translations myself, but shall only be the editor."[22] But nothing came of this project. His financial position was as precarious as ever; his letters to Looström that winter and spring are full of requests for loans.

The strain of writing *Swedish Destinies* was beginning to tell. On 2 May he complained to Looström that he was overworked and needed rest, and he did no more on the book for six months. "To save the spark of sense that flickers in my brain," he wrote to Daniel Fallström, "I am going to Dalarö . . . Thérèse Raquin!!!!! I must!"[23] Presumably he meant he must read the play, which Zola had adapted from his own novel ten years earlier, for he begged Looström: "Zola Théâtre (Thérèse Raquin etc.) is within the gates of Stockholm so for God's sake get them for me."[24] It is surprising that Strindberg had not read it earlier in view of his interest in Zola. But the effect of *Thérèse Raquin*, which six years later Strindberg was to name as a keystone of the new movement, and of Zola's naturalistic theories about the theatre, was not immediate. For several more years the drama was to remain low on Strindberg's list of priorities.

His distaste for the theatre remained deep-seated; he regarded it as a place for amusement, and the drama as an inadequate medium for psychological study. Pehr Staaff tried to convert him. "Goncourt is wrong," he wrote to Strindberg on 25 June, "in saying that the drama is an unsatisfactory form, * even if, as I think, he is right that five acts cannot comprise a complete soul-history. But this is not for the reason you gave, that drama exists to amuse; it achieves far more than one of Goncourt's excellent novels which only the élite can read. Ideas must be spread; surely that is at least as important as that psychological questions be exhaustively treated . . . Plays are alpha and omega, the beginning and the end, and in that sign shall we conquer . . . Each must choose his own form, as best he can, and I feel that until we find better, Ibsen's is the best—as yet."[25]

That month, Staaff visited Strindberg at Kymmendö, to which he had moved in mid-May, and they discussed the subject. On 3 July, Strindberg wrote to Staaff: "You go ahead and write plays! . . . but . . . for me the theatre is omega . . . You know how one has to lie once the curtain is up and how little one is allowed to say. The theatre is a clique set-up for Stockholmers, and scripts don't get read unless you write like Ibsen and we can't do that. But you carry on. Under present circumstances the theatre is a good weapon."

This letter is doubly revealing about Strindberg as a dramatist. It shows that even at this early stage of his career, he sensed that Ibsen's classical manner was not for him; and it suggests that he also sensed that the kind of play he wanted to write, and was eventually to write, would prove unacceptable to the theatre of his time.

---

*In his foreword to *Henriette Maréchal* (1879), Goncourt had protested against Zola's theory of naturalism in the theatre, saying that such things were better suited to the novel. Having himself had a series of fiascos in the theatre, Goncourt dismissed the drama as *"cette boîte à convention, cette machine de carton qu'est le théâtre . . Dans cinquante ans, le livre aura tué le théâtre."* Strindberg at this stage of his career supported Goncourt. Three years later, in *Time of Ferment*, he wrote that theatre was a spent force and that future writers would choose another medium to discuss important questions.

That summer Sarah Bernhardt visited Stockholm and appeared at the Royal Theatre in, among other things, Sardou's *Fédora*. Strindberg did not come in from Kymmendö to see her, another instance, perhaps, of his feelings about the theatre at this time. However, he asked Looström (26 May) to send her a copy of *Sir Bengt's Wife*. "To arouse her interest," he added, "give her these four photos of my wife; simply to show that the play has been performed (with a certain success!) and to get her excited about the costumes, which will suit her splendidly." But Bernhardt was never to show interest in Strindberg's plays, any more than in Ibsen's. When, in the nineties, the Norwegian painter Christian Krohg asked Lugné-Poe whether Bernhardt had ever played Ibsen, Lugné-Poe replied, "She will not. She says contemptuously of him, Strindberg and everything new: '*C'est de la Norderie.*'"[26]*

Kymmendö had its usual invigorating effect on Strindberg. "I am gradually recovering," he wrote to Gustaf af Geijerstam. "I go to bed at 9, sleep for three full hours in the middle of the day and stroll in the forest." Stockholm by contrast seemed a nest of enemies. "God, how I've been abused!" he told Carl Larsson (a case, if ever there was one, of the pot calling the kettle black). "And the things they say! But how stimulating it is! I'm so piss-full of ideas after this last load of shit they've thrown at me that I'll need a lifetime to write them all down."[27] Poetry, he decided, was to be the medium. "The tumour in my brain has burst," he informed Looström the next day (8 June), "and now only verse pours out. So beautiful and angry! . . . Don't talk about the *Destinies*. The longer they wait, the better. They are to be my great masterpiece and mustn't be hurried." On 10 June he told Staaff that he had completed a hundred pages of this volume.

Some of these poems that Strindberg wrote on Kymmendö that summer of 1883 were lyrical, but many were satirical, attacking the various objects, human or impersonal, of his contempt. A selection was printed in the magazine *Ur Dagens Krönika*; Karl Otto Bonnier, who had met Strindberg on the boat to Dalarö three years earlier, read these and suggested to his father that they should publish them. "They will certainly be a big success when they appear," he wrote to Albert, "which I would grudge Looström or Oscar [Lamm] or Fritzes, and it would be a pleasure to publish them. I wonder, assuming he hasn't already signed a contract with someone, whether we might not get them if we offered him really good terms (e.g., 50 crowns per ark [of 16 pages] per 1,000 copies)?"[28]

*"Oh, that Northern stuff."

Albert Bonnier consented, and on 22 June, Karl Otto made Strindberg an amended offer of 200 crowns per ark per 5,000 copies, totalling 4,000 crowns for twenty arks, the estimated length of the book. Strindberg demanded more, and Karl Otto took the boat to Kymmendö. Strindberg received him courteously and showed him proudly round his orchard and vegetable garden, though "I remember how overstrained and unwell he looked."[29]

It was only a year since Strindberg had promised Looström that he could have "all my next books" if he settled Strindberg's debt to Isidor Bonnier and enabled him to "escape the clutches of the Jews," but his prejudices did not extend to his rejecting a good bargain when he saw one. On 8 August he wrote to Karl Otto telling him he could be his publisher "for life" provided he repaid Looström the 7,000 crowns which Strindberg owed him. "I am not the trouble-maker people think," he explained. "I left Seligmann because he cheated me on *Old Stockholm* (after *The Red Room*), Isidor because I had sold myself for little money, Fritzes because they became insolent and wanted to censor *The Swedish People* but mostly because they wouldn't take *The New Kingdom*. Now I'm tired of running around."

Albert Bonnier agreed to these terms; so Strindberg changed publishers yet again, by no means for the last time. On 19 August he wrote to Looström: "A ridiculous stroke of fate ordains that after a year's association with you Albert Bonnier comes and frees me from Looström & Co. just as a year ago you freed me from Bonnier. Well! As an author I seek only one thing in a publisher, capital—and freedom. I sell my work, not my soul. You were the nicest and most agreeable I have had, but you were not free from fear and influences and hadn't enough capital to be able calmly to accept a bout of illness or a writer's whim. And you didn't believe in my poems; Bonnier believes in them . . . Besides, Bonnier is paying more . . . Bonnier is more fearless than you and a little freer from prejudice. He had for example no objection to an anti-Semitic poem [*Isaac's Christmas Eve*]." Four days later he wrote again to Looström: "We shall see how long Moses and I get on together. I cannot think of a more vivid illustration of the omnipotence of the Jews than that to save my life and my future I have to cast myself into Abraham's bosom."

However distasteful Strindberg's attitude in this matter, Albert Bonnier's seems scarcely less cynical. Karl Otto, in his history of his family's publishing house, contents himself with the remark: "My father did not love Strindberg as a person—rather the contrary—but he respected him greatly as an author."[30] But Strindberg was publicly known at this time to be a virulent anti-Semite; he had reiterated his contempt for the race in

The Red Room, The Swedish People, The New Kingdom and now in his poems.

His Uppsala friend Eugène Fahlstedt wrote two newspaper pieces about him that summer. In *Handelstidningen i Göteborg* (30 June) he described him as "considerate, almost gentle, communicative . . . his conversation strongly spiced with humour. Only when political or social questions arise does one suddenly glimpse the fanatical libertarian . . . If one accompanies him into the forest and fields or out to sea, one notes his undiminished physical resilience and hardiness."

On 25 July, Fahlstedt published another profile of him in the Uppsala magazine *Fyris*, and told how "when Strindberg was anonymously reviewing plays for *Dagens Nyheter,* one of our leading actors . . . had been the target of this new writer's sharpest criticisms. One day he was invited to a dinner and learned that this fierce critic was to be among the guests . . . Imagine his surprise when, instead of the strident, loud-voiced figure of his imagination, there appeared a young, pale, fair man who bowed shyly, looked much embarrassed and was presented as Herr Strindberg. Before long . . . the wounded *artiste* asked him why he had chosen thus to pillory him. Herr Strindberg bowed diffidently and begged that no mention should be made of that insignificant article. He had not then acquired much knowledge of theatrical matters, and his views were worth little consideration."[31]

At last Strindberg's plans to emigrate were maturing. "We are definitely going abroad in September," he wrote to his brother Axel on 25 July. "Do you feel inclined to have my library, with bookshelves, in your home for a year or two? It is big, as you know, but it might amuse you to have these books to leaf through. Otherwise I shall have to store them in barns to be eaten by rats." (Axel took some of the books, the remainder being left at Kymmendö; three years later, all of them were to be sold by auction.) Lest Albert Bonnier should suppose that his departure might delay the delivery of the volume of poems, Strindberg assured him on 31 August: "I don't think the trip will distract me. I hate museums and art exhibitions, and shun big towns with theatres. I am simply changing my abode." Siri cannot have felt wholly pleased at his decision, since it meant, temporarily at least, abandoning her acting career. If one of Strindberg's motives for the move was to remove Siri from the permissive atmosphere of the theatre, his decision was to rebound against him.

On 12 September they left Kymmendö and spent only twenty-six hours in Stockholm before taking the train south. The next day, en route, he wrote to Ludvig Josephson, who was preparing the production of *Lucky*

Peter's Journey: "If you want to alter and do things to the play, you have my full permission. I have not only lost all interest in the theatre but will go far to avoid hearing about it. If the play gets performed, no harm; if not, I don't care. I say this as an expression of my general indifference." They stopped off at Lübeck and Bremen, where he was disappointed in the beer-cellars but "in my capacity as a purveyor of filth" made notes on the hotel lavatories.[32] They stayed two days in Paris and on 22 September arrived at the little town of Grez, near Nemours, a few miles south of Fontainebleau. It had been recommended to him by Carl Larsson, who was one of a number of Scandinavian artists who had formed a colony there.

Like Ibsen nineteen years earlier at almost the same age, Strindberg was to spend several years in voluntary exile (though only ten compared to Ibsen's twenty-seven). Like Ibsen and so many other writers before and after him, he was first truly to discover himself in exile. Again like Ibsen, he went abroad resolved to turn his back on the theatre and stayed abroad far longer than he had at first intended. Hitherto, his interests had been primarily social and cultural, his main target the establishment in all its forms. He had written ten plays, but none of these except the early *Master Olof* is of real quality or interest. Ibsen likewise had written ten plays when he left Norway, but although only the last of these, *The Pretenders*, remains theatrically valid today, the signs of the great dramatist are clearly to be seen in them: the complex characters and relationships, the ability to keep a story moving and, above all, to bring it to a powerful climax. By contrast, Strindberg's early plays, *Master Olof* excepted, show little evidence of what was to come. They contain lively scenes, good dialogue and the occasional interesting character, but are ill constructed, end feebly, and many of the characters are thinly sketched and of small interest. His women in these plays, especially, are sentimentally idealised. The reason for this last failing is simple; his marriage was still happy, or anyway, he was still happy in it; whether Siri was remains unsure. It was not until he became disillusioned with marriage, and the sex war replaced social and political matters as his primary theme, that he became a major writer.

Part Two

THE FIRST EXILE
(1883–1889)

Chapter Nine

FRANCE AND SWITZERLAND

Strindberg did not intend to stay long abroad. "I do not think I shall extend my exile beyond one year," he wrote to Albert Bonnier on 26 September, adding, which cannot have pleased Bonnier, that he was planning to abandon creative writing for more of those didactic exercises which so repeatedly distracted him from what he did best. "I have come to the conclusion that one cannot inform and entertain at the same time," he explained, though one would have thought that Dickens and Ibsen, to name only two, had proved that one could. "If you debase yourself to play the clown, the public will take you for a clown." He would write a series of "Letters about Sweden," dealing with religion, economy, education, the theatre, etc. "I think such work would be most useful and the biggest thing I could attempt, and the young expect this from me now."

He gave a further reason for not wanting to write plays (as opposed to novels and stories) in a letter to an author named Georg Nordensvan on 2 October. *The New Kingdom*, he says, brought him 2,400 crowns, whereas "Writing plays in Sweden is such a lottery that with my present family I cannot afford it. For *The Secret of the Guild* I got from the Royal Theatre about 250 crowns, and for *Sir Bengt's Wife* at the New Theatre 160. From the publisher one gets hardly anything for a play, as nobody buys it to read. For *Master Olof*, which did very well, I got 750 crowns." For his forthcoming volume of poems, by contrast (though in fact it did not do well), he was to receive 4,333 crowns.[1]

Grez, he told his old editor Rudolf Wall, was "homely, cosmopolitan, mostly Scandinavian and American"; he and Siri were "very happy among nice unpolitical Swedes." He joined a vocal quartet and "an orchestra of cornet, flute and guitar," playing the last-named instrument. His next work, he proclaimed, "will be my biggest . . . to survey all branches of Swedish development since 1865 . . . I cannot spend the rest of my year here to better effect, for France interests me not in the least."

After only two weeks in Grez, the Strindbergs moved to Passy, on the outskirts of Paris. The change did not suit him. "I am miserable in Passy," he informed Albert Bonnier on 13 October. "It is warmer outside, but not indoors. Am buying a stove today; found a big hole in my bedroom wall overlooking the yard, blocked with three months' issues of *L'Evénement*; the floor beneath the carpet has sunk two feet. The tobacco is appalling, and matches 20 centimes a box. I do not love this people, but will endure my year of hard labour here resigned to the inevitable."

To Ibsen, in 1864, Italy had been a revelation, and escape from his homeland a liberation. Strindberg was already longing to return to the country he had so longed to leave. His letters from Paris that October are full of grumbles. "This is a damnable land," he wrote to Claes Looström on 15 October, "and the people are all rogues. Butter costs 1 crown 70 öre a pound, a bus journey 30 centimes. A hundred francs lasts only five days, so I shall have to write hard. No aquavit, no beer. To piss costs 5 centimes, to shit a franc at least, and Paykull and the Drawer who were here a few days ago say you can't fuck for less than 10 francs. This last doesn't concern me, but I still think it's too dear." Even the restaurants did not please him: "We can't eat the local dog-food without getting ill. Otherwise we lead a quiet and peaceful life. Go to bed 8–8.30; my pen is busy from 8 a.m. to 6 p.m. I miss Grez more than Sweden, which I have actually forgotten."[2]

He visited the Triennial Art Exhibition, but "found not a single work of significance," and an exhibition of Manet, who, he thought, "must have something wrong with his eyes or be touched in the head. He has employed colours which do not exist in nature and is, consequently, in my view, a bad painter."[3] Nothing seemed to please him. "Saw Sarah Bernhardt in *Frou-Frou*. Horrible! Just tricks and mannerisms. For me there is only one yardstick in art—realism. Here and there she had studied this, and then she was surprising. Otherwise, shit." Thus to Pehr Staaff on 19 October; and eight days later, again to Staaff: "To live in a republic! I've never before seen people wear medals in the street except army buffers. And on *both* their jacket and their overcoat, so that when they open the latter you can see two red ribbons. They're so narrow and bloody I can hardly sit in a café for a beer with Siri without being nauseated. Humbug, sir! Humbug!* And how they stink! They don't wash, just scent themselves. Christ Almighty! And how they rob you! Jesus! And when they're not stealing, they're begging." "There's no proper bookshop (except for pornography)," he informed Looström. "You can't find a German or English book . . . They're such a bumptious, discourteous rabble that one can't talk to them."[4] On 29 October he assured Rudolf Wall: "I shall never leave Sweden again once I have returned." He missed Swedish food, asking friends to send him such items as split peas and dill, which he could not find in Paris.

On 10 November he moved from Passy to Neuilly, and six days later his *Poems in Verse and Prose* were published in Stockholm. Advance interest in the book was considerable, and the bookshops had ordered large quantities, but on balance, it was ill received. *Aftonbladet* said Strindberg ought to be whipped and warned the public not to buy "this dangerous book," much of which was "infamous" and "repugnant." *Figaro*, noting that for once a book by Strindberg contained no anti-Semitism, concluded that Strindberg had been bribed by Bonnier not to write against the Jews. *Nya Dagligt Allehanda* found "nothing literary or unusual worth remarking," though admitting that "a genuine poetic element can occasionally be glimpsed," and *Kasper* commented: "There is much here that redounds to the writer's honour, but more that he would have done better to consign to the fire." On the other hand, *Dagens Nyheter* found it "brilliant, individual and hair-raising," Karl Warburg in *Handelstidningen i Göteborg*, while regretting the coarsenesses and cynicisms, praised it for its "genius and power," *Budkaflen* thought it "brilliantly witty," *Arboga Tidningen* named it "the most remarkable book of the year" and *Kristianstadsbladet* wrote: "Herr Strindberg is a pioneer, the creator of a completely new school. Whether one enjoys or hates what the man writes, one must read him." But by the end of the year, less than 2,000 of the edition of 6,000 had been sold.[5]

Strindberg was never a skilful versifier, though he sometimes said interesting things in verse, and the best poems in the book are the least formal. In some of them he anticipated the free verse which such poets as Ezra Pound and T. E. Hulme were to pioneer in the English-speaking world thirty years later. They are an expression of doubts, doubts about beauty, science and philosophy, a confused yet stirring demand that his age should awake. Strindberg himself does not seem to have rated the book very highly, and anticipated that it might be attacked. "As far as

*Strindberg wrote these three words in English.

possible," he asked Bonnier, "please keep me completely uninformed about any censure or abuse, as it serves no purpose, it just disturbs my work and irritates me . . . Good and cheerful news, on the other hand, we are all grateful for . . . They look nice, but I haven't had the courage to read them. They're a mixed bag, anyway, and will probably prove more valuable as [auto]biography than as poetry"[6]; a fair verdict.

He thought of visiting England that autumn. On 13 November he asked Leopold Littmansson, a friend from the *Red Room* days who now lived in Versailles, to "accompany me (*en garçons*) to London, just for a couple of days—I want to see the South Kensington Museum, but am prevented for lack of company." But the trip never materialised, and it was to be another ten years before he went there. "I lead an exemplary life," he told Albert Bonnier later that month. "But rest, I shan't get that till I'm in the grave. And even if I could afford it, my restless brain would not allow it."[7]

He had put aside the projected *Letters from Sweden*, and instead wrote a sequence of four long poems entitled *Somnambulist Nights* (five years later he was to add a fifth). They are a kind of "Home Thoughts from Abroad," though, characteristically, they incorporate much of the criticism he had intended to put into the *Letters*. They rattle along briskly in a loose, often dactylic metre, and are admired, sometimes extravagantly, by those who admire Strindberg's poetry. It is always dangerous to judge poetry in a language not one's own, but I find them technically unskilful, like most of Strindberg's formal verse, and banal in content.

Early that December he met, for the first time, the Norwegian writers Bjørnstjerne Bjørnson and Jonas Lie. Both were older than he (Bjørnson was fifty-one, Lie fifty) and firmly established, Bjørnson as dramatist, poet and novelist, Lie as a novelist. Nine years earlier, Bjørnson had written two plays, *The Editor* and *A Bankrupt*, which dealt with contemporary themes in ordinary everyday prose, thereby anticipating Ibsen's *The Pillars of Society* and *A Doll's House*, and, though they do not read very well today, they represented at the time an important breakthrough in drama; Georg Brandes had hailed them as the first genuinely modern realistic plays. Lie was an excellent, sensitive, realistic novelist, whose works have lasted rather better than Bjørnson's. They were living in Paris, knew and admired Strindberg's work, and came to call on him in Neuilly. Bjørnson, within the year, was to quarrel violently and irreparably with him, but Lie was to remain Strindberg's friend for the rest of his life. His abiding memory of him was of "the magnificent, lofty forehead . . . the so expressive, sometimes strangely beautiful mouth; the vitality that lurked hidden there as in his whole slim, tense, lithe body, so like his writing . . . As I came to know him, [his face] seemed to me more and more like a divided mirror in which one sees two faces, two expressions. I began to glimpse in it something of an evangelist . . . [but] instead of burning violins and worldly books he cries Woe! Woe! over art, aesthetics, power, riches, all that makes the modern Jerusalem, and instead of sermons and psalms he uses stories and verse. Yet he was no irresistible, fearless fanatic, but one of those hypersensitive, thin-skinned, refined beings whom the manifestations of this world fill with fear and alarm . . . But there is another profile to this face in the mirror—an expression glowing with life and joy, almost satyr-like. Is it that all the *joie de vivre* which the ascetic in him censors has fled thither? These two, the preacher and the Mephistopheles, wrestle within him, mould and colour his writing, rend this restless spirit."[8] The following spring Lie was to write an eloquent eulogy of Strindberg in the Norwegian magazine *Ude og Hjemme*, summing him up as "this unquiet soul, this feverish, rebellious 'damned heart.'"

Like most of his contemporaries, Strindberg succumbed immediately to Bjørnson's famous charm. "I have now met Bjørnson, whom I love," he wrote to Albert Bonnier on 17 December. "This is the man I have sought for so long; mostly, perhaps, because I am so unmasculine myself. It is not the blows I receive that hurt me most, it is the blows I inflict; honestly! So that I am not fitted to be a battler." And on 20 December he told Pehr Staaff: "I am seeing BB and Jonas Lie. Splendid fellows both, and so human and true." He dedicated *Somnambulist Nights* to them. In his autobiography two years later, Strindberg told how as a young man in Uppsala he had "feared and avoided" Bjørnson: "He heard people emerge from his lectures stunned, as though they had witnessed a birth or a death-struggle. Johan [i.e., Strindberg] felt that here was a powerful ego, more powerful than his own, which might sow seed in his own soul. He shrank from this as though he sensed a victor in the strife . . . For the same reason he had refused to see or read *The Editor* or *A Bankrupt*." But since those days, Bjørnson's star had declined; his latest play, *A Gauntlet*, had been rejected everywhere in Norway and had failed when staged in Hamburg, so that "Johan felt himself on a level with the dethroned god, set aside all criticism, ceased resisting and submitted totally. He felt an uncommon peace in the presence of this powerful man and could not repress a feeling of filial love." Thus Bjørnson "became my father confessor and soon my conscience." Strindberg perceptively noted the complexity of Bjørnson's character: "the minister (an inherited trait)* who preached to his congregation and brooked no appeal; the peasant with his

*Bjørnson was the son of a pastor.

small hint of cunning; the theatre director searching for effect; the people's tribune seeking to rouse, move and convert. But behind everything lay a good child . . . He did not easily understand a joke and at first always listened suspiciously, but then laughed without restraint." Jonas Lie, by contrast, "with his lively, phosphorescent mind, his gentle and conciliatory temperament, was seductive rather than overpowering and thus exerted a stronger influence than Bjørnson."[9]

Bjørnson was as attracted by Strindberg as Strindberg was by him. "A splendid fellow, deeply honest," he wrote to Ludvig Josephson on 4 January 1884. "Jonas Lie and I have both fallen completely in love with him. He is as noble a nature as one could wish to find . . . His wife doesn't want to stay abroad long because she wants to go home to act in comedies. Swedes here say she can't, that she hasn't the grace or the voice (too dry) for the stage. If so, why don't you tell him so, Josephson? Firmly, strongly, incessantly. He thinks she has a considerable acting talent and has made a great hit. He thinks it's the King and his friends' friends who want to block her career and that she's being persecuted for her husband's sake."[10] Josephson prudently declined the invitation. Bjørnson, highly sensitive to criticism himself, had a blustering way of imparting home truths which made him enemies throughout his life.

Ironically, while he was in Paris Strindberg enjoyed his first popular theatrical success in Sweden. *Lucky Peter's Journey*, the play he despised and claimed to have written in a fortnight,[11] received its premiere at Ludvig Josephson's New Theatre on 22 December. The reviews were mixed, but the public liked it, reactions which have been repeated whenever the play has been revived in Sweden. It ran for 76 performances, a great number in those days. On 8 January 1884 *Göteborgsposten* reported: "The high priest and standard-bearer of the young, August Strindberg, has the wind of success in his sails. No play at any theatre in human memory has achieved such a triumph." On 17 January the same paper reported that it had already taken over 30,000 crowns at the box office. Strindberg received the news cynically. "So my old suspicions that *Lucky Peter* would be bad enough to succeed on the stage have been true," he wrote to Josephson on 3 January. "It's just a mess of rubbish." He was not far wrong; it is *Peer Gynt* with water, the tale of a boy who has his dreams fulfilled and finds that all is vanity except love. But it brought him 2,200 crowns, temporarily easing his financial problems.

In the second half of January 1884 Strindberg left Paris and moved with Siri and the children to Ouchy in Switzerland, just outside Lausanne. Siri's distaste for housekeeping, even with help (they had brought a maid, Eva Carlsson, with them from Sweden), was such that they always, whenever possible, and even when they could least afford it, lived *en pension*. It is perhaps not surprising; she had been born into an aristocratic family, where everything was done by servants, and had married into another such family. (After she was divorced from Strindberg, according to her eldest daughter, she became an excellent housekeeper.) They settled, in some style (so he informed Karl Otto Bonnier), in "a chalet on the shore of Lake Geneva with a view of the lake and of the Savoy Alps." This cost no more than 12 francs a day for the whole family, which left him enough to ride each day. [12] He was not planning to stay more than two or three months; he told Pehr Staaff (25 January) that "we shall return home in March or April to increase the population, probably direct to Kymmendö, under no circumstances to Stockholm." Siri was expecting a child that spring.

Occasionally he became depressed, as reformers do, at how little he had accomplished. "Yesterday I read *The Red Room*," he wrote to Bjørnson and Lie (25 January). "And I found that I said there all that needed to be said; I also found how wretchedly unrewarding it is to address dead ears. What has that noteworthy book achieved? Since 1879? Five years! Nothing. Yes, irritation and reaction. The young who should have begun to write as a result of it pen little stories about nothing more shocking than what our aunts and uncles wrote thirty years ago."

"Here in Ouchy," he reminded Carl Larsson on 29 January, "Byron wrote *The Prisoner of Chillon*. Chillon itself lies only an hour's unforgettable journey by steamer from here, with its dungeons and torture instruments intact . . . Ouchy is not a town but a village as rural as Grez—five minutes from Lausanne and two to the lake and the gulls." He ended ominously: "We have developed such a taste for living *en pension* that we plan to do likewise on Kymmendö this summer instead of keeping house ourselves."

Each day he climbed a thousand-foot hill, and learned fencing "under a French fencing-master." [13] Oysters cost only a few centimes each. To complete his satisfaction, he learned that a wax model of his head based on a bust by the Finnish sculptor Ville Vallgren had been installed in the new Panopticon in Copenhagen; [14] and on 12 February Bjørnson wrote a eulogy of him in the Norwegian daily *Verdens Gang* which was reprinted three days later in the Stockholm paper *Dagens Nyheter*. His impression of Strindberg interestingly complements Jonas Lie's:

> He has been a Pietist and, despite much soul-searching, is so still—not religiously, but morally . . . "The false film that obscures all Swedish imagination must be stripped away, layer by layer"—such things he says calmly and in a gentle voice, full of charm, but in his eyes something dark

and almost fox-like burns. He is a tall fair man, handsome; his brow
occupies half his head. His body is lithe and fine. But he is overworked and
sick, so that both his conversation and his emotions seek muted expression.
His love of his country is his religion. It torments him to be away from
Sweden; all our suppositions that this is what he needed seem to be
mistaken. He must be in Sweden; but he wants to live apart, preferably in
the skerries. And he must have a garden.

Somnambulist Nights was published in February. It received excellent
reviews; Hjalmar Branting in *Tiden* thought it Strindberg's richest work to
date, and *Dagens Nyheter* found it "unquestionably the most remarkable
work of one of the most honest and indomitable 'doubters' that any
country can boast." Karl Warburg in *Handelstidningen i Göteborg* much
preferred it to Strindberg's previous volume of poems, but *Aftonbladet*,
Stockholms Dagblad and *Nya Dagligt Allehanda*, three powerful dailies
which had disliked *Poems in Verse and Prose*, all ignored it.[15]
Strindberg decided to visit Italy that spring, and on 12 February he
addressed an appeal to Bjørnson and Lie which confirms that his hostility
towards Ibsen does not date from the publication of A *Doll's House*:
"Surely I should visit Ibsen in Rome! Will you be so kind as to ask him to
receive me, since if he shows me the door, I shall feel hurt. I want to see
the angriest man in Europe before I die." Strindberg did not yet regard
Ibsen as the Enemy (an essay he wrote about Bjørnson early this year
refers to Ibsen as "the great Norwegian dramatist" and praises *An Enemy
of the People* as "brilliantly executed").[16] One must reiterate: Strindberg
was still happy in his marriage. "Without my wife," he told Bjørnson on
21 February, "I cannot live. She is a good wife; she is my only friend, and
I have wept myself back to health and strength many times with my head
in her lap. If she does not fully understand my aims, and does not exhort
me to battle, she always gives me comfort when I come to her beaten and
miserable, for she has inexhaustible resources of generosity and kindness." Bjørnson, replying, apostrophised him as "O warm, strong, weak,
O trusting-suspicious, brave-timid, loving-hating, poetic-prosaic, solici-
tous-uncaring Strindberg!"[17] Strindberg and Siri had enjoyed six years of
married happiness; but the idyll had not much longer to run.
On 23 February he told Karl Otto Bonnier, who must have welcomed
the news, that he had decided "to divide my writing into two parts and not
mix polemics with creative work." Unfortunately, his immediate inclination was not to write the fiction or drama which Albert Bonnier had urged
him to do. "I think," he informed Carl Larsson (29 February), "of
devoting some summers of my life to discovering Europe, as Stanley
discovered Africa. Everyone writes about the capital cities, museums,

monuments, newspapers and police, but nobody has written about the people and their life on which the whole city and society rests. I don't want to write about how the peasant celebrates his wedding or how he dances or what name he uses for a wood-louse. I want to write about how he lives and thinks . . . I don't want to travel by barge but by rail, and then wander around on horse, donkey or foot . . . Normandie, Bretagne, Les Landes, Auvergne, Côte d'Or, Provence . . . The next summer we'd take England Scotland Ireland . . . I speak French German English and Italian badly now, but I would take lessons and study the dialects before I start."

Albert Bonnier, had Strindberg known it, was beginning to lose faith in him, and on 5 March he wrote to his son Karl Otto about the possibility of getting Strindberg's contract shifted to another publisher. "If when he returns he doesn't get some steady job on a newspaper or in a government office with a regular salary, he will go to ruin and things will end badly, both for us and for him." Karl Otto resisted this suggestion. "Strindberg's stock is rising," he replied to his father. "That is clear from the sales of *Somnambulist Nights* and the undivided [sic] praise it has received everywhere, and also from the success of *Lucky Peter* (yesterday he was even quoted in Parliament!)."[18] So Albert Bonnier kept him, little knowing how deeply he was to regret this decision before the end of the year.

Not all Strindberg's friends liked *Somnambulist Nights*. Bjørnson dismissed them as "scribbled in haste" and "lectures in verse," not an unreasonable judgement, and perceptively added: "He is best fitted to write plays, and will do fine things for the theatre,"[19] an opinion with which not many would have agreed at that time. "I regard you as the greatest dramatist in Scandinavia," he assured Strindberg on 3 June. ". . . You know how to write plays, and by God you shall. What you write on the side (as I do about politics) I don't value at all."[20] Bjørnson had little sympathy for Siri. "She is stage-struck," he told Albert Bonnier, "and apparently has no acting talent. It should be enough for her to be August Strindberg's wife, and she should devote herself to this calling—I have told him so myself at the risk of losing his friendship."[21] Poor Siri; to be Strindberg's wife was both less and more than enough, as she was shortly to decide.

On 1 March, with Siri eight months pregnant, Strindberg took her and the children to Italy for what was to have been a month. But the kind of ill luck that pursued him almost everywhere haunted him here too. The weather turned so bad that after a fortnight, having got no farther than Genoa, he turned for home. "All water is blue when the sky is blue," he wrote to Carl Larsson (8 March). "Eva [their maid] and I have searched in vain for that damned blue in both sky and water. Humbug, sir! The olive trees are horribly grey. The landscape like a garden and uglier than the oil paintings. Pine trees are the same everywhere. And the people! Moleskin and slouch hats! Not at all picturesque, old chap! The old houses daubed with red, green and yellow! . . . The whole coast here is so occupied by factories and wharves that one can't get to the beach. The hills covered with villas! Nature is dead here. No walks possible. The roads dusty. Oh, how dusty it is here!"

"I saw all of Savoy," he told Karl Otto Bonnier (22 March), "stayed in Modane by Mont Cenis; 10 days on the Riviera; was in Turin, Savona, Pegli, climbed Scoglionero; saw Genoa; Como; Airolo; climbed the great Gotthard; saw Lucerne; saw the whole of Italian, German and French Switzerland . . . Switzerland is number one." So he never got to Rome, and never met Ibsen. One feels they might have got on rather well; Strindberg was the kind of emotional individualist, like Georg Brandes, whom Ibsen found stimulating, and Ibsen, when he liked anyone, was a great charmer. By August, sadly, Strindberg's hostility towards Ibsen as a supposed champion of feminism had become set, and he was describing the latter's writings as "swinish."[22]

On 3 April, Strindberg's and Siri's third and last child was born; a boy, whom they christened Hans. Strindberg was overjoyed; and after the disappointments of Italy, Switzerland seemed better than ever, though he was still homesick for Sweden. "One loves Sweden from afar," he wrote to Gustaf af Geijerstam on 14 April, "but hates her at close quarters . . . Here I live in the most beautiful country in the world . . . Imagine, living among a people that has no literature, art or theatre! That is medicine for the soul. If only I could overcome my longing for Kymmendö . . ." He wrote in a similar optimistic mood on 4 May to his cousin Oscar: "After four months of blissful peace, with no housekeeping or society or pub-crawling, no newspapers, no socialising, no drop of spirits, going to bed at 8–9 and getting up at 6–7, cold water and walks in a landscape as beautiful as heaven, I and my nerves are at last to rights . . . *Lucky Peter* has been accepted for production in Copenhagen and is being translated into French free by an admirer, to what end I know not. *Swedish Destinies* is published in Danish, and is being translated into French, German and English. I have been taken on to the editorial board of a French magazine, with the best young authors of France. *Sir Bengt's Wife* is translated into French . . . Jonas Lie has written a text to my portrait (the 8th!) in Denmark's leading magazine." Not all of these translations were to be published or performed.

A new work of fiction was germinating in his mind, but his distrust of creative as opposed to didactic literature inhibited him. "My distaste for art as a falsification," he wrote to Bjørnson, also on 4 May, "has taken on a quasi-religious character . . . This is the dilemma. To be useful I must be read. To be read I must write 'art,' but I regard art as immoral . . . I have plans for the most splendid works of art but am unwilling to write them, although I know they would make me and give me a 'reputation.' And what tempts me to art is, I fear, the prospect of gaining a big 'reputation,' since reputation gives force to what one says. But that would involve me in contradictions from which I could never extricate myself. Yet I long to gain such a reputation that there would no longer be any doubt about my art; then I would like to break my pen and say: 'See, now I abandon play and turn to serious business.' . . . The world is so damned ruined by your bloody art and aestheticism that it spews back naked truth. Had I been born a couple of centuries ago I would have become a monk and gone forth to preach. Calvin began by throwing works of art out of the church, thus showing that he knew where falsehood lay . . . Bjørnson! Do as Ibsen does, utter one word a year, and speak cunningly so that no one understands what you say, for then the people will lie down on their faces and worship the Sphinx. Do you know, I begin to hate Ibsen in a small way after *An Enemy of the People*. There is something so insufferably *aesthetic* [the modern word would be "uncommitted"] about him. And *The* [sic] *Doll's House*! Ibsen the woman-hater! . . . Yet he has written *Ghosts*. I mustn't hate him. No. I will follow his example and become Moses on the mountain . . . What the devil does it matter if my soul goes to hell if thereby I can save 10,000; and I can, if only I can get the people to listen to me. And that they shall do."

Exactly what he would write that spring, and how, he was unsure; his plans were confused and various. "Henceforth I shall write my books in French," he informed Jonas Lie on 19 May. ". . . I have three French teachers. One who has taught himself Chinese can also teach himself French. It may take a year, two years, five years, but it will happen." Three days later he told Hjalmar Branting, a young radical journalist who in due course became Sweden's first Social Democrat prime minister, that he was going to Geneva to "interview Russian nihilists and get the background for a story," and on 24 May he wrote to Lie: "I have discovered that I am not a realist. I write best when I hallucinate"—a prophetic remark, for much of his greatest work was to be written in a more or less hallucinatory state of mind. But the following day he began a sequence of short stories of the straightest and most realistic kind, writing them (he told Lie on 27 May) "sharply, calmly, analytically, beautifully, coarsely, indecently, just the way life is."

He composed them, as usual, at great speed. "I sit and write like a sleepwalker," he told Karl Otto Bonnier on 12 June, "and must not be awakened, or it may stop in the middle. *This and That* [a projected volume of essays] tempts me and threatens in the background. I think it immoral to write fiction and my conscience weighs on me. So I am writing as fast as I can. One day I wrote 16 printed pages . . . I dare not read through my MS, for if I do, it so revolts me that I might break it off. And I have always a strong inclination to burn it." He shelved his plans to spend the summer at Kymmendö. "I certainly won't come this summer," he had told Karl Otto on 2 June, and four days later: "My wife longs to go home, but that can't be helped."

At the end of June they moved from Ouchy to Chexbres, between Lausanne and Vevey. They stayed at first at the Hotel Victoria, but soon left it for a small *pension* outside the town owned by a Swede named Welinder. After a few days they moved into the annexe, a ramshackle old house containing two small rooms, a big kitchen with an open range and a dank, dark attic. The whole place was in tumbledown condition, "but during the summer the luxurious wild vine hid its blemishes, and in the autumn it shone like a purple jewel." The description is by Welinder's Swiss wife, Hélène; she got to know Strindberg well during the following weeks:

> Instead of the brash and ruthless person I had expected, I saw a man whose whole appearance and manner suggested delicacy and consideration. He did not look downcast, but the exceptionally sensitive expression around the finely chiselled lips, the sad smile, something indefinable that he exuded, made me feel at once that he belonged to those who are predestined to more than the common measure of suffering . . . During a full month's acquaintance, I never found him otherwise than calm, mild and agreeable; sometimes absent-minded and a little melancholy, but never morose; considerate and withdrawn, and never boorish; very neat in his appearance, but totally unsnobbish; courteous to us ladies, but in a simple and natural manner which seemed not to cost him the least exertion. Never did I hear an inelegant word from his lips.[23]

Hélène noticed his reluctance to speak French, "although he had already mastered it." (Although he could read it well and in time was to write books in it, he never learned to speak it fluently; in *Time of Ferment* he confesses to "insuperable difficulty in making speeches and speaking foreign languages.")[24] He spoke to her of the compulsions which forced him to write. "I cannot rest, however much I might wish to. I have to write to eat, to keep my wife and children, and even apart from this I cannot stop. If I go on a train or whatever I do, my brain works ceaselessly, it grinds and grinds like a mill and I cannot make it stop. I find no rest till I have got it down on paper, but then something new starts at once and the same misery ensues. I write and write and do not even read through what I have written." His idea of happiness, he told Hélène, was "a little home in the country, an orchard to cultivate, animals and flowers to tend." Of Siri, Hélène noted: "She was not unpractical—she took sole charge of their financial affairs, and sewed most of her clothes and their children's —but she did not like housekeeping and preferred to live *en pension.*"[25]

Hélène's impression of Siri is confirmed by a Norwegian lady who met the Strindbergs at this time. "Hers is a heavy fate, but in spite of everything I still pity her husband more and cannot but blame her for many of his weaknesses and prejudices. He judges other women by Siri, which is unreasonable. For all the goodness and warmth that is in her, she is not suited to be a wife, or a mother, however much she loves her children."[26] (Their eldest daughter Karin contradicts this and says she was a wonderful mother.)[27] The Finnish sculptor Ville Vallgren, who had met them in Grez the previous year, supports Edvard Selander's observation, quoted above,* that she sometimes drank too much, and "gave Strindberg much cause for painful thoughts."[28] Living *en pension* with a nanny she must, like so many married women of her day, have found time heavy on her hands, the more so since she knew what it was to have a career.

Within a few days of moving to Chexbres, by 4 July, Strindberg had finished his new book of stories. He called it *Getting Married.* "I am depicting," he told Pehr Staaff, "twenty marriages of every variety."[29]† It was one of his best books, perhaps the best outside his major plays and *Inferno,* and its reception was radically to change his life, though not in any way he could have anticipated.

---

*See p. 99.
†Although the book contains only twelve stories, it describes more than that number of marriages.

Chapter Ten

∽∽∽∽∽∽∽∽∽∽∽∽∽∽∽∽∽∽∽∽∽∽∽∽∽∽∽∽

THE TRIAL

The first volume of *Getting Married*—he was to follow it with a very different sequel*—contains twelve stories, some of them dealing with more than one marriage, and a long preface. Anyone who reads this book expecting an uninterrupted display of misogyny is in for a surprise. Strindberg's claim to have depicted marriages of every variety is not far from the truth. Some of the stories take the woman's side, some the man's. "Compensation" is about a selfish husband; "Bad Luck" about a monogamous man who finds himself married to a polyandrous woman. "The Reward of Virtue" treats of the dangers of asceticism and celibacy; "Just to Be Married" shows how a man may find himself wedded not only to the girl he loves but to her family too; "Needs Must" tells of a seemingly confirmed bachelor who finally and grudgingly marries and for whom marriage works out surprisingly well. "A Doll's House," a deliberate riposte to Ibsen's play, is an attack on feminists; a young wife, under the influence of a feminist friend, tells her husband that their marriage has been no real marriage, but later she realises the error of her ways and ends happily in his arms.

*This was not the only time he was to write an unpremeditated sequel bearing the same title as its predecessor. He was to do it with *The Dance of Death* and *To Damascus* (twice) and, as with *Getting Married*, the sequels proved awkwardly inconsistent with the originals.

Strindberg's preface to *Getting Married, Volume One*, is, like so much even of his best work, a curious mixture of good sense and blind stupidity. His criticisms of the campaign for emancipation strike one as generally fair; for example, he points out that the problem does not exist among many working-class families since (e.g., with farmers, small shopkeepers, cobblers, etc.) the husband works at home and the wife shares his work "so that each plays the part indicated by nature and the one is not master of a subject which the other does not understand."[1] Even his ill-reasoned critique of Ibsen's *Doll's House*, of which Pehr Staaff observed that it attacked "a caricatured *Doll's House* of which Ibsen never dreamed,"[2] is qualified by the admission: "This much was gained. The folly of regarding marriage as a divine institution was exposed, the demand that marriage should generate absolute bliss was modified, and divorce between people who could not agree was recognised as justifiable. And that was a good thing."[3] "One partner develops in one direction, the other in another, and their marriage breaks up. Or one of the two remains stationary while the other develops, and they drift apart. Incompatibility may arise when two strong spirits clash . . . Some are born monogamous . . . others polygamous."[4]

"Among people who live close to nature (the peasants) the woman does not suffer so much from prolonged motherhood. This is firstly because the children have to be useful by the age of seven or eight, and secondly because the home does not grow musty, since the husband only uses the cottage when he eats or sleeps and spends the rest of his time in the open air. In the towns people of standing live packed together in small cells, and a more pitiable creature than a young girl it would be hard to find. Her lot closely resembles that of a prisoner." Strindberg observes that this is particularly so in northern lands, as opposed to southern countries, where people can spend much more time out of doors and can anyway keep the windows open for most of the year. In a section headed "Women's Rights" he recommends:

> The right to the same education as men . . . Boys and girls shall attend the same schools, so that both sexes learn to know each other early in life. Things will not then be as they are today, when boys imagine that girls are angels, and girls that boys are knights . . .
> The girl shall have the same freedom to "run wild" and choose what company she pleases.
> There shall be complete equality between the sexes . . . A girl will not expect a boy to get up and give her his seat . . . and a brother will not get into the habit of expecting his sister to make his bed or sew on his shirt buttons, for these are things he must do for himself.

Women shall have the vote . . .

Women shall be eligible for all occupations . . .

By a just distribution of the combined riches of nature, the community of the future will ensure that all who are born receive sustenance and instruction. Marriage as a guarantee for these advantages will therefore become unnecessary. Man and wife will conclude a contract, verbal or written, for a union of any length they may decide, which they will have the right to dissolve when they please, without reference to law or gospel . . .

A woman shall come of age at 18 without any restrictions . . .

A woman . . . shall have the right to fill any post and practise any profession she pleases . . .

A woman shall keep her own name . . .

Separate bedrooms shall be the rule from the beginning . . . This rule will make a woman's position freer and will give her the right to possess her own body . . .[5]

Finally, in an imaginary interview with a critic who says, "Your attack on the champion of the Woman Question [i.e., Ibsen] is inexplicable considering that you are yourself a radical," Strindberg replies: "I have attacked the indefensible way in which the question has been handled . . . I have attacked woman's attempt to emancipate herself from child-bearing, not her attempts to emancipate herself from the cradle and the kitchen." In other words, he was attacking extreme feminist demands, which he believed hampered recognition of the moderate demands he thought should be granted. He concluded his preface: "The freedom she is now demanding is the same freedom that all we men demand too. We must get it together, as friends, not as enemies, for as such we shall get nothing."[6]

What could be more reasonable than this? But when the book appeared, none of these liberal suggestions atoned, in the eyes of the emancipationists, for the attack on Ibsen; rather as though someone were to recommend Christianity while denouncing the Sermon on the Mount. Strindberg had suddenly developed a violent personal antagonism towards Ibsen, the more surprising when one considers that on the question of female emancipation Ibsen was, if anything, more moderate than Strindberg at this time; Ibsen would have baulked at several of Strindberg's recommendations, such as the verbal or written contract to be dissolved at the whim of either. Yet to Staaff's complaint that he had caricatured *A Doll's House*, Strindberg replied: "You are a doctrinaire where Ibsen is concerned. Read that swinery once again! I have been duped too," and went on to complain that women "want office, rank, to drink and smoke—all the shit that we men should give up. Are they to have it?"[7]

Strindberg's sympathy with the movement for female emancipation was of long standing; it was part of his general sympathy for the oppressed. In December 1868, in a letter to a friend, Fredrika Roos, he had declared: "I deeply deplore the oppressed condition of women, which does not allow them to concern themselves with the loftier interests of life and the pursuit of truth." In April 1872, as we have seen, he wrote a piece for the femininist-oriented magazine *Svalan* about the novelist Wilhelmina Ståhlberg praising her for following George Sand's lead in denouncing what he called "female slavery"; and this sympathy is evidenced in several of his early plays. Karl, in *The Freethinker*, urges Agda to free herself from "the ingrained prejudices and superstitions in which she has hitherto slumbered" and come with him to America. Antigone in *Greece in Decline*, the early draft of *Hermione*, is stronger than Agda and defies these prejudices, though in the end she fails and finds herself unable to commit the necessary murder. In *The Outlaw* Strindberg portrayed two bravely independent women, Gunlöd and her mother Valgerd. Kristina in *Master Olof* wanted to share Olof's problems but found him unhelpful. "He wants me to be a holy image standing on a pedestal," she complains, and she says to the Whore in the last act: "You and I have shared the same fate." And in an unfinished story, "Tale from the Stockholm Skerries," which he wrote in the spring of 1872, he bewailed the fact that women could do nothing useful unless they married and became mothers, which affected men badly too, since they became plagued with women's unfulfilled longings.*

Strindberg's first flickers of doubt about female emancipation appear in *Sir Bengt's Wife* and *The Swedish People*, the former written in 1882 and the latter completed the same year; in both, he expressed strong reservations about the damage excessive female demands could cause to marriage and motherhood. These fears found their most unequivocal expression in his story "A Doll's House," and in his attack on Ibsen's play in the preface to *Getting Married*. In the eyes of the supporters of female emancipation these outweighed his arguments in favour of what they regarded as moderate reforms.

In *The Author*, the fifth† volume of his autobiography, Strindberg says he began *Getting Married* "while living in happy eroticism" and venerating women, but that halfway through he found the book was not turning out as he expected. In *A Madman's Defence* he says he wrote the whole

---

*Cf. Ulf Boethius, *Strindberg och kvinnofrågan* (Halmstad, 1969), pp. 84 ff., an admirably thorough and balanced study of Strindberg and the woman question.

†*The Author* was published in his lifetime as Volume 4, because its predecessor, *He and She*, was rejected as libellous.

book in the midst of a fearful row with Siri. But there is no evidence of any such row in his letters of the period, and the former explanation seems the more likely. Anything Strindberg claims in *A Madman's Defence*, the most venomous and unbalanced of all his works, should be regarded with more than usual suspicion. On 17 August, only six weeks after he had finished *Getting Married*, Siri thanked him for "seven happy years."[8]

Strindberg was not one of those writers who regard the completion of a book as an excuse for idleness. When the writing mood was on him, he could not stop. He told Karl Otto Bonnier (27 July) that he was planning a second volume of *Getting Married*, more volumes of *Swedish Destinies*, the aforementioned book of essays *This and That*, a further volume of stories set in Switzerland to be entitled *Utopias in Reality*, and a verse trilogy "dealing simply [sic] with world history, from India, Egypt, Palestine, Greece, Rome, the Mediaeval Reformation and ending with the French Revolution . . . I shall portray Jesus of Nazareth as simply a good socialist without any theological claptrap." Bonnier was alarmed and asked him not to publish so much and so quickly. "The public will be surprised by such fertility (imagine, seven books in a year!); people will think that under such circumstances not everything can be meaningful, interest in your work will lessen, their desire and perhaps even more their ability to buy will not suffice."[9] This counsel had no effect on Strindberg, except that he postponed writing the verse trilogy (and this was probably not in deference to Bonnier).

Getting Married was published on 27 September 1884, in an edition of 4,000 copies. Strindberg knew that the feminists would attack it. "Soon the autumn storm will break," he wrote to Looström two weeks before publication. "This year it will be worse than ever, for when women go to war, all hell breaks loose."[10] And on 16 September he warned his cousin Oscar: "The hermaphrodites will tear me to pieces." But what happened was worse than he had expected.

On 3 October a representative of the Ministry of Justice called on Albert Bonnier to inform him that there was to be a prosecution and that all unsold copies of the book, amounting to 320 in stock and a further 141 in the shops, were meanwhile to be confiscated. The offence was not, as might have appeared most likely, obscenity, in the open references to sexual intercourse and venereal disease, but blasphemy; a passage about holy communion in the opening story, "The Reward of Virtue," mocked "the impudent deception practised with Högstedt's Piccadon* . . . and Lettström's wafers . . . which the parson passed off as the body and blood

*Communion wine.

of Jesus of Nazareth, the rabble-rouser who was executed over 1,800 years ago." Strindberg had in fact half jokingly wondered whether this sentence might cause trouble. "Will they prosecute me for that Piccadon?" he had asked Albert Bonnier on 13 September. But neither Bonnier nor his son had been bothered by that possibility.

On 4 October, Albert Bonnier informed Strindberg, who three days earlier had moved from Chexbres to Geneva, of the forthcoming trial. "I assume," he wrote, "that you will wish to return and defend the case. Liberal and enlightened opinion is unanimous that the authorities have perpetrated an enormous gaffe which will redound to your advantage. If the defence is conducted with spirit and energy, and the liberal press unites in your support, I think it very likely that either the jury will acquit you or at worst you will be fined." The charge brought was "blasphemy against God or mockery of God's word or sacrament"; the maximum penalty for this was two years' hard labour. The authorities would have liked to prosecute for obscenity but could find no legal grounds. The ban took several days to be enforced in Stockholm, since the governor of the province, whose signature was required, had left the city for a long weekend, and on 6 October, *Dagens Nyheter* reported a rush to the libraries and bookshops. [11]

It is not certain who instigated the prosecution; probably, it is now believed, the feminist Society of Married Women's Property Rights and a moralistic body, also feminist, called The Federation. To quote Mary Sandbach's admirable account of the background of the trial: "Both bodies were led by influential members of the upper classes, supported by the right-wing press. Though not numerous, these were powerful people, and they hated Strindberg—the feminists for his suspect views on the emancipation of women, the moralists for his outspokenness about sex and religion and, more particularly, for the satirical attack he had made on them in *The New Kingdom*. As the government of the day and the Minister of Justice were both liberal, many people believed that Queen Sophia was at the bottom of it. She was an ardent Pietist, and many members of the court circle belonged to The Federation."[12] A Finnish journalist, J. F. Hagfors, later recalled that it was "generally agreed" in Stockholm at the time that the Queen had been actively involved, though recent research suggests that she was not. [13]

Bonnier had expected that the book would be condemned by the right-wing press. But to his surprise and alarm, it was also attacked in the liberal newspapers and magazines. "Repellent to every healthy mind" (*Vikingen*). "Painful reading . . . crazy ideas . . . We doubt if anything more corrupt . . . has appeared in Swedish" (*Göteborgsposten*). "Often

coarse and vulgar—one is ashamed to open it" (*Ny Illustrerad Tidning*).
"The unlovely and unchaste scenes which he portrays are beyond
description" (*Tidskrift för Hemmet*). "Stinking and repellent rottenness
. . . almost worse than Zola" (*Folkets Tidning*). The only praise came
from *Nya Dagligt Allehanda* ("undoubtedly the most remarkable work
that Strindberg has written"), *Handelstidningen i Göteborg*, *Budkaflen*
and *Aftonbladet*—in which paper, after the trial (31 December), Georg
Brandes thanked Strindberg for having "awakened new life in his country's literature" and acclaimed his "freshness and boldness," while noting
the confusion of radicalism and conservatism in him, and his sometimes
reactionary views.[14] In Denmark, quixotically, the left-wing reviewers
were especially hostile because they felt it gave radicalism a bad name,
while several conservative papers welcomed it as a healthy, if belated,
counterblast to Ibsen's *A Doll's House*.[15]

Albert Bonnier himself was the target of abuse almost as much as
Strindberg. He and Karl Otto received unpleasant letters, and some of
their friends went so far as to return gifts that the Bonniers had sent
them.[16] Hitherto suppressed anti-Semitic feelings began to manifest
themselves.

Several of Strindberg's friends, including Hjalmar Branting and Pehr
Staaff, wrote urging him to return and face the music with Bonnier. But
Strindberg hated the rough-and-tumble of open debate, and the prospect
of defending his views in the dock terrified him. "I shall probably stand
quite alone," he wrote to Albert Bonnier on 4 October from Geneva,
"against judges, newspapers + hermaphrodites and pederasts and Ibsen-
ites and the radicals (my friends!). When I worked in the Royal Library I
was openly told that half the judges of the Supreme Court are pederasts. Is
it they who will now judge me?" Three days later he wrote: "I shall of
course come home if you are threatened with prison. Otherwise not. An
autumn journey with my family and my youngest child ill with toothache
is impossible, and I can't come alone," though he does not explain why
not. The same day he informed Carl Larsson: "I want to show my
contempt for this stupid law by not going home . . . The worst thing is
that my friends send telegrams telling me to go back and make myself
popular by orating on railway platforms. Damned old-fashioned nonsense!" And on 8 October he wrote to Albert Bonnier: "I spoke today with
the Russian nihilist Elpidine. He said it was mere idealism to go to prison
and would be tantamount to admitting I was guilty . . . that to martyr
oneself was just romanticism. One must enjoy one's freedom, use it and
do one's duty. He is right! My reply to this accusation will resound no less
if penned from Geneva."

During the next two days he received two communications from Bjørnson which, surprisingly from such a fighter, confirmed this view. "This [prosecution] is the biggest and best advertisement for the book there could be," he wrote from Paris on 7 October, and three days later on a postcard: *"Don't go back to Sweden! Face your exile like a man and create a kingdom for yourself.* But you need people, Strindberg; much of what you write gives the impression of a man talking in the wilderness." He also, while condemning the action of the authorities, criticised *Getting Married* somewhat sharply and expressed the fear that Strindberg's nervousness might create a bad effect if he were to appear in person.[17]

But suddenly this support fell away. On 10 October, Albert Bonnier wrote that a judge had told him that if Strindberg did not return, he, Bonnier, would be arrested. He also urged Bjørnson to throw his weight onto the scales. "If he [Strindberg] stays away, will not his whole future be destroyed? So think all his friends . . . Who will then listen to or believe in him?"[18] Bjørnson was convinced by this argument and on 13 October offered Strindberg new advice: "You must go home . . . You cannot opt out of life . . . You must return to face the judgement, you must submit to it if you would achieve more in Sweden . . . Thus you will advance by ten years everything for which you are fighting."[19]

This abrupt change of heart by Bjørnson infuriated Strindberg, who replied abusively on 14 October: "Your Majesty! I am in receipt of your imperial decree . . . If you talked less and read more, you would have got as far as I have! . . . Don't be old-fashioned and romantic. (People laugh at your newspaper proclamations.) Be true! Bjørnson! You are as false as an after-dinner speaker." Then, in a wounding reference to Bjørnson's recent and unsuccessful play *A Gauntlet*, which urged among other things that men, like women, should observe chastity before marriage, Strindberg added: "Be immoral, Bjørnson, as you were in your youth, for the virtue one learns at fifty is not worth preaching. Avoid alcohol and drink water like me, and your mind will become clear and you will understand my book." He concluded, sadly and significantly: "I am as lonely as a man could be, for my wife is against me."

This letter was to cause a permanent breach in their friendship. "He is a wretched coward," wrote Bjørnson to S. A. Hedlund of *Handelstidningen i Göteborg* on 18 October. ". . . He is attacking me in the coarsest, most lying, swinish letters I have ever read, let alone received . . . He is a craven, wretched, lying creature . . . Beware of him! In all my long experience I have never met anyone so repulsively self-worshipping and perfidious and cowardly."[20]

Meanwhile, Karl Otto Bonnier was on his way to Switzerland to try to persuade Strindberg to return. He arrived in Geneva on 14 October and visited Strindberg at his *pension* in the suburb of Plainpalais. At first Strindberg refused point-blank to return, agreeing only to sign an affidavit that he was the author of the book, a legal necessity which would relieve Albert Bonnier of having to bear sole responsibility for its publication. Karl Otto, who noted that Strindberg was happy in Switzerland but that Siri was "in poor health, unhappy in the *pension* and homesick for Sweden," went back to his hotel convinced that he had failed. But next morning Strindberg came to Karl Otto's room to say that he would, after all, go to Sweden, since he had received several telegrams from friends saying that not to do so would be cowardly. So they set off together. As they left, Strindberg told Karl Otto: "The doctor has told me that my wife is very sick and can live only a few more years. But I can't live without her. If she dies, I shall shoot myself."[21]*

Throughout the long train journey, Karl Otto records, Strindberg was in a state of deep depression. But when they reached Kiel and saw that the ferryboat waiting to take them to Copenhagen was called *Victoria* (after the Kaiser's consort, Queen Victoria's daughter), Strindberg cried: "Look! *Omen accipio* . . . Auguste Victoria! Victory! August!" Karl Otto comments: "He was as though transformed and throughout the lengthy sea voyage was in capital humour."[22]

They arrived at Stockholm central station on the morning of 20 October. A large crowd was there to greet him, and as Strindberg stepped out of the carriage, reported *Aftonbladet*, "every hat flew up and a great cheer rang forth." Strindberg made a brief speech, unfortunately, as with so many of his public utterances, inaudible except to those within a few feet of him. He was escorted triumphantly to his hotel, where "the throng that had accompanied him remained beneath his window, until he appeared to receive their plaudits." *Aftonbladet* concluded: "That a private citizen should be received and acclaimed as though he were a monarch, that a thousand people should gather merely to set eyes on this man and comfort him by assuring him of their sympathy is, in such a case as this, of the utmost significance and well worth the notice of the authorities. For it is an expression not merely of sympathy for Strindberg but above all of disapproval of this prosecution."

*Strindberg, in his book *Sequestration Journey* (*Kvarstadsresan*), asserts that Karl Otto came to him with these telegrams, but Karl Otto says this was not so and that Strindberg came to him—another instance of Strindberg's tendency to fictionalise. Strindberg's version of what the doctor had said seems equally improbable, since Siri was to live for another twenty-eight years.

That evening Ludvig Josephson staged a special performance at the New Theatre of *Lucky Peter's Journey*. The house was full and vociferously enthusiastic; such lines as "What form of government exists in this country? Constitutional despotism!" and "God preserve mankind from politicians!" were greeted with prolonged cheering. Strindberg took several curtain calls and was crowned with a laurel wreath; flowers rained onto the stage. Outside the theatre he was greeted by another cheering crowd, including many members of the working class who, ironically in view of the imminent change in his political thinking, regarded him as their especial champion.

These demonstrations seem to have surprised and somewhat alarmed the authorities. Most newspapers, including several which disapproved of the book, attacked the prosecution as an infringement of free speech. These included the two powerful Stockholm dailies, *Aftonbladet* and *Dagens Nyheter*, the latter (24 October and 1 November) naming no less than nineteen provincial papers and magazines as sharing its view. Comparatively few newspapers and magazines appear to have supported the prosecution.

"The King is said to be dead scared," Gustaf af Geijerstam wrote to Siri once the trial had started. "Public sympathy for August has expressed itself so strongly that his reception has exceeded all expectations. When we go to and from the court, we have to fight our way. August is accompanied back to the Grand Hotel each day by a huge crowd, and it is with difficulty that people are restrained from cheering in the courtroom itself. Indignation against the prosecution is colossal . . . August himself is remarkably calm and well . . . And in court, I assure you, he does us proud. Discreet, controlled and refined; as always in his public appearances, he makes an impeccable impression even on strangers. Be happy that he is staying here. He *cannot* go to prison. There would be a riot . . . The King is said to have ordered that a liberal jury be empanelled so that the affair may be concluded with a minimum of embarrassment."[23] A medal was struck showing a profile of Strindberg's head and a sentence from *Master Olof*: "The truth is always audacious." (Strindberg wanted a longer device: "You were born to provoke; you were born to strike. I am called the liberator who came too early. I am called Satan, my name is Johan August Strindberg. The truth is always audacious." But all that could hardly have been got legibly onto a medal, so only the last sentence was used.)[24]

Strindberg's enemies were no less active than his supporters. The right-wing press attacked him vehemently. A divinity teacher named John Personne, who three years later was to publish a famous and damaging denunciation of him, asserted (over a pseudonym) in *Nya Dagligt Allehanda* (14 October) that Bonnier had paid Strindberg a large sum to return in the hope of boosting the book's sales. A well-known doctor offered, in the event of an acquittal, to buy up the whole edition so that it could be burned.[25] Even the liberal *Handelstidningen i Göteborg*, while recommending an acquittal, published a leader deeply hostile to Strindberg. Among the many letters and telegrams which he received were abusive (often anonymous) ones, sometimes containing excrement. "I was watched the whole time by detectives," he told Jonas Lie, "and people were more frightened of me than I of them. . . . Had I been sent to prison there would have been a riot. Cartridges had been distributed and the cavalry alerted."[26]

On 17 November the nine-man jury, after a four-and-a-half-hour retirement, returned a verdict of not guilty. The enthusiasm both in and outside the court was tremendous, "a display of jubilation," Karl Otto Bonnier recalled, "that none of us present will ever forget."[27] That evening a celebratory banquet was given for Strindberg at the Grand Hotel. Next day he left for home. In Malmö he was met by his old Uppsala friend Nathan Hellberg, who found him "in the best of humour . . . His marriage appeared to be quite happy and his economic situation comparatively good. His devotion to his small children was apparent from the beautiful little presents he had bought for them."[28]

Victory seemed total. But the forces of reaction were not to be denied. The acquittal resulted in an immediate and widespread demand from the bookshops for copies of *Getting Married*, but for legal reasons it took time for the sequestrated copies to be released. Several of Albert Bonnier's friends in the Jewish community begged him not to reprint because of the anti-Semitism that such a course would foster. The conservative *Nya Dagligt Allehanda*, which had reviewed the book sympathetically on publication, nevertheless published two long articles, on 18 and 19 November, deploring the verdict and expressing the hope "that our booksellers may feel impelled to refuse to co-operate in distributing a book of such content, and that they will sufficiently respect decency and morals not publicly to display this offensive work on their shelves." One of Bonnier's leading authors, the poet and novelist Zacharias Topelius, threatened that if Bonnier reprinted the book he would find another publisher.[29]

Bonnier sought to compromise by suggesting to Strindberg that he should reprint, only omitting the story, "The Reward of Virtue," which contained the offending sentence. Strindberg refused, to which Bonnier replied that in that case he dared not publish. "You cannot imagine," he wrote, "the quantity of uncontrolled and base abuse to which my son and I have been subjected, both in the newspapers and in anonymous letters, as a result of a rumour that a large new edition of *Getting Married* has been printed and is ready for distribution. People are behaving like madmen, and one wonders when the tumult will cease." He offered to relinquish his rights in the book so that Strindberg could sell it to another publisher. Strindberg offered it to his old publisher Claes Looström, but Looström refused because he "would risk losing the clients of his bookshop." One J. G. Leufstedt wrote that he was willing to publish it, provided Strindberg agreed to certain deletions. His suggested fee of 2,000 crowns tempted Strindberg; but while he demurred, another publisher offered anonymously through an intermediary to republish it unabridged. Strindberg accepted this offer. It turned out, to his surprise, to have come from Albert Bonnier's nephew Isidor, though Isidor pardonably kept his name out of it, the title page carrying only the name of the printer and the bookshop which distributed it. Karl Otto Bonnier recalled that it was fourteen years before his father and he learned the truth. By the time the new edition appeared, which for some reason was not until November 1885, interest had faded, and although Isidor, to Strindberg's disappointment, printed only 3,000 copies instead of, as he had hoped, 4,000 to 5,000, it did not sell out until 1900. [30]

Among the letters of support and congratulation which Strindberg received on his return to Geneva was one from the Scandinavian community of Providence, Rhode Island, and another from a young Swedish poet, ten years his junior, Verner von Heidenstam, which inaugurated a long correspondence and a warm, though prematurely terminated friendship. Heidenstam, like Carl Snoilsky (who had publicly declared his support for Strindberg both before and during the trial), was a nobleman and, much as Strindberg denounced the ruling class, his old attraction to the aristocracy remained.

Strindberg spent the last weeks of 1884 writing an account of his journey to Sweden entitled *Sequestration Journey*. Subtitled "Letters to a Compatriot Abroad," it is one of his least rewarding books. It begins with observations on socialism, patriotism, and so on, then deals with his visit to Sweden, but says practically nothing of interest about it—there is, amazingly, no account of the trial—and rides to death various hobbyhorses such as the woman question. Albert Bonnier refused it, telling Strindberg (30 December) that he thought it "not worthy of your talent." It appeared in the magazine *Budkaflen* the following year but never in book form until after Strindberg's death.

"I am spiritually bankrupt," Strindberg informed Jonas Lie that Christmas Eve. "I have studied the problem of society in French, German and English, and as a result find myself in the same nihilistic situation as when I wrote *The Red Room*. My view now is: everything is shit. No way out. The skein is too tangled to be unravelled. It can only be sheared. The building is too solid to be pulled down. It can only be blown up." Switzerland, too, was beginning to pall. He felt in no mood to complete *Utopias in Reality*, though Albert Bonnier was still willing to publish it. "I don't think this idyllic life suits me any longer," he wrote to Isidor Bonnier as the year ended. "I would achieve more in Sweden as a newspaper editor . . . We shall see."[31]

At least he was not doing too badly financially. Albert Bonnier alone had paid him 7,749 crowns that year, and he had received various sums from other sources. Had either he or Siri had any notion of economy, they could have lived quite comfortably on this. "It is better to sleep well and not eat well than to eat well and not sleep well," Ibsen had told his son fifteen years earlier[32] when his financial situation was worse than Strindberg's was now, but Strindberg enjoyed the good things of life, and Siri liked to live *en pension*. So they remained in debt, moving from one boardinghouse to another, staying in each until the sum owing was so large that it had to be paid, then raising the money by loans or advances on future books.[33] When the bill was paid the family moved to a new town and a new boardinghouse, and the business of sliding further into debt started again. A few months previously Siri had thanked him for "seven happy years." But this happiness had not long to run.

Chapter Eleven

THE BEGINNINGS OF MISOGYNY

Unlike Ibsen, who neither knew nor corresponded with any of his peers outside Scandinavia, Strindberg in his gregarious way was to enjoy many such contacts, either in person or by correspondence, and the publication of *Getting Married* brought about the first of these. "Zola has read it!" he informed Pehr Staaff excitedly on 7 January 1885. "Was prevented by the bad translation from fully enjoying it! Used strong expressions such as 'Master.'"* These first letters between Strindberg and Zola have been lost,[1] but others were to follow.

Shortly before Christmas, Strindberg had published an article in the Swedish radical paper *Tiden* entitled "My Anti-Semitism" which seemed to indicate a change of heart on that subject. Some Jews, he declared, had become conservative and chauvinistic; their true mission was to be not insular patriots but Europeans, as the Brandes brothers in Denmark had realised. The Jew, he continued, "has no fatherland, he has become an

---

*Zola's enthusiasm may have been less than Strindberg supposed. According to one source, an admirer of Strindberg asked Zola to write a preface to the French edition of *Getting Married*, Vol. I. Zola replied, "This is just rubbish, coarse without any purpose to its coarseness, immature and adolescent. But if I can do a poor author a service, I will write something. Tell me what you want me to write that may help him and I will do it." But the French edition did not materialise. (*Cf.* Olof Molander, *Harald Molander*, Stockholm, 1950, p. 321.)

Ishmael in every land, has kept free from all narrow national prejudices, is not fettered by the deadening dogmas of Christianity, is brother to all men, always speaks a cultural language, has kinsmen in every European country. This is an advantageous situation, and has in truth made the average Jew an intelligent man, perhaps the most intelligent race in Europe."

Unfortunately, some letters which Strindberg wrote that January scarcely reflected this new attitude. Writing to a provincial newspaper editor, Isidor Kjellberg (12 January), about *Aftonbladet's* championship of a Jewish politician, Moritz Rubenson, in opposition to the official left-wing list, Strindberg complained: "You see! Persecution of Jews is always followed by kow-towing to Jews. Upper classes and Jews!" And the next day, in reply to a plea by Pehr Staaff that he write another play: "A play! Yes, when I have become very rich. If I write crap, Joseph[son] accepts it but it fails and I fall on my face; if I write bold stuff, which one can't do for that theatre, then that shit-aristocrat hasn't the guts to take it . . . I shit on him and his theatre and all other theatres . . . Beware of the Jews! . . . People talk about 'persecution of the Jews'! That is their strategy! 'Persecuted' the moment people stop kissing their arses!" Apparently remembering his recent article on the subject, he added: "But hate them as reactionaries, not as Jews!"

At least his marriage was stable, or so he thought. "Now my wife and I," he assured Kjellberg on 14 January, "are, after seven years of marriage, happily in love with each other, although we differ on many (but unimportant!) questions, and no one comes between us. She has never been swallowed up by me, and has never taken on the ape-role of the 'great man's wife' (as Fru Bjørnson has done). Despite her stage career she has remained a woman, but a free woman, and we have built a new reformed marriage (with a two-bedroomed system which keeps love alive and fresh, so that demonstrations of tenderness are only the result of deep inner tenderness and not of a strong supper)."

He spent that month completing the final story of *Utopias in Reality*; then, in early February, accepted an invitation from his new admirer Verner von Heidenstam to join him and his wife on a two weeks' trip to the Tyrol, Venice and Rome. This, although he liked the Heidenstams, turned out little better than his previous visit to Italy. "I expected little, found less," he told Kjellberg on his return (15 February). "It evoked only a homesickness—for the Swedish countryside—not the people! If you knew of any little house at Kolmården or Bråviken with a garden, hunting and fishing rights, I would trudge there incognito and hide myself. I no longer read the Swedish papers. My wife is my secretary, opens and answers my mail." At least he wrote the Heidenstams (18 February) a letter of thanks for their good companionship: "My memories of the trip are grey and porridge-like, but against this background Venice shines bright and, comparatively, coloured, a happy impression." Four days later he told them: "The thrush and bullfinch have begun to sing. I long so damnably for the Stockholm skerries." Unable to rest from writing, he informed Albert Bonnier that he was starting a new book of stories, *Sagas*—"a completely new development in my writing. Amusing, beautiful, satirical, and above all, new."[2] Pursuing his plan of writing in a language better known than Swedish, he wrote these in French.

Isidor Bonnier sent him 4,000 francs (2,880 crowns) advance on the second volume of *Getting Married*, which eased his financial situation. At the end of March he moved with Siri and the children to Neuilly, where in April he began work on that volume and a series of articles in French for *La Nouvelle Revue* on "La Société de Stockholm," over the fanciful pseudonym Comte Paul Vasili. In May he attended Victor Hugo's funeral, and Albert Bonnier returned the French manuscript of *Sagas*, saying that he would have to read them in Swedish before he could decide—a thin excuse, for there were enough people in his firm who could read French. In the event, they were not published in Swedish until 1891, under the title *Fables*, though they appeared that August and September in Danish in a new Copenhagen newspaper, founded the previous year, *Politiken*.

Strindberg's letters around this time contain frequent complaints about the "upper classes," and God also joined the ranks of the enemy. "I am on the way to becoming an atheist," he told Albert Bonnier on 25 May. "The world is ruled by idiots, so God is an idiot." Towards women in general he was not, as yet, unfavourably disposed, but feminists were another matter. "Strindberg . . . is firing away on the Woman Question," wrote Jonas Lie to Edvard Brandes on 3 June. "Whether for or against I cannot, from what he says, make out. His latest discovery and target are the unsexed representatives of the female sex, which he asserts to be a new development . . . His life is a fever and can hardly last long."[3]

Despite the advance from Isidor, money was still a problem. "Siri wants to sell all my furniture in Stockholm and Kymmendö and my books," he told Albert Bonnier on 7 June, typically putting the blame on her for this sensible suggestion. Yet he was not pessimistic about the future. In reply to a letter from Heidenstam suggesting that pessimistic books were more truthful than optimistic ones, he declared (11 June): "It is false just to show the ugly side of life, just as it is false to show only the beautiful . . . Pessimism is the aristocrats' best friend. It robs the lower class of all hope and makes them resigned, if not contented. Pessimism is a stage which we have passed and to which we may some time return, but not to stay there . . . The main thing is to rip down! Rip down heaven, the Bible and art! Leave not a stick standing!" This denunciation of pessimism sounds curiously from the man who a year and a half later was to write *The Father*.

A letter arrived from Edvard Brandes—the first in three years—congratulating him on his article recanting his anti-Semitism. "You have erased all that could wound in that chapter of *The New Kingdom*."[4] "Everywhere I see the Jew as the salt of the earth," Strindberg replied around 12 June. "I didn't see that at home in rotten Sweden." It was lucky that Brandes had not seen Strindberg's letters to Kjellberg and Staaff. "I am educating myself to become an atheist," Strindberg added in a postscript, "but am finding it horribly difficult."

On 19 June, finding Paris too hot and also too expensive, the Strindbergs left for Luc-sur-Mer in Normandy. Although busy with the new volume of *Getting Married*, Strindberg was, as usual, full of other plans. The theatre, which he had so denounced in his letter to Staaff of 13 January, had now, for no obvious reason, returned to favour. "I think I must now sit down and write a bunch of plays," he informed Albert Bonnier on 23 June. Perhaps he was heeding Bonnier's advice not to risk wearying the public with a flood of books. Luc-sur-Mer turned out to be a bit dull, so he asked Heidenstam to join him there. "Come and drink Pale-Ale [*sic*] and talk and let's damn the sea together. Don't you think that deep conversations (*à deux*) are as good as fucking?"[5]

On 30 June he wrote a letter to Albert Bonnier which must have made that cautious man glad he had opted out of publishing the second volume of *Getting Married*. "My new stories," Strindberg told him, "are ugly, though not in their language. They deal with pederasty and lesbianism and all the less common forms of 'marriage.'" The first stories in this volume, which he had written in the spring, are not of this nature; they are not even hostile to women; they express rather the resigned sadness of a husband accepting that the toil to make ends meet takes the shine off married life. But the later stories are bitter and disillusioned, reaching their climax in the final tale, "The Breadwinner." This tells of a writer who wears himself out trying to keep his family while his wife, idle and licentious, neglects the children, spends all her time with a woman friend and regularly comes home drunk. Strindberg was to assert in the fourth volume of his autobiography, *The Author*, that he had based this story on a couple he had met in Switzerland; but few people who knew him believed his.

At the end of July the family left Luc-sur-Mer and returned to Grez, where they were to stay for a fateful nine months. "The sea was driving me mad," he told Jonas Lie on 1 August. "Sterile. Nothing done. Sick. Moved. The summer has passed without my accomplishing anything, and without rest." The next day he wrote to Albert Bonnier: "With *Utopias* I have now said all I have to say and regard myself as old . . . [but] am divinely happy in Grez although my room lacks two window panes and has no lock or desk or water jug and no furniture but a wicker chair." On 3 August he told Albert Bonnier that he was "sleeping 12 hours a night and 6 each day. Am only awake around mealtimes." "I am content and find things ordered," he assured Edvard Brandes on 11 August, "since as an atheist I have given up the demands of the ideal* and therefore begin to forgive everything, since I am beginning to understand." In this euphoric mood, he finished the second volume of *Getting Married* and sent it, on 21 August, to Isidor Bonnier.

Utopias in Reality, his book of stories set in Switzerland, was published in early September, but it was poorly received and the edition of 3,000 copies did not sell out until 1900.[6] The Swedish poet and novelist Oscar Levertin summed up what Strindberg's admirers felt in a letter to Edvard Brandes (10 September): "Have you read *Utopias*? As usual with Strindberg, this eternal mixture of good and bad. I think it is tragic to see such a genius as Strindberg's wear itself out in this Ixionic struggle to improve society. Poor Strindberg, his health is delicate and he has scarcely any income; and, nervous and overworked as he is, one must be very gentle in criticising him."[7]

The subject of Utopia was not new to Strindberg. Six months earlier, in the spring of 1884, he had written, for *Swedish Destinies*, a story called "The Island of the Blessed," a kind of *Robinson Crusoe*. A group of colonists is shipwrecked on the way to America. At first they enjoy the primitive life; then a volcano erupts and they have to move to another island, where conditions are less favourable. Here they go through the stages of creating a civilised society, moving from pastoral life to the concept of private property, and finally establishing a social order to protect the rich against the poor. Strindberg pokes fun at everything in the story, as in *The New Kingdom*, and it fails for the same reason: Strindberg's heavy-handed way with satire.

The stories in *Utopias in Reality* are more serious in their treatment. One, called "Remorse," deals with a true story Strindberg had read about

---

*"The demands of the ideal" is a phrase which recurs frequently in Ibsen's play *The Wild Duck*, which had appeared the previous November, and Strindberg may well have got it from there (later he was to believe that Ibsen had maliciously based the character of Hjalmar Ekdal on him).

an incident in the Franco-Prussian War, when a young officer was ordered to execute twenty-five *franc-tireurs* and as a result lost his reason. It begins well but declines into sentimentality; living in the free atmosphere of Switzerland restores the officer to health. The same naïve optimism pervades the whole book; another story seeks to show that all family problems can be overcome by living in a commune. In his foreword to the collection, written in July 1885, Strindberg claimed socialism as a panacea, but he was as naïve when writing about politics and sociology as when writing about science—and there is a good deal of undigested science too in *Utopias*; the main characters tend to be geologists, doctors or chemists. His belief in socialism had not yet begun to waver; but before long he was to abandon it and deride his enthusiasm for it as a hangover from adolescence, though he was to recapture his old faith in it later in his life.

On 28 September and 15 October, Strindberg's and Siri's possessions still in Sweden were auctioned in Stockholm. This did little to ease his financial situation; the first auction realised 1,183 crowns, but after the payment of debts, interest, and the like, he was left with only 130 francs, and the October auction brought him only another 550 francs. During the first week in October he spent a few days with Siri at a family commune in Guise, a socialist collective founded in 1859, whence on 4 October he wrote to Edvard Brandes that they were studying "a realised Utopia." On his return to Grez on 9 October he told Heidenstam that they had had "an agreeable honeymoon; as happy as newlyweds. The commune was terrific." He wrote three articles about the commune which Edvard Brandes published in *Politiken*, of which he was co-editor.

Brandes, though accepting the articles, begged Strindberg to abandon polemical for creative writing. "Write a great novel, a mature *Red Room*," he urged him, "and you will achieve more than by any number of articles on economics, and earn a few thousand into the bargain. How can a man forfeit so fine a talent? Till my dying breath I shall repeat to you: write a novel, write a play . . . But it is useless preaching to deaf ears."[8] And to Jonas Lie, Brandes wrote on 29 October: "It is a real disaster that with all his power, that man wants to turn his back on creative writing. He understands far less than he thinks about economics. And he could write such excellent novels if he wished."[9] Again, on 19 November, he begged Strindberg: "Write a great novel. You sin against nature if you castrate your talent."[10] Strindberg did not respond to this appeal immediately, for he was to spend most of the next year writing the first four volumes of his autobiography (though he was to categorise that as "part fiction," which indeed it is). But writing that seemed to clear his head for creative writing, and he was to follow it with four plays, a novel and a volume of stories which between them contain some of his finest work.

His eldest daughter, Karin, was now five, and over forty years later she recalled her father during this time at Grez. "He was quiet and rather sombre, often in a bad mood, spoke in a soft voice and had a disturbingly piercing glance. But both he and Siri made it a rule to keep us children out of their domestic troubles." Of Siri, Karin had nothing but happy memories; she was clearly a devoted and solicitous mother. Nor was she as impractical as Strindberg liked to make out. "The general view of Siri as a housewife seems to be that she was impractical and disliked housework. Admittedly, she was not by nature practical . . . but, and it is a big but, her strong sense of duty and the thoroughness which distinguished everything she did made her a good housewife when the occasion arose." Thus, she made her own clothes, and the children's, skilfully, and although she had never learned to cook (or do anything else) at home or in her first marriage, she became adept at that too. When Strindberg liked a dish at a *pension* or a hotel, Siri would go to the kitchen and get the recipe. And she managed all the practicalities of moving, which happened so frequently—packing, ordering the carriage, registering the baggage. Strindberg bothered with none of this and would become impatient if any meal was not ready on time amid such preparations.

Curiously, Karin remembered, neither Strindberg nor Siri ever called their children *"du,"* so that the children did not call each other *"du"* either. Karin says she was sombre like her father and unwilling to say either "Thank you" or "Sorry"; Hans was "a nervous child, who often twisted and turned as he slept with half-open eyes, something that the maids said presaged an early death." Greta, by contrast, was merry and outgoing. Karin also recalled that during this second stay at Grez, after a period of complete temperance, her father began to drink absinthe.[11]

Strindberg's marital contentment was disturbed by an unpleasant rumour which reached them from Sweden. On 15 October he wrote to Isidor Kjellberg that he had heard that abusive lampoons were circulating there about him and Siri, "imitations of *The New Kingdom*," referring particularly to their sexual life. "We understand that my wife is accused of infidelity . . . we need to know with whom. I know that at the theatre she was accused of running after girls, but that's true of all actresses who don't give themselves to the first man that asks. Pamphlets have been circulating, but I haven't read them, don't want to know their content except on this one point . . . To spit on this slow-match before it catches fire I must know precisely where to spit . . . If I kept silent, I would be appearing to concur . . . Luckily we are still as much in love with each other as on the day we married, and nothing, not even the foulest accusations, affects our mutual trust, which nothing can destroy."

On 19 October he informed Jonas Lie that he was "working on ten different projects," though the same day, in reply to a query from Albert Bonnier as to whether he was writing a play, he declared: "I hate plays."* In a third letter written that day he told Heidenstam: "I begin to hate Frenchness and France . . . We are homesick for Switzerland . . . I am miserable here but must stay put because of debt."

A verbal portrait of Strindberg at Grez that autumn, confused but prolific, comes from the Swedish painter Karl Nordström. "He still thinks mainly about social problems," Nordström wrote to his brother Anders, "but has by no means abandoned creative writing; on the contrary, his head is full of new plans, plays, his autobiography, etc. He is a person whose head is so crammed with everything that one reels before such mental activity." A month later he wrote again to Anders: "Strindberg wanders around with his head full of every kind of rubbish which he ought not to be bothering about . . . I like Strindberg very much, he's good company—but no one can survive being a socialist 24 hours a day for months on end. It's too much to take, like playing whist every evening with three women who will never be able to learn."[12]

The Strindbergs had found pleasant lodgings in a pension owned by a family named Laurent, in a park by the river where they were able to bathe. "We live a gregarious life," Strindberg informed Heidenstam on 22 November. "Old friends from Paris come out on Saturdays, and last Saturday we had a respectable orgy which lasted for 2 days with song, guitar, tambourine, pipe and wild *joie de vivre*; theatrical sketches (by me), dancing, billiards, late supper, herring breakfast at the girls' (the Danish ones!), lunch with our own cabaret and dancing at the Chevillons'. It was almost Decameronian and everyone of any talent contributed songs (I a French chansonette!!) . . . On Wednesday I am giving a lecture in Paris: 'On the Literary Reaction in Sweden.'"

The Danish girls were Sofie Holten and Marie David. Sofie was twenty-seven and had studied painting in Paris, where she shared a room with a cousin of Siri's; she was also a contributor to Edvard Brandes' paper *Politiken*, for which she had written articles about the contemporary art scene in France. Strindberg was much taken with her and suggested that she should accompany him on a cycling trip to illustrate essays he was

---

*An acquaintance recalled Strindberg's hatred of culture at this time, and how, when someone mentioned the theatre, he burst out: "Ugh—people in masks among painted paper." (Ögonvittnen, I, pp. 187–8.)

planning to write about French peasant life. Marie was twenty and Jewish, the daughter, or anyway the presumed daughter, of a failed landowner who had lost the family fortune. Her parents' marriage had failed, though they remained together for a while, and Marie's mother became the mistress of Georg Brandes. Marie did not resemble her brothers and sisters, and according to Strindberg's daughter Karin, "knew that she was illegitimate";[13] she claimed to be Brandes' daughter, though Brandes denied it.

In due course Marie's mother left her husband and took Marie and her other youngest child to Naples. There she soon died of tuberculosis. Under these circumstances Marie, while still in her teens, became a heavy drinker, and Karin (who later knew her well) states that "an unhappy love affair with a young Dane set a permanent mark on her, so that she never again loved any other man."[14] Her mother's unhappy experience of marriage cannot have helped in this respect. Marie had intended to become a doctor and took a course in anatomy, but abandoned her medical studies and decided to write. She regarded herself as an "enlightened atheist"; her small library included Darwin, Spencer, Mill, Buckle and Comte.[15] In a little over a year she was to become one of Strindberg's great enemies.

For the time being, however, and indeed for the first year of their acquaintance, Strindberg enjoyed her company. He described her and Sofie to Edvard Brandes (12 November) as "2 lively Danish girls," and asked them to write a piece on "La Société de Copenhague" for *La Nouvelle Revue* in the series for which he had written a corresponding essay on Stockholm. His letters of this autumn contain several warm references to them. Sofie later recalled how he wrote small roles for her to act in their evenings of cabaret "and himself, though in another way, partook actively in these entertainments. He liked to sing Mendelssohn duets to his own accompaniment on the guitar, wearing a black velvet beret and cloak."[16] She returned the compliment by painting a portrait of him.

The unconventional manner of the two girls offended the more conservative members of the Scandinavian community. "There is something brutal and impudent about them," wrote one such that winter. "Their whole mode of being is pervaded by a contempt, a malignant hatred of all convention and of all the millions of people who accept convention. And for them, as for Strindberg, everything is convention. Imagine being married to such women! Fru Strindberg tries to imitate them."[17] Another guest at one of their parties remembered, fifty years later: "Fru Strindberg was rather disagreeable, smoked a cigar, seemed a little drunk. She insisted on singing. When she began, Strindberg got up and went out."[18]

The bad reception of *Utopias* had, if possible, increased Strindberg's animosity towards Sweden. "I don't regard Sweden as my fatherland," he told Albert Bonnier on 22 November, "which won't stop me from visiting it as a tourist . . . No one can stop me from setting my writings in Sweden. I know that country and its language best and hate it most." He thought vaguely of undertaking a lecture tour there the following January. A few days later he delivered his lecture "On the Literary Reaction in Sweden" in Paris. Jonas Lie attended it and reported to Edvard Brandes: "It was good and individual, but was delivered to a not very sympathetic audience, who had expected more of the firebrand. He suffers, as you say, from the madness of not wanting to be what he is—a creative writer. He drapes his reading and arguments around his characters instead of expressing his ideas by creating human dramas out of them. I told him this when we last met; but the prophet in him is too dominant, and I suppose that is how he has to be, his country's nipple for the New Ideas. It is an axiom with him that Art is somehow frivolous."[19]

On 11 December, Strindberg's brother Axel wrote to him that the actor Emil Hillberg, who was also editor of a Saturday magazine called *Stockholm*, had opened a fund to provide a stipend for him, the aim being to get promises from well-wishers which would ensure an income of 3,000 to 4,000 crowns a year for the next ten years. Among others, he had contacted such writers as Snoilsky, Levertin and Geijerstam. In the issue of 26 September Hillberg, disturbed by the news of Strindberg's enforced auction of his possessions, had declared: "He has never swerved from the beliefs of his youth. But when the world turned against him, he became bitter, more bitter than was needful, and far more so than his best friends thought right. As a result, he has for some time not been the doughty champion of what is right and noble that he would be were he able to create in peace and calm."

This proposal was attacked from several quarters. *Vårt Land*, *Figaro* and *Smålandsposten* all opposed it. Hugo Nisbeth in *Figaro* wrote: "Herr Hillberg's foolhardy attempt to inaugurate a nation-wide subscription for Herr Strindberg has, as is well known, aroused the deepest indignation and disgust in all right-thinking people."[20] None the less, on 12 December, Hillberg announced a forthcoming "Strindberg number," which duly appeared on 19 December, containing various tributes. But that same day Strindberg wrote to Axel rejecting the idea, on the ground that he would then be forced to praise the writings of anyone who subscribed; besides which "Hillberg surely knows that after such a revelation the victims never have a happy moment, never ride in a carriage, never drink a glass of wine, never visit a restaurant . . . All social intercourse is ended. Who wants to accept an invitation from a pauper?"

An unpleasant shock came shortly before Christmas; *La Nouvelle Revue*, for which he had so proudly written "La Société de Stockholm" in French, ran into financial trouble and could neither publish the articles nor pay him. "Four months wasted," he told Albert Bonnier on Christmas Eve. "A Christmas present which is far from welcome." Begging Edvard Brandes (29 December) to help him with his project of a book about European peasants, he wrote: "This plan will save me from creative writing and Sweden. Help me, in the name of Jesus Christ the Nazarene, for otherwise I'll have to go back to writing plays, which I hate and do badly." 1885 had been a bad year. Apart from the final story of *Utopias* and some occasional pieces, he had written nothing but the second volume of *Getting Married*. 1886 was to be a fertile and, in general, a happy year, the last happy one that he was to know for some time; arguably, the last that he was ever to know.

Such was his financial plight that the most improbable projects received serious consideration. "Siri wants to go to Neuchâtel," Strindberg informed Geijerstam on 20 January, "to start a *pension* for the many Scandinavian gentlemen who live there, studying French because the town is cheap. I shall go with her and become chief gardener, my doctor having declared that unless I exercise or take some form of bodily exertion, the fever in my brain will not slacken. On his advice I have taken up drinking and billiards, playing cards and being sociable. We are stuck here since we owe 2,000 francs and our debts grow like an avalanche." Four days later he told Hjalmar Branting: "To be able to work as incredibly as I do, I am following [Herbert] Spencer's counsel and enjoying myself. I dance, play billiards with young ladies, strum the guitar and write songs. I cannot be happy except in female company, however much of a misogynist I may be. My wife and I have argued ourselves to a standstill over the woman question and are as much in love with each other as before, though we quarrelled so bloodily that we nearly split up. Thank God it passed and that assassination attempt concerning her fidelity towards me failed."

The pressure of debt forced him to reconsider his attitude towards the collection that had been planned for him in Sweden. On 18 February he wrote to a lawyer friend, Theodor Frölander, accepting the proposal, though stipulating: "I must absolutely reject every penny that has been subscribed by authoresses and women in general, since we must for the present remain enemies." He added a note of regret concerning his new-found and uneasy atheism. "I sometimes wish I still believed in God and heaven. That was at least a refuge. Now I see none. Or that I had become an atheist when I was younger. Then I could have adjusted my life accordingly. Now my life is ordered by a fixed reference to heaven —which means everything is to hell." A month later he was to write: "I am an old-fashioned Christian idealist and live in an eternal feud with my former self, a feud which is destroying me. I am split quite in two."

At the end of January, Strindberg had published an intemperate article in Hillberg's magazine *Stockholm* entitled "Capital and Literature," attributing his economic plight to the treatment he had had from publishers and abusing them as unnecessary middlemen, parasites and self-appointed censors. Albert Bonnier, not unreasonably, took offence; since the trial, hardly a Swede could have been unaware that he was Strindberg's publisher. He wrote to Strindberg suggesting that they should cancel the contract existing between them, at the same time generously offering to waive Strindberg's debts to him, amounting to 8,000 crowns. Karl Otto, however, persuaded his father not to send this letter, and on 15 February Albert drafted a new one merely offering to cancel the debt.

Strindberg, characteristically, was reluctant to accept Bonnier's gesture at its face value. "The great Shylock!" he wrote to his brother Axel (24 February). "There is some devilry behind this!" Still, he accepted the offer, and even wrote a letter to *Stockholm* acknowledging Bonnier's generosity, describing him, however, merely as "one of my publishers" without having the grace to name him. [21]

In his letter of acceptance, Strindberg asked Bonnier: "What would you say if I wrote my autobiography?" The possible implications of such a book alarmed Bonnier, who replied evasively, querying whether "writing your life story might not be excessively polemical." [22] But Strindberg was not to be deterred. He sensed, correctly as it turned out, that to delve into his past might release some of his inhibitions concerning the writing of fiction. In any case, he did not intend his autobiography to be strictly factual. "I regard myself and my talent as dead," he informed Edvard Brandes in early April, "and am now writing the saga of my life in a curious novelistic form (Secret!). I think I can thereby disentangle myself and discover the key to my scale." [23] The book progressed so quickly that he was able to post the manuscript of Volume I to Bonnier on 24 April. He entitled it *The Son of a Servant*. Next day he wrote to him: "When you have read this first instalment . . . you will doubtless ask yourself, as the public will: 'What is this? Is it a novel? No.   Biography? No.   Memoirs?

No.' I reply: 'It is a book which is what it says it is—"The Development of a Soul, 1849–1867." ' "

Bonnier was delighted with *The Son of a Servant*, and proposed an edition of 4,000 copies—a thousand more than Strindberg had anticipated—and an advance of 3,000 francs. Strindberg was exhilarated. "When I receive the 3,000 francs," he replied on 7 May, "I shall leave this tedious and expensive Grez for the cheap environs of Zurich, where I shall drink myself stupid with beer and my wife will take a midwifery examination (my daughters shall become midwives), since I don't expect to live long and someone must work for the children till they're able to work themselves." On 11 May, a bare fortnight after receiving the manuscript, Bonnier was able to send him the proofs.

Strindberg received these not in Grez but in a Swiss castle. Verner von Heidenstam, his companion in Venice and Rome, had leased, as befitted an aristocrat, Schloss Brunegg near the village of Othmarsingen in the canton of Aargau. "A mountain castle from Roman and mediaeval times," Strindberg informed Bonnier (14 May). "We toss coins in the Grand Hall, fence with lances in sixteenth-century armour, act the aristocrats, drink beer, play backgammon and talk socialism . . . The change of air and surroundings have braced me, and once Volume II [of the autobiography] is finished I shall immediately write two modern plays which I have long planned; one for the New Theatre and one for the Royal."

The castle was so small that there was insufficient room in it for Siri and the children, so Strindberg found lodgings in the village, and on 20 May they joined him there. "Here I live in Arcadia," he told Edvard Brandes the next day, "with my flock for 3 francs 50 centimes full pension per day (five rooms, a bowling alley, a balcony, the Alps, lightning conductors, etc.)." The lightning conductors were important, for though he was fascinated by electricity, and was later to experiment with it, it, and especially lightning, frightened him, like dogs.

Heidenstam recalled Strindberg as "well-built, slim, on the tall side"; his head, with its curly hair and upbrushed moustaches, reminded Heidenstam of Molière. He noted the fine, high, wide forehead, the tired and melancholy light-blue eyes with their small, compressed pupils, the broad face with its protuberant cheekbones and the painfully deep lines around the full, well-shaped mouth. But he found Strindberg's habitual expression "challengingly severe, almost cruel. When he is annoyed it is such that, if you met a man wearing a similar expression on a remote forest path, you would hand him your purse before he asked for it." But "Strindberg's face lights up during conversation. His demeanour, at first austere, even shy, gradually becomes not courteous or compliant, but unaffected and approachable. His smile is beautiful and warm, but transient and silent. I can never remember having *heard* Strindberg laugh."[24]

On 29 May, five weeks after he had completed it, *The Son of a Servant* was published. "An attempt at the literature of the future," Strindberg called it in a letter to Edvard Brandes two days before publication. "No action, no 'style.' Psychology, and the story of an epoch in a person's life. No landscapes, no furniture, no *style.*" He went on to explain how the project was to develop. "There will be five parts, the whole story from 1849 to 1886. It will be the story of Sweden: the story of how an author comes into existence; the story of the development of a soul during a particular period . . . I think that literature should totally emancipate itself from art and become science. Writers must learn their craft by study; psychology, sociology, physiology, history, politics. Otherwise we shall be just dilettantes . . . Now I am finishing with journalism, I can't afford that any longer. Everything must go into the story of my soul's development."

Bonnier's optimism in printing a larger edition than usual proved unfounded. *The Son of a Servant* was violently attacked by most of the critics in the predominantly conservative press. "New Example of Sordid Writing" was the headline in *Stockholms Dagblad*, and Carl David af Wirsén wrote in *Vårt Land*: "The whole book is stamped with immodesty and coarseness . . . One lacks words to express one's disapproval of the publisher who paid for, and circulates, so impudent a work." Most of the reviews were in this tone, though Karl Warburg in *Handelstidningen i Göteborg* described it as "a remarkable book" and praised the "mood of sensitive and gentle melancholy which makes it the aristocrat among Strindberg's works." Importantly for Strindberg, however, it was admired by some discriminating friends. Edvard Brandes praised it in a letter to Strindberg as "important, rewarding, profound and honest,"[25] and Hjalmar Branting assured him that "it will be a monument in our literature."[26] Several Norwegian papers praised it, but in Finland it was banned by the censor. Oscar Levertin passed a shrewd judgement on the book in a letter to Edvard Brandes: "Starts well, ends weakly, I think. Up here [in Sweden] there is pious indignation at the way he has portrayed his whole family, which I feel he might in some respects have done a little more graciously. And the book wavers unhappily between autobiography and fiction, though parts are fascinating and brilliant."[27] Sales were poor. The Finnish writer Zacharias Topelius, who had threatened to leave Bonnier if he reprinted *Getting Married*, summed up many people's attitude when he wrote to Bonnier: "I have heard too much about *The Son of a Servant*, even from impartial readers, to wish to soil my hands by touching this book."[28]

The Son of a Servant has since come to be regarded as one of Strindberg's better non-dramatic works. It contains some of his most vivid descriptive writing: life in the overcrowded childhood home, the early death of his mother, the different schools which the young Strindberg attended, the excursions into the countryside. But it also contains, like so many of his works, passages of social commentary which, admirable in their intent, now read tediously and suffer further from the self-conscious slant of the writing. Strindberg was never wholly successful in integrating his political beliefs into his non-journalistic writing, perhaps because his belief in socialism was always diluted by an admiration of the aristocracy. He was not a scientific historian any more than he was to be scientific in his approach to physics and chemistry, and *The Son of a Servant* is least successful when, as so often occurs, he twists his memories to prove a sociological point. His attitude towards women when he wrote the book provided another obstacle. Strindberg remembered his mother much more affectionately than he remembered his father, but he felt bound to portray the one as an indolent woman drinking her morning coffee in bed with wet nurses and servants to do the work, and the other as an overworked breadwinner. In particular, he sought to identify himself with the working class from whom his mother sprang, but his distaste for much that the working class stood for continually blurs this attempted self-portrayal. "I think I'm too much of an aristocrat amid all my demagogy to write for the masses," he confessed to Edvard Brandes (9 June).* Like *The Red Room, The Son of a Servant* is a deeply flawed book, sometimes brilliant, often tedious; and like *The Red Room*, and indeed most of Strindberg's non-dramatic works, it is much overrated in Sweden today.

Its hostile reception did not, however, deter Strindberg from proceeding with its sequel, which dealt with his years at Uppsala and his first efforts as a dramatist and actor. He began this four days before *The Son of a Servant* appeared, and completed it in a month, entitling it *Time of*

---

*This opinion of himself was confirmed shortly afterwards by Heidenstam, who, after they had taken a short excursion together that month and quarrelled about various small matters, wrote to Strindberg (22 June): "You, the 'son of a servant,' turn up your nose at what hundreds of spoiled tourists consume with relish. Your nervous fussiness has turned into monomania; you brood over your obsession that most things are bad and unenjoyable. You began by expressing discontent with society and end by complaining about beefsteaks, trout, and billiard balls that are too mauve."[29] Strindberg defended himself (23 June) on the ground that fussiness was evidence of a refined sensibility.

Ferment. He described it to Edvard Brandes (16 June) as being "much tauter and richer than Part I," and so it is, not least because, unlike the earlier book, it does not set out to teach sociology. Strindberg sent the manuscript to Albert Bonnier on 20 June, and the following day informed him that the writing of these two volumes had cleared his head and made it possible for him to return to creative literature. "In a week," he had told Edvard Brandes (9 June), "I'm going to sit down and write two plays." Bonnier liked *Time of Ferment* and promised an edition of 4,000 copies despite the poor sales of its predecessor. He also encouraged Strindberg to go ahead with his plays: "Sweden needs a dramatist."[30]

On 27 July Strindberg completed the third volume of his autobiography, *In the Red Room*, an account of his Bohemian years of teaching, casual journalism, poverty and conviviality between his final departure from Uppsala and his joining the Royal Library. A few days later he moved from Othmarsingen to Weggis, near Lucerne, where he at once started work on the first of his promised plays. "I feel splendid," he assured Albert Bonnier on 3 August, "if only my brain and nerves could rest, but they chafe incessantly and the only rest I know is hard work. Hence I write too much." But the urge to explore his past proved too strong, and he quickly abandoned the play for a fourth volume of autobiography, *He and She*. This merely comprised the letters that he and Siri had written to each other during their period of courtship, together with a few of Wrangel's letters, so he was able to send it to Bonnier as early as 9 August, stating that there would be "no foreword and no notes." He had, he explained, lost his desire to write anything creative "until I have completed this pilgrimage through my tormented past. I began a play but couldn't be dishonest enough to write for the stalls. 'One must be a little stupid to write for the theatre,' Gondinet (I think) said.* Simply being an artist nauseates me. My intelligence has developed from fantasising to thinking. The conjuring of voluntary hallucinations at one's desk is like self-defilement. The novel and the theatre are only for women. Let us leave these diversions to them . . . I have seen through 'creative writing' and lack the illusions—so I can no longer pursue it . . . Have been reading Tolstoy [Bonnier had sent him *War and Peace*]. Can anyone endure this unending female chatter? And one needs an index for all these masses of characters. Pierre was good but evaporated. The battle scenes were inartistic and leave no real picture."

Despite these protestations, he informed Heidenstam only three days

---

*"Pour faire du théâtre, il faut être un peu bête" (*Le Figaro*, 22 December 1885). *Cf.* Torsten Eklund's note, *Brev*, VI, 20n.

later: "Now I am working on the play again. Am enjoying it! Subtle psychology, sceptical, irreverent, I'm afraid a bit improper, quite the old Strindberg again!" This play was *The Marauders*, which he was eventually to rewrite as *The Comrades*; it was to be the first of his dramas of sexual realism, the forerunner of *The Father, Miss Julie* and *Creditors*. But his interest quickly lapsed again. On 20 August he wrote to Bonnier: "For a whole month I've been struggling with the first act of a play; I actually finished it, but so badly that I've scrapped it. Just debate, no characters."

He turned instead to another well-intentioned but time-wasting project, a study of the working conditions of the French peasantry. A young Marxist sociologist named Gustaf Steffen, later to become a professor, had started a correspondence with him in February and visited him in Othmarsingen during the summer. Strindberg liked him and invited him to join him on a three weeks' study trip through France. They left on 30 August and travelled through Châlons-sur-Marne, Rheims, Lille, Rouen, Tours, Nantes, Brittany, Bordeaux, Toulouse, Sète and Nîmes, mainly by train but sometimes on foot. "Full of notes, photographs, drawings," he told Heidenstam (15 September). "I feel rich. No stomach catarrh, no nerves, no fussiness. I got up at 4, 5 a.m., ate rancid pork and drank warm beer on an empty stomach at a farmers' alehouse, travelled 3rd class, was jostled, insulted as a supposed German, but adapted after a couple of days." Mixing with the working class, which he so proudly championed, never came easily to Strindberg.

He handed over the money side of the trip to Steffen, giving him 100 francs at a time to cover all expenses, an arrangement which must have seemed sensible at the time but which turned out most unfortunately. In a letter to his old mentor Gustaf Klemming, Strindberg's boss at the Royal Library, Steffen told an alarming story.

> [In Toulouse] Strindberg began to reproach me for having squandered the money . . . and when he found that some days had cost over 100 francs and others no more than 50 he began to speak of treachery and theft!! . . . I had destroyed the hotel bills so as not to be bothered with a mass of, as I supposed, unnecessary papers. Herr Strindberg now asserted that it was *impossible* that any day could ever cost us 100 francs . . . Finally at the station in Nîmes Herr Strindberg threw 100 francs at me for my ticket back to Berlin, said we should part and overwhelmed me with the crudest insults: I had "exploited" him or, "even worse," I was a Jew and had a hereditary tendency to betray him, an Aryan . . . I began seriously to fear that Herr Strindberg was temporarily out of his mind. This suspicion received unpleasant confirmation by way of a postcard which I have just received, dated the day after we parted in Nîmes, in which Herr Strindberg suggests that I "took 100 francs" from his wallet and threatens "legal proceedings" unless I "return the 400 francs of which I have swindled him"!!![31]

Strindberg continued his journey alone. On 20 September, after his return to Weggis, he sent a triumphant account to Albert Bonnier. "We travelled third class, where we interviewed peasants, got off at country halts, tramped overland with our baggage, sometimes more than six miles; interviewed people in peasant inns and cottages. Photographed and drew peasant houses and landscapes. Sometimes travelled twelve hours at a stretch, third class; got up at 2 a.m. to continue our journey . . . gathered plants, which we pressed . . . were abused as Prussians, insulted by gendarmes, treated like tramps at the hotels, since we had no luggage but our grips . . . My eyes are as red as a roach's and the lining of my coat is rotted with sweat; my feet were raw from walking and were assuaged by a glass of cognac poured into my socks." He did not mention the contretemps with Steffen.

Bonnier, meanwhile, had rejected *He and She* as libellous; Karin comments that the portrait of Siri in the book bore no relation to the mother she knew. *Time of Ferment* appeared at the end of September but, like *The Son of a Servant*, was sharply criticised and sold poorly. Strindberg's attacks on the Swedish classical poets Bellman and Geijer provided further ammunition for his enemies; and he was now so unpopular with the establishment that any book by him stood little chance of acceptance in the conservative-dominated press. He informed Bonnier on 22 September that the *Neue Freie Presse* in Vienna had asked him if he could let them have a new novel not yet published in Sweden, and that he was considering, among other things, "a new Pick-Wick" or "Adventures of a Travelling Salesman in Sweden" or "Adventures of an Actress (my wife's career, starting where *He and She* ends)." Neither of these projects materialised.

On 1 October they moved from Weggis to the smaller and pleasanter town of Gersau, where they stayed until early the next year. Karin recalled how at this time:

> He used to take little Hans on his knee at his desk and show him pictures in *The Flower Book* or *The Book of Wild Animals* or *The Monkey Book*, while I and Greta stood beside him. How his beautiful hands carefully turned the pages in his herbarium, and gently stroked the flowers into place, how his soft voice would say, "Come here, children," or "Stop, children," how his eyes suddenly widened with an indescribably amused expression when one of us children made some precocious observation. When we kissed him good night, he always turned his cheek and looked gentle and earnest, and then often stroked our hair with a beautiful gesture as though to console us for his having shrunk from our kisses. His violet copying ink, which glowed with the colours of the rainbow once it had dried, the yellow copying-jelly

with *Getting Married* on it in mirror-writing which tasted sweet when we tried to lick a corner of it and squeaked when the paper was pulled off, his white lamp of glass-flux, his big glass inkwell, his woollen loose-cuffs, which Eva darned, and his velvet beret, are all intimately interwoven with my memories from our time at Gersau. His fencing foils interested us deeply, and in merry moments we would try on his fencing-mask.[32]

She says he busied himself much with photography, including several self-portraits which he took by remote control with "a long cord and an ingenious shutter . . . He developed his photographs himself, and we loved to be allowed to join him in the red glow of the dark room and wait there for the ten minutes that the developing required . . . But it was not a happy time at Weggis and Gersau, and with those bright memories are mingled sombre ones, which I already began to sense if not to understand."[33]

Relations between Strindberg and Siri had been generally good since the *Getting Married* trial—or at any rate, he was happy; his letters over this period frequently refer to his marital bliss. But at the end of October 1886 Isidor Bonnier at last published the second volume of *Getting Married*, which Strindberg had completed over twelve months before, its appearance having been delayed by the difficulty of finding a printer and distributors willing to risk being associated with such a controversial book. This second volume was very different from its predecessor. Volume One had on the whole been sympathetic to women and to some at least of their demands for emancipation, and Volume Two is by no means wholly misogynistic; several of the early stories are as sympathetic to women as anything he wrote. This is especially true of the two first stories, which he wrote in French: "Autumn," which tells of a marriage that has drifted into boredom and resignation, and "Bread," which shows how financial difficulties can destroy love. Similarly, "It Is Not Enough" portrays a mother wearing herself out for her egotistical and ungrateful sons.

But as the book progressed, Strindberg's hatred of feminism turned into something not easily distinguishable from misogyny, however much he was to protest to the contrary. The later stories contain a series of portraits of malignant and shrewish women, of the kind he was later to create so memorably in his plays, women who regard man as their natural enemy and the sex act as unclean and degrading, vampires who drain the blood from their honest and hard-working husbands. Worse, he prefaced the book with a foreword denouncing women as responsible for all of history's monstrosities, including religious persecution and war, and summing up marriage as a form of prostitution by contract which, as a consequence of woman's indolence and ambition for power, has imprisoned the husband in a condition of complete slavery.*

Some of these stories show Strindberg at his most powerful; as the plays were to prove, anger, even of the most irrational kind, tended to bring out the best in him as a writer, as sentimental woman-worship brought out the worst. But the effect on his marriage was disastrous. The publication of the book brought to a head for Siri the frustrations of living in permanent debt with an impossibly jealous and suspicious husband who had forced her to abandon her career. Everyone who read it would, she knew, identify her with these spendthrift, selfish and domineering wives, as indeed most readers did. Karin says that her mother "felt incurably wounded by the book, insulted in front of the whole world. People must reason: What kind of a wife must this writer have had to speak thus about women and marriage?"[34]

Siri's resentment was fuelled by her two Danish friends, Sofie Holten and Marie David. Marie especially encouraged Siri to stand up to her husband and demand that she be allowed to return to the stage, which of course would necessitate their returning to Sweden or going to live in Finland. To this end she joined Siri in urging him to reconcile himself with his fellow countrymen. To make matters worse for Strindberg, his children were very fond of Marie. As late as January 1886 he had been well enough disposed towards her to suggest to Edvard Brandes that she might translate his articles "La Société de Stockholm" into Danish for *Politiken*.[35] She now became the personification of all that he dreaded and loathed in feminism, the Enemy.

In *A Madman's Defence* two years later, Strindberg described Marie as "red-haired and thin, with a crooked nose, a double chin and yellow eyes, cheeks swollen by drink, flat-chested with crooked hands . . . the most horrible type one can imagine; a farm-lad would have run from her."[36] This picture seems to be as far from the truth as almost everything else in that book. Harry Jacobsen, who interviewed several of her relatives and friends, says she had golden hair, an attractive profile, a small, well-shaped mouth, beautiful hands and a soft and delicate skin,[37] and a contemporary painting of her bears out this description. But Strindberg was to describe his method of portraying women in his plays as: "Accuse them, blacken them; abuse them so that they haven't a clean spot—that is dramatic!"[38] and it was the method he used, against not only Marie but also Siri, in *A Madman's Defence*. Another example concerns the "respectable orgy" about which he wrote so enthusiastically to Heiden-

*Cf. Martin Lamm's penetrating analysis (*August Strindberg*, ed. and translated by Harry G. Carlson, New York, 1971, pp. 157–9.)

stam on 22 November 1885.* In A *Madman's Defence* he gives a very different account of this occasion, among other things accusing the Danish girls of lesbian activities, including attempts by Marie on Siri, as a result of which, he claims, he took Siri to the river intending to drown her and was prevented from doing so only by the thought of their children.

Karin remembered Marie with nothing but gratitude and affection. She says Marie had "no trace of 'emancipated fashions' or masculinity in her dress, but was simply free from affectation, that special kind of small affectation that was then regarded as a sign of femininity. Accustomed to travel and managing for herself, parentless as she was, there was something independent and 'continental' in her whole way of life." Karin sums her up as a freethinker sympathetically tolerant to those who thought otherwise, calmly objective in her judgements and a convinced but not exaggerated supporter of women's emancipation; small, with especially beautiful hands, happiest with simple and natural people and disliking smart society. She "sometimes yielded to an overwhelming desire for alcohol, whether inherited or not I do. not know," but could go for long periods without it. [39]†

Strindberg's letters in the weeks surrounding the publication of this second volume of *Getting Married* reveal an extraordinary duality in his attitude towards Siri and women in general. On 22 October he sent Albert Bonnier a paranoiac letter asserting his conviction that some of his letters and manuscripts had been intercepted (an obsession which was to find repeated expression in his plays, from *The Father* to *To Damascus*) and commenting: "The theft of the manuscripts began when they started employing women at the post office." On 14 November, in reply to a feminist writer, Anna Wahlenberg, who had rashly sent him a novel by her about a woman who, like Ibsen's Nora, breaks with her conservative background, he wrote: "So you find it reasonable that a woman should intrude into the breadwinner's field of work without his being freed from the intolerable burden of keeping a woman, her children and servants, just because they share a child." Yet five days later he assured Heidenstam: "At my request, my wife never reads my books and accordingly we live, for the present, like turtledoves," and on 29 November he told

*See p. 150, above.

†In old age, Karin recalled that Marie had "occasional but irresistible" lapses into alcoholism, but that this happened only twice in all the years Karin knew her, once in Stockholm and once in Helsinki. She added that Siri and Marie never shared a bedroom, was sure there was never sex between them, and says that there is nothing in their letters to suggest it; and Karin was unprejudiced enough about homosexuality to write a play about it. (Karin Smirnoff, *Så var det i verkligheten*, Stockholm, 1956, pp. 36, 80, 86–7.)

Alexander Kielland: "My hatred is purely theoretical, especially towards ladies, whom I still worship . . . If you had any idea of what an idyllic family life I lead, after completing my term of strife, you would perhaps envy me." On 3 December he assured Edvard Brandes: "After many domestic storms, I now live the most delightful family life with those I love . . . our love blossoms as when we were newlywed and never a hard word is said . . . But I must first cleanse my house of these damned modern women, who for a time made my marriage unendurable." This was, of course, a reference to Sofie and Marie.

The second volume of *Getting Married* was attacked even more fiercely than its predecessor. Even some of his old supporters, such as Carl Snoilsky, Gustaf af Geijerstam and Hjalmar Branting, criticised it for its lack of balance and seemingly obvious and unflattering references to Siri. These hostile comments irrationally increased his suspicion that she had been unfaithful to him; she, not unreasonably, consulted doctors about his state of mind. He discovered this, and that autumn and winter of 1886 they came near to breaking point. Karin says that the publication of this book marked a watershed in their relationship, and that from now on their marriage was doomed.

> Siri was not a rabid emancipationist . . . but she objected passionately to the new stories in *Getting Married*. "For the sake of domestic peace" she begged henceforth to be allowed not to read what he wrote. He did not extract this promise from her; she requested it. The second volume of *Getting Married* became an incurable cancer in their domestic life . . . She began to keep silent . . . Strindberg found this mute hostility more painful than when it was overt, and could not refrain from continuing to provoke her until she burst into sobs or violent retorts . . . If *The New Kingdom* had driven them into exile and the first volume of *Getting Married* had caused a scandal, the new volume would not, she realized, open the way for them to go home. She felt bitterly and clearly that her artistic career was finished. [40]*

Moreover, the book vehemently publicised another source of distress to Siri, Strindberg's increasing contempt for religion, which had so dominated his childhood and adolescence and which, in a few years, was to save him when he hovered on the brink of insanity. On this subject Karin shrewdly notes: "It seems to me that Strindberg's whole lifelong struggle had to be so difficult because at root it was a struggle against his inmost

*He now refused women the right either to vote or to inherit. Henceforth young liberals regarded him as a radical reactionary; they supported Ibsen on the woman question, Strindberg attacked him.

longings. He had been born into an age, and been drawn into a way of thought, which suited his reason but not his general needs."[41]

All this hostility did not, however, deter Strindberg from continuing to write. He returned to his unfinished play, and on 30 November was able to send the completed manuscript of *The Marauders* to Albert Bonnier. "A comedy in 5 acts," he explained, "the last 4 written in the past 8 days, which doesn't mean it's not good, because I can't write slowly. The piece is, I think, very actable, but so as not to fall foul of the ladies (it deals, of course, with ladies), certain precautions should be taken. It needs to be staged at all the Scandinavian theatres simultaneously, so that the New Theatre won't come first and frighten off all the others."

The Marauders is set in Paris. A painter, Bertha, who wears a man's tie, has her hair short and smokes cigarettes, does not want to compromise her career by "becoming a man's slave," but marries another painter for economic reasons and also in the hope of curing her chlorosis, an illness symptomised by irregular menstruation. She gets a painting accepted in a competition, while her husband's is refused. She tries in various ways to humiliate him until at length he sends her away and takes a mistress, revealing that the accepted picture is in fact his and that he had changed the numbers so as to provide his wife with a success. Other characters include an emancipated and bisexual girl named Abel, a poet and a Dr. Östermark (who was to reappear in *The Father*). Strindberg later asserted that the two main characters were based on an American painter at Grez named Francis Brook Chadwick and his Swedish wife;[42] but Bertha is clearly a malicious portrait of Siri, and the plot stems from her success and his failure in the New Theatre production of *Sir Bengt's Wife*.

Though sometimes wittily written, it is an unconvincing story, and Albert Bonnier told Strindberg (7 December) that he found it "undramatic" and "painfully bitter and cynical . . . only a variant on Volume Two of *Getting Married*, and people have long been weary of and bored by this eternal 'woman question' . . . If you decide to instruct me to halt the printing and destroy what has been set I shall not be at all sorry."[43] He suggested that the play be shortened and "some violent passages" deleted, but generously offered to print ten copies for distribution to the theatres. Strindberg, complaining that the play was "more dramatic than *Ghosts*," grudgingly accepted this offer; but *The Marauders* was rejected by both the New and the Royal theatres in Stockholm, as well as by leading theatres in Copenhagen and Helsinki. The only theatre to show interest was, surprisingly, the Casino in Copenhagen, which went in mainly for operettas; Hans Riber Hunderup, its director, requested changes, and Strindberg agreed, deleting the first act and, equally surprisingly, providing a happy ending. Then he repented of this and wrote a grim one, but Hunderup rejected it. None of the three endings really works.

Although *The Son of a Servant* and *Time of Ferment* had both been ill received, and Bonnier rejected *The Marauders*, yet Strindberg's belief in himself as a writer remained as resilient as ever, and he seemed unaware of the storm clouds gathering over his marriage. "I have now worked myself through and out of the woman question," he assured Bonnier (around 10 December), "as regards both my writing and my domestic life . . . It is now repellent to me, and now that I am no longer daily reminded of it, I abandon it and talk of other things. After my autobiography I shall probably write a rustic Swedish novel, into which I shall pour the great fund of material from Kymmendö which I have been storing while I had hopes of returning there." In reply to Bonnier's offer to send him the latest plays of Ibsen (*Rosmersholm*) and Kielland, he declared: "Ibsen and Kielland have nothing to teach me, two ignorant women's writers." He concluded: "To live and rule one must, I suppose, write for the theatre, and I have an old portfolio of theatrical ideas which I shall dust off."

Consolation for the failure of this year's books came to him in the shape of praise for the second volume of *Getting Married* from those fearless consolers of rebellious genius, the brothers Brandes. Edvard wrote to him on 13 December: "I admire the foreword most. Some of the stories I find too carelessly written, but others are very remarkable."[44] And Georg, reviewing the book in *Politiken* on Christmas Day, though critical of Strindberg's general hostility to women, praised him for having the courage, unlike other Swedish writers, to speak plainly, and denounced Swedish publishers for their unwillingness to publish the book. "It makes a pitiable impression," he wrote, getting his facts slightly wrong, "to see this latest book by Strindberg published at the author's own expense. Is it conceivable that no Swedish publisher has dared?"[45] And on New Year's Eve, Edvard wrote to Strindberg: "This year has made you well known in Denmark. Six years ago, when we first corresponded, you were un-known—now you are read and discussed and denigrated and praised, as must be. . . . You are the man who will awake the literature of Sweden, who will be the leader for the new age."[46]

That same day, sending the manuscript of *The Author*, covering his life since 1877 to Bonnier, Strindberg wrote: "I shall have *The French Peasant* ready in a week. Then, with my dearly bought experiences, I shall start a new year and a new life as a human being. To that end we are leaving for Bavaria, a village on the Bodensee, to study the German peasant, set up home in a cheap country and reduce our living expenses by half so that I won't have to write quite so fast and so much . . . I must think of the theatre and write Plays 1 and 3* of my *Marauders* trilogy . . . It may happen that my comedy [*The Marauders*] will take off, if not this year then next (like *Ghosts*), and it will most assuredly be a monument or a milestone marking a stage in my literary development." In this at least he was to prove a true prophet, even though the play had to wait seventeen years for its premiere.

---

*"Play 1" (*The Father*) was to be about Bertha as a child; "Play 3" was never written.

Chapter Twelve

THE FATHER

On New Year's Day 1887, Strindberg was noticed in England, seemingly for the first time. His compatriot Arvid Ahnfelt, editor of the magazine *Ur Dagens Krönika*, contributed a section on Sweden to a survey entitled "Continental Literature in 1886" which appeared in the magazine *Athenaeum* that day, disparaging the second volume of *Getting Married* (which he had already attacked in his own pages) as "a mistake even as a work of art. The wit and knowledge of life which were so happily displayed in the first volume . . . are here sought in vain." However, he went on to say that in *The Son of a Servant* and *Time of Ferment* Strindberg "has given many proofs of his brilliant talents as a painter of character, describing the state of things in the capital and in the university of a small town. Here he is so much in his element that he even advances the somewhat hazardous proposition that autobiography ought henceforth to be the only form of *belles-lettres*." There is no suggestion in the article that Strindberg was anything of a dramatist; it was to be over five years before the British public would be informed of that. Nor was this the only mention of him in a foreign periodical that week. In Vienna, according to *Nya Dagligt Allehanda* (4 January), a new anti-woman magazine called *Der Frauenfeind* appeared, its purpose being "to counter the exaggerated passion for worshipping women," and its opening issue contained a story from *Getting Married*.

Meanwhile Strindberg began work on his new play, about the parents of Bertha in *The Marauders*. His motive was, he declared, polemical. "I am writing now for the theatre," he told Geijerstam on 4 January, "because otherwise the bluestockings will take it over; and the theatre is a weapon . . . It's easier than novel-writing once you get the knack . . . Gondinet says that one needs to be a bit stupid to be able to write plays.* I think that's true of all creative writing. Once I started to think, my art went to pot. We'll have to see if I can come back . . . My wife no longer reads what I write, partly because she doesn't understand it, and it doesn't concern her what I write, since she has her department as wife and mother . . . so I write as ruthlessly as I please."

This euphoria was disturbed by a letter from Albert Bonnier expressing doubts about *The Author* as being too argumentative and polemical.[1] Bonnier was right; the book is a strained attempt to attach Strindberg's new views to books he had written before he held them, and contained reactionary attacks on the younger Swedish writers which, had the book appeared, would have lost him most of the few disciples he still had. "In Volumes 3 and 4 of *The Servant*," he wrote to Heidenstam on 9 January, "I have openly abandoned socialism and German philosophy, and have declared myself—a revolutionary," but this abandonment had been emotional rather than rational, and his efforts to rationalise it make heavy reading. Not content with playwriting, he assured Heidenstam that he had "discovered a new and higher form of writing which I shall now try out on the Germans." This was scientific analysis of human behaviour in an uneasy mixture of the essay and the short story, the short book which he was to call *Vivisections*; it was to prove hardly more satisfying than *The Author*.

That same day he left Gersau with his family for Issigatsbühel in Germany, a little town near Lindau on the Bodensee, where he shared a house with a bookseller, Wilhelm Ludwig, who had translated some of his stories. It was the first time Strindberg had actually lived in Germany, and in his new undemocratic and anti-feminist mood he found it much to his liking. An infantry regiment stationed nearby particularly aroused his admiration. Germany, he wrote enthusiastically to Heidenstam a week after his arrival, was "patriarchal and male-dominated; army recruits six feet tall with fat cheeks; France is absinthe and self-abuse; Switzerland matriarchal sentimentality. Here there still exist live cocks with organs on their bodies. I admire Bismarck's speeches. He is a realist, the modern spirit . . . If nations are to continue, then let them be soldiers; if there are

---

*See p. 158, above.

to be soldiers, then let them live in barracks and train from 5 a.m. to
8 p.m." The Germans had the right attitude towards the Enemy. "In
Germany, women are forbidden to study at university. In England the
medical association is discussing whether they should be allowed to
attempt higher studies, in Paris a book has appeared attacking emancipation. Reaction on every side." He penned a hysterical attack on the
Enemy, entitled "The Last Word on the Woman Question"; it appeared
at the end of the month in a small Swedish periodical, *Jörgens Stockholm-
brev*. It is significant that he had to turn to so humble a paper to get it
published.

Further bad news came from Bonnier to the effect that Ludvig
Josephson had rejected *The Marauders*. "His refusal does not surprise
me," Bonnier commented, "for, as you know, I have already expressed a
similar opinion, which I still hold. I fear that these last months you have
been living too isolated a life to be able to stay acquainted with public
opinion and really understand it, and if you are not willing even to read a
country's newspapers, I think it must be difficult to go on writing for that
country and to partake in literary polemics."[2]

Other theatres in Stockholm, Copenhagen and Helsinki refused the
play. Nobody shared Strindberg's enthusiasm for it. "Technically it's not
bad," Edvard Brandes wrote to him on 18 January, "and it's amusing, but
right and wrong are too melodramatically confronted. Bertha is a pure
villain and Axel a pure angel; such a pillar of virtue suffocates me. Dear
God, can't he have one little fault? . . . Only equal battles are artistically
interesting."[3] Strindberg's reply on 22 January, his thirty-eighth birthday,
unconsciously confirms Brandes' judgement: "That I have now portrayed
a mean and dishonourable woman is no more unjust and unaesthetic
than Ibsen's and the sisters' scandalous attacks on the male sex. It is now
becoming evident that woman is by nature mean and instinctively
dishonest, though we ruttish cocks have not been able to see it; so, I have
drawn a typical woman . . . I shall fight for as long as my nerves hold out,
and if they gnaw me to death, you can write a play about 'the last man.'"
But he ended: "Actually, my misogyny is purely theoretical, and I can't
live a day without deluding myself that I warm my soul in the glow of their
unconscious vegetable existence."

By 6 February he had completed the first act of his new play, *The
Father*, and the two remaining acts took him only nine days—two and a
half weeks in all. Brief (its three acts add up to barely a hundred minutes of
playing time), savage, as unbalanced as *The Marauders* in its treatment of
the sex war, as melodramatic in the climaxes of its last two acts as though
Ibsen had never written, masochistic and self-pitying, it must have

seemed even more likely than most of Strindberg's writings of this unhappy period to sink without trace. He was so depressed by Bonnier's rejection of *The Marauders* that he did not even offer him *The Father*. Other Stockholm publishers refused it, and he could find no better outlet for it than, in due course, a printer and small newspaper owner in the southern town of Hälsingborg, Hans Österling. The play's faults were obvious; less so its scenic power and deep understanding of that twilight area where sanity and insanity merge.

Woman had not completely displaced the Jews as the Enemy. On 15 February Strindberg wrote his brother Axel as violently anti-Semitic a letter as any that he had yet penned.

> If only you knew what a net the Jews have spun round the whole of Europe . . . I have praised them, partly because I was duped, partly from necessity. In France last year there appeared a book in two volumes called *Jewish France*. It is frightening to read. And in Germany they have divided up the country so that eighty per cent of it belongs to them. It is their right, since they have the power, but then we too have the right—to flee from them, since we cannot beat them. Alb. B's tactic is to suck blood (i.e., money), slowly, and so "torment me to death." Remember: a Jew never forgives! He will not kill you, but he will take your job. He refuses to publish my books, so as to reduce their circulation—my editions are now down to 2,000 (from 7–9,000). His waiving of that 8,000 crowns [Strindberg's debt to Bonnier of the previous year] was to preclude my writing further articles about him in the press . . . Jews do not believe in friendship or gratitude . . . Read my play *The Father*! For Laura read Albert Bonnier and you will understand what a devilish fight I have on my hands.

Yet eight days later, he wrote a warm letter to Bonnier assuring him that he wished to stay with him as an author, and telling him (which Bonnier must have welcomed) that he was now abandoning social questions and returning to "the neutral ground of the creative writer and thinker."

Strindberg's attitude towards Siri was equally schizophrenic. He wrote to Axel asking for information concerning rumours which he supposed to be circulating about his marriage and the legitimacy of his children.[4] But a few days later he assured Axel that "we have been very happy . . . As a creative writer I blend fiction with reality, and all my misogyny is theoretical, for I couldn't live without the company of women . . . So don't get depressed when you read *The Father*, for it is a fiction. Like *The Marauders*!" And on 4 March he told a journalist friend, Georg Lund-ström: "I am living quite idyllically here on a farm, alone in the house with six women . . . My wife and I sing student songs, play backgammon, drink beer and live like newlyweds. We aren't petty-minded, and so never nag each other." This spring was the last brief period of happiness that Strindberg and Siri were to share.

The campaign of vilification against Strindberg in Sweden reached its peak that spring of 1887. John Personne, the divinity teacher who had anonymously accused Albert Bonnier of paying Strindberg to return and face trial so as to boost the sales of *Getting Married*, now published a booklet of 93 pages entitled "Strindbergian Literature and Immorality among Schoolchildren" denouncing him at length as a corrupter of youth. Summarising his theme as "the demoralising influence of Strindberg literature on society and especially on young people, and the duty of the authorities to protect us from the dissemination of this poison," Personne was already by page 4 on the *bête noire* of Victorian moralists, masturbation—"an evil which can lead to the spiritual and bodily ruin of our children if it is not discovered and cured in time . . . I refer to the secret sin which has been called 'the most dangerous enemy of youth.'" Even more worrying was the growing tendency of schoolboys to associate with prostitutes. "I know through boys' own admissions that they have not only used the *afternoons* but even the lunch break from 11 to 1 to visit the houses of vice."

By "Strindberg literature" Personne explains that he means principally "the wretched outpourings of August Strindberg's own pen," though there have, sadly, been many followers. He proudly repeats a sentence from his anonymous article of 14 November 1884 in *Nya Dagligt Allehanda*: "The wording of these rotten ideas, the coarse and filthy expressions with which they abound, the descriptions of these adulteries, indecencies and bedroom scenes, are such that I shall not soil my pen with them even as quotations."[5]

Strindberg's incitement of the young to disobey parental authority naturally comes in for castigation, as do those reviewers who in any way praised *Getting Married*, such as Hjalmar Branting who had confessed to finding "pearls among the sand" and Georg Nordensvan, who had likewise discovered "moments of illumination." Especially severe treatment is reserved for Albert Bonnier. "He must bear the greatest blame. Without him, these books would not have appeared." A possible reason for his acquiescence is suggested. "In *The New Kingdom*, Herr Strindberg devoted a chapter entitled 'Moses' to a ruthless satirising of the Jews. In his later filth-writings, however, published by Herr Bonnier, things are quite otherwise. In these he not only writes most favourably of the Jews but even represents them as fellow enthusiasts and fellow campaigners in the great new cultural movement seeking to 'remove the boulder which holds us down' [a quotation from Strindberg's *Time of Ferment*]. . . . One hears of a kind of agreement between Herr Bonnier and Herr Strindberg by which the former agrees to act as the latter's publisher, allowing him more or less uninhibited freedom to write what he will, provided he leaves 'Moses' in peace . . . For my part I cannot see the moral distinction between such a publisher and someone who hires thieves to steal for him, or runs a brothel."[6]

Personne summarises Strindberg's teaching thus: "That marriage is simply legalised prostitution; that man should conduct himself like an animal if he wishes to lead a natural life; that the young have no reason to love their parents and obey them, since their father is but a cock and their mother but a hen who bears chickens; that masturbation is neither wrong nor dangerous; that schoolboys should 'go with girls' because their unmarried teachers do and their fathers did." If Herr Strindberg were to utter these opinions in the street, Personne concludes, would he be allowed the "freedom of expression" which he enjoys in print?[7]

It soon became apparent that Personne was speaking for the majority of Swedes. The right-wing press joined gleefully in the attack on Bonnier as well as on Strindberg. On 1 May *Stockholms Dagblad* declared: "Herr Strindberg has written, Herr Bonnier has published . . . one volume after another of this new gospel, which really stands for the erasure of the Ten Commandments." One of Bonnier's most respected authors, Zacharias Topelius, wrote to him: "A worried mother asks me from Vasa: 'What shall I do with Herman? The boy is now 15 and his classmates in school are not the choicest. The form has clubbed together to buy Strindberg's works, which they study eagerly. One of his friends recently said to his father: "Shut up, you're a fool." Another has said terrible things to his sisters. A third laughed in his Scripture teacher's face and said: "There is no God!" What shall I reply to this mother?'"[8]

Karl Otto Bonnier recalled that Personne's book "became the starting point for an unprecedented persecution of my father and our firm, the effects of which it took a generation to erase,"[9] and that it sparked off "a hatred and fear of Strindberg which the right-wing press did everything in its power to spread."[10] Hostility towards Bonnier was such that that spring five leading publishers resigned from the publishing union of which Bonnier was chairman. "It is difficult to convey," wrote Oscar Levertin to Edvard Brandes on 23 July, "how widely this moralising fervour has taken hold here. It is a Black Death, castrating the land."[11] Strindberg's sales were naturally affected. Apart from *Getting Married*, big stocks of his earlier books such as *Town and Gown, The New Kingdom, Swedish Destinies* and *Utopias in Reality* were returned from the bookshops to join the piles lying in the warehouses.[12] It says much for Albert Bonnier that despite this open antagonism, the poor sales of Strindberg's recent books, the abuse he received at intervals from Strindberg himself and Strindberg's debts to the firm, he remained willing to continue as his publisher. Would he, had it been offered to him, have recognised the virtues of *The Father*? Within the year he was to reject *Miss Julie* as being too "risky" and "naturalistic," but *Miss Julie* is explicit about sex as *The Father* is not.

Having finished *The Father*, Strindberg returned to that "higher form of writing" which he had mentioned to Heidenstam, the quasi-scientific stories-cum-essays, *Vivisections*, which he had begun earlier in the year. The seven pieces which the book contains explore the theory of "suggestion" which lay behind *The Father*, the ability of one human mind to control another and drive it into submission. During the previous autumn and winter Strindberg had read and been fascinated by two recent books on this subject, Hippolyte Bernheim's *De la Suggestion* and Max Nordau's *Paradoxes Psychologiques*; Nordau stressed that brilliant individuals can influence masses, and his idea that there exists an aristocracy of the intellect especially attracted Strindberg, who developed from it a theory that human beings consisted of two kinds, the "great" and the "lowly." This was a long way from the socialism which he had embraced so passionately earlier; it anticipated, indeed, the enthusiasm which he was to develop the following year for Nietzsche's theory of the superman (although Strindberg's brand of Nietzscheanism was very much his own). Strindberg's heroes fail (as in *The Father*) because they are over-refined; they are humbled by the "lowly," who are better equipped for the rough struggle for survival. Strindberg's attempts at scientific analysis are seldom convincing, and *Vivisections* is no exception; obsessions can result in powerful drama, but they make boring essays. The last in the book, "Soul Murder," deals with the power of suggestion as exemplified in Ibsen's *Rosmersholm*, in which Rebecca West drives Beata Rosmer to suicide, but Strindberg, who might have written fascinatingly about this, says disappointingly little that is original.

Vivisections at least found a publisher, if not in book form and not in Sweden. It appeared in three issues of the Vienna newspaper *Neue Freie Presse* and aroused considerable interest among the intellectual elite. Strindberg made the short journey from Issigatsbühel to Vienna during the last week in April and, he happily informed Edvard Brandes, found himself "a celebrity with a reputation and disciples."[13]

On 20 May Edvard Brandes wrote to Strindberg praising *The Father*: "I admire it greatly. The dialogue is excellent, the build-up brilliant, the interest deep and powerful. If only you weren't a monomaniac [i.e., making Laura an incarnation of evil] . . . Just a few lines to modify her character and a few cuts here and there. But what a brilliant work!"[14] Next day Strindberg left for Copenhagen, a trip he had been considering for some time. He spent two weeks there, during which time he became aware of a new movement in European theatre which was fatefully to influence his work.

Seven weeks previously, on 30 March 1887, a young employee of a Paris gas company named André Antoine had started an experimental theatre in the Place Pigalle. Using amateur actors like himself, and with the most meagre material resources, he aimed at a simple but extreme naturalism as opposed to the fashionable theatricality of the day. A decade earlier Zola had demanded that playwrights should write naturalistically, as novelists did but as the popular dramatists of the day such as Dumas, Sardou and Augier did not; Zola himself had attempted to write such a naturalistic play himself in *Thérèse Raquin* but had failed for the simple reason that he was not a good playwright. Ibsen, of course, had succeeded, but Ibsen was as yet unknown in France except to a very few (and would not be performed there until Antoine staged *Ghosts* in 1889). But the demand for naturalistic plays and acting was there and Antoine articulated it:

> In view of the hoped-for generation of new playwrights, there will be needed a new generation of actors . . . The actor will no longer "speak his lines" in the classical manner; he will say them naturally, which is just as difficult to learn . . . Purely mechanical movements, vocal effects, irrational and superfluous gestures, will be banished. The old stagy effects will be replaced by effects produced only by the voice. Feelings will be expressed by familiar and real accessories; a pencil turned round, a cup overturned, will be as significant and have an effect as intense on the mind of the spectator as the grandiloquent exaggerations of the romantic drama. Is it necessary to note that this apparent revolution is nothing but a return to the great traditions, and that the most famous actors of the French stage got their finest effects from simple means? Has not Salvini himself moved us deeply by his sobriety of gesture? . . . Did not Molière himself, in two or three instances, take care to affirm the necessity of "acting as one speaks"?[15]

Edvard Brandes, in his capacity as literary editor of *Politiken*, read the Paris newspaper *Figaro* each day. *Figaro* carried a full report of Antoine's activities at the Théâtre Libre, and Brandes showed this to Strindberg, who was greatly excited. Antoine's ideas about what the theatre should be were very close to his own, and Antoine's theatre was the kind of which Strindberg dreamed, as opposed to the theatres with which he had hitherto had to deal. While in Copenhagen he met August Lindberg, who had directed *Master Olof* in 1881 and, in his production of Ibsen's

The Wild Duck at the Royal Theatre in Stockholm in 1885, had anticipated several of Antoine's experiments in naturalistic staging, making his actors move and talk as though unconscious of the audience, not like actors but like human beings such as one might meet outside a theatre. On 3 June he wrote to Lindberg, who was acting just across the Sound in Malmö:

> Do you feel inclined to create (?) with me a Swedish theatre on the following principles? Starting on a small scale and touring, later perhaps to settle in Stockholm, where we anyway would wish to end our days. Only plays by August Sg will be performed and none of his older ones . . . by 1 September this year I shall have five new plays . . . A company of only eight . . . Max. 30,000 crowns! I'm sure I could scrape together half of that . . . We'd never be short of plays, for I can write a one-acter in two days . . . If you want to have your wife in on it, I'll write alternate roles for her and for my wife, always with one for you. You can't go on long with Ibsen; he probably won't write much more, and his kind of play is on the way out.* You should read the Germans on *Rosmersholm* . . . N.B.: The theatre will be used only for artistic ends with no political, social or sexual aims.

Lindberg, however, was unenthusiastic. He knew the situation between Strindberg and Siri and sensed that this would cause problems; nor did he feel that a repertoire comprising only plays by Strindberg would pay its way.

On his return to Germany in June, Strindberg moved from Issigats-bühel to a nearby farmhouse named Eichbühl. Karin later recalled that summer as the most idyllic of her childhood;[16] ironically, for it was now, after that illusory spring, that Strindberg's relationship with Siri at last reached the point of no return. Marie David wrote urging her to leave him. "The worse of the two ladies," Strindberg informed Carl Larsson on 9 July, "is still pestering my wife with love letters urging her to abandon her husband and children." But they remained together.

To compound his troubles, Albert Bonnier wrote to him on 25 July that he had decided not to publish *The Author*. His letter reveals how unpopular Strindberg had become with the Swedish public:

> That your writing, for various reasons, not merely malicious attacks by your adversaries, but also beyond doubt certain excesses on your part, labours under a regrettable and quite unprecedented unpopularity, is a fact which cannot be unknown to you, although living as you do at a distance, you cannot conceive how intensive this is. To publish under such circumstances Volume 4 [of the autobiography] would in my view only further

---

*In this Strindberg was, as so often, a bad prophet. Ibsen, though fifty-nine, was still to write *The Lady from the Sea*, *Hedda Gabler*, *The Master Builder*, *Little Eyolf*, *John Gabriel Borkman* and *When We Dead Awaken*.

Carl Oscar Strindberg

Eleonora Ulrika Strindberg

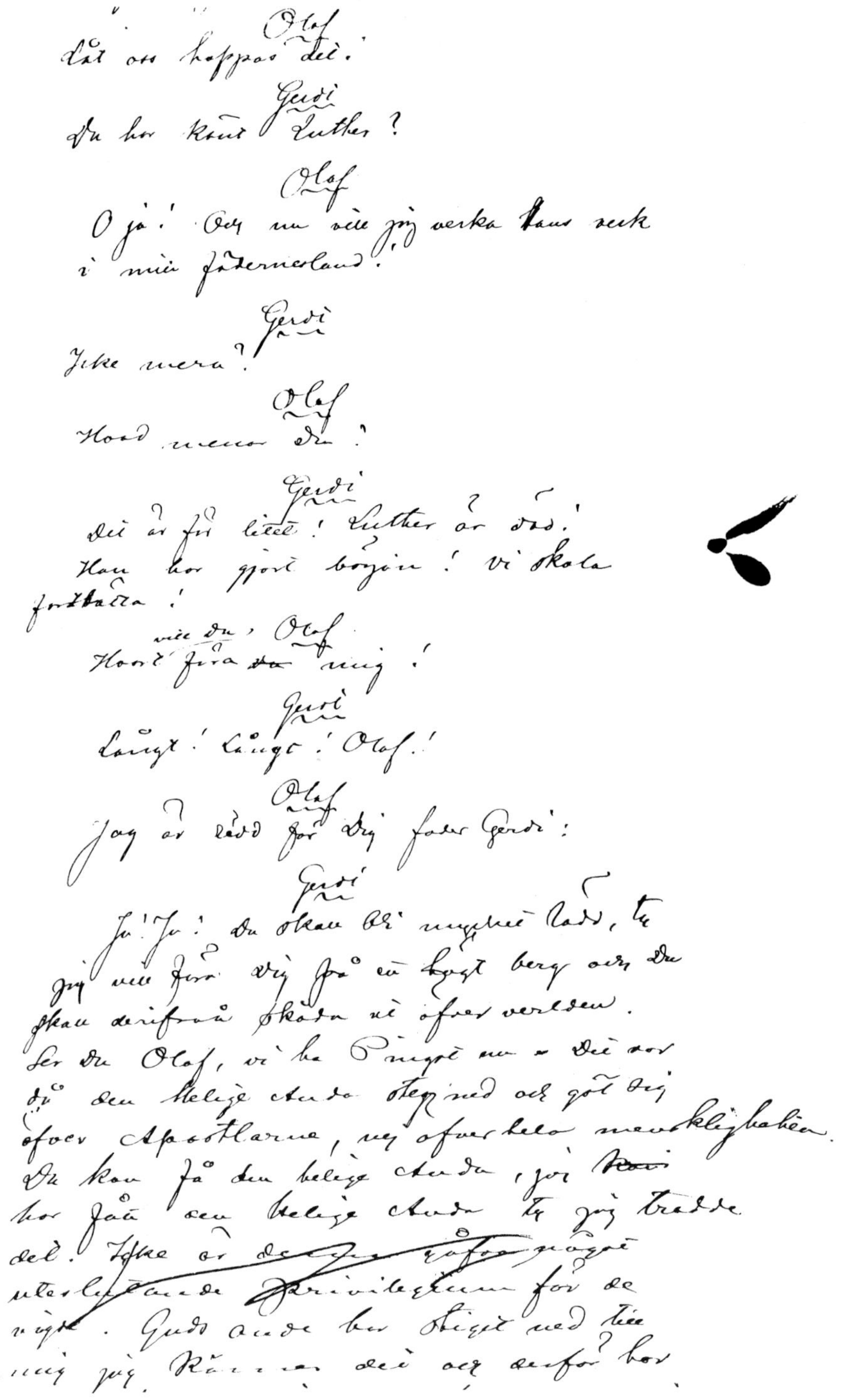

Strindberg in 1874, aged twenty-five

Siri, 1877

Drawing by Strindberg of
Gustaf Klemming

Albert Bonnier

Från o. E. Drottninggatan 14

Himmeln 1000000098 före Chr. f.

Darling, My Love!
Ophelia!

You are sorrow and I have been very cruel to You! Forgive me! My head is sick and I cannot tame my wild thoughts when I think You would leave me!

I love You by all my heart and therefore You must not be angry with me!

Love me but for a little and I am not unhappy as I have been't for long, long years! Peace to You!

Your
Hamlet.

Älskade Julia!

O jag måste säga att jag älskar Dig innan jag går att arbeta i min ensamma cell! Jag känner mig stark som en Afrikansk lejon; jag tycker mig skola vilja ta ett språng mellan Blåbergen och Himalaya; jag känner mig som en Cocospalm vid Amazonfloden; blås Cyclonen så att det knakar i Anderna, jag står ändå, ty det finnes en ung björk däruppe vid mellan Kolmården och Städjan som jag älskar och som älskar mig. Älska mig alltid eller jag biter Dig i strupen så att Du dör!

Din
Romeo

Rom är 31 före slaget vid Actium!

Cleopatra!

Tror Du att Kärleken bara är intet! Den är en naturkraft som åskan! Lek icke med den, ty den dödas dig! Låt dina blixtar ljunga och molnen skola dela sig och gråluft flyr!

Vågar ännu att älska mig eller jag sticker dig en korg med Smyrnafikon och en äsping, en svart en med citrongula ringar omkring ögonen! Han skall hitta den röda Jungfrukällan under ditt venstra bröst och han skall dricka dig och min hämnd olöstiga!

Quod bonum fortunatumque sit Tibi omnibusque amantibus!

Tuus
Antonius

Thérèse!

Comme je suis heureux! Mon cœur s'est enivré, j'ai été aux abois et je vis, je vis det toute ma vie! Est-ce que cela est un crime que de m'aimer; alors soyons des forçats, mais soyons heureux! Et j'ose dans ce moment provoquer le bon dieu, le dieu des amants comme témoin et je ne baise point mes yeux! Aimez toujours votre pauvre petit enfant et amant!

Votre excessivement affectionné
Léon.

Letters from Strindberg to Siri in English, Swedish and French, 1876

Self-caricature by Strindberg, 1882

Strindberg in 1884, the year
of his trial

Strindberg's arrival in Stockholm
to face trial, 1884

"Jag kommer hem!"

(Illustration till August Strindbergs mottagande i Stockholm.)

Så helsas han, en sanningstolk,
   af tusenstämmig röst.
Och hyllningen utaf vårt folk
   går djupt utur dess bröst.
Det vet, att han är öppet *sann*,
det känner, tänker, tror som han.

På tankens stora, fria fält
   ej kommenderas man,
som nummerkarlen i sitt tält,
   ej anden bindas kan.
han tål ej våld och barbari,
han sväfvar ljus och glad och fri.

Så helsas »gudsförsmädaren»,
   så helsas han i dag,
den sakramentets »hädaren»,
   som dömas skall af lag.
En stark och mäktig opinion,
som tränger genom vår nation!

Skall man mot denna sätta lag
   och tunga samvetsband?
Nej, fritt man andas vill i dag
   uti vårt fosterland.
Ej våldets makt ger samvetsro,
men fritt man tänka vill och tro!

Karl Otto Bonnier and his wife Lisen

Gustaf af Geijerstam

Strindberg with Greta, Hai
and Karin, Gersau, 1886

Siri, Gersau, 1886

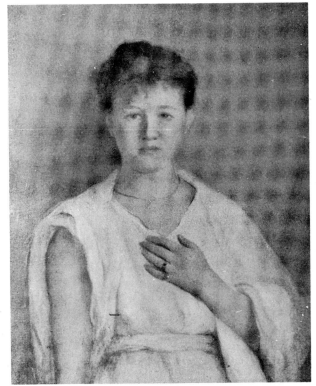

Marie David,
painting by Mme. Mackay

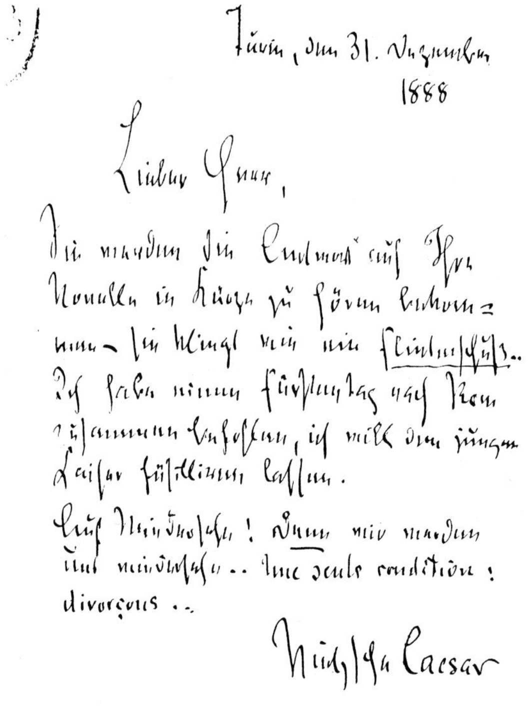

Turin, den 31. Dezember
1888

Lieber Herr,

Sie werden die Antwort auf Ihre Novelle in Kürze zu hören bekommen — sie klingt wie ein Flintenschuß.. Ich habe einen Fürstentag nach Rom zusammenbefohlen, ich will den jungen Kaiser füsiliren lassen.

Auf Wiedersehn! Denn wir werden uns wiedersehn.. Une seule condition: divorçons..

Nietzsche Caesar

Letter from Nietzsche to Strindberg, 1888

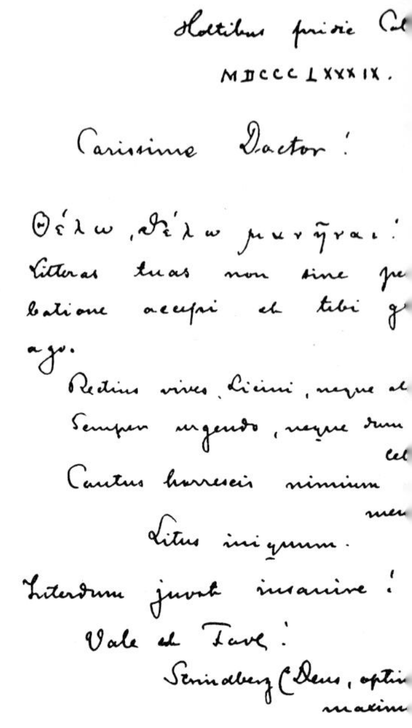

Holtibus pridie Cal
MDCCCLXXXIX.

Carissime Doctor!

Θέλω, θέλω μανῆναι!
Litteras tuas non sine pe
batione accepi et tibi g
ago.

Rectius vives, Licini, neque al
Semper urgendo, neque dum
cel
Cautus horrescis nimium
men
Litus iniquum.

Interdum juvat insanire!

Vale et Fave!

Strindberg (Deus, optir
maxim

Letter from Strindberg to Nietzsche

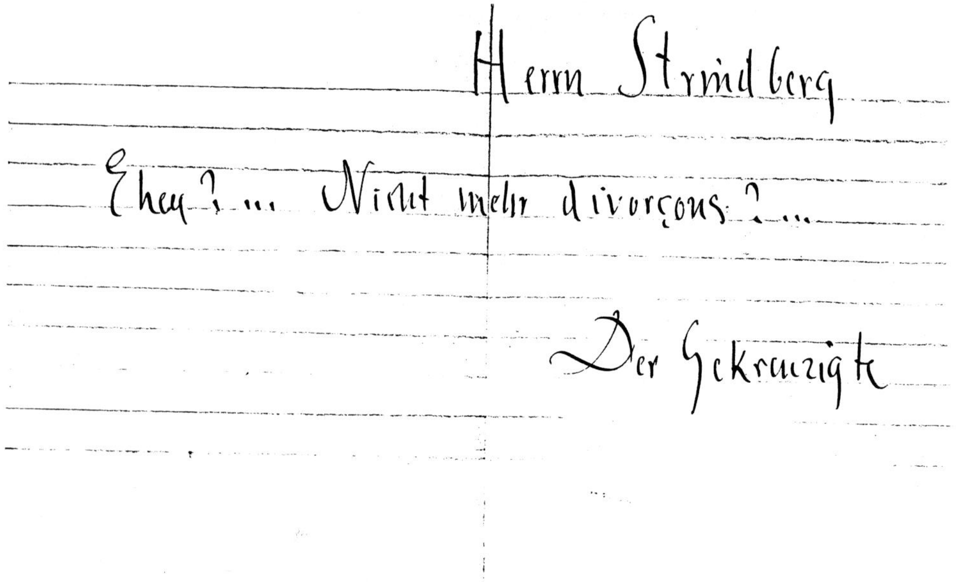

Herrn Strindberg

Eheu?... Nicht mehr divorçons?...

Der Gekreuzigte

Nietzsche's last letter to Strindberg

Strindberg, *c.* 1891

Frida, 1892

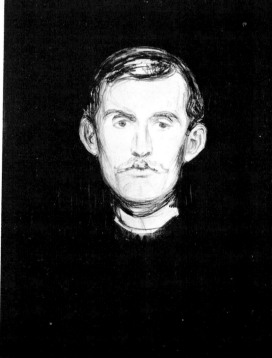

Edvard Munch,
self-portrait

Stanislaw Przybyszewski,
lithograph by Edvard Munch

Jalousi: lithograph by Edvard Munch showing
Przybyszewski, Dagny Juel and Strindberg

Dagny Juel

Kerstin, aged eight

Strindberg in Paris, 1894

Hôpital de St. Louis, Paris

Hôtel Orfila

Lithograph of Strindberg by Edvard Munch, 1896

Mme. Charlotte in her *crémerie*

Strindberg in Lund, 1897

Harriet Bosse as the Lady in *To Damascus*, 1900

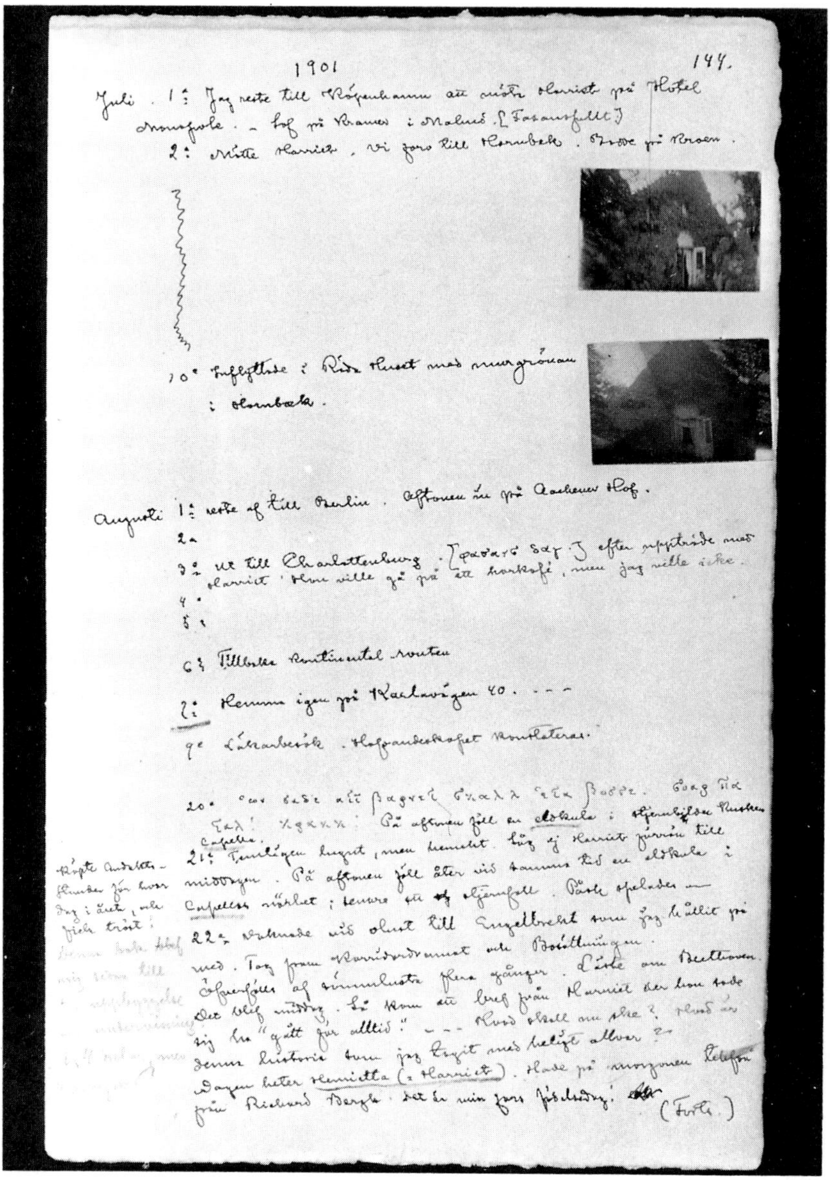

1901 144.

Juli. 1: Jag reste till Köpenhamn att möta Harriet på Hotel Monopole. – Log på Kramer i Malmö. [Fasanfället]

2: Mötte Harriet, vi foro till Hornbæk. Bodde på Kroen.

10: Inflyttade i Röda Huset med murgrönan i Hornbæk.

Augusti 1: reste af till Berlin. Aftonen ... på Aachener Hof.

2.

3: Ut till Charlottenburg. [...] efter uppträde med Harriet som ville gå på ett kafé, men jag ville icke.

4.

5.

6: Tillbaka Kontinental routen

7: Hemma igen på Karlavägen 40. ...

9: Läkarbesök. Havandeskapet konstateras.

Page from Strindberg's *Occult Diary*, 1901

"The White Mare." Painting by Strindberg, 1901. Upside
down the painting shows Strindberg's head in profile.

"The City." Painting by Strindberg, *c.* 1900–07

Strindberg at Furusund, 1904, with Harriet, Anne-Marie,
Hugo and Anna Philp

Photograph by Strindberg of Stockholm at night, 1908

Self-portrait, 1906

Interior of the Intimate Theatre

The Father at the Intimate Theatre, 1908

Fanny Falkner

Strindberg with Greta, Hans and Karin in the Blue Tower, 1911

Strindberg acclaimed at the Blue Tower by the Stockholm Workers'
Commune on his sixty-third birthday, 22 January 1912. From *Social-
Demokraten* (left) and *Stockholms Dagblad* (right).

Strindberg, *c.* 1911–12

Max Reinhardt's production of A *Dream Play* at Dramaten, Stockholm, 1921. Gustav Molander as the Advocate and Jessie Wessel (left of cradle) as Agnes.

Wilfrid Lawson in Peter Cotes's production of *The Father* at the Arts Theatre, London, 1953

Michael Gough, Mai Zetterling and Lyndon Brook in Casper Wrede's
production of *Creditors* at the Lyric Opera House, Hammersmith, 1959

Johan Bergenstråhle's production of *The Ghost Sonata* for Swedish TV, 1972.
Allan Edwall (kneeling) as Hummel.

Maggie Smith and Albert Finney in Michael Elliott's production of *Miss Julie*, at the Old Vic Theatre, London, 1966

damage your reputation and profit neither of us . . . You said yourself that you wanted once more to be popular in Sweden. For that you need to write something which deals neither with yourself, your friends and enemies, nor the woman question. [17]

Strindberg replied abusively that he felt disinclined to write books "suited to the little heads of your wives and sons."[18] He offered *The Author* to other publishers, but without success, and it was to remain unpublished until shortly before his death.

Sometime this summer, doubtless as a result of his excitement about Antoine, Strindberg translated *The Father* into French. He sent a handwritten copy to Zola, describing the play in grammatically peculiar French, as "a piece composed with a view to the experimental formula, aiming to show the full effect of the inward action at the expense of theatrical tricks, to reduce decor to the minimum and to preserve the unity of time as far as is possible."[19] He was to have to wait a long time for a reply, though when it finally arrived, it was worth waiting for.

In August, Strindberg reluctantly decided to apply for a divorce. "The comedy of my marriage is over," he told Pehr Staaff on 5 August, "after ten years of happiness and misery . . . Motto: never get married! for you can, like Monsieur Bovary, live your life out without knowing to whom you are married. The moment a man enters marriage, both sexes become his wife's accomplices, and he must walk like a clown to death and immortality."

He bombarded the unfortunate Staaff with six very long letters on the subject within eleven days, followed by a further five in the next fifteen days, all hideously unbalanced and containing the wildest suspicions about Siri's supposed infidelities. "She complained ceaselessly about my sensuality—to me! That I would not leave her alone!" Was his sexual organ, he wondered, as men commonly do in such circumstances, too small to satisfy her? "Irritated to the roots of my testicles, I visited Geneva and took a doctor with me to a brothel . . . I had my semen investigated which proved fertile, and was measured at full cock (16 × 4 centimetres [6.3 × 1.6 inches])."[20]

He sought refuge from his torment in writing, not another diatribe on the sex war, but "a novel about life in the Swedish countryside and skerries, the first genuine novel I have written . . . If my name is as unpopular, as hated, as that old villain Albert Bonnier has for years been trying to make me believe, then I may as well try to make myself popular again."[21] And in another long letter, to the same friend on the same day: "The ways of humanity are strange! Here I sit in my good concubinage writing my splendid novel about the Swedish skerries and sleep the well-earned sleep of the strong and the conqueror in the same room as my woman!"[22]

But such euphoric moods were the exception. "Her witchcraft was stupendous," he assured Staaff on 3 September. "She succeeded, despite her crimes, her immense culpability, in deluding everyone she met into thinking that I was the criminal. She deluded me for three years into believing that I was ill, deluded me and others into supposing I was mad, and won sympathy and belief everywhere. I have been unusual, bizarre, talked nonsense . . . perhaps on the way to being mad, but I have never been it . . . It will be interesting to see the outcome of this drama; it will probably be tragic. But I won't let her go so soon, for otherwise she'll raise an army against me, and woman's power is greater than our understanding. To part for ever? Yes! Then I'll have to sit masturbating, with no sex, and pay her so that others can whore with her. That hardly tempts me. And her capacity for blackmailing money out of people is monstrous!"[23]

Two days later Staaff received another huge letter detailing Strindberg's needs: "Help me . . . to obtain a young woman who has recently had a child; by a more or less unknown father who has skulked off. But a young woman with hip-muscles and breasts; an ex-maidservant would do as long as she has served in a superior household and has upper-class sympathies, so that she won't ally herself with the rustic farm-hands and skivvies against me, for I count myself upper-class and am happy to be thus connected. If she looks good, so much the better. Not above 25. Careful about her appearance and clean. She will be my housekeeper and I shall bring up her children in our home, and take care of the mother of course. I must have children because I can't work without the sound of children's voices. A whore would serve the same purpose but they are so unfaithful that she'd be false to me and wouldn't enjoy the loneliness. The best thing would be a fallen upper-class girl, but those bitches have all the instincts of lesbians and neglect their children. Above all I want a woman who loves children and wants to rise in the social scale and not sink . . . By the beginning of October my novel will be ready." There follows a page of hysterical abuse of Siri, ending: "She has even got together with my translator [Wilhelm Ludwig], a Prussian reptile, Prussian and Jewish (the Jews hate all blond people)."[24]

On 15 September, *The Father* was published. It was unfavourably received; *Svenska Dagbladet* mocked it as an exaggerated expression of Strindberg's well-known views on women, *Figaro* thought it worth reading "mostly as a literary and social curiosity" and even Karl Warburg, one of his admirers, declared in *Handelstidningen i Göteborg* that

Strindberg's misogyny had by now become "pure monomania."[25] That same month, and in the same frame of mind as when he wrote the letters to Staaff, he began in French—for he knew it could not be published in Sweden in Siri's lifetime—the venomous and grossly untruthful account of their marriage entitled *Le Plaidoyer d'un Fou—A Madman's Defence*.

Yet by 6 October he had completed his skerries novel, *The People of Hemsö*, a delightful work full of robust humour and containing no trace of misogyny or any other of his obsessions, as though he had deliberately turned his back on them. He sent it to his brother Axel for the latter to find a publisher for it. "Where can it be sold quickly? . . . I promised Isidor long ago that he could have a novel after *The Red Room* . . . But will he take it? . . . Is this rumoured boycott a fact? I don't care who buys my book, but Alb. B. is as repellent to me as a slimy reptile, and I don't want to correspond with him even if he takes it . . . The book contains coarsenesses, but nothing actionable."[26] Axel offered it to Isidor, but he was scared by the naturalism of some of the writing, and refused it, as did Seligmann. Strindberg himself, shortly before completing it, had offered it to Österling, who had published *The Father*: ". . . it contains nothing in the least polemical, no socialism, protectionism or female emancipation, a purely literary work, good-humoured, a lot of natural description, and happy people, coarse happenings admittedly, but nothing dangerous."[27] But before Österling came up with an offer, Axel showed it to Albert Bonnier, who found it "good and amusing" and offered a generous advance of 2,000 crowns, representing a royalty of 18 per cent, provided Strindberg allowed him to make "necessary and suitable cuts and alterations, which would not affect the content and would make the book more readable and saleable."[28] Strindberg at first accepted, then refused ("I thought it was just a question of coarse words. Now that I see it involves changing my truthful depiction into a false idealistic book for shop accountants and unsexed women, I withdraw")[29] and told Axel to submit it to Claes Looström, but Looström likewise demanded cuts, and Strindberg, desperate for money, grudgingly agreed to Bonnier's terms.

Now came an unexpected and exciting piece of news. A Danish actor-manager, Hans Riber Hunderup, offered to stage *The Father* that autumn in Copenhagen. Hunderup, who was only thirty, had long been an admirer of Strindberg, having written him a fan letter as long ago as 1882, and had met him briefly in Stockholm in the summer of 1883; more recently, when assistant director at Dagmars Theatre in Copenhagen, he had wanted to direct, and play the lead in, Strindberg's early play *The Outlaw*, but Strindberg had not wished to be introduced to the Danish public by this immature work. In April 1887 Hunderup was

appointed director of the Casino Theatre, which was principally associated with farces, light musicals and melodramas; he was keen to raise its
standing and, only three days after his appointment, *Morgenbladet*
announced that he intended to present a Strindberg there, hopefully *The
Secret of the Guild*. But Strindberg felt the same about this play as about
The Outlaw.

In contrast to its reception in Sweden, *The Father* had, on publication,
been widely reviewed in the Danish press. *Social-Demokraten, National-
Tidende* and the weekly magazine *Piraten* all criticised it as sick monomania, but, unlike the Swedish press, agreed that dramatically it was
masterly and, if adequately performed, could work powerfully on the
stage. Then, on 5 October, Edvard Brandes reviewed it in *Politiken*,
praising its power and psychological insight and insisting that the play
must be judged as a work of art, regardless of whether or not it mirrored
the author's marriage. Hunderup reacted predictably, and a week later
Politiken announced that he was to stage it at the Casino. [30]

Hunderup commissioned a young Swedish writer, Axel Lundegård, to
translate it, and asked him to try to persuade Strindberg to attend the
premiere. On 17 October, Strindberg wrote Lundegård a lengthy and
detailed letter in which the precision and clarity of his observations about
the play contrast astonishingly with the wildness and woolliness of his
remarks on political, sociological, scientific and sexual subjects. After a
characteristic opening ("I rejoice to hear from one of the younger
generation, who understand what I write and realise that I represent the
spirit of the age . . ."), he continued:

> But who is to be the Captain, and what woman is prepared to act Laura?
> The play can easily be destroyed and become ridiculous. I suggest, though I
> don't usually interfere in such matters, that the Captain be given to an actor
> of normally healthy temper who, conscious of his superiority, goes loftily
> and cynically, almost joyfully, to meet his fate, wrapping himself in death as
> in a spider's web which he is impotent to tear asunder. A deceived husband
> is a comic figure in the eyes of the world, and especially to a theatre
> audience. He must show that he is aware of this, and that he too would
> laugh if only the man in question were someone other than himself. This is
> what is *modern* in my tragedy, and alas for me and the clown who acts it if he
> goes to town and plays an 1887 version of the Pirate King! No screams, no
> preachings. Subtle, calm, resigned—the way a normally healthy spirit
> accepts his fate today, as though it were an erotic passion. Remember that a
> cavalry officer is always a rich man's son who has had an education, is
> exacting in his demands upon himself as a social animal, and behaves like a
> civilised human being even when addressing a common soldier. He
> mustn't be caricatured into a hidebound military reactionary. He stands
> above his profession—has seen through it, and has turned to science. In

particular he symbolises for me a masculinity which people have tried to pound or wheedle out of us and transfer to the third sex! It is only when he is with the woman that he is unmanly, because that is how she wants him, and the law of adaptation forces us to play the role that our sexual partner demands. Yes, we sometimes have to act chaste, naïve or ignorant, simply to get our marital rights! . . . As regards appearing personally, I don't believe in that. I've tried it and it hasn't worked. My presence has usually injured my cause, and I am content to stay at my desk. I am gauche, stupid and tactless in company, and too cynical to play the blushing author.

Despite these and further protestations, however, Strindberg eventually agreed to attend the premiere, and on 4 November, together with Siri and the children, he set off for Denmark, where he was to spend a harassing eighteen months. He did not want to go alone; besides, if *The Father* went well, other productions of his plays might follow, and since he was more admired in Denmark than in any other country, it might be advantageous to settle there for a while. But Copenhagen was Marie David's home town. Before leaving Eichbühl, he forbade Siri to contact her and also, with unusual tactlessness even for him, wrote to Siri's two aunts who lived in Copenhagen asking them to charge Sofie and Marie with homosexual conduct, at the same time schizophrenically sending a friendly letter to Sofie. Not relishing the prospect of accusing two women whom they had never met on dubious hearsay evidence, the old ladies asked their brother-in-law for advice; he replied that after this he would never again let Strindberg set foot in his house. Siri persuaded her relatives to forget the matter, and she does not seem to have met Marie in Denmark, although in due course their relationship was to be resumed with dramatic consequences.[31]

En route, Strindberg left the train at Roskilde to visit the big hospital at Bidstrup and consult a specialist about his mental health, since he was convinced that Siri was planning to have him certified, like Laura and her husband in *The Father*. "Whether his fears were genuine," writes Karin, "or whether he merely wanted a document with which to resist his wife, who had never in fact dreamed of having him confined, is unsure."[32] He got a clean bill of health. His young translator Axel Lundegård came to meet him and was at once embarrassingly quizzed as to the identity of Siri's lovers. "He mentioned name after name. I knew none of the persons and said so, but I saw he did not believe me. 'But you have heard rumours?' I replied that I had heard none, and thought this would please him, but he looked as though I had failed him." They lunched at the hotel and Strindberg's mood mellowed until "through the empty dining-room walked a tall, slim, blonde lady accompanied by three children and a maid. Strindberg ate his dessert and did not blink an eyelid. In innocent curiosity I said: 'I wonder who that can be?' He replied sombrely: 'It is my former wife.' . . . 'Are you divorced?' I stammered. 'Well,' he said, 'not legally divorced, that isn't necessary. But I no longer regard my former wife as my wife. Only as my mistress. Henceforth she must rest content with that. I do not intend to be seen with her in public.' "[33]

On arrival in Copenhagen, then still a small and idyllic walled city, Strindberg dutifully attended at least one rehearsal, and agreed to various cuts. Unlike almost all other dramatists he was, throughout his career, willing to give his directors *carte blanche* to delete anything that might offend the censors or simply not work. (By contrast, he hated any alterations being made to any printed work.) On 12 November, two days before the premiere, he wrote to Lundegård, to whom he appears to have taken a fancy, warning him that he might "in a fit of romanticism" absent himself (i.e., commit suicide), and asking the unfortunate young man to act as his executor, listing a series of extraordinary requests:

> Rehabilitate my wife by throwing a cloak of obscurity over everything that has happened, for the children's sake . . . Force Albert Bonnier to publish Part 4 of my autobiography . . . See that my collected writings are published, when the time is ripe, in Flensburg, Leipzig, Copenhagen or Chicago; *everything* that I have written, every word, from newspapers, almanacs, abroad and at home, including my letters . . . Arrange pensions for my children, who, whether they are mine or not, were adopted by me (we don't need to mention my wife). . . Urge Zola to get a publisher for *The Father*, or have it printed in Copenhagen in French . . . try to get it acted in Paris. Get in touch with my brother Axel at the Royal Theatre* in Stockholm, but don't obey him, for he doesn't understand me and has been talked over by Albert Bonnier and the Younger Generation . . .

He goes on to the impossibility, if one is a romantic, of living without an ideal:

> Mine was incarnated in a woman, because I was a woman-worshipper. When it fell, I fell. In my letters you will see . . . a trusting and credulous fool, who allowed himself to believe anything, even that he was trash, which he wasn't at all—believe anything, so that the crimes of others might be concealed . . . It seems to me as though I walk in my sleep—as though reality and imagination are one. I don't know if *The Father* is a work of the imagination or if my life has been; but I feel that at a given moment, possibly soon, it will cease, and then I will shrivel up, either in madness and agony, or in suicide. Through much writing my life has become a shadow-play; it is as though I no longer walk the earth, but hover weightless in a space that is filled not with air but with darkness. If light enters this darkness, I shall fall,

---

*Axel was a member of the Royal Theatre orchestra.

broken. What is curious is that in a dream which often recurs to me at night
I feel that I am flying weightless, and I find this quite natural, as though all
conception of right and wrong, true and false, had ceased to exist for me, so
that everything that happens, however strange, seems inevitable.

On 14 November 1887, *The Father* had its premiere at the Casino
Theatre in Copenhagen and, against the odds, was quite a success. The
left-wing papers, *Politiken* and *Social-Demokraten*, had managed to
drum up a full house, informing their readers that it was the duty of all
liberal-minded men and women to support this boycotted Swedish writer.
Hunderup himself played the Captain, with his future wife, Johanne
Krum, as Laura. There was warm applause at the end, and the reviews
were good; even conservative papers such as *Berlingske Tidende* and
Avisen admitted the power of the play, while expressing fears lest its
technical merits might blind audiences to its doubtful morality. The cuts
in the text must have been considerable, for *Avisen* (16 November) noted:
"He has deleted all the lines which could be said to go too far . . . He sticks
his head in the sand, tones everything down and pretends he is quite
innocent of it all."[34] Georg Brandes, who, at Strindberg's request, assisted
with the rehearsals, relates: "At first the actors didn't understand much of
it. But gradually I got everything arranged as I wished, so that the cast,
despite somewhat weak abilities, achieved a good and sometimes considerable performance." On meeting Strindberg for the first time now,
Brandes noted: "He revealed himself to be serious and of an original
talent, and more lucid in conversation than I had expected. But he was
not conversationally rewarding, and I thirsted after that."[35]

The Father nowadays plays for barely a hundred minutes, and even
allowing for the much slower tempo of those days, it was regarded as
insufficient for an evening's fare. Audiences expected four or even five
hours, and Ibsen had even had to request theatres not to make *Ghosts*,
which runs for two and a half hours, part of a double bill. So Hunderup
rounded the evening off with a farce, telling the story, ironically, of a
husband who is locked up as insane. Audiences fell off for the next few
evenings, then revived. But after eleven performances, in itself a good
number for so serious a play, the malignant fortune that was to dog
Strindberg throughout his career struck in typical fashion. Hunderup
went bankrupt, and the play had to come off.

Before the decision was taken to end the run, Hunderup suggested to
Strindberg that he should give a talk at the theatre to gain publicity and
sustain interest in the production. Strindberg was unwilling, since he
hated speaking in public, but eventually agreed, as a compromise, to give

a reading. On 2 December he duly appeared, smartly dressed in grey trousers and black tails. There was a fair attendance, but he disappointed them by reading them nothing new, only his old poem, *Somnambulist Nights.* "Had he given a lecture," complained *Politiken*, "the house would have been full." An eye-witness recalled: "The programme contained no information as to what he was to read, and there were not many who discovered what he did read, or indeed whether he read anything at all. We saw him, yellow-faced and pale, stare down at the book and move his lips, but heard nothing. He turned page after page, then suddenly raised his head in acknowledgement and disappeared." The applause of his admirers was mingled with hissing.[36]

Meanwhile, another Strindberg production had opened abroad. On 30 November, *Master Olof*, in its original prose version, was staged at the Swedish Theatre in Helsinki. It was directed by Harald Molander, one of the finest talents of his time, but aroused little interest and managed only five performances. Strindberg only heard about this production from August Lindberg, who was acting in Copenhagen, and wrote to Molander to ask for "a little conscience money, as the Germans call it when they steal a play."[37] Molander replied with 100 crowns, telling him of the play's failure. Strindberg took the news philosophically: "I'm not surprised. It's almost twenty years old, is an opera libretto, apprentice work, now only of literary interest."[38] The judgement seems strange, but one can appreciate that the play must have seemed inadequate to one who had just written *The Father*.

Strindberg's face had been well known in Copenhagen for two years before he arrived there, for since 1885 there had been a waxwork of him in a permanent exhibition called the Scandinavian Panoptikon, showing him seated in a café with other notables, the rest in groups, Strindberg alone in a corner, with crossed legs. But people expecting to meet a gloomy recluse were sometimes surprised. One evening during a symposium at a restaurant with Hunderup and others, he produced a revolver and fired a volley of shots "to see [he explained] the psychological effect it would produce." He then ran through the streets to Kongens Nytorv, where he tried to mount the statue of a horse which stands outside the Royal Theatre. The police started to arrest him, but desisted when it was explained that he was a foreign celebrity.[39] By contrast, when his former publisher Claes Looström invited him to dinner to meet Paul Gauguin's Danish wife, Mette (whose sister was married to Edvard Brandes), the Danish writer Henrik Pontoppidan and the American minister in Copenhagen, Strindberg arrived drunk, took offence at Mette Gauguin's short hair, and launched into a tirade against women who pretended to be men. Pontoppidan tells that the first thing Strindberg asked him was where the nearest pawnbroker was.[40]

Hunderup, despite his bankruptcy, contrived within a few months to take his production of *The Father* on a tour of the Danish provinces, without Strindberg's permission and paying him nothing. They played to full houses in Odense; then a heat-wave descended, which cut attendances badly; a newspaper advertisement announced that children (!) would be admitted at reduced prices. Everywhere some people walked out, but the play's power was widely admitted; a reviewer in Aarhus praised the curtain calls after each act because they reminded the audience that it was only a play.[41]*

Notwithstanding the premature closure of *The Father* and the failure in Finland of *Master Olof*, 1887 concluded on a hopeful note. Not only had *The Father* proved its worth on the stage; before the end of the year, two powerful voices from abroad expressed their admiration of it, albeit privately. In December, Strindberg at last received the longed-for reply from Zola to the letter he had sent him on 29 August enclosing his own French translation of *The Father*:

> Sir and dear colleague,
> I must beg you to forgive me for my long silence. But if you knew what a life I lead, how much work and worry! I did not want to return your manuscript without having read it, and I have only now found the necessary time.
> Your play has greatly interested me. The central idea is most audacious, the characters very boldly conceived. You have drawn powerful and disturbing effects from the theme of doubt regarding paternity. Your Laura is woman incarnate in her pride and ruthlessness, and in the riddling mystery of her virtues and her faults. She will remain implanted in my memory. In short, you have written a curious and interesting work, with some very fine things in it, especially towards the end. To be frank, your analytical shorthand troubles me a little. You may know that I am not one for abstraction. I like characters to exist in the round, one should be able to elbow them, they should breathe our air. And your captain who has not even a name, your other characters who are virtually abstract creations, do not give me the full sensation of life that I demand. But that, between you and me, is certainly partly a question of race. Accepting it for what it is, I repeat that your play is one of those rare dramatic works which have profoundly moved me.
> Believe me, your most devoted and sympathetic colleague,
> Emile Zola[42]

*Hunderup kept *The Father* in his repertory for several years. In 1891 the company visited Christiania, where, one very hot evening, the sparse audience (the evening's takings were only 33 crowns) included Henrik Ibsen in a box, "staring at us in lonely majesty." Ibsen's opinion of the performance is, sadly, not on record.[43]

The other letter was written in Norwegian to Hans Österling, the publisher of *The Father*:

> Munich, 15 November 1887
>
> During my visit to Stockholm in September you were so kind as to send me a copy of Strindberg's recently published play *The Father*, and I beg you to accept my sincerest thanks for this most valuable gift.
>
> One does not read a new work by a writer such as Strindberg during the restlessness and changing moods of travelling. I have therefore postponed the perusal and study of this work until now, when I have returned to the peace of my home.
>
> Strindberg's observations and experiences in the sphere of which *The Father* principally treats do not accord with my own. But this does not prevent me from recognising and being gripped by the author's violent strength, in this as in his earlier works.
>
> *The Father* is soon to be performed in Copenhagen. If it is acted as it needs to be, with merciless realism, the effect will be shattering.
>
> Gratefully,
> Henrik Ibsen[44]

Joining Strindberg for a meal in Copenhagen around this time, young Lundegård found him full of optimism. All manner of payments, he explained, would soon start flooding in. There was interest in *The Father* in Stockholm, Bergen and Helsinki, Hunderup wanted to do *The Marauders*, a Danish translation was being made of *Sir Bengt's Wife* which would probably be staged at the Royal Theatre in Copenhagen. His earnings from all this would, he reckoned, come to around 16,000 crowns, in addition to which he could borrow 1,000 crowns from Edvard Brandes and a further 1,000 from another friend. "But," he concluded glumly, "I can't afford to buy myself a dinner."[45]

"I must write for those who understand me," he wrote to Albert Bonnier, "and in the way I feel I must, even at the risk of staying unpublished. As no ephemeral political or so-called social questions any longer tempt me, I hope I may be able to achieve some artistic psychological writing which may interest me and my public, and hope soon to produce an example."[46] This seems to be a reference to *A Madman's Defence*, into which he was now pouring his spleen.

On 9 December, Albert Bonnier published his skerries novel, *The People of Hemsö*, only two weeks after signing the agreement. The omens were not favourable. Such was the antipathy towards Strindberg in Sweden, Bonnier told him, that the booksellers scarcely dared display it on their shelves. "God, how I love it!" Bonnier told Carl Larsson. "My main difficulty will be getting anyone to read it, for Strindberg has become so unpopular that one scarcely dares mention his name."[47] But the reviews, partly perhaps thanks to Bonnier's bowdlerising of the gutsier passages, were unexpectedly favourable. *Dagens Nyheter* called it "a stylistic masterpiece"; *Handelstidningen i Göteborg*, "a delightful surprise"; *Nordisk Tidskrift*, "one of the best portrayals of rural life in our literature." *Budkaflen*, *Figaro* and *Ny Illustrerad Tidning* also praised it. Admittedly, the conservative press remained aloof or hostile. *Stockholms Dagblad* complained that the book portrayed only low feelings and actions; *Aftonbladet* grudgingly welcomed the fact that for once he had not appeared as a "world-improver" and hoped he would continue thus; and *Nya Dagligt Allehanda* and *Post- och Inrikes Tidningar* both ignored it. A really bad review came, ironically, from a new left-wing daily, *Arbetet*, which protested that the book turned a blind eye to social problems and held "little joy for the masses."[48]

Edvard Brandes, reviewing the book in *Politiken* (15 April 1888), rebuked the Swedes for their treatment of Strindberg: "Let us hope that the misunderstanding between Sweden and her greatest writer will disappear, and our sisterland realise what a remarkable and fructifying spirit she possesses in someone whom Strindberg's compatriots persist in regarding as an immature adolescent. It is too ridiculous that Sweden now cold-shoulders him through a privy conspiracy between the press and the public. But especially ridiculous are the publishers who will not print his work. In a few years his will be the most respected name in Swedish letters; his sheaf will grow and ripen, while the little sheaves around him will bow to the ground."

The People of Hemsö reads wonderfully well today. It tells of a devious farmhand, Carlsson, who comes as bailiff to a smallholding in the skerries, worms his way into the affections of the owner, a widow much older than he, marries her, thus further antagonising the already hostile natives, and is finally, to the general delight, drowned. Strindberg knew his skerries, the people as well as the landscape, and the book is full of splendid Brueghel-like scenes, lyrical, as with a midsummer mowing, and savage, as in the account of a wild saturnalia. Coarseness and rough humour are not qualities that most people normally associate with Strindberg, but they are in full evidence here, a far cry from the feline comedy of *Creditors* and *Playing with Fire*. But nothing, except lyric poetry and puns, is more difficult to render into another language than dialect humour, and *The People of Hemsö* has, like so much of Thomas Hardy's work, hitherto defied its translators.

"Everyone who has read the book," Albert Bonnier wrote to him on 28 December, "expresses joy that you have returned to realistic descriptive writing in place of that, from every point of view, distressing conflict about the mutual relationship between the sexes."[49] Strindberg replied indignantly two days later, assuring Bonnier that "whatever the papers write . . . will not lure me into laying down my arms in the battle of the sexes now that I have just won my greatest triumph since *The Red Room* on that very battlefield with my tragedy *The Father*, which is very far from having had its last production."

He had spent the last weeks of 1887 rewriting *The Marauders*. Hunderup had intimated an interest in staging it but wanted certain changes, and Strindberg, during a brief period of reconciliation with Siri, made these alterations, deleting the first act and even giving it a happy ending. But he repented of this and rewrote the climax brutally, making the husband throw out his wife and bring a mistress to live with him. He retitled the play *The Comrades*. Hunderup rejected it. Strindberg offered it to Hans Österling, who published it the following April.

He also sent Österling his French translation of *The Father*, with the curious explanation: "My reason for wanting this published is so that I can get it read by Dumas, Sarcey, Pailleron, etc. And perhaps staged at the Théâtre Libre."[50] It is amazing that he should seriously have supposed that those three pillars of the old drama would like *The Father*, and that he should have wished them to; in 1883 he had seen and hated a play by Pailleron, and in an essay he was to write in 1889, "On the Modern Theatre," he spoke disparagingly of Dumas and dismissed Sarcey as decadent. And he should surely have known that Zola's letter of admiration, which he printed as a preface to the French translation of the play, would antagonise all three men, since Zola had attacked them all in his *Le Naturalisme au Théâtre*.[51] Österling published the French version that January; and the Swedish version sold well enough for him to print a second edition in March, albeit of only 500 copies.

On 12 January 1888, *The Father* received its Swedish premiere, at the New Theatre in Stockholm, one of whose directors was August Falck, father of the more famous actor of the same name who twenty years later was to be the leading spirit of Strindberg's Intimate Theatre. Falck must have been relieved to receive a letter from Strindberg (23 December) which, together with much sensible advice ("Don't take it too quickly, as we did here at the Casino. Rather let it creep forward quietly, evenly . . . except the Captain's lines when his obsession has manifested itself. They should be spoken quickly, abruptly, repeatedly breaking the atmosphere"), gave Falck *carte blanche* to amend the text. "You'll have received a copy showing the cuts. Cut more if you wish! You'll hear at rehearsal what doesn't work."

A tradition has developed among Strindberg commentators (myself unhappily included) that this first Swedish production was a disaster and was uniformly dismissed by the critics. Recent research has shown that this was by no means the case. Most of the conservative newspapers rejected the play out of hand: *Nya Dagligt Allehanda* called it "simply a dramatised pamphlet," *Stockholms Dagblad* said it contained "several scenes and lines so painful or repellent as scarcely to be acceptable even on the printed page, let alone in a theatre," and *Post- och Inrikes Tidningar* wrote: "It can suitably be epitomised in Hamlet's exclamation: 'O horrible, O horrible, most horrible!' Any other comment seems superfluous." On the other hand, the newly founded *Svenska Dagbladet* summed it up as: "From several viewpoints a confusion, but a confusion that only a writer of more than usual powers could create." *Dagens Nyheter* wrote that it made a terrifying impression, even more frightening than when read; *Budkaflen*, while feeling that Strindberg had gone too far, admitted: "It is written with a passion and a strength which draw the spectator irresistibly with it, and contains several moments of deeply gripping power." *Ny Illustrerad Tidning* called it "a wild shriek of revenge, a battle-cry"; one was bewitched and gripped, but on sober reassessment the characters were incredible, "the awful imaginings of a sick brain." *Söndags-Nisse* felt that one was being addressed by a genius, if one who had sometimes strayed.

Georg Nordensvan in *Aftonbladet* wrote a vivid description of the atmosphere at the premiere. "Part of the large audience received the play with enthusiasm, and the applause after each act was loud and long, though far from unanimous. The longer the passionate play proceeded, the more one noticed in the audience an unrest, a surge of emotion which, from the disturbing scene when the old nurse tricks the sick man into donning the straitjacket, took the form of a continuous murmur which mounted after almost every line. It was, no doubt about it, indignation at the content of the play, at its furious assault upon the whole female sex, at expressions such as one has not hitherto been called upon to hear in a theatre, which whipped up our normally calm audience to fever pitch." But Nordensvan concluded that the play, though written with immense energy, finally proved nothing except that "its author is monomaniac in his attitude to these subjects . . . One cannot predict much future in our theatre for Strindberg's tragedy."[52] The noes had it; the play was withdrawn after nine performances, and Strindberg's royalties amounted to 40 crowns.[53]

Chapter Thirteen

MISS JULIE

On 20 March 1888 Strindberg finished A *Madman's Defence*.* Its main interest today is as an illustration of how much better Strindberg was as a dramatist than as a novelist (for the book purports to be a novel), or as a would-be straight narrator. If the dialogue alone of A *Madman's Defence* had survived, it would offer dramatic opportunities comparable to those of *The Father* or *Miss Julie*. But the linking commentary, hysterical and puerile, makes it impossible to believe the dialogue. Any one of his best plays would be equally incredible had he written it as a novel.

Writing A *Madman's Defence* did not expunge the poison from his system. He continued to abuse Siri to anyone who would listen. "I still have a letter from her when she was Baroness Wrangel," he informed Rudolf Wall on 23 March, "confessing her passion for the present Baroness [Sophia In de Betou]. . . . After a year of marriage I surprised her with our maid . . . In Germany we barely escaped punishment when she accosted schoolgirls and, in the middle of a musical soirée, attacked the town-major's daughter." His paranoia became extreme that spring. "Herr Lundegård is now my enemy," he told his brother Axel on 25 March,

---

*Even Strindberg realised that A *Madman's Defence* could not be published during Siri's lifetime, nor was it officially until as late as 1925, though a pirated edition translated from the German appeared in 1893–4.

"and so is August Lindberg." Yet the same day he was able to report to Hans Österling that Guy de Maupassant had written to him that he found *The Father* "powerful and profound." If only Strindberg had been born in a more liberal country than nineteenth-century Sweden, he would surely have received, if not general acclamation, at least the kind of elitist recognition which he had in Denmark and which Ibsen was about to gain in England. As it was, the compliments of Zola, Ibsen and Maupassant can scarcely have counterbalanced the abuse and mockery levelled at him by the majority of his compatriots.

On 28 March, Strindberg's "enemy" August Lindberg gave a public reading in Copenhagen of *Master Olof*, at the request of the Brandes brothers. It was a great success; *Morgenbladet* commented that the Royal Theatre there should long ago have regarded it as an honour to present something by Strindberg,[1] and *Aftonbladet* in Stockholm complained: "Our own Royal Theatre has still not staged this remarkable play. How long shall this continue?"[2] But Strindberg's increasing reputation in Denmark did not prevent this from being a most miserable spring. He wondered fitfully about seeking other sources of income, often wildly impractical: starting a daily paper in Stockholm,[3] and even "studying foreign banking correspondence so that in the autumn I can apply for a place here [in Denmark] in a big bank for a salary of 4,000 crowns . . . If necessary, I shall spend three months this summer at a commercial college."[4]* Yet he could not abstain from writing even for a few weeks, and within days of finishing *A Madman's Defence* he had embarked on a successor to *The People of Hemsö* in the form of a volume of short stories, *Men of the Skerries*. In little more than two weeks, by mid-April, he had completed half of these, and sent them to Bonnier, who was as delighted with them as he had been with *The People of Hemsö*—more so, since they contained no "coarsenesses." They contain some of Strindberg's finest work outside his plays, yet, because they dealt with themes other than his obsession, the sex war, he despised them, and himself for writing them.

At the beginning of April, Österling published *The Comrades*. Unsurprisingly, it was greeted with little enthusiasm; Edvard Brandes summed up the general reaction when he wrote to Strindberg that he found it "good on female psychology but badly constructed."[5] *Svenska Dagbladet* (14 April) called it a social and aesthetic error and hoped it would have no successors. Georg Brandes, reviewing it anonymously in *Politiken* (28

---

*Axel Strindberg passed this news on to the writer Oscar Levertin, who wrote to Edvard Brandes: "I have heard from Strindberg's brother the most pitiful account of his poverty. Are things really that bad? That we Swedes do nothing for such a genius is outrageous."[6]

April), praised Strindberg's critical approach to the kind of woman idealised by Ibsen and Bjørnson, but found the play in some respects "the outcome of a pathological rather than an artistic viewpoint. The bitterness remains like a bitter taste on the tongue."

That spring Strindberg made a literary discovery which greatly excited him: Friedrich Nietzsche. For this he had to thank Georg Brandes, whom he had got to know during the rehearsals of *The Father*. Seven years older than Strindberg, and a more formidable and less sympathetic character than his younger brother Edvard, Georg Brandes had, like Edvard, immediately recognised Strindberg's gifts. "I value this man's talent highly," he had written to Jonas Lie on 2 January in reply to a letter from Lie praising *The Father*. "It is sad that an unhappy marriage of the most peculiar kind—he clearly feels both the strongest physical attraction towards her and the greatest spiritual loathing—makes this great talent almost monomaniac. He belongs to the not small army of the unpredictable. But he is a man of genius."[7]

Georg Brandes delivered a series of lectures on Nietzsche in Copenhagen that spring, and, on being discovered by Strindberg in a city square reading one of Nietzsche's books, told him: "This is a man for you." Strindberg was tremendously excited by what he found. "Buy a modern philosopher called Nietsche [*sic*]," he told Heidenstam (17 May). ". . . Everything is there!" At the same time, Brandes wrote to Nietzsche drawing his attention to Strindberg, describing him as "Sweden's only genius."[8] Before the end of the year, Nietzsche and Strindberg were to conduct a brief but remarkable correspondence.

Since January the Strindbergs had been living in a fishing village, Taarbaek. Late that April Albert Bonnier visited them and reported, surprisingly, that Strindberg was "in unusually good health and looked fine. All that divorce story is just nonsense. He can't exist without his wife and children, not for two days."[9] Strindberg seems to have been one of those people who, however unhappy their marriage, dread living alone; in any case, their financial situation at this time would have made this scarcely practicable.

They wanted to move into the countryside for the summer, and an old gipsy woman, Fru Hansen, who sold them vegetables, told them that her son Ludvig was bailiff at an ancient castle called Skovlyst at Lyngby, some rooms of which were available for rent. Strindberg expressed interest, and Ludvig, a handsome fellow with black moustaches, came to collect them in an antique carriage drawn by two thin horses and drove them to the place, where they were greeted by the owner, a middle-aged lady named Countess Frankenau. She had a reputation for eccentricity, which she at once demonstrated by lying on the floor and playing a concertina while Hansen brought in his young sister Martha and gave an exhibition of levitation, leaving her suspended in mid air without visible support. Magnetism, he explained, had rendered her unconcious. One might suppose that Strindberg, who had already shown an interest in magnetism and hypnotism, would have been fascinated by this, but he became alarmed and (according to his daughter) glanced towards the door. However, the rooms were attractive, apart from dirty and uncurtained windows which the Countess promised to see to, so he agreed to rent them.

On 30 April Siri came out with the children to take possession, mercifully without Strindberg, who was to follow later, for they now discovered that the Countess owned eight dogs, an animal about which Strindberg had a phobia, that the windows were still filthy and curtainless, and that a foul smell from beneath the bed proved, on investigation, to emanate from a pile of dogs' excrement. Siri had not only to remove this but to open the bolsters and pillows and boil the feathers to get rid of the smell. Karin remembered how thankful they were that Strindberg was not present.

At first the summer went well. Strindberg regarded the Countess and Hansen with suspicion; the Countess's quarters were unbelievably squalid, and he had the door between their living-room and her bedroom (which he suspected that she shared with Hansen) locked, and forbade the children to enter her rooms or let her or Hansen kiss them, since after the levitation experiment he believed them to possess occult powers. Numerous livestock wandered around the house, including two peacocks. Dogs, rabbits and even ducks shared the Countess's bedroom. Hansen was frequently drunk and mismanaged the estate almost ostentatiously. Yet Strindberg became fascinated by him and soon began to enjoy his company.[10]

Years later, it transpired that Hansen was not the Countess's lover but her half brother, being the illegitimate son of her late father, a fact they kept secret out of respect to the dead man's memory. But Strindberg did not know this, and their supposed relationship formed a starting point for the great play which he was to write that summer about a high-born lady and her passion for one of her servants.

Strindberg described his new apartment to Heidenstam (9 May) as "a whore-palace which used to belong to Fredrik VII—four rooms and a kitchen for 50 crowns a month, furnished in Empire style. I live in a tower room." His hatred of Siri at this time, and of women in general through her, together with his increasing disillusionment with socialism and his discovery of Nietzsche and the latter's theory of racial elitism, put him in a state of more than usual confusion. Sending the manuscript of *A Madman's Defence* to Heidenstam on 25 May, he writes of "disharmony through changed circumstances; from having been 'small,' with sympathy for the small, to acknowledged greatness (?) and persecution *by* the small, resulting in antipathy towards Brutus and increasing sympathy for Caesar . . . I don't love the ones who sit up there, because they are small through too much power . . . but I don't like the stupid tyrants down there either. It is Christ, the little degenerate unsexed sophist, who is responsible for the little ones both up there and down there . . . [But] don't confuse the little ones down there with the unjustly oppressed! . . . If I had to define my present standpoint it would be: Atheist. Christ-hater. Anarchist. . . P.S.   Woman, being small and foolish and therefore evil . . . should be suppressed, like barbarians and thieves. She is useful only as ovary and womb, best of all as a cunt."

"What you tell of Strindberg is sad," Oscar Levertin wrote to Edvard Brandes on 12 July. "An unlucky star rules over him, and my dear country has done everything to add to his troubles. One despairs to think of it . . . It is remarkable that he can produce anything in his distress."[11] Ten days earlier, however, Strindberg had completed the last and longest of his stories for *Men of the Skerries*, "The Romantic Organist of Rånö." While midway through this, he had described it unflatteringly to Heidenstam (17 May) as "an idyll even more idiotic than *The People of Hemsö*," explaining that he was writing it "from necessity, so that I can then write unperformed plays and unpublished novels." He now, so he told Albert Bonnier, found it "fine, less idiotic than I hoped."[12] It is one of his best tales, the story of a poverty-stricken young musician searching for fulfilment, and it foreshadows his later experimental dramas in that the main character, as we learn in the final sentences, finds it difficult to distinguish between reality and fantasy.

Towards the end of July he started on a new play, which he completed in a couple of weeks. Unlike anything else he had written, with the exception of *In Rome* and *The Outlaw*, it was a one-act play. Of the merits of this work Strindberg had no doubts. "I take the liberty," he wrote to Albert Bonnier on 10 August in a letter accompanying the manuscript, "of hereby offering you the first naturalistic tragedy of the Swedish drama, and I beg you not to reject it without serious thought, or you will later regret it, for, as the Germans say: *Ceci datera*—this play will be remembered in history. P.S.   *Miss Julie* is the first of a forthcoming series of naturalistic tragedies."

Strindberg wrote a long preface to *Miss Julie* in which he developed his theory of what modern drama should attempt to be. This important document echoes, not surprisingly, many of Antoine's sentiments on the subject, but it is written with a passion and clarity that make it one of the seminal theatrical statements of its century. Noting, correctly, that "in those cultural strongholds which have nurtured the greatest thinkers of our age, namely England and Germany, the art of writing plays is . . . dead," he goes on:

> In other countries, men have tried to create a new drama by pouring new ideas into the old forms. But this has failed . . . we have not succeeded in adapting the old form to the new content, so that the new wine has burst the old bottles . . . I find "the joy of life" in life's cruel and mighty conflicts; I delight in knowledge and discovery . . . Since they are modern characters, living in an age of transition more urgently hysterical at any rate than the age which preceded it, I have drawn my people as split and vacillating, a mixture of the old and the new . . . My souls (or characters) are agglomerations of past and present cultures, scraps from books and newspapers, fragments of humanity, torn shreds of once-fine clothing that has become rags, in just the way that a human soul is patched together . . . I have avoided the symmetrical, mathematically constructed dialogue of the type favoured in France, and have allowed their minds to work irregularly, as people's do in real life . . . I believe that what most interests people today is the psychological process. Our prying minds are not content merely with seeing something happen—they must know why it happens . . . I have . . . eliminated all intervals . . . which give the spectator time to reflect and thereby withdraw from the suggestive influence of the author-hypnotist. My play will probably run for about one and a half hours, and if people can listen to a lecture, a sermon or a parliamentary debate for that length of time, I think they should be able to endure a play for ninety minutes . . .

In his opening stage directions to *Miss Julie,* Strindberg stresses that neither side wall of the kitchen is visible, so as to eliminate

> those tiresome exits through doors; for stage doors are made of canvas and flap at the slightest touch; they will not even allow an angry father to express his fury by stumping out after a bad dinner and slamming the door "so that the whole house shakes." (In the theatre, the door simply waves.) I have likewise confined myself to a single set, both to enable the characters to accustom themselves to their milieu, and to get away from the tradition of scenic luxury. But when one has only one set, one is entitled to demand that it be realistic . . . Even if the walls have to be of canvas, it is surely time to stop painting them with shelves and kitchen utensils . . . Another perhaps not unnecessary innovation would be the removal of the footlights . . . Does not this under-lighting annihilate all subtle expressions in the lower half of the face, particularly around the mouth? Does it not falsify the shape of the nose and throw shadows up over the eyes? . . . Pain is caused to the actor's eyes, so that any realistic expression is lost . . . When anyone on the

stage wishes to speak to the audience with his eyes, he has no alternative but to look straight at the audience, thereby entering into direct contact with them outside the framework of the play—a bad habit, which, rightly or wrongly, is known as "greeting one's friends." Would not sidelights of sufficient power (with reflectors, or some such device) endow the actor with this new resource, enabling him to reinforce his mime with his principal weapon of expression, the movement of his eyes?

I have few illusions of being able to persuade the actor to play *to* the audience and not with them, though this would be desirable. I do not dream that I shall ever see the full back of an actor throughout the whole of an important scene, but I do beseech that vital scenes should not be played opposite the prompter's box as though they were duets milking applause.

A word about make-up; which I dare not hope will be listened to by the ladies, who prefer beauty to truth. But the actor might well ponder whether it is to his advantage to paint an abstract character upon his face, which will remain sitting there like a mask. Imagine a gentleman dipping his finger into soot and drawing a line of bad temper between his eyes, and suppose that, wearing this permanently fierce expression, he were called upon to deliver a line smiling! . . . In a modern psychological drama, where the subtler reaction should be mirrored in the face rather than in gesture and sound, it would surely be best to experiment with strong sidelights on a small stage and with the actor wearing no make-up, or at best a minimum.

If we could then dispense with the visible orchestra, with their distracting lampshades and faces turned towards the audience . . . if we could get rid of the side-boxes (my particular *bête noire*) with their tittering diners and ladies nibbling at cold collations, and have complete darkness in the auditorium during the performance; and, first and foremost, a *small* stage and a *small* auditorium—then perhaps a new drama might emerge, and the theatre might once again become a place for educated people.

Such was Strindberg's view of what modern drama should be. It contains no direct reference to Ibsen, though no doubt Strindberg had him especially in mind as the chief of those who had sought "to create a new drama by pouring new ideas into the old forms." During the past eleven years Ibsen had written *The Pillars of Society*, *A Doll's House*, *Ghosts*, *An Enemy of the People*, *The Wild Duck* and *Rosmersholm*, and had thereby revolutionised drama by writing tragedies about ordinary middle-class people in everyday prose, instead of the poetic dramas about kings and queens, or at the least Montagues and Capulets, which had previously been regarded as the only possible medium for tragedy. Ibsen had, too, drawn people as "split and vacillating," a phrase which fits all his major characters in these plays, to say nothing of his earlier works such as *Brand* and *Peer Gynt*. And he showed, at least as much as Strindberg, the "psychological process." Where Strindberg broke new ground in *Miss Julie* was, firstly, in the "irregularity" of his dialogue; secondly, in dramatic concentration; and thirdly, though he does not mention this, in his boldly realistic treatment of sex.

Ibsen's characters think and speak logically and consecutively; Strindberg's dart backwards and forwards. They do not think, or speak, A.B.C.D.E., but A.Q.B.Z.C. (I remember that when we were rehearsing the National Theatre production of *Miss Julie* in 1965, Maggie Smith and Albert Finney, two most experienced and intelligent interpreters, asked me if I had not omitted some sentences or got things in the wrong order; the answer was, of course, that people in an over-heated state of mind do not think or speak consecutively.) Strindberg, like Dostoevsky and D. H. Lawrence, excelled in depicting men and women in a condition of emotional turmoil; and, like them, he tended not to be good at portraying people in a state of calmness; his finest characters, such as the principals in *The Father* and *Miss Julie* and *Creditors* and *The Dance of Death* and *Erik the Fourteenth*, are all thus frenzied when we see them.

Ibsen had gradually reduced the length of his plays; apart from *Ghosts*, all his prose plays up to and including *The Wild Duck* play for a minimum of three hours (even *A Doll's House*), but the later plays, such as *Rosmersholm*, *The Master Builder* and *John Gabriel Borkman*, play for two and a half or even two hours. But Strindberg achieved an economy beyond Ibsen's; he proudly pointed out that the plots of *Miss Julie* and *Creditors* would each have sufficed for a five-act play, but that he had reduced each of them to a single act of ninety minutes or less. Take a lamb cutlet, he said; it looks large, but three-quarters of it is bone and fat, containing a kernel of meat. I strip off the bone and fat and, like the Greeks, give you the kernel. [13]

As regards sexual realism, Strindberg, unlike any dramatist before him, showed that men and women can hate each other yet be sexually welded, as he still was to Siri. Before Strindberg, sex in drama is something in which only married people or wicked people indulge. (Even Romeo and Juliet do not sleep together until Friar Laurence has married them.) Miss Julie's tragedy is that she does not want to make love with Jean; she does not want to sleep with him; she wants—there is no other word for it—to be fucked by him, like an animal. When it has happened, she despises herself for having allowed it, and him for having done it; but she knows she will want him again; so she sees no alternative but suicide.

Miss Julie also expresses Strindberg's divided feelings about the aristocracy and the working class, his unwilling sympathy for the former and inability to associate himself, as he would have wished, with the latter. As his letter to Bonnier shows, he felt a sense of achievement in this play as in no previous work; and within a few days he embarked on a successor, of

similar length and ferocity, *Creditors*. He was surprised not to receive an
immediate reply from Bonnier, and eleven days after sending him *Miss
Julie* he wrote again, telling him that "in a week I shall be sending you a
new naturalistic tragedy, even better than *Miss Julie*, with three characters, a table and two chairs, and no sunrise!"

But Karl Otto Bonnier had already written to Strindberg the previous
day rejecting *Miss Julie*, and their letters crossed. "It is much too risky,
much too 'naturalistic' for us," Bonnier explained. "We therefore dare
not publish the play, as likewise I fear you will find difficulty in getting it
produced."[14] Bonnier later described this decision as the most unfortunate ever perpetrated by that distinguished house;[15] though he was right in
his prognostication. Strindberg accordingly offered *Miss Julie* simultaneously to both Hans Österling and Joseph Seligmann, who had
published *The Red Room*. "It is nearly ten years," he wrote to Seligmann
on 22 August, "since the first naturalistic Swedish novel appeared under
your imprint, with the consequences that we know. Today I send for your
perusal the first Swedish naturalistic drama, written as I think it should
be, for the reasons I have given in the foreword." He added the exciting
news that he had heard at last from Antoine about *The Father*, which
Strindberg had sent to him in French as long ago as March. Antoine was
full of enthusiasm for the play. He would, he said, have produced it at
once but for the fact that he had committed himself to staging *Ghosts*; he
would, however, do his best to present it in the near future. Seligmann at
once accepted *Miss Julie*, on condition that he was allowed to make
certain cuts and amendments; Strindberg agreed, and it appeared in this
abbreviated and adulterated form. The full version, based on Strindberg's
original manuscript, was not published until 1984.

"I have finished a bunch of shitty stories for Albert the Great,"
Strindberg wrote to Heidenstam the same day, "and with the money have
written 2 naturalistic tragedies which are the flower of my authorship
and of Swedish drama. Naturally refused by the same Albert." Soon after
finishing *Creditors*, he had to leave his castle at Lyngby in melodramatic
circumstances. He had a brief affair with Hansen's sister Martha; she
promptly accused him of raping her, on the grounds that she was under
sixteen and thus a minor. Two days later she withdrew the charge,
admitting that she was legally of age; but by this time Strindberg, as he
sadly reported to Edvard Brandes on 4 September, had been "driven out
by revolver shots, unlawful entry, gipsy dances and eight dogs, after I had
paid my September rent in advance. However, my spiritual uterus has
found a tremendous fertiliser in Friedrich Nietzsche, so that I feel
distended like a bitch in heat. He is the man for me!" He was especially

attracted by Nietzsche's theory of the Superman, which offered some consolation against the impending domination of the world by women; here at last was a fellow spirit to support him in the battle against Ibsen and the feminists. Of *Miss Julie* and *Creditors* he told Brandes: "I feel that in them I have written my stage masterpieces."

Strindberg retaliated against Hansen by accusing him to the police of having committed certain burglaries out at Taarbaek, where they had stayed before moving to Lyngby. On, it seems, no stronger evidence than Strindberg's word, Hansen was arrested and confined to prison pending trial. Meanwhile, the Danish newspapers learned about the "rape" and gave the matter great publicity. To escape from this, Strindberg departed with Pehr Staaff on a short trip to Berlin, without informing Siri, leaving her to face the music. From Berlin, on 19 September, he sent Siri a characteristic explanation of the affair. "You knew about my relationship with the girl Martha. I never had any intentions towards her, but Hansen sent her over on errands in the evenings after I had gone to bed and in the mornings when I was getting up, and so—! I only went with her once, and then with a sheath, so that I am (almost) sure she didn't get pregnant; if she is, I shall pay for the child's upkeep, though I think other men [*sic*] are the father. But not until a doctor has certified that she is pregnant . . . I regarded our marriage as dissolved, you agreed, and I kept the matter no more secret from you than delicacy demanded."

After only a week in Berlin, he had to return to Denmark to give evidence in Hansen's trial. By this time, the true thieves had been discovered; Hansen's nightly wanderings in Taarbaek turned out to have no more sinister explanation than that he was carrying on an affair with a girl. Towards the end of the year Strindberg wrote Hansen and the Countess out of his system in an indifferent and disagreeably racist *nouvelle, Tschandala,* about a professor of science who, after being humiliated by a gipsy, manages by suggestion and the use of a magic lantern to get him killed by his own dogs.

Siri seems not to have been greatly bothered by Strindberg's infidelity. He appears, at any rate temporarily, to have resigned himself to the prospect of divorce, for he advised her to use the incident as evidence to speed the process, but (she later told Karin) she refused to do this, since "it would have been shabby to accuse him of something I didn't care about."[16] "My friend and I are friends again," Strindberg wrote to his cousin Oscar on 27 September. "Jesus, how tough love is!"

They moved to a house in Holte. *Creditors,* like *The Father* and *Miss Julie,* had taken him only two weeks to write. A three-hander skilfully constructed in three dialogues, it tells of a sensual woman novelist past her prime and how her embittered ex-husband returns to avenge himself on her and her present husband. He offered it to Seligmann so that the latter might publish it simultaneously with *Miss Julie*, but Seligmann refused on the ground that it was too obviously descriptive of Strindberg's own marriage and deeply libellous about Siri. Strindberg begged him (16 October) to reconsider: "It is a great favourite with me, and I read it again and again, continually discovering new subtleties . . . *Miss Julie* is still a compromise with romanticism and painted flats. But *Creditors* is modern right through, humane, lovable, all three of its characters sympathetic, interesting from start to finish," an extraordinary judgement, except for the opening and closing remarks. But two weeks later he wrote: "Upon mature consideration I have decided not to publish *Creditors* in Swedish and I beg you to return it,"[17] thus taking the same decision about the play as he had concerning *A Madman's Defence*. He began forthwith to translate *Creditors* into French; though in fact he allowed it to appear in Danish the following spring, and in Swedish a year later.

That autumn Albert Bonnier published *Men of the Skerries*. In his preface, Strindberg wrote that what fascinated him about the archipelago was its "mixture of black melancholy and rough humour, poverty and wealth, civilisation and savagery, inland and coast," adding that, while in *The People of Hemsö* he had dwelt mostly on the lighter side of the islanders' life, he had set his new stories mainly "in the half-shadows." Thus, "The Romantic Organist of Rånö," the longest piece in the book, tells of a young musician full of ideals who becomes organist to a church on a tiny and remote island and gradually drifts away from reality; "A Criminal" deals with a man who murders his wife cruelly after years of marriage and refuses to offer any explanation or defence, something that the sophisticated young judge from the mainland finds incomprehensible but which the islanders regard as natural. Islanders, it has been said, tend to be manic-depressive, and it was not only for its deceptively peaceful landscape and seascape that Strindberg loved the archipelago. He felt more affinity with its inhabitants than with the townspeople of Stockholm. Except when he digresses into quasi-scientific theories, *Men of the Skerries* shows Strindberg at his best as a short-story writer, and is one of his most powerful works outside the plays.

Several critics, while praising the book, thought it less good than *The People of Hemsö*, and most of them deplored the "coarseness" of one of the best stories, "The Tailor's Ball" ("Why can Strindberg not forgo this curious love of coarse cynicism?" asked J. A. Runström in *Ny Illustrerad Tidning*, though admitting that he was "one of our most original writers"). But Georg Nordensvan in *Aftonbladet* praised its "unadulter-ated truthfulness . . . one of the most original talents among our younger writers . . . In several of the shorter stories the author is at the peak of his narrative power," and *Dagens Nyheter* and *Handelstidningen i Göteborg* likewise rated it among the best of Strindberg's works. [18] The Danish press were enthusiastic; Edvard Brandes wrote in *Politiken*: "He is like a leaping spring in Scandinavian letters. Cerebral natures may shrink from the current . . . but they cannot stem the source."

Strindberg, however, continued to disparage the book. "I haven't sent you my latest work, *Men of the Skerries*," he told Georg Brandes on 2 October, "since you need not read it. It is worth nothing." He repeated his gratitude to Brandes for introducing him to Nietzsche's work, "an acquaintance for which I am most grateful, for I find him the most liberated, the most modern of us all (not least, of course, as regards the woman question)." Brandes replied that he was "happy to have brought two such significant men together," but warned Strindberg that he himself found much to object to in Nietzsche's teaching, despite his general admiration of him: "Much in him seems to me less new than you think."[19]

But however great his theoretical hatred of the other sex, Strindberg needed women. "I am fast approaching epilepsy as a result of celibacy," he informed Heidenstam on 13 October. ". . . I could, I suppose, get girls, but where sex is concerned I am an aristocrat. I demand that they use soap and a toothbrush. If I fuck once I shall have to pay the slut a hundredfold. And I don't want to sow my seed in bad soil . . . My Aryan sense of honour forbids me to steal other men's wives. Can you under-stand my misogyny? Which is only the reverse image of a terrible desire for the other sex. My fainting fits during sleep and my chewing of the tongue are simply the consequences of celibacy—not of masturbation, for that helps a little and dissipates my melancholy. Without that I should now be mad! Rousseau recommends it in his *Confessions*, but he ranks it above coition with women. I don't! Buggery is nothing for me—my seed is too strong, and seeks eggs—unfortunately!"

This confused mood of hating women yet wanting them, so vividly expressed in the two plays he had written that summer, was a contradic-tion that brought out the best in him as a dramatist, if not as a novelist. He knew that *Miss Julie* and *Creditors* represented, with *The Father*, his best dramatic writing to date; equally, he despaired of any director ever accepting them for the stage. There was only one solution. He must do as Antoine had done and found his own theatre.

Chapter Fourteen

THE EXPERIMENTAL THEATRE

"Yesterday," Strindberg wrote to Gustaf at Geijerstam on 15 November 1888, "the anniversary of the first performance of *The Father*, and of modern Swedish drama, I founded the Scandinavian Experimental Theatre (Th. Libre). The roles are written for my wife, who can return to acting now that the children are grown up [*sic*] . . . As in Paris, the theatre will be run by amateurs with a performance once a month (Sunday afternoons) by subscription. It will subsequently tour the Scandinavian capitals except Stockholm. The few (3) persons I need apart from my wife I shall seek through advertisement. They should be mature, educated, possess smart outdoor clothes and enough to live on for a month. They can live here in this pretty hotel, with free lessons in mime, song, fencing, declamation and billiards . . . Will you write a one-act play? . . . Only one act, please. We don't want big spectaculars. We shall only play for the elite and don't need the bourgeoisie—who will in any case follow suit in ten years!"

Siri was excited at the prospect of creating *Miss Julie*; nor does she seem to have been bothered by the unflattering implied portrait of her as Tekla in *Creditors*. "My wife has read both plays," Strindberg informed David Bergström on 16 November, "is thrilled with the parts and can, and wants to, act them. So no problem about them being too intimate, and who could judge that better than she? . . . We shall open with two subscription performances in Copenhagen, then Gothenburg, Christiania, Bergen, Hälsingborg, Malmö, Kristianstad—n.b. not in Stockholm. High prices and small houses—so that only the elite can come—we shall sell only the stalls and dress circle—the upper galleries will be blocked off, so that we shan't get any mocking rabble." It was hardly to be a people's theatre; but, he might have argued, nor was Antoine's.

The next day he inserted an advertisement in *Politiken*:

> Since I intend at the earliest opportunity to open a Scandinavian Experimental Theatre on the pattern of the Théâtre Libre in Paris, I hereby announce that I invite plays of whatever kind to be sent to me for reading. Preferably they should have a contemporary setting, be of not too great a length, and not require elaborate machinery or a large cast.

Seldom can a theatrical enterprise have been planned with such limited resources. "We live now in complete misery," he told his cousin Oscar on 19 November. "Christmas and the New Year approach and the winter is cold. We don't even have clothes. I haven't a winter coat nor a pair of winter trousers. The children's clothes are five years old." Nor did he find the support he had hoped for from his admirers. Edvard Brandes, like August Lindberg the year before, did not believe that Strindberg was sufficiently practical to run a theatre, and nobody was prepared to back him. His advertisement evoked no worthwhile response. "I have now read twenty-five submitted plays," he told Geijerstam on 1 December, "and have found only one that is actable." He would have to provide the repertoire himself.

He intended to use amateur actors, like Antoine, ignoring the fact that Antoine had worked a good deal with his actors before exposing them to the critics at the Théâtre Libre. His impracticality is apparent from his letters; the money to start things might be raised "in ten- or five-crown notes"; they will tour "twenty cities in three months."[1] But if friends such as Edvard Brandes doubted his ability to run a theatre, what chance had he of finding support elsewhere?

When Seligmann published *Miss Julie* on 23 November, the reviews proved to be no help: "A filthy bundle of rags which one hardly wishes to touch even with tongs" (*Stockholms Dagblad*); "A heap of ordure . . . language that is scarcely used except in nests of vice and debauchery" (Karl Warburg in *Handelstidningen i Göteborg*); "Makes a most disagreeable impression even on reading, and will surely nowhere find a public that could endure to see it" (*Ny Illustrerad Tidning*); "Totally repellent" (*Aftonbladet*); "Repulsive. . . . Displeasure at its content can be but little mollified by the suspicion that the man who wrote the play, and a foreword in which he states the most irrational theories, must, while writing them, have been troubled by some affectation of the brain which rendered him for the nonce not wholly normal" (Carl David af Wirsén in *Post- och Inrikes Tidningar*). The only exception was an anonymous critic in *Svenska Dagbladet* who found the treatment of the conflict masterly, the dialogue natural and the preface "especially rewarding."[2] Bjørnson denounced it; and when Edvard Brandes suggested to August Lindberg that it was a play that the latter ought to stage, Lindberg replied, "My best actress . . . says she would rather break her contract than appear in this."[3] The Danish press, usually more sympathetic to Strindberg, was equally hostile. *Avisen* called it "one long protracted foulness," and *Dagbladet*, "water from the same dirty sewer in which Herr Brandes and his supporters wish to re-baptise the art of dramatic writing." *Dagens Nyheder* declared: "Not a thought is genuine, not a feeling true."[4] Edvard Brandes himself admired the play; he had doubts about the ending but concluded that it would "act brilliantly."[5]

Ironically, Strindberg's little pot-boiler of reflections on country life, *Flower Paintings and Animal Pieces*, which contains essays on such subjects as the art of angling and how to grow melons and which appeared at the same time as *Miss Julie*, received uniformly excellent notices. Georg Nordensvan, in the same article in *Aftonbladet* as that in which he dismissed *Miss Julie*, found it "as fresh and delicate as though he had never done anything but dig in his garden, cultivate flowers, and study the habits of dogs, hares and perch, in a word, lived in intimate communion with nature far from big cities and from everything to do with human beings."[6]

But however depressed Strindberg must have felt at the wretched plays being submitted to him and the hostile reception of *Miss Julie*, encouragement came at the end of November in the shape of a fan letter from Nietzsche himself. As a result of the letter which Georg Brandes had written to Nietzsche about Strindberg the previous year, Nietzsche asked Brandes in October for Strindberg's address so that he might send him *The Twilight of the Gods*, adding that he had read *Getting Married* in French and had been "entranced."[7] Strindberg had sent Nietzsche *The Father* in French during the spring, care of his publisher; now, having heard nothing and fearing it might not have reached him, he sent him a copy of his own French translation of the play, containing Zola's letter as foreword.[8] Meanwhile, Nietzsche sent Strindberg *The Twilight of the Gods*, inscribed: "Herr August Strindberg. Should this not be translated? It is dynamite. The Antichrist." On 27 November he wrote to Strindberg in German from Turin:

Most honoured Sir,

I think our messages crossed? I read your tragedy twice with deep emotion; it has astounded me beyond measure to find a work in which my own conception of love—with war as its means and the deathly hatred of the sexes as its fundamental law—is so magnificently expressed. Your play is surely certain to be staged in Paris at M. Antoine's Théâtre Libre! *Demand* this of M. Zola . . .

Strindberg replied in French around 4 December:

Without any doubt, you have given to mankind the most profound book that it possesses and, not least, you have had the courage, the means perhaps, to spit these superb words at the rabble! and I thank you! . . . And you want to be translated into our Eskimo tongue! Why not into French or English? You may judge of our intelligence when I tell you that they wanted to commit me to an asylum because of my tragedy, and that as rich and flexible a spirit as M. Brandes has been reduced to silence by this rabble majority. I end all my letters to my friends: read Nietzsche! That is my *Carthago est delenda.* *

Yet the moment you are known and understood, your stature will be belittled and the sacred and revered rabble will address you familiarly as their equal. Better to preserve your distinguished solitude and allow us ten thousand elite to make a secret pilgrimage to your sanctuary to draw inspiration. Let us protect your esoteric teaching by keeping it pure and inviolable and not divulge it except through your devoted disciples, among whom I sign myself

August Strindberg

On 4 December, Strindberg wrote to Georg Brandes:

To me Nietzsche is the prophet of the overthrow of Europe and Christendom, the awakening and re-entry of the East into its rightful inheritance . . . Christendom is to me a barbarism . . . a backward step, the religion of the small, the paltry, the castrates, women, children, because it is in direct conflict with our evolution which wants to protect the strong against the weak species, and the current aggressiveness of women seems to me a symptom of the regress of the race and a result of Christendom. Nietzsche is therefore to me the modern spirit who dares to preach the right of the strong and the wise against the foolish, the small (the democrats).

Nietzsche was much moved to receive this tribute from a fellow spirit as lonely and unrecognised as himself. On 8 December he thanked Strind-

---

*The Latin words "Carthage must be destroyed" (actually *Delenda est Carthago*) were those with which, according to Plutarch, Cato the Elder ended every speech he made to the Roman Senate until that action was taken.

berg for "the first letter in my life which has really *reached* me," praised
Strindberg's translation of *The Father,* which he had assumed to have
been done by a Frenchman, and asked if he would care to translate his
own autobiography, *Ecce Homo,* into French. "It is annihilatingly
anti-German," he proclaimed. "I treat all German philosophers as
'unconscious' coiners, I call the young Kaiser a scarlet hypocrite."
Strindberg explained (11 December) that it was a question of money. "I
am a poor devil (wife, three children, two servants, debts, etc.). . . If the
considerable expense does not deter you, you may count on me and my
talent!" Concerning the possibility of Nietzsche's getting translated into
English: "As regards English, I must plead ignorance now that it is a
country 'priest-ridden' by the arrival of women who stand for absolute
decadence. Morality in England, sir, you know what that means! The
Library of Young Women, Currer Bell, * Miss Braddon, etc. That is not
for you! In French you will reach even the world of Negroes and can raise
your fingers at the English matriarchy!"

Nietzsche on 21 December offered further encouragement about *The
Father*: "M. Antoine's Théâtre Libre exists to take risks. Your play is quite
innocent compared with what they have dared to present there lately.
This caused A. Wolf, in a leading article in *Figaro,* publicly and in the
name of France, to blush . . . I advise you not to involve M. Zola further
but to send scripts and letters direct to M. Antoine. They like to stage
foreign plays." He went on to comment on some remarks Strindberg had
made about the awfulness of trying to be a writer in Sweden: "How
envious you have made me! You underrate your luck: '*O fortunatos
nimium, sua si bona norint* [If you only knew, you are over-blessed with
luck]'—namely, that you are not German." Strindberg then sent him
a short story, entitled "Remorse," which he had written in 1884, evoking
a brief and cryptic letter of thanks: "It rings like a rifle-shot . . . *Auf
Wiedersehen.* This will be our *auf Wiedersehen* . . . Une seule condition:
divorçons [one condition: let us divorce] . . . Nietzsche Caesar." Strindberg, uncertain whether to take this seriously, replied the next day (1
January 1889) in similarly ambiguous vein in Latin and Greek. "I want, I
want to be mad," he began in Greek, then quoted in Latin a verse from
Horace: "'You would live better, Licinius, if you did not always either
seek the open sea or, in fear of storms, keep too close to the perilous coast.'
But we rejoice in being mad. Farewell and think well of me." Nietzsche
answered this with an even briefer note than his last: "Alas . . . Nicht

---

*The pen-name of Charlotte Brontë.

mehr divorçons? [Let us no more divorce?] The Crucified One." So their correspondence ended. *

"I think our friend Nietzsche is mad," Strindberg wrote to Georg Brandes on 3 January, and indeed it was during their correspondence that Nietzsche's reason finally abandoned him. "My health is really quite normal," he had told his sister two and a half years earlier. "Only my soul is so sensitive and so full of longing for good friends of my own kind. Find me a small circle of men who will listen to me and understand me—and I shall be cured." Like so much that Nietzsche wrote, the words could have been penned by Strindberg. Even more than Strindberg, Nietzsche lacked followers and disciples; only during the last year of his conscious life was he praised by a critic of note, Georg Brandes.

It has often been asserted that Nietzsche influenced Strindberg's writing. It seems likelier that Strindberg merely found confirmation in Nietzsche of what he already believed, as Ibsen had with Kierkegaard. Nietzsche despised "the humble, the feeble, the subjected, the peace-loving," values which, he claimed, came from the Jews, the slave people of antiquity; the Jews corrupted the master morality into the slave morality, bequeathing these values to Christianity and leading to the triumph of the common man. Nietzsche also believed that these "debased" instincts dominated all modern movements, such as socialism, feminism and pacifism, that the emancipation of women could only lead to defective offspring, and that mankind's fate depended on the success of its higher types and the creation of a new ruler caste. "The aim should be," he wrote in *The Will to Power*, "to prepare a transvaluation of all values for a particularly strong kind of man, most highly gifted in intellect and will, and, to this end, slowly and cautiously to liberate in him a whole host of slandered instincts, hitherto held in check . . . I am writing for a race of men which does not yet exist: for the lords of the earth."[9] Like Strindberg, he despised the mob, whether below or, as in politics, above. In all these respects Strindberg found his own beliefs mirrored, though Nietzsche, unlike Strindberg, foresaw that he would attract unwanted disciples; rather than them, he declared, he preferred his adversaries.

Strindberg's daughter Karin believed that her father turned from

*Karl Strecker, in his *Nietzsche und Strindberg, mit ihrem Briefwechsel* (Munich, 1921), pp. 30 ff., prints a further letter from Nietzsche, allegedly addressed to Strindberg, in which he says that he "hardly regarded loneliness as a hardship, but rather felt it a priceless distinction and at the same time a purification." These words would have comforted Strindberg, but Walter Berendsohn has convincingly demonstrated that Nietzsche wrote them not to Strindberg but to Jean Bourdeau. (*Cf.* Berendsohn's "Strindberg och Nietzsche," pp. 9–15.)

socialism to Nietzscheanism partly out of boredom with an ideal that was no longer an inspiration (boredom, she says, was always an important factor with him), and partly from a need to armour himself against all the hatred directed against him. "The mantle of the Superman became his coat of mail." Siri, she says, "hated Nietzsche with all her heart," especially his theory that the small must suffer so that the strong can live, that they should provide a kind of subsoil for the Supermen, and that Christianity is "the religion of women, castrates, children and savages."[10] Inevitably, Strindberg's embrace of Nietzscheanism widened the rift between Siri and him.

The two men were further drawn to each other by their common loneliness, lack of recognition and fear of madness. As their correspondence ended, Strindberg discovered another kindred spirit, albeit a dead one. "On Boxing Night," he told Ola Hansson (3 January), "I read Edgar Poe for the first time. And noted it in my diary. I am astounded. Is it conceivable that he, who died in 1849, the year I was born, could have smouldered through the various media to me! What are 'The Battle of Brains,' 'Short Cuts,' even *The Secret of the Guild* . . . but E.P.!" "This genre (Edgar Poe)," he assured Karl Otto Bonnier, "will dominate the next ten years . . . Zolaism with its naturalism looks like becoming a spent force."[11]

Strindberg's identification of himself with Poe is not surprising. "True! —nervous—very, very dreadfully nervous I had been and am; but why *will* you say that I am mad? . . . I heard all things in the heaven and in the earth. I heard many things in hell. Now, then, am I mad?" Thus Poe begins "The Tell-Tale Heart"; and in *Eleonora* he wrote: "I grant, at least, that there are two distinct conditions of my mental existence—the condition of a lucid reason, not to be disputed . . . and a condition of shadow and doubt." In his prefatory note to *Eureka*, Poe said it was intended for "those who put faith in dreams as the only realities." He shared Strindberg's interest in science, mesmerism and the occult, his neat handwriting and detestation of democracy, his tendency to keep moving home, his combination of quarrelsomeness with elaborate courtesy, his mania for composition, and his belief, as expressed in *The Fall of the House of Usher* and *William Wilson*, in the division of personality. They were even the same height (five feet eight inches, 1.73 metres), and of the same slim build. They had the same attitude towards science; Julian Symons, in his biography of Poe, has written: "The right way to regard *Eureka* is to discard the science with its occasional brilliant guesses . . . emerging from a sea of nonsense, and to regard it as a vision," which might be said of Strindberg's *Antibarbarus*, and has summed up Poe's work as "an expression of personal obsessions which articulate universal fears and horrors . . . The shriek of a man possessed by demons . . . His various obsessions strike chords of fear and longing in us all . . . his perceptions of a different world that existed in the imagination, into which one might enter like Alice through the Looking-Glass." "You speak of an 'estimate of my life,'" Poe wrote to James Russell Lowell. ". . . I have none to give. I have been too deeply conscious of the mutability and evanescence of temporal things to give any continuous effort to anything—to be consistent in anything"; and when he died, his cousin Neilson Poe wrote (and it could serve as an epitaph for Strindberg) that he "had seen so much of sorrow—had so little reason to be satisfied with life—that to him, the change can scarcely be said to be a misfortune."[12]

A few days before he discovered Poe, Strindberg's name was presented to the American public for, as far as one can ascertain, the first time. On 20 December 1888, the Chicago weekly *America* printed an article in praise of him by the young Norwegian novelist Knut Hamsun, who that year had published his first, extraordinary novel, *Hunger*. Hamsun's tribute was eloquent and perceptive.

> His circumspective mind attends to everything, comprehends every-thing. With an unswerving, and even fanatic, logic he thrusts himself everywhere . . . August Strindberg has formed no party, he stands alone. But there is an eminent power in this uneasy-minded man . . . As he is the brutish rebel who overthrows temples and fights Philistines, he is also the tender, sensitive spirit who fights the evil principles in life . . . Strindberg is a complex nature, coarse and tough as a butcher, delicate and tender as a child, as a woman . . . I have found in no literature such a velocity as Strindberg's. It is no tempest, it is a hurricane. He does not speak; he does not say his opinions, he *explodes* them . . . What is called his "contradic-tions" seems to me psychologically consistent. He uses no deliberate planning, and not the method of positive criticism; he *guesses* his way, throws about ingenious forebodings, bold paradoxes . . . He is a far-seeing observer of a rare sort.

But Hamsun's words fell on stony soil. A further five years were to elapse before the next recorded article about Strindberg appeared in America, and that was to be by a Swede.

At the turn of the year 1888–89, Strindberg wrote a short play for his new theatre, *The Stronger*. Antoine had introduced plays lasting as little as fifteen minutes into his repertory, and *The Stronger* is this length. It contains two characters but is a monologue: a wife meets a woman friend in a café and, as she chats to her without reply, realises that the friend is, or was, her husband's mistress. Within six days of completing this he had

written another two-hander, of half an hour's duration: *Pariah*, this time
with two male characters, based on a story by Ola Hansson about two
petty criminals, unconvincing in its attempt to portray the victory of "a
stronger intelligence." Like *The Stronger*, it offers powerful opportunities
for a stage duel, but only works if acted by two skilful and equally matched
actors.

Hansson, later to become a close friend and then an enemy of
Strindberg, visited him at Holte and noted his "slim, supple figure . . .
small feet and small white hands . . . small aristocratic Mongolian face"
(he repeats elsewhere this adjective "Mongolian"), and his eyes with their
changing expression "shining and smiling like sunshine through the mist,
then threatening like a pair of pistol barrels."[13]

A thirty-three-year-old Danish author and amateur actress, Nathalia
Larsen, who had written five plays, two of which had been performed,
offered her services as general assistant to the Experimental Theatre, and
Strindberg, amazing as it seems, left the preparation of his season entirely
to her and Siri, bombarding Nathalia with letters (one of them facetiously
headed: "General Orders from Headquarters"),[14] telling her which actors
to approach and so forth. Nathalia also undertook the translation of his
plays into Danish. The fears of August Lindberg and Edvard Brandes
proved justified, for seldom if ever can the founder of a theatre have taken
so little active part in its organisation; indeed, Strindberg found time that
January to adapt his novel *The People of Hemsö* for the stage, not for his
own theatre (it required too large a cast), but for Lindberg. He also found
time for scientific experiments; Ola Hansson reported that he was more
interested in the crystallisation of egg-white than in his theatre. He had
another look at Shakespeare and, as befitted his elitist outlook, decided
that the plays could not have been written by a lad from grammar school.
"I read *Lear* and *The Tempest* after 15 years," he told Hansson on 15
January. "Everything good is by Bacon, all the rubbish by the provincial
actor. . . . Who is Shakespeare? Bacon, of course, with his atheistic
smile, superior, aristocratic." In similar vein he described a Swedish
newspaper editor as "a knowledgeable man but duped by socialism."[15]

In February he wrote another fifteen-minute play, *Simoom*, a banal
three-hander about revenge set in a burial chamber in Algeria, and a
curious article, "On Modern Drama and the Modern Theatre," which
appeared in the magazine *Ny Jord*, and which deserves to be examined in
detail.

The theatre, Strindberg asserts, is either a dying art or needs to be
"modernised to meet the demands of the age so that it may once again take
its rightful place as a medium of education." Archaic as it is now, "big as a

circus, opening out into a stage with a Greco-Roman triumphal arch, decked with emblems and grotesque masks . . . the red drapes, the brilliant curtain, the orchestra in its ancient and traditional place . . . all lead the memory back to olden times when the theatre was the place for religious and national feasts. . . . This hardy popular notion of the theatre as principally a festive arena where grandly dressed warriors, lords and ladies appear *en masse* and where cryptic and preferably unintelligible events take place in castle halls, wild forests or trenches." He tells how in Copenhagen he saw a play written in 1852 by Paul Féval in the tradition of Dumas *père*, and condemns the romantic dramatists for neglecting psychological study and replacing the bare stage of Shakespeare with ostentatious decor and mechanical effects; also for the poverty of their supporting characters, thus condemning the majority of actors and actresses to second- and third-rate roles for most of their lives, and for the expense such plays involve. He praises Molière for the economy of his effects and his smaller casts, and deplores the decline of the French comic tradition as exemplified by such writers as "the decadent Sardou," with his "jaded characters and threadbare plots. All trace of human life has disappeared from Sardou's plays, in which everyone talks as though they were editors of comic magazines."

He traces the birth of the new drama, which "some date from the Goncourt brothers' *Henriette Maréchal*, in 1865," but Strindberg thinks that this is not a truly realistic play and that the key work was Zola's *Thérèse Raquin* eight years later. He tries unconvincingly to make this play fit his theory of the Small and the Big, but rightly observes that it loses by being an adaptation of a novel rather than having been conceived as a play, and by the passage of a year between Acts One and Two; he suggests, interestingly, that it would profit by dropping Act One completely. But *Thérèse Raquin*, in Strindberg's view, had no successors; he will not allow Henri Becque's *Les Corbeaux*, written in 1876 but not staged until 1882 and generally regarded as a pioneer work of the new movement, to be truly naturalistic. "This is photography, which registers everything, even the dust on the camera lens . . . the little art, which cannot see the wood for the trees; this is misconceived naturalism, not the big naturalism which seeks the crucial points where the great battles take place, which loves to note what one does not see every day . . . the great art which we find in *Germinal* and *La Terre* and which for a moment we glimpsed in *Thérèse Raquin* and hoped to see continue in the theatre, but which did not come with Becque's *Corbeaux* or Zola's *Renée* but which should gradually emerge through the opening of the new theatre which under the name of the Théâtre Libre practises its craft in the heart of Paris."

Strindberg deplores the fact that no play can be staged in the traditional Paris theatres unless it contains parts suited to their stars—"and the repertory which has grown to feed Sarah Bernhardt and Ristori is completely worthless. But every time a dramatist has had a theatre at his disposal, a true drama has resulted, as with Shakespeare and Molière, and the plays have given birth to actors, which is the right way about." He praises Antoine for his belief that once you have the plays the actors will emerge who can act them, thus continuing the tradition of Lessing who "feared the great actors with their fixed traditional methods more than he feared amateurs ignorant of the secrets of the craft." In the Théâtre Libre "there is no superb decor to blind the audience to the emptiness of the plot . . . Only a simple *mise-en-scène*, and the performers are a handful of young pupils who combine the naïveté of inexperience with the conviction and fervour of youth. Shakespeare was not better interpreted when he wrote his masterpieces." This has resulted in a form "which seems to lead the new drama in a somewhat different direction to that suggested by its faltering steps in *Thérèse Raquin* and which breaks completely with Zola's adaptations of *L'Assommoir* and *Germinal* with their mass effects and complicated devices. Hardly a full-length play is seen, even Zola making his bow with a one-act piece; and where three acts are given, one notes a strong leaning towards the unities in time and space. At the same time all attempts at plot are regarded as secondary, and the main interest is focused on psychological development."

On the question of length, Strindberg observes how rare good five-act plays are; from the twenty-five submitted to him of that length, he found none good, though by contrast "every beginner seems to me able to write one good act . . . As soon as he tries to write long plays, everything becomes strained, calculated, artificial, and untrue. Two-act plays are a genre by themselves, not too fortunate; there is a head and a tail, but the body is missing—before and after the catastrophe, usually with a year in between . . . The best constructed are the three-act plays which observe the unities of time and place—when the subject is big, that is; for example, Ibsen's *Ghosts*, as contrasted with *Rosmersholm*, which was found to be much too long . . .* One scene, a *quart d'heure*, seems the most likely model for modern drama, and it has an ancient tradition, for it can trace its ancestry—why not?—to Greek tragedy, which contains a concentrated action in a single act." Via the French eighteenth-century dramatists Carmontelle and Leclerq, this genre "finds its highest achieve-

---

*Rosmersholm, a subtler and more elusive play than *Ghosts*, had failed everywhere it had been performed in Europe.

ment in the accepted masterpieces of Feuillet and Musset . . . With the aid of a table and two chairs one was able to present the strongest conflicts that life has to offer."

Finally, Strindberg praises Antoine for "proclaiming no dogmas, promulgating no theories, seeking to create no school . . . The Théâtre Libre's programmes offer the most varied types of play, old and new side by side . . . including the breaking of the rule that no play should be set in a past age. . . . We have renewed our acquaintance with Pierrot, but a nineteenth-century version who knows his Charcot;* Jesus Christ—he of the Bible—has appeared as a lover . . . tragicomedies are presented—in verse—imagine, in verse, which was lately banned from the stage! . . . This is true freedom; one might almost say anarchism! Is not this perhaps . . . a liberation from a dreadful aesthetic which . . . sought to turn the theatre into a political riding-school, a Sunday school, a chapel?"

The oddest thing to a modern reader about this essay is its almost total disregard of Ibsen; *The Pillars of Society*, *A Doll's House*, *Ghosts*, *An Enemy of the People*, *The Wild Duck*, *Rosmersholm* and *The Lady from the Sea* were of a naturalism beside which *Thérèse Raquin* seems contrived and melodramatic (though often adapted today, it is never performed in Zola's original version). One can only suppose that Strindberg's dismissal of him was due to his hatred of him as a (supposed) champion of feminism, coupled with the fact that in four of Ibsen's last six plays—*A Doll's House*, *Ghosts*, *Rosmersholm* and *The Lady from the Sea*—the leading character had been a woman, as was to be the case in his next play, *Hedda Gabler*.

Around this time, Strindberg managed to quarrel with Edvard Brandes. The Danish novelist Henrik Pontoppidan had written a piece in *Politiken* (28 January), to which Strindberg took offence. He penned an intemperate reply, which Brandes refused to print "because I found it unworthy of you. A few days' reflection should have made you realise that one cannot conduct private conversations in a newspaper."[16]

Despite, or perhaps assisted by Strindberg's absence (he did not even visit Copenhagen during the preparations for the season), Siri and Nathalia Larsen managed better than might have been expected. They succeeded in leasing Dagmars Theatre, somewhat bigger and less centrally situated than they would have liked, and planned to open on 2 March with a double bill of *Miss Julie* and *Creditors*. Hunderup, who had staged

---

*Jean Martin Charcot (1825–1893), the great neurologist whose writings on hysteria and hypnotism fascinated Strindberg and other writers of the time. His study of medicine in art in *Nouvelle Iconographie de la Salpêtrière* had appeared in 1888 and caused widespread interest.

The Father, agreed to play Gustav in the latter play; F. A. Cetti, as Adolf, dropped out during rehearsals and was replaced by Gustav Wied, later to make a name for himself as a comic writer. But the day before the premiere, police arrived at the theatre with the news that the censor had, somewhat belatedly, decided to ban *Miss Julie*.

Edvard Brandes in *Politiken* and C. E. Jensen in *Social-Demokraten* both protested against this action, but Brandes felt bound to express doubts about Strindberg's plans, writing reasonably enough that he thought the project insufficiently prepared in contrast to Antoine's, and wondering if it was wise to play in so big a theatre without a properly trained company. He concluded, however, with characteristic generosity: "Even should the enterprise fail, it will not in the least affect Herr Strindberg's reputation, which rests upon other things than his ability to run a theatre." *Dagbladet*, referring to uncertainties about the venue and the casting, was less charitable: "A theatre without a building, an actress without lines [a reference to the silent role in *The Stronger*] and male roles without actors . . . Who can henceforth call Herr Strindberg a realist?"[17]

Strindberg and Siri had to make new plans. They decided to replace *Miss Julie* with *The Stronger* and *Pariah*, postponed the opening for a week, and opened with these two and *Creditors* in a triple bill on 9 March. Tekla was played not by Siri, as originally intended, but by Nathalia Larsen, presumably because it would have been an excessive burden to act both Tekla and Miss Julie in the same evening. Wied's performance as the weakling husband in *Creditors* was apparently most unfortunate. V*ort Land* wrote: "People laughed until the tears sprang to their eyes as the tiny, slender author writhed like a snake in a monster of an armchair up there on the stage. There was no question of hearing his lines; he practically whispered, partly from stage fright, partly through lack of voice." Nathalia Larsen was too young and inexperienced for the difficult role of Tekla, who is anyway meant to be a woman approaching, and fearful of, middle age. Yet surprisingly, the evening was a fair success. The plays were greeted with applause sufficient to justify several curtain calls and unmixed with hissing. *Aftonbladet*, which had mocked the enterprise, had the grace to write: "We must respect the truth and admit that he won." The only bad reviews were in *Dagbladet* and *Avisen* (which demanded that Strindberg be deported), though even the favourable notices expressed disappointment at the lack of originality in the staging and decor.[18]

Next day, as a postscript to a hysterical letter to Ola Hansson ("Emancipated women are like an army of whores and would-be whores—professional whores with abnormal inclinations—had they been poor and uneducated"), Strindberg, who had not attended the premiere, wrote: "Have just received the following telegram from Wied: '8:30 p.m. Unanimous applause for *Creditors*. Curtain call . . . great success. Fru Strindberg called five times. Calls for the author. Speech by Fru S. Great applause, a few whistles.'" This euphoria soon turned to depression. Three days later he wrote to Siri: "It is sad to see how all our hopes, our decisions to begin afresh, our striving for freedom and independence and our children's future, the establishment of our reputation, have failed."

Meanwhile, they hit on the idea of circumventing the censor's ban on *Miss Julie* by presenting it privately at the Copenhagen University Student Union. Accordingly, on 14 March 1889, it received its premiere before an audience of a hundred and fifty students, their friends and a handful of critics. The scene was described by the Malmö correspondent of the Stockholm *Dagens Nyheter*:

> We find ourselves in a depressing little room on the first floor of a building in Bath-house Street in Copenhagen. The window-shutters are screwed shut, and only a single lamp illuminates the stage in front of us. The room is packed, and when our eyes have accustomed themselves to the relative darkness, we are able to study the people sitting or standing under the low ceiling. Most of them are students, only six or seven are women, but not so few of the *coryphées* of Copenhagen are seated in the front rows. But we search in vain for August Strindberg, though it has been announced that he is to attend the performance . . .
>
> In front of the chairs a long, blue, half-transparent curtain hangs from ceiling to floor. The bottom of it is concealed by a broad board, behind which are the footlights. A gas-light shines through at one side (later in the evening it was to serve as the setting sun).
>
> "Nine o'clock" it said on the tickets, for which the students have been fighting for two days. The academic quarter* has already passed, the hall—if one can so describe this large room—is more than full, and people are beginning to grow a little impatient. Feet are stamped, and a cry of "Ring it up!" is heard.
>
> "Shut up those galleryites!" shouts a witty citizen to those sitting behind him.
>
> "Galleryite yourself!" is the retort, and the stamping of feet continues until at length a few faint sounds of a teaspoon being tapped against a toddy glass make themselves heard. There is a deal of hushing, and then, after another teaspoon-tap, the blue curtain is drawn aside. A deathly silence reigns in the "auditorium," where the heat begins to be oppressive. The ceiling is not so high that a man standing on his chair might not touch it with his hand, and there is no ventilation.
>
> The play, as is known, takes place in a kitchen, and completely new decor

*In Scandinavia, academic events, such as lectures, normally begin fifteen minutes after the advertised time.

has had to be bought for the evening's performance. To our surprise, it resembles a real kitchen. A plate-rack, a kitchen table, a speaking tube to the floor above, a big stove with rows of copper pots above it—in short, everything is there, presenting the living image of a real kitchen.

From the little programme sheets which have been handed out we see that the title role is to be played by Fru Essen-Strindberg, Christine by Fru Pio and the servant Jean by Hr. Schiwe. As regards the first-named, her performance appears to be precisely opposed to what the author intended. She is too cold, much too cold, and one gets no impression at all of the kind of woman who would seduce a man like Jean. Hr. Schiwe hardly suggested a servant; his manner was much more that of a gentleman and a *viveur*. Fru Pio, however, spoke her lines excellently.

Although the play was performed before an audience almost exclusively male, the author had been compelled to accept several deletions. The promised midsummer romp by farm-hands and serving-girls did not materialise; we merely heard a violin playing a dance.

And so, after rather a tame final scene, the curtain fell, or, more correctly, the sacking was pulled across the stage. There is resounding applause and the actors are called to take their bows.

Then we gather round the tables, and our theatrical evening ends like any student party.

The author himself, we are told, "stood half-hidden behind a door, his face pale and twisted with jealousy."[19] He was convinced that Siri and Schiwe were having an affair. Next morning he rushed into her aunt's house, where she was staying with the children, and forced his way into her bedroom hoping to find the two together.[20] "I don't understand Strindberg," Schiwe wrote to his fellow actor Gustav Wied. "Must he, a genius of the first order, really conduct himself like a complete lunatic? . . . Not just that he wildly accuses me; by destroying his wife's good name, he demeans himself."[21] Siri demanded that Strindberg apologise to Schiwe; he refused.

On 16 March the company crossed the Sound to Sweden and performed the triple bill of *Creditors, Pariah* and *The Stronger* in Malmö. It received a mixed reception; *Sydsvenska Dagbladet* disliked the plays and complained of "the acting style of these dilettantes, which is very different from what we are accustomed to seeing and hearing. (Among other things, we are used to hearing the actor speak louder than the prompter and not, as here, vice versa.)" But other newspapers, while complaining of "prolixity" and "lack of action," acknowledged the power of the writing, even though they found it "misdirected" and "unhealthy."[22] Strindberg had hoped to present further performances in Hälsingborg and Christiania, but that was plainly beyond their means. "I feel," he wrote to Siri on 17 March from Holte, "that we must now take stock—regather our strength after the battle—assess our resources—and find new ones —But this means that you must come home—and stay at home while I arrange money—we two must find our way back alone to that first atmosphere of hope and initiative . . . If we stay together and as long as we do that—everything will work out—and we are irresistible." From the absence of any letters from him to her over the next month, one must assume that she complied; it was to be a long and painful process for both of them to make the final break.

This ended Strindberg's first brief attempt to create an Experimental Theatre. The doubts of Edvard Brandes and other well-wishers as to the practicability of the enterprise had proved sadly justified. Brandes set out his objections in two letters he wrote to Strindberg later that year (7 and 23 June) in reply to an accusation by Strindberg that Brandes had destroyed his theatre:

> I destroy your theatre! I was your only conspirator. August Strindberg's worst enemy bears the same name as himself, and he will carry him whithersoever he goes in all his enterprises. You could have made yourself master of these three small countries had you used your talent wisely. You could have been a mighty man . . .
>
> Perhaps you forget the facts. You did not ask my advice when you decided to found an Experimental Theatre; nor, later, did you discuss with me the company and repertoire. I didn't even see you. You were quite right, since you didn't consider me a suitable adviser. When the whole thing was set up, you asked me for a play. I hadn't one, and anyway, to whom should I have given it? To a director of whose ability I knew nothing, and a company of whose inadequacy I was convinced? To you—who took not the least interest in your own theatre because you can never be interested in anything on this earth but yourself? . . . I did not lay your theatre in ruins; you never seriously worked at the enterprise, which consequently fell apart after the first experiment.
>
> I wish you all luck. You have so much in you. But your genius does not seem to comprehend the existence of us poor ordinary mortals.
>
> With every good wish,
Yours,
Edv. Brandes[23]

As though to underline his continuing admiration of Strindberg, Brandes wrote an article for the Swedish periodical *Ur Dagens Krönika* deploring the cold-shouldering of him by his compatriots, asserting: "His plays are and must remain classics," and provocatively concluding: "Is one sure that *The Father* will not be reckoned among his most brilliant works?"

Part Three

THE FIRST RETURN
(1889–1892)

Chapter Fifteen

A HUNGRY LANDSCAPE

Strindberg stayed in Holte for a further month, then left alone for Sweden and, after a few days in Malmö, proceeded to Stockholm, thus ending his six years of self-imposed exile. Someone who met him in Malmö for the first time was surprised to find him, at the age of forty, "young in appearance, well-proportioned and wiry; but the defiant head with the mighty brow and the brushed-up abundant chestnut hair bore in its lower half a most discordant contrast. Beneath the half-dreamy, half-sarcastic grey-blue eyes was a vulgar nose, and beneath the prominent cheekbones his cheeks were sunken, I think through the loss of his molars. But his mouth was attractive despite his discoloured and ill-shapen front teeth" —a reminder that no photograph exists of Strindberg with his mouth open. But the observer noted, as so many did, his "beautiful smile," and in that small gathering as the punch flowed he resembled "rather a merry carefree artist from Montmartre or the Quartier Latin than the misanthrope that most people supposed him to be."[1]

On 26 April 1889, two days after his arrival in Stockholm, he begged Siri to join him. "Siri, come to me with the children and I shall protect you! Protect you from my friends who want to save me by my losing you! Siri, Siri, how shall I get you here?" That afternoon he went out to Sandhamn in the skerries, which at once cast its old spell on him. "I am determined in spite of everything to stay in Sweden," he assured Siri two days later, "for the effect that the landscape of the skerries has made on me is ten times stronger than when I last saw it . . . People are glad I am home and want to win me back to the land which I love to distraction." Four days later: "If you don't return now when I send for you, with money, let the divorce go ahead at once, and I shall seek a new wife and new children, however dear the old ones have been."

He began a new novel set in the skerries, *By the Open Sea*, about a young scientist who is sent to improve fishery techniques among the primitive inhabitants, and on 1 May sent Albert Bonnier the first two chapters as security for a requested loan of 1,000 crowns to get his family and possessions from Denmark: "I shall gladly accept deserved or undeserved rebukes if only I can, after six dreadful years, settle peacefully again in my native land, where I shall surely end my restless days." He wrote Siri four very warm letters in four days, begging her to return to him. "I am dying slowly—and yet I cannot hate you . . . Come here with the children and let me live myself once more back into the illusion of happiness, then . . . die happily by your hand, not knowing when. I shall leave evidence that I have done it myself . . . Three months of summer by the sea under the birches with the children, and then— *finis*."[2]

Two days later he began another letter to her in a lyrical mood. "I am sitting in a fisherman's hut in the skerries, alone as in my student days, reliving the first archipelago memories of my youth. This grand silence, this beautiful, hungry landscape, the simple people who have no locks on their doors, this bad coffee, these sour pipes when I am out of cigarettes, this enforced half-voluntary celibacy, delight me so that my past married life seems almost unclean. When I think that this peace could be permanent if we parted . . . I would be willing to bid you a friendly farewell. I have no thoughts of remarrying, for I have emptied that bitter cup to the dregs." But, his daughter Karin relates, that letter then became so revolting that she destroyed it after her parents' death: "One insult follows another, . . . he begs her to keep away from him and at least let his name be unsullied by hers, he feels as though chained to filth . . . And so this curious missive ends: 'Leave me, evil woman, and I shall become good again to all men, even to you.'"[3] Yet the next day, as though oblivious of having penned all this, he wrote to her: "Life seems to smile on me again. Lindberg's enthusiasm for [the play of] *The People of Hemsö* increases; Albert B. has sent me 1,000 crowns, *Unsere Zeit* has published a glowing biography of Aug. Sg. [by Ola Hansson] . . . Welcome here and let us agree on one thing at least—the children. We have played out our game—let us think of those who come after us."[4] And the day after that he assured Heidenstam: "I feel 20 years younger, at rest, in peaceful, mad dreams, loathing every minute my memories of abroad."[5]

Within a few days, Siri and the children joined him at Runmarö, to which he had moved from nearby Sandhamn. The reason for their coming together seems to have been purely financial; they could not afford two establishments. On 29 May, August Lindberg staged the premiere of *The People of Hemsö* at Djurgårdsteatern in Stockholm. It had a fair reception. The critics regretted that the dramatisation reflected only the comic and not the tragic aspects of the novel (it ends with the wedding of Carlsson and the widow, thus omitting the last, tragic quarter), and complained that the language was often coarse and that it was less a play than an assembly of amusing characters. *Budkaflen* summed up the general reaction: "The novel was masterly, the play but a smudged mirror-image." "The more discriminating members of the public," declared *Post- och Inrikes Tidningar*, "must feel repelled by such crudities . . . which make one shrink in displeasure from even the better sections of the play." Nevertheless, *Dagens Nyheter* and *Stockholms Dagblad*, two of the leading dailies, praised it for its realism, and the acting and direction received praise greater than Lindberg had ever previously had in Stockholm.[6] But after the first three nights, attendance dropped calamitously, partly because of the unusually hot summer, and he had to withdraw it after only eight performances.[7] Strindberg took the failure philosophically; he had never believed in the novel's theatrical possibilities. "You see!" he wrote to Lindberg on 5 June. "When one is untrue to oneself, the result is shit."

The great Meiningen company visited Stockholm that month. They were already famous as the pioneers of a new and exciting method of stage presentation; Antoine and Stanislavsky have both described how the Meiningen productions opened their eyes to the possibility of a theatrical realism of which they had never dreamed. Ensemble acting, intelligent and searching characterisation, new ways with decor, crowds and lighting; all the things that Strindberg demanded from the theatre and admired in Antoine (except simplicity of decor) he could have seen for the price of a short boat trip from his island to Stockholm. What might he not have learned from them, and what plays might they not have inspired him to write? But he did not bother, any more than he bothered to see Eleonora Duse when she visited Stockholm twenty years later.

His new novel went slowly. "Creative writing nauseates me and I shall gradually go over to science," he told Ola Hansson on 6 July. "Practising that is an incomparable joy. But it doesn't make any money!" In the same letter he complained that lesser writers such as Geijerstam and Staaff were more admired than he. "Strindberg is dead, belongs to a past age, is a spent meteor." Six days later to his brother Axel: "I am probably written out . . . I dare say I shall survive for a few years; but during that time I must study and get myself a Danish doctorate, which only requires a thesis. And then, when I'm 50, apply for a Professorship." An article about him in *Dagens Nyheter* on 28 September announced that he "plans to complete a wide-ranging thesis with a view to becoming a Doctor of Philosophy at Uppsala," later correcting this to "not Uppsala, but Leipzig."

There was little comfort for him that summer apart from the company of his children. Albert Bonnier refused *Tschandala*, as did his nephew Isidor. *The Red Room* was published in German in Budapest, and *The People of Hemsö* was serialised as a novel, likewise in German, in the *Neue Freie Presse* in Vienna. *Men of the Skerries* appeared in Danish, but brought him only 120 crowns. He had to borrow again from Albert Bonnier on the strength of his new novel, though by the end of the year he had completed only five chapters. "Troublesome summer after the failure of *The People of Hemsö* [on stage]," he told Ola Hansson on 20 October. "Sterility, thoughts of retreat, unsuccessful begging. All doors shut, theatres and newspapers barred to me, envy, abuse, insults." Three days later, in reply to a request from Gustaf Wied for the balance of his salary as an actor, he detailed how little he was earning by his pen. "Fru Mann [his German translator], who sold *The People of Hemsö* to *Neue Freie Presse* for 900 crowns, kept 800 and gave me 100.* *Ny Jord* [which had published several essays and stories by him] paid nothing in the end [it had gone bankrupt]; *The Red Room*, to look further back, got me nothing for its serialisation in *Politiken*. The stage version of *The People of Hemsö* in Stockholm brought 150 crowns in royalties . . . Not a penny from Germany for *The Red Room*, *Getting Married*, *The Father*, etc." At least he received some praise in France. René Fleury lauded his plays in *Revue de l'Art Dramatique*; *Aftonbladet*, reporting this, expressed surprise that Fleury had dealt only with *The Father, Miss Julie* and *Creditors* rather than his earlier plays such as *The Secret of the Guild* and *Lucky Peter's Journey*, "which are of indisputable worth and at least as characteristic."[8]

In November, Strindberg moved with Siri and the children to Stock-

---

**The People of Hemsö* (as a novel) proved a lasting success in German. By 1919 Fru Mann's translation had sold 20,000 copies. Whether Strindberg received anything more than his original 100 crowns is uncertain.

holm, leasing a seventeenth-century house at Hornstull—supposed, like many others of that period, to have been Queen Christina's hunting-lodge—for the modest rental of 10 crowns a week. That month Albert Bonnier published *Among French Peasants*, which was well received; its openly anti-socialist arguments endeared it to the conservative press, and only the two left-wing dailies, *Arbetet* and *Social-Demokraten*, demurred. "An anti-socialist pamphlet," complained Hjalmar Branting in *Social-Demokraten*, adding with justification "his arguments are often paradoxical."[9] The descriptive passages show Strindberg's sharp eye for rustic character and landscape; the sociological comments read much less attractively. Bonnier also issued a miscellany of Strindberg's recent writings entitled *Published and Unpublished Works*, containing *Creditors*, *Pariah*, *Simoom*, a sequel poem to *Somnambulist Nights* and several essays, for which Strindberg received 325 crowns (400 crowns less 75 crowns for books purchased from Bonnier). *Stockholms Dagblad* published a report from its Vienna correspondent that the serialisation of *The People of Hemsö* in the *Neue Freie Presse* had been a success despite poor translation, many appreciative letters having been received from the paper's readers. But domestically, financially and creatively, 1889 had been a bad year.

By the Open Sea had ground to a halt—it was to take him over twelve months to complete, an unusual time for him—and it is a measure of his creative barrenness at this period that he could find nothing better to do than write more stories for his old collection *Swedish Destinies and Adventures* for Looström to publish in the summer. His marriage was dead, and his loneliness emerges in a sad little note to his brother Axel (11 January): "Do you think I could come to your mandolin club as a guitarist? I practised when I was abroad and could always sit in a corner, to get some diversion and be among people." Moneywise he had never been worse off. "I have brought financial embarrassment on both my brothers," he told Geijerstam on 16 January, "plundered Eva's [his servant's] savings book, am flooded with unpaid bills, cannot pay the children's school fees, have been drinking since 2 January, must associate with dubious persons who hang about alleyways and street corners, outside pawnshops and moneylenders, have in a word so degraded myself that I am giving up all hope of seeing a position in government service fall to me in the next ten years." Strindberg in government service! On 11 March: "Last night . . . I went to whores, in the same house where my marriage was celebrated. It was for me an exquisite pleasure to soil the most joyful memory that life should have to offer."

Yet that same month he had two successes in the theatre. On 15 March

the Dramatic Theatre in Stockholm staged *Master Olof,** not in its
original prose version but in the inferior verse text which they had
encouraged him to write eighteen years previously and then rejected.
Strindberg, for once attending a premiere, was called six times, garlanded
with two laurel wreaths and entertained as guest of honour at a public
supper attended by a hundred and fifty people. The reviews next morning
were unanimously favourable; even *Stockholms Dagblad* had to admit
that Sweden had no dramatist to match Strindberg, and J. A. Runström,
who a year earlier had damned *Miss Julie*, wrote a three-page survey of his
career in *Ny Illustrerad Tidning*, ending by wishing him "a calm day after
his long stormy morning." *Budkaflen* regretted the reactionary climate
which had hitherto prevailed in Sweden and wondered whether Strindberg's appetite for battle might have waned, but felt there was no real
danger of this; Strindberg was "created for storm" and was only temporarily seeking harbour. *Figaro* noted that at his curtain call his appearance
was "broad-shouldered and virile."[10] Any comfort this may have afforded
Strindberg seems to have been temporary, for ten days later he informed
Geijerstam: "I am in a state of nervous sickness—agoraphobia, persecution mania, paralysis."

Master Olof was performed fourteen times that spring, a fair run for so
serious a play, and on 25 March, *Creditors* and *Simoom* were performed
in a matinée double bill at the Swedish (formerly the New) Theatre.
They, too, were well received; *Aftonbladet* found *Creditors* "unreservedly
brilliant," *Dagens Nyheter* wrote, "No one can deny the genius of this
tragedy" and the newly founded *Stockholms-Tidningen* called it "a small
dramatic masterpiece."[11] Nevertheless, public interest was not reckoned

---

*On 1 July 1888, the Royal Theatre had gone private and become the Dramatic
Theatre, though it continued, for snobbish reasons, to be referred to by its old title. Since
then it has always been known as Dramaten, an abbreviation which had come into use
when it was still officially Royal. *Master Olof* was staged there despite the opposition of
Strindberg's old adversary Erik af Edholm, who had sacked him as an actor in 1869 and
rejected the original prose version of *Master Olof* in 1872. "I told the author then," he
now wrote to the head of the theatre, Gustaf Fredrikson, "my reasons for this refusal,
namely, that in my view religious questions are not suitable to be aired in a theatre, and I
still believe this. Since the author has, in addition, by his repulsive contributions to the
literature of filth, acquired a bad name among people of judgement, I think many would
be indignant to see it on the posters of Dramaten, and that the play's appeal would
seriously suffer and, despite the puffing by his political and literary associates, from whom
I surmise that the aforesaid pressure originates, that it would not enjoy many performances. I therefore advise against the acceptance of this play which, despite its obscurity
and longueurs, could be interesting, but no more." But Edholm's influence was on the
wane and his recommendation was overruled. (*Cf.* Stig Torsslow, *Dramatenaktörernas
republik*, Uppsala, 1975, pp. 281–90.)

sufficient to justify more than one further matinée. This was to be the pattern for the future: the historical plays, at any rate when they dealt with Swedish history, were to succeed where the plays with a modern setting would fail or at best achieve a very limited success.

That spring of 1890 Strindberg met a young student from Uppsala, Birger Mörner, with whom he was to have a lasting friendship and with whom, almost uniquely, he seems never to have seriously quarrelled. In an affectionate and perceptive memoir, Mörner recalled that his first and strongest impression was of "Strindberg's wonderful mouth. I have never seen anything like it, nor have I since. It could express anything, scorn, pride, distrust, more quickly and immediately than his speech or eyes. It could contract to a small dot, and expand into the most lovable and childishly kind smile that I have ever known. His glance was more difficult to analyse. It was piercing, and unusually bright, yet at the same time, from beneath that gigantic brow, suspicious, almost suggesting a shining rifle-barrel peering out from the loophole of a fortress." Later, seeing on the street a poster advertising the collected works of a minor writer of the time, Strindberg asked "Do you think my children will ever be able to read that August Strindberg's collected works have appeared?" and, on Mörner's replying in the affirmative, said "No, my boy. But perhaps my grandchildren." He also told Mörner of a dream that kept recurring. "He was seated in the back of a carriage driving full tilt, and close behind him ran a shining white horse which tried to bite him. He could see the yellow teeth glisten threateningly."[12]

"Between Fru Sg. and me," he told Geijerstam on 12 April, "there is nothing but spiritual indifference and physical repulsion." Yet still they took no steps towards a divorce. He began to read Knut Hamsun, whose anti-democratic sentiments appealed to him; Hamsun, unlike Strindberg, was to retain these feelings and to end as a supporter of Hitler even during and after the Nazi occupation of his country. Strindberg wrote a long letter on 12 April to Georg Brandes explaining his rejection of democracy and Christianity:

> As early as 1885, following my trial, I began to cut myself away from theism, deism and democracy . . . I also reconsidered socialism, in which form my old Christianity reappeared during my period of sickness, and purged myself of it . . . Then when I found in Nietzsche, whom I had partly anticipated, this whole movement formulated, I embraced his standpoint, and intend henceforth to experiment to see where that leads. The next consequence was an infinite loathing of Christianity which led to a love of Voltaire, not least in his capacity as a spiritual aristocrat. Hence, too, my reaction against petty realism, *Die Kleinkunst*, as expressed in [Becque's]

> soulless *Corbeaux* with its sympathy for the "little people," including
> Women; hence my apostasy from the Catholic Sisters-of-Mercy-
> worshippers Goncourt in *Soeur Philomène*. The extent to which I have
> changed direction manifests itself in my enthusiasm for Hamsun's book on
> America, in which all the opinions for which I have suffered near-death
> over the past five years are openly and frankly expressed. And it now seems to
> me that I was only forced down to democracy by the pressure of the masses
> from below and the treading of envy from above. I was born an aristocrat but
> have never had the money and opportunity to show it . . . So it must be my
> lot to be ground alive between these two millstones—as I have always been.

He had changed a lot since, only four years earlier, he had proudly
entitled his first volume of autobiography *The Son of a Servant*.

Brandes replied, warning him not to accept Nietzsche uncritically:
"There is an element in him which is fruitful, and another which leads
one's thoughts and emotions astray. As a poet, you are insufficiently
sceptical about philosophy." He added that he thought Strindberg
"experimented" too much with different viewpoints. [13] Strindberg replied
praising a remark Brandes had made that one should be fructified by
Nietzsche and then cleanse oneself of him, but defending his own
attitude with a confusion that reflected the division within him.

In April, Strindberg moved with Siri and the children to the skerries,
first to Värmdö and then Runmarö. "It is dead out here," he told Ola
Hansson on 24 April. "No interests, no questions. So I have limited
myself to drinking punch, going to parties and even dancing. This has
provided a kind of rest." It was the last time the family lived together, and
his second daughter, Greta, then nine, later recalled, shortly before his
death and her own, that during this summer he was "the gentlest and most
considerate father one could imagine." He had at this time a particular
interest in snakes. "He would catch them in a fly-net . . . Then he would
play the flute to them. They would stand on their tails and sway back and
forth in time to the music. I especially remember one time when he
caught a big adder which he brought home and put under a glass bowl. It
lived there for several days, fed with insects which Father caught." She
remembered how keen he was on gardening and how he even grew
melons, "which is not so usual in the skerries." [14]

He settled down grudgingly to complete his novel *By the Open Sea*, and
on 7 June he posted the manuscript to Karl Otto Bonnier. "It is," he
explained to Ola Hansson, "about the persecution of the strong individual
by the little people, who instinctively hate the strong . . . and defends the
indisputable right of the stronger (= the wiser) to oppress and use the
Little Ones as dung for their best good, which they do not understand.
Among the Little Ones I include the Little Ones up there who sit above us

with the acquiescence of the majority (the Little Ones) and the support of the army and the priests."[15] The novel, which had begun so promisingly, had changed course when he took it up again, and ends unconvincingly and disagreeably as a plea for the Superman; the islanders and even the girl with whom the hero has fallen in love turn out to be treacherous, and drive him to suicide. Nietzsche and Hamsun had proved an unfortunate influence; Strindberg was becoming one of those "unwanted disciples" whom Nietzsche had feared he would attract.

His misguided admiration of Nietzsche, coupled with his marital unhappiness, naturally led to an increasing hatred of Ibsen, the champion of human rights. "How ghastly," he complained to Ola Hansson on 10 July, "that Ibsen's sick and ageing spirit should oppress young Germany for a generation and that virile Germany should be Nora'd and sink into woman-worship . . . Now since you are a man you must see what Ibsen is: the poet of the women and consequently of the young. That is why he is hated by grown men! That is why I hate him, especially since he caused the young to rebel, together with their equals, the married women, against the lords and aristocrats of creation—men! I have now at the age of 41 begun at last to read Balzac. Voilà un homme! who writes for men." Six months later he was to declare that he was reading "no literature but Balzac . . . always Balzac!"[16]

A new quasi-scientific project now occurred to him: "a physical-geographical description of Sweden . . . to be dealt with in a comprehensive journey from Skania [in the south] to Lapland."[17] "I am so taken with my travel project," he wrote ten days later, "that I have decided to do it with no means beyond my ticket to Malmö, where I shall buy a stick and hike, making a nuisance of myself to, and borrowing from, newspaper editors and wandering actors . . . Master Olof, which is playing at Dramaten, must feed my family the while."[18] He planned a journey of three months and, surprisingly, managed to raise the money for it from well-wishers. But after six weeks, during which time he covered two and a half thousand miles, he returned exhausted to Stockholm.

The twelfth of October 1890 saw the first production of a Strindberg play outside Scandinavia; the Freie Bühne in Berlin, which Paul Schlenther and Otto Brahm had founded the previous year on the model of the Théâtre Libre, staged The Father. The title role was played by Emmanuel Reicher, who subsequently created several of Strindberg's leading characters in German. Social-Demokraten's Berlin correspondent noted "loud applause after Act One, hostile demonstrations during Acts Two and Three . . . The audience seemed in no way to understand the problem being debated on stage."[19] Politiken summed up the reaction: "Despite the German press's hostile criticism of the play's philosophy, all news-papers agree in recognising the great talent of the author, while asserting that the type of woman characterised by Laura is incomprehensible in Germany."[20]

Strindberg was still immersed in Balzac—"my only company," he told Ola Hansson on 13 October. He tried Tolstoy but found him less sympathetic. "Have read *Kreutzer Sonata*. Fine observations but rub-bishy reasoning; above all, I don't think the old man understood the philosophy or philogyny of love-hatred." (Among other things, Tolstoy recommended sexual abstinence.) Strindberg had to borrow another 700 crowns from Albert Bonnier, making a total of 3,650 crowns for the year.

He could not settle in Stockholm and, unusually for him so late in the year, went out to Brevik in the skerries. En route, on the steamer, he wrote to Siri on 6 November asking her to bring the children to live somewhere in the vicinity so that he could see them once a week. She found accommodation in the wing of an old manor house, Lemshaga, just outside Gustavsberg, an hour and a half's journey by horse from Brevik. "Since I shall never remarry," he assured her, "I am in no hurry to go through the scandal of a divorce. But if you want it, I am ready." His landlady at Brevik, Anna Dahlqvist, recalled his routine. He began his day at eight a.m. with an hour's walk, then breakfasted substantially on four boiled eggs, roast reindeer, cheese and coffee, after which he would work with the curtains drawn, since "he never liked to write by daylight . . . He asked me please to see that he changed his collars and to put out his socks, etc. I also had to remind him to brush his abundant bushy hair. 'I haven't time to bother about myself. Please look after me.'" She found him kind and courteous and was amazed when people asked her, "How can you put up with that dreadful creature?"[21]

On 7 November, Albert Bonnier published *By the Open Sea*, but it met with a chilly reception. It is a broken-backed book; as a modern critic has remarked, "the Strindberg who wrote the second half of the book was not the same as the one who wrote the first."[22] The Nietzschean figure of the early pages becomes, as its author had, uncertain, and longs for prayers and comfort. The girl he falls in love with never comes to life, and long before the end of the book one ceases to care what happens to either. Karl Warburg in *Handelstidning i Göteborg* observed that Strindberg meant to make his principal character sympathetic but failed because the great lacuna in Nietzsche's teaching is the absence of love and indifference to the welfare of one's fellow mortals. *Nya Dagligt Allehanda* felt that Borg was "a marionette constructed to serve the needs of Strindberg, Nietzsche & Co." Anna Branting in *Social-Demokraten* wrote that Strindberg had acquired so many seeds of thought from his new god that they had grown into a wild mass of thistles in his brain. *Aftonbladet* found Strindberg "more than ever subjective and embittered with the world. He attacks not only women but humanity in general, and not only Swedish society but every society." *Svenska Dagbladet* noted that nowhere does Strindberg hint that he disapproves of Borg, and "God preserve us from so self-important and egocentric a man."[23] With none of these judgements would one disagree. Yet this portrait of a man driven to extreme loneliness and paranoiacally isolating himself was to find at least one distinguished admirer in Franz Kafka.

The bad reviews renewed Strindberg's old dislike of Sweden, which a few months previously he had declared he never wished to leave again. "I have," he told Ola Hansson on 20 November, "begun to long so dreadfully for abroad."

Siri compounded his depression by telling him that she wished to go ahead with the divorce. He did not protest. "Incompatibility is sufficient ground," he wrote to her on 11 December, "and the court does not bother itself with who is to blame. So no accusations and no defence. *The children will go to you.*" In the same letter he says he is sending Karin the camera which one of his well-wishers gave him for his study trip around Sweden, with instructions on how to develop the film: "no need for a dark room at this time of year, since one can work in the evening in one's own room with a red lamp." He sought refuge from his unhappiness in various scientific experiments, such as trying to devise a method of colour photography, and investigating the content of nitrogen in milk. Birth control, too, attracted his attention. Brevik, he informed a friend, was overpopulated, "relatively, of course . . . The upper class has failed with pessaries and is in despair, the middle class has failed with withdrawal, and the lower class doesn't give a damn . . . Everyone asks my advice and I have nothing to suggest but expensive pessaries, since French letters are the dearest of all. But I have heard that some cheap Chinese pills are around . . . Some people have got wind of Tolstoy's rubbishy novel [*The Kreutzer Sonata*] and are considering abstinence and even divorce!"[24]

On 19 December 1890 Strindberg and Siri went together to see the pastor on Värmdö, the first stage towards the formal dissolution of their marriage. "After eight years of torment," he wrote to his cousin Oscar that afternoon, "my divorce is at last under way."

Life was hard for Siri and the children at Lemshaga that winter. There was little warmth in the old wooden house, they were poor and short of everything. The children's clothes were patched and they had grown out of them; Siri's own clothes had become threadbare and her worries had made her worn and thin. (A doctor diagnosed her the following spring as suffering from chronic lung catarrh, anaemia and general nervousness.)[25] She tried to supplement her small income by offering acting and language lessons and seeking work as a translator and proofreader, but without success. Karin remembered her sighing as she sat over her accounts with her pencil each evening. Of her father at this time, she says: "We children liked him in our way, but he frightened us." His expression told her when a storm was about to break, so that "the thought of losing him was no great grief to me." When Siri told her that they were to be divorced, Karin asked, "Won't Father ever come home again?" and when Siri replied, "Never," Karin was silent, feeling that she "could not show the sudden calm and peace which possessed me . . . It was not until many years later that I realised the tragedy underlying my happiness."[26] She recalled how the children had disliked visiting their father at Brevik that winter.[27]

On Christmas Day, Strindberg wrote to Ola Hansson an insane attack on various publishers. "Seligmann . . . is a louse-ridden cur whose doors I never open . . . I never visit Albert Bonnier, my ordinary publisher, but deal with him by post . . . Looström commissions translations and then refuses them without reason." How he was to keep two households going, he could not imagine. "Last year I made 2,000 crowns, and for the coming year the former Fru Strindberg demands 3,000 crowns for herself and the children under the threat (already part-fulfilled) that otherwise she will go into town and borrow the money." 1889 and 1890 had been bad years; 1891 promised to be even worse.

Chapter Sixteen

~~~~~~

THE END OF A MARRIAGE

In January 1891, an old adversary of Strindberg dramatically reappeared. Marie David joined Siri at Lemshaga. Although they had not met or even corresponded for five years, Siri had written to her to ask for a loan to help them through the winter, and Marie turned up without warning one snowy evening. She came, Karin remembered, "like the sun itself after the dark days that had passed. It was not only her kind help that brought a feeling of infinite relief into our home; her whole personality was like a bright and warming fire." She so enchanted the children that they clung to her wherever she went. She saved them from "total disaster," and she was to stay with them, on and off, for five years. [1]

On hearing of her arrival, Strindberg lost all self-control. He wrote on 29 January to the pastor before whom he and Siri had appeared, telling him that Marie was famous in Copenhagen "for such conduct as by Swedish law . . . is punishable by two years' imprisonment" [i.e., lesbianism], and that he had already been forced to seek police protection while in Denmark for his children, since Marie had tried to seduce them and their mother from him. He added that she was known to be "addicted to alcohol, to such a degree that her inebriation aroused public disquiet," and asked the pastor to have her ordered from the house, to forbid her further contact with the children, and to warn Siri that she was housing "a woman of bad repute." [2] Next day he wrote a hideous letter to Karl

Nordström: "The former Fru Sg. appeared before the church committee drunk and talked gibberish. Was silenced! Offered her hand in reconciliation. I refused it. She received a private warning from the priest, who calls her a whore. She tried to flirt with him . . . Now Fröken David is living with Fru Sg. and my children. I am condemned by the court to keep a lesbian menage until they die . . . I have thought of going to see the King."

He had mad ideas of supplementing his income by obtaining "a humble position which could keep me and my three children. E.g., a tutor in German to a family; reader of German, English, Italian and Scandinavian in a French ditto . . . if needs be, porter at a large hotel, needing to speak Fr. G. Eng It and Scand.; a porter earns good money . . . I must take a rest from writing—otherwise I am finished. I have now during the past year . . . taught myself to play solo on the guitar, beautiful adagios and andantinos and to accompany excellently. If I could now find a violinist, I could play at variety shows in duets for mandolin and guitar."[3]

His debts were heavy. He owed, he told Pehr Staaff (13 February), "nearly 3,000 crowns," over half of it to Albert Bonnier. He was still borrowing from their maid, Eva; by July he owed her 400 crowns.[4] He plotted further measures against Marie, commanding Karl Nordström: "Arrange for the following to be written in a woman's hand. 'Fröken David! Go! Strindberg is at this moment circulating in Stockholm copies of all your letters since your time at Grez. Your friend, B. L——g.' Then she will go! If Fru Sg. and the children leave with her, the pastor will have the children returned to me."[5] Remembering that Marie was partly Jewish, he began trying to find a publisher willing to consider an anti-Semitic book. "Who published *The End of Sodom* [a recent play by the German dramatist Hermann Sudermann, which Strindberg regarded as anti-Semitic]?" he asked Ola Hansson (20 February). "Which of the bigger [German] publishers are anti-Semites? Have they any magazine? And which powerful men are at the head? Are Hallberger and Kurschner [Stuttgart publishers] Jews?"

At the end of February, Marie returned to Paris. "David has left the house," Strindberg informed Karl Nordström on 4 March, "but that means I don't have the children. Fru Sg's lawyer has advised her not to send them to me on the ground that I could not maintain them. And now they are denied the right to visit me! And I may not visit them in the house where their mother lives." He then swung into a demented attack on Ibsen, whose *Hedda Gabler* had appeared three months earlier. "Two years ago on my way back to Sweden I met Herr and Fru Lange in Malmö. That night I told them much about my sad state . . . *Hedda*

Gabler is based on this! And it's obvious that Ibsen has just patched this together from gossip, not observed it at first hand . . . How can a man of talent be 'destroyed' because he gets drunk, whores and fights with the police? It seems to me that Ibsen realises that I shall inherit the crown when he is finished. (He hates me mortally and had the impertinence to refuse to contribute to Jacobsen's tombstone unless my name was struck off the list.)* And now the decrepit old troll seems to hand me the revolver a second time! But his shit will rebound on him. For I shall survive him and many others, and the day *The Father* kills *Hedda Gabler*, I shall stick that gun in the old troll's neck!"

Strindberg repeated the accusation in another letter four days later, to Ola Hansson, adding the charge that "Hedda Gabler is a bastard of Laura in *The Father* and Tekla in *Creditors.*" Querying whether Løvborg could have been destroyed by a night's drinking, he commented irrelevantly: "For my part, I have always felt refreshed by a good debauch!" On 10 March he wrote to Birger Mörner: "Do you now see that my seed has fallen into Ibsen's brain-pan—and fertilised! Now he carries my seed and is my uterus!" In the same letter: "As regards my scientific studies . . . I am working on big things but with small means; I blow my own glass, do my own soldering, and have to use all my inventive talent to turn a spinning wheel and a raincoat into a powerful electrical machine."

Mörner suggested editing a book about Strindberg, to contain tributes by well-known writers from Sweden and elsewhere. Strindberg was flattered, and asked that it should contain essays about him as a Sinologue, scientist and cultural historian as well as about his plays, novels and poetry. He also proposed that an anthology might be compiled of his various writings, "absolutely 'clean,' so that the book will be acceptable in families, schools and private circles of young people."[6] The latter project did not materialise, but the former did, though not for three years and only after many vicissitudes. New and increasingly improbable ways of supplementing his income occurred to him. "Most of all," he assured Mörner on 12 March, "I would like to be a lighthouse keeper . . . It provides food, lodging and clothes, and the opportunity for scientific investigations. I mean this seriously!"

In mid-March, Marie returned to Siri and the children. Fearful lest she might take them abroad, Strindberg wrote again to the church committee at Värmdö naming Marie as "a woman of bad repute" and begging that the children be removed from Siri's care and placed in the protection of

---

*The accusation about Ibsen and the tombstone was, of course, wholly without foundation.

other persons. This was refused, and on 24 March the court took the next formal step towards the final dissolution of the marriage by ordering that Strindberg and Siri be "divorced from bed and board" for a year, and that Strindberg should give Siri 100 crowns a month for the children's up-keep.

Mörner visited Strindberg at Brevik and found him in a state of extreme paranoia. He believed that other people lodging in the house were trying to poison him. Several times he had made chemical analyses of the food but could find nothing wrong with it. "And he had enemies who wanted to break into the house. So he had all the doors carefully bolted and tied up some of the locks with string and sealed them with wax." Another enemy had sent him a box of special cigarettes; whoever it was knew that he loved this brand but could not afford any but the cheapest, and had sent these so that once they were finished he would no longer be satisfied with humble ones. Mörner had the embarrassment of explaining to him that he had sent these himself but must have forgotten to enclose a covering note.[7]

Alarmed at Strindberg's mental condition, Mörner invited him to accompany him back to Lund for a short holiday. They arrived in Lund on 8 April. To Mörner's surprise, Strindberg seemed to have no desire to discuss literature or politics but only scientific matters ("I got a firm impression that he was brooding over not one but fifty problems simultaneously")[8] and wanted to talk only to scientists. He now met for the first time a young botanist named Bengt Lidforss, whom he was to see much of, and write enormous letters to, over the next few years. Lidforss, an admirer of Strindberg's plays and novels, was fascinated by some of Strindberg's theories but amazed at his ignorance of elementary prin-ciples, especially in chemistry, and at the blind frenzy of his feelings about women. He informed Lidforss that woman was no more than a bird's nest for man's eggs. "She can be replaced, dispensed with. One needs only a constant temperature of 37° and a suitable nourishment fluid. Then man will be emancipated. Completely!"[9] Nevertheless, Lid-forss was sufficiently intrigued to agree to help him with a scientific book which Strindberg had now begun to plan under the title of *Anti-barbarus*. Strindberg conceived this as a study of chemistry theories, but it was to change its character considerably before it was published more than two years later.

One morning Mörner was surprised to find Strindberg working at his desk in bedroom slippers and a top hat. He explained that he wore the latter merely to keep warm. "That is why I wear my hair as long as I conveniently can. My brain needs warmth to be able to work. I should like to be like the Bedouins and wear a turban wound twenty times round my head." Mörner noted how unusually small the lower half of his face was. "Strindberg was very proud of his cheekbones. He once told me that they were an inheritance from Lappish ancestors; he was from the wilderness, a Mongol."[10] On the subject of Ibsen, he told Mörner: "I always have a curious sensation when I read Ibsen. I think involuntarily of a pair of old, black trousers, somewhat shiny and with patches at the knees."[11]

After six days in Lund, Strindberg set off for a holiday in Paris, but got no farther than Copenhagen, where, he wrote to Mörner, "the street noises deadened my mind, caused persecution mania and general unrest, fear of and longing for the land where my children live."[12] He returned to Sweden and spent a few days with Ola Hansson and his wife, Laura, at Skurup in Skania. Laura, who had not met him before, noted the smallness of his feet and his short, dignified steps.[13] In the garden of the local hotel Strindberg met, and stroked the cheek of, the proprietor's baby niece, Fanny Falkner. Eighteen years later she was to become his fiancée.

That spring Strindberg wrote a number of letters to the servant, Eva Carlsson, asking her for information about Siri which he might use against her. Eva complied, and on 24 April Siri sacked her. The following day Eva presented a written statement to the church committee testifying that Siri had "shown herself both unskilful and uninterested in the bringing up of her children . . . allowed several days to pass without the children having lessons, partly because Fru Strindberg is very changeable in her moods and behaviour, probably because she consumes more beer and other even more intoxicating drinks than can be regarded as compatible with a sober way of life; partly because she keeps daily and even nightly company with a foreign woman who lives in her house and who clearly consumes even more strong drinks than Fru Strindberg and is consequently somewhat intoxicated, partly because Fru Strindberg one day towards the end of January said she intended to leave the children in the care of the above-mentioned woman."[14]

This statement sounds suspiciously as though it may have been dictated by Strindberg, the more so since the same day he wrote to Karl Nordström asking him to sign with others an affidavit to the pastor at Värmdö, to be worded thus: "The undersigned beg to attest that Fr. David, who is living in the home of the Strindberg children, should be regarded as a highly unsuitable companion for young girls, since Fr. David has acquired a reputation for drunkenness, which we the undersigned can confirm, since we ourselves have had opportunity to witness her disturbing behaviour and crude excesses when, during our sojourn abroad, we lived in the same place as Fr. David."

On 7 May, Strindberg presented these two testimonies to the church committee, together with further evidence from Nordström that Marie "drinks alcohol in ever-increasing quantities . . . cognac with her breakfast coffee, absinthe before lunch and cognac again throughout the day. She is constantly half intoxicated."[15] Strindberg also offered much evidence from various sources, all of it hearsay, about Marie's alleged lesbianism.

Astonishingly, this evidence seems to have convinced the church committee, who on 22 May ruled that Marie should cease all contact with Siri and the children. Strindberg was triumphant. But he had picked a formidable opponent. On 10 June, Marie sued Strindberg for libel, with a string of witnesses to support her. A Paris hotelier at whose establishment she had been living since the previous December except during her short visit to Sweden testified that she had always behaved with the utmost propriety, and no less than fifteen people at Grez signed a letter describing her as "a very proper lady of excellent habits . . . Far from having a bad reputation in Grez, she has given proof of her kindness and neighbourliness, and we remember her not with contempt but with respect." She also presented a letter from Edvard Brandes stating that, contrary to what Strindberg had suggested, he had "never expressed any adverse comment on your character, morals or conduct." Siri meanwhile presented five affidavits to rebut Eva Carlsson's evidence about Marie's supposedly bad influence on her and the children, including one from the children's former schoolteacher stating that they were well-educated and well-behaved, and another from her landlord at Lemshaga, a respected local figure named Eklund, who denounced Eva's testimony as "not truthful" and avowed that Siri was "a tender mother to her children, who behaves as a respectable woman should."[16]

One of those who had agreed to testify against Marie on Strindberg's behalf was an old lithographer named Pettersson, who had known her at Grez. On 24 June, Midsummer's Day, Marie went with two witnesses to a house where he was staying on the island of Runmarö, apparently to ask if he seriously held the views he had expressed about her, since they had been good friends in France. It so happened that Strindberg was, unknown to her, also living there. When she asked for Pettersson and the maid went to fetch him, Strindberg emerged instead and, as she later testified in court, "without the least cause commanded me immediately to leave his house, and when I replied that I wished to see someone else who was living in the house, which I did not know belonged to

Strindberg, he first gave me a hard push in the back which caused me to fall against the wall, then seized me violently by the shoulders and threw me headlong down the verandah steps." She consequently put in a new action against him for assault, demanding 1,000 crowns in damages, to which he retaliated by charging her with trespass. "My domestic misery seems to have reached a crisis," he wrote to a friend that evening. "In brief: today Fröken David was so shameless as to seek me out in my home and insult me; whereupon I literally threw her down two flights of steps, without her managing to kill herself. Then she went into the town and told everyone I was mad."[17] The two cases were set to be heard, together with Marie's action for libel, in September.

"A year's celibacy," he wrote to his cousin Gotthard Strindberg on 4 August, "has come close to robbing me of all masculine powers of decision and strength to act—I am almost back in my childhood—am fearful in broad daylight—fearful of travelling, fearful of staying—fearful of everything and everyone—so an end to celibacy—but no new bonds!" At the end of August he set off for the north of Sweden to complete research for his "physical-geographical description" of the country which he had begun the previous year. Anxious to assure himself of comfortable lodgings on his return (the archipelago becomes chilly in late September), he asked Gotthard to "be so kind as to advertise for four *furnished* rooms with kitchen at Djursholm [a newly built suburb north of Stockholm]. I shall be a hermit there but shall receive on Saturday evenings and Sundays (with tambourines). Abroad I shall die . . . To live in a hotel in Stockholm again will kill me, for I hate the city."[18] He wrote to his unmarried sister Elisabeth, eight years his junior, asking if she would come and keep house for him; that was why he needed the extra rooms.[19]

Marie's forthcoming actions weighed heavily on him. "I am so nervous," he informed Gotthard on 1 September from Sollefteå, "that, due to my revulsion against appearing publicly at dinner with the other guests, I have sometimes gone without food. In Åre I got up and went home from a lavish spread to a jug of milk." But there were also manic periods of high spirits, including "6 days and nights of continuous Roman *fin-de-siècle* orgies in Sundsvall, superb of their kind, with good wine and bad women."[20] He became friendly with the band leader in the Tivoli restaurant there, and on one occasion even took over the bass drum.[21] On 4 September, *Jämtlands-Posten* published a lively interview with him. Strindberg said that in the past ten years he had earned altogether about 100,000 crowns (about £600 a year). "I write a book a year and get 2–3,000 crowns for it but I need at least 6,000 crowns a year to keep myself and my family. And my travels and my expensive library cost a lot." He spoke of the things he loved: "The ring of tambourines and guitar music, coloured lights and beautiful women, jewels and expensive clothes . . . the wonders of our changing, colourful world fill me with an indescribable joy." Of his solitariness, he said: "I seek loneliness because I love people too much . . . I have to tear myself away from them, otherwise I can't work independently."[22]

If Strindberg was correctly reported, and there seems no reason to doubt it, it shows how exaggerated his complaints of poverty were. Ten thousand crowns was by no means a bad income in Scandinavia then. Ibsen's annual income during the eighties, when he was being widely performed in Europe (admittedly in sometimes pirated productions), averaged only a little more.[23] Ibsen also had a modest civil list pension, but he had to pay for the education of his son, who did not start earning until 1884. On this income Ibsen, in Italy and Germany, lived perfectly comfortably, so much so that he was regarded in Norway as a well-off man. If Strindberg had had any idea of economy, he could have managed easily, but he was always buying books, visiting restaurants, eating expensive food, drinking good wine and living in hotels.

On 7 September, the day before the court hearings at Värmdö, he broke off his trip, still without having seen the extreme north of Sweden, and went south to Djursholm. He had decided not to attend the hearings, nor even have his case put by a lawyer. Gotthard had not succeeded in finding him a house, so he lodged with a florist friend named Carl Sachs in the latter's summer villa, then took an attic room for a month and in October, when Sachs moved back to Stockholm, leased his villa.

On 8 September the three cases involving Strindberg and Marie David received a preliminary hearing at Värmdö. Since Strindberg did not appear, his case against Marie for trespass was dismissed and he was ordered to pay the costs of the two witnesses, totalling 41 crowns, plus a penalty of 10 crowns for his non-appearance. Marie's two cases were postponed until the following year.[24]

In Djursholm, Strindberg planned, of all things, another experimental theatre. It was, he explained to a painter, Richard Bergh, another of the circle at Grez, to be in a restaurant. "The room is 23 paces long and 9 broad, holds a couple of hundred people . . . New programme for the premiere. *Miss Julie*. Epilogue to *Master Olof*."[25] Not surprisingly, he could find no one to back this project. He tried to arrange a lecture on Swedish nature, based on his study trip to the north, but could excite no enthusiasm for this either. Instead he started work on a new play, his first in two and a half years. Ten years previously he had written a saga-play, *Lucky Peter's Journey*, and it had proved a commercial success. He now decided to attempt the genre again; he called his new work *The Keys of Heaven*. He told Birger Mörner (28 October) that he was writing it "for my children."

At a party given in Djursholm that autumn by an insurance agent, Sven Palme, Strindberg met for the first and only time a young man whose fame, both in and outside Sweden, was for some years to exceed his own. Sven Hedin was then twenty-six; five years earlier, he had wandered on horseback through Persia and Mesopotamia and had written a book about his adventures, illustrated by himself, which had earned him a world-wide reputation. (He was later to write equally vividly about Tibet, India, China and Mongolia, and was to end his days, like Knut Hamsun, as a passionate disciple of Hitler.) He had lately returned from Chinese Turkestan, and Strindberg questioned him closely about the country, surprising Hedin by his knowledge. "But it was not long before Strindberg switched to the subject which clearly interested him most, namely the Chinese language and its relationship with other languages. Our conversation now became more of a lecture than a dialogue . . . He talked with conviction and passion as though he had made some great linguistic discovery and put contemporary Sinological research to shame. He believed that he had found the key to all these riddles and in good time he would reveal to the scholarly world his revolutionary findings. He supported his theories with evidence based on a certain similarity of sound . . . I expressed doubts as to the correctness of his findings, on historical, geographical and ethnographical grounds. But such reasoning meant nothing to him; the similarity of sound overcame all arguments." Hedin found Strindberg "extremely sympathetic and friendly . . . Of the suspiciousness, envy and hatred which was later [*sic*] to embitter his life I found in that late autumn of 1891 no trace. The only memory I retain of Strindberg's personality is wholly attractive and I have often regretted that our paths crossed so briefly."[26]

Sven Palme's wife, Hanna, saw much of Strindberg at Djursholm. They went on long walks, and "he spoke mostly of *Antibarbarus*, of chemistry and gold-making, and the bad luck that gold brings." Her abiding memory was of an infinitely lonely man desperately longing for his children.[27]

On 17 October, *Arbetet* announced that Swedes in the United States were negotiating for Strindberg to make a lecture tour there, delivering fifty talks in areas with Scandinavian populations; but nothing came of this. Three days later he begged Fredrik Vult von Steijern, who had succeeded Rudolf Wall as editor of *Dagens Nyheter* and had been largely responsible for financing his study trip to the north, for a loan of 2,000 crowns, explaining that if he did not pay Siri her 100 crowns per month he would not be able to see the children each Sunday at his home. "Work? Yes, but there isn't a newspaper which will employ me, nor even a shop, much less any government department." Elisabeth had come to keep house for him, but he refused to do without his luxuries. Gotthard's wife, Martha, was another whom he asked for a loan: "Our most urgent need—for tobacco, will be relieved by 200 Brousse, 50 Khedive and 100 caporal—from Svensson at Stureplan, but you mustn't mention my name for I owe him 60 crowns. Elisabeth needs her luggage . . . and if we could have six decent handerchiefs and a woollen or silk scarf for me we can get through till Monday; though I think Elisabeth needs 5 crowns partly to get home, partly to get something to cook, for we live in a state of siege without a penny in the house."[28]

On 2 November he wrote more cheerfully to Vult von Steijern of plans for a play, a novel and a book of stories, "for now the plug is out and with a year's gathered strength things begin to flow." Ten days later he was in despair again. "Yesterday I wrote my last will and testament—for I was quite determined to shoot myself . . . All illusions regarding my play are absolutely finished. And all others too." Another nine days, and "my prospects in Paris are excellent, I have a publisher for my novel written in French [*A Madman's Defence*] . . . Am now selling Act 1 of my saga-play. Have sold my lecture on Swedish nature to *Aftonbladet*. Am also selling my library and instruments. Nothing left then but to go to the Hall of Anatomy and sell my corpse!" But news came that Mörner was having difficulty in interesting any publisher in his book of tributes to Strindberg, and *The Keys of Heaven*, after its promising start, was not going well. "I dragged myself up from my despair by the hair and wrote in a frenzy and three hectic sessions the second act—which I must now destroy! It is hollow, black, empty. Unworthy! I am spiritually and economically bankrupt."[29]

But at least he had his admirers abroad. Georg Brandes wrote a piece in *Berliner Tageblatt* calling him "for all his oddnesses and unpredictability the greatest of living Swedish authors and one of the most interesting writers in Europe." Knut Hamsun delivered a eulogy on him to the Liberal Society of Trondhejm, to an audience of six hundred, hailing him as a great poet of protest; a motion that he should be sent a telegram of homage was passed amid acclamation. Paul Ginisty acclaimed him, albeit mainly for his novels and stories, in *La République Française*.[30] And in Russia extracts from *The Son of a Servant*, some stories from *Men of the Skerries* and the novel *The People of Hemsö* had recently been published, without of course any payment to Strindberg. The last-named, serialised in a magazine, had proved an especial success.*

1892 began badly with his sister leaving him. "Elisabeth has gone," he told Gotthard's wife, Martha, on 2 January, "without saying where to. She left with taunts and slammed the door behind her. There is gratitude for you!" He finished his saga-play *The Keys of Heaven*, but August Lindberg, who had been enthusiastic about the first act, refused it —rightly, for the remaining four acts have little to commend them, being full of heavy-handed satire on Christianity, Swedish democracy, and the like. Other theatres were no more enthusiastic, and it had to wait seventy years for its unsuccessful Swedish premiere.

He wrote an article in French entitled "What is Russia?" which appeared in *La Nouvelle Revue* that January, a superficial piece declaring, among other things, that Russia needed no parliament since the Tsar "rules in accordance with the wishes of the majority." On 9 February *Handelstidningen i Göteborg* published an account of the article, noting that it made no mention of pogroms, famine or the persecution of all opposition, facts of which Strindberg, as a one-time supporter of the nihilists, must have been well aware. This further weakened his standing among the young Swedish writers, which had been so damaged by the publication of the second volume of *Getting Married*; Heidenstam and Levertin had by now replaced him as the leading figures. For his article, *La Nouvelle Revue* paid him 16 crowns 85 öre, less than £1.[31]

On 3 April, however, *Miss Julie* received its German premiere, when the Freie Bühne in Berlin, which eighteen months earlier had staged *The Father*, presented it for a single performance at the Residenztheater. The audience contained several distinguished literary figures, including Gerhart Hauptmann, and the cast was strong, with Rosa Bertens as Julie and Rudolf Rittner as Jean. Adolf Paul reported in *Dagens Nyheter* that the play was preceded by a "long and informative" lecture by Paul Schlenther† and, contrary to Strindberg's expressed wish, was split by an

---

*But few people in Russia thought of Strindberg as a dramatist until 1894 when a theatre magazine, *Artist*, printed an article on *The Father*, *Miss Julie* and *Creditors*. The first Russian performance of a Strindberg play was not until 1901. (*Cf.* Nils Åke Nilsson, "Strindberg på rysk scen," in *Meddelanden från Strindbergssällskapet*, Stockholm, December, 1956, pp. 5 ff.)

†It was as well that Strindberg was not present, for Schlenther ventured the criticism that "the author has not wholly succeeded in transmuting his ideas into the attitudes of the characters, and often puts his own words into their mouths. . . . The imperfect German translation is partly to blame. But the fault lies chiefly with the author, who has not yet quite achieved the perfection which we have so often seen from the master Henrik Ibsen." (Adolf Paul, *Min Strindbergsbok*, Stockholm, 1930, pp. 198–9. Paul's book reproduces the full text of Schlenther's lecture.)

interval; otherwise, the performance was "the best imaginable," and at its conclusion nothing but applause was heard; those who disapproved sat silent, which "is not customary at the Freie Bühne."

Strindberg wrote four one-act plays for Dramaten between March and May—*The First Warning, Debit and Credit, In the Face of Death* and *Motherly Love*—but these, too, were justifiably rejected. All save *Debit and Credit* stem from his hatred of Siri and are imbued with the same blind admiration of "the strong man" which led him to adulate the Tsar. *The First Warning* is about a jealous husband whose wife suddenly feels that she is growing old and becomes jealous herself, whereupon the husband nobly dispels her suspicions. *Debit and Credit*, a return to his old admiration of the Superman, concerns an explorer who returns to Sweden, finds his former friends unworthy of him and leaves them. *In the Face of Death* is a ludicrous melodrama about an old man with three daughters, whom he cannot support; he burns down his house with himself inside it so that they can claim the insurance. *Motherly Love* is not quite as bad as these; it shows a divorced mother of forty-two (Siri's age when he wrote it), her feminist companion and her twenty-year-old actress daughter. The mother keeps her daughter isolated lest she should hear good of her father; the daughter knows her father to be a good man, yet is unable to break free and remains the prisoner of the two older women. It contains three excellent roles without being a convincing play.*

Strindberg's financial position was now desperate. Some friends in Gothenburg tried to raise money to help him, "enough," as one of them wrote to another, "for him to be able to enjoy reasonable maintenance for three years."[32] They did not succeed that far, but at least helped him to survive these difficult months. As is the case with manic depressives, explosions of high spirits broke his gloom. An old friend who had not seen him for twenty-four years met him at a party and found him in splendid form. "He played skittles, danced a can-can and sang various songs with the others, including 'John Brown's Body.'"[33]

That spring Sweden nearly had its first chance to see *Miss Julie*. Some actors planned to present it, and Strindberg agreed to co-direct, but the project had to be abandoned because no actress could be found who would risk her reputation by appearing in the title role.[34] At the end of April, he went out to Dalarö in the skerries and devoted himself feverishly

---

Debit and Credit and *The First Warning* were at first accepted, and got as far as the first read-through, but were then dropped because the actors objected to some of the lines as immoral. (Torsslow, *op. cit.*, pp. 282–3.)

to science, painting and a new venture, sculpture. He painted over thirty canvases during the next few months, mainly seascapes, some of considerable accomplishment and power. Several of their titles reflect his loneliness: "The Recluse" (an isolated tree on the shore), "The Flying Dutchman," "The Flower by the Shore," "The Lonely Thistle," all small objects in or on the edge of a tumultuous sea. He wrote long and affectionate letters to his children:

8 May 1892

Beloved Karin!
I have now seen on the map where you are going to live, and as it isn't more than ½ kilometre from Sigtuna, I may take a temporary place in the town; if I can only see you all for a few hours without our being able to walk, fish, botanise and play together as before, it is hardly worth my moving completely . . . I shall get the camera things if you tell me what you need . . . Greta shall have her stove; but does she need a saucepan for it? . . . And Putte [Hans] his dog, though I have already bought him an electric machine which hums and buzzes worse than the steam machine.

Cheering news reached him in mid-June. One of his French translators, Moritz Prozor (a Lithuanian), wrote from St. Petersburg that M. de Veyran, the editor of the *Revue de l'Art Dramatique*, had informed him: "I have met M. Antoine. He has promised me that he will stage *Mademoiselle Julie* at the start of the season. He would rather introduce M. Strindberg to the French public through a one-act than a three-act play. Depending on the reception of *Mlle. Julie*, he will stage *The Father*." Thus, at third hand, did Strindberg receive the news which above all else he wished to hear. (It was to be another four and a half months before he heard from Antoine.) The news of the project aroused interest in Strindberg in Paris. In July the symbolist magazine *L'Ermitage* published an essay by Jean de Néthy on "The Woman Question in Recent Scandinavian Literature" containing a good deal about Strindberg, and in August, Arvède Barine (a pseudonym for Madame Vincens, who ran a celebrated literary salon) wrote a eulogy of *The Father* in the *Journal des Débats*.[35]

The *Revue de l'Art Dramatique* had published three articles about Strindberg during the spring and early summer by Charles de Casanove, and on 26 June Strindberg wrote him a letter setting out his views on marriage: "I love women and I adore children; although divorced, I recommend marriage as the only form of intercourse between the sexes. But I detest hermaphrodites, among whom I include emancipated women, and the war I have waged against M. Ibsen for ten [sic] years has cost me my wife, children, fortune, and career." He recommended Casanove to read *Creditors*—"my most mature work . . . You will find the vampire wife, charming, conceited, parasitical (spiritual trans- fusion!), loving (two men at once), tender, falsely maternal, in a phrase, woman as I see her!"

On 19 July the court at Värmdö announced its findings on Marie David's actions for libel and assault. Strindberg was found guilty on both charges, but was let off with comparatively light penalties. For the libel, he was fined 25 crowns, plus 50 crowns damages to her, and her costs, amounting to 209 crowns. For the assault he was fined 15 crowns, plus 120 crowns costs, but was not required to pay damages, since she had suffered no physical harm. Altogether, the fines and costs, including his own, totalled 498 crowns, a considerable burden to him, since he already had other debts to meet.[36] Marie must have been satisfied with the outcome; she did not need financial reparation, and had cleared her name.

It was as well for Strindberg that he did not counter-claim against her as he had originally intended, for one of his chief witnesses had admitted, albeit privately, that her testimony had been false. On 23 May, Eva Carlsson wrote to Siri asking her to forgive her for having lied. "This year I have come to know the master and realise I have been very unfair to Madam . . . The master went so cleverly about it that I believed everything he said . . . He wouldn't give me a receipt for the 200 crowns which you remember he borrowed from me, or my salary which is still owing. When I asked for a receipt he replied that they cannot be demanded between servant and master, but I am still working for him as the work is very easy and I am not well and have a lot of free time. But I am very sorry for all the harm I caused you by believing the master."[37]

In July he exhibited some of his paintings at a gallery named Birger Jarls Bazar. The critics were generally sympathetic. *Dagens Nyheter* found "fine and poetic understanding, surprising technical skill . . . The whole provides new and fascinating evidence of the restless creative talent of one of our most notable and gifted contemporaries." *Stockholms-Tidningen* likewise praised his "uncommon technical skill" and his poetic, if usually melancholic feeling for landscape, and *Nya Dagligt Allehanda* thought the paintings "interesting for their own sake . . . not just because of their authorship." Naturally, there were scoffers. "Strindberg is merely making fun of the public," wrote the weekly *Från Birger Jarls Stad*. "Whether 'Snow Fog at Sea' is meant to represent a dirty sheet hung up to dry or a new way of painting barn doors is hard to say." None of the paintings was sold during the exhibition, though afterwards a doctor named Gustaf

Brand declared himself interested and took eight, plus another two which Strindberg gratefully gave him. Unfortunately Brand defaulted on the payment, and Strindberg received only 200 crowns for the lot.[38]

To help pay his debts, he wrote on 25 July to the publisher Hugo Geber offering to translate Zola's novel *La Faute de l'Abbé Mouret*—"his most beautiful book—I don't want my name to appear as translator but would like to write as a preface an essay on Zola, whose works I am now rereading." Strindberg had often praised this novel and tried to get Swedish publishers to issue it, but Geber refused, like the rest, and it did not appear in Swedish until 1902. Reviewing his long list of rejections since the beginning of the year—*The Keys of Heaven*, the book on Swedish nature, the four one-act plays and now this—he wrote to Ola Hansson on 5 August: "It seems as though Sweden will get no peace until I am dead."

That late summer, alone on Dalarö, he wrote two more plays, and although they interested no one at the time, they have since come to be ranked among his best. *Playing with Fire* and *The Bond* are both one-acters of about the same length as *Miss Julie*, around ninety minutes. *Playing with Fire*, a black comedy, tells of six people on summer holiday, all of them, except the old mother, lusting after someone not their rightful partner. *The Bond* is a courtroom drama, based on the hearings at Värmdö: a couple seeking divorce and disputing the custody of their children. It is a bitter and moving reflection on how love can turn into hatred and the two can exist side by side; hatred, says one of the characters, is "the lining to the dress." It was to wait ten years for its premiere (in Germany, under Max Reinhardt's direction), and a further six years before it was staged in Sweden, at Strindberg's own Intimate Theatre. *Playing with Fire*, though it was performed briefly in 1893 in Berlin, was not seen in Sweden until 1907. According to Karin Strindberg, it was so obviously and libellously based on former friends that no theatre or publisher in Sweden would consider it.[39]

Despite the failure of his exhibition, Strindberg continued to paint and sculpt and to experiment in ever varying fields of science. "All my cooped-up lust," he wrote to his sculptor friend Per Hasselberg on 19 August, "seems to burst out in inventive ability and intelligent will. *L'homme chaste est fort* [The chaste man is strong] says—unexpectedly —Zola. But one can be so strong that one explodes." Three weeks later he wrote again to Hasselberg: "I cannot deny that the resurgence of my first youthful love, natural science, seems to me an autumn blossom which must flower before winter, just as my old flame, painting, must rise again before I die. What battles have I not fought to suppress this passion for research, which was ruining my writing and bringing my loved ones to ruin! But now it burns so as to consume me. To appease a bad conscience that survives from earlier days I am at the same time writing plays." He goes on to describe experiments he is making in colour photography. "Development with liquid is wrong; I shall develop with gases." He had constructed his own camera, replacing the lens and diaphragm with a disc of paper or metal in which he had bored a small hole. He concluded: "One day of life is so rich for me, divided between writing, science and painting, but I have no peace, for when my brain is emptied by work it becomes so empty that I am left nauseated by life."[40]

On 21 September 1892 his marriage with Siri was formally dissolved. They never saw each other again. Some of their acquaintances blamed Siri as much as Strindberg for the failure of their relationship, saying that he needed a calm and practical wife, like those of Bjørnson and Jonas Lie, who could have given him a home as Siri could not. But Karin, who loved both her parents, observed:

> Strindberg would never have chosen such a wife. Strindberg would never have fallen in love with Caroline [Bjørnson] or Thomasine [Lie], as is shown by his later involvements, all of which were with women who were artists. His nerves demanded radiance and stimulation, resistance to conquer, beauty to worship. Could one picture the woman who "should have been" Strindberg's wife, she would be roughly as follows: a beautiful, elegant and refined lady . . . stronger than he when he was weak, but weak when he wanted to feel that he was strong . . . witty in company, a subtle mistress, but also the pure virgin, the warm mother and the practical housewife. She would be endlessly patient, but not excessively so, since over-submissive patience "nauseated" him. She would understand him without seeing through him, ever ready to alter her views to meet his, yet at the same time she would be intelligent and have opinions of her own. She would be calm and harmonious, but lively and unpredictable so that she would not bore him. She would like the people he liked and become their "enemy" when he did . . . Many women have imagined that they could fill the role of Strindberg's wife. Three have failed. Not one in ten thousand would have succeeded.[41]

Karin added that, while Siri was repelled by Strindberg's hatred of feminism "which often spread to embrace the whole female sex," and by his embrace of what he believed to be Nietzscheanism, with its worship of the strong, contempt for "the small" and mockery of Christian ideals, what finally killed love in her was his "terrible suspiciousness"—opening her letters, laying traps for her, and constantly accusing her, not only to her face but to others, and thereby ruining her good name. Later she told Karin: "I was never unfaithful to your father."[42]

Karin painted an equally fond portrait of Strindberg. For all his cruelty, she said, "he had, when calm prevailed, a marvellously sensitive tenderness, a sympathy with all suffering things . . . He suffered more than balanced people when he reflected on his own shortcomings. He hardly ever verbally confessed that he had done wrong, but would admit it by some small action . . . Despite everything, he was a good man."[43]

That September the London *Fortnightly Review* published the first appreciation of Strindberg to be written by an Englishman—or rather, an Irishman. The author was Justin Huntly McCarthy, an improbable person to admire Strindberg; aged thirty-two, he had been a Member of Parliament since the age of twenty-four and was a popular historian and writer of romantic novels and plays, one of which, *If I Were King*, was to become a famous hit both in London and on Broadway and was later to be adapted into an even more popular musical, *The Vagabond King*. His analysis of Strindberg was, none the less, perceptive. "A new star," he began, "has arisen in the North . . . A very little while ago* the name of Strindberg was unknown in England . . . He deserves to be studied almost as much, if not quite as much, as Ibsen . . . Pessimism has its profound influence upon modern thought and modern action. If that phase of the thought and action of our age is to find its expression in the drama, it could scarcely be expressed more ably than it has been expressed by Strindberg." After summarising Strindberg's life and career to date, McCarthy continued: "He is intensely impulsive, passionately following high ideals, passionately fighting all that he holds unjust and evil in the world's business." Unlike some of Strindberg's admirers in Denmark and France, and indeed Sweden, McCarthy especially admired *The Father*, *Miss Julie* and *The Comrades*. "*The Father* is terrible . . . as *King Lear* is terrible. If Mr. Irving, who is about to put *King Lear* on the stage, would also put *Fadren* [sic] on the stage he would be rendering us simple service. But the convention which allows people to be base, comical, horrible, so long as they wear fancy costumes and belong to a past period, would shudder at the idea of showing that the passions of a Goneril or a Regan exist beneath the garments of the nineteenth century." Praising the preface to *Miss Julie*, McCarthy described the drama as "perhaps the most remarkable of all Strindberg's plays . . . Even the most persistent vaudevillist ought to be able to recognise the extraordinary power of *Fröken Julie*." He went on to quote a long passage in translation, presumably by

*Presumably a reference to Arvid Ahnfelt's article in the *Athenaeum* five years earlier (see p. 168).

himself. This article elicited a letter of thanks from Strindberg, to which McCarthy replied in French (4 November), asking for a signed copy of "your latest comedy [i.e., *Playing with Fire*] . . . I would prefer it in Swedish, which I read more easily than German." Strindberg obliged; and McCarthy responded by translating *The Father*, though his translation seems never to have been performed or published. *

Ola Hansson was now in Berlin and was actively promoting Strindberg's reputation through articles in the German press. He begged Strindberg to leave Sweden and settle in Berlin, assuring him that he had many admirers there and that several theatres were planning to stage his plays (which turned out to be true). Strindberg was tempted; but "How to get out of this Hell?" he asked Hansson on 13 September. "If I had the 200 marks I need for the journey, I would run . . . I have thought of becoming a photographer to save my talent! as an author!" Hansson and his wife started a fund to raise the money, and succeeded. On 30 September 1892, Strindberg left Sweden for Berlin to begin his second and, ultimately, more terrible exile.

---

*McCarthy's letters to Strindberg are in the Library of the Swedish Academy; Strindberg's letters to him seem not to have survived. Alix Grein, in her biography of her husband J. T. Grein (London, 1936), tells (pp. 127 ff.) how keen Grein was to stage *The Father* at his Independent Theatre in London, but he could find no one to play the Captain.

Part Four

THE WANDERER
(1892–1898)

Chapter Seventeen

~~~~~~

FRIDA

Strindberg arrived in Berlin on 1 October 1892. Ola and Laura Hansson met him at the station, together with a young Finnish writer and admirer, Adolf Paul, whost first impression of his idol was disappointing. "I had naturally expected to hear a resonant, virile voice—the voice of one crying in the wilderness. But it was squeaky, tired and peevish, somewhat strained even when he was trying to sound friendly. And that weak, almost feminine handshake!"[1] Strindberg's luggage comprised one small case of clothes and an enormous green flannel sack stuffed with manuscripts and fastened by a cord.[2]

The Hanssons had acquired a small flat for him in the same house as themselves in the neighbouring town of Friedrichshagen. Shortly after his arrival they gave a party for him, where he met another foreign admirer, the Polish writer Stanislaw Przybyszewski,* known to those who could not or would not pronounce his name as Stachu. Stachu was twenty-four, and though he, like Adolf Paul, was to become a hated enemy, his first impression of Strindberg was more favourable than the Finn's.

> He talked the whole evening, dazzled us with his astounding paradoxes, impressed us with his scientific theories, turned hitherto accepted scientific

*Pronounced Pshibishevski.

dogmas inside out. Of literature he spoke with contempt; only Balzac found favour in his eyes, and perhaps Zola, and he spoke of his private life with such unabashed frankness that we looked at each other in some embarrassment. At length—it was already morning—he took his guitar, from which he never allowed himself to be parted, and, standing on one leg, began to sing some Swedish songs.[3]

A new magazine, *Die Zukunft* (*The Future*), had just been founded by Maximilian Harden, one of the leading figures behind the Freie Bühne, which had staged *Miss Julie* in Berlin the preceding spring. Its first issue happened to appear on the day Strindberg arrived in the city, and Ola Hansson had arranged for it to include Strindberg's letter to him of 13 September detailing his financial plight, accompanied by a bitter commentary by Hansson on the way Sweden treated her writers. Strindberg professed embarrassment at its publication, protesting that it made him appear to be coming to Germany as a beggar, but it brought in contributions totalling 1,500 marks, which enabled him to pay off most of his debts without leaving him enough to support himself. In the absence of any substantial income from his writing he was to remain a beggar for some time, the more so since he was to abandon literature for science; his seven months in Berlin were to be devoted to chemistry, painting and photography. The respected *Magazin für die Literatur* also welcomed him with a lengthy article, announcing that three of his plays were shortly to be performed in Berlin and that he was planning to write in German to avoid the need of a translator, and expressing the hope that the "brilliant author" might find in Germany the peace and appreciation that had been denied him in his homeland.

Ironically, Strindberg now learned that one of his books had become something of a best seller in the United States. A young Gothenburg journalist, Gustaf Uddgren, recently returned from America, met him in Friedrichshagen. He tried to infect Strindberg with his own enthusiasm for Walt Whitman, but

> Strindberg was not interested. He was far more concerned to learn about the Red Indians whom I had met the previous summer in the Wild West. . . . In later years he thought he had discovered that the Indians were probably descended from the Phoenicians and that their language had its roots in Hebrew and Greek . . .
>
> I also told him of a success he had had out there in the unsophisticated United States. He was not popular among the Swedish Americans, they being mostly church people of the narrowest character, and so quite unappreciative of any critique of the established order of things . . . After reading *The Red Room*, most of those I spoke with had decided that Strindberg was a dangerous anarchist and had determined never to read

another line by him. . . . All the more curious that one of Strindberg's least popular works in Sweden, *The Swedish People*, had recently enjoyed a great success among these immigrants. This came about through the founder and sometime editor of [the Stockholm magazine] *Vikingen*, who had settled in Chicago as a publisher. He called himself, over there, Mr. Strand, and had taken it on himself to print the entire book and copy the illustrations. * This project had been so successful that *The Swedish People* had achieved wider sales in the States than any other book in Swedish except the Bible. The publisher had earned 20,000 dollars, and when I told him that Strindberg was living in the utmost poverty Mr. Strand declared that he would gladly send him 2,000 dollars if he could have his address. [4]

Unfortunately, the next book Strand published lost him all he had earned from *The Swedish People*, and Strindberg never received a cent. Uddgren adds: "The strongest impression I got of Strindberg at this time was how strangely happy he was at having forsworn creative writing." [5]

The Scandinavian artistic community in Berlin and their admirers gathered regularly in a small wine cellar at the corner of the Unter den Linden and Potsdamerstrasse. Its name was Türkes, after the proprietor, but because of a stuffed Bessarabian wine sack which it used as a sign and which resembled a pig, it came to be known as Zum Schwarzen Ferkel, the Black Porker. Stachu remembered it as "so small that scarcely twenty people could drink there at one time; by six in the evening there was not an inch to spare, so full had it become once Strindberg was a habitué." [6] Here Strindberg met for the first time a tall, controversial young painter approaching his twenty-ninth birthday, Edvard Munch.

A few weeks earlier, on 14 September, Munch had opened his second one-man exhibition in Christiania. It had been violently attacked by the critics, but it resulted in an invitation from the Verein Berliner Künstler to bring the exhibition to their city, and on 5 November it opened there, the first one-man exhibition in the society's fifty-year existence. † It created even more controversy in Berlin than it had in Christiania. Impressionism was virtually unknown there, and the reaction was one of shock and horror. *National-Zeitung* complained that every traditional value and ideal was ignored by "Blunch [sic] and his friends." Another critic demanded that the exhibition be closed immediately. The respected art historian Adolf Rosenberg in *Kunst-Chronik* called the paintings "naturalistic excesses, the like of which have never been seen in Berlin before." *Frankfurter Zeitung* published a headline "Art in Danger," and

---

*His real name was Algot Liljestrand, and his edition of *The Swedish People* was a photocopy of the Swedish one. (*Cf.* Torsten Eklund's note, *Brev*, IX, p. 306n.)

†Munch had shown four pictures at an exhibition in Munich in 1891, but they aroused so little interest that none of the critics mentioned him.

back home in Christiania, *Aftenposten* gloatingly headlined its report: "Munch's Berlin Fiasco." Hostile elements within the Berlin Artists' Society forced a general meeting six days after the opening at which, after a stormy debate, it was decided by 120 votes to 105 to close the exhibition.[7]

Munch's biographer Ragna Stang comments that this short-lived exhibition "set light to the glowing embers of discontent that smouldered beneath the surface of German art, bringing into the open the conflict between the traditionalists and the modernists."[8] Its effect on Strindberg was considerable. Like Munch, he disliked the French Impressionists, not for their method but for their subject matter of pretty dancers, picnics, people bathing or knitting, leading comfortable, untroubled bourgeois lives. Munch, like Strindberg and Knut Hamsun, who joined the Porker circle early in 1893, believed that art should depict the agony and suffering of human existence. Two years earlier, in an essay entitled "From the Subconscious Life of the Soul," Hamsun had written of the need to concern oneself with "the secret impulses that exist unheeded in the hidden areas of the soul, or the disorderly confusion of our senses . . . the fragile world of fantasy within us . . . the whisperings of our blood, the prayers of our bones."[9] The words could be used to describe almost any of Strindberg's major works.

In Munch, Strindberg found a kindred spirit of his own calibre, such as he had never been lucky enough to encounter before, if one excludes his brief correspondence with Nietzsche. He met him often that autumn and winter at the Black Porker, together with seven other gifted Norwegians: Hamsun, the sculptor Gustav Vigeland, the lyric poet Sigbjørn Obstfelder, the novelist Hans Jaeger, the dramatist Gunnar Heiberg, the composer Christian Sinding and the painter Christian Krohg. Also among the group were two distinguished German writers, the dramatist and novelist Hermann Sudermann and the young poet Richard Dehmel, then on the threshold of his breakthrough. Adolf Paul was trying to persuade his compatriot Jean Sibelius to join the circle, but unfortunately Sibelius did not come to Berlin until Strindberg had left.

Another habitué of the Black Porker was a young German doctor, Carl Ludwig Schleich, who was later to make his name as a pioneer of local anaesthesia. "On first meeting [Strindberg]," Schleich recalled, "I involuntarily thought: 'Beethoven!' His high brow had something in it of Prometheus; the same spirit spoke from his curiously sharp yet at the same time sorrowful grey-blue eyes, seemed to ruffle his unruly hair like flames and even expressed itself in his short, energetic moustache, which lent a defiant and ironic touch to his very soft and beautiful mouth, femininely small and finely pursed. Strindberg was of medium height and very well-built, with almost excessively muscular arms and legs. He had a broad chest, often proudly held high as though by a deep breath, and his monumental head was held consciously erect; one could not imagine it humbly bowed. His movements were almost pedantically measured and deliberate, stiffly grave. Those analysts who seek psychological traits in people's way of moving and holding themselves would soon have found in Strindberg's bodily rhythm that he lacked natural ease and flexibility. . . . He looked as though Thor's hammer would have seemed right in his hand, and only the weak lines of the mouth and the undersized lower jaw hinted at this strange man's extreme sensitivity and mimosa-like fragility."[10]

But the leading member of the circle was the Pole, Przybyszewski. He was not only a talented writer but a brilliant pianist who, Strindberg later wrote, "played Chopin, the great pieces, by heart like a gipsy. No beat, no tempo, and when he was drunk he would insert an explanatory passage here or there. He had arms like a gorilla and hands two feet long. In the end we discovered that he had just cobbled bits of Chopin together, but how!"[11] And Edvard Munch remembered Stachu's "large eyes burning in his pale face, young, enthusiastic, brimming over with courageous optimism."[12] Stachu lived with a Polish mistress, Martha Foerder, and their three children; but there was a darker side to his nature. He dabbled in black magic and proudly declared himself a Satanist.

In the Black Porker, Strindberg found himself among admirers of his work, and to be surrounded thus instead of being the object of public denunciation was a refreshing experience. "Fate seems for the moment to have wearied of persecuting me," he wrote to Birger Mörner on 5 November, and three days later he was able to tell Adolf Paul: "I have just received a letter from Antoine himself saying he will stage *Miss Julie* 'towards December,' i.e., this month. He is already into rehearsals." The premiere was in fact to be delayed until mid-January.

Sometimes Strindberg's fame led to bizarre incidents. Schleich tells how the Danish poet Holger Drachmann came to the Porker one day with "one of the most beautiful women I have ever seen. Hardly had she entered the crowded room . . . before she took a champagne glass, looked around and cried: 'Where is August Strindberg?' Everyone pointed to where he sat in a corner. 'Strindberg, come here and give me a kiss,' she said, stretching out her arms. Then an amazing thing happened. The famous woman-hater rose, gravely removed his coat, climbed over the table through all the bottles and glasses, and kissed this woman so vigorously and lengthily that Drachmann took out his watch and laconically remarked: 'Over two minutes!' At last the embrace was concluded, and Strindberg returned to his seat by the way he had come and put on his coat. No one could understand why he had removed it." Schleich adds that "Strindberg drank quietly and a great deal and could take surprising quantities, and never once did I see this remarkable and fascinating man lose his customary dignity."[13]

Adolf Paul noted that "though only 43 he looked at least 50 . . . a noticeable plumpness lent his movements a certain vicar-like dignity." He would not let a barber come near him; he shaved himself and cut his own hair. "If allowed to sit in peace for an hour and strum his tune and sing inaudible songs, toneless and wordless, he would suddenly become alive and as happy and cheeky as a street urchin, and one could not wish for a better drinking companion. But only if two or three of his closest friends formed the company. If it became too big or any 'outsider' came, his humour would sour and he would sit silent in his corner as menacing as a thundercloud, saying nothing, pulling at his moustache and drawing at his cigarette." Paul adds that Strindberg repeatedly declared, "I cannot lie," and if caught out would cheerfully say, "I am a poet."[14] Sometimes his old suspiciousness would manifest itself. A doctor named Asch who specialised in mental illnesses invited Strindberg to visit an asylum. Strindberg agreed but, halfway there, at Charlottenburg, jumped out of the train and caught the next one back to Berlin. "I was too clever for him," he told Adolf Paul triumphantly.[15]

Six weeks after his arrival, Strindberg fell out with the Hanssons. A shortage of letters led him to suspect, as he so often did, that his mail was being intercepted. A young German, Max Dauthendey, visiting the Hanssons, was surprised to find Strindberg standing in the garden in the November cold. When Dauthendey mentioned this to Laura Hansson she replied "red with anger: 'You see! Strindberg mistrusts everyone. He wants to take the letters from the postman himself. He won't even trust his best friends.' "[16] Przybyszewski completes the picture: "His brain began to whirl feverishly; he forgot the desperate appeals he had written to Ola Hansson and began to suspect that Hansson had seduced him to Germany—him, the great and famous man, hoping to grow in his shadow and become a famous writer too. He forgot that he had given Nietzsche's letters . . . to his brother in Stockholm for safe keeping and, since he could not find them, suspected that Laura Marholm [Hansson] had stolen them. . . . Hansson was, he was convinced, a deeply dubious intriguer and Laura a detective who had trailed him night and day to worm his deepest secrets from him and publish them in the Scandinavian press."[17]

In mid-November Strindberg left the Hanssons' and turned up at

Stachu's flat with only 50 pfennigs and his green sack of manuscripts, not even his clothes or his suitcase. Stachu organised a consortium of Strindberg's friends to help him, "and strangely, they were all Jews except three," namely, Dehmel, Schleich and Stachu himself. "For the time being, Strindberg's existence was assured. We found him a pretty room in a quiet hotel off the Unter den Linden, we bought him a suit and underwear . . . Each week Seligsohn [a Jewish sympathiser] came and paid the hotel bill, which was usually rather large—Strindberg denied himself nothing." A year later, when Strindberg had fallen out with Stachu, "he began to write to my friends that I was a Jew and my father the leader of a Jewish secret society."[18] Stachu noted when they went swimming the following summer Strindberg's "complete lack of body hair," and how when he combed his hair "one clearly heard an electric crackling, and in the dark his hair glowed with a phosphorescence like that of a cat when one rubs its fur." He says that Strindberg's German became more fluent the more he drank, so that "by the tenth toddy he was speaking pure literary German," and confirmed that when he sang to his guitar, as often happened at the Porker, he did so standing on one leg. He brooked no opposition; when people argued, he would reply "That's just metaphysics. I don't want to know about it."[19]

Strindberg stayed at the hotel on Neue Wilhelmstrasse for two weeks. Adolf Paul, who was also living there, tells that as at the Hanssons Strindberg busied himself with photography, painting (usually with a palette knife) and chemical experiments. He also got involved with a young Norwegian girl who was a guest. "The tragicomic husband has become the ridiculous lover," he explained in French to Stachu on 1 December, "and since that role is impossible for me, I am fleeing to the Black Porker to deaden my zoosperms with bad alcohol." At Paul's suggestion, he fled to Weimar, planning to proceed to Dresden. But Strindberg, unlike Goethe, found no joy in Weimar. "Came to the hotel and froze," he complained to Paul on 5 December. "Went to bed. Had no lunch, as I had foreseen, since I don't fancy keeping company with a head waiter, three waiters in tails, etc. Have lain here till now, 5:30 p.m., starving, frozen. Increasingly petrified at the idea of freezing to death in this room through being unable to press the bell and say what I want. I knew from previous experience that this would happen. Panic at the thought of the mounting bill paralyses me . . . I can hold out here for two days, no longer." Next day, again to Paul: "My fears are fully justified. I remember the German law which condemns to prison anyone who enters a hotel without the means to pay on first demand. Imagine if the manager sees that begging article in *Zukunft*! I am indignant that I let myself be fooled into this and didn't obey my instinct which is always right. Now I am painting." He peppered Paul with four similar letters in the next two days. Paul sent him 125 marks, which proved insufficient and elicited an ultimatum: "50 marks tomorrow morning and I shall return to Berlin." Paul obliged, and so Strindberg's brief and unhappy stay in Weimar ended. Dresden no longer tempted him and by 10 December he was back in Berlin.

There, good news from Sweden greeted him. Birger Mörner, who had found the task of editing the book of tributes to Strindberg too much for him, had handed over the task to the poet Gustaf Fröding, who had at last found a publisher for it, albeit a small provincial one in the town of Karlstad. ("Strindberg hopes for so much from this project," Fröding wrote to Georg Brandes. "He seems to regard it as a kind of reparation for all the ignominy he has suffered in Sweden.")[20] "Now I am about to be properly honoured, Ibsen being finished," Strindberg assured Mörner on 18 December, "but the contrast to my lack of funds is the more painful." Still, his painting, photography and chemical experiments and occasional evenings at the Porker filled his time agreeably. "I, a recluse," he wrote on 23 December to Karl August Tavaststjerna, a Finnish author whom he had met through Mörner, "am living a tremendously intensive life." Edvard Munch completed the almost full-length portrait of him which he had begun before the flight to Weimar, and gave it the place of honour, on an easel in the middle of the hall, when he re-opened his banned exhibition in the Equitablepalais. Jens Thiis, a young Norwegian friend of Munch (and later his biographer), records:

> I was standing before this painting one grey Christmas day when two men entered, both dressed in the blue silk raincoats with wide sleeves which were a fashion then. It was Munch and Strindberg . . . Strindberg made a decidedly sympathetic impression on me. There was a certain stylish Swedish *grandezza* in his manner which contrasted markedly with Munch's Norwegian straightforwardness, but the two got on excellently.[21]

On 7 January 1893, Hermann Sudermann's play *Heimat* (known in the English-speaking world as *Magda*) had its premiere in Berlin; it was to be a vehicle for many of the great actresses of the age, including Bernhardt, Duse and Mrs. Patrick Campbell. Afterwards there was a reception at the home of the critic Julius Elias, the friend and later the executor of Henrik Ibsen. Strindberg attended it; so did a twenty-year-old Austrian journalist, Maria Friedrike Cornelia Uhl, known as Frida. Her father, Friedrich Uhl, was the wealthy editor of two Vienna newspapers, *Wiener Abendpost* and the official court publication, *Amtliche K.u.K.*

Wiener Zeitung. To both of these Frida contributed literary and art criticism and drama reviews.

Forty years later Frida wrote a book about her relationship with Strindberg entitled (in English) *Marriage with Genius*. Her account needs to be treated with reserve; she adds to and cuts letters which she quotes and sometimes joins two or three letters into one, usually without indication. How much she romanticised is difficult to judge. But her writing, if often florid, is sometimes vivid, as in her description of their first meeting:

> . . . in the shadow emerges a startling new figure. He wears what seems a loose storm-coat. Stands there like a rugged grey rock. Stone grey the coat, stone grey the hair, hewn of grey stone the powerful head, of a flickering grey the iris of the eyes, grey are the hollows of his cheeks. Melancholy and romantic he stands there, a picture of the Flying Dutchman. I cannot turn my eyes away.
> Frau E. introduces him to me: "Herr August Strindberg."
> So that is he, the lover of Truth who unmasks the Lie. He who adores woman and lashes her for not being divine. . . .
> He steps out of the shadow. Seen now in the full light, he is most reassuringly real. . . . His hair is not grey but blond . . . the severity of his cheeks is softened by the gentleness of the mouth and coquettish little moustache . . . He carries his head high; there is power and dignity in his poise . . . The eyes are like doors of eternity. They are a deep sapphire blue, like the distant skies above my native mountains. I never knew or imagined that so much light could radiate from a human being. [22]

A month elapsed before they met again.

On the evening of 16 January 1893 the twice-postponed Paris premiere of *Miss Julie* at last took place at the Théâtre Libre. It shared a triple bill with a new play by Edmond de Goncourt, *À Bas le Progrès* (the main item of the evening), and a one-act curtain-raiser by Romain Coolus, *Le Ménage Brésil*. It was a curious combination, for Goncourt had made no secret of his hostility towards the new wave of Northern dramatists, and on the morning of the premiere he published a violent attack on them in *L'Echo de Paris*. "I am convinced," he concluded, "that one should leave the Slavonic [*sic*] fog to Russian and Norwegian minds and not attempt to force it into our clear heads . . . Great heavens, if we need a guiding star for our modern theatre, it is neither to Tolstoy nor to Ibsen that French thought should turn, but to . . . Beaumarchais." Goncourt lumped all Northern writers together; a note in his diary reveals that he thought Strindberg was a Dane. The irony of this is deepened by the fact that in his preface to *Miss Julie* Strindberg had declared that he had learned more from the Goncourt brothers' novels than from any other modern writers. "How curious!" Antoine wrote in his diary. "This great champion of life and truth, this revolutionary, talks of Swedes and Norwegians with the same lack of understanding, the same prejudice, as do his hated rivals Sarcey and Pessard."[23]

The evening was by no means an unqualified success. The Coolus play aroused little interest; *Miss Julie* evoked isolated whistles and hisses; and several people left before the end of the Goncourt. The press reaction to *Miss Julie* was mainly hostile. *La Liberté* called Strindberg a charlatan and humbug from the North Pole, and the *Revue des Deux Mondes* dismissed the play as "a Scandinavian indecency." Francisque Sarcey in *Le Temps* complained: "Every morning we are invited to admire some new exotic master. M. Strindberg is the latest." He found the "Norwegian [*sic*] genius" totally incomprehensible. Jules Lemaître wrote in *Journal des Débats* that the play was cooked "in a pseudo-Ibsen sauce," and concluded that Strindberg was "ten years behind the Norwegian, as he is behind us." Worst of all, Paul Ginisty, who had so praised Strindberg's novels and stories in *La République Française* eighteen months earlier, now wrote in the same magazine: "The disaster was total . . . Ibsen's work is shot through with poetry. M. Strindberg by contrast seems to wish to ban poetry from his theatre, eject it as something dangerously seductive and unworthy of one whose mind is full of bitter truths." Yet the play found half a dozen defenders. Ayraud-Degeorge in *L'Intransigeant* declared it a masterpiece, and an anonymous critic in *Revue d'Art Dramatique* wrote that it was not surprising that the Paris public had been repelled by the play's theme. "There is in this downfall of a girl of good family something which we find repellent and unacceptable. Yet accept this situation, and a magnificent drama unfolds before you. Never before has anyone so brilliantly dramatised the licentiousness and terror of a restless, wild and sick spirit." Antoine noted in his diary: "*Au fond, Mademoiselle Julie* has created an enormous sensation. Everything has gripped the public—the subject, the background, the concentration into a single act of ninety minutes of enough action to fill a full-length French play. Admittedly, there was laughter and protests, but one found oneself in the presence of something completely new."[24]

Strindberg spent the evening in Berlin as a guest, with his fellow Scandinavian writers, of the Freie Literarische Gesellschaft. He read one of his stories in German, inaudibly as at all his public readings, "in a tired, monotonous voice," recalled Adolf Paul, "like a schoolboy reading his lesson."[25] "No one understood a word," Strindberg reported to Karl August Tavaststjerna five days later, "but we were loudly cheered.

Drachmann wore velvet tails and the Order of Dannebrog and made us seem respectable."

On 22 January, Strindberg's forty-fourth birthday, *Creditors* was presented at the Residenztheater in Berlin as part of a triple bill. It was strongly cast, with Rosa Bertens, Rudolf Rittner (as Adolf) and Josef Jarno; the last-named was to direct the Theater in der Josefstadt in Vienna for a quarter of a century from 1899, and was to be a great pioneer of Strindberg in Austria. "The theatre did not really believe in the play," Adolf Paul remembered. "At the read-through the actors shook their heads and expressed grave doubts as to the theatrical viability of the three long dialogues which comprise it. At the dress rehearsal, which Strindberg attended, doubts remained . . . But once the curtain rose on the opening night, victory was assured . . . Whether or not the audience fully comprehended the powerful content, it was held speechless by the elemental power which reverberated across the footlights. When the curtain fell, a storm of applause broke forth which seemed as if it would never end, and Lautenburg [the director] had to take repeated calls and thank the audience on behalf of the absent author."[26] As was his custom, Strindberg refused to watch his play in the presence of an audience. Lautenburg, together with, among others, Otto Brahm and Paul Schlenther, the founding spirits of the Freie Bühne, tracked him down in the restaurant where he had hidden and assured him that the production would earn him at least 30,000 marks. It ran, indeed, for seventy-one performances and was invited at the end of March for a special gala performance in Vienna, where it was equally acclaimed. But Lautenburg's prediction proved over-optimistic. At the end of the Berlin run he demanded the German rights to the play for a lump sum of 3,000 marks. Strindberg at first agreed, then changed his mind and returned the money. Lautenburg, piqued, now reneged on an offer he had made after the premiere to stage *The Comrades*. So even this success turned sour.

These disappointments, however, lay in the future. For the time being, things seemed rosier than ever before. On 18 January J. T. Grein, the founder of the lively Independent Theatre in London, where in March 1891 he had presented the sensational British premiere of Ibsen's *Ghosts*, wrote offering to stage *The Father* "in private, for I fear the play will never pass the censorship . . . during the course of this year with a very good cast."[27] Strindberg was ecstatic. "This New Year of 1893, after *l'année terrible* 92," he wrote to Birger Mörner on 26 January,

> seems likely to prove a turning-point in my tragicomic life. In Berlin I am decidedly up through *Creditors*, and am so sure of my two new plays, *The*

Bond and *Playing with Fire*, which are soon to be done at the Lessing Theater, that I regard myself as "saved"; economically too. Last Sunday there was a moment in the Rathskeller, where we dined in a large mixed gathering after the performance and I was toasted, when in a rebirth of childlike and Christian humility I wondered whether I had deserved this good fortune, so that I almost began to doubt the genuineness of the acclaim and sympathy which everyone poured over me. I became almost sentimental, perhaps not least because I had not dined for three days and had been walking around in summer socks in the fearful cold. Odd, lovable nation, this, that abases itself before foreign talent, honest, irresistible, without envy.

We—Drachmann, Heiberg, Munch, Paul and I—attended a banquet recently at Leman's,* Suderman's [sic] publisher, the day after Suderman's premiere [of *Magda* on 7 January]. Drachmann proposed a toast to Suderman—the great Suderman—and Suderman, thanking him, acknowledged the big debt he owed to the Scandinavians, his teachers . . . From Paris I hear that . . . *Mlle Julie* . . . has for eight whole days—a long time in Paris—been the main subject of argument in conversation and the press; much enthusiasm and much hatred . . . My name is made there . . . In London I have an offer to stage *The Father*, and an agent is taking my plays for England and the colonies . . . In Rome my best plays are being translated into Italian; so I am hard on Ibsen's heels . . . I probably won't see Sweden again for a long time. This is a good place to be.

On 30 January he wrote to Karin, Greta and Hans: "My dear children, this time fortune has favoured me. I have been played in Berlin and Paris which will mean us getting a lot of money so that you can look forward to an adolescence as calm as your childhood was when you were secure without knowing how difficult things often were for your parents. But I must stay abroad to complete what I have begun and to make sure that people don't take our money from us. But this will not prevent my coming home to you . . . I may visit Stockholm as early as Easter." He added proudly that since leaving Sweden he had sent them more than 1,000 crowns. The letter reached them in Finland, where they had gone with Siri for a holiday. But events during the next few weeks were to result in a drastic change of plan, and were to cause Siri to settle in Finland for the rest of her life.

Frida had not seen him since their first encounter, but could not forget him. "I hear about him every day. The whole town is telling anecdotes of him. He sounds through Berlin like a clarion."[28] Otto Neumann-Hofer, the editor of *Das Magazin für die Literatur*, took her to see Strindberg "on his own ground" at the Black Porker, and the experience depressed her.

*Strindberg meant Felix Lehmann.

Bottles line the walls. Tables and again tables. Thick cigarette smoke
and loud voices. Then, suddenly, silence. I see Strindberg sitting behind a
big table and talking. I cannot catch his words, his voice is low and quiet.
He holds himself erect, his head high, sitting squarely and heavily, almost
majestic in his ponderousness . . . A dark slim young man jumps up.
"That's the insurance agent, Richard Dehmel." Otto smiles. "He does
accounts in the morning and composes poems at night." He does not think
of accounts now! His cane lashes through the air, cuts off the golden neck of
a green bottle. The guests are jubilant. Champagne sparkles in the glasses,
champagne streams across the floor . . . Strindberg is presiding over this
Witches' Sabbath as calmly as if it were a committee meeting. The
handsome young Pole, Stanislaw Przybyszewski, is sitting to his right in the
attitude of the favourite disciple at the Last Supper. He is the only one who
has not a wine glass but a water glass standing in front of him. This large
glass is full to the brim with cognac. He is bent forward, his eyes riveted on
the glass; greyish-bluish, slanted, half-closed eyes, a greyish skin, a thin
blond Henry IV beard; on his blood-red, finely chiselled lips is a voluptuous
and tortured smile. Now he comes closer and slowly kisses the two hands of
August Strindberg, who, surprised, and with a blush, withdraws them.
"What do we want here?" I ask, and turn away, sad and depressed . . .
Otto gently guides me out into the street.[29]

Neumann-Hofer told her how he had been "present at a bout a few
nights ago. It was 6 in the morning when I took three of the guests home,
dead drunk. Strindberg had stayed behind and I felt uneasy about him
. . . I called on him after I had had a little sleep. I was ready to fetch a
doctor . . . He had not even been to bed. He sat at his writing desk in his
grey flannel jacket with his velvet cap on his head—he says his brains
need warmth—and was busy noting down some fresh mathematical
dogmas which had occurred to him, just accidentally, on his way home.
His hand was firm and his writing stood out like an etching on the
parchment paper he is using. Quite close to him on the floor rested his
famous 'green bag'—ready for a new conception."[30]

On 5 February, Neumann-Hofer and his American wife, Annie,
invited Frida to a small dinner party at which Strindberg was the guest of
honour. She was hurt to discover that he had no recollection of having
met her before. But he escorted her home and accepted an invitation to
dine with her next evening in her flat. "He likes the food, he likes the
wine, he likes my harmless prattle."[31] She gave him a rose, which he left
behind. The following day he wrote his first letter to her, in French,
thanking her for the evening and admitting that "I did not forget the rose,
but left it behind on purpose, so as to have an excuse for calling to get it
next day, although I lacked the courage to do so when the time came."
She invited him to dinner again, on 11 February, this time at a restaurant,

but when she tried to pay he took offence and "throws down a banknote worth three times the amount with an impatient and final gesture."[32]

He was sitting for his portrait to two Norwegian painters, Christian Krohg* and Severin Segelcke, and was being sculpted by Max Levi. "All goes well for me," he informed Birger Mörner on 19 February. ". . . Strindberg is discussed here in societies and clubs and is quoted in newspapers and magazines. Offers of publication and performance, requests for autographs and photographs . . . Now Krohg is painting my portrait, grandly . . . I live here in the centre of Berlin, a life so rich and intensive that I sometimes think I shall crack, but I don't. I am simply renewed." News of his success filtered back to Sweden. Gustaf Fröding, who had worked so hard to find a publisher for the *Festschrift*, wrote to Georg Brandes: "The book now begins to seem less necessary, since Strindberg appears to be finding recognition without our help. But one must complete what one has begun."[33] By the time it appeared the following spring, Strindberg's star had already begun to wane.

On 20 February, Strindberg wrote to Frida, again in French: "I do not know how to tell you how our walk in the Park has tamed the bad spirits which persecute me . . . Now I must see you every day at the risk of compromising you, and supposing that I have compromised you—be sure of this—I would be ready to give you the honourable satisfaction that one expects from a man of honour. Does that suffice?" On 26 February: "I would like to walk by your side, always, forever, beneath the trees, beside the sea, up hill and down dale." He still addressed her formally as *Chère Mademoiselle*. On 1 March he wrote to her for the first time in German, the next day in mixed German and French. On 4 March he sent her a proposal of marriage. Meeting him that evening, she handed him a letter in which she declined, explaining that she was in no position to feel anything resembling passion or love. Fearing a desperate reaction, she gave him a hasty kiss as they parted before he could read her reply.[34] A few days later she left to visit her father in Austria.

Bewildered by all this, Strindberg wrote to her almost daily, sometimes oftener; he sent her nineteen letters between 20 February and 16 March. In his frustration he returned to the Black Porker, which Frida had begged

---

*Krohg painted seven portraits of Strindberg at this time, one of which was bought in 1895 by, of all people, Henrik Ibsen, who hung it in his study, explaining to astonished acquaintances that it helped him to work to have "that madman staring down at me." Ibsen especially liked the "demonic eyes," and once remarked, "He is my mortal enemy, and shall hang there and watch while I write." August Lindberg tells how Ibsen, never having met Strindberg, once asked him if it was a good likeness, and "in a whisper that he perhaps did not intend to be heard, muttered, 'A remarkable man!'"[35]

him to stop visiting and which had begun to bore him. A new and striking girl had joined the circle, a twenty-five-year-old Norwegian music student named Dagny Juel. Edvard Munch, who had not met her until now, was to use her as his model in several of his most famous paintings. A writer of some talent, tall, thin and red-haired, she drank quantities of absinthe without noticeable effect and was an exponent of free love; she rapidly acquired the nickname Aspasia, after the famous mistress of Pericles. "She was by no means beautiful," one of the Porker circle remembered, "yet few women were more seductive . . . A much too large mouth with narrow lips, which gleamed so redly over her pointed weasel teeth that those who did not know her swore they were artificially coloured, which was not the case . . . She needed only to look at a man, and put her hand on his arm, and he at once found himself able to express something he had long carried within him without previously having been able to give it form."[36] Whether she was ever Munch's mistress is doubtful; the absence of any reference to this in his diaries, which tell frankly of his sex life, and in his letters to her, suggest that she was not.[37] But she quickly became Przybyszewski's mistress and now, briefly, Strindberg's, though the affair was to end, like so many of his relationships, in his abusing and denigrating her.

Frida gives an account of this affair which, since she had it from Strindberg and neither was the most reliable of witnesses, needs to be regarded with double suspicion. But it is too good a story not to be repeated:

> It had started by his talking to her about me. She, too, was a woman, and he had spoken to her about me for hours and hours . . . They had been drinking, beer, wine, toddy, Swedish punch, absinthe. He had not been drunk, he declared, he never was drunk; but he had not been sober either. In a semi-fog he had taken her home—"Strindberg knows what's proper!" She had invited him in and he had gone with her to her room [at a hotel] . . . When his senses had cooled, he became conscious. He suddenly found himself in bed in an unknown, untidy room. He caught sight of hairpins on the carpet and of ugly powder spots on a drab red plush sofa. Disgust rose in him. Then he perceived the woman lying by his side. He was unable to reason, he obeyed an urge which ordered him to break away from the vulgar situation. He jumped up. He dragged Aspasia out of bed and pushed her out of the room and bolted the door. He had lived in so many hotels during the last few years that it had not occurred to him that he had done all this not in his own room but in Aspasia's. Physically and morally relieved, he had again gone to bed and slept until late in the day . . . "In the morning, she gave me another rendezvous for the next night."[38]

Strindberg (so he told Frida, or so she claims) went to the rendezvous, but brought Schleich with him. In the *chambre séparée* where Aspasia greeted them, there was a piano. "Schleich had one weakness, his tenor voice. Aspasia was a great accompanist. The two made music like angels." Strindberg slipped away. "She and Schleich made music again yesterday and they are making music again tonight. They will continue for quite a while yet, until the fear of his wife possesses him. But by that time she will have found another singer."[39]

It seems likely, however, that Strindberg's affair with Dagny was less brief than Frida thought. Later that spring Strindberg wrote to Birger Mörner that Dagny had been his mistress for three weeks.[40] And the German art historian Julius Meier-Graefe, after describing Dagny as having "the figure of a 14th-century Madonna and a laugh that drove men wild . . . She drank absinthe by the litre without getting drunk," recalled occasions when "One man would dance with Ducha [i.e., Dagny], while the other two sat at the table and watched; one would be Munch and the other, as often as not, Strindberg. The four friends there were all in love with Ducha, each in his own way, but they never let it show. Stachu was perfectly happy with the situation. Munch called Ducha 'Lady,' and always addressed her very politely and correctly, even when he was drunk." Stachu would hold forth on "pathological eroticism . . . Strindberg spoke about chemical analysis, while Munch just sat and listened."[41] The fourth "friend" was Dr. Schleich.

Frida as yet knew nothing of all this, and on 12 March, in response to Strindberg's volley of adoring letters, she wrote to him suggesting that they should become engaged "without a ring and without witnesses," but should delay the announcement until his financial situation was stable and his debts paid, which she thought should not take longer than six months. Strindberg agreed (16 March), "provided you let me remain independent." By now she had returned to Berlin and replied the same day: "As regards your independence, my dear friend, of course you will *always* have that—without limit. You are free to do what you please. Above all, do not feel obliged to remain faithful to me."[42]

On her return to Berlin, she set about reforming his wardrobe, and Gustaf Uddgren noted with some horror his new appearance in "large check patterns, trousers with high turn-ups, a short yellow-grey overcoat, a garish cravat, a grotesque walking stick and a shiny top hat which he had difficulty in keeping on his abundant lion's mane."[43] Strindberg meanwhile described his new fiancée to Adolf Paul, now back in Finland, as "a completely new type for me—gentle, buxom, dark. And an utter rogue!"[44] Rumours of their engagement appeared in the Swedish press, and on 27 March, Strindberg told Siri, adding that it would probably not be officially announced until the autumn and assuring her that he would not neglect his obligations to the children. It was the last message that passed directly between them; henceforth he wrote only to the children. That spring, Marie David went to live with Siri in Helsinki.

One unfortunate result of this secrecy was that Frida's father first learned of the engagement through a newspaper. His reaction was such that Frida panicked and bombarded Strindberg with telegrams blaming him for leaking the news and suggesting that they break it off.[45] But Frida's mother persuaded Friedrich Uhl to relent, and on 11 April they exchanged rings and became officially betrothed. Next day they had a row and she returned his ring, writing: "It seems to me that after yesterday's scene we have no more to say to each other. You did not need to demonstrate this in so blatant a manner, such as I would not have thought possible, and fit only for the cheapest of women."[46] Frida's eldest sister, Marie Weyr, who had come to Berlin for the wedding bringing with her a dowry of 4,000 marks,[47] sent her husband, a sculptor and professor in Vienna, a description of her future brother-in-law:

> Strindberg is fundamentally a noble person, good to the point of weakness. What his heart says is gold, but as a result of sad experiences he has learned to follow his head, which leads him astray and is filled with fixed obsessions. Physically he is very healthy, has no bad habits, is said to have lived like a monk since his divorce[!] and long before it. For ten years he has not read what the newspapers write about him, reads no books but scientific works or Balzac and the French psychologists. He cannot do business with any publisher or theatre manager, it makes him nervous. So he has hardly earned anything up to now. He has piles of manuscripts lying around, completed works, for he has always been incredibly industrious, but he doesn't know what to do with them . . . When he isn't writing, he paints, as well as he writes. He has sold some paintings but has never had any training. He sculpts, too, plays the guitar charmingly, he can do anything he sets his hand to, could create a paradise on a desert island, but is overwhelmed by a mixture of gaucheness, fear of people and of mockery and above all shyness. He doesn't understand jokes, never jokes himself, thinks himself perpetually persecuted and despised, cannot walk on the shady side of the street, speaks eight languages including Chinese, most of them badly, but writes them fluently, except German, which he has the most difficulty with, but at the same time he has an obsession to "reform" German and is the despair of his translators.
>
> He lives here in a "furnished room," has nothing to call his own except a trunk, has left all his furniture to his first wife, cannot bear the thought of settling anywhere for any length of time, never knows if he has any money or how much. Goes to bed at 9, gets up at 5, lives on almost nothing—fish, vegetables, a little red wine. Blushes like a young girl, this happens quite

often and makes his face flower into a bewitching beauty. His mouth and eyes are wonderful, the latter blue like a clear morning at sea. His hair is already much greyed, his face deeply lined—a figure of catastrophe. He worships flowers, is starving, but buys a plant. He can, when seized by some delusion, be horribly coarse to men, never towards a woman, whom he dares not even contradict[!]. When he and Frida have a misunderstanding, he says, "I can't stand this," and runs away—without his hat. Then when he comes back he asks, "Was it you who wounded me, or I you?" He does not remember next morning what he has done today; no longer knows even what he has written; creates everything under hypnosis; as soon as it is down on paper it has, as far as he is concerned, disappeared. By contrast, his head is always full of lucid and detailed plans of things he intends to write.

A few days later she sent her husband a second and less enthusiastic report:

> Strindberg . . . would be apt to drive an ordinary being like myself insane. I have never in my life met such a man before . . . I shall not be able to stand it much longer. He weighs on my nerves like lead. At first he seems far better-looking and more attractive than in his portraits and there are moments when he looks much younger; but then his face will change brusquely to that of an old man when he often starts to brood all of a sudden and entirely forgets in the middle of a sentence that anyone is listening . . . At the same time he impresses me more and more as a great genius . . . It is terribly strenuous to hear him talk. You almost see how his thoughts work and rush ahead and he cannot follow with his speech and suffers martyrdom. Half of what he says you must really guess. He also paints; there, too, he is a law unto himself, naturalistic symbolism, he calls it. He finishes a picture in two or three days . . . But his is not a joyful way of creating. It is more like the savage impulse driving a murderer to his crime . . . I cannot understand Frida, nor how she risks entrusting her future to the hands of such a man. But these two can no longer be separated; I must, on the contrary, do all within my power to marry them as quickly as possible. I am afraid his love for her is mere passion, intellectually she is not his equal, nor will any woman ever be . . . Her love for him, by contrast, seems utterly of the mind, she admires, nay, she idolises his genius. I believe she would never dare to embrace him unless he permitted or demanded it first. God alone knows how this will end in the long run.

In a third report, Marie concluded: "She must renounce any personality of her own . . . otherwise she may drive him into a lunatic asylum."[48]

To avoid having to wait six weeks following publication of the banns, they decided to get married on the island of Heligoland, which Britain had ceded to Germany three years earlier (in exchange for Zanzibar), but where British marriage regulations still applied and no banns were required. On their way back from the railway station, having booked their tickets, they saw two men, one rather portly in a white suit. Strindberg chased after them, and returned a quarter of an hour later looking, to Frida's alarm, "like a dead man rising out of a grave." The portly man, he informed her, was Carl Gustaf Wrangel, Siri's first husband. "He has married again and is going with his young wife on a trip like me. I had a strange feeling just now when he shook my hand and congratulated me on my new marriage. He displayed as much sentiment on the day when he congratulated me on my first marriage, despite the fact that it had robbed him of his wife . . . Perhaps it was not a wish that he repeated, but a curse."[49]

On 27 April they left Berlin for Heligoland, Strindberg protectively clutching his green sack—"about one yard in length [Frida noted] with gentle billowing summits and valleys . . . It contains Strindberg's new theory that plants have nerves. It contains the evidence that an element can be split. In this bag Newton is refuted, famous astronomers are led on *ad absurdum* . . . The day before, it had been an effort to close the sack, the hundreds of large sheets and hundreds of small slips of paper have no longer room in it . . . 'Why do you write on these little slips and not on a full-sized page?' I asked . . . He explained . . . 'The beautiful parchment paper is very expensive. A scientist as well as a poet must be economical.' He insisted that the green sack must stay with us in the carriage and not go into the luggage-van," into which, however, he allowed his chemical instruments and "a green-and-white footbath which accompanies him like cleanliness itself from one hotel to another."[50]

Strindberg and Frida Uhl were married on 2 May, with two local pilots as witnesses. In reply to the parson's question to Frida, "Do you swear that you do not carry another man's child under your heart?"

> although it was exclusively my affair, August Strindberg placed one hand upon the Bible and raised the other hand for the oath and swore most solemnly and in truth, with utter defiance of German grammar and with indescribable dignity: "I state upon my oath that I carry no child from no other man under my heart." Utterly forgetful of where I am, I surrender to the explosion of a most hilarious laughter. The parson and August Strindberg turn to stone and stare at me . . . But the only result is a still wilder gush of laughter.[51]

Chapter Eighteen

AN ENGLISH HONEYMOON

The new marriage did not begin promisingly. At dawn on their wedding night, Frida relates, Strindberg "brusquely started from a dream" and attempted to throttle her. "Although he soothingly reassured me that the attack had nothing to do with me, but was probably intended, as a mere matter of habit, for his first wife, I did not get to sleep again for quite a while."[1]

They stayed on Heligoland in "a lovely little white house, after Strindberg's own heart, with three rooms, a white verandah, a flower bed, a lane and trees in front." Frida noted that "he writes without a pause, almost without stopping, does not even read over what he has written, let alone correct it." After a week—"If anyone should ask me: what kind of a man is he, who is he?—I should not know . . . I ought to know Strindberg, but it is his greatest charm that you never get to know him. I know him as one knows the world at the end of a week's tramp . . . Take his hatred of women; yesterday he began a poem in which he praises woman's body as the great wonder of creation."

As they unpacked his trunk, "he pulled out two faded photographs from a mass of papers, importantly, as one lays hand upon valuable possessions. In the tone of a proud owner, he said, 'That's how she looks; she is aristocratic, beautiful, slender and refined.' The pictures were of his first wife and were taken in Switzerland . . . 'Slender' he calls it. Worn out and emaciated is what she is; in the eyes of my 21 years, she, at 40, is a faded and spent woman. There is no human being that I am so boundlessly sorry for as this woman. I can feel no jealousy, only a pang of guilt, as if I were a thief. It hammers on my brain: 'She is old, faded and weary. And the man who made her so now belongs to me.' Of course I am innocent, they were parted before ever I came, nothing on earth could have brought them together again. And yet—"[2]

After a couple of weeks, Strindberg's new novel ground to a halt. His early-morning hour walk now stretched out till noon. Frida felt that they must move from this isolated spot. A Scandinavian paper announced that the London publisher William Heinemann had already set up a translation of the poetic sequence *Somnambulist Nights*. More importantly, J. T. Grein invited Strindberg to come to London to discuss his projected production of *The Father*. Strindberg was unwilling to visit a country where, though he could read it with some difficulty, he could not speak the language. But Frida's English was fluent (she had completed her education four years earlier at a convent school in Hampstead), and she persuaded him to make the journey. They booked berths on a collier from Hamburg which would land them in the Port of London after two and a half days at sea. "I was attracted by the cheapness of the passage, Strindberg by the length of the voyage." They left Heligoland on 17 May, and had a bad day in Hamburg, where in oppressive heat "the town glowed like a furnace" and Strindberg alarmed Frida by an attack of agoraphobia which prevented him from crossing the square back to their hotel so that they had to take a cab round it. On the ship, Frida spent the whole voyage below seasick while Strindberg stood on the bridge with the captain, surprising him by his knowledge of things nautical and making observations with a telescope to confirm his conviction that the earth was flat.

When they reached Gravesend in the Thames estuary, Frida was too ill to proceed immediately to London, and at the captain's suggestion they rented rooms in a house at 12 Pelham Road, a front sitting-room and back bedroom on the ground floor. The latter contained "a shameless married English double bed with shining brass knobs. It brazenly defies our notions about modern marriage." So they took a third room upstairs where Strindberg could work during the day, since he was offended by the furnishings of the sitting-room, and which contained a lumpy old divan where Frida could sleep at night.

Strindberg found it difficult to work in Gravesend. He lost interest in his new novel; "the rosy pink shells, the polished mahogany, the Leighton and Alma-Tadema pictures, all make mock of the glorious wildness of his

dreams."[3] They went reconnoitring in London and found things less
promising than they had hoped. William Heinemann was not, after all,
planning to publish *Somnambulist Nights* and was anyway in Italy, and
although J. T. Grein was indeed hoping to stage *The Father*, he would
not be able to do so during his current season. Strindberg described his
first impressions of England in a letter to Adolf Paul on 23 May, four days
after their arrival. "Today I have seen London! It's horribly big and quite
unlike Berlin and Paris. I didn't see the famous chimney-smoke . . .
England is a Mediterranean land. Roses up the walls, now at Whitsun,
laurels twice the height of a man and chestnut trees reaching to the sky!"
Two days later he wrote again to Paul: "England is good, the ale is strong,
the gin half-strong," no doubt comparing the latter unfavourably with
schnapps.

One afternoon in Gravesend, when Strindberg had retired for his
siesta, a book arrived in the post. It was an advance copy of the German
translation of *A Madman's Defence*. He had made Frida "promise him,
solemnly vow to him, that I would never read the book." But—

> In my drowsy condition I had not glanced at the title but had begun
> straightway to turn the pages. Now it was impossible to stop, to remember,
> to lay the book aside. I was caught in the wheels . . .
> He was right, I ought not to have read it. It cast an evil spell between him
> and me. I experienced his love and his hatred for the mate of his early
> manhood. I saw him embrace her and then pelt her with dirt in front of the
> whole world. From being his wife, I had become one of the many thousands
> before whom he stripped this woman naked and whom he allowed to
> penetrate into her soul . . . Then, in a curious change of feeling, quite
> another kind of terror took forcible possession of me. It was no longer Siri
> von Essen whom he exhibited, but myself. No doubt it would soon be my
> turn . . . Were these frightful accusations true, or were they a betrayal of
> reality by imagination? If so, they might happen again any day and would he
> then besmirch me too?

Grein was due to go abroad at the beginning of June, and offered the
Strindbergs his flat in Pimlico at Fairmantle House, 84 Warwick Street
(now Warwick Way), just behind Eccleston Square, ten minutes' walk
from Buckingham Palace to the north and the Thames to the south.* The
weather on the day of their arrival, as Frida describes it, was dramatically
untypical for an English summer.

> When we took the train at ten o'clock in the morning, there was not a
> cloud in the sky. When we got out in London, the air was full of black smoky
> fog. As we went along Pall Mall, we could see it getting thicker and thicker.
> Then it descended suddenly like an iron curtain, just as we turned into

*The house, now a hotel, still stands.

Trafalgar Square. The one-armed Nelson who had perched in the centre a few minutes before seemed to have taken wing, along with his telescope. Only his column was there, abruptly cut off. The darkness swallowed up more and more of the daylight; some subterranean monster must be spewing up this darkness. Then of a sudden all the lamps were lit and now the sea of fog seethed wildly, sulphurous yellow, in a dusky and threatening glow. Strindberg stood spellbound. Drawn up to his full height he stood, his head thrown back and his eyes aflame . . .

I shall never forget it. As though consecrated to the fire we stood, amidst the uncanny swathes of reddish-yellow smoke and greedy gleam of flame. It was impossible to distinguish the point where the neighbouring streets reached the square, but we felt them cowering in the darkness like the open jaws of wild beasts. We felt as if these maws might open wider at any moment in order to spew out still more bloodthirsty flames, still more conflagrations and funeral pyres.

Strindberg drank in the picture. In the wild glow of destruction he seemed to see only the resurrection from the ashes.

Grein and his wife Alix greeted them; Alix remembered that Strindberg arrived carrying his large sack over his shoulder, explaining that it contained "all my unacted plays." He did not mention, or she did not recall, its scientific contents. They conversed in a mixture of French and German. Grein explained that he was keen to stage *The Father* but could find no actor suitable for the Captain. (He never did.) He installed them in the flat with his Irish housekeeper, Bobby Jeffreys, to look after them.[4]

Frida was fascinated by Pimlico:

Mountains of food of all kinds, clothes, old books, household goods and rubbish piled higgledy-piggledy are on sale a few paces from us in the open street market. A sharp and brutal smell of raw meat hangs in the air, of fish, winkles, rotting fruit and vegetables, pitch, salt water and human sweat, exciting and intoxicating. Torches flame and flicker late into the night. Dark figures in fantastic costume flit across the patches of light as in a lurid scene from Dickens. Tipsy beggar women wear great hats with nodding plumes, poverty has bought up the glories of past fashions from the rag-and-bone man's barrow and trails them through the dust. Bobby looks after the housekeeping, her provisions kept strictly within the limits of national taste. Three times a week we get chops, three times steaks, and on Sunday, the seventh day of creation, there is roast mutton. As accompaniment we have marrow, beans, spinach—spinach, beans and marrow. Salad every day, but without oil and vinegar. Salt is only to be tasted in the tang of breezes from the sea.

Strindberg rebels, he has the Swede's highly developed sensibility to appetising food and, as every disturbance of his physical well-being puts a brake on his intellectual activities, he regards unsuitable diet as an attack on his genius. The dry, dusty heat, too, is a torture to him. And the narrowness of two rooms which he must share day and night with a woman, and the millions of people in the vast city, all of them strangers to him . . . And then there is something worse. Strindberg can sit at J. T. Grein's table and sleep in J. T. Grein's bed, but he finds it hard to work at J. T. Grein's desk. The drawers of this desk are full to bursting of other people's intellectual labours. Young Shaw and old Browning have already leapt out of them . . . Is August Strindberg to sit quietly by, until other people's dramas shall be born and buried? Strindberg is Youth, knocking at Master Solness's door. But here Ibsen is only just coming into the world.

He decided that he must found another theatre of his own, not in London but in Berlin. "To be called the Strindberg Theatre," he explained to Adolf Paul on 12 June. "No decor needed; just a room! . . . Might not be a bad idea to start with *The Bond* and *Pariah* . . . No light on the stage. No music. We should be able to raise a few hundred here." But this project, like so many others, was to remain still-born.

One Sunday Bobby announced that they must lunch out that day, since she was going rowing on the river. Frida decided to show him the convent school where she had finished her education, near Hampstead Heath. They wandered happily for miles among the gorse.

> At last we see an inviting inn. Strindberg, who has for some time been playing with the idea of a glass of ale, laughs delightedly over the charming name, the Dickens Inn. He is laughing too soon. The giant figure of the landlord blocks the entrance. He regards us darkly and penetratingly and then asks "Where did you sleep last night?"
>
> "Where did we—?" I repeat indignantly.
>
> I had no idea, and Strindberg still less, that this question, which we regard as an outrageous insult, was due merely to a legal provision. Since the sacred peace of Sunday may not be disturbed, no inn might serve a wanderer with meat and drink unless he were at least three miles removed from his legitimate home or the place where he had last spent the night. Strindberg thinks the question reflects on our honour. His cane switches through the air. I throw myself between him and offender just in time.
>
> "Drunk again, first thing in the morning, you ought to be ashamed of yourself, young feller," shouts the landlord indignantly and slams his door in our faces.
>
> We wander back over the heath like Adam and Eve driven out of Paradise . . . thirsty and depressed, until the streets are about us again, in the grey of the evening. One bus after another gallops invitingly past us. But every time I want to jump up, Strindberg shakes his head silently. He stands obstinately still. Agoraphobia has him in its grip again . . . It seems an eternity before at last a four-wheeler comes crawling along. The bony old mare takes two hours to rattle us home to Pimlico.
>
> Scarcely have we arrived home than Strindberg begins to look out once more cheerfully for his supper. Alas, the bony old nag has swallowed the last of our ready cash. I have no choice but to fetch the ill-omened cold mutton from the larder. I know exactly what will happen. And it happens. My poor

husband gulps down two glasses of whisky neat, thrusts the mutton aside and goes sulkily to bed, hugging a huge astronomical tome.

It was a pity that Grein was not in London to introduce Strindberg to writers and artists who could have talked with him in German or French, such as Bernard Shaw, Oscar Wilde, Henry James and Thomas Hardy, or Ibsen's two pioneers, Edmund Gosse and William Archer, who could have spoken Norwegian to him and understood his Swedish. All of these were patrons of Grein's Independent Theatre and would surely have been impressed and intrigued by Strindberg. As it was, his dislike of going to the theatre, coupled with the poorness of his English, inhibited him from seeing any plays during his stay. It so happened, by the sort of misfortune that dogged Strindberg, that those first two weeks in June 1893 were a period of intense Ibsen activity in the London theatre. *Rosmersholm*, *Hedda Gabler* and *The Master Builder* (with Act 4 of *Brand*) were in repertory at the Opéra Comique in the Strand with Elizabeth Robins and Lewis Waller, Eleonora Duse was playing A *Doll's House* at the Lyric, and Herbert Beerbohm Tree was appearing in his own lavish production of An *Enemy of the People* at the Haymarket. This must have intensified Strindberg's feeling that the city was hostile to him, a feeling of which Frida was painfully aware.

> Strindberg certainly had the right to demand peace and quiet, and it was the only thing in the world which he did demand. But everyday life would grant him none. There was no protection from the noise of the traffic, from the disgusting stenches of the street market, no protection from the dusty heat, no protection from me. Our being together, which should have been happiness, had become torture . . . He was crushed by my continual presence. I felt ashamed of existing every time I caught his reproachful glance, seeking in vain the concentration that only solitude can bring. I was continually thinking of a story by Gogol. A bachelor has a dream on the eve of his wedding. He dreams that he is already married and sees his wedded home and his wife in it. He sees her everywhere. He looks at the bed, there lies his wife. He goes to the table, there sits his wife. He opens the cupboard, his wife springs out of it into his arms. He draws out his handkerchief to wipe the sweat of fear from his brow—his wife slips out of his pocket. I feel as if I were this appallingly ubiquitous wife. But how am I to get rid of myself?

One thing Strindberg must surely have done in London, though we have no direct evidence of it, is visited the National Gallery. Six years later he was to name Turner as the English painter whom he most admired and, despite his close acquaintance with Munch and later with Gauguin, Turner had a much greater effect on his painting than either. As a modern critic, T. G. Rosenthal, has written: "The only close affinity

Strindberg had with any other painter was with . . . Turner . . . It was really only the Englishman who influenced his style . . . It is not only a question of the fascination for both of them of sea and sky and all the terrible, beautiful havoc they could create. It is rather in this use of a seemingly insignificant 'storm centre' such as we find in Turner's *Snow Storm*. . . . There was a wildness of temperament in both men which made their response to the wildness of nature so powerful and so similar."[5] The following year Strindberg was to start painting very much in the manner of Turner, and it seems unlikely that he could have seen any of Turner's work during that period anywhere but in London. (The Tate Gallery, which was to house the finest Turner collection in the world, did not open until four years after Strindberg's visit.)

Meanwhile, he began to work on a theory of world history, that all things were directed by a Conscious Will that favoured certain repetitions and correlations.[6] But Frida decided that the best course was for him to leave London while she remained to try to negotiate the sale of his plays to Grein and the possible publication of his plays and poems by William Heinemann when those two returned. To pay for his ticket, she pawned her leopard-skin coat, lace, dresses, linen and wedding ring, all for £5. That night, 17 June, Strindberg took the steamer to Hamburg and proceeded to Sellin, on the Baltic island of Rügen, south of the tip of Sweden, where Adolf Paul, Karl August Tavaststjerna and other Scandinavians from the Black Porker circle were spending the summer. Frida would join him there as soon as she had completed her business in London.

"Our English trip was a crazy idea," he wrote from Hamburg to Adolf Paul on Rügen on 22 June. "Expensive as hell, we over-estimated the possibilities and I nearly got rabies with the heat and that coal they use. So that we shouldn't come away empty-handed, my wife has to stay to work on theatres and publishers and I had to go ahead and find rooms." He took the opportunity to abuse Dagny Juel, who by now had replaced Laura Hansson as The Enemy. "One can pity her and her family when, having been Aspasia, she sets up as a common whore. I fucked her so had no revenge to seek, but she, having been fucked, everything!"*

---

*Adolf Paul thought that Strindberg's war against women was "the battle against the feminine element in himself. His misogyny was less a hatred of women than a feminine man's expression of the need to stress his own virility." Przybyszewski shared this view; in his memoirs, he suggests that Strindberg's view of woman arose from his having an excess of female hormones; that he was "a brilliant woman," and that his hatred of the female sex was thus directed against himself. "The sadistic tormenting of the woman in himself . . . was a battle against a demonic Satan that dwelt in him."[7]

Including his stay in Hamburg, it took Strindberg eight days to reach Rügen, "the time [Frida noted in her diary] it took him in lucky days to write a play."[8] "For the moment, the natural sciences obsess me," he wrote to her on 26 June, "to the extent that I can no longer bother with belles-lettres or my theatrical affairs. Here everything is peaceful, the sea, the forest, the men (and even the women), except me." He wrote affectionately to her almost daily; but Rügen soon began to pall. "Life here is dreadfully monotonous," he complained on 8 July. "Tavaststjerna is deaf and his wife not here, Paul is busy writing, and we meet no one else." To add to his worries, the Stockholm weekly magazine Budkaflen had pirated A Madman's Defence, which had appeared in German at the end of May, and was serialising it in an unauthorised Swedish translation without paying Strindberg anything and in defiance of his wish that it should not appear in Swedish during his lifetime. "The whole country," he wrote to Frida, "is convulsed with rage and shame—and rightly. Thus cursed by everyone, I shall not be able to return home for years."[9]

Adolf Paul describes how, during a swimming expedition that summer, Strindberg inadvertently ducked himself and came up looking like "no man any longer but an old woman. His head had lost half its size, the lion's mane stuck fast to his skull, the angular furrowed face with its tiny pointed chin and small gossip's mouth were one with the narrow arms. The old woman who day in and day out complained of the petty hardships of life stood suddenly before us." Paul also tells how Strindberg would stand all day over his crucibles "usually dressed only in a nightshirt and slippers, a belt around his waist and a straw hat on his head." His room was "hot as hell and stank of pitch and sulphur."[10]

On 11 July, Frida informed him that an unnamed rich lady in London* had agreed to finance a Strindberg performance that very month, and that there was a good chance that they might be able to start their own theatre there that autumn. She, Frida, would be artistic director, choose the plays and actors; and with a singular lack of tact, she added that in addition to his plays she would present some by Ibsen and Bjørnson. Since Strindberg so hated London, she proposed leasing a small house in the country outside. These suggestions evoked a frosty reply. "I am happy that, young and ambitious as you are, you have found the opportunity to exploit your vitality and talent . . . You dump me

*Probably Annie Horniman, the tea heiress, who entered into a fortune on the death of her grandfather this year and backed a season in London early in 1894 which included the first production of Shaw's Arms and the Man. Within the next decade she was to co-found the Abbey Theatre in Dublin and the Gaiety in Manchester, the first repertory theatre in Britain.

without ceremony because you think you have acquired an imaginary fortune. It is a little too soon to write me off . . . I forgive you because I love you; and I am ready to return to London, provided the necessary money is available and on condition that I am spared concern with anything theatrical. But an hour and a quarter on a train is no doubt too much for you, assuming that you wish to live with me. And to live alone in the countryside in England where I don't know the language does not appeal to me."[11]

Frida, still ensconced at Grein's flat with Bobby Jeffreys, was enjoying herself. William Heinemann had returned from Italy and lunched her several times at the Savoy. She found him "keen, young, easily enthusiastic," but unwilling to publish Strindberg until he had had a success on the English stage. Bobby took her to see *Rosmersholm*; she found Elizabeth Robins "a thought too literary, perhaps too honest for the world of illusion, but with talent and a superb stage presence. Would be the thing for us." Among the audience she spotted Bernard Shaw "like a Whistler harmony in reddish brown . . . What vitality, what eyes!" He greeted Bobby but, to her disappointment, "takes no notice of me."[12]

She had begun to teach herself Swedish so as to be able to translate Strindberg's plays into English, and on 17 July he wrote her a short letter in Swedish, depressed by the cool reception of his scientific writings in Berlin and by his loneliness. "Alone I shall die," he concluded, "alone without you." Her optimism about prospects in London was beginning to cool. The rich lady's enthusiasm had quickly faded and, although Frida was still living in Grein's flat, he was no good either; her letters to Strindberg that month are full of complaints about the Dutchman's unreliability, meanness and behaviour towards women. Nevertheless, she begged her husband to join her. "Everything will be better, I swear to you. Everything will be good . . . We will go to the country—it will be beautiful there as in Heligoland—more beautiful—for this reunion will be our new marriage, a marriage perhaps happier than the first . . . August, I will do everything for you to make you feel happy." Alternatively, if he could not overcome his repugnance for England, she suggested that he should go and stay with her parents on the shore of Mondsee, near Salzburg, where they would receive him with open arms. "See that he gets there before Father," she urged her mother. "You will have a wonderful time together . . . He cannot come here. Because of the heat, you know, the terrible heat." Marie Uhl sent him a warm invitation.[13] But Strindberg demurred. "You think I want to go alone to Mondsee," he wrote to Frida on 22 July. "No! I only want to be where you are, but not in Fairmantel [*sic*] House."

At length, however, on 28 July, he decided that Mondsee, even without Frida, was a lesser evil than life on Rügen. He took the train there and, to his surprise, quickly established a rapport with her parents. "Your father and I are very good friends," he informed Frida on 3 August. ". . . I have fallen in love with your mother." Friedrich Uhl was impressed by Strindberg; he had, he reminded Frida, met many great men, including Wagner and Brahms; but, he felt bound to add, "such a man has his place on a pedestal. One does not marry such men." Among other things that disturbed him, Strindberg had torn all his curtains from the bedroom window because they kept out the light.[14] Strindberg repeatedly begged Frida to join him there; she insisted that if his plays were to be staged in London, she must remain there. Eventually, after he had been two weeks at Mondsee, she yielded but, owing to a misunderstanding, when she arrived at Mondsee she learned that he had gone to meet her in Berlin. Finding she was not there, he retired in a depression to the suburb of Pankow, where he alarmed the owner of an open-air restaurant by injecting an apple hanging from a tree by his table with morphia to observe its reaction. As the *patron* stared at the syringe, Strindberg explained, "I am a botanist." The *patron* took him to be an out-patient from the local asylum.[15]

By 15 August he and Frida had at last met up in Berlin and settled in a pension on Albrechtstrasse, where several of his old associates lived. Przybyszewski had now abandoned his common-law wife, Martha, and their two children for Dagny Juel, whom he married that month. They had two children, who were both alive as late as 1977; the other characters in this drama were less fortunate. Martha killed herself shortly after Przybyszewski's marriage, and Dagny was murdered five years later in Tiflis by a Russian lover.

Strindberg now gave up painting for nearly a year and concentrated on the scientific experiments he had begun in Rügen. His main interest at this juncture was to prove that sulphur was divisible and was not, as generally supposed, an element. The horrible smell of sulphur, which had so distressed Adolf Paul on Rügen, became a familiar part of Frida's life. He also tried to make gold by mixing copper and sulphate of iron. "Unwearying, he stands bowed over his retorts, operates with balances, looks up old books and the very newest; the whole room is crowded with books and papers, chemicals, lamps, glass and porcelain. Only the bed stands up above the flood like Noah's Ark . . . Gold, gold! The bills are unpaid, the last ready money gone."[16]

Strindberg's doubt that sulphur was an element was not as far-fetched as it seems today. A number of scientists in the 1890s were sceptical about the atomic theory and leaned towards the old hypothesis that hydrogen, the element with the least atomic weight, was the source of every other supposed element. To prove that sulphur was a combination of hydrogen and carbon, as he believed, would considerably reinforce that hypothesis. But the apparent evidence he discovered seems to have been the result of impurities in his material; and his impatience with modern scientific methods led him to follow the outdated methods of the ancient scientists.[17] His approach to science was strikingly imaginative, but unscientific. Bengt Lidforss, the botanist whom he had met in Lund in the autumn of 1890, commented that to Strindberg the whole of modern structural chemistry was a closed book and that he seemed to have no idea of the meaning of a rational formula.[18]

Another aspect of Strindberg which troubled his young wife at this time was his apparent clairvoyance. One evening, after she had gone for a walk, he accused her of having met Hermann Sudermann at 4 p.m. on the corner of Karlstrasse, wearing a green dress which he had not seen her go out in. Sudermann, he added, had remarked that it reminded him of something. She admitted having worn the dress but assured him that she met no one. A week later, wearing the same dress, she did meet Sudermann at the spot named by Strindberg, and the dress did remind him of something. When she told Strindberg of this, he asked why she had not admitted the truth when he first asked her.[19]

On another occasion, he asked Frida one morning in Schleich's presence what she had dreamed about that night. When she denied that she had dreamed at all, he insisted that she had. "You moved in your dream like our little dog when it wags its tail. You stretched your arms and tossed your head in ecstasy. Confess: whom were you dreaming about?" When Schleich said that no one could be held responsible for their dreams, Strindberg replied, "It is not a question of responsibility. I am merely asking if I observed correctly." Frida repeated her denial, whereupon Strindberg shouted, "You are lying!" and left, banging the door behind him. Frida began to cry, and when Schleich tried to comfort her she said, "The dreadful thing is, it was all true." Schleich adds, "Strindberg quoted this as an example of the total and meaningless mendacity of women: 'They play with truth as with their dolls.' "[20]

During the summer an anonymous writer denounced A Madman's Defence to the German police, signing herself "A German Mother."*

---

*Torsten Eklund suggests that the letter may have been written by Marie David (Meddelanden från Strindbergssällskapet, 1961–2, p. 28n).

Strindberg published a reply in the German press on 10 September, but
the authorities now belatedly banned the book under the Lex Heinze, a
new law against immoral writings named after a prostitute and her pimp
husband. The case was due to come to court the following spring, and the
prospect recalled to Strindberg all the anxieties of the Stockholm trial
nine years earlier. "There are times now," wrote Frida, "when he will sit
and stare in front of him, seeing visions of himself in convict's garb."[21]
His mood became even more difficult and suspicious. One morning he
found that his breakfast coffee was not hot enough. He rushed into the
street and, on returning, shut himself in his room. "Instead of a verbal
explanation, soon afterwards a long white sheet of paper came gliding in
from under the door, like an evil snake, with hateful and extraordinary
things written upon it. Extraordinary things."[22]

On 15 October Frida discovered that she was pregnant, but this did
nothing to soften Strindberg's mood. Perhaps he suspected, as with Siri,
that someone else was the father; she had, after all, spent a month away
from him in London. She left to stay with her sister Marie Weyr in
Vienna and, while there, applied to have a legal abortion. This the
authorities refused; but she wrote to Strindberg asking for a divorce. In her
absence he paid a five-day visit to Lund in the south of Sweden to seek
advice from a lawyer there about the possibility of taking legal action
against *Budkaflen* for its pirating of *A Madman's Defence*; but he was told
that he had no case, since Sweden was not a signatory to the Berne
Copyright Union. He bombarded Frida with telegrams begging for a
reconciliation. Marie wrote to him that Frida was willing to live with him
again provided he stopped accusing her of imaginary crimes, and at the
end of October they were reunited in Brünn (now Brno), the ancient
capital of Moravia. Unable to settle their account at the pension in Berlin,
they had to leave some of Frida's belongings behind as security. On 10
November Strindberg gloomily reported to Adolf Paul that the woman
who owned the pension had now pawned them, uncharitably adding:
"Blackmail seems to be her speciality." Although they were only two
hours' journey from Vienna, where he had many admirers, especially
since the performance of *Creditors* the previous March, lack of funds
prevented him from going there. This, he told Paul in the same letter,
"has surprised the Viennese and I suppose people will think they have
banned me. Had I the money, I would long ago have gone there."

During October, *The Father* had been staged in Amsterdam, where it
achieved the respectable number of twenty-three performances, and
now, on 14 November, it was performed in Rome. But its reception there
was less sympathetic; *Aftonbladet* reported on 23 November that "The

Romans listened to the pathological drama in silence; at the end of the play . . . they greeted it with loud whistles."

Strindberg was working on his scientific treatise *Antibarbarus*, dictating to Frida each evening in German what he had written during the day in Swedish. "His day's work lasted ten hours," she recalled, "yet he showed no trace of fatigue when he laid down his pen." The book took the form of four discourses between a teacher and his pupil. "Every objection was dealt with before it had been made. Every misconception had been foreseen and stifled. It was a crossing of lightnings, a sparkling whetting of thoughts, which clarified themselves, were steeled and sorted even as they shaped themselves in words." She summarised the book's content. "In the First Letter, Strindberg strove to prove that sulphur is not an element, but analogous in nature to a fossilised resin—that it therefore consists of carbon, hydrogen and oxygen. The Second Letter, the most important in the book, proclaimed the theory of transmutation, as applicable to all the elements. Here Strindberg affirmed that mercury also was no element, but, subject to fitting conditions, could be transmuted into silver and gold. In the Third Letter, he cast doubts upon the ruling theories as to the composition of the air and the indivisibility of nitrogen. And in the Fourth and last Letter, he sought to explain many of the substances which we call elements as combinations of hydrogen and oxygen."[23]*

On 21 November, Strindberg sent Albert Bonnier the first ark, or sixteen pages, of the book, describing it as "a work which I started in 1883 and have been working on for the past three years . . . The whole should fill ten volumes, each of four large octavo arks, and should be ready in a year or so. It should not be too difficult for you to decide whether you want it or not, since it is a natural-scientific-philosophical work." Bonnier replied that he did not wish to publish a work the scientific worth of which he could not assess, and that it would be better suited to a scientific journal. To Strindberg's request for an advance, Bonnier pointed out that he already owed the firm 1,655 crowns.[24]

The rejection of *Antibarbarus* was a bad blow, both psychologically and financially. Strindberg was having difficulty keeping up his payments to Siri and the children, and some of Frida's belongings were still in pawn in Berlin. There was, however, one place where, in Frida's words, "food and drink are always to be had in plenty and where one need not work in order to eat."[25]

---

*Dr. Michael Yudkin, of the Department of Biochemistry at Oxford University, comments in a letter to the author: "Strindberg was writing balderdash. Sulphur and mercury are undoubtedly elements; mercury cannot be transmuted into silver and gold; and no elements are made from combinations of hydrogen and oxygen."

Her maternal grandfather, Cornelius Reischl, was a retired public notary. By industry and speculation he had acquired a considerable fortune, with which he had purchased a country estate at Dornach in Lower Austria, on the banks of the Danube between Mauthausen and Grein. He was a great huntsman, who every day "shot more venison, pheasants, partridges, hare or wild duck than would have provisioned a small army." His wife, Maria, a famous Viennese beauty in her day, looked after twenty-seven cows, fourteen dogs and twenty cats. To the original single-storey house Reischl had added another storey and two wings. "For many leagues all round, the land belonged to Grandfather, and he could hardly reach the boundaries of his hunt . . . in a day's march."[26]

Frida was not fond of the place. It resembled, she felt, "a bewitched harbour, enemy to Hymen, out of which no ship of marriage escapes quite unharmed back to sea. There gather widows whose husbands are still alive elsewhere and orphans whose fathers are not dead. It has always appeared to me like a negation of love. It is the last place that I should freely choose—but I have no other choice."[27]

She and Strindberg arrived at Dornach at the end of November, so short of money that the sledge-driver who took them from the station at Amstetten had to pay the porter who carried their bags, and they had to ask the innkeeper on the bank by the house to pay the sledge-driver. (Strindberg was to recall the humiliation bitterly in the first part of his dramatic trilogy, To Damascus.) But the grandparents made them welcome. They were allotted a floor of the wing over the stables, so that they had not only separate bedrooms, which Strindberg liked, but separate sitting rooms and a fifth room which he turned into "a regular alchemist's den," where the fumes of sulphur filled the air. He played chess with Reischl, who always won, and enjoyed the freedom of the enormous library which Reischl had acquired as a default payment on the death of an eccentric debtor who owned nothing but books.[28]

Strindberg found peace and contentment at Dornach, where he was to stay eight months. "I am now living on the Danube," he wrote to Adolf Paul on 3 December, "so close that I hear the lapping of the water as I lie in bed. I work much, think more, read an incredible amount. The landscape is beautiful . . . the house large, 15 rooms, etc. Friendly people, lots of food and early to bed. So I am saved."

That evening, 3 December, the Lessing Theater in Berlin staged the world premiere of Playing with Fire (it was to be another fourteen years before it was performed in Sweden). It concluded the evening after three one-act farces, and was performed as a farce instead of as the subtle black comedy which it is. But black comedy was not an accepted form then. It was not well received, though in time it became one of Strindberg's most frequently performed plays in Germany. The news of this failure pleased his detractors in Sweden, who resented the warmth of his reception on the other side of the Baltic. His one-time friend Verner von Heidenstam wrote a piece in *Dagens Nyheter* on 23 December complaining of the way in which foreign works were overrated in Sweden, and adding: "We see a Swedish prose writer cause a stir in Germany while his earlier and better books are already old-fashioned here." Another friend who was to become an enemy, the botanist Bengt Lidforss, concluded the year with some gossip from the Black Porker; he informed Strindberg that Dagny Juel was now to be seen there regularly with Edvard Munch and, less accurately, that Przybyszewski was "completely finished with Aspasia and is only waiting for money to kick her out."[29]

Chapter Nineteen

THE END OF ANOTHER MARRIAGE

1893 had ended for Strindberg and Frida in apparent peace and reconciliation. 1894 was to see the collapse of their relationship. She would recall:

> The New Year did not keep the promise which the old had made. We went through grey days. As the Danube fog often shut us out from the light with impenetrable walls, so impenetrably Strindberg's past often stood between himself and me. This murderous past had burrowed itself deep into his mind, as the river burrows its bed . . . The past devoured the present, the Shadow devoured the Reality. At times Strindberg imagined conflicts between himself and me which never took place, but for him they were as real as his plays. It came about then that he would speak words to me that I was already familiar with, that I had already read and heard. In his eyes I wore the garb of his first wife, and behaved as, in his mind, she would behave. And he hated me then as he hated her, visioned crimes of which I was guilty (that I had never committed) and forgave me for them and loved me again—as he had loved her. Sometimes I no longer knew—was it I at all that he loved and hated or was it the other, still the other, only the other? Or were we both but a poet's fiction, a larva, out of which she had crept and which I was now wearing? . . .
>
> There were unwritten laws in our marriage, neither he nor I had laid them down and yet we both respected them. One of them was that we never explained things to one another when we had been parted by misunderstanding or quarrel. We feared the weakness of the spoken word—in its

incompleteness, it might fail. Always a silent kiss was my refuge—from him, from myself, from fate. And Strindberg always put his arm about me, kindly and protectingly, as if some third person had threatened us. I was full of fear, he of sadness and sympathy. This strange feeling of impending fate gave to our love something ethereal and winged. It was a death ride over crackling ice and bottomless depths, but these sunny winter days were beautiful.[1]

Frida's mother, Marie Uhl, visited the house and found Strindberg in a highly nervous state:

One day we were all seated at the dining table when the postman rowed across the Danube with the latest news from Vienna. My father opened his newspaper and began to read the news aloud to the family. Strindberg's face became more and more sombre, and finally furious. In a loud voice he declared that he had nothing to do with the disturbances in Vienna and was quite innocent . . . It was with the greatest difficulty that we succeeded in calming him and assuring him that no one for a moment associated him with what was happening there . . .

One evening Strindberg was served soup as usual. He seemed much angered at this and asked loudly why he was served soup when we knew that he did not eat it. When we remarked that he had eaten soup up to now, he became so angry that he rose and left the room—returning, however, for the next course. Next day he was given no soup. He then asked irritably why he had been excluded from this course, and the scene from the previous day was repeated. A little later the maid came to my mother in tears and complained that "the gentleman" had thrown a heavy brassbound missal at her head.[2]*

He took refuge in new scientific experiments. One was to photograph the moon by a system he had invented which used no camera or lens, only a plate covered with bromide of silver which he lay on his writing desk in a bath of developer, exposed to the moon's rays. A book by the eighteenth-century French naturalist the Comte de Buffon which he found in Reischl's library set him speculating on the subject of progeniture. "Do you know what *sansclou* are?" he asked Bengt Lidforss (10 January). "Buffon writes that fructified eggs have been found in men's penises. *Sansclou* are a *Dröppel*. A *Dröppel* is a heap of male semen found in a vagina. Now, if one mounts a woman over-filled with semen, a man can get another man's semen in his penis or testicles, and so the seeds grow and the *sanscloued* man finds himself in a perverse state of pregnancy which, however, is stopped by the lowering of temperature (ice-bags!)

*Siri once told her daughter Karin that Strindberg "was not happy without scenes and literally provoked them" (Smirnoff, *Så var det i verkligheten*, p. 100).

. . . Everything is in everything, and everything moves, even semen. Wombs are only birds' nests in which the cock lays his eggs. Ergo: if the cock has his eggs ready, he can lay them in a receptacle warmed to a temperature of 37° Celsius!"

His painter friend Carl Larsson wrote urging him to return to Sweden, where he was "greatly missed." Strindberg was not convinced. "In Berlin," he replied on 16 January, "where I was much bigger than I knew, I was supported by admirers of my writing, so that I was able to send the children what I earned from theatres and publishers. It was a rich and stormy life, through which I grew unbelievably, learning much. But what good does that do me in Sweden, where people put out their tongues and say Bah to everything they don't want to understand? I have got wind in my sails, and at last the time has come when I no longer need Sweden. I have publishers in Berlin, Paris and Milan, and am acted and read all over the world . . . Of course I long for pines and grey rocks when the spring comes, but my loathing for the country and its air and people is greater . . . Is there really anyone except you who misses me? I doubt it . . . I have not spoken my native tongue for three months." Ten days later he wrote again to Larsson: "To [Viktor] Rydberg and the other grand Swedes I am the Black Baldur at whom they have been shooting for fifteen years. When will they find the mistletoe?"*

Bengt Lidforss, whom he was bombarding with enormous letters full of scientific formulae, informed him that some of the old habitués of the Black Porker were planning to establish a new Porker elsewhere in Berlin. The news made Strindberg nostalgic. "When you write to Strömgren [the fiancé of Lidforss's sister] ask him to send my guitar to you. † Leave it at the new Porker so it'll be there when I come, and keep a table for me. Ask Anton [Przybyszewski's half-brother] to build a pagoda as an artist cell to contain portraits (not caricatures) of us all. Prepare a travel book and advertise it in *Dagens Nyheter*. If he wants to call the Porker 'Chez August Strindberg,' he may. But it must be *fin de siècle*. In the pagoda must hang a real human skeleton, of a woman showing her supernumerary bottom vertebrae. On the altar a Bible, with a condom as bookmark and a candle (no. 9) as pointer . . . Shouting, fireworks and music shall be permitted, and respectable women ejected."[3]

The first three volumes of *The Son of a Servant* appeared in German

*Baldur, in Scandinavian mythology, was a son of Odin. His mother persuaded all things to vow not to injure him, but overlooked the mistletoe. His enemy Loki induced the blind god Hödur to shoot a branch of mistletoe at Baldur, and this killed him.

†Strömgren lived in Lund, where Strindberg had left his guitar during his visit the previous October.

that February. Lidforss published an article in *Dagens Nyheter* about Scandinavian writers in Berlin, dealing principally with Strindberg and pointing out that he dominated the bookshop windows with displays not only of *The Son of a Servant* but also of novels and stories published earlier such as *The People of Hemsö* (which had appeared in two different translations), *By the Open Sea* and *Tschandala*. Lidforss added that news of the forthcoming "immorality" trial concerning A *Madman's Defence* had stimulated interest in Strindberg's works.

The preliminary hearing of this trial was fixed for March, and a bailiff duly presented himself at Dornach with a summons for Strindberg to report to the police station in the neighbouring town of Grein. Old Reischl, as a former public notary, was appalled. Never, at least in his time, had the house harboured anyone wanted by the law, and he declared that Strindberg must leave. Frida's grandmother came to the rescue. She had bought a tiny hut, scarcely more than a hovel, not far off, in which to keep a donkey that troubled the cows. Strindberg and Frida might live in that, and she would build a stable for the donkey. Surprisingly, Strindberg took to this unpromising residence. "The hut did not strike him as poverty-stricken, damp, dismal nor unhealthy [wrote Frida]. It seemed to him glorious, beautiful beyond compare . . . At our feet was the river, behind us the dark masses of the forest, a field spread out to the right. An old pump stood under the pear tree before the door, it had not been working for a long time but it looked most decorative. The roof was of thatch and a grave-looking crow flew up from it slowly as we entered. Lumpi [the donkey] screamed shrilly for joy and bade us welcome."[4]

Strindberg departed for Berlin, to hurry up the printing of *Antibarbarus*, but before he left, advance copies of the *Festschrift*, which had been in preparation for nearly three years,* arrived from Sweden. Entitled A *Book about Strindberg*, it had an impressive list of contributors, albeit mainly Scandinavian: they included Georg Brandes, Knut Hamsun, Bjørnson, Jonas Lie, Holger Drachmann and Gustaf Fröding, who had finally taken over the editing. The only non-Scandinavian piece was a reprint of the essay by Justin Huntly McCarthy (spelt in three different ways) from the *Fortnightly Review*. The best things in the book are the contributions by Fröding himself (on Strindberg as a poet), Brandes and Hamsun.

---

*Strindberg himself was largely responsible for the delay in its appearance. "The book will never be ready," Fröding wrote to Georg Brandes on 24 October 1893, "for Strindberg keeps coming up with new *addenda* from foreign journals. But the publisher is now fed up and intends to publish it as printed."[5]

"Strindberg," Fröding wrote, "is usually regarded as above all the poet of antipathetic feelings. And surely hardly any of his predecessors have succeeded in giving such energetic expression to hatred, defiance, repulsion and contempt—the only possible exception being Jonathan Swift, whose loathing and contempt for the human race developed into real madness." Ironically, a few years later Fröding himself was confined to an asylum for the remainder of his life. After praising Strindberg's "profound and many-sided depiction of love—not merely tenderness and self-sacrifice, but also its frailties, vanity, jealousy and every kind of madness," he observed perceptively: "Unluckily Strindberg has lived in a country and age in which pedantry, observation of the rules on the one hand, and empty rhetoric on the other, have been too highly admired. It was not therefore strange that his first collection of poems displayed an open and unconcealed contempt for this literary form . . . He seems now and then almost deliberately to have written worthless verses, sometimes thereby destroying the effect which he intended to create. Several of his satires, excellent in themselves, have thus suffered grievously, and several of his best pure lyrics have blemishes which devalue them." Of his poem "Loki's Blasphemies" (1883), Fröding wrote: "No one who was alive and young when this poem appeared will forget the powerful impression it created. The younger generation recognised in it the long-awaited declaration of war against the prevalent stagnation and slavish obedience to every kind of usurping authority."

Brandes praised a characteristic "especially needful in Sweden—ruthlessness in the face of convention and generally accepted prejudice." While agreeing that Strindberg's anti-feminism sometimes led him astray, he reflected that in plays like *The Comrades* and *The Father* (and he might have added *Miss Julie*), "female characters are merely subjected to the same ruthless and sceptical observation which we have long accepted in the creation of male characters." And Hamsun wrote: "For me he is the most remarkable writer of his country, perhaps of his age: a superior talent, a mind on horseback riding his own path and leaving most others far in the rear . . . He has investigated most things and attacked everything, from science to art and inventions, from culture to religion and God; with a kind of jubilant rage he has flung himself at everything in this life and the life to come . . . One would be naïve to take all Strindberg's paradoxes for gold; but one would be foolish not to see that one is in the presence of an energetic and uncommonly sharp observer who, by searching everywhere and sweeping away the rubbish, has produced a wealth of observations in a multitude of fields . . . He does not approach the reader with short, careful steps, to win him over inch by inch; he storms wildly ahead, blind with conviction, and either conquers or falls." Hamsun concluded by reminding his readers that "Strindberg is almost the only writer in Scandinavia who has made serious efforts to utilise modern psychology . . . But what is perhaps even more important is that Strindberg understands the inadequacy of modern psychology to portray the split and unharmonious child of today."

Strindberg arrived in Berlin on Easter Monday, to find everything shut, and next day had to pawn his watch and wedding ring to buy necessities. He settled in Friedrichshagen, where Bengt Lidforss lived, and which had unhappy memories of his row with the Hanssons there a year and a half previously. His lawyer was at first pessimistic about the forthcoming case, but comforted Strindberg by explaining that German law differentiated between deliberate and "accidental" obscenity, the latter covering instances when a book had not been intended as pornographic. Strindberg replied that he could establish that he had asked his cousin Oscar not to publish *A Madman's Defence* until after his death, in order to clear his own name as regards his relationship with Siri. This, he felt confident, would settle the matter.

He revisited the Black Porker with Schleich, but found it changed. The owner had expanded it with a smart saloon upstairs and had raised his prices. It had become a rendezvous for young officers and their ladies. In an effort to make up for this, Dagny Juel had, according to Frida, who presumably had it from Strindberg, founded a salon consisting of "one room, rather shabbily furnished," where she and Przybyszewski were regularly joined by Munch and Lidforss. "Aspasia danced enchantingly, Stachu played the piano ravishingly; he often played the whole night long. In order to keep the neighbours from protesting, the instrument had been inventively insulated and dampened with cardboard."[6]

Antibarbarus was published that May. Not surprisingly, the notices were almost universally contemptuous, in both Germany and Sweden. Bengt Lidforss, who had supervised the translation into German, took the surprising and one might think unethical step of reviewing it critically in *Dagens Nyheter* several weeks before publication on 13 April. After describing it as "a declaration of war on modern science," he recalled that in *Flower Paintings and Animal Pieces** Strindberg had "put forward personal ideas which he unpretentiously called experimental theories and fantasies, and which he seemed to be proposing half seriously and half in jest. The Strindberg whom we meet in *Antibarbarus* is no longer the gentle gardener who seeks to interpret the song of the nightingale and is

*See page 204.

moved to the depth of his heart by seeing again the pelargoniums of his childhood. The author of *Antibarbarus* is a truculent reformer . . . storming the fortresses of modern science . . . The most revolutionary chapter is that on alchemy . . . Strindberg's old adversaries will doubtless seize the opportunity to capitalise on the many eccentricities of the book, and most professional scientists will reject it with a shrug of the shoulders and a few words about genius and madness without taking a closer look at the suggestive pointers which a perceptive reader will discover. . . . [But] *Antibarbarus* proves above all one thing: that Strindberg is neither a reformer nor a philosopher but solely and exclusively a poet and one of the purest water. In him, imagination has reached the pitch where the frontier between fact, hypothesis and fantasy has been obliterated; a seed of thought which the wind of chance has blown past his head returns, takes root in his brain as truth and grows into a dogma in defence of which he is prepared to live or die."

The following year Lidforss was to expand his view of *Antibarbarus* in a signed notice of the book in the magazine *Nordisk Revy*, and it is worth quoting because, like the review in *Dagens Nyheter*, it is a very fair assessment of Strindberg as a scientist. "The truth is that Strindberg's theories are of greater interest to the psychologist than to the scientist. But to the psychologist with a grounding in chemistry and botany, *Antibarbarus* offers as much of interest as do his other works. For the Strindberg whom one meets in *Antibarbarus* is at root the same as the one who appears in *Tschandala* and *By the Open Sea*, but the medium he employs is different and . . . much that was vague and indistinct in the earlier books can now be seen more clearly. This unusual mixture of genius and barbarism, so much a part of Strindberg's character, is apparent here too; but whereas in Strindberg's creative writing the genius is dominant and the barbarism only occasionally perceptible, in his scientific writing the reverse is the case." Lidforss adds that when he tried to explain to Strindberg the meaning of a rational formula, Strindberg interrupted: "No, old chap, it's no good. All these drawings of atoms you've just made are simply metaphysics and sophistry which I mustn't allow to confuse me. I don't understand it and I don't want to understand it."

Lidforss also tells how in Lund in 1891 Strindberg had propounded a theory that "the moon was a disc of quartz which the earth had cast off, that the landscape of the moon with its dead craters was a myth and that the man in the moon was . . . America, reflected in the quartz. When Birger Mörner . . . objected that in that case we ought surely to see the reflection of Europe, Strindberg hummed and replied with his strange smile: 'When one evolves theories, one must not bother with trivialities.'"[7]

This view of Strindberg as a scientist represents a considerable change of heart by Lidforss, for three months earlier, on 30 December 1893, he had written to Strindberg that his first impression on reading *Antibarbarus* had been "intense and overwhelming," and that "every line carries so clearly the stamp of genius that, despite one's professional reservations, the whole must be regarded as a tremendous breakthrough." But supervising the translation may have dampened his youthful enthusiasm; or, as Mary Sandbach suggests, he may, on the threshold of what was to prove a distinguished scientific career, have belatedly realised that to be associated uncritically with a book of dubiously scientific value might well be damaging for him.[8]

Strindberg was furious at the *Dagens Nyheter* review, and Lidforss joined the swelling ranks of his enemies. A hostile review in *Aftonbladet* on 28 April summed up the book as "78 pages full of incomprehension, misrepresentation and precipitate conclusions. Had this been written by Strindberg the young medical student, one would have laughed at the naïve errors. But knowing as one does that *Antibarbarus* is the most recent work of a man once regarded as one of this country's leading writers, one can laugh no longer." This notice was signed H.B., and Strindberg assumed it to be by his old friend Hjalmar Branting, who accordingly also briefly joined the ranks of Judases; but it turned out to have been written by Helge Bäckström, a docent in mineralogy who was married to a sister of Dagny Juel, so Branting was forgiven.

Strindberg returned to Dornach in early April, and there received a letter from a twenty-one-year-old German named Emil Schering who the previous year had seen *Creditors* in Berlin, and had been so excited by it that he decided to learn Swedish and devote his life to translating Strindberg's works and furthering his cause in Germany. He was to fulfil this mission so conscientiously that, although his translations are over-literary and not easily speakable, Strindberg's plays were, in the early years of the next century, to be performed and admired far more widely in Germany than in any other country, and the resultant fees and royalties were to ease Strindberg's financial position considerably during the last decade of his life.

This, however, lay in the future. His income at this time was minimal, and he was defaulting on his monthly payments to Siri. Frida, by now eight months pregnant, had suggested that his daughter Karin might come to live with them; apart from helping with the baby, she could teach Frida Swedish. He put this to his brother Oscar, the children's guardian:

"She will have her own room, 200 francs in pocket money, plus clothes and whatever else she needs." But Karin rejected the idea. "I really do not understand," she told Oscar, with some acerbity for a fourteen-year-old (but perhaps Siri dictated the letter), "how Pappa can afford to offer me 200 francs in pocket money, with clothes and everything found, when he cannot afford to give 200 francs a month for the three of us. If his wife wants to help us, why cannot she do so by paying us the 150 crowns a month which he owes us for our upkeep?"[9] Strindberg wrote to her on 18 May excusing himself: "Since I left Sweden I have sometimes suffered privation, gone without dinner, something that has never happened to you . . . I have gone hungry for you, and I have sold books, watches, everything I could sell so that for as long as possible I might send you birthday presents, but then everything ran out."

In their hut by the Danube, Strindberg and Frida prepared for the coming of the child. They painted the doors and window-frames, and he executed seven canvases to cover the bare walls, including a fine "Alpine Landscape" and a powerful chiaroscuro, "Golgotha." He planted roses and clematis on either side of the entrance and, in the little garden and the field that ran up the hill, "practically every flower and vegetable that could endure the climate . . . He created a blossoming garden where a wilderness had been." Her grandmother gave him an English tropical suit which an explorer had presented to Friedrich Uhl years before, "probably the first ever seen in Vienna"; it had hung in a cupboard at Dornach for years, occasionally being shown to visitors as a curiosity. Strindberg liked it for its exotic appearance as well as for its coolness. He worked on his theory that flowers had nerves like human beings, injecting them with morphia and thus alarming the locals as he had the restaurateur at Pankow.[10]

On 26 May 1894, Frida gave birth to a daughter, Kerstin. Strindberg was present at the accouchement, watching "coldly and scientifically." He mentioned the birth as a postscript to a letter he wrote the next day to Adolf Paul, full of vindictiveness about two former friends, Lidforss and Przybyszewski. "They will destroy themselves, for they know that he who touches me dies, as when one carelessly fingers an electric accumulator. But without my needing to raise my hand . . . They attack me in Stockholm and I am dead one day, then pop up in Karlstad;* then they kill me in Christiania [where at the end of the previous year *The First Warning* had lasted for only two performances] and I pop up in Paris . . . I

---

*The Swedish provincial town where *A Book about Strindberg* had been published a few weeks earlier.

fell in Rome, was whistled in Naples, rose like a sun in Copenhagen; was hissed in Berlin by Aspasia and the cuckolds, and popped up at once in Moscow [where *The People of Hemsö*, having been serialised in a magazine, had just appeared in book form] . . . No, they won't extirpate me, but I can extirpate my enemies . . . Today [*sic*] my wife has presented me with a daughter." More cheerfully, he informed Leopold Littmansson, his one-time companion on Kymmendö: "I am now damned big; have a bust in the Finnish National Museum by Ville Vallgren, and sit in two waxwork exhibitions with a whorelike mane of hair and stained clothes."[11]

He had indeed "popped up" in Paris. The previous November he had been the subject of a long and laudatory article in *Revue des Deux Mondes* by a member of the Académie Française, Victor Cherbuliez,[12] and now, on 21 June 1894, the young actor-manager Aurélien Lugné-Poe presented *Creditors* at his Théâtre de l'Oeuvre, which he had opened the previous year with *Rosmersholm* and *An Enemy of the People*.

This strange and eventful evening began with a lecture by Lucien Muhlfeld, the editor of *Revue Blanche*, who had praised Strindberg five years earlier in *Revue de l'Art Dramatique*. As well as introducing the play and another by Herman Bang which was to precede it, he launched a bitter attack on Sarcey and the other critics present in the audience. Bang's play was coolly received; a symbolic poem by Henri de Régnier was then recited in semi-darkness from behind a gauze, which evoked irreverent comments from the audience, including some of the critics, causing Lugné-Poe to rebuke them from the stage, Sarcey replying from his stall. During the interval that followed, rows broke out between the opposing factions in the corridors and outside in the street. The omens for *Creditors* seemed unpromising. But it was listened to with attention and greeted with loud applause. The reviews were generally favourable. Even Henri Fouquier, a confirmed opponent of Scandinavian writing, was comparatively sympathetic; though describing Strindberg as a Norwegian and asserting that the play owed a debt to Dumas *fils*'s *Une Visite de Noce*, he confessed that it had gripped him. And Sarcey, while complaining that it was obscure, allowed that it was significant, and was less hostile to it than he had been to any Ibsen play. Some of the critics preferred it to *Miss Julie*.[13]

Lugné-Poe sent the good news to Dornach in two brief telegrams: "TRIOMPHE" after the public dress rehearsal and "GRANDE TRIOMPHE" after the premiere. Strindberg was overjoyed. "This is happiness," he wrote to Leopold Littmansson in Paris, "this sense of power, sitting in a hut on the Danube among six women who regard me as a semi-idiot, and knowing that in Paris, the intellectual centre of the world, 500 people are sitting in an auditorium silent as mice, stupid enough to expose their brains to my powers of suggestion."[14]

Unfortunately, the lawsuit concerning A Madman's Defence had not been settled as he had hoped. "On 17 July," he informed Richard Bergh on 26 June, "I have to stand trial in Berlin and am liable to arrest if I don't appear and to be expelled from Austria. A wretched piece of ill luck is that as judge I have the famous Brausewetter who was so brutal towards writers last spring and whom even my lawyer fears. So I intend to flee, especially since the whole trial is illegal and in Sweden, says Professor Winroth [the lawyer he had consulted in Lund the previous October], they can't touch me . . . Among other things I have painted a whole roomful of big symbolist canvases—some bad, some excellent! Have worked in laboratories and experimented and finished Antibarbarus, so that I find myself with nothing to do on this earth and think I have nothing more to do down here, the more so since I have already received a hundred times more honour than I ever dreamed of."

Life with Frida alternated, as usual, between happiness and gloom. "My life is as stormy as before," he wrote to Littmansson on 30 June. "But sometimes it has been beautiful, damned idyllic, but sometimes hellishly agonising. I am often content. I have had everything I asked from life and more." He toyed, as so often, with the notion of taking some job, "a sinecure," he suggested to Richard Bergh on 9 July, "which will not bind me to anything . . . The customs officer at Sandhamn will soon retire . . . I could have the job . . . and in a year will be earning money with a house and salary for the rest of my days! If that isn't possible, then give me a first-class lighthouse . . . Korsö lighthouse . . . is disused and could be furnished to provide five rooms and a kitchen . . . could be equipped to serve as a meteorological station and a job created for me there! as superintendent, with my own telegraph machine. I have been a telegraphist!* So there! Ask around. But no begging lists or anything of that sort." Despite his hatred of Sweden, he could not escape nostalgia. "Foreign countries are enemy territory," he concluded, "and not speaking one's own language makes one's thinking superficial."

Even more ironically, he wrote to Littmansson around 15 July suggesting that they might start a monastery for intellectuals in the Ardennes "combating the beast in man . . . suppressing the vegetative and animal functions to advance those of the emotions and intellect. Development of the spirit by isolation and shutting off contact with the impure; emancipa-

*See p. 51.

tion from expensive and unfruitful habits. Simplicity in food and drink
. . . No servants; no cooking . . . The monastery shall be subsidised by
voluntary gifts, and by the work and legacies of the brothers. All sciences,
arts and literatures may be studied . . . When we have so trained
ourselves as to produce the highest type of human being, then and not till
then shall we reveal ourselves! As the army of salvation! We shall build a
white dragon-ship, gold and coloured; clothe ourselves in white ceremo-
nial dress and row a pilgrimage down the river Aisne; sail with blue silken
sails when the wind is with us down into the Oise and to the Seine;
traverse Paris without disembarking, playing new instruments which I
have invented, new melodies which I shall allow nature (chance) to
invent . . . and so we shall sail into the Marne and back to the Aisne
where we live!"

These high-minded dreams did not prevent him from writing a
disagreeably racist letter a couple of days later to Littmansson (himself a
Jew) about an acquaintance of theirs named Adolf Hirsch and his sons
Hjalmar, Ivan and Philip. "Hjalmar has negro blood in him, you don't
know that. But I saw it in Philip's lips, old Adolf's legs and Ivan's hair;
even Hjalmar's hair which he used to have was nigger,* i.e., half-ape . . .
To squander, to pinch, to pilfer, to be disloyal and show one's eyeteeth
. . . that is nigger! Black man is bad man! Vanity without ambition!"[15]
On 11 August, writing to another correspondent, he expanded this
unpleasant theory: "If I rate the black race below the white, it is grounded
on experiences which have shown that the black are inferior to the
white."[16]

Strindberg now began a correspondence which was to continue for over
a decade with a young French scientist, François Jollivet-Castelot, who at
the age of twenty had published a book, *La Vie et l'Âme de la Matière* (*The
Life and Soul of Matter*), in which he declared his belief in the unity of
matter and in the capacity of elements to be transmuted. Strindberg was
much excited to find his own beliefs thus echoed. "I have just read your
book and am stupefied," he wrote to Castelot on 22 July. "At the same
time, I am comforted to see that I am not alone in this folly, which has
cost me domestic happiness, my good name, everything!" Castelot was
soon to become one of the leading occultists in France; he founded, in his
home town of Douai, an alchemist society, and in 1896 was to start a
magazine, *L'Hyperchimie*, to which Strindberg became a prolific contributor. In two books, which Castelot wrote about alchemy in 1896 and
1897, he devoted much space to Strindberg, quoting him freely.

---

*Strindberg uses the English word.

Another fellow spirit in the field of science appeared in the unlikely person of Torsten Hedlund, publisher of the newspaper *Handelstidningen i Göteborg*. Hedlund, six years Strindberg's junior, had written to him in 1891 shortly after the publication of *By the Open Sea*; he was a keen theosophist and thought he detected echoes of that teaching in Strindberg's novel, but Strindberg denied this (he had in fact written disparagingly of theosophy in a story, "Short Cuts," in 1887). Now, four years later, Hedlund wrote congratulating Strindberg on *Antibarbarus* and raising again the question of the occult. A year later he became what we would now call Strindberg's guru; in *Inferno*, Strindberg refers to him as "my occult friend who was to play a decisive role in my life."

"Not to have found my destiny," he lamented to Littmansson on 13 August (one of four letters he wrote to him on that day), "that is the tragic thing. And this terrible discord between what I am and what I am supposed to be; the disproportion between my powers and what I achieve; my shame at unfulfilled obligations; the unjust hatred, persecution, chafing, the eternal harassment, the encroachment of material needs. I am sick, nervously sick, hovering between epileptic attacks of workomania and general paralysis."

The relationship between Strindberg and Frida was worsening. The child was sickly, wet-nurses came and went, and a lengthy row developed between Strindberg and his in-laws over whether she should be baptised into the Roman Catholic Church. Forty years later Frida wondered: "What was it that had slipped between us, tearing us apart so cruelly, creating so much hatred, making us so blind that neither of us any longer saw the other or even himself in a true light? Perhaps it was our being too close, the brutal untrammelled intimacy of family life." Strindberg suggested to her that natural laws applied also to the emotional life of human beings. " 'If any object approach too near the magnifying glass, it becomes indistinct. . . One can lose the true aspect of a loved one if he or she come too near' . . . The child also had something to do with it . . . 'There is a physical repulsion as soon as a third body is propelled between two others.' "[17]

He felt they should part for a while. He would go to Paris, where his name now stood high and Lugné-Poe was talking about staging *The Father* to follow up the success of *Creditors*. Frida might join him as soon as the baby was strong enough to travel. Leopold Littmansson invited him to stay at Versailles in a house he owned next to his own, and sent him the fare. On 15 August Strindberg left by the night steamer from Grein to Linz, whence he sent Littmansson a card: "I haven't got drunk for a year and a half and long to see what it feels like." From Linz he took the slow train via Salzburg, Munich, Ulm and Strasbourg, a journey of nearly forty-eight hours, and by 17 August was in Versailles.

There was ample space for Strindberg in the house in the Boulevard Lesseps: it had fifteen rooms, including three kitchens. Almost immediately after his arrival, Littmansson left for Aachen, and Strindberg's consequent loneliness, combined with a shortage of money, exploded into hideous abuse of Albert Bonnier. In the last two years Strindberg had published nothing in Sweden except *The Keys of Heaven* and a volume of one-act plays. His royalties had consequently dried up, and characteristically he suspected that Bonnier was swindling him by concealing the true nature of his sales. "If Albort [*sic*] believed in Jehovah," he wrote to Littmansson on 19 August, "I would go into a synagogue one Sunday and pray for him. But he has got his deserts. His wife died barmy in an asylum . . . his only daughter was confined as a lunatic; Karl Otto is ailing and the old man has a concubine who is unfaithful to him and has already cheated him out of one villa; he wants to marry the woman because they have (she has) a child, but Karl Otto doesn't want that . . . I have said openly: if there is ever a revolution, I shall join it and put Albort and Karl Otto on a bench; and I shall personally pull out their eye-teeth until six million crowns lie on the table, the seventh they can keep."*

Despite the proximity of Paris, and the fact that he had had two plays staged there during the past nineteen months, Strindberg visited it only twice during the three weeks he was to stay in Versailles. "I must live in the country, for reasons of sanity," he explained to his French translator Georges Loiseau on 24 August, complaining the next day to Frida: "I live slowly and nothing interests me." Suddenly, however, things changed, through a meeting with two curious young men named Willy Grétor and Albert Langen.

Grétor (born in 1868 with the more commonplace surname of Petersen) was a Danish painter. Despite a bad limp, he was a tremendous womaniser, with a gift for living off other people. On his arrival in Paris in 1889 he had begun an affair with a young German artist, Marie Schorer. Marie had for some years been supported by a wealthy admirer, Rosa Pfaeffinger, whom she now somehow persuaded to set Grétor up in a six-room apartment on the Boulevard Malesherbes. In 1891 Rosa joined Grétor and Marie there; shortly afterwards, Marie bore Grétor a daughter, and before the end of the year he married Rosa. With Rosa's money, he kept as mistress an Italian dancer named Severina, and collected paint-

---

*Extracting teeth was a torture formerly used to make Jews reveal their hidden treasure.

ings with a shrewd eye; by the time Strindberg met him in 1894 he owned works attributed to Rembrandt, Velázquez, Hals, Fragonard and Corot. By 1894 he had almost dissipated Rosa's fortune.[18]

Albert Langen, a German from Cologne, had inherited a large estate, settled in Paris and, in 1893 at the age of twenty-four, had started a publishing house with Grétor. Within a year, his list included Henri Becque, Knut Hamsun, Georg Brandes, Paul Hervieu and Anatole France. Grétor had met Strindberg briefly in Denmark six years earlier, and on 28 August Langen invited Strindberg to join him and Grétor for dinner at the fashionable Restaurant Laurent on the Champs-Elysées. Also present was Becque, whose most famous play, *Les Corbeaux*, Strindberg had severely criticised in his essay "On Modern Drama."* It was to prove a fruitful meeting. "Langen lives like a rich man," Strindberg reported next day to Frida, "with a *valet de chambre*, etc. He has definitely accepted *Le Plaidoyer* [A *Madman's Defence*]. . . . Becque will revise the translation . . . B. proved a merry fellow, witty and amusing, and said some charming things to me about *Creditors*. He had expected to hiss the Scandinavians [at the premiere of *Creditors*] like everyone else, and admits he is conquered. He knew very well what I had written about him and was amused by it. He has invited me to La Plume Society.† On my return home I found a letter from Zola, who is waiting to shake hands with me. Now I am throwing off my paintings one by one, and they plan to establish me as a painter and sculptor (of busts)."

Grétor saw Strindberg's paintings and was impressed. On 31 August, Strindberg was able to inform Frida that Grétor "today bought 'Wunderland' and 'Alpine Landscape' for 400 francs and has told me that I am a painter. So I'll send you 200 francs, and you'll come? Remember that on 15 September I get paid for *Plaidoyer*. And shall paint more. My friend here [Grétor] said I should exhibit at the Champ de Mars, that 'Alpine Landscape' is a masterpiece but the 'Meadows' picture nothing. O God, what is what? What?"

Grétor's enthusiasm and encouragement seemed to know no limits. Having persuaded Rosa to sell the Boulevard Malesherbes apartment with most of its contents to Langen and move to a smaller place on the rue

---

*See page 211.

†*La Plume* was a symbolist magazine, which also held literary evenings. Zola's letter to Strindberg is reproduced in facsimile in Birger Mörner's *Den Strindberg jag känt* (Stockholm, 1924), facing page 106. Strindberg never accepted Zola's invitation to meet him, probably because of his fear of powerful personalities who might influence him (see page 121). He did not mind meeting dominant characters in other walks of life, such as Gauguin, but dominating writers daunted him.

Ranelagh in Passy, he now offered the latter to Strindberg. "4 rooms, kitchen and maid's room, *furnished free* till 1 October," Strindberg told Frida excitedly on 3 September, "two minutes from the Bois de Boulogne. Thereafter 900 francs a year if we so wish . . . Also: he has sold two more of my paintings for 500 francs this year, making a total of 900 francs. And he will guarantee me as a painter (!) 6,000 francs a year. He says he will arrange a Strindberg exhibition at Durand-Ruel's with 20 paintings and will sell them for 1,000 each! These are fairy tales, I tell myself, but his friend, a Dane, a blond youth,* says yes. A famous German has seen my paintings and is going to write about Sg. as a painter. And if no one wants them he will buy them himself . . . But: ultimatum! Come with our little one into my paternal home and be my wife, the mother of your child!"

The "famous German" was probably Frank Wedekind, who three years earlier, at the age of twenty-seven, had burst upon the German theatrical scene with his play *Spring Awakening*, and who this month became Langen's secretary. He had met Strindberg eight years earlier in Switzerland, through his parents' belonging to the circle based on the Schloss Brunegg where Strindberg had visited Heidenstam. Wedekind was to make Grétor the model for the chief character in his play *The Marquis of Keith* and in due course, after she had parted from Strindberg but before her divorce, was to become the father of Frida's second child.

The Littmanssons had by now returned to Versailles, but on 3 September they left again. Strindberg's elation at the prospect of living luxuriously in Passy straightway changed to depression. He became nostalgic for Dornach; what could they not do to the cottage with the money that was about to pour in from his paintings? "Paris is so depressing, depressing like London . . . With money one can have the books, reviews, magazines, the little things that make life tolerable. Imagine! Tiled stoves, beautiful lamps, curtains, carpets, above all, nurses!—a glass of wine in the evenings, happy evenings *à deux*. Here, you would sit alone in the house with terrible servants, endlessly exploited . . . In the country of the enemy, where people do not understand what you say, where people mock everything. Here, we shall have a muddy, damp autumn. Tramways, lorries, railway stations, street-organs, counterfeit money, bad tobacco, adulterated milk. I miss the Danube, in spite of everything. A Home† in spite of everything! Here: the street. Think about it."[19]

---

*Sven Lange, a popular playwright of intellectual pretensions.
†Strindberg uses the English word.

Perhaps the memories of Passy, where he had lived unhappily with Siri in the autumn of 1883, influenced him. However, it must have seemed preferable to be there, where he could meet his new friends, rather than to stay alone in Versailles, and on 5 September he moved into Rosa's apartment, on the ground floor of an elegant detached house in a large private park. On the day of his arrival he fired off no less than four letters to Frida, followed by five more in the next five days. "I have everything I want and I want to leave everything," he assured her, "—to rejoin you, and recommence an existence *à quatre diables*. Remember my words of yesteryear: better an unharmonious marriage than nothing. It is too calm here. No one harasses or torments me; I long to endure a good matrimonial quarrel in which you are ever the undisputed master. Dear master, call me back!"[20]

He painted furiously; within four days of his arrival in Passy he was able to tell Frida that he had completed ten canvases, landscapes and seascapes, painted, like so many of Munch's, from memory and imagination. Rosa had left painting materials, of which he availed himself; also her collection of modern paintings, including, according to Frida, a Cézanne which Grétor had bought from Gauguin, and Van Gogh's *Ronde des prisonniers*.[21] Strindberg was cheered by a letter from his old Uppsala friend and benefactor Gustaf Eisen, now a professor of science in San Francisco, telling him that he and two chemist friends had read *Antibarbarus* and had found it "good, and not mad."[22] But Frida was unwilling for him to return to Dornach; not unreasonably, remembering that she was still only twenty-two, the prospect of being the wife of a famous man in Paris seemed more attractive than the resumption of daily rows in the cottage. On 11 September he sent her 250 francs for the journey, and a few days later she joined him in Passy for the last six weeks that they were to spend together.

Frida was delighted to be in Paris again, the more so since Langen and Grétor both paid assiduous court to her. "They are both quite young and good-looking," she noted, "with bright, wholesome faces, dressed with a touch of dandyism. I never saw so much 'shine' as upon these two young heads, sleeked with brilliantine, and on these patent-leather shoes . . . They treat Strindberg with ceremonious deference." Grétor she found "a splendid *causeur* . . . strong white teeth and the figure of a sportsman. A pity that he is lame on one side." Langen offered her work translating German authors into French.

Sarah Bernhardt was appearing in Dumas *fils's La Femme de Claude* at the Comédie-Française, and Langen arranged for Strindberg to see the performance from a box and then meet her. He gave a dinner first in his apartment, with Becque and Paul Hervieu among the guests. But when the carriage arrived, Strindberg refused to enter it and wandered away instead into the city.[23] Bernhardt, like Zola, was someone whom Strindberg chose not to meet.

The Norwegian painter Fritz Thaulow and his wife, Alexandra, cycled from Dieppe and invited the Strindbergs to dine.

> As we approached the hotel, Strindberg said "Let me go up first and tame the wild animal." We waited patiently, expecting to see an alarming creature. We were to be surprised. With Strindberg entered a poor, pretty little dark-haired lady, her eyes red with crying. She did not look a day more than seventeen or eighteen. She had been sitting alone all day waiting for him. Now she smiled radiantly, overjoyed at being allowed to be with him and his friends . . . She told me she had a little child. . . . She had left it with her parents, for Strindberg had demanded that she choose between him and the child to show which she was most bound to—and now she longed so dreadfully for her little one.[24]

Strindberg spoke Swedish to the Thaulows, and Frida remembered that she "had never seen Strindberg so animated. He speaks in his native tongue, like a man released after being sentenced to silence. Now for the first time I realise what a torture exile means to him." Afterwards, although they had only 20 francs in the world, they took a carriage and she realised that "for the first time since I have known him, Strindberg is blissfully drunk . . . Every five minutes or so the coachman has to halt. The fare gets out of his cab and stands for another five minutes lost in contemplation of the pitch-dark night." The trip cost 10 francs and Strindberg gave the coachman his remaining 10 francs as a tip.[25]

He now became jealous of, as he saw it, the way Frida flirted with Langen, Grétor and Wedekind. For once his jealousy may have had grounds. Later Frida admitted to Grétor's daughter: "I was strongly fascinated by Willy Grétor that autumn in the nineties and did everything to win his friendship, even proposed visiting his studio for coaching—but I was greeted with a sustained and demonstrative coolness which caused me to form a close friendship with Frank Wedekind to make Grétor jealous. This too failed."[26] It seems unlikely that she and Wedekind became lovers until later; her book about Strindberg, not surprisingly, gives no clue.

As a change from painting, Strindberg executed a bust of Becque. He visited the Morgue to study the corpses. "Extraordinary how happy they looked," he wrote to Littmansson on 2 October, "and, above all, good! except a woman who was evil." He read that Lugné-Poe had staged

Maeterlinck's *Pelléas et Mélisande* in Copenhagen and that Herman
Bang had delivered a lecture there criticising naturalism and hailing
Maeterlinck as the harbinger of a new wave. Strindberg had admired
Maeterlinck's early plays, but found his more recent work self-conscious
and mannered. "Naturalism is not dead," he wrote to Birger Mörner on
7 October. "It lives grandly here in Zola, Goncourt, Hervieu, Prévost,
Huysmans, Becque, etc. Naturalism or the poetic portrayal of nature can
never die until nature dies. But Maeterlinck, a caprice, a curio which
amuses me in a weary moment, is still-born . . . Anyone who follows
Maeterlinck's unknown echo-form is lost as an independent writer . . .
He . . . has lost his naïveté and is an old coquette . . . I have three plays
accepted here for the winter. *The Bond* by Antoine, *Père* by l'Oeuvre and
Playing with Fire by les Escholiers."

Only the second of these projects was to materialise; Antoine never
staged another Strindberg play, and although Lugné-Poe had planned to
direct *Playing with Fire* for les Escholiers he instead gave an extra
performance of *Creditors*. He also, during his Scandinavian tour that
October (which included a triumphant visit to Christiania, where his
Solness was praised by Ibsen himself), presented *Creditors* in Stockholm,
but it had an undeservedly chilly reception. Strindberg's old friend Pehr
Staaff complained in *Dagens Nyheter* that this leading figure of the
French theatre was treated by the Swedes as "a common second- or
third-class actor."[27]

Their stay in Rosa Pfaeffinger's apartment was rudely cut short by the
appearance of bailiffs; whether Rosa owed merely the rent, or for the
furniture and paintings, too, they never discovered. "Strindberg, who
always fears the worst, trembled for his most sacred possessions and stood
protectively in front of his green bag." But the bailiffs dismissed that, and
the Cézanne, as worthless, and showed more interest in the furniture and
carpets.[28] They moved to the small Hôtel des Américains in the rue de
l'Abbé de l'Epée near the Luxembourg Gardens, recommended by the
Thaulows, where they met a Norwegian actor and actress, Johan and
Alma Fahlström. Seven years later, by his third marriage, Strindberg was
to become Alma Fahlström's brother-in-law.

He continued as feverishly as ever with his painting and scientific
experiments, sitting up half the night over the latter while Frida, lying in
bed, watched "the flame glowing and flickering under the retorts and how
he disintegrates and transmutes his materials. I see them changing from
yellow to blue and red like the mysteries of a new world at birth."[29] A
young Danish poet, Sophus Clausen, offered to introduce them to Paul
Verlaine, who, he said, admired Strindberg's work. He took them to

Verlaine's favourite haunt, the Procope, but unfortunately Verlaine was not there.

A letter now arrived from Anna, their nurse at Dornach, saying that Frida's grandmother had insulted her by accusing her of looking at men in the street and that as a result she was giving notice. The next day, 21 October, Frida took the train to Austria. She and Strindberg bought toys in the Printemps department store and, since he had a dinner engagement, kissed farewell in the street outside. "It is not the first time that we have parted hugging each other on the pavement of a foreign town. The first time was in London, and passers-by regarded us disapprovingly as lost souls . . . Then he jumps on top of a bus . . . Over the heads of the people on top of the bus, his white fluttering handkerchief in his hand, half laughing, half crying, staring after me with all his eyes and waving, always waving his white kerchief—while the black crowds that fill the streets coil around me and carry me away—I see August Strindberg vanish."[30] The plan was that she should return with Kerstin to Paris, but Frida and Strindberg were never to meet again.

Chapter Twenty

TOWARDS INFERNO

Most people, however miserable their marriage, are more miserable alone, and Strindberg was no exception. He wrote Frida twenty-two letters in nineteen days after their parting, the familiar mixture of nostalgia, dependence and accusation. The day after she left Paris he accepted an invitation from the Thaulows to visit them in Dieppe. Alexandra Thaulow tells how each day there he asked if any letters had arrived from Frida, eventually declaring: "Six days without a letter. I shall divorce her." When Alexandra asked if he had given Frida his change of address, he replied, "Certainly not. Must I account for everything I do?"

"Then there will be a pile of letters waiting for you in Paris."

"That does not alter my decision. I have been caused suffering and disquiet by this vain waiting."[1]

Thaulow had to leave for Norway to attend his mother's funeral, and Strindberg returned to Paris on 1 November, lodging again at the Hôtel des Américains. "What a wretched existence!" he complained to Frida on 4 November. "I detest mankind and I cannot be alone—thus, bad company, alcohol, late nights, Chat Noir, despair and the lot—above all, paralysis. What purpose have I in Paris? . . . Littmansson has been to see me and we have a plan to found a Chat Noir or a Procope

Strindberg . . .* Then we'll be back at the Porker, with chronic alcoholism and all that. To sink so as to rise, to die in order to live! The tavern
replaces the family. *Joie de vivre!* I'm already a wreck after four days on my
own. A six-hour lunch with Becque; a whole day from morning to night
with Littmansson; an evening and half the night with Geissbart [his
translator, Georges Loiseau]. Yes, it's nasty, and yet, alone in a city, the
tavern saves me from suicide, or leads me towards it, so much the better."

On 7 November an exhibition was held in Gothenburg of the paintings
which Strindberg had done at Passy, thanks to an admirer, Algot
Colander, to whom he had sent the canvases shortly before leaving for
Dieppe. A respectful notice appeared in *Handelstidningen i Göteborg*,
describing them as "new and singular proof of the famous author's great
versatility . . . the more or less comprehensible products of a rich and
restless spirit." Some of the paintings were even bought, albeit for only 30
crowns apiece. [2]

But by now Strindberg had become disillusioned with Willy Grétor
and his promises to promote him as a painter, and he abandoned art to
return with a dreadful single-mindedness to his misguided forays into the
byways of science.

> Back once again in my miserable student's room in the Latin Quarter [at
> the Hôtel des Américains] I delved into my trunk and drew forth from their
> hiding place six crucibles of fine porcelain which I had robbed myself to
> buy. A pair of tongs and a packet of pure sulphur completed the apparatus of
> my laboratory. All that remained was to make a fire of furnace heat in the
> stove, secure the door, and draw down the blinds; for since the execution of
> Caserio, only three months earlier, it had become dangerous to handle
> chemical apparatus in Paris. †
>
> Night fell, the flames of hell rose from the burning sulphur, but towards
> morning I had ascertained the presence of carbon in sulphur, previously
> regarded as an elementary substance. By doing this I believed I had solved
> the great problem, overthrown the prevailing chemical theories, and won
> the only immortality accorded to mortals.
>
> But from my hands, roasted by the intense heat, the skin was peeling off
> in scales, and the pain caused by the mere effort of undressing reminded me
> of what victory had cost. Yet alone, in my bed, where the odour of woman
> still lingered, I was blissful. A feeling of spiritual purity, of masculine
> virginity, made me regard my past married life as something unclean. [3]

*The Chat Noir was a cabaret in Montmartre founded by the painter Rodolphe Salis
which specialised in shadow plays, using zinc silhouettes against a background lit through
shades of coloured glass and accompanied by spoken dialogue. Strindberg considered
adapting *The Keys of Heaven* for performance there but the plan fell through. The Procope
on the Left Bank specialised in literary cabaret.

†Caserio, an Italian anarchist, had assassinated President Carnot on 24 June 1894.

On 8 November he wrote Frida an insanely jealous and hysterical letter: "M. Langen has insulted me by visiting me towards nightfall; you say you asked him to stop these visits and I know you have invited him in the evenings to read manuscripts, even at midnight, four o'clock, leaving at eight and this on the very day when you swore you would not do this. You offer to be his secretary and declare yourself willing to visit him every morning . . . Do you act thus consciously and by design or is it your immoral nature that drives you on? In London your bad reputation was confirmed by your dining with an unmarried man [William Heinemann] in public, you a young wife; in Berlin you are notorious, in Vienna too, and in Paris you have made a fine start. What is the use of our acting the comedy of love when we hate each other? You hate me as the superior being who has never done you wrong, and I hate you because you behave like an enemy . . . Divine unconcern has led me into a marriage in which I have been treated like a beggar, lower than the servants, and to the point where my children curse me." He followed this the next day with an even wilder letter ("your cruelties, your sordid conduct in England, in Berlin, everywhere, have aroused my disgust"), and another the following day. "I only want," he told Littmansson on 9 November, "to lie in a bed and hate everyone else, rejoice in their reverses and think how my successes will rile them—if not before then after I conk out, for I shall conk out bloody soon." To make matters worse, on 15 November Siri's lawyer in Helsinki wrote to Frida's father asking him to "save your son-in-law from dishonour" by paying the 2,100 crowns which Strindberg owed her for the children's upkeep.

"I don't really know about my marriage," he wrote to Richard Bergh on 26 November. "It was never taken seriously, as you must have noticed in Berlin, and is probably moving towards its end—but I don't know for sure. Sometimes it was great fun and very good, but language, race, moral differences and different habits sometimes created great tensions."

Frida wrote that she would seek a divorce unless he withdrew his accusations. "No," he replied on 3 December.

> I won't withdraw a word, and there is more I could add but that can wait for another time . . . Be humble; repent and mend your ways . . . Fortune has favoured me and if you wish to continue to live with me, and for your family, I will place at your disposal the two rooms on the ground floor where Thaulow used to live . . . But all this on condition
>
> that you cease arranging rendezvous behind my back
>
> that you never see either M. Grétor or M. Langen, whom I have sent packing

that you never make propaganda here for your German friends and
lovers, in view of the unpopularity of Germans in Paris

that you do not wander the town alone or with people who will
compromise you . . .

Frida predictably refused. "You are the filthiest human beast I have
ever known," he retorted on 8 December. ". . . I shall never introduce
you as my wife, I shall never escort you in society . . . I shall not take
revenge. To write a second volume of *Plaidoyer* would be to rewrite the
first. And to what purpose? A vulgar common type like you does not
interest me."

Consolation offered itself in the form of a repeat performance of
Lugné-Poe's production of *Creditors* on 10 December at the Cercle St.
Simon on the rue Serpente. More importantly (and it must have been this
to which he was referring when he wrote "Fortune has favoured me"), on
13 December came the much delayed premiere by the Théâtre de
l'Oeuvre of *The Father*, at the Nouveau Théâtre on the rue Blanche, one
of the largest theatres in Paris, holding over a thousand people. Lugné-
Poe had cut the final scene of the Captain's stroke and instead had him
helped out, broken, through a door. Strindberg was unbothered by this.
When his translator, Georges Loiseau, nervously told him of the change
after a rehearsal, Strindberg replied, "Be sensible and let things be. I've
given Messieurs Poe and Bauër permission to change the end, make cuts,
etc. And why not? In return M. Poe will perform the play for a whole
week."[4] One is reminded of how on the occasion of the first Swedish
production of the play he had told the director to "cut what doesn't work."

Philippe Garnier and Lucienne Dorcy played the principal roles, with
Lugné-Poe as the Pastor. The performance was received with rapt
attention, apart from an elderly lady who interrupted it so repeatedly with
hawking and coughing that she had to be ejected; this turned out to be one
Bertha Straube, who had made an earlier translation of the play and was
angry that Loiseau's had been used instead. The critics were enthusiastic.
Henry Bauër, who had helped Poe with the adaptation but found it not
unethical to review it in *L'Echo de Paris*,* described it as "the first
unquestioned and indisputable victory which Scandinavian literature has
gained in Paris," which must have delighted Strindberg by its implication
that the play was better than any of Ibsen's which had been seen there.
Francisque Sarcey in *Le Temps*, though he described the Captain as a

*Bauër had taken part in the Paris commune uprising of 1871, and subsequently served
ten years in exile in New Caledonia. Strindberg dedicated the French edition of *A
Madman's Defence* to him.

"naval commander" and found Laura contrived and unreal, thought Strindberg much superior to Ibsen and Bjørnson, praising his stagecraft and his ability to conceive and write effective scenes. The younger critics, such as Paul Ginisty (who had condemned Miss Julie in Le Petit Parisien as "total disaster"), Edmond Stoullig in Le National, Achille Segards in La Plume and Romain Coolus in Revue Blanche, were favourable, and Camille Mauclair in Revue Encyclopédique, echoing Henry Bauër's words, wrote: "Last night we witnessed the Scandinavian theatre's first great and unquestioned success in Paris. We have had excellent evenings before, Antoine's Ghosts, A Doll's House at the Vaudeville [with Réjane], but these were successes for the actors or for tragic effects. Strindberg has achieved his triumph through his ideas, through the irreconcilable violence of his piercing and brutally realistic genius." Some of the older critics remained sceptical; Jules Lemaître, in Journal des Débats, complained that the play was unpleasant, monotonous and patently indebted to Dumas fils, Laura having been clearly cribbed from the faithless wife Césarine in La Femme de Claude.[5]

Strindberg attended a late rehearsal of the production on 11 December but absented himself from the dress rehearsal as well as from the premiere. "If I have sinned against convention," he wrote to Lugné-Poe the next day, excusing his absence, "I say: Forgive the foreigner. I am neither ungrateful nor unmannerly, but what do you want with my poor body when you have my work? Please think of me as a sick person and believe that I have good reasons to seek solitude." As a result of the production's success he received, according to Julien Leclerq, numerous invitations to meet celebrities but refused them all, partly because of his embarrassment at being unable to converse fluently in French, partly because of a recurrence of a skin disease, which was shortly to become serious.[6]

Among the audience at the premiere, which included Auguste Rodin, the columnist for Le Figaro noted "an unknown gentleman in an astrakhan bonnet." This was Paul Gauguin, who had made Strindberg's acquaintance a short while before on returning to Paris from his first visit to Tahiti. William Molard, a composer with a Norwegian mother, and his wife, Ida, a Swedish sculptress, lived on the rue Vercingétorix; Strindberg knew them and met Gauguin when the latter moved into a studio above their apartment. (He had dined with Gauguin's Danish wife, Mette, in Copenhagen in 1887, when he had been offended by her close-cropped hair.)* He and Gauguin seem to have taken an immediate

*See page 184.

fancy to each other. Both were strong individualists, separated from their wives, tormented by the absence of their children, under continual rebuke for not meeting their obligations and denigrated as artists; Gauguin's exhibition of his Tahiti paintings in Paris had been harshly criticised and had sold poorly.

Another celebrity whom Strindberg met at this time, on the day before the premiere of *The Father*, was Alexandre Dumas *fils*, then aged seventy-one (he was to die the following year). A young Finnish painter, Sigurd Wetterhof-Asp, was present, and recalled that Dumas began the conversation by praising Tolstoy, which made Strindberg nervous—"it was a characteristic of his that he did not really like to hear other people praised. Luckily, Dumas did not mention Ibsen." Mostly, however, they talked, as serious writers tend to when brought together, about money. Dumas said that as a member of the French Society of Dramatists, Strindberg was entitled to 10 percent of the gross receipts from *The Father*, that Lugné-Poe had asked him, Dumas, if he needed to pay Strindberg that much, and that he had told Lugné-Poe that he must; if necessary, the society would fight Strindberg's cause in the matter. Finally, "Dumas rose and wished Strindberg luck with his play. Strindberg rose too, numbed, as though from a lethargic sleep. '*Eh bien, mon cher confrère,*' were Dumas's last words, '*nous lutterons ensemble*' [Well, my dear colleague, we shall fight together]."[7] But although Lugné-Poe gave ten performances of the play, compared with the single performance which *Miss Julie* had received at the Théâtre Libre the previous year, and subsequently toured it in the provinces and in Monte Carlo, Strindberg's reward amounted to only 300 francs, and he was not to be staged in Paris again until 1920. Lugné-Poe further annoyed him by giving a series of lectures in which he linked *The Father* with *An Enemy of the People*. "Why must I act as Ibsen's hunting dog?" he complained to Lugné-Poe on 16 December, adding that people still accused him of having based Laura on Hedda Gabler, "whereas the reverse is the case."

On Christmas Eve Julien Leclerq visited Strindberg and found him "sitting alone in an enormous winter coat . . . The desk was bare save for a photograph of his children, and a revolver . . . Strindberg explained that since the age of seven he had suffered from a compulsion to kill himself. Feast days such as this made him melancholic."[8]

On 7 January 1895 he published a long article, "On the Inferiority of Woman to Man," in *Revue Blanche*; it occupied the first twenty pages of the issue. The old arguments were trotted out, bolstered by "scientific" evidence as fanciful as his theories about sulphur and gold. The article provoked a long and impassioned controversy. Paul Ginisty, who, despite his disappointment with the performance of *Miss Julie*, had pioneered Strindberg's writing in France for some years, commented in *Le XIX Siècle* that the piece aroused "more attention in Paris . . . than he has done with all his plays . . . This wild misogynist declares, less courteously than anyone has done before, that woman is an inferior being, that man's great fault has been to allow her to seek equality with him, that she must be returned to a state of passive obedience . . . One might say of him what was said of the dinner guest who rejected with revulsion the dishes offered to him: 'If you don't like this, that is no reason to infect others with a distaste for it.'" Ginisty concluded: "If man is 'superior,' he has a duty to show charity, help and protection to the woman, who fights so desperately to survive . . . True superiority consists in the broadest conception of one's duties."

A photograph of Strindberg at this time, taken a few weeks before his forty-sixth birthday, shows him looking much older than his years, his hair greying and receding, his face pale, his eyes tired. He had experienced a return of an unpleasant skin disease of the hands known as psoriasis which had afflicted him several times before, usually at periods of severe mental or emotional stress. In *Inferno*, which he wrote two years later, Strindberg claimed that his chemical experiments were solely to blame for this:

> My chapped hands became poisoned, the cracks widened, were filled with coke dust, blood oozed from them, and the agony became intolerable . . . Almost mad with pain, I avoided and neglected my fellow-men, refused invitations, drove my friends from me. Silence and solitude encompassed me, the stillness of a desert, solemn, terrifying, in which I defiantly challenged the unseen Power to a wrestling match, body against body, soul against soul.[9]

In fact, the prime cause was probably a combination of worry about the impending trial in Berlin, his suspicions about Frida, the failure of *The Father* to bring him any real money, and his months of absinthe drinking, though the chemicals may have exacerbated his condition. Moreover, psoriasis was popularly believed at that time to be a venereal disease (though as long ago as 19 June 1891 he had written to Fredrik Vult von Steijern that "the skin eruption on my hands from which I have suffered for three years has been certified by Dr. Anton Nyström on oath as not being of a syphilitic nature"). Another school of thought held that it was a form of leprosy. Strindberg seems to have dismissed such alarming theories; Frida tells that in February 1893, when he came to dinner at her flat in Berlin, he showed her his hand and described it as "an innocent eczema, I have had it since I was a child . . . When anything happens to me, the wound opens and bleeds."[10]

But so low was his general state that his friends decided he must go to hospital, and Nathan Söderblom, then Swedish pastor in Paris (and later to become Archbishop of Uppsala), organised a whip-round to cover his expenses. Thus, less than a month after his triumph with *The Father*, Strindberg had to depend on charity to recover his health. On 7 January 1895 he became an out-patient at the Hôpital de St. Louis, which specialised in skin diseases. Four days later, Strindberg became an in-patient, and remained there until the end of the month. It was the only time of his life that he spent in a hospital.[11]

"It is not much fun here," he wrote to Frida on 16 January. "A kind of prison. This morning the porter refused to let me go out without a note from the director, and the director refused to sign one. Two policemen are here every day and the company—mostly without noses—is discouraging."

> My hands were swathed in bandages, so that any sort of occupation was out of the question . . . The bell sounded for lunch and at the table I found myself among a company of spectres. A nose missing here, an eye there, a third with a dangling lip, another with a crumbling cheek. Two of the individuals at the table did not look ill at all, but their expression was sullen and despairing. They were master thieves of a good family who, thanks to their powerful relatives, had been let out of prison on the grounds of illness . . . In the midst of this delightful company of criminals and those doomed to die there moved our kind mother, the Matron, in her austere habit of black and white . . . How wonderful it was to use that word "mother," a word that had not crossed my lips for thirty years . . . She was gentle as resignation itself, and she taught us to smile at our sufferings as if they had been so many joys, for she knew how salutary pain can be. She never uttered a word of reproach, she never admonished us, she never preached to us.[12]

A few days after entering the hospital, Strindberg was interviewed there by reporters from *Le Matin* and *Le Temps*, who found him with both hands "completely smothered in cotton wool and bandaged up to the wrists." He declared that the theatre now held second place in his interests: "I am returning to science, which I have never totally abandoned; now I shall devote myself exclusively to it."* He explained his method of photographing the sky, and how he had succeeded in tracing

---

*Albert Langen published the French edition of *A Madman's Defence*, under its original title of *Le Plaidoyer d'un Fou*, while Strindberg was in hospital, and *The People of Hemsö* began to appear in *Revue Hebdomadaire*, but Strindberg showed no interest in them apart from what money they might bring him.[13]

the presence of carbon in sulphur. The *Le Temps* reporter concluded: "Les auteurs dramatiques scandinaves ne sont pas les auteurs dramatiques ordinaires [Scandinavian dramatists are not like other dramatists]."[14]

Strindberg left the hospital on 31 January, partly because his psoriasis was pronounced incurable, though not in the long run dangerous, and partly because the fund raised by his well-wishers had run out. He took rooms in a *pension de famille* at 12 rue de la Grande Chaumière, in the heart of Montparnasse. In *Inferno* he suggests that he now lived the life of a recluse, but that, like so much else in *Inferno*, is a distortion of the facts. Over the next year and a half he mixed freely with the Molards and their circle, which included in addition to Gauguin, two promising younger talents, the Czech painter Alphonse Mucha, whose first famous poster of Sarah Bernhardt had appeared on the Paris streets that month, and the English composer Frederick Delius.

Gauguin had by now finally broken with his wife and this, together with the failure of his exhibition, made him decide to sell his possessions in France and return to Tahiti for good. He arranged an auction of his Tahiti paintings at the Hôtel Drouot and asked Strindberg to write a foreword to the catalogue. The success of *The Father*, the controversy aroused by the essay "On the Inferiority of Woman to Man," and the publication in late January of *A Madman's Defence* in the original French (which elicited an enthusiastic review from Julien Leclerq in *Revue Encyclopédique*), meant that Strindberg's name would draw attention to an event which otherwise might pass virtually unnoticed. Strindberg refused, in a long and eloquent letter: "I cannot understand your art and I cannot like it . . . But I know that this avowal will not surprise or hurt you, for you seem to me to be strengthened by other men's scorn; your personality takes pleasure in the antipathy which it arouses, determined to remain intact. And perhaps rightly, for the moment when, approved and admired, you find yourself the centre of a cult, people will pigeon-hole and classify you, will sum up your art in a word which within five years the young will use as a catchword to describe an out-of-date art which they will do everything to make seem more out-of-date."

He went on to recall his first visit to Paris in 1876, when the Swedish circles in which he mixed had never heard of Zola, and a young artist had taken him to see paintings by Manet and Monet, which at first made little impression on him but which he found interesting when he revisited the exhibition next day; and his subsequent visits in 1883 and 1885, when he saw a posthumous exhibition of Manet's work but when the name on everyone's lips was that of Puvis de Chavannes, the precursor of symbolism.

It was to Puvis de Chavannes that my thoughts turned yesterday when, to the midday strains of mandolin and guitar, I saw on the walls of your studio this medley of sun-drenched paintings which haunted me last night as I slept. I saw trees which no botanist would recognise, animals of whose existence Cuvier never dreamed, and men whom you alone could have created. A sea which ran from a volcano, a sky in which no god could dwell. Monsieur (I said in my dream), you have created a new earth and a new heaven, but I am not happy in this world of yours, it is too sunny for me, who like chiaroscuro. And in your paradise there dwells an Eve who is not my ideal—for I too have an ideal or two of how a woman should be! . . . No, Gauguin is not a rib from the side of Chavannes, nor from that of Manet, nor Bastien Lepage! Who is he? He is Gauguin, the savage who hates the encumbrance of civilization, a kind of Titan who, jealous of his creator, creates in his lost moments his own little world, the child who dismantles his toys to make new ones, who challenges and defies God, preferring to see the sky as red rather than, like the mob, as blue. Upon my soul, as I warm to these words, I begin to feel a certain understanding of the art of Gauguin.

People have reproached a modern writer for not portraying real human beings but *simply* creating ones of his own. *Simply!*

Bon voyage, Maître! only come back to us and come back to find me. By then I may perhaps have learned to understand your art better, which would allow me to write a true preface for a new catalogue in a new Hôtel Drouot, for I too begin to feel an immense need to turn savage and create a new world.

Strindberg wrote this letter on 1 February, the day after leaving the hospital. Gauguin was delighted and penned an equally vivid reply.

I had the idea of asking you to write this preface when, the other day in my studio, I saw you playing the guitar and singing; your blue Nordic eye studied attentively the pictures on the walls. I had a kind of presentiment of revolt; of a head-on collision between your civilisation and my barbarism. Civilisation, from which you suffer. Barbarism, which is for me a rebirth . . . The Eve whom I have painted (and she alone) truthfully can remain naked before our eyes. Yours, in this natural condition, would not know how to walk without shame. To enable you to understand what I mean, I will compare not merely the two women, but the Maori or Turanian language which my Eve speaks with the tongue which your chosen woman speaks, an inflected language, a European language. In the languages of Oceania, reduced in their simplicity to bare essentials . . . everything is naked, vivid and primordial . . . Forgive this philological digression; I think it necessary to explain the primitivism [*dessin sauvage*] which I have used to portray a country and a people that speaks Turanian.

It remains, my dear Strindberg, for me to thank you. When shall we meet again? Then, as now, yours with all my heart.

Paul Gauguin[15]

Gauguin printed Strindberg's letter in its entirety as foreword to his catalogue, and sent it and his reply to the critic Arsène Alexandre, who arranged for them to be published in the newspaper *L'Eclair* on 15 and 16 February, immediately prior to the opening of the exhibition. The veteran Impressionist Camille Pissarro read them and wrote to his son Lucien (in English): "I asked Rodolphe to send you the newspapers in which you will see the letter of Strindberg, the Norwegian [*sic*] dramatist, to Gauguin, and the latter's reply. This author has a poor impression of the impressionists, he understands no one but Puvis de Chavannes." But Strindberg was ahead of his contemporaries in appreciating what Gauguin was trying to do,* even if he could not wholly sympathise with him. That May he tried to persuade the German painter Hermann Schittgen, whom he had known at the Black Porker, to arrange an exhibition of Gauguin's paintings in Munich; but nobody in Germany seemed interested in Gauguin. [16]

Strindberg's new lodgings in the rue de la Grande Chaumière stood opposite a *crémerie*, or small restaurant, run by an Alsatian lady named Madame Charlotte Futterer, described by the Swedish sculptor Carl Milles as "a strongly built woman of around fifty with a full face and beautiful eyes." [17] Gauguin had patronised it for some years, and now held court there. It had a small garden at the back, shaded by acacias. "Artists received unlimited credit," Frederick Delius remembered. "It was a little place of the utmost simplicity where hardly ten people could sit down at a time and where one's meal generally cost a franc, or a franc fifty including coffee." [18] In addition to Gauguin, who did not leave for Tahiti until the end of June, Delius and Mucha, the circle included the young poet Julien Leclerq, a Polish painter, Wladislaw Slewinski, who presented the restaurant with a large and not very good pastel of Strindberg, and a Czech *maître de ballet* from the Folies Bergère. "It was a family circle," Strindberg wrote in *Inferno*. "They loved me there." [19] Delius continues:

> I would sometimes fetch Strindberg for a walk in the afternoon and we would go through the Luxemburg Gardens and around the Panthéon, again up the Boulevard Raspail and down the Boulevard St. Michel, turning down the Boulevard Germain towards St. Germain des Près, then up again through the rue de Tournon, the Galeries de L'Odéon and back through the Luxemburg Gardens. Another favourite walk of ours was to the Jardin des Plantes. Strindberg seemed extremely interested in monkeys at that time. He had a theory that the gorilla was descended from a shipwrecked sailor

*Only nine of the forty-seven paintings at the Paris auction were sold, two of them to Edgar Degas.

and an ordinary female monkey. One of his great proofs of this was the similarity between the inside of the paw of the gorilla and the palm of the hand of an old sailor. He showed me photos of both, and indeed there was a great resemblance.

Strindberg was then also greatly occupied with alchemy, and claimed to have extracted gold from earth which he had collected in the Cimetière Montparnasse, and he showed me pebbles entirely coated with the precious metal. He asked me once to have one of these samples analysed by an eminent chemist of my acquaintance. My friend examined it and found it to be covered with pure gold. He was hugely interested and expressed the desire to make Strindberg's acquaintance. So I arranged a meeting in my rooms for a certain Wednesday afternoon at three o'clock. My friend arrived quite punctually, but we waited an hour in vain for Strindberg. At a quarter past four a telegram arrived with these words: "I feel that the time has not yet come for me to disclose my discovery—Strindberg." The scientist went away very disappointed, saying to me, "I am afraid your friend is a practical joker" . . . Another day Strindberg told me that he had discovered a way of making iodine at half the usual cost, and that he had inspired an article in *Le Temps* about this new method. This article created an immense sensation, especially in Hamburg, where iodine seemed to be monopolised; in one day iodine dropped 40 percent on the Hamburg market. Unfortunately, nothing further was ever heard of this affair. [20]

That February of 1895, Strindberg had received encouragement for his scientific ideas in a letter from André Dubosc, an engineer at a chemical factory in Rouen who sat on the board of the periodical *La Science Française*. Dubosc had read an article there about Strindberg's experiments with sulphur, and another in *Le Figaro* about Strindberg as a chemist. "If the hypothesis you have propounded is justified," Dubosc wrote in a second letter of 6 March, "it probably explains hitherto unexplained phenomena in the manufacture of sulphuric acid and sulphides." Strindberg visited Dubosc in Rouen in April, and corresponded actively with him for the next fifteen months. [21]

His dream of conquering Paris as a man of letters was fast fading; as, indeed, was French interest in Scandinavian writing. In his favourable review of the French edition of *A Madman's Defence* in *Le XIX Siècle* (11 February), Paul Ginisty noted: "The great enthusiasm for Scandinavian literature is beginning to decline somewhat and, curiosity having abated, reaction is setting in against the Swedes and Norwegians who for two years have almost tyrannised over us. Some are even beginning to burn the idols they worshipped and to discover that these ideas from the land of the fjords were at bottom nothing but French ideas, but so shrouded in mist that at first people did not recognise them." For the remainder of his time in Paris, Strindberg virtually gave up seeing Lugné-Poe, Becque, Hervieu and even his translator Georges Loiseau, and concentrated solely on science.[22]

Another subscription was started for Strindberg at this time by Scandinavian writers and artists living in Paris. On 7 March an appeal signed by, among others, Knut Hamsun and Jonas Lie, appeared in a number of Scandinavian newspapers. "Things are not going well with Strindberg," Hamsun wrote to Adolf Paul on 19 March.

> . . . The Swedish papers to which I sent the appeal will not print or mention it. He is living here most insecurely, now and then writing an article which may or may not get accepted. He is ill paid too. *Figaro* paid 40 francs for his latest piece about sulphur, of which his translator got 20, so that Strindberg received only 20. He is in debt at his lodgings, has lived there on credit the whole time and doesn't know how long he will be allowed to stay. He has one tiny room, where he also has to sleep. He lacks clothes. This winter he has been walking around in a light grey summer suit which, reasonably enough, embarrasses him. Nor can he visit people dressed like that, not even editors . . . You say he bears a grudge against you. I hardly know anyone he doesn't bear a grudge against. He can't easily endure me either, he says I am "too powerful a personality" for him. He is virtually impossible to be with. But I overlook that—as, I gather, do you. He is, despite everything, August Strindberg.
>
> He should be enabled to do whatever he wishes. If he wants to write creative literature, good. If he wants to dabble in chemistry, good. If he wants to do nothing, good. This man has done so much and is so important that he should be allowed to live just as he pleases. One evening we went out for a meal. We stopped outside a place which didn't look too smart and where other shabbily dressed people were going in. But Strindberg said, "No, this is too bright for me, this is too dear—let's go somewhere else." But the way he said "This is too bright for me" moved me deeply. He said it without complaint but simply as a fact.[23]

A separate appeal was started at the same time in Sweden on the initiative of Birger Mörner and F. U. Wrangel, a writer and artist (no relation to Siri's first husband), who had met Strindberg twenty years earlier when the latter was a tutor at Dr. Lamm's. A letter dated 22 March appeared in several Swedish newspapers that April, signed by twenty leading figures in Swedish literature, including some, such as Heidenstam, Viktor Rydberg, Frans Hedberg and Oscar Levertin, whom Strindberg regarded as enemies. But the response was poor: 1,795 crowns, or 2,468 francs, and even this small amount took until the end of the year to raise.[24]

Strindberg at first welcomed these appeals, but reacted angrily when people began sending money direct to him instead of to the organisers. On 2 April Hamsun visited him to hand over the first instalment from his appeal. Strindberg was out, so Hamsun left a note and followed it with a letter, to which Strindberg replied with a single sentence: "Keep the pieces of silver and let us be finished with each other for life." On 17 April Hamsun told Jonas Lie that he had tried again to see Strindberg but had been refused admittance. Undaunted, Hamsun arranged for the Deutsches Theater in Berlin to put on a special performance for Strindberg's benefit. Strindberg agreed to this, but refused to accept any proceeds, asking that the money be sent to his daughter Kerstin. "But they will scarcely wish to give a performance to benefit this child, the granddaughter of a rich judge," Hamsun wrote to Jonas Lie on 27 May; and Cornelius Reischl was furious when he read of the performance. [25]

Strindberg's letters to Frida during these months were a mixture of affection and reproach. As early as January he had rejected the idea of continuing their marriage; then he invited her several times to return to Paris; in February, he begged: "Do not be my enemy! Only leave me in peace! Leave me with my sorrows!"[26] In the spring he often spoke of going to Dornach to see Kerstin. "The divorce suit," he recalled in *Inferno*, "made very slow progress. It was held up from time to time by a love letter, a cry of regret, or promises of reconciliation, always followed by a curt, irrevocable farewell. I loved her and she me, yet we hated each other with the savage hatred of a passion that was intensified by separation."[27] Frida's account of this period confirms this. Eventually, however, probably in April (her letter is undated), she decided to end the relationship and wrote to him asking that proceedings for the divorce go ahead. She had, she admitted, caused him suffering but had never been unfaithful, nor done any of the things of which he accused her. "Goodbye, then," she concluded, "you whom I have thought I loved, whom I am trying to forget, who do not live for me. Goodbye, and without bitterness. We shall never see each other again on this earth."[28] Although she stopped writing to him, he continued to write to her until September 1896. Her denial of infidelity may be true; but by the beginning of June she had become Frank Wedekind's mistress. [29] *

In order to be allowed to work in the research laboratory of the Sorbonne, Strindberg enrolled as a student in the Faculty of Natural Sciences. "The morning on which I betook myself to the Sorbonne was a holy day," he writes. ". . . After about two weeks I had obtained incontrovertible evidence that sulphur is a ternary compound, composed of carbon, oxygen and hydrogen. I proffered my thanks to the director of

---

*Gunnar Brandell believes that Strindberg "never took the divorce proceedings quite seriously; perhaps one can say that he regarded them as natural developments in the marital cold war" (*Strindberg in Inferno*, p. 71).

the laboratory, who pretended to take no interest in what I had been doing."[30] On 12 May he told Birger Mörner he had "discovered the structure of iodine . . . Were I a businessman I would now take out the patent, but I won't, but will write an article in *La Science Française*, to which I contribute and where I have disciples . . . I think this will ensure my future more quickly than I had supposed. But, fellows, if you are arranging any stipend* for me, let me have it now, tomorrow, for I am imprisoned by debts, can't move from Paris, have only one pair of trousers with a hole in the knee so that I had to hold my hat over it when I was up at the legation. I'll have finished the iodine article this week and then I'd like to get out of town, for it's so hot here that I can't work, can't eat, much less drink, and my bed burns. I'm not ungrateful, but I think I deserve to be allowed to live. I'd like to go home to Sweden, but don't know if I'm married or divorced (the marriage is invalid in Austria and there I'm a bigamist!). I'm waiting to know! We'll see where fate tosses me next. I'm tired of these tossings, with my belongings scattered over half Europe."

"I am overworked, have open sores in my hands and sulphuric acid in my lungs," he complained to Mörner on 16 May. The same day he asked Frida to send his various papers to his brother Oscar in Stockholm, but "as regards my books and instruments you can chuck them in the Danube. As regards our correspondence, keep it or burn it." He concluded: "You have charmed the boredom of my glum life, despite your cruelties. That is a great deal, and I am not ungrateful. Sincerely, you have sweetened my existence, which you have made so bitter." He began to look for new scientific fields to conquer. "When I have finished with iodine," he told Frida on 22 May, in the third of three letters he wrote to her that day, "I shall return to botany for the summer. I have made progress, thanks to my friends who have given me a handsome microscope and some books. And I have proved the existence of nerves in plants. Then I shall start on astronomy. I have been elected a member of two astronomical societies, and there are so many people waiting for a bold man to stop the old earth in its mad course through the void."

Staying in the same *pension* as Strindberg in Montparnasse was a young Finnish art student, Esteri Kumlin. He took a liking to her and for three months they met daily. Once he took her to a café, La Maison Blanche, famed for its ice cream, and read aloud to her Georg Brandes' accounts of Byron and Shelley in *Main Currents of Nineteenth-Century Literature*. Then they took a walk by the Seine.

*The question of organising a government stipend for Strindberg had arisen several times, most recently following the publication of *A Book about Strindberg*. But he may here be referring to the appeal of 22 March (see page 319).

Strindberg talked at length and fascinatingly of what he had just read to me. In his reflections on the conflicts and disappointments of life, he repeatedly named Byron and Shelley. Gradually Byron and Shelley became "I," his voice grew more bitter and harsher as he described the reverses and humiliations which he had endured as a human being and as an artist . . . He told me that he had begun as a full-blooded idealist and had wanted "to bring the stars down from heaven so that men might see them and rejoice in them" . . . That he had given the best of himself and had found no understanding had wounded him so deeply that a great anger and desire for revenge had awakened in him, and he decided hereafter to leave the glittering stars of heaven where they were and instead pour out his hatred and spit out his anger at his contemporaries . . . I felt as though I was strolling beside a wounded lion, a chained titan, who raged because, though conscious of his strength, he knew that he had always been a prisoner.[31]

Earlier that spring, Strindberg had received a friendly letter from Anders Eliasson, a doctor in Ystad, on the southern tip of Sweden, whom he had met during his visit to Lund in April, 1891. Eliasson had read of the various appeals that had been launched on Strindberg's behalf and wrote that he would be happy to help in any way he could. Strindberg now took up this offer. On 1 June he wrote asking if Eliasson could "bring me home to rest for a couple of months, for I'm sick with overwork and iodine and sulphur . . . While I have been firing my ovens I have burned my ships behind me and can't get away from here for less than 300 crowns, but I must leave before the 7th to avoid paying for the new month . . . I don't want to live at a hotel, only in your cottage in the country, alone, and incognito!" Eliasson must have sent the money at once, for on 7 June Strindberg wrote to thank him, adding: "There was one thing in your letter which rather disturbed me: you spoke of my broken spirit. My spirit is not broken, has never been so clear and lucid, on the contrary I have broken spirits of lower degree who threatened my soul's more legitimate freedom. And I have also broken down old prejudices in science, and have penetrated into the Sorbonne itself, lit torches of doubt there, won followers, admirers, slanderers. Disciples are now working in four different laboratories to determine the formula of iodine: in Paris, Rouen, Havre, Douai and the fifth [sic] in Lyons. I have followers in Prussia, Austria, England, Italy, and used to have a disciple in Sweden who called me Master, and he of course ended as Judas, since he was a bad man and led a bad life. He is called B.L. and is the translator of *Antibarbarus* . . . I don't like luxury and hate immoderation. I shan't burden your home much or for long, as they claim to have arranged a stipend for me in Sweden to guarantee my existence!"

Strindberg's sister Anna, who was in Paris in the first days of June with her husband, Hugo, tells how "his artistic friends in Paris learned of his impending departure and arranged a series of farewell parties for him." At one such party, organised by the Molards, "the dancing even overflowed into the street, a cul-de-sac. Coloured lanterns, hung between the houses, spread their motley light over the revellers. August took part in these festivities with evident pleasure."[32]* Those present included Gauguin; it was the last occasion on which the two were to meet, for by the time Strindberg returned to Paris, Gauguin had gone back to Tahiti for ever. On 11 June, Strindberg took the train to the German port of Stralsund on the Baltic coast, and on 12 June landed in Malmö.

He planned to spend three months in Ystad, but as things turned out he stayed only one. "I am living at Dr. Eliasson's," he told Birger Mörner on 18 June. "I have a kitchen to work in, but very few utensils." He enclosed a list of twenty pieces of chemical apparatus he needed. "It looks a lot, but the things are quite cheap." "I have completely given up creative writing and am devoting myself to chemistry," he informed Fredrik Wrangel on 23 June, and he addressed enormous letters on the subject to his "disciples" in France, giving details of his theories and experiments. He also, on 25 June, wrote his first letter for over a year to his children in Finland: "I have been ill, have had reverses, but also big successes, the fruits of which we shall share. Never despair and do not think that I have forgotten you although I do not write often. You have had to share the evil days with me, but you will also share the good ones." On 13 July, thanking Wrangel for a second instalment of 732 crowns from the Stockholm appeal (the first 500 crowns had been given to him in Paris in May), he asked him to send the remaining 450 crowns to his children, a contribution which Siri must have welcomed considering how little she had received from him of late; Karin reports that even in January of this year he owed them seventeen months' support.[33] Otherwise we know little of the month in Ystad; Strindberg does not mention it at all in *Inferno*. A letter he wrote to Eliasson on 15 July, the day after leaving, suggests that he read with him, surprisingly for the first time, Nietzsche's *Thus Spake Zarathustra*; Eliasson, like Strindberg, was a great admirer of Nietzsche.

On his return to France, Strindberg spent a week with Julien Leclerq at Palaiseau, to the south of Paris, then returned to his old *pension* on the rue de la Grande Chaumière. He settled down to write in French his

---

*Anna misremembered these parties as having taken place the following June, but by then Gauguin, whom she met at them, was no longer in Paris and Strindberg had broken with his friends at the *crémerie*.

Introduction à une Chimie Unitaire (Introduction to a Unitary Chemistry) for the *Mercure de France*, and addressed eleven letters on the subject to Eliasson in August, including one on each of the last five days of the month.

> I reckon the summer and autumn of 1895—in spite of everything— among the happy resting places in my turbulent life [Strindberg wrote in *Inferno*]. All my undertakings prospered, unknown friends brought food to me as the ravens did to Elijah. Money came to me of itself. I was able to buy books, natural history specimens, and, among other things, a microscope that unveiled for me the secrets of life. Lost to the world by renouncing the empty pleasures of Paris, I lived entirely within my own quarter of the city. Each morning I visited the departed in the cemetery of Montparnasse, and afterwards walked down to the Luxembourg Gardens to say good morning to my flowers. Now and then some countryman of mine, on a visit to Paris, would call and invite me out to luncheon or to the theatre on the other side of the river. I always refused, as the Right Bank was forbidden territory. To me, it represented the "world" in the true sense of the word, the world of the living and of earthly vanity. [34]

This idyllic picture is not borne out by his letters of the period. "Things are horrible as usual," he wrote to Richard Bergh (around 18 September), "but I intend to apply for a job as a gardener in the Jardin des Plantes so as to be able to continue with my scientific studies. I spent six weeks [*sic*] in Sweden recently but found that I was a foreigner, not even that, the enemy in the land of enemies . . . One starves better here than in Sweden, and can live on tick too! . . . It has been 40° [Celsius] here and 50° in the attic where I have been heating the stove for the iodine. Wearing nothing but spectacles! . . . I've been celibate since last November when my money ran out and I fled from the Danube,* analysed by three doctors because I didn't believe sulphur was an element. Fled to Paris where no professor even believes in elements!"

Strindberg never, of course, seriously pursued the idea of becoming a gardener, any more than those other jobs he had mooted in the past, of hotel porter, lighthouse keeper and the rest. Instead, he wrote various begging letters: to Carl Wahlund, professor of French at Uppsala, for a loan of 500 francs, to Torsten Hedlund the theosophist: "I beg you, save me very soon from this torment . . . They are demanding payment for last month and harass me every moment of the day."[35] Since he wrote this letter on 20 October, it does not seem unreasonable of the *pension* to have

---

*Strindberg in fact left Dornach in August 1894, and Frida parted from him in Paris in October.

wanted payment for September. To add to his worries, the court in Berlin was about to deliver its verdict on A *Madman's Defence*. "I am no bugger," he assured Eliasson, "and will surely not be scourged like Oscar Wilde" (who had been sentenced to two years' hard labour in England that May).[36]* Mysterious news arrived from Barcelona. "Unknown friends, literary Spaniards, are sending a sculptured silver inkhorn weighing 1,000 (One Thousand) grams, and a gold pen in a gold stand! Which will probably have to go to a *mont de piété* [pawnshop] in Montparnasse. (Pity silver has depreciated.)"[37] "Now it is winter," he told Eliasson on 26 October. "Please send my winter overcoat in a wax cloth—express, so that I can be ready to travel! If you could put a twist of tobacco in the breast pocket I shall be happy." The same day he begged Torsten Hedlund: "Ask those who can to rescue me from distress, humiliation and degradation. Everyone has abandoned me, the evil ones persecute me and seek to bring me to despair in order to force me to return to what was worse. Get me help or I shall perish."

Hedlund replied with 700 crowns, a gift which initiated a long and intimate correspondence which was to last, apart from one short break, for thirteen months, during which time Hedlund was Strindberg's principal confidant, although the two were never to meet. "Your letter has made me very happy and strong," Strindberg replied on 30 October. "You are giving me two months of life and do not ask for my soul in return. Thank you! . . . I do not regret my past life, for I have not been responsible for my fate . . . I pray only that my temptations may cease! The loneliness and the suffering are immense, but I would rather burn than return to sinning, whether it be blessed or not." The same day, the court in Berlin wrote to him announcing its verdict on A *Madman's Defence*; the book was declared immoral, but Strindberg was found not to have written it with immoral intent and was accordingly acquitted.

His yearning for female company, and fear of it, found expression in a long letter he wrote to Hedlund on 10 November:

> . . . I often ask myself: Why do you not found a monastery, a refuge for all those weary of the world, a free city offering solitude in comradeship, where one might by a strict regime, asceticism, symbols, follow the hermit's life? But that brings temptations from which the desert could not shield an Anthony.
>
> I want to get away from the milieu into which isolation, persecution and

---

*On 6 April 1897, Wilde included a volume of Strindberg's plays in French in a list of books which he asked Robert Ross to have ready for him on his release.[38] Unfortunately, his opinion of them is not on record.

poverty have driven me, but I don't know where to. I have thought of a Catholic monastery, but that would involve confession and an obedience which I loathe . . .

It is a miserable age we live in. The old positivism, which we tired of, assured the young: "The universe contains no more secrets. We have solved every riddle." And the young believed it and became dejected, despaired.

I remain sceptical about Theosophy. It is said to derive from Buddha, and I was educated by three Buddhists: Schopenhauer, von Hartmann and, finally, Nietzsche . . . As a Buddhist I am, like Buddha and his three great disciples, a woman-hater . . . Woman is for me the earth with all its splendours, the bond that binds . . . They are sweet illusions, dear God, too sweet. But shall I never learn to subdue the flesh? It is still too fiery, but may perhaps thereby come to burn itself out. But the spirit may die with it! . . . I shall never escape from this. Bachelor life strikes me as dirty. Family life is the most beautiful—but! but! even dirtier when one stirs it. Outside —absolute degradation, and then the beast appears.

He sent Hedlund the manuscript of a fanciful short book of scientific speculation which he had completed, *Sylva Sylvarum* (the title is from Francis Bacon). * Hedlund disliked it, told Strindberg so and pressed the claims of theosophy by sending him a devotional manual translated from the English called *Light on the Path*. Strindberg reacted with a hysterical and abusive letter on 5 December accusing Hedlund of wanting to steal his soul, "to debase and humiliate me, force me to bow the knee to your gods and goddesses . . . You could not bear that I know more than your ignorant professors, who know nothing . . . Our ways must now part." Next day he regretted this letter and wrote in more conciliatory terms, but Hedlund was not to be placated and withdrew his support. For seven weeks the correspondence lapsed.

During this period Strindberg underwent another bout of extreme tension and persecution mania. He believed that he was being deliberately disturbed by hostile neighbours. "Three pianos in adjacent rooms were all being played at the same time. I told myself that this must be an intrigue on the part of the Scandinavian females with whom I had refused to mix." Then people began hammering nails on either side of his bed, and "the behaviour of my friends at the *crémerie* changed towards me. Their muffled hostility was shown by the hints they dropped and the sidelong glances they gave me."[39] He concentrated ferociously on his

---

*Strindberg mentions Bacon in his letters as early as 19 January 1889, and two years later, in a letter to Bengt Lidforss on 1 April 1891, quotes him extensively as an authority on natural philosophy. A page of a manuscript dating from Strindberg's days in Germany (1892–3) contains excerpts from Bacon's *Sylva Sylvarum*. (*Cf.* Brandell, *Strindberg in Inferno*, p. 165.)

scientific experiments, firing off a series of enormous letters to Anders Eliasson packed with formulae.

Towards the end of January 1896 he briefly entered a calmer period and made his peace with Hedlund, who generously responded by sending him money and even offering to publish *Sylva Sylvarum* himself in Sweden (where it appeared later that year in an expanded form under a French title, *Jardin des Plantes*). He suggested that Strindberg should return and settle near him in Gothenburg or some small neighbouring town. Strindberg was tempted ("A cottage with two rooms and a garden to plant in. To be able to borrow books from Gothenburg library, if that is permitted").[40] In the end, however, he decided to remain in Paris, but to move from Montparnasse. On 21 February he left the pension on the rue de la Grande Chaumière, leaving his books and various other possessions as security against his unpaid bills, and moved to the Hôtel Orfila on the rue d'Assas in the Latin Quarter.

Chapter Twenty-One

∽∾∽∾∽∾∽∾∽∾∽∾∽∾∽∾∽∾∽∾∽∾∽∾∽∾∽∾∽∾∽∾∽

INFERNO

The Hôtel Orfila took its name from a French chemist, Mathieu Orfila (1787–1853), the author, as it happened, of a book which Strindberg had stumbled on the previous spring and which had excited him by its declaration that sulphur was not an element. In *Inferno* he writes that it "looked like a monastery," but "was in fact a boardinghouse for students of the Roman Catholic persuasion. It was supervised by an abbé, a gentle, kindly man. Science, order and good habits were the order there, and, a thing that was particularly comforting to me after so many vexations, women were not admitted. It was an old house with low rooms, dim corridors, and a labyrinth of winding wooden staircases. The whole building . . . had about it an atmosphere of mysticism."[1]

Young Gustaf Uddgren, visiting him there, found it less impressive. "The lobby in which I sat was damp and cold, the old Catholic gentlemen who came and went seemed like gliding eels, and I felt much depressed that the Master Olof of my youth should have been condemned to such a place. A more unsuitable residence for someone of melancholic temperament could scarcely be imagined."[2]

Despite the excitement of his supposed discoveries, and the respect with which these were regarded in France if nowhere else, science was not wholly satisfying him. "If only," he wrote to Hedlund around 22 February, "I could see the possibility of abandoning physics, so as to be

able like Aristotle to pass on to metaphysics, mankind and God and the
secrets of creation. You say Karma. Why not say plainly: God? That needs
courage, for it isn't fashionable . . . none of the existing religions can
satisfy me, least of all Christianity—I am closer to the God of the Old
Testament, for He too can hate and strike, but also forgive, and He
comforts us in our sorrows by making us understand the purpose of the
evil that happens to us. I have been systematically scourged these last
months; at first I raged and shook my fist at heaven. But then I read Job
and bowed my knee to God, not men, and I bore my fate with more calm,
expecting no reward but the sublimation of the senses which sorrow
brings. Tears nourish like spring rain, leading to growth later." True to his
illiberal political beliefs of the past few years, he rejected theosophy for
(among other things) its humanitarianism.* The letter continues: "I
believe theosophy's dabbling in human improvement and social problems to be an interference in the rule of God, since what exists, especially
evil, exists by His will, either as punishment or as a therapy. He ordains,
and no one has the right to complain at what He ordains."

Shortly after he moved into the Orfila, Strindberg began to keep a
diary. He named it his "Occult Diary," and was to keep it intermittently
for twenty-two years, noting strange coincidences, dreams, clairvoyant
experiences, the flights of birds (especially magpies), movements of dogs,
cats and spiders, playing cards and their significance, even the numbers of
railway tickets; also bad nights, storms, Bible quotations and extracts from
other books, usually without comment. He pasted in newspaper cuttings
about supernatural happenings and public events that interested him,
such as the Dreyfus case and the Andrée balloon expedition to the North
Pole, but included nothing (even in later years) about his plays, except
sometimes the dates on which he began or finished them and their
acceptance by theatres or publishers. In due course, it was to contain a
vivid running commentary on his third marriage. The diary opens with
undated jottings, of which the following are typical:

> . . . the recovery in the card game. Dreams. The Dominican monastery
> in Sthlm [Stockholm]. The song when mother died.
>
> The microscope: the walnut: the Christmas rose.
>
> The crab . . .
>
> The goblin cracks in the sun as the trolls crack.
>
> The pillow. Mandragora. Verlaine . . .

*He was also worried by the fact that several of the leading figures of the movement,
such as Madame Blavatsky and Annie Besant, were women.

Madhouse: God. Caesar (Shakespeare) . . .

Neglected visits. Conflicts. Shirked dangers. Broken acquaintances. The black poodle in Luxembourg.

*Envoûtement . . .**

I walk on the street between two people who speak to each other and cause unease as though a tree were between them.

Or between the master and his dog.

Between married people.

One's voice when one cries and wakes oneself.

In Brünn when my soul had left my body . . .

The walnut and the crab, as *Inferno* makes clear, refer to the similarity Strindberg noticed between the patterns of the nut and a crab shell and the human brain. The pillow and Verlaine are explained by a passage in Frederick Delius's memoirs:

> Paul Verlaine had just died [in January 1896], and Strindberg had in his possession a rather large photo of the poet on his deathbed. He handed me the photo one day and asked me what I saw on it. I described it candidly, namely, Verlaine lying on his back covered with rather a thick eiderdown, only his head and beard visible; a pillow had dropped on the floor and lay there rather crunched up. Strindberg asked me did I not see the huge animal lying on Verlaine's stomach and the imp crouching on the floor? At that time I could never really make out whether he was quite sincere or trying to mystify me. However, I may say I believed implicitly in his scientific discoveries then. He had such a convincing way of explaining them and certainly was very ambitious to be an inventor. For instance, Röntgen rays [X-rays] had just been discovered, and he confided to me one afternoon over an absinthe at the Café Closerie des Lilas that he himself had discovered them ten years ago.[3]

In considering what happened to Strindberg during these last months in Paris, it must again be stressed that one should be wary of taking his account in *Inferno* at its face value. He wrote it a year later and, as in his earlier autobiographical works, dramatised his experiences, though without the malice which makes *A Madman's Defence* so distorted a version of the truth. A comparison with the Diary also makes it clear that in *Inferno* Strindberg sometimes altered the chronology of events.

*A word used by the French occultists to describe murderous attempts made from afar by persons adept at black magic. The theosophists as well as the occultists believed in this, and early in their correspondence Hedlund had warned Strindberg against practising black magic. (Brandell, *Strindberg in Inferno*, pp. 108–110.)

His financial situation now improved considerably. Hedlund had found a Gothenburg businessman named August Röhss who fancied himself a Maecenas and who promised 1,200 crowns to support Strindberg over the next eight months. This was more than a town clerk's annual salary. "The room costs 30 crowns a month," Strindberg informed Hedlund on 25 February, "food, fuel, lighting and laundry 120 crowns = 150 crowns." At Strindberg's request an appropriate amount was sent each month direct to the hotel and Madame Charlotte's *crémerie*, which he still frequented, and to which he was much in debt. Although the stipend met his immediate requirements, it left little over for books, clothes and absinthe. He hoped to make something by sending scientific articles to *Handelstidningen i Göteborg*, but after two had appeared there, they were found to be unpopular and no more were printed. Nor did the French or the Swedish edition of *Sylva Sylvarum* bring him anything, and although he had several pieces published in Jollivet-Castelot's *L'Hyperchimie* the magazine could not afford to pay him for them.

The range of his scientific explorations is remarkable. "When the moment comes that people take my research seriously," he wrote on 22 March to Birger Mörner, "found a Free Laboratory for me! All I need: a big cottage outside Stockholm, with cheap apparatus . . . There I would concentrate on completing the inventions which I have half ready: e.g., colour photography. The telescope. Air electricity as motor power. Iodine from coal. Phosphorus from sulphur. Sulphuric acid from alum slate. Nickel plating without nickel (transmutation of metals). New ideas in iron and steel metallurgy. Etc. etc." To this list, writing six days later to Hedlund, he added: "To make silk from a liquid without silkworms. To transmute cotton thread into silk. To transmute linen thread into silk." But the letter continues:

"I have today finished reading a book about India,* and I no longer know where I am. It seems to me as though the author of *Sylva Sylvarum* is someone other than I, and that this 'I' is a Hindu. (I suspect my mother to have been a gipsy, for my uncle was an absolute gipsy type whose living likeness I have seen in Denmark, in East Prussia and by the Danube.)" Quoting a description of a copper jar, he asks: "What do these chasings represent? At first one has no idea; one sees only a web of tangled lines, flung together haphazard. Gradually the skein unravels, and dim figures appear: gods, genii, fish, dogs, gazelles, flowers, plants, not grouped according to any plan but flung together higgledy-piggledy like a lump of

---

*André Chevrillon's *Dans l'Inde* (Paris, 1891).

mud dragged from the seabed from the shapeless mass of which emerge glimpses of a claw, a scale, a fin."* Noting that Siva is "a lord of death, but also of life. He is love and terror, good and evil, he is the great ascetic . . . a drunken Bacchus," and that Krishna is "an Orpheus, Adonis, Hercules, Jesus, ascetic and libertine," he concludes: "This is mankind, I, you, he, she. . . I cannot root out my egos—I scourge the one with the other . . . You know how fearfully I guard my Self, that I would rather suffer the pains of loneliness than rub against other people. But now I am sick and must seek a cure among human beings! So, back to earth, for a while—then out into the desert again, to return once more to earth." Five years later he was to dramatise these ideas in *A Dream Play*.

In *Inferno*, Strindberg tells how during these months in 1896 he became aware of a power, or powers, guiding his destiny, usually, it seemed to him, perversely. His window looked on to numerous outdoor closets; "if at that time I had known anything about Swedenborg, I should have realised that the Powers had condemned me to the Hell of Excrement." Pieces of coal from his fire assumed fantastic shapes and, when he put them on the roof, frightened away the sparrows. A letter arrived addressed to a student bearing his wife's name of Uhl, another to "a Swedish name that reminded me of an enemy in my native land," a third from a firm of analytical chemists which showed that "someone was spying on my synthesis of gold." Most alarmingly, an experiment he performed in witchcraft was followed by a letter from his children in Finland saying that they had been seriously ill. "By playing with those mysterious powers out of pure folly, I had given the reins to my evil desires. But they, guided by the hand of the Unseen, had struck at my heart."[4]

The first dated entry in his diary, apart from that of his arrival at the Orfila, reads: "29 March. Swedenborg. Séraphita." In *Inferno* he tells how that Sunday morning, Palm Sunday, he picked up in the arcades of the Théâtre de l'Odéon a copy of the novel *Séraphita* by his beloved Balzac, which he had read years before but had practically forgotten. *Séraphita* contains numerous references to Emanuel Swedenborg, the Blake-like mystic (1688–1772) whom William Blake admired and who lived much of his life and died in the East End of London, where a square is named after him. One of the leading physicists and anatomists of his time (he invented the first mercurial air pump, and anticipated by more than a century several modern discoveries relating to the function of the brain and the spinal cord), he eventually, in his fifties, abandoned science

*Strindberg adds a note: "The great disorder and the eternal pattern."

for psychical inquiry (as Newton, during Swedenborg's youth, had abandoned mathematics for biblical inquiry, and as Immanuel Kant, shortly before Swedenborg's death, was to abandon physics for philosophy). Swedenborg experienced many visions, in which angels and dead mortals spoke to him, and attached particular significance to dreams. The following year, 1897, he was to excite Strindberg greatly. *

A long letter which Strindberg wrote to Hedlund around 10 April confirms how the physical and the metaphysical simultaneously obsessed him:

> . . . my work quietly pursues its appointed course. I had a visit from the Secretary of Science Française who said: Scientists discuss you; some say: you are mad; others: not mad; one cannot discuss his chemistry, but one can use it . . . Well, that seems to be my fate . . . I have celebrated Easter as suffering should be celebrated, with my disciples. There are two who have already had their eyes opened, and we "see" together, but without trying to summon visions. We simply wait quietly, and then that is seen which was long forbidden and perhaps should be, for every time I have seen anything, evil spirits at once attend and play their game. I am not a visionary, for I don't believe that spirits can be seen, but I believe that if one does not harden one's soul much can be revealed . . .
>
> Where are our souls at night? Do we lead a double life, one life here by day and another when there is day on the other side of the world?
>
> Not a word of this or I will be put away by my relatives!

That spring, Strindberg became deeply involved with the Paris occultists, about whom he had written to Torsten Hedlund in February. In several European countries, and nowhere more than in France, the interest shown during the previous decade in hypnotism and "suggestion," which had influenced the writing of such plays as *Rosmersholm*, *The Lady from the Sea*, *The Father*, *Miss Julie* and *Creditors*, had logically led to the study of occultism and magic. The occultists fascinated the new symbolist poets such as Villiers de l'Isle-Adam and Stéphane Mallarmé by their mysticism and research into such things as telepathy, ghosts, doppelgängers, exorcism and black magic. Strindberg became a regular reader of their magazine, *L'Initiation*, and in due course a contributor. He did not have much personal contact with them, though he met their leader "Papus" (Gérard Encausse) a few times; but according to *Inferno* he became acquainted that May with the elements of black

---

*But Strindberg seems to have taken his time about reading *Séraphita*. Although he says in *Inferno* that he began the book that same day, noting that it was the anniversary of Swedenborg's death, there is no mention of it or of Swedenborg in his letters until six weeks later; and his references to Swedenborg in *Inferno* are equally misleading.

magic and appended to the book when it appeared a select bibliography of
works by various members of the group. This occultism, and especially
the idea that we have astral bodies or dream selves which exist independently of our ordinary selves, was considerably to influence his future
plays.

We should not sneer at Strindberg's interest in occultism. "For a time
around 1890," Gunnar Brandell has written, "it appeared that occultism
might become the unifying outlook for the entire younger generation.
Thus, it was not an obscure Parisian sect with which Strindberg became
associated in 1896, but a trend that had been the focus of literary debate
for years."[5] Nor was alchemy the obsession of an eccentric minority;
according to a contemporary newspaper, there were in 1883 no fewer
than 50,000 alchemists in Paris alone,[6] and for decades to come it was to
appeal to serious researchers and creative writers and artists, as it had to
Goethe. C. G. Jung tells in his autobiography how as late as 1926 "my
encounter with alchemy was decisive for me, as it provided me with the
historical basis which I had hitherto lacked . . . Grounded in the natural
philosophy of the Middle Ages, alchemy formed the bridge . . . to the
future, to the modern psychology of the unconscious." Jung was fascinated by the way "alchemists talked in symbols," and how "in a most
curious way, analytical psychology coincided with alchemy . . .
Through understanding of alchemical symbolism I arrived at the central
concept of my psychology."

Jung goes on to describe the problems facing the mediaeval alchemists
who could not unreservedly accept Christianity, and they correspond
remarkably to those which Strindberg and so many of his contemporaries
now faced:

> The alchemists ran counter to the church in preferring to seek through
> knowledge rather than to find through faith . . . they were in much the
> same position as modern man, who prefers immediate personal experience
> to belief in traditional ideas . . . there have always been people who, not
> satisfied with the dominants of conscious life, set forth—under cover and by
> devious paths, to their destruction or salvation—to seek direct experience of
> the eternal roots, and following the lure of the restless unconscious psyche,
> find themselves in the wilderness where, like Jesus, they come up against
> the son of darkness . . .
>
> The problem of the opposites called up by the shadow plays a great
> —indeed, the decisive—role in alchemy, since it leads in the ultimate
> phase of the work to the union of opposites in the archetypal form of the
> *hierosgamos* or "chymical wedding." Here the supreme opposites, male and
> female (as in the Chinese *yang* and *yin*), are melted into a unity purified of
> all opposition and therefore incorruptible . . . The alchemist was forced to
> represent the incorruptible substance as a chemical product—an imposs-

ible undertaking, which led to the downfall of alchemy . . . When he [the alchemist] spoke of a union of the "natures," or of an "amalgam" of iron and copper, or of a compound of sulphur and mercury, he meant it at the same time as a symbol: iron was Mars and copper was Venus, and their fusion was at the same time a love affair. The union of the "natures" which embrace one another was not physical and concrete, for they were "celestial natures" which multiplied "by the command of God."[7]

The editor of Jung's autobiography, Aniela Jaffé, sums up: "The more serious alchemists realised that the purpose of their work was not the transmutation of base metals into gold, but the production of a . . . philosophical gold."[8] Likewise, when we read of Strindberg's seemingly futile and time-wasting efforts in this field, we should see them as a symbol of his defiant unwillingness to accept the existence of a God, and of his search for an alternative explanation of the human condition.

Although he gives the impression in *Inferno* that he was leading a solitary existence at this time, Strindberg was still seeing a good deal of his friends from the *crémerie*, who had now been joined by Edvard Munch. Frederick Delius gives an amusing account of Strindberg's obsession with the occult:

> His interest in spirits caused Leclerc [*sic*] and me to play a joke on him. I asked them both to my rooms one evening, and after dinner we had a spiritualist séance in the form of table rapping. The lights were turned down and we joined hands around a small table. After ten minutes' ominous silence the table began to rap and Leclerc asked it what message the spirits had for us. The first letter rapped out was M, and with each letter Strindberg's interest and excitement seemed to increase, and slowly came the momentous letters "MERDE" [shit]. I do not think he ever quite forgave us for this . . . He was extraordinarily superstitious, for often on our walks he would suddenly refuse to go up a certain street on the pretext that some accident or misfortune was awaiting him there . . . He was extremely touchy and often imagined he had been slighted without any cause whatever, as the following incident will show.
>
> We would often gather at night at the studio of one of our mutual friends [Molard], a very amusing and bohemian interior. When we left, our hosts would use the occasion to accompany us downstairs into the yard in order to empty their *"boîte à ordures"* [dustbin] and give Bob, their little bastard dog, a chance of getting a breath of fresh air. Strindberg had been great friends with this couple and had been taking his meals with them for a couple of months at least. It appears Strindberg was there alone one night and it was getting very late and they were evidently very tired, when the hostess suggested *"si nous descendions la boîte à ordures"* [Let's get rid of the rubbish], a ceremony which had become quite a known institution. Strindberg went down with them and said good night in the wonted friendly way; but he never entered their house again, taking the allusion to the *boîte à ordures* as a personal insult to himself.[9]

Another member of the group was less sceptical than Delius about the occult. Alphonse Mucha's son Jiri tells how his father and Strindberg took part in alchemical experiments and "discussed the Hidden Truth in long walks through the old Montparnasse cemetery where Strindberg had tried to capture the emanations of the dead in a phial and subject them to chemical analysis . . . To the end of his life he [Mucha] continued to practise automatic writing, convinced that he was receiving messages from dead friends and great men."[10] These occult experiments sometimes caused inconvenience. Madame Futterer told Carl Milles how one morning at seven she came down into her restaurant and found Strindberg standing in the middle of the floor, having moved the chairs against the walls and arranged all the pots and pans in a circle. "Wearing only underpants and a shirt, he was performing a dance of exorcism around them. He explained he was doing this to chase away the evil spirits which might poison the food. During the hot weather he would usually climb in through the window, since evil spirits stood watching in the doorway; and one day everything in the kitchen exploded just before lunch was to be served. This was a consequence of Strindberg trying to make gold in a saucepan, and the whole meal was ruined."[11]

On 14 April he wrote excitedly to Mörner: "Here is a specimen of gold which I have made. Look at it through a magnifying glass by sunlight or lamplight. It is microscopic, but so is the gold in the Transvaal, though mine is cheaper, irrationally. But it isn't ready, since it contains iron oxide. Hold it over an open ammonia bottle and it will become apparent. This gold could be produced in large quantities at Dylta [a Swedish industrial plant noted among other things for its production of sulphur]." Ten days later he informed Dr. Eliasson: "Yesterday in the Luxembourg Gardens I found hanging by the fountain a scoop of rustily tinned sheet iron. It bore stains of gilding. This morning I took my chemicals along, since I didn't dare steal the scoop. The gilded stains did not react to saltpetre acid or hydrochloric acid, but did to the two together. It is gold!"

It was probably at this time that Strindberg met W. B. Yeats. Yeats is unrevealing about the occasion; in his autobiographical volume, *The Tragic Generation*, he says only: "I am sitting in a café with two French Americans, a German poet Douchenday,* and a silent man whom I discover to be Strindberg, and who is looking for the Philosopher's Stone." He does not even specify the year. Later, in *The Bounty of Sweden*, Yeats wrote that he seemed to remember Strindberg as "big and

---

*Yeats, a notoriously careless speller, presumably meant Max Dauthendey (see p. 258), who was a member of Strindberg's circle at the *crémerie*.

silent," although Strindberg, at five feet eight inches, was considerably shorter than he, adding in a fine phrase: "I have always felt a sympathy for that tortured self-torturing man, who offered himself to his own soul as Buddha offered himself to the famished tiger."[12] Another distinguished Irish dramatist was resident in Paris at this time, but Strindberg did not meet John Millington Synge; nor Oscar Wilde, who came to live there in February 1898, six weeks before Strindberg left the city for good.

At the beginning of May, Strindberg was called to the police station to sign papers relating to his forthcoming divorce. 2 May was the anniversary of his wedding with Frida, and that day he wrote her a sad little note: "Three years gone! Begun in Heligoland and ended in front of the commissioner of police, rue l'Abbé St-Gregoire [*sic*]. *C'est la vie!*" He asked her how much he owed her and her parents; she replied that he owed them nothing and invited him to visit Kerstin that summer at her grandmother's in Saxony. "Why can I not endure a marriage?" he wrote next day to Eliasson. "I cannot bow to a woman's foolish whims. Anyway—love should be enjoyed as an intoxicant—quick, transitory and new! To rot side by side is stupid and ugly. There were great moments, in Act One as it were, superb, and the memories remain. *Requiescat!*"

During the six months from May to November of 1896, Strindberg seems to have come very close to madness. From May he began to keep his diary more regularly, though by no means daily, noting especially dreams of the most terrifying nature, and waking experiences when normal sights and sounds became distorted into visions of equal horror. He was to describe these experiences vividly enough in the chapter of *Inferno* entitled "Purgatory," but there they are dramatised; the naked diary entries are even more alarming:

> 13th, letter from Frida. Night of 14th dreamed that a severed head was fixed on a man's trunk and began to speak. The man like a drunken actor haunted me: he was behind a screen which I knocked down over him . . . At night I killed a mosquito so that my hand was bloody in the morning . . ./ The sound of the cricket in my pillow. The sound of grasshoppers in general; they have to me always sounded as though they came from an empty hall underground with a strong echo. / The night of Whit Sunday I dreamed: I was bullied and threatened with prison by a railwayman's son who had teeth like fish hooks. / Whit Sunday: 11 a.m. a buzzing in the lock of the door as though a great moth was caught in it.

During this crisis he at last got down to reading the Balzac novel he had bought on 29 March. *Séraphita*, written in 1833–35, must rank with Herman Melville's *Pierre* as the worst book ever written by a major novelist. Set in Norway—the magnificent opening section describing the fjord landscape is almost the only part worth reading—it tells of an androgynous creature with whom a young girl and a young man are simultaneously infatuated—to no avail, for Séraphita-Séraphitus is not interested in earthly things. This the local pastor explains to the frustrated couple in an after-dinner speech of twenty-eight pages, telling them the life story of Swedenborg (Séraphita being the daughter of one of Swedenborg's cousins), and expounding the seer's philosophy in merciless detail, noting that "within the space of thirty years this man published twenty-five quarto volumes on the truths of the spiritual world, written in Latin, the shortest containing five hundred pages, and all in small print; he left twenty more, it is said, in London in the care of his nephew . . . His followers now number more than seven hundred thousand souls . . . there are seven thousand Swedenborgians in the city of Manchester alone." Séraphita then invites the three of them to tea, and regales them with more details of Swedenborgianism for an uninterrupted twenty-six pages. The final expression of humanity, they are told, is when "the spirit is supreme over the form, and the form still contends with the divine spirit; it is this supreme conflict which gives rise to the inexpressible anguish which the heavens alone can see and which Christ endured in the Garden of Olives." The novel ends with Séraphita-Séraphitus, after a last gigantic address, being taken up to heaven, leaving the young people converted by "a glimpse of the higher mysteries."

Dreadful as *Séraphita* seems today, it had an immediate and powerful effect on Strindberg. "How great and wonderful it is!" he wrote to Hedlund on 15 May. The idea that "everything here below has its hidden meaning" particularly appealed to him, as did Swedenborg's unorthodox mystical reasoning for a belief in God. Strindberg did not, in fact, start to read Swedenborg properly until towards the end of the year, though he suggests otherwise in *Inferno*, but Balzac's novel opened the door.

> *Séraphita* became my gospel. It caused me to renew my ties with the beyond to such an extent that life filled me with repugnance and Heaven drew me to it, so that I yearned for it with the irresistible yearning one has for home. I doubted not that I was already prepared for a higher existence. I despised the earth, this unclean world, man and all his works. I saw in myself the righteous man upon whom the Eternal has visited temptations, but whom the purgatory of this earthly life would make worthy of imminent deliverance.[13]

But this comforting belief that persecution was a sign of grace came later. That spring and summer of 1896 it seemed perverse and meaningless, as is evidenced by a letter he wrote to Hedlund on 17 May assuring him that "if a man is actually persecuted so that everything he does is torn to shreds, mocked, smeared with filth; if he is persecuted with lawsuits, threats of imprisonment, false accusations of anarchism, hunted from country to country; threatened with the madhouse, hounded by debts, harassed in public places; and when enemies turn up at the hotel where he lives and warn the landlord, etc.; if this man, who is persecuted, gets the idea that he is persecuted, then this is no illusion or mania." It was not until the following year, when he had digested Swedenborg, that he would proudly proclaim these sufferings as proof that he was one of God's elite.

Strindberg's sister Anna and her husband, Hugo, visited him in Paris that June, as they had the previous summer. After showing her his specimens of home-made gold on the window-sill, he accepted her invitation to dine at a restaurant, but on seeing that no prices were marked on the menu, he declared that they might be charged anything and insisted on leaving. "August was tired and wanted to go and eat dinner alone in his monastery, which he did." He agreed to collect her the following evening at her hotel on the Right Bank, but did not come. "The next evening I received by post a note of apology from my brother. He explained that he could not bring himself to cross to the Right Bank of the Seine."[14]

It was at this time that Munch executed his famous lithograph of Strindberg. He designed an ornate border for the portrait, incorporating a naked woman and the sitter's name, mis-spelt "Stindberg," thereby causing double offence.* Relations between the two became strained. "Munch got nervous," Strindberg noted in his diary on 2 June, "grew hysterical when he put on my coat; got up and went home to bed! Returned. Talked about women, like a woman . . . Sunday 7 June. Munch became nervous when I visited him. Made his bed and got into it." Munch, writing to his sister Inger later that summer, described Strindberg as "now rather old."[15]

The summer days of 1896 were, for Strindberg, if we are to believe his

*Munch later corrected the spelling and replaced the naked woman with a linear motif. He tells that Strindberg "never said a word on arrival but merely laid a revolver on the table in front of him and stayed silent throughout the session." Despite their differences, Strindberg wrote a sympathetic, if obscure, introduction in *La Revue Blanche* (1 June) of an exhibition which Munch held that month in Paris, describing him as "le peintre ésotérique de l'amour, de la jalousie, de la mort et de la tristesse." They had little contact after 1896, though Strindberg lived on in Munch's mind. Once, when Munch was painting a woman on the beach at Warnemünde and the wind blew away his easel, he immediately packed away all his equipment, exclaiming, "That wind is Strindberg, trying to disrupt my work." (Ragna Stang, *Edvard Munch*, London, 1979, pp. 98, 294.)

diary, scarcely less terrifying than the nights. On 15 June: "When I reached the quay before the Pont des Saints Pères the quay swayed under my feet . . . I still felt the swaying in the courtyard of the Louvre and today I felt it up in the Avenue de l'Opéra. Is Paris undermined by sewers, gas, water and telephone cables and catacombs?" On 18 June he heard that "Psbysechewski [*sic*] has been arrested for the murder of his wife. Soot in my absinthe," and expressed his alarm by underlining the entry in red.

The news of Przybyszewski's arrest, for the poisoning of Martha Foerder, came to Strindberg from Edvard Munch, who had it in a letter from Richard Dehmel. Strindberg had no doubt who was the prime mover. "There is your beautiful Dagny, whose knight you still long to be!" he wrote to Munch on 1 July. "If you wish, with my help, to do something for her victim, Pby, I am ready." It transpired, however, that the unfortunate woman had committed suicide, and Przybyszewski was released. Strindberg now, according to *Inferno*, became convinced that Przybyszewski was in Paris, seeking revenge on him for having been Dagny's lover. He heard Schumann's "Aufschwung" being played on a piano as only Stachu could play it, "my *famulus* who had called me 'Master' and had kissed my hands because his life had begun where mine had ended. He had come from Berlin to kill me . . . It must have been he who had annoyed me by sending all those letters with faked addresses that I had found in the porter's lodge . . . He played every afternoon between four and five for a whole month."[16] The discovery in the Luxembourg Gardens of two twigs "shaped like the Greek letters for P and i," the first and last letters of the Pole's name, made Strindberg "sure that it was he who was persecuting me, and that the Powers wanted to open my eyes to the danger."[17] A few days earlier, on 26 June, he had written to Hedlund: "My life has had the peculiarity that it unfolds like novels, without my really being able to say why. I don't meddle in other people's destinies, since from early youth I realised that this was criminal and brought its own punishment. But I have always been a kind of lime-twig; it attracts small birds, they finger my destiny, stick fast and then complain."

Nils Strindberg, the son of August's cousin Oscar, had been making several balloon ascents in France this year as preparation for a voyage to the North Pole with S. A. Andrée, an event which was to lead to the death of all concerned. Several newspapers supposed it to be Strindberg himself who was involved, and Frida wrote to him blaming herself for this, as it seemed to her, suicidal project: "Is it I who have so harassed you, is it I?"[18] Strindberg replied abusively: "Who has lost the game? You, for opinion here is convinced that you are the abandoned mistress of my publisher . . . to make me ridiculous, you have degraded yourself to the point of questioning the legitimacy of your child." He concluded: "I thank Providence that I am delivered from you."[19] "My misogyny," he confessed to Eliasson the next day, "knows no limits." Yet his longing for Frida remained. An entry in his diary at this time (23 June) runs: ". . . saw a hind over the Luxembourg Gardens which beckoned to me in the southeast (Danube!)."

He poured out his feelings and fears in a succession of letters to Eliasson, some of enormous length. His old fear of insanity had returned; he believed he was the victim of *envoûtement,* * and on 11 July asked whether Eliasson did not think that such attempts "are very common without our knowing it . . . I do not especially fear the madhouse, for it would be interesting to see these people whom I believe to be possessed by demons and not sick or senile. And I would regard it as a new education for a new life, if the maltreatment was not too severe; for people are maltreated by doctors, who are almost all godless and greedy for wealth. How many dangerous witnesses, heirs, 'inconvenient' people are not incarcerated there? The world doesn't change!"

That month he broke with his friends at the *crémerie*, where he had been eating regularly for seventeen months. "The company was too disagreeable even for me," he told Eliasson on 17 July, "and people there wanted to influence my destiny." His old fear of powerful personalities, which had caused him to break with previous friends such as Georg Brandes and Bjørnson and avoid meeting Zola, had returned.

One day Munch and Delius visited him at the Orfila. "We found him," wrote Delius, "poring over his retorts, stirring strange and evil-smelling liquids, and after chattering for five or ten minutes, we left in a most friendly manner. On [my] fetching Munch next day to go to lunch, he showed me a postcard just received from Strindberg, worded something in this wise, as far as I can remember: 'Your attempt to assassinate me through the Müller-Schmidt method (I forget the real names) has failed. *Tak for sidst* [Thank you for that].' It appears the method to which he alluded consisted in turning on the gas from the outside so as to suffocate the person within, or some such proceeding."[20]† In *Inferno*, Strindberg tells how "a torpor, such as I have seldom experienced,"

*See p. 330.

†Strindberg's postcard to Munch is postmarked 19 July, 1896 but, as Lionel Carley points out in *Delius: A Life in Letters*, I (London, 1983, pp. 109, 406), Delius was in Norway from early June until mid-September, returning to Paris only after Strindberg had left. Mr. Carley thinks that Munch probably showed Delius the postcard that autumn in Paris and that Delius, writing twenty-four years later, confused the visit by Munch which provoked it with one which Munch and Delius had made to Strindberg earlier.

assailed him. "With a great effort I got up and made haste to get into the open air . . . I could hardly drag myself along . . . I was poisoned, that was my first thought." His immediate suspicion was that Przybyszewski, who had been reported as having killed his common-law wife with gas, had made the same attempt on him, as revenge for his having slept with Dagny. Munch, who had just visited him, was a friend of Przybyszewski's and had obviously acted as his instrument. On returning to the hotel, "for three hours I lay awake unable to get to sleep, a thing that does not usually take me long. An uneasy sensation began to creep over me. I was being subjected to an electric current passing between the two rooms on either side of mine . . . I had only one thought in my mind: 'Someone is killing me! I will not be killed!' Waking the proprietor, I alleged that the fumes from the chemicals in my room had made me feel unwell, and I asked him if he could let me have another room for the night."[21]

On 19 July, Strindberg left the Hôtel Orfila and moved to another hotel at 4, rue de la Clef, near the Jardin des Plantes, whence he immediately wrote a huge letter to Hedlund unsigned and with no salutation. It made alarming reading:

> Escaped with my life, as long as I don't die of my wounds. So much the better [if I do]!!!
> It had been quiet on the floor where I live [sic]. Suddenly I noticed that I had a neighbour in the next room, but was surprised by the fact that he occupied both rooms on either side. I heard him to the right of my writing-table every day; at 10 p.m. he left that room and went to bed in the room next to my sleeping alcove, where I had him a foot away with the wall between us. But then I was amazed to hear someone else in the room he had left take off his clothes and go to bed. So there had been two people in there all day in a small room without talking to each other. Why? Because they wanted to be hidden—from me. At night between 2 and 3 I was extremely nervous, heard a rattle on the wall, woke many times, felt I would suffocate, thought it was my chemicals, but it could not be for they were standing on the stove.
> Yesterday Saturday I had bought a furnace (50 centimes) and crucibles (30 centimes each). I would now attempt a synthesis of gold in the fire through lead oxide which is already on the way to being gold. Despite the heat I felt fine and although I was working with soda and potassium cyanide I noticed no discomfort. But each time I left the stove and the furnace and sat at my writing-table I felt an unease, partly because on the other side of the wall the unknown one sat a yard from me and moved his chair, and partly because I had attacks of suffocation. A great discomfort came over me, fear of something silent, hostile. At noon I ate from a tray, standing at the chest of drawers. Read newspapers. Lay on the bed to rest, but found none; heard a man's and a woman's voice in the next room but deliberately speaking in the carefully low tones that conspirators adopt . . .

Read Isaiah Chapter 54, opened at random and I thought it was as though it had been written to me:

The Lord saith: "For a small moment have I forsaken thee; but with great mercies will I gather thee. In a little wrath I hid my face from thee for a moment; but with everlasting kindness will I have mercy on thee, saith the Lord thy Redeemer."

Around 10 I went to bed, and immediately the other one crossed over and went to bed beside me. But now the other awakes and makes a noise.

I lay awake and heard them both signalling with coughs and certain knocks. Lit the lamp again after feeling as though I were tugged between the poles of a powerful electrical machine or as though I were being suffocated between pillows . . .

Shut in between two probable murderers, I made a decision; got dressed, went down to the landlord, said that the chemicals in my room had made me feel ill and asked for another room.

He was friendly, gave me something to drink, and another room, directly beneath that of the unknown one, without my so much as mentioning the unknown one.

I now hear the unknown one jump from his bed:—He plans to flee, I thought, he thinks we have sent for the police.

But he did not flee, but banged once with a chair on the floor and let something heavy fall as though in a knapsack. I fell asleep, awoke and remembered only that I had dreamed about Ola Hansson.

It was a grey, gloomy morning; yellow-grey! like murder and the fear of detection.

At 11 I packed and fifteen minutes later fled, giving my address as: Dieppe.

And now I lie on a bed in a garden pavilion on the ground floor, the doors stand open; hollyhocks outside and acacias. It is the first feeling of summer that I have had. And now I am waiting for something new, or the end, or some new persecution.

Whom are you to believe? you ask! Yes, not the godless ones, but believe me, for I am so terrified that I dare not commit any bad act, for it will straightway be punished . . .

The hotel here gives full pension for 135 francs, so much less expensive than Orfila and Chaumière, but it became dear there because when I first went there evil people said I was mad, and it is expensive to be regarded as mad. My lungs and heart are destroyed: not by this last occurrence, but by two years' handling of poisons, Sulphur, Iodine, Bromine, Chlorine and Cyanide. I have grown thin, hate food and strong drinks, and will probably become paralysed.

Don't tell anyone my address, for if people come here and poison the minds of the owners, they too will give me putrid food, steal my laundry and salt the bills!

If I die here, I have no one to take care of things. I beg you to telegraph and reclaim my body, for I regard it as a punishment to be cut up in the anatomy hall and have the janitor sell my pieces to shops. The cheapest method is burning (50 francs). Otherwise, I have had a childish wish, since I was young, inexplicably, to be buried in Montparnasse. It costs 500 francs but that could surely be got from Bonnier as an advance on my Collected Works. I don't want to lie in Swedish soil, since it is cursed and I do not wish to have my grave defiled by enemies. Do you not notice that Sweden is the land of the banished, the accursed, who must sit in darkness and see how the world is governed without heed to their advice? The land of the unfranchised, the voteless, the silenced. Hence the demonic hatred, the envy, the clawing; devils whose purpose is to torment each other.

After describing various signs he has seen which indicated that God wishes him to leave Paris—a cock on a steeple "flapping its wings as though exhorting him to fly," the Pole Star in the sky ("I wondered: is it northwards you must go!")—he concluded: "I do not yet know what God intends with me. Must I go to Ystad, where the asylum in Lund awaits me? Perhaps I must endure this Golgotha too? To continue my lessons."[22]

He explained his belief in signs and portents such as these in a letter he wrote a few days later to Fritz Thaulow: "I have long heard speak of something called occultism, the study of all those phenomena the existence of which cannot be denied, yet which cannot be explained. A year ago I glanced at the subject, somewhat sceptically. But I saw at once that there was something in it. I threw myself into the subject more deeply and when everything confirmed itself I ended by becoming an occultist; that is: I received factual proof through the natural sciences that the soul was the all-important thing, the body only a transitory dress, that we are immortal, created, guided according to a certain plan etc., all things long known. To confirm this I withdrew into isolation . . ."[23]

That July, Strindberg published an article in the occultist magazine, *L'Initiation*, entitled "The Irradiation and Extensibility of the Soul." During the spring he had read an essay by Albert de Rochas which postulated that people's sensibility could be "exteriorised," enabling them to contact each other from a distance, either sympathetically or for the purpose of torment. This seemed to offer an explanation of some of his recent experiences and, going beyond de Rochas, he declared himself "certain that the soul is capable of extending itself and that it extends very far during ordinary sleep, finally to leave the body altogether at the moment of death but by no means to be extinguished." He lists various conditions which might be explained by this irradiation of the soul, such as collective behaviour, the power of actor over spectator, and the erotic bond between lovers, adding that certain metaphorical expressions such as "My thoughts wandered" or "I am absent-minded" might be literally true. "The soul shrinks with fear and expands with joy, happiness or success." He was to develop this exploration of the astral plane in *Inferno* and in several of his subsequent plays.

"If I live long enough," he told Hedlund on 23 July, "I shall translate the Book of Job and illustrate it from an occult standpoint . . . The illustrations would look like a piece of paper which one has crumpled and over which one has broken charcoal. The uninitiated would see nothing, but the seers would . . . Read the Book of Job! 'O blessed is the man whom God chastiseth!'"

But if Strindberg supposed that his troubles had ended with his departure from the Orfila, he was to be rapidly disillusioned. The day after writing the above letter, he wrote to Hedlund: "After sleeping calmly for a whole week I was awakened last night at 2 a.m. by a door slamming above my head and feet tiptoeing as at the Orfila, but half a minute later I jumped up almost stifled and with my heart threatening to burst. I stood on the floor and now felt as though I were standing beneath an electricity machine; and that I would fall dead if I did not hasten away. Once in the garden, I felt better. But each time I went back into the room I was stifled. So I stayed outside for three hours. Now this morning after going out and returning home, I feel the same sense of being stifled and the same pressure on my shoulders especially the left and strains in my upper arms, pains in the pit of my stomach . . . Is it the Pole with his gas apparatus or is it the electrical engineer with his accumulators and reflectors? . . . What does it matter if I die? My spirit will be the more vital and a greater torment to my enemies. But, but . . . Do you now see that I am not suffering from any mania but am persecuted?"

He had decided, at last, that he needed medical help, and since he does not seem to have trusted any doctor in Paris, he left that same day, 24 July 1896, to seek advice from his friend Dr. Anders Eliasson in Ystad. En route he stayed with the Thaulows in Dieppe. Alexandra Thaulow records that he told them how, on leaving his Paris hotel, in order to deceive his "pursuers," he hailed a cab and told the driver to go to the Gare du Midi on the other side of the city. As they approached the station he left the cab, stopped another and told the new driver to take him to the Gare St. Lazare. Not until the train began to move did he jump on, and then not into a carriage but onto the engine beside the fireman, losing his hat in the process. "Next morning we saw candle-wax on all the stairs and entrances. Strindberg had gone round tapping the walls and ceilings with a broomstick to make sure there were no machines hidden there." He insisted on knowing who lived in all the neighbouring houses, and changed his room each night. One morning he said, "Now they have found me. I know they are here and even if I fall dead on the spot, I shall show you I am right." Alexandra suggested that they should go round the house with an electric compass which would react to any electrical impulse. When it did not, Strindberg said, "They have discovered that I am not alone. Look at that red wall—there is a man sitting on it making signs to someone outside." Alexandra had to explain that the wall belonged to a home for retired seamen who sat there watching the ships enter and leave the harbour.[24]

He left Dieppe on 28 July and two days later was in Ystad. He had been in France for just under two years. "Strindberg has gone home to Sweden," Edvard Munch wrote to his aunt, Karen Bjølstad. "He is under treatment for mental illness—he had so many strange notions—made gold, and found that the earth was flat and the stars were holes in the vault of heaven. He had persecution mania and once thought I wanted to poison him with gas."[25]

Chapter Twenty-Two

"DO I FIGHT WITH DEMONS?"

Dr. Anders Eliasson, Strindberg's host in Ystad, was an autocratic character separated from his wife and living alone in a large house enclosing a quadrangular courtyard which his guest likened to a Buddhist monastery. "The pitch of the roof, and the Chinese tiles that covered it, reminded one of the Far East. An apathetic tortoise crawled about on the paving stones, or buried itself in the weeds in a state of Nirvana which seemed likely to endure for ever."[1]

Strindberg was immediately alarmed to find that his bedstead was of iron, "surmounted by brass knobs that resembled the conductors of an electric machine," and the mattress of copper wire. "It was quite impossible to ask for another bed, as that would have aroused suspicions about my sanity. To convince myself that nothing was hidden above me, I went up into the attic. There, just to make matters worse, I found precisely one object, an enormous coat of chain mail, placed exactly over my bed. 'That is an accumulator,' thought I. 'If a storm breaks, a thing that very often happens in these parts, the network of iron will attract the lightning and I shall be lying on the conductor.'" He was further disturbed by what sounded like the steady roar of a machine ("I had been plagued by a buzzing in my ears ever since I left the Hôtel Orfila"); but this turned out to be a press in a printing house next door.[2]

That night in bed he felt "someone watching me, someone who

touched me lightly, groped for my heart and sucked." He ran to the doctor's room and told him of this, and of the attempts in Paris to kill him by electricity. Eliasson informed him that he was suffering from a mental disorder. "I persisted in demanding that he listen to me, but he refused to let me speak." Strindberg then remembered that Eliasson had that evening "expatiated upon the unfortunate effects that mankind would suffer should it prove possible to manufacture gold. Universal bankruptcy . . . the end of the world. There would be nothing for it but to kill the gold-makers. Those had been his final words . . . Every circumstance combined to make me suspicious of my good friend."[3]

Such is Strindberg's account in *Inferno*, written a year later. He may have dramatised it, as he did so much else in that book, but his private diary suggests that at least the waking nightmares were true. "Had an attack on the night of 30–31st [the night of his arrival]. Repeated less violently the following nights: 2 a.m., midnight. Night of 1–2 August, no attack, but I awoke at 3.45 a.m. but fit and rested . . . Sun 2 Aug. The telegraph pole sings: I approach to listen; a horseshoe lay at the foot of the pole in the grass of the ditch . . . Dr. E——n gave me Strophanthus [a drug extracted from a poisonous plant and used as a cardiac tonic]. Strophanthine [*sic*] causes death by paralysis of the cardiac muscle . . . Friday 7th night: bad attack 2 a.m."

On 1 August he wrote to Torsten Hedlund enclosing a newspaper cutting which quoted a passage from William James's *Principles of Psychology* about a preacher who in 1887 lost his memory, disappeared for several months and reappeared as a quite different person. This, Strindberg suggested, might explain "the strangeness of our existence, our double life, obsessions, our nocturnal life, our bad conscience, our groundless fear, our persecution mania, which is perhaps not a mania but we are persecuted—by what you and the occultists call elementals or lower beings, which envy us our existence, drive us to suicide so as to be able to possess our, as you call them, Astral Bodies . . . What happened to me in Paris must remain a riddle; and should not be investigated. That I wrestled with death is certain. Dr. Eliasson has examined my body thoroughly and found it free of fault and strong. Whether he says this out of kindness I don't know. I cannot judge. And my spirit has never been so clear-sighted as now, so solemnly calm when I am not disturbed—by others."

Later that same day he wrote again to Hedlund: "Is it possible, I ask now, that the evil principle is dominant in me? I have evil in me and I hate it! And do you know, I would choose to be buried, to be burned —alive, to cleanse me from evil! Am I more evil than other men? No! But I have been wrong in avenging myself on the demons whose mission was to torment me into goodness. That was my error. But don't suppose they were better than me!"

Dr. Eliasson prescribed cold douches, took away his missal and Bible, and told him to "read things which do not excite you, things of secondary interest, world history or mythology, and take leave of these chimerical dreamers. Above all, beware of occultism . . . We are forbidden to pry into the Creator's secrets." He also urged him to leave chemistry alone. Strindberg's suspicion that Eliasson was ill-disposed towards him was strengthened when he saw that the grain of wood in a cupboard resembled "a goat's head, executed by a master hand, upon which I instantly turned my back. Pan himself! . . . whom the Middle Ages had transformed into Satan . . . After this adventure my friend and I openly declared our hostility to each other."[4]

On 15 August he received a letter from Frida telling him that she pitied and loved him, and inviting him to visit not her, but their daughter, who was living with her grandmother. This letter, he told Hedlund three days later, "recalled me to life." (He still imagined that Frida wanted him to return to her, despite her repeated insistence on a divorce; he was of course ignorant that she was now living with Frank Wedekind in Munich, whither Albert Langen had removed his publishing house.) "The latest crisis I have undergone," Strindberg's letter continued, "I have not told you about, but I shall in a book—a novel, if you wish to call it that . . . I thought I was being punished either because I had probed into the forbidden, but science has always done that . . . or because I sought to evade life's 'toil without reward' and because I tried to sever the bonds that *should* bind me to the earth and the human race: should—the rebel! Often in my researches I met the hand that blew my papers into chaos, obscured my solutions, and in the blowpipe bubble on the charcoal I saw a grinning face that poked out its tongue, mocking me. But I began the experiments again, telling myself: These are enemies who must be overcome." He concluded by reiterating that he had decided, for a time, to abandon science.

Two days later he wrote again to Hedlund: "Did I not tell you that I regarded my researches into the hidden as forbidden activities for which I should be punished . . . that my occultism cost me my health and almost my personal freedom and that I regard it as criminal to continue? . . . I suddenly realised that I was no Job; no righteous man who must be tested but a robber who had ended on the cross because his deeds deserved it and who had to be punished." He still shrank from meeting Hedlund. "My instinct tells me that we should not see each other now—we have given each other the best of ourselves; the worse or meaner part of us we can keep for ourselves or for those who are meaner." On 23 August he told Hedlund: "You said recently that people are looking for the Zola of occultism. That I feel is my vocation. But in the grand manner. A poem in prose: called *Inferno*. The same theme as in *By the Open Sea*. The destruction of the individual when he isolates himself. Salvation through: working without honour or gold, duty, the family, consequently— woman—the mother and the child! Resignation through the discovery of each one's task allotted by Providence." By the time he came to write *Inferno*, however, he was to interpret his experiences differently in the light of what he had learned from Swedenborg.

In *Inferno*, Strindberg gives the impression that his month in Ystad was a time of unrelieved tension and horror, and that apart from Eliasson he met no one except the local medical officer, to whom he complained that Eliasson regarded him as a hypochondriac. But a forestry commissioner named Eugen Hemberg tells how Eliasson asked him to take Strindberg on walks and "talk to him about botany, zoology and archaeology." Hemberg adds that Strindberg clearly enjoyed these almost daily excursions and talked eagerly about everything they saw. "Only in nature," he told Hemberg, "can I find peace of mind." Eliasson organised a "beer evening" with a number of guests, and Hemberg "watched Strindberg forget his worries and smilingly partake in the conversation and singing, sometimes leading the discussion in sparkling humour," until the party broke up at dawn.[5] Even when things seemed at their worst, there were calm and happy interludes, though no one would guess it from *Inferno*, any more than from *A Madman's Defence*.

On 28 August, Strindberg left Ystad for Austria. The local newspaper described him on his departure as looking "fit and strong, and longing only to be active again."[6] "I parted from my friend the Tormentor without bitterness. He had only been the instrument of Providence."[7] He stayed at first in the village of Saxen with his mother-in-law, Marie Uhl, with whom Kerstin was living. He had not seen his daughter since she was six weeks old; now she was two and a half. But after three days there he moved to the house of Marie's twin sister, Melanie, in the neighbouring village of Klam. In *Inferno* he says that Marie's mother, Great-grandmother Reischl, threatened to disinherit Marie if he remained with her and the child, and a letter which the old lady wrote that November to a third party tends to confirm this.[8] However, he was allowed to see Kerstin regularly, and found great happiness in her company.*

---

*A letter which Strindberg wrote to Hedlund on the day he left Ystad suggests that he was hoping for a reconciliation with Frida, and although in *Inferno* he denies this, the Reischls no doubt feared the possibility.

At Melanie's, he was given the "rose-red" room in which Frida had stayed during their two years of separation. It seemed to him to suggest hope. "This rose-red I saw in Malmö when I woke in the morning. Saw it in Berlin in the morning [on the train journey to Austria]." The fact that there was red ink in the inkwell, and that a packet of cigarette papers contained a single rose-coloured one, also encouraged him. [9]

His resolution, expressed to Hedlund three weeks earlier, to abandon science did not last long. On 7 September he wrote that he had found in Klam "1,000 (One Thousand) pages of notes on chemistry and the other natural sciences and have rediscovered there lost trails; vistas reopen revealing the general coherence of things and I have grown yards in a few days. But I have 700 pages on chemistry in Ystad and 700 pages on other sciences in Paris. Do I fight with demons?" He added a postscript: "Here Swedenborg's writings fell into my hands for the first time. They contain wonderful things."

For this he had to thank Marie and Melanie. Strindberg describes them in *Inferno* as "identical twins, exactly alike in character . . . If I talked to one of them when the other was not present, the absent one always knew what I had said, so that I was able to confide in either without having to repeat myself. I don't therefore distinguish between them in this account." [10] When he told them of his recent "inexplicable experiences," they (or one of them) told him that they too had studied occultism and had suffered similarly: "sleepless nights, mysterious happenings followed by mortal anguish, and finally nocturnal attacks." They had found salvation in Swedenborg, expressed astonishment that Strindberg had not read his great compatriot at first hand, and lent him a book of extracts from his writings in German.

On 8 September he excitedly recorded in his diary Swedenborg's account of Hell. As described by Swedenborg, the landscape of Hell precisely resembled that around Klam, with its enclosed valley, hills and dark woods, manure heaps and puddles of filth. As for its inhabitants, the damned:

> The unblest cannot endure daylight and clean air. Self-love, hatred, jealousy . . . Hell's fire: to wake passions which are never satisfied, flare up again . . . When the heavenly light reaches the unblessed, an icy cold runs through their veins and their blood congeals . . . To each other they look human but in the light of heaven they wear a horrible corpse-like aspect. Some black, others like firebrands, others with warts and boils; some with tufts of hair on their face; others have bones without skin, others only one row of teeth . . . Seeking sensual pleasure, honour and wealth. They get it too, only to lose it again. They wander about lonely and sad, they hunger

and have nothing to eat . . . get a whore for company. Despair, hatred of the good and of God . . .

In *Inferno*, Strindberg explains: "I had been brought up to regard Hell with the deepest contempt as an imaginary conception . . . [But] we are already in Hell. It is the earth itself that is Hell, the prison constructed for us by an intelligence superior to our own . . . Hell-fire is our desire to make a name for ourselves in the world. The Powers awaken this desire in us and permit the damned to achieve their objectives. But when the goal is reached and our wish fulfilled, everything is found to be worthless and our victory meaningless . . . It is not unappeased hunger that plagues us most but gratified greed, which leaves us with a loathing for everything . . . I was in Hell and damnation lay heavy upon me." Human suffering "could be explained in no other way than by assuming that we have had a previous existence, from which we have been removed and sent here to suffer the consequences of misdemeanours of which we ourselves have no recollection."[11]

Swedenborg brought him the peace he needed. "I spent eight days and nights in my roseate chamber. My daughter's daily visits brought peace to my soul . . . I spent my days reading Swedenborg and was overwhelmed by the realism of his descriptions . . . It was unfortunate that the volume I now had contained only extracts. It was not until later, when the complete edition of *Arcana Coelestia* fell into my hands, that I was able to discover the answer to the principal riddles of our spiritual life."[12]

He wrote several times to Frida asking her to join him, but without success. His diary records how he dreamed of Sarah Bernhard [*sic*], his father, who gave him a packet of cigarette tobacco, and Frida, "young, brilliant, light with a boy's hat; I asked to be allowed to introduce her as one of my relations"; and how one night the church clock struck thirteen. "Heard noises in the attic. Went up. Saw spinning-wheels and a sewing-machine . . . saw four black sticks forming a pentagram; re-arranged them better." His translator Mathilde Prager wrote that the new Freie Bühne in Munich was planning to open at the Deutsches Theater there with an unauthorised production of *Creditors*. Strindberg accepted the news indifferently. "Since experience has taught me that it is better to be staged without getting any money than not to be staged, I think one should leave the Deutsches Theater in peace until the production has opened, for it is a great honour to open the new theatre."[13] It worried him that his possessions were scattered. "At the rue de la Clef," he told Hedlund on 17 September, "are the papers that must be saved. At the Orfila my books, chemicals, winter clothes and all my laundry. They'll have to stay, for I owe 50 francs there—I don't know what for . . . I am now reading Hoffman's *The Devil's Elixir* and every word is true. Also Schiller's *Visionary*. But Swedenborg is greatest and first!"

Hedlund tried to help by sending him Madame Blavatsky's *The Secret Doctrine*, but Strindberg's aversion to theosophy remained. "You know my feelings about her since 1884," he replied around 26 September, "namely, that she has had no visions; that she read in libraries and used other people's writings." Later he was to condemn the theosophists as "these devils who like the Jesuits shun no means."[14] In *Inferno* he was to dismiss *The Secret Doctrine* as "that hotch-potch of all the so-called occult theories, that rehash of every scientific heresy, ancient and modern . . . the work of a virago who wants to beat men at their own game and plumes herself that she has . . . set up a priestess of Isis on the altar of the Crucified."[15]*

On 25 September, Melanie returned to live with Marie in Saxen, and Strindberg rented a small cottage close to the house. His diary over the two months he spent there records mainly dreams and "signs"—a jackdaw chases him, screeching, then follows its dead master's funeral procession and perches on the coffin in its grave; he hears rustling in the lock of his door, as in Paris, dreams again of his father, who this time gives him a gold bracelet, a ladybird flaps its wings northwards as the cock on the weather-vane had done in Paris, he sees the Venus de Milo in his coffee cup.

He wondered if his unease was not being cunningly engineered by his enemies. "Assuming that *envoûtement* (magical assassination)† is possible," he asked Eliasson around 30 October, "would it be a sin to *envoûter* one's enemies? The other ones may murder without hindrance, but I may not be counted among the other ones. Why? . . . I believe that people are tormenting me from afar, and others believe the same of me; but unjustly." A week later he assured Dr. Eliasson: "I am well, working keenly and successfully (*Ne audiat Nemesis*, Linnaeus ['Let Nemesis not hear me']), and enjoy life through my lively two-year-old daughter."[16] He wrote huge letters about chemistry to Hedlund, Jollivet-Castelot, Eliasson and others.

Marie Uhl recalled Strindberg's extreme eccentricity during these days. Once, when an organist came to visit them, "Strindberg became distraught and explained that this was the Bosnian, Pole or African who

---

*Professor Gunnar Brandell observes that the philosophy of occultism provided Strindberg, as theosophy did not, with a theory to explain his suffering without his having to confess personal guilt (*Strindberg in Inferno*, p. 121).

†The parenthesis is Strindberg's.

had persecuted him all his life. From this hour Strindberg went everywhere armed with a big bowie-knife [*sic*] and often stabbed around him so that we feared for our lives. His old obsession that we wanted to poison him returned, and he often changed his plate with little Kerstin's, whose food he thought less likely to be dangerous." On another occasion they found him lying motionless on his bed dressed in black with his feet on a cushion. To their anxious questions he replied "I am dead," asserting that "he had been murdered by men who had broken into the room through the wall, assisted by my sister. He demanded that the burgomaster and the police be summoned to conduct an investigation. My sister immediately went to the telegraph office and telegraphed to my husband to send male nurses from Vienna and find a place for Strindberg in a mental hospital." Luckily, this proved not to be necessary. Marie concluded: "My sister and I have often wondered whether these dramatic and often theatrical scenes were not staged to make a theatrical effect or to study its effect on the public, i.e., ourselves, to whom these scenes were played. It is difficult to decide how much was fantasy and how much reality."[17]

Irrationally, Strindberg came to the conclusion that Torsten Hedlund, his "confessor," was the instigator of these attacks. In *Inferno*, he states that his rejection of theosophy ("the idea of the collective deity, Karma, did not appeal to me and . . . for this reason I could not join a sect that denied the existence of a personal God") "changed my upright and noble-minded friend into a vengeful demon. He flung a sentence of excommunication at me, threatened me with the occult powers . . . and uttered prophecies like some heathen, sacrificial priest."[18] It seems most unlikely that Hedlund could have written as Strindberg claims, but on 23 November, Strindberg sent him a violently abusive letter: "Your lust to dominate, your egoism, your prophet-like megalomania, are the grossest I have ever come across . . . Have I ever interfered in your spiritual life?" Thus concluded this lengthy and intimate correspondence, apart from a terse note from Strindberg asking Hedlund to forward a manuscript to a newspaper and a transitory renewal three years later.

Frida's father, perhaps at her instigation, decided that Strindberg had overstayed his welcome, and wrote from Vienna telling him to leave. On 26 November he went with Kerstin and Marie Uhl to visit Great-grandmother Reischl, who was living in the cottage by the Danube in which he and Frida had been when Kerstin was born. "Two years, two eternities had passed since we said our farewells . . . Which of us was responsible for the rupture? I was, who had murdered my own love and hers. Farewell, white house of Dornach, field of thorns and of roses. Farewell, Danube. I comfort myself with the thought that you were never more than a dream, brief as summer, sweeter than reality, and that I do not mourn you." Next day he left for Sweden, "there to face the fire of the enemy at yet another station on the road to atonement."[19]

He spent the night of 30 November in Copenhagen, where he saw Georg Brandes for the first time in seven years. Brandes described their meeting in a letter to Gustaf af Geijerstam a week later. "The other day . . . I had a curious encounter. Strindberg, who was in Copenhagen that evening, sent a card asking me to spend the evening with him. I went at once; he was already in bed and had been asleep for a while, but got up and we drank a glass of wine together at a café. He has never looked better, more considerable, more serious, yet more careworn. Soon he told me that his death was imminent, and he returned to this again and again. He is suffering from persecution mania, explained to me that an enemy had driven him from France and was now, by magic, driving him from town to town, by sticking nails in his portrait and thus ruining his night's sleep, giving him raging palpitations of the heart, etc. He talked incessantly of magic. Magic was the latest phenomenon of the age and of the future. It was a natural power akin to those discovered by Charcot. But it was secret, terrible, a power that could work from afar. He is writing for the Magic Magazine in Paris. Literature no longer exists for him. A great mind broken."[20]

Seventeen years later, in his memoirs, Brandes gave a fuller account of the evening:

> When I returned home at 10:30 p.m. I found a note on my desk from Strindberg saying that he was spending that one night in Copenhagen, didn't want to leave without seeing me, but asked me to meet him *at some modest place, not smartly dressed* . . . When I came to the hotel . . . he was in bed asleep. I put my hand on his shoulder. He woke, said, "I have taken a sleeping pill, I didn't think you were coming," but dressed quickly, much more smartly than I. While still half dressed, he said, "Do you know, my coming is foretold in classical French literature?" "Where?" "In Balzac's *Séraphitus-Séraphita.*" He looked for the book in his bag and showed me the passage: "Once more the light will come from the north." "He means me." "How do you know he doesn't mean Ibsen?" I asked to tease him. "No, it's me, there can be no doubt."

Strindberg went on to speak of occultism. "We live in the age of occultism, it is occultism that now rules in literature. Everything else is out of date." Brandes told him how Huysmans had accused the Marquis de Guaita of causing him chest pains in the night in Paris by black magic. Strindberg replied, "I too suffered chest pains which a man in Sweden caused me while I was in Paris . . . My benefactor who wished to avenge himself on me for my ingratitude* . . . I wasn't really ungrateful; I had caused him pain without wishing it." Then abruptly: "You have enemies, I would like to do something for you. Do you want me to kill your enemies? . . . We can blind them, we needn't kill them, it would render them equally harmless . . . Get me a photograph of the person. Then with the aid of magic I will put his eyes out by piercing the eye in the picture with a needle" . . . As they walked along the harbour, Strindberg said: "All the good sense of olden times has been chucked out under the guise of progress. With all my heart I wish we could go back to the time when people burned wizards and witches without mercy. They serve the devil and deserve their punishment." "'Be glad,' I replied, 'that they no longer burn wizards, otherwise you and I would both have been burned long ago.' "[21]

Next day, 1 December 1896, Strindberg took the ferry to Malmö.

What was the cause of these repeated fits of alarm and hallucinations from which Strindberg suffered? Diagnoses have varied: schizophrenia, manic depression, paranoia, alcoholism. He had been drinking absinthe steadily for at least eight years (Jonas Lie noted with concern that he was already addicted to it when they met in Paris in 1884).[22] Dr. Sven Hedenberg records that a French doctor named Lancereaux described in 1880 how absinthe poisoning leads to hallucinations of a tormenting and terrifying nature: shimmering lights, bloodthirsty animals threatening to swallow you; standing on the edge of huge abysses, fearful of falling; nocturnal cramp, especially in the calf muscles; a skin irritation as though ants were crawling on it; audial hallucinations such as singing in the ears, screams, wailing and threatening sounds, usually at night but also during the day; and the illusion of being insulted and persecuted.[23]† The French poet Marcel Réja, who saw much of Strindberg in 1897–98, believed that alcohol "probably played a not unimportant role in his *Inferno* crisis."[24] Several modern doctors concur with this view. A. W. Anderson states that the symptoms described in *Inferno* are very suggestive of toxic poisoning, such as might come from an over-indulgence in absinthe,[25] and Torsten Frey believes that his absinthe drinking, combined with the sulphonal which he had been taking in "big doses" in 1894 and which Dr. Eliasson prescribed for him again in August 1896, plus the effect of his experiments with sulphur, were in themselves enough to account for his *Inferno* symptoms and that "his brain was definitely damaged . . . Thujon, the

*Torsten Hedlund.
†The manufacture and sale of absinthe was banned in France in 1915.

hallucinatory substance in absinthe, can, even in minute doses, give the sense of electrical attacks."[26]

A German psychiatrist, Dr. S. Rahmer, believed that Strindberg suffered from deep melancholia, *"melancholia agitata et daemonimaniaca,"* with the typical symptoms of a compulsion to be alone, vague fears, thoughts of death and suicide, and delusions of having committed crimes, followed by hallucinations. Rahmer dismissed paranoia on the ground that Strindberg blamed himself as much as others.[27] Dr. Hedenberg likewise rejects paranoia, since paranoids believe in a single injustice and fight against that, while Strindberg kept imagining different injustices; he believes, however, that Strindberg had a paranoid tendency, in that he was so imprisoned in his illusions as to be dominated by them. Two eminent Swedish authorities on Strindberg, Martin Lamm and Torsten Eklund, have concluded that he suffered from schizophrenia; but Dr. Hedenberg states that he cannot have, otherwise he would not have enjoyed, as he did, calm and balanced periods.[28] Torsten Frey, writing in 1980, declares: "Hardly any Scandinavian psychiatrist writing today regards Strindberg as schizophrenic."[29]

To a layman, absinthe poisoning seems the most plausible theory; but the debate is never likely to be resolved. What is sure is that, as Brandell remarks, from the time of Strindberg's return to Sweden in December 1896 "his feelings of persecution diminished and finally disappeared altogether." During his first weeks in Sweden he was still haunted by "demons" and tormented by electric currents; but these gradually subsided, and thereafter he "was never again subject to concentrated attacks that caused him to decamp." He himself was to attribute this discovery of comparative peace to his "atonement with the Powers."[30]

Chapter Twenty-Three

THE ROAD TO DAMASCUS

Strindberg reached Malmö in poor physical as well as mental condition. "I have taken sulphonal these last four nights, with varying success," he wrote that evening to Anders Eliasson in Ystad. "Met a Danish doctor on the train who (1) said that the sulphonal dose is 1 gram (you wrote 3 grams) (2) advised against sulphonal as bad for the heart. He had given a man sulphonal with the result: that the man leaped up out of his sleep half mad and out through the window." A young journalist named Emil Kléen, later to become a good friend to Strindberg, interviewed him for *Malmö-Tidningen* and saw "a pale furrowed face, with a hint of the preacher, the fanatic. Two deep, piercing, noble eyes; a brow of astonishing height and beauty topped by unruly grey-flecked hair. A slim and supple body with small hands and feet. And when he speaks, a soft and gentle voice accompanied by a sensitive and sympathetic smile. But he so seldom smiles."[1]

Next morning Strindberg left for the neighbouring town of Skurup to visit another doctor, Lars Nilsson, whom he had met there while staying with Ola and Laura Hansson in the spring of 1891. He no longer had faith in Eliasson. Nilsson had already received a letter from Marie Uhl warning him of Strindberg's persecution mania and suspicions that people were trying to kill him, and saying that Nilsson was the only person whom Strindberg now trusted, since he believed him to have undergone the same travails as himself.[2]

He stayed five nights with Nilsson, who could do little for him. Like Eliasson, he prescribed sulphonal, with no good effect. "What is it with me," Strindberg wrote to Marie Uhl on 4 December, "that I am now so tormented night and day? My doctor has given me medicine so that I sleep through the nights, but then fear comes in the day instead. Fear of everything and everyone. So I am planning a trip round Sweden to pass the time." Three days later he wrote again to Marie: "My peace is gone and I must start my journey today, always journey to seek what I cannot find—peace." That same evening he wrote her from Malmö: "Either I am persecuted or I have persecution mania. But no matter. It even gladdens me to think that higher powers torment me so that I shall long for the hereafter. And the world tempts me no longer. I say to myself continually: '*Adieu, pauvre terre, adieu!*' "[3]*

That month Strindberg began to write letters to his daughter Kerstin, a one-sided correspondence (she was only two and a half) that was to last continuously for three years before he abruptly terminated it at a time when she most needed him. She was living with her grandmother, Frida having already begun to lose interest in her. "Your old daddy," he informed her on 11 December, "has become a young sportsman. He has got new teeth which don't hurt; a new suit with knee-breeches and bicycle stockings, yellow shoes and gloves," accompanying this with a cartoon of himself thus dressed, captioned: "Prince Hamlet, or the sick dandy." His projected trip was blocked by the weather. "The snow," he informed Kerstin a week later, "has made the roads so frightful that the acrobatic activities have for the moment been postponed."[4] The letter went on, as most of his letters to her would, to reflect on the possible reasons for his anguished state of mind; just as, in *Inferno*, he was to treat Marie and her sister Melanie as a single person, so now he was to regard Marie and Kerstin as one, addressing impossibly gloomy thoughts to the tiny child. Small wonder, with such a father and such a mother, that she was eventually to meet a fate as tragic as that of any of his created heroines.

The torments, or illusions of torment, that had plagued him in Paris followed him to Sweden. "As soon as I had settled in a hotel, an uproar would break out . . . People walked about, dragging their feet and moving furniture. I changed my room, changed my hotel; the noise was always there, just above my head." He was also "attacked by those currents of electricity that lifted me off chairs and out of bed . . . My thoughts returned to the occultists and their hidden powers."[5] On 13 December he left Malmö for the old university town of Lund, a few miles inland,

---

*A quote from Balzac's *Séraphita*.

"where I had friends, doctors, psychiatrists, even theosophists, on whose support I counted for my spiritual salvation."[6] He was to remain there for eight months. "An oasis of civilisation," he was to call it in *Legends*, "on the great south Swedish plain." Among other advantages, it had a splendid library.

One of the first acquaintances he renewed there was with, of all unlikely people, Bengt Lidforss, who had helped to translate and then publicly criticised his *Antibarbarus* and whom he had since repeatedly abused in his letters. This Judas now atoned for his crime by lending Strindberg a book which hugely excited him. "I am reading Swedenborg's *Arcana Coelestia*," he told Marie Uhl on 17 December, "and am terrified. It all seems to be true, and yet is cruel from the God of Love . . . Today the sun is shining but Swedenborg is so terrible that everything seems wrong. Is my own hell not enough? Must I have others' too?"

Arcana Coelestia is an immense work, thirteen volumes in the standard English translation. Much of it is simply Bible commentary, but what most intrigued Strindberg was the detailed account Swedenborg gives of his communication with spirits. This Swedenborg relates partly in the form of diary entries, sometimes copied directly, sometimes trimmed and arranged, as Strindberg was to do with his own diary when writing *Inferno*. Moreover, to quote a later scientist-spiritualist, Sir Oliver Lodge, Swedenborg "teaches that heaven and hell are not in space but that they are internal and spiritual states, so that entrance into the spiritual world is only the opening of an interior consciousness."[7] He relates how spirits informed him about the after-life, and sometimes even tried to get physical satisfaction through him, making him greedy for food and sexual pleasure. They tormented him in other ways, too. "Spirits have produced on my body effects entirely perceptible to sense . . . have scattered disagreeable and sweet odours often enough . . . have maltreated my body with grievous pain . . . have most manifestly induced cold and heat, and cold more frequently; have, as it were, driven along blasts of wind; I have felt the wind plainly, yea so as to cause the flame of the candle to flicker." He tells how he sometimes felt lifted up by spirits when passing over steep places, and how when he looked in a mirror and spoke with spirits, his face would be changed so as to resemble the faces of those with whom he spoke.[8]

Strindberg had not spoken thus directly with spirits, but many of the torments Swedenborg describes closely mirrored those which he himself had experienced in Paris. "Everything that had befallen me I found again in Swedenborg."[9] He must equally have been excited by Swedenborg's conviction that the soul could exist separately from the material body and thus could survive apparent death; that space and time as we know them do not obtain in the world of the dematerialised, and that thought there can be directly communicated without the need for speech. Swedenborg insists, too, that the pangs of conscience are not the pangs of hell, since those who retain a conscience are not spiritually dead, and therefore are not in hell. Moreover, Swedenborg's diary of his dreams, which was not published until the middle of the nineteenth century (when it caused an uproar), includes frank descriptions of his sexual dreams. He once confessed that women had been his chief passion all his life ("this most pleasant and delicious violence and necessity"), but he interpreted these dreams as being symbolic of spiritual aspirations, either intellectual or religious or both. His visions would often be preceded by a great shivering, and "unaccountable sweats and tremblings."[10] It is easy to imagine the comfort Strindberg must have found from learning that nightmares similar to those he had endured, waking and sleeping, had been experienced by his great compatriot and interpreted by him as a sign of grace. *

Strindberg had not been happy in his own university town of Uppsala, and although he mixed to a certain extent with some of the younger teachers and postgraduate students, on the whole he found Lund equally dispiriting. He did not like the general run of academics, and the sight of so many students made him feel old. "I have often asked myself why I have come to live in this little town, where I don't belong. What business have I here? But . . . it is so that I may come into contact with the sciences and with new moods of thought among the young."[11]

He made this remark to Johan Mortensen, a young docent† in literature who made his acquaintance that December and saw a lot of him over the next eight months. He first met Strindberg at a dinner party and was surprised at his appearance. "He was dressed in a sporting suit, which was not so common then as now, at least in a dining-room; yellow shoes,

---

*It is interesting to note that Swedenborg in his youth was a lover of the theatre, and when in Paris was a regular visitor to the Comédie-Française. Another thing that must have endeared him to Strindberg was that censorship prevented him from having his works published in Sweden in his lifetime, or even imported except with difficulty, because of the unorthodoxy of his views. But Strindberg's comprehension of Swedenborg always remained inadequate; Professor Gunnar Brandell rightly remarks that their differences are greater than their similarities. For example, Strindberg rejected Swedenborg's central belief that the individual is free and bears full responsibility for what he or she does; and Swedenborg believed that we enter hell after death, Strindberg that we endure it during our life on earth. (*Strindberg in Inferno*, pp. 125–6; *Strindberg: ett författarliv*, III, pp. 234–5.)

†University teacher.

broad check stockings, knee-breeches and a blouse fastened with a strap."
His hair was "already flecked with silver-white threads," although he was
not yet forty-eight; Mortensen thought he looked like "a burned-out
volcano . . . He always spoke with such earnestness, so slowly and softly,
as though he wanted to say something momentous. He later told me he
had developed this way of speaking when training to be an actor. If he
raised his voice, it sounded harsh and broken."[12] Waldemar Bülow, the
owner of the radical newspaper *Folkets Tidning*, found him "like a
helpless child, grateful for the smallest act of friendliness."[13]

Since mid-October a revival of *Lucky Peter's Journey*, the first Strindberg production in Sweden since 1890, had been playing successfully at
Vasa Theatre in Stockholm, staged by the brilliant Harald Molander with
a rising young star of the Swedish theatre, Anders de Wahl, in the lead.
The critics had complained that it was overlong and undramatic, but the
public liked it and it ran for sixty-five performances. Knowing how far
behind Strindberg was in his payments to his children in Finland,* the
owner of the theatre, Albert Ranft, organised a benefit performance for
them, from which nearly 2,000 crowns resulted. A move was also afoot to
get Strindberg a state pension. Hjalmar Branting had planned to put such
a proposal before Parliament but postponed it so as not to clash with a
campaign by David Bergström, Strindberg's old companion at the Royal
Library, to move that state pensions to writers should be (a) doubled to
12,000 crowns and (b) awarded jointly by the Swedish Academy and the
Writers' Union, instead of, as hitherto, simply by the Academy, which
was hostile to everything that Strindberg stood for. Unfortunately, neither
project came to anything, and Strindberg, unlike Ibsen, was never to
receive the pension which would have so eased his problems.

"Daddy works hard, hard, and drinks tea and milk in the evenings with
cakes," he wrote to Kerstin on 3 January 1897. "Smokes less tobacco and
drinks extraordinarily little schnapps." Many of the invitations which
came his way seem to have been for the kind of lavish gathering which he
disliked. "I, who would be an anchorite," he complained to Marie Uhl on
22 January, "am forced to choose between champagne dinners or none at
all! To be starved to death or feasted to death . . . I brood over my fate,
without understanding what its Master wishes of me. I want to be a decent
human being but must lead a swine's life; I am already so fat that my
clothes strangle me." But two days later he told her: "Funny! All this
feasting, so that I am never at home, has restored my health. As long as I

---

*According to Karin, he was now three years behind in his payments (Karin Smirnoff,
Strindbergs första hustru, p. 362).

sat at home, I was tormented." The same day he confided to Karl Staaff*: "I have dreadful debts in Lund."

Another former acquaintance, Gustaf af Geijerstam, had now become literary adviser to the Stockholm publishing house of Gernandts. He wrote to Strindberg expressing the hope that they might become his publisher and inviting him to come to Stockholm, or to Frösunda, where Geijerstam lived. Strindberg was unwilling to return to the city which had so many traumatic memories for him and which he had not seen since 1892. "I never want to live in Stockholm again," he told Mortensen, [14] yet he knew that with this new opening offered to him, he ought at least to pay the capital a visit. "I know I must come up to Stockholm," he replied to Geijerstam on 24 January, "though I don't long to . . . I can't live at a hotel nor in town, nor in complete solitude. So is there any summer house available at Frösunda, with 2 rooms and a kitchen? Or some forestry inspector or bailiff who would board me without my having to eat at his table, for that I can't? I'd thought of Saltsjöbaden, but that must be so dear and full of sportsmen."

On 5 February, Frida made a new application for divorce, and Strindberg agreed. She was, though he did not know it, pregnant by Frank Wedekind. "I have fought with God and Fate," he wrote to Marie Uhl that day. "Sought the good God and found the foul Fiend. What does it mean? Will He not traffic with us? Remain unknown? Incognito? Only children see the Angels, we old ones only the Fiends."

His New Year resolution to drink less had not lasted long in the face of solitude, insomnia and celibacy. "Attacked day and night by 'electric currents' which squeeze my breast and sting my heart, I leave my torture chamber and visit inns, where I meet friends. Fearing to sober up, I drink unceasingly, the only way to find sleep at night."[15] He thought of returning to Paris to concentrate on science. "I shall rent a laboratory," he told Marie Uhl on 16 February, "where I shall have the right to work, and to train disciples if I find any. In this laboratory, surrounded by friends and disciples, I would like to aim at the Nobel Prize [for chemistry]. My Paris friends, the chemists, expect this of me! . . . My heart remains in Dornach but my head must go to Paris. Here I give of my spirit, in Paris I receive. And if ever I seek a wife, she must be French, for reasons . . . † And without a wife and home I shall go under! Condemned to alcoholism! Imagine that three days ago my nights of terror began again, after I

---

*Younger brother of Strindberg's old friend Pehr Staaff. He was at this time ombudsman to the Writers' Union. In 1905 he became Sweden's first Liberal Prime Minister.
†The dots are Strindberg's.

had spent three quiet evenings alone. So back to the cafés, and when I come home half-drunk at 12, 1, 2, 3, I sleep like an angel and am up and fresh at 8 a.m. But mark that in the evenings and mornings I drink milk like a cat. But how will this end? In the hospital? I don't know. Anyway, don't worry. Let us await what fate and the spring will bring."

That February, August Lindberg acted Ibsen's latest play, *John Gabriel Borkman*, published only two months previously, in Lund. Strindberg, naturally, did not attend, but after the performance he met Lindberg at a party given by Waldemar Bülow which lasted the whole night. They persuaded Lindberg to do some scenes from his most famous parts, including the graveyard scene from *Hamlet* with Yorick's skull. "Lindberg [recalled Bülow] had to play the scene three times before Strindberg was satisfied." At 5 a.m. they ate breakfast (Strindberg lit the fire and made the coffee), and the conversation continued until 7 a.m.[16]

The Nobel Prizes were much on Strindberg's mind. "What would I most like?" he wrote to Marie Uhl around 22 February. "To be allowed to spend the spring in Klam with my child, and there, in two months, write my most beautiful book—*Inferno*, so beautifully written that I shall win the Nobel Prize for Literature. That is 300,000 francs. But then it must be written with love and not with hatred." He was of course never to win the prize, any more than Tolstoy, Ibsen or Zola.

"I have shunned people, and people shun me," he wrote of this period of his life in *Legends*. "In my longed-for solitude I am visited by a whole flock of demons, and in the long run I begin to prefer the meanest of mortals to the most interesting of spirits."[17] An English novel alarmed him by the reflection it presented of his own situation. "I have read Bulwer's *Zanoni*," he told Marie on 23 February. "With terror! Everything is there: I, Frida, the child. Moreover: the demon persecutes the unfortunate Zanoni (a reincarnation) whenever he seeks to raise himself above material things and bury himself in solitude and pious thoughts. But when he mixes with happy people, the demon flees. Just as with me! And Zanoni has an occult child who always looks at him with great calm eyes. Her mother flees Zanoni from fear of 'the Unknown' in him. He is a Rosicrucian, makes gold, is two thousand years 'young,' cannot die because he has drunk the elixir of life. He seeks his Viola eternally, and she flees although she loves him. Read this book! Fillide (Aspasia) is there too."* On 28 February he started planning *Inferno*, although he did not begin to write it for another nine weeks.

---

*Strindberg had probably had his attention directed to *Zanoni* by Frederick Delius, who had dramatised it and written incidental music for it in 1888.

That March he happened on three more of Swedenborg's works in a secondhand bookshop: *The Marvels of Heaven and Hell, On Conjugal Love* and *The Book of Dreams*. "Read today and yesterday in Swedenborg," he noted in his diary for 21 March, ". . . and was thereby enlightened about many wonderful things which happened to me last year. E.g., *esprits censeurs et correcteurs*, which torment man from evil to goodness by tormenting him in the hand (cf. my hand disease), in the foot . . . or around the abdomen . . . also *esprits contradicteurs*, which oppose and destroy what the *esprits correcteurs* have achieved; these appear as *feu volant* . . ." His diary for the ensuing weeks contains many such references to Swedenborg.

In April the famous Italian actor Ermete Zaccone played *The Father* in Venice. "You noble ladies who witnessed last night's terrifying perform-ance" commented the *Gazetta de Venezia*, "will come to hate this Nordic writer who nourishes such a ferocious aversion to you."[18] Zac-cone was to achieve a triumph in the role the following year in Milan.[19] But Strindberg did not receive a penny from either production. The same month, as though to underline the diversity of his interests, he was elected a Fellow of the Alchemists' Association of France.[20]

He told Johan Mortensen of his belief that "women and animals are of a lower order than men. They have done wrong and are punished for it. Animals are often very cunning and wish to conceal their secrets, as proof whereof he told of a gorilla which he had often observed in the Jardin des Plantes. It was unwilling to reveal the lines in its hands . . . 'And what crime have I committed in some past existence,' he suddenly cried, 'that I should be compelled to lead the wretched life I do? . . . I have often thought of rejecting the world and entering a monastery, but there are certain small things I could not easily give up: for example, cigarettes.' He put up the hood of his blue cape. His earnest head perfectly suited this improvised headgear, and he quoted: 'Robber in Act One, monk in Act Five.' "[21]

He liked to make an ink blot on paper which he then folded and unfolded, so that the blot appeared like a butterfly "and, with luck, a death's-head butterfly, that mystic creature of which he wrote in *Jardin des Plantes*." (Several examples of these butterflies adorn his diary at this time.) He lived in a two-room flat, "Spartanly simple, like a student room; the bed was small and narrow, fitting for a monk." He used to quote Dante's remark in the *Commedia* that gold-makers were punished by damage to their hands; he had given up gold-making because the Powers did not wish it. Mortensen thought it a pity that he did not use his experiences to write a novel about alchemy. "Now and then his interest in gold-making would blossom afresh, despite the disapproval of the 'Powers,' especially when he met a chemist who would listen to this theories and analyse the results. Then for some days it was as if his old friends did not exist. He would talk only with chemists . . . But it always ended the same way; the chemist, if he was a true chemist, would demur, and the friendship would end." He gave Mortensen a piece of filter paper with some home-made gold on it; but over the years it lost its glitter and turned to a rust "which revealed its source in copper and iron salts."[22]

Once as he lay reading in Lund, Mortensen continues, Strindberg saw a rat appear and begin to jump up and down on the floor. "The worst thing was that he didn't know if it was a real rat. He chased it for a full hour without catching it. It simply disappeared. In the end he decided to get two students who lived on the other side of the hall to help him, but only after much hesitation, for what embarrassment if it turned out not to have been a real rat. Together they hunted the rat and finally killed it, thus happily proving that it actually existed. There followed a series of learned and profound explanations. Although proved to have been a real rat, it had nevertheless been a warning, sent by the 'Powers.' Rats and flies are vermin that live in dirt. Swedenborg and other occultists explain that these creatures are, thanks to their delicate senses, drawn to alcoholics. They scent, as it were, inner rottenness." He told Mortensen of Bulwer-Lytton's story "The Haunted and the Haunters," in which a man spends a whole night in a haunted house and sees nothing but senses a horrible atmosphere which invisibly fills the room, and the dog with him dies of terror. Mortensen adds that Strindberg "suffered from the most Swedish of all traits, envy," and "seldom said anything good about contemporary writers"[23] (though posterity is on his side as far as his fellows are concerned, for none of them has lasted well except Snoilsky and Fröding). His diary shows that he dreamed of Hyde Park in London, made copious notes about Napoleon, and "saw Edvard Munch on the wall when I awoke. He had as it were a black wad in his mouth, a wreath on his head with a red poppy."[24]

"On the First of May," he informed Kerstin, "there were great student celebrations. I was invited by the young people; wore a white student cap with a black band and a yellow-blue cockade—felt young again and drank punch for 14 hours."[25] *The Father* was performed in Vienna with Emmanuel Reicher in the title role, but had a mixed reception. On 3 May Strindberg began to write *Inferno*, and as early as 25 June sent the completed manuscript to Geijerstam. "It is," he assured him (untruthfully), "what it says it is, a genuine diary with digressions . . . If you are unsure of the book's authenticity I can send you reports by two impeccable authorities (docents) that it is taken from my diary and not faked."

Strindberg wrote *Inferno* in French; occultism was widespread in France, Swedenborg was revered there more than in Sweden, and Strindberg himself was taken seriously there as a scientist. Beginning with his last farewell to Frida in Paris in October 1894, it tells, partly as reminiscence, partly in the form of purported diary entries, the story of his tribulations up to the spring of 1897 when he began to write the book. Dishonest in the sense that it dramatises and partly fictionalises what it presents as fact, it remains one of Strindberg's finest works, perhaps his best outside the great plays, an extraordinarily powerful and convincing portrait of the interior of a distraught mind, worthy to stand beside the self-portraits of Van Gogh, the poems of Hölderlin or the novels of Dostoevsky. Its theme is that mortal life is a time of chastisement and expiation. "These are the Mills of God, that grind slow but grind exceeding small—and black. You are ground to powder and you think it is all over. But no, it will begin again and you will be put through the mill once more. Be happy. That is the Hell here on earth, recognised by Luther, who esteemed it a high honour that he should be ground to powder on this side of the empyrean . . . Let us rejoice in our torments which are so many debts repaid, and let us believe that it is out of pure compassion that we are kept in ignorance of the primordial reasons for our punishment."[26]

It was an agonising, if salutary, ordeal for Strindberg to relive those three years. "Shut up in that little city of the Muses,* without any hope of getting away, I fought out a terrible battle with the enemy, my own self. Each morning when I took my walk along the ramparts shaded by plane trees, the sight of the huge red lunatic asylum reminded me of the danger I had escaped and of the future, should I suffer a relapse . . . Swedenborg . . . had shown me the only way to salvation; to seek out the demons in their lair, within myself, and to destroy them by repentance. Balzac, as the prophet's adjutant, had taught me in his *Séraphita* that 'remorse is the impotent emotion felt by the man who will sin again; repentance alone is effective, and brings everything to an end.' "[27]

This change in Strindberg's attitude towards suffering was to be permanent, and was strongly to influence his future work. Gunnar Brandell observes that the guilt feelings which characterise almost everything Strindberg wrote after his decisive experience with Swedenborg that spring do not exist anywhere in his previous works; they are not even present during the early stages of the *Inferno* crisis. In an essay, "Sensations Détraquées," written (in French) in October 1894, he

*I.e., Lund.

had written: "It is not the evil we have done, not our crimes . . . that we are ashamed of, but our follies." But (to quote Brandell): "After 1897, it was his crimes that concerned him . . . In *Inferno, Legends, Jacob Wrestles* and *To Damascus*, the basic problem concerns such problems as: What shall I regret? How much remorse should I feel? What is the relation between the crimes I have committed and the punishment I have been subjected to? How should I live my life in order to satisfy God? The obstinate attitude towards God that was so characteristic of the latter part of Strindberg's life—his bookkeeping system of guilt and punishment, his revolt against his God at moments when he thought the punishment too hard—all these reactions were determined by his new moralistic outlook."[28] But the struggle within him was not immediately resolved by writing the book. "The last three chapters of *Inferno* and the Epilogue constitute a network of contradictions. Their tone is one of self-criticism and passionate doubt."[29] This doubt was never wholly to be resolved; during 1897 he ceased to think of himself as Job, the passive seeker after God, and identified himself with Jacob, who submitted to God only after fierce defiance.

On 10 July he noted in his diary: "Have today finished with chemistry and occultism and planned *Merlin.*" At a later date he added a phrase in brackets: "(which became *To Damascus*)." Despite "finishing" with occultism, he continued nevertheless to note details of his dreams.

"My financial situation is improving," he told Marie Uhl on 25 July, "since they are beginning to stage my plays again. I have managed to send 3,000 francs to my children this year and have also repaid large debts." Paris again beckoned to him, partly because he was relying on the occultists there to publish *Inferno* in French, partly because, despite his averred rejection of chemistry, he believed that the French alchemists would help him to fulfil his dreams of founding his own laboratory; partly, too, perhaps, to have a closer look at Roman Catholicism. On 24 August he left Lund. Next day in Hamburg, he noted in his diary, he "saw Frida's double weeping, dressed in light blue and white," and the same evening in Cologne "saw Frida everywhere." By 26 August he was back in Paris, where he booked in at the humble little Hôtel de Londres on the rue Bonaparte, parallel with and close to the Boulevard St. Michel. His room there cost him 37 francs (less than £2) a month.

He did not re-establish contact with the Molards or their circle at the *crémerie,* and life proved lonely. "One day like another," he wrote in his diary on 6 September, and the next day told Waldemar Bülow: "It looks as though my task here will soon be done, so I shall probably soon be back in Lund. I can see no other purpose in staying here, and a long autumn in dirt, cold and noise doesn't tempt me; and to stoke a fire twelve hours a day has no attraction." He was attempting again to make gold. But placing *Inferno* proved more difficult than he had anticipated. The occult publishing house of Chamuel rejected it; the Paris occultists, indeed, seemed disturbed by it. Papus refused to support it, and even Jollivet-Castelot reacted tepidly.

His diary for September and October contains repeated complaints of loneliness and of all days being alike. On 22 September he began, again in French, *Legends*, a sequel to *Inferno*, describing his eight months in Lund and his return to Paris. Like *Inferno*, it contains purported diary extracts which do not appear in his diary or are much altered, but is nothing like as powerful or interesting as its predecessor. His actual diary of the time is more vivid:

> 4 Oct. Irrationally depressed sometimes but I am not tempted to seek company. 5th. Home each evening; in bed by 10. Am reading Dickens! Have ceased to drink in the evenings since I came to Paris. 9th, night of: dreamed that I fell off a high wall because I had gone too far. With my head sticking into space: saw an infinite light, experienced a feeling of indescribable bliss, in the knowledge that I was dead. Light, cleanness, freedom, in a moment and I cried "God" in the certainty that suffering and sin were finished and that only bliss awaited me . . . 13th . . . On my left side inside my coat *there is often a ticking* like the beetle called the Death Watch. It is not my watch. *Shall I die soon?* . . . 17th. Finished *Legends*; which I began 22 Sept. 23–26th. Alone! All days alike!

By good fortune, however, he now found a new champion in a young poet and medical student, Marcel Réja, who succeeded in placing *Inferno* with his own publishers, Mercure de France, and also undertook to revise the French text, which he did to Strindberg's satisfaction. Réja seems to have been the only person whom Strindberg saw at all regularly that autumn and winter. Seventeen years later Réja recalled their relationship:

> [Strindberg] lived in an unpretentious hotel and devoted his day mainly to writing (or chemical, not to say alchemical, broodings), and it was not until the sacred hour of the apéritif that I used to come and collect him. Then we ate a less than humble dinner in some little café, a "good wine" being the only luxury permitted, then spent the evening wandering tirelessly through Paris with an occasional pause at a café for American toddies. Despite the biting cold we stayed out of doors, since the promiscuity of café life was too much for the great man's nerves. Five or six such pauses during the evening, and as many toddies; it is time for bed; we have touched on all the big questions concerning magic, metaphysics and even literature . . . He had a positively physical aversion to visiting places he did not know . . . [30]

On 11 October, Strindberg wrote Kerstin one of the most extraordinary letters that can ever have been addressed to a child of three:

> Some nights ago I had a vision in a dream which made me long to cross to the Beyond; but I do not need to arrange that myself. It seems as though I have gradually dwindled away. In six weeks I have become as thin as a skeleton, and that pleases me. I have neuralgia, am poisoned with carbon monoxide. And long to see the Alps . . . I live here like a monk in a cell with a window under the roof as in Marie Antoinette's prison, with bars to the windows too . . . In a week my "Inferno" will appear in Swedish. Then it would be better that I should lie in my grave than live under the shadow of the gallows! I shall be called a charlatan or a madman.

Gernandt did not publish *Inferno* until 1 November, the French edition following eight months later. Strindberg's fears regarding its reception in Sweden proved correct. "One is left with the feeling," wrote Carl David af Wirsén, the Secretary of the Swedish Academy, in *Vårt Land* (19 November), "that the author's negative, destructive and paradoxical activity which spurns every curb has led to the suicide of his talent . . . Herr Strindberg has never possessed the learning claimed for him by his admirers. Aesthetically the book is preposterous . . . His talent has now collapsed." Even those who admitted the book's power were repelled by its content. Tor Hedberg, the son of Strindberg's old mentor Frans Hedberg and later to become a successful playwright himself, summed it up in *Svenska Dagbladet* on 5 November as "a gripping but at the same time unpleasant and ridiculous book . . . ridiculous as everything must be in which a sense of proportion and harmony is lacking . . . the ridiculousness of a stormer of heaven who lets himself be scared by a bounding hare, and of a man condemned to death who complains that his shoes are tight . . . the story of a powerful and seething mind crumbling into pieces." Many of his admirers regretted his abandonment of free thought for religion. Georg Nordensvan complained in *Aftonbladet* on 25 November: "He has passionately and restlessly embraced one viewpoint after another, burning what he has admired and admiring what he has burned . . . *Inferno* portrays a spiritual bankrupt who stares appalled at the dregs of his misery and with a last despairing effort reaches for a hand to save him . . . One is tempted to laugh at the childishness of his discoveries, for they sometimes seem pure parody, but one is more tempted to weep at the pass which Strindberg's long career as an author has now reached. Yet one cannot but admire the brilliance of the analysis, the sharpness of the logic and the clarity with which the spiritual abnormality is described." Even Strindberg's old friend Pehr Staaff wrote to Gustaf af Geijerstam: "I cannot possibly regard the book . . . as anything but the beginning of the end. And what an end! The most nauseating form of madness I can imagine, the most sordid craziness, grins out from every tenth page."[31]

But *Inferno* found at least one discriminating admirer. Henrik Ibsen, in Stockholm the following spring for his seventieth-birthday celebrations, was asked by a Swedish journalist what he thought of Strindberg. Ibsen described him as "a very great talent. I don't know him personally—our paths have never crossed—but I have read his work with *great* interest. Not least, his latest book, *Inferno*, has made a powerful impression on me."[32] Alas for Strindberg that Sweden contained no critic of such authority and perception. Yet the book sold well enough for Geijerstam to inform Strindberg that they were reprinting it and to offer him better terms for *Legends* than Strindberg had expected. "This is good news," Strindberg replied on 15 November, "and reminds me of the great time when *The Red Room* and Karin entered the world together." The same day he wrote again to Geijerstam suggesting a brief but eloquent single-sentence epilogue to *Legends*: "I should not have related these banal and in themselves repulsive stories did they not by their illogicality suggest the existence of a reality which is neither real nor a vision, but, as it were, a phantasmagoria evoked by the invisible ones with the determined purpose to warn, teach or punish." The passage could equally serve as a description of *The Ghost Sonata*.

He accepted the critics' abuse of *Inferno* with resignation. "My destiny," he wrote to Waldemar Bülow on 17 November, in words which might have been uttered by Gregers Werle in *The Wild Duck*, "is seemingly to be allowed no friends but to walk alone like the hangman, whose hand no man will touch." But at least some of his earlier plays were being revived. The success of *Lucky Peter's Journey* at Vasa Theatre the previous autumn had moved the owner of that theatre, Albert Ranft, to revive *Master Olof* in its original prose version, which had not been seen in Stockholm since its first production in 1881. The team was the one that had triumphed with *Lucky Peter*, Harald Molander directing and Anders de Wahl in the title role. The production was acclaimed and ran for 53 performances. Moreover, *Lucky Peter*, newly cast, was touring the Swedish provinces, while in France, Lugné-Poe was touring his production of *The Father*, achieving a particular success with it in Monte Carlo. This considerably eased Strindberg's financial situation, enabling him to send extra money and presents to the children in Finland.

Perversely, however, he continued to regard himself, despite his earlier protestations on the subject, as a scientist rather than as a creative writer.

On 4 December he offered Geijerstam an uninviting project—"my *New Cosmos*, sketches for which have appeared in *Jardin des Plantes, Antibarbarus, Sylva Sylvarum, Introduction d'une Chimie Unitaire, L'Initiation, L'Hyperchimie*, etc. It is all there in the piles of paper you saw in Lund. But I will write it up popularly, poetically, and with illustrations." When Geijerstam begged him to return to fiction, Strindberg replied on 23 December: "I can't write plays and novels, have lost interest and therefore the ability. I have only one book left unwritten and that is my occult natural philosophy." He would have been astonished if one of those seers or astrologers in whose prescience he believed had told him that during the next four years he would write no fewer than twenty plays, including several of his finest.

The next day, Christmas Eve, he noted in his diary: "Concerning absinthe, several times this autumn I have drunk absinthe with Sjöstedt, but always with unpleasant results." These he describes: the café "became filled with horrid types," ragged people "covered with filth as though they had come out of the sewers" appear on the street and stare at him. "I have never seen such types in Paris, and wondered if they were 'real' or 'projected.'"

That month, although Strindberg seems never to have known of it (there is no mention of it in his diary or letters), one of his great enemies died: Marie David, at the age of thirty-two. A long period in hospital, Karin tells, had greatly altered her. "She had suffered greatly, brooded deeply, and seemed to have lost some of the intellectual sharpness which had previously characterised her. On returning home, she had returned to her childhood faith and had lost her atheism, her passion for free thinking and also much of her infectious humour. She had changed, and if her need for alcohol remained, it was no longer apparent. Religion had given her a strength she had previously lacked, a steadfast faith had replaced her scepticism, but she was no longer as nice as before . . . She no longer said anything disparaging about others, as she had used to do in her inimitably humorous way, she chose her words so as not to lead the children's minds astray, corrected us gently for things that had previously amused her, rebuked Siri for speaking mischievously, and no longer said 'Damn!' . . . Siri and she gradually and imperceptibly slid apart. It was useless to argue with her; she now had her 'faith,' and wanted nothing more than to be allowed to work for it. About a year later she became a novice in an order of nuns, but died of consumption before she could take her vows."[33] Shortly before entering the nunnery, she burned all of Siri's letters to her.[34]

Strindberg was now working on a sequel to *Legends* entitled *Jacob*

Wrestles, * describing his spiritual struggles since his return to Paris. Though better than *Legends,* with vivid accounts of "occult" experiences (finding himself stared at by men "covered in filth as though dragged up from the sewers," he reflects that he has only seen such figures before at "the mouth of London Bridge, where the throng bears a truly occult appearance"), it is blurred and confused like his own religious position, which he summarised more accurately and concisely in a letter to a young Lund friend, Axel Herrlin, on 31 January 1898:

> Were I to attempt to define my standpoint, I don't think I could succeed. Since our last exchange of letters I have been working on *L'Imitation*† and Swedenborg's *Vera Religio Christiania,* which I found completely identical with Protestant pietism. Both these books, instead of giving me peace, inspired an irreligiousness like that of my youth; and when Swedenborg ended by allowing *(sic!)*‡ the heavenly beings to indulge in theological disputations and put Calvin in a brothel, etc., what I would like to call my godly self rebelled, and a war of extirpation began. I had less difficulty with the *Imitation,* for that is for monks and those to whom spiritual matters are a calling. I, who am earthbound by earthly duties, to the children, may not "despise the world" but am doomed to root about in the earth with a small but steady surreptitious glance upwards. Religion as I practised it before Christmas degenerated into a vice. So I closed Swedenborg and the *Imitation* and found a relative peace, with a certain sober pleasure in life.
>
> I don't yet know if these are temptations set in our path; I don't know if there exist several powers which fight against each other, but so it sometimes seems to me, and as though the Protestant God has got hold of you and the Catholic God of me. For since the Solesmes scandal last August§ everything I have seen of Catholicism and its adherents has only drawn me closer to it. It is a religion for children, and if we are not prepared to become as children . . . etc. ¶ Protestantism seems to me the religion of the rebel, the freethinker's bottomless reasoning about belief, dogma, theology, but not religion . . . Often the idea returns to me which Eliasson expressed: that religion is occultism and forbidden, for as soon as one seeks to probe the secrets of belief, and one has the right to demand to know what one shall believe, one is tormented by *angst* and loss of grace, and madness beckons.

By the time he wrote this letter, Strindberg had decided that reflective narration was not the medium best suited to expressing his spiritual

---

*He began it in French but wrote the final section in Swedish. This marked the end of his years of attempting to establish himself as a French author.

†*De Imitatione Christi,* by Thomas à Kempis, a German Augustinian monk (1380–1471), which traces the gradual process of the soul to Christian perfection.

‡The parenthesis is Strindberg's.

§The abbot of the Benedictine monastery there had been ejected for immorality.

¶The dots are Strindberg's.

struggles. Early in January 1898 he abandoned *Jacob Wrestles* and on 19 January began, for the first time in over five years (since *The Bond* in September 1892), to write a play. In less than seven weeks, on 8 March, he sent the completed manuscript to Geijerstam: "Herewith a play—I have no inkling of its worth. If you find it good, chuck it in at the theatre. If you find it impossible, hide it away."

He called it *To Damascus*. It is Part One of the trilogy as we know it, but Strindberg had no intention, even by the time he finished it, of writing a sequel, let alone two. It is an attempt to state in dramatic form what he had failed adequately to describe in *Jacob Wrestles*: his strife with God and his eventual grudging acceptance of God's existence. "The fact was," he had written in *Inferno*, "that a kind of religion had developed in me, though I was quite unable to formulate it. It was a spiritual state rather than an opinion founded upon theories, a hotch-potch of impressions that were far from being condensed into thoughts . . . In my boyhood I had borne the Cross of Jesus Christ, but I had repudiated a God who was content to rule over slaves cringing before their tormentors."[35] Strindberg wanted to settle his accounts directly with God and not through some intermediary.

He described the play to Geijerstam on 17 March as "a fiction with a terrifying half-reality behind it." A famous writer in "a strange city" feels damned and persecuted. He meets an unhappily married woman and takes her away from her husband, but lacks the money to support her and is humiliated by having to seek help from her relatives. He has an accident and wakes in a monastery which is also a madhouse; here his feelings of guilt become living figures, people whom he has injured in the past. His mother-in-law, a pious Catholic, explains to him that these torments are a necessary part of the process of salvation; he must be humbled to see the light, like Saul on the road to Damascus. Gradually, though unwillingly, he comes to accept that his fate is directed by a benevolent, if stern, power. Yet he remains defiant. At the end of the play the Lady tries to persuade him to come with her into the church. The closing lines are:

THE STRANGER   Well, I can always go in with you. But I won't stay.
THE LADY   You don't know. Come. In there you will hear new songs.
THE STRANGER (*goes after her to the church door*)   Perhaps.
THE LADY   Come.

Strindberg constructed *To Damascus* like a circle; the Stranger passes through seven stations before reaching the asylum, then returns to each of them in reverse order before ending on the street corner where he began. Several of the scenes reflect episodes from his marriage with Frida. Those by the seashore stem from his honeymoon on Heligoland. The visit to the Lady's parents is a more or less straight account of the visit which he and Frida paid to her grandparents in Dornach, and the central scene in the Abbey of Good Hope reflects his experiences in the Hôpital St. Louis. The doctor who is the Lady's husband, though, is clearly based on Anders Eliasson. The play contains, inevitably, several of Strindberg's more or less permanent obsessions: his old sense of guilt at being unable to support his children (one of the chief supporting characters is a mirror image of himself dressed as a Beggar), his lack of recognition as a scientist, his agoraphobia, his fear of darkness and his fear of madness. The contrast between *To Damascus* on the one hand and *Legends* and *Jacob Wrestles*, which treat the same theme, on the other, is marked. It is not merely that he is writing again in his native language instead of in his painfully acquired French. Instead of trying to analyse, as in the two earlier books, he is dramatising; he has turned from his weakness to his strength.

Writing the play had at least partly clarified his understanding of his position. Two days after completing it, on 10 March, he wrote to Axel Herrlin: "My crisis of nearly seven months had not made me any more certain except on some points . . . Alchemy and occultism, looking into the future and probing the occult, are completely forbidden, but not speculative chemistry. On the other hand, I seem to have regained the grace of being able to write for the theatre . . . a gift which can be taken from one if one misuses it. As regards religion, I have had to stop at a moderately warm connection with the beyond, which it seems one may not approach too intimately, or one will be punished with religious fanaticism and led astray. But I am not sure whether it is a temptation to be withstood or a call to be obeyed." He developed this theme in a letter to Waldemar Bülow on 1 April: "In 1867 Renan and Taine and Zola (Darwin was no atheist) began this flouting of the Powers . . . But now the return of the Powers is approaching, now people light candles and seek God . . . Those who probed through arrogant inquisitiveness too deeply into forbidden secrets, such as the occultists (and I), saw more than they wanted to and the Sphinx rent them one after the other. But occultism led men back to an understanding of God and the certainty that there are others who control our destinies. That is the standpoint that I have reached, and I have reached no further, but it seems to me that with the return of the Powers there return old demands, for order and discipline, etc. I even believe that the old morality will return, but with much stronger demands."

Geijerstam, meanwhile, had written enthusiastically, accepting *To Damascus* and promising a fee of 1,000 crowns for the first edition, far more than Strindberg had expected. He received the money in Paris at the end of March and at once made preparations to return to Sweden. He was no longer an object of much interest in France. When, that July, the French editions of *Inferno* and *By the Open Sea* appeared, they passed almost unnoticed. He, who had hoped to conquer Paris as a writer, and especially as a dramatist, remembered it later as the place where he had triumphed over himself. He planned to spend Easter at a Belgian Benedictine monastery in Maredsous, to which he had been recommended: "I want to see who Christ is and find if I belong to his flock."[36] But he put this off until the summer. On 3 April he left Paris for the last time, and by 7 April he was back in Lund.

Part Five

THE HOMECOMING
(1898–1912)

Chapter Twenty-Four

ᵒᵒᵒᵒᵒᵒᵒᵒᵒᵒᵒᵒᵒᵒᵒᵒᵒᵒᵒᵒᵒᵒᵒᵒᵒᵒᵒᵒᵒᵒ

"PLAYS AND NO MORE ALCHEMY"

Despite his previous complaints about Lund, Strindberg stayed there for fourteen months on this second visit. It was a period of intense literary activity, during which he wrote five plays and another quasi-autobiographical novel.

His sister Elisabeth, who had kept house for him at Djursholm in 1891, had sunk into another deep depression (later in the year she was admitted to a mental hospital).* She wrote to Strindberg asking if she could come and stay with him, and received a chilling reply. "I live like a student in one room in Lund," he informed her on 12 April, "and have no home to offer you. Nor would my company profit you, since I am in the same state as yourself. It is our fate to suffer . . . It must be so; and for some hidden purpose, which is probably not evil. Accept your fate! That is my only advice. You must have seen that changes of abode do not help; and that one cannot escape one's destiny. What is the use of trying?" Eleven days later he continued: "As regards your feelings that you are persecuted, they are like the ones I had when I was ill; and they lack any foundation; though not wholly so, since one is said to persecute oneself. If you have read my book *Inferno*, you can see the causes of my sense of persecution,

---

*According to Karin, Elisabeth was suffering from severe persecution mania, and believed that people were trying to poison her (Smirnoff, *Så var det i verkligheten*, p. 152).

consisting mainly of self-reproach . . . Whether your case resembles mine I don't know and I have no right to question or admonish; but one piece of advice I can give you: try to search out the purpose of Providence in punishing you with these torments. Do not leave your place of abode so hastily, for that doesn't help. One cannot escape oneself—or Him who scourges you . . . Here is a little money. When I get more you shall have more." In the same state of gloom, he told his German disciple Emil Schering, who had written to suggest some kind of *Festschrift*: "I beg you, for reasons that I should like to call religious, if I were more religious than I am, not in any way to commemorate my fiftieth birthday, nor even to mention it. I would like to be completely forgotten; let the few of my works which may possess the power of life find their path quietly and without obtrusion." On 12 May he wrote to Gustaf af Geijerstam: "I wonder where the grass grows where I may some time rest my weary bones, where the wild hunt of my Eumenides will cease!" He had additional cause for depression that month; on 27 May he noted in his diary: "The last front teeth in my upper jaw (apart from the two middle ones which remain) fell out."

But at least *To Damascus* was in the press, and in an almost cheerful mood he assured Karin: "My prospects are quite good. I have just completed a big five-act play, the best I have written and which has given me and my friends who have read it great hopes. Since it is a new genre . . . it may be that it will prove our salvation, but it may also be that the public will find itself a little disorientated at first."

On 16 May, *Legends* was published to hostile reviews. Oscar Levertin in *Svenska Dagbladet* (1 June) dismissed it as "a weak repeat of *Inferno* . . . stupid anecdotes, undisciplined impressions . . . Both these books are depressing proof of a great, sick mind's hysterical compulsion to degrade itself . . . These 'Powers' who conduct everything without plan or libretto like boys making a shadow play, how contemptible do they not seem, how ridiculous with their little omens and meaningless punishments, how vengeful and full of hatred!" Carl David af Wirsén in *Vårt Land* (20 May) was equally mocking, and Georg Nordensvan in *Aftonbladet* (28 May) concluded: "The whole book leaves an impression of a weak character trying to inject himself with courage, an exhausted man longing for change, a truth-seeker irresistibly yearning to bury himself in his own ego, yet also of a vain man's complacency at listening to his own voice and feeling sure that it is interesting." Sadly, this is a view of *Legends* with which it is difficult to disagree.

The book also aroused not unreasonable indignation among those friends and acquaintances of Strindberg who at his request had told him about their private supernatural experiences and now found them related with little or no attempt to conceal the identities of those who had undergone them. Waldemar Bülow tells how, when he expressed amazement at some of the things written about himself and others in *Legends*, "Strindberg threw his arms wide and cried 'Yes, well, you know, when I get a pen in my hand, the Devil gets into me.' "[1]*

Gustaf Fröding, the poet who had edited A *Book about Strindberg* and written so perceptively about him, read *Legends* with particular interest for its account of hallucinations. He wrote to Strindberg about his own problems in this field. Strindberg replied on 5 June:

> Do not use the word hallucination (nor even the word delirium) as though it expressed something unreal. Hallucinations and delirium possess a certain kind of reality—or they are phantasmagoria consciously designed by the Invisible One to terrify us. They all have a symbolic meaning. For example, the projections of alcoholic delirium are always the same: flies and rats. The direct progeny of filth . . . I am sure that your visions are to be found in Swedenborg, and if you could write them down from memory, you would do yourself, me and many people a great service. I would interpret them for you; you would see that there is a consistency in them, a meaning and good intent. When I chanced to find my hallucinations described in Swedenborg, I was liberated. Now, when in the night they attack me, I lie and balance these torments against the evil things I have thought and done. I at once reason: "Serves you right! Mark well, and don't do that again." And so I regain peace; till I sin again. But don't suppose that I am punished simply for wine and women; no, every harsh word I have spoken of others, even if it is true and well known; hubristic thoughts; and much else of the like, all come under scrutiny. I don't believe in any Hell but this, though I don't know. And Swedenborg's Hell is a precise description of life on earth; I don't believe we leave this world until we have had our measure of suffering. But we, we seem to have a task to fulfil, and it is no use throwing oneself into the sea like Jonah to escape one's calling. We must stand forth and prophesy, and risk being disavowed like Jonah. My development is not as absurd as it appears. "Pull down," said the Spirit, and I pulled down. "Now build!" says the Spirit . . . And now I shall try to build.

Strindberg invited Fröding to visit him in Lund; but Fröding, now fast approaching madness, was, like Strindberg's sister Elisabeth, committed later that year to an asylum for the remaining thirteen years of his life, and

---

*Johan Mortensen recalled that the previous summer, in Lund, Strindberg had asked everyone if they had had any mystic experiences and that some had made up such experiences because "we saw he was in great need of material . . . Both *Inferno* and *Legends* are full of such fake experiences, and the victims, easily identifiable, were far from pleased at finding their supposed inner life bared to the world."[2]

Strindberg never met the one contemporary Swedish writer whose genius was comparable to his own.

Karin wrote to him that she wished to become a Roman Catholic. A few years earlier Strindberg would have greeted this news with alarm or contempt; now, attracted himself by the discipline of that religion, he replied on 20 June with an enthusiasm which must have surprised her:

> I find it difficult to say how happy I am that you are thinking of adopting some religion. You know that I have always allowed you full freedom regarding spiritual matters, partly because I myself was unsure, partly because I didn't feel I had the right to influence you. I am especially happy that you have discovered Catholicism, since I regard it as the only religion for us Westerners, and since I have found Protestantism to be no religion but merely theology, intellectual argument, free thinking which only results in godlessness and doubt. "Our fathers' faith," that is Catholicism, and the Protestants now seem to be returning to it in droves . . . But, Karin, let your religion be a living thing, a guiding rein for your thoughts and actions. Look at my undisciplined and vacillating life grounded on a lack of religion . . . And do not believe that He who decides our destinies is evil. Those seemingly "evil powers" that torment us when we have done wrong cannot be evil, since they persecute and punish evil with pangs of conscience and the like. Were these powers evil, they would encourage our vices and persecute what is good in us, but we have seen no example of that. So, they too are ruled by Good. Whether I shall ever bind myself by any formal religion I don't know, but if so, it will be Roman Catholicism.

Some time during the summer (we do not know exactly when), Strindberg began to write a sequel to *To Damascus*, entitling it simply Part 2; but, with characteristic inconsistency, he made it less forgiving and resigned than Part 1. "I have several times ground to a standstill in my new play," he wrote to Emil Kléen on 9 July. "Decided to burn it, as totally worthless, although I'm near the end of Act 4. But I'm going on. It is conceived in hatred and deals with hateful people. Although it's strongly constructed and has a number of good things in it, it upsets me and makes me ill. *Tristis sum!* [I am sad!]" But eight days later he finished it.

Part 2 of *To Damascus* opens with the marriage already on the rocks. "Half the day like angels," says the Lady's Mother, "the other half they torment each other like devils." The Stranger has become preoccupied with his scientific research. While she is in the pangs of childbirth, he finds a letter which she has intercepted confirming that his efforts to make gold have been proved successful and offering him membership of the Academy in Stockholm and a decoration. The next scene is at the Academy's banquet; the Stranger is the guest of honour. Some of the diners are in full evening dress; some, strangely, are in suits, and some are dressed as tramps. Gradually the well-dressed diners leave and he finds himself with only the tramps, who mock him. The barmaid demands payment from him for the banquet, since he is the only member left. Unable to pay, he is taken to prison, where he finds himself sharing a cell with the Beggar who is his doppelgänger. Released, he hurries back home, where he is amazed to find that the child is not yet born. He asks, "Can it take so long? . . . How is the mother?" to which his mother-in-law replies, "The same as she was when you left, a minute ago." Everything that we have seen in the last two scenes has taken place in his mind, aroused by a suspicion that his wife *may* have intercepted a letter to him. He goes to a whore "to degrade myself. Dirt hardens the skin against the thorns of life," but even she will not have him. The Doctor, the Lady's former husband, plays on his sense of guilt to break him. The Beggar tells him, "You must preach against yourself from the rooftops . . . you must flay yourself alive at every street corner." Finally the Beggar reveals himself to be the Dominican who had received him in the abbey-asylum —"your terrible friend," says the Lady, "who has come to collect you." As she cradles their baby, he is tempted to stay with her instead of going to the monastery, as he knows he must if he is to find peace. The final words of the play are: "Come, priest, before I change my mind."

Part 2 of *To Damascus* is, like Part 1, a splendid play, and Strindberg never wrote a better scene than that of the nightmare banquet, or the episode with the whore. Three years later he was to write a third part. Even with cuts, the three parts can scarcely take less than five hours; but in 1975 the little Traverse Theatre in Edinburgh found a way round by performing Part 1 on some evenings, Parts 2 and 3 (with cuts) on others, and on yet other evenings the three parts together over five hours with a supper interval. It proved an enthralling experience; Allen Wright in *The Scotsman* (10 April 1975) summed it up as "a play so packed with ideas and invective that it makes most contemporary dramas seem trivial."

Lund had begun to bore Strindberg. Mortensen relates of that summer:

At this time Strindberg was very alone. Most of his acquaintances had left town, others did not wish to meet him because they had been portrayed in *Legends*. What perhaps hurt him even more was that "they no longer told him anything," as he once complained when we began to talk about this. All Strindberg was in this remark. He lived to write, and when he could no longer suck anything out of a person he usually lost interest in him. He had, too, an attack of temperance and withdrew occasionally to the School of Domestic Economy, where it was not possible to drink punch.* But his

*Swedish punch was, and is, a lethal drink, not to be confused with the gentle stuff handed out under the same name in Britain and the United States.

longing for alcohol would return. As he confessed, he needed alcohol to be able to write . . . He said . . . "One must have ragged nerves to write. Last Easter when I lived ascetically and drank no punch I couldn't write anything" . . . He was tired of Lund and wanted to return to the continent to gather impressions . . . "I'm just twiddling my thumbs," he said. "I have outlived my usefulness." I was afraid he was right. I thought Strindberg had written himself out.[3]

In August, Strindberg decided to visit the Benedictine monastery at Maredsous in Belgium, as he had intended to do the previous April. After spending four days in Brussels and five in the seaside resort of Heyst-sur-Mer (where he jotted in his diary half a page of dialogue about Napoleon on St. Helena, which he was never to develop), he reached the monastery on 24 August, but stayed only one night. The trip was a failure in every respect, as he described to Kerstin on 29 August, the day after his return to Lund. "After five days of torture in Heyst—where I was compelled to live with 200 people and eat six different courses for dinner, seated at table for over an hour, I was ready for monastic life. Went to Maredsous, a place of extraordinary beauty . . . Was amiably received as a guest, slept there, ate in the refectory with the 100 monks. All was peace and calm, except for me. For there, too, each guest got five courses at table with beer and wine, and that was too much for me, so I came back here . . . The night I slept in the monastery was—St. Bartholomew's Night! 24 August! Imagine! But I was not afraid, since I had attended night mass and been forced to accept consecrated water and even make the sign of the cross, otherwise they would have killed me as a Huguenot. The fathers were very friendly, but drank wine and took snuff, which I didn't like. I thought them a little too worldly." Thus ended Strindberg's brief flirtation with the Catholic Church. But the indifference to religion and general Laodiceanism of his contemporaries in Sweden depressed him. "I almost think the eighties were better," he wrote to Emil Kléen on 20 October. "Then we lived; now they talk. Then we wanted to do something all the time; loved, hated, sinned and blasphemed. But these armchair atheists do nothing, are neither hot nor cold."

In France the Dreyfus affair had now resurfaced, four years after Dreyfus had been sent to Devil's Island, and radical opinion, led by Zola and Picquart, was demanding that the case be reopened. Strindberg's diary that autumn of 1898 is full of cuttings and handwritten entries relating to the case, the latter all testifying to his certainty of Dreyfus's guilt, often irrationally, e.g.: "9 Sept. All godless people are convinced of Dreyfus's innocence. *Est-ce assez?* [Is it enough?]" Anti-Semitism may have influenced his attitude, but Johan Mortensen gives another explanation: "If Dreyfus was not rehabilitated, Zola's star would decline, and then the great turnabout in literature would come—the way would be open to mysticism." Strindberg had changed a lot since the days when he had revered Zola as the pioneer of naturalism and had proudly described *Miss Julie* as "the first naturalistic tragedy of the Swedish drama."*

That he was still beset by drink problems is evidenced by an entry in his diary for 18 September. "Having lived soberly, with no schnapps with my meals or evening visits to cafés for a week, and since, as a result, I felt well, and found calm and a capacity for work, I went last night to Åke Hansson's [restaurant] with Gillberg. A cat came three times and looked through the door. Slept horribly badly! Today I promise *myself* never again to touch schnapps, cognac or whisky! May God help me to keep this vow! Including rum, arrack, absinthe."

Gernandt published Parts 1 and 2 of *To Damascus* in a single volume towards the end of October, to a mixed reception. Karl Warburg in *Handelstidningen i Göteborg* thought the plays lacked action and consistency; Hans Emil Larsson in *Nordisk Tidskrift* found "the whole thing weak and confused," and Edvard Alkman in *Dagens Nyheter* had "an impression of confusion and grandeur." But Tor Hedberg praised it in *Svenska Dagbladet* for its "exuberant, new-born creative power," and acclaimed Strindberg as "what he was before, the unknown one whose ways we cannot predict and whose resources we cannot measure, the greatest creative writer we have today." And Georg Nordensvan, who likewise had damned *Legends*, wrote a very sympathetic notice in *Aftonbladet*: "In these two plays, Strindberg treats the theme he dealt with in *Inferno* and *Legends* . . . having erred hubristically, he now in penance turns his hostility against himself. He sets himself in the pillory with an energy that testifies to an undiminished power of conviction . . . Technically, both these plays are highly original, and more than one surprising and brilliant treasure is to be found. The dream, or ghost, scenes are executed with a sharpness and graphicness of a very rare kind; they are almost more real than the other scenes." But he concluded: "Dare one hope that in his next work he will concern himself with something other than his eternal ego?" And the poet and short-story writer Per Hallström (who died at the age of ninety-four in 1960) wrote to Georg Brandes: "He now seems to have worked himself clear of the worst of his 'queer' period and can perhaps take his place again amongst us here, where in many respects he is much needed." Brandes replied briefly: "I have long since lost all interest in Strindberg."[4]

*See page 194.

Not surprisingly, no Swedish theatre was keen to stage *To Damascus*, and it was not until after his successes the following year with a very different kind of play that it was to receive its premiere.

One complimentary copy of *To Damascus* must have surprised its recipient. Henrik Ibsen had celebrated his seventieth birthday in March, and Strindberg had been invited to contribute to a *Festschrift* in his honour, but had refused. He now (23 October) wrote to Geijerstam at Gernandts: "Would you please send Ibsen a copy of *To Damascus* and just say this: Strindberg is ashamed that as a prominent Swedish author he did not join in the homage to the Master, from whom he learned much. But he was in a state of depression and did not think his homage could honour or gladden anyone." Fearful lest this might be taken to imply a modification of his antagonism to Ibsen's general view of life, he assured Geijerstam that his homage would have been "to the master of dramatic art, not the philosopher."

It had been a busy year. In addition to the two parts of *To Damascus*, he had written a short story that summer entitled "The Silver Marsh," set in the Stockholm skerries, about a loner who, against the advice of the locals, goes fishing in a "forbidden" lake; sadly, after a haunting start, the tale tapers off into anticlimax. He had also, in July, begun to plan a historical play set in the fourteenth century entitled *Magnus the Good*. But he abandoned this to write another quasi-autobiographical novel, *The Monastery*, to fill the gap between *A Madman's Defence* and *Inferno*, beginning with his arrival in Berlin in 1892 and ending with his departure from Mondsee for Paris in 1894. He completed this on 23 November* and immediately started work on another symbolic play, *Advent*.

"Plays and no more alchemy!" he assured Kerstin on 1 December, and eight days later asked Jollivet-Castelot to "forgive my silence, for my thoughts are elsewhere, far from chemistry and even farther from alchemy. This is because I have earnestly returned to the art of the theatre, it is my *métier* and I *ought* no more to busy myself with magic, forbidden by my religion." Sending *Advent* to Geijerstam on 19 December, he wrote: "Herewith the Mystery in the spirit of Swedenborg. Never have I been so unsure whether I have succeeded or failed. No idea whether it is good or awful."

Advent tells how an unjust judge and his malignant wife come to see

---

The Monastery was not published until 1902, when he reworked it so as, untypically, to avoid identification with living people, setting it in Denmark, making Frida a Dane and himself a Norwegian, and cutting the opening chapter about the Black Porker. He retitled it *The Quarantine Master's Second Story* and included it in the collection *Fairhaven and Foulstrand*.

the evil of their ways. Like *To Damascus*, it combines realism with fantasy, sometimes with powerful effect. When the Judge unthinkingly invokes the Devil, the latter appears dressed as a poor schoolmaster with a red neckerchief, carrying a cane, one of Swedenborg's "corrective spirits." There is a macabre ball, at which musicians with chalk-white faces play, and the Judge's wife finds herself partnered by a hunchbacked prince who abuses her. In the final act, the wife freezes to death in a marsh, while the Judge is stoned to death by people whom he has unjustly condemned. They meet in Hell, where, it being Christmas, each is given a peepshow in which they see their past life, even love appearing as "two cats on an outhouse roof." At this moment of greatest humiliation, the Advent star shines. Knowledge of their guilt has cleansed them and gives them hope of redemption. *Advent* was not performed until after Strindberg's death (in Munich in 1915), nor in Sweden until as late as 1926. Realism and fantasy are not as skilfully blended as in *To Damascus*, and the didacticism to which Strindberg was always prone sometimes intrudes uncomfortably. It is not often performed, even in Sweden; but I have seen it work powerfully on the stage. It is a play that deserves greater attention than has been given to it, though it needs tremendous presences in the two main roles, and in several of the minor ones.

On 22 December, Strindberg sent his sister Elisabeth 25 crowns for Christmas, accompanied by another harsh letter: "You are not persecuted by people, but by Someone Else, the same who persecuted me with the good intent that I should forget myself and think a little of others; reduce my demands of mortals and rethink my duties towards life"—cold words, one might think, to address to someone in an asylum. He spent Christmas Eve, he informed Geijerstam, "alone in my room with a jug of milk, thinking without bitterness but gratefully of all the beautiful Christmas Eves which Providence has granted me. Despite everything, I have had the best that life can offer, with my own children around the Christmas tree. One's demands lessen with the years, my friend! I did not and do not want to come to Stockholm."[5]

His daughter Greta, now seventeen, wrote to him that she had decided to become an actress; having appeared in several amateur productions, she was to start in the New Year as a professional at the Folkteater in Helsinki. "Strange," he replied on 26 December. "I always thought Karin would hanker for the theatre and you for a life at home. But as you see, I was wrong! I have now put aside everything else to devote myself exclusively to writing for the theatre, so as to fulfil the promise I showed in my youth as a dramatist . . . So you appreciate that I am not sad that you are entering the theatre, since the stage is my own art."

The three plays that he had written in 1898 had all been highly symbolic, and no theatre would touch them. In 1899 he was to write four predominantly realistic plays, which brought him money and acclamation, although, as in Paris, the acclamation was to prove short-lived.

Gustaf Uddgren, the young journalist who had become friendly with Strindberg in Berlin and Paris, met him in Lund early in the New Year.

> How he had changed in these years! When I saw him in Paris he was still in the full vigour of manhood, worn by his troubles but not yet aged. Now it was a gentle grey-haired old man who stood before us. The grey tufts of hair stuck out in all directions, his face was sunken, and he did not hold himself erect and proudly as in former days . . . He was full of indignation that nobody wanted to stage his plays in Sweden . . . "It is impossible for a man to go on writing plays when no one ever puts them on. What could I not have learned by seeing my plays on the stage? How has this not inhibited my development as a dramatist?" He said there was nothing for it but that he must start his own Strindberg theatre in Stockholm. But where was the Maecenas who would support such a project? Of all the injustices he had suffered, this seemed to him the bitterest.[6]

But when Uddgren met him later the same day in a restaurant,

> he was quite different . . . He had put off his aged appearance with his dressing-gown. His hair was still grey, but there was a youthfulness about him—something of the student as we sat down to dinner like three young men who have slipped their reins and are out on the spree . . . He read old mediaeval books to calm himself in the evenings. The Bible and Swedenborg he merely dipped into when he was uncertain and needed counsel. He opened them at random but always found the answer to what he was asking. In one respect he was quite different from before. All the bitterness and suspiciousness had been erased . . . He sat there, big, wise and good, addressing us with worldly wisdom.[7]

On 21 January, *Folkets Tidning* declared in a leader: "Tomorrow will be August Strindberg's fiftieth birthday. It is an important day not merely for Swedish literature but for the nation as a whole. Since Tegnér and Almqvist* no name has had such impact in our literature as that of Strindberg. Nothing would have seemed more natural than that August Strindberg as our leading writer should tomorrow be the object of congratulations that would unite the nation in enthusiasm, overlooking his weaknesses and seeing only the greatness of this great man. But Swedes are envious, and patriotism runs thin." Strindberg spent the day

---

*The poet Esaias Tegnér and the novelist C. J. L. Almqvist who had died, respectively, in 1846 and 1866.

quietly at Waldemar Bülow's. "Pleasant dinner," he recorded in his diary. "But then Anna Norrie [an operetta singer] arrived and it became horrible, dancing, shouting, etc." In Stockholm his friends and admirers held a banquet at Berns' restaurant, where twenty years earlier they had gathered with him in the Red Room; he was invited, but declined. "I said no," he told Kerstin on 14 January, "since no man should be praised before his death, perhaps not after it, either." Those present included Hjalmar Branting, Pehr Staaff, August Lindberg, Gustaf af Geijerstam, Carl Larsson and Richard Bergh, all now eminent in their chosen fields. They sent him a telegram: "Old friends from the early eighties whose life and view of life you have indelibly influenced empty on your fiftieth birthday a glass to your future." *Svenska Dagbladet* published half a page of tributes to him, including a poem of homage by Verner von Heidenstam, one of the many friends who had become "enemies," and *Dagens Nyheter* referred to him as "Sweden's greatest living writer." The only theatre to celebrate the occasion was the Swedish Theatre, which revived the production of *Master Olof* which had been so successful two years earlier; and the only gesture by any of his various publishers was a reprint by Gernandt of *Swedish Destinies and Adventures*, so ill proofread and so badly produced that Strindberg complained that the dust jacket looked like "a boulevard *pissoir* plastered with advertisements."[8] A photograph taken of him at Bülow's that day, in tails with an enormous buttonhole, shows him looking spruce but decidedly portly.

In a letter to Carl Larsson two days later, the first that had passed between them for five years, Strindberg underlined his bitterness at the original rejection of *Master Olof*, which had deflected him from the theatre at a critical stage in his career, plus the fact that so many of his best plays remained unperformed. "My life is a cripple lacking a foot of spine. The years between 20 and 30 are missing; the best years . . . Imagine yourself painting enormous canvases which never get accepted for exhibition but which you must roll up and carry to the attic where they must lie until they grow old-fashioned. That is what I have had to do repeatedly."

On 26 January, Strindberg at last revisited Stockholm, for the first time for over six years, to discuss the publication of his collected works with Gernandts. He stayed four days, living in a small boardinghouse, but was persuaded to attend a party in Carl Larsson's studio, where he met several of those who had graced the birthday banquet at Berns'. "Stockholm was bright and gay," he reported to Kerstin on 1 February, "too gay, but it was nice to see again all my good old friends from the eighties gathered together. But sad to wander the streets where I passed my childhood, youth and middle age. Pompeii and Herculaneum beneath the ashes; no house which I could enter as my home . . . Now I am writing another play; an all too human drama in which all the people are angels and do the most horrible things—just as in life. The villains are too cunning to break the law." This was a modern drama set in Paris, *There Are Crimes and Crimes*.

An issue of the German magazine *Quickborn* containing Munch's illustrations of various of his works reached him, and his old enmity towards Munch reawoke. "Tomorrow I shall send you Munch's latest horrible masterpieces," he wrote to Richard Bergh on 5 February. "In seven years he hasn't had a new idea, nor even found a new subject to caricature." He himself had, however, discovered a new English writer who excited him: "I have been reading Kipling for the first time. The man is a complete expression of the present age. He is 'half-crazy,' and all his heroes are 'crazy'; even the whisky is everywhere. But Kipling is occult, i.e., he believes in the soul in man and touches lightly on the Inferno problems which I encompassed." On 24 February he told Geijerstam: "I have read eight volumes of Kipling with increasing admiration. On reading 'The Brushwood Boy' I became scared! for there the author believes, and so tricks the reader into believing. *The Jungle Book* is dreadful . . . Here everyone reads Kipling and talks Kipling. 'The Mark of the Beast' and 'The Conversion of Aurelian McGoggin' give rise to many reflections." "The Brushwood Boy" tells how two people have the same dream in which they meet; "The Mark of the Beast," how a man defiles the statue of an Indian god by making "the mark of the beast" on its forehead and is turned into a beast himself; and "McGoggin," how a freethinker, in the midst of a speech denying the existence of God, loses his speech and memory. Of these, only "The Mark of the Beast" is anywhere near Kipling's best; Strindberg was inclined at this time to overpraise anything that dealt with the occult, like *Séraphita* and *Zanoni*. It is curious that he does not mention Kipling's most famous achievement in this genre, "The Finest Story Ever Told," in which a modern man repeatedly dreams of a previous existence in which he was a galley slave; perhaps *Many Inventions*, in which it appears, was not one of the eight volumes he had read.

He completed *There Are Crimes and Crimes* in a little over three weeks, on 24 February. Set in Paris, it tells how a dramatist, Maurice, living with his common-law wife, Jeanne, has a success with a play, falls in love with a sculptress, Henriette, and wishes his little illegitimate daughter dead so that there will be no obstacle to his marrying Henriette. The child dies, Maurice is arrested on suspicion of murder, his play is withdrawn and his friends turn against him. It transpires, however, that the child died a natural death. He returns to public favour, and gives up Henriette; but Jeanne will not forgive him, and the play ends with him going into a church, like the Stranger at the end of Part 1 of *To Damascus*, to settle his conscience with God. It is an attempt to breathe new life into French boulevard theatre, the genre which he so despised; *To Damascus* and *Advent* had failed to interest the managers, and he needed to be performed. *There Are Crimes and Crimes* works well in its way until the last act, when it falls apart; but, like *Lucky Peter's Journey*, it was to succeed in the theatre where so many of his best plays were rejected or failed.

On finishing it, he took a month off from writing, as he needed to after his outpourings of the past twelve months, then on 1 April returned to his historical play *Magnus the Good*, which he had begun but abandoned both in the previous July and again in January. He retitled it *The Saga of the Folkungs*. By 9 April he was able to report to Geijerstam that he had reached the middle of Act 3 "without understanding how I got there," and five days later: "Tomorrow I begin Act 5. Can you imagine! But it is like sleepwalking . . . Alas! If only the Selected Works could come about! The children need so much. Grown ladies who must have clothes." On 20 April he posted the completed manuscript to Geijerstam, telling him: "Send Karin 330 marks (not crowns) and me the crumbs."

The Saga of the Folkungs tells the story of Magnus the Good, the last of the Folkung dynasty, King of Sweden from 1319 (when he was three years old) until 1365, the first man to be ruler of both Sweden and Norway. When the play opens, all is well with Sweden; the Russian invaders have been expelled, the slaves freed, laws have been passed establishing human rights, and Magnus is hailed as the "saviour and prince of peace." He recognises this as hubris, and the nemesis he dreads descends on him in full measure. His wife betrays him, his son plots to replace him, revolt threatens, he is excommunicated, and the Black Death reaches the land. Finally, the people depose him in favour of his son. Magnus, like Shakespeare's Henry VI, is portrayed as a good man but an ineffectual monarch; he sees himself as one destined to suffer for the sins that others have committed. It is a splendidly powerful and vivid play, with powerfully realised characters and magnificent crowd scenes; and, like Strindberg's other historical plays, it is virtually unknown outside Scandinavia. For some reason, Strindberg later disowned it; on 12 August 1905 he wrote to Emil Schering: "The play is among the worst constructed I have written, and the characters weak," a judgement which strikes a modern reader as unduly harsh. But he did not feel thus when he finished it, and at once began work on another historical play set two centuries later, about the great Gustav Vasa, whom he had shown as a young ruler learning his way in *Master Olof*.

The Dreyfus case continued to obsess Strindberg that spring and summer of 1899, and he pasted numerous cuttings into his diary with comments which show that his anti-Semitism was far from dead. "14 April. The Jews now call Devil's Island the Isle of Salvation, *Ile du Salut*. In other words Dreyfus is the Saviour! . . . This is Satanism! The Antichrist (= the Jew) cannot be Christ! . . . 4 June. Ever since 1894 I have believed Dreyfus to be guilty and I still believe it . . . No one suffers innocently and D. must be guilty to suffer so immeasurably." He also dreamed about him.

Late that April, Geijerstam wrote to Strindberg that Gernandt wanted to publish a collected edition of his novels and short stories, having agreed terms for their release from all the original publishers. Strindberg was delighted, but (29 April) "couldn't you also think about Collected Theatre (my plays!) . . . As you see, I have found my way back to my path which the theatre once promised to be . . . The dramatic form tempts me most and I have many plans laid. The question is whether I ought not to live nearer the world of the theatre, or in it. I wouldn't object to being dramaturge for Ranft for 1,800 crowns. Will you ask him? An inexplicable longing draws me to Kymmendö this summer. Perhaps because in *Gustav Vasa*, which I am now writing, Master Olof appears as an old man, and I wrote *M. Olof* on Kymmendö."

Geijerstam's news, added to Schering's energetic proselytising in Germany, meant that Strindberg's financial position was now more promising than it had ever been, despite the unwillingness of any Swedish theatres to accept his recent plays. "Good news at last!" he wrote to the children in Helsinki on 5 May. "My writings scattered among many different publishers are now gathered and belong to me; after my death, to you. For this we have to thank Uncle af Geijerstam, and this you should never forget." (Strindberg himself was soon to forget, and was to revile him publicly and unforgivably.) His letter continued: "But we cannot expect much money at once, only gradually. It will cost me 7,000 crowns to buy back the existing stocks of books and I shall have only 3,000 crowns left . . . I am reserving 2,000 marks for you and am sending you now 1,000 marks." On 16 May he sent them a further 2,000 marks, the result of various items which Schering had managed to place in German newspapers and magazines, adding: "I shall probably send more at midsummer."

A Danish writer, Georg Brøchner, put a series of twenty-nine questions to him that month, apparently with a view to publishing the answers in an English newspaper or magazine, though for some reason they did not appear until *Svenska Dagbladet* printed them on the day of Strindberg's funeral. Some of the answers are revealing:

1. *What is the main trait in your character?*
   This strange blending of the deepest melancholy and the most astonishing light-heartedness.

2. *Which characteristic do you prize most highly in a man?*
   Absence of narrow-mindedness.

3. *Which characteristic do you prize most highly in a woman?*
   Motherliness.

4. *Which talent would you most like to possess?*
   To find the key to the world's mystery and the meaning of life.

5. *Which fault would you least like to possess?*
   Narrow-mindedness.

6. *What is your favourite occupation?*
   To write dramas.

7. *What would be the greatest happiness you could imagine?*
   To be nobody's enemy and to have no enemies.

8. *What position would you most have liked to have?*
   To be a dramatist whose dramas were always being played.

9. *What would you regard as the greatest misfortune?*
   To be without peace of mind and conscience.

10. *Where would you most like to live?*
    In the Stockholm skerries.

11. *Your favourite colour?*
    Zinc-yellow and amethyst violet.

12. *Your favourite flower?*
    Cyclamen.

13. *Your favourite creature?*
    The butterfly.

14. *Which books do you like most?*
    The Bible; Chateaubriand's *Génie du Christianisme*; Swedenborg's *Arcana Coelestia*; Victor Hugo's *Les Misérables*; Dickens's *Little Dorrit*; Andersen's *Fairy Tales*; Bernardin de Saint-Pierre's *Harmonies de la Nature*. Kipling: various.

15. *Which paintings do you like most?*
    Théodore Rousseau's "Paysages Intimes." Böcklin: various.

16. *Which musical compositions do you like most?*
    Beethoven's Sonatas.

17. *Which English writer do you admire most?*
    Charles Dickens.

18. *Which English painter do you admire most?*
    Turner.

19. *Which male historical personages do you admire most?*
    Henri IV of France and Bernard of Clairvaux.*

20. *Which female historical personages do you admire most?*
    Elizabeth of Thüringen and Marguerite de Provence (consort of Louis the Holy).†

21. *Which historical personage do you most despise?*
    One has no right to despise anybody.

22. *Which fictitious male characters most attract you?*
    Balzac's Louis Lambert‡ and the Bishop in *Les Misérables* by Victor Hugo.

23. *Which fictitious female characters most attract you?*
    Margaretha in *Faust* and Florence in *Dombey and Son*.§

24. *Which name do you like best?*
    Margaretha.

25. *Which fault in others do you find it easiest to forgive?*
    Extravagance.

26. *Which social reform would you most like to see accomplished?*
    Disarmament.

27. *Your favourite drink and your favourite food?*
    Beer and fish dishes.

28. *Which season and which weather do you like best?*
    The height of summer after warm rain.

29. *Your motto?*
    Speravit infestis.¶[9]

---

*The twelfth-century Cistercian abbot and saint who has been described as the embodiment of mediaeval monasticism.

†St. Elizabeth (1207–1231), daughter of Andrew II of Hungary, famous for her generosity to the poor. Marguerite de Provence (1221–95) was the wife of Louis IX of France, known as Louis the Holy or St. Louis, though he was never beatified.

‡In the novel of that name.

§Strindberg evidently got someone to translate his answers into English, since the Royal Library in Stockholm contains a manuscript of them in an unidentified hand, which Strindberg altered and then copied. This other manuscript names Balzac's Séraphita as his second female choice, but Strindberg deleted her and substituted Dickens's Florence.

¶"He was hopeful in adversity" (Horace).

Although he was never to know it, Strindberg had acquired two distinguished admirers in Russia. That May of 1899, Anton Chekhov was sent a translation of *Miss Julie*. He replied to the translator: "I read *Miss Julie* back in the eighties (or early nineties), I know it, but I read it now again with great pleasure . . . He is a remarkable writer. He has a quite unusual power." A little later he wrote again: "Undoubtedly it will not be possible to perform *Miss Julie*; cuts and deletions would not help. But it can and must be published." He sent the play to Maxim Gorki, who echoed Chekhov's admiration: "He is bold, this Swede. Never have I seen the aristocratism of serfs [i.e., Jean] so lucidly portrayed . . . The idea of the play struck me forcibly, and the author's power awoke in me feelings of envy and surprise."[10] What a contrast between the dismissal of Strindberg by his contemporary midgets in Sweden and the respect accorded to him by his peers, Chekhov, Gorki, Ibsen, Zola and, within a few years, Shaw, Kafka and Thomas Mann.

On 12 June he completed *Gustav Vasa*. It had taken him less than eight weeks, and he at once began to draft its successor, *Erik the Fourteenth*, about Gustav's mad son. On 15 June he noted in his diary: "I was serenaded by the students . . . I wept and was seized with a terrible longing for Stockholm." The city that he had left nearly seven years previously as an impoverished divorcé no longer seemed hostile. Not only were his novels and stories to be published in a collected edition; more importantly, he sensed that his historical plays would appeal, as *Master Olof* had and as his modern plays had not, to theatre managers and audiences. But it was midsummer and the capital would be empty for the next six weeks. The skerries of his beloved archipelago beckoned to him. On 20 June he left Lund for ever, and by 23 June he was with his sister Anna at Furusund.

"Here I live in the most beautiful landscape in Europe," he wrote on 8 July to Kerstin who, at the age of five, had been packed off from her home to a boarding school in the Austrian village of Haag. ". . . Young people and children wander around in light-coloured clothes, beneath oaks and birches, on green meadows, on the grass in quiet groves, in the forests and by the shore. And the sun shines hotly. The sea is warm. In the evenings I sit on the verandah with my sister. Steamers and sailing ships pass on their way to Russia, Finland and Lapland, which enlivens the picture. My sister often plays Beethoven, the loftiest music I know, while my brother-in-law and I smoke and drink punch." The same day he wrote to Haakon Gillberg, a lawyer in Lund with whom he had become friendly: "I am definitely becoming a Stockholmer. My years of wandering seem to have come to an end." And five days later, to another Lund friend, the city notary Nils Andersson: "Now that I have come back to my country and landscape, I am making contact with the past and with my youth, am finding myself more and more, dropping new roots, and the stump is gradually beginning to blossom."

Anna's daughter Märta told me seventy years later, when she was over ninety, her memories of this summer: how Strindberg loved to sit in the evening sunlight with a glass of wine and listen to her playing classical music on the piano, "though he himself could only pick out a tune with one finger." "He must have been a very difficult guest," I suggested, but she said, "No. He was charming, and so gentle." Then she was silent for a moment, and added, "Of course, when the black mood was on him, then he was terrible." After another pause: "My mother was the same."

His daughter Greta wrote to him that she was coming to Stockholm to be confirmed into the Catholic Church. On 24 July she visited him at Furusund, and again on the twenty-eighth, when she stayed for three days. She was just eighteen and he had not seen her since she was a child of eleven. "I feared seeing her again," he wrote to Carl Larsson on 2 August, "but found only joy. The same kind blue eyes; traces of dimples in her cheeks; pure friendliness and consideration for others; and I heard again her 'dear father,' which I had not heard for 7 years. Yes, life seems less irreconcilable than I had supposed . . . My sister Nora has arrived here too with her husband and seven-year-old son. The sisters play duets, Mendelsson [*sic*]; and the affluent brother-in-law opened champagne; skittles were felled; the vasty deep was sounded and pure harmony reigned. These five weeks are to me a beautiful dream from which I dread to wake." He had worked well too, for on 1 August he was able to post *Erik the Fourteenth* to Ernst Gernandt. The effort of writing four full-length plays in seven months had exhausted him, though his head was still full of ideas. "I have a Swedish saga-play planned in detail," he told Geijerstam on 5 August, "which intoxicates me and I burn to write it down. But I must have six months' rest." And unusually for him, he did take at any rate seven weeks off. The "saga-play" was probably *The Virgin Bride*, though he was not to write that until the end of the following year, by which time he had completed five other full-length plays and a one-acter.

Albert Ranft accepted *Gustav Vasa* for production at the Swedish Theatre, sending him an advance of 1,000 crowns. On 8 August, Strindberg took the steamer into the capital for a day to fix lodgings for the autumn. "Received a terribly strong impression of something new, bright, which lit up Stockholm," he noted in his diary. "All the old dark houses from the seventies and eighties looked dirty." On 15 August he left Furusund ("This sojourn seems to me like a beautiful Midsummer

Night's Dream, now that I look back on it")[11] and, after spending three days at a hotel in the outlying resort of Saltsjöbaden, moved on 19 August into lodgings at Narvavägen 5, a few minutes' walk from where he had first lodged at Grev Magnigatan on leaving Uppsala thirty-seven years before. "The rooms are very handsome," he wrote that day in his diary, "and the landlord is a court chamberlain; but down in the café where I eat, lower-class people sit and insult me. Upstairs above my head lives someone who repeats my movements and 'rolls furniture' just as in Paris."

Stockholm, as he feared, was full of ghosts and disturbing memories. "Ever since I left Furusund," he noted in his diary on 26 August, "I have been hunted and made uneasy by several 'warnings.' " Two days later he told Kerstin he was "calm but not especially happy. I see a lot of my sister Anna and her daughters. Yesterday we all played skittles . . . My sister plays Mendelsson [sic] and Bethoven [sic] to me . . . In a month we shall start rehearsing my Gustav Vasa. And in February, Erik XIV will be staged. Sweden is not hostile to me. Almost the reverse." On 9 September he wrote to Nils Andersson in Lund: "There are moments when I long to be back in Lund, but it's only an illusion; for it is not as it was; was already changed before I left; and it doesn't matter where I am, for I can't escape myself. So I shall stay where I am! and dream of three rooms and a kitchen with my own housekeeper—if only I could find an Elna*—then I wouldn't need to go to the café in the evening. I don't enjoy the theatres." He was to remain in Stockholm for the remaining twelve years of his life.

On 12 September, Geber published a seventh edition of The Red Room, and on 19 September Strindberg began to plan a new historical play about the great seventeenth-century warrior king Gustav Adolf, the father of Queen Christina. The reopening of the Dreyfus case infuriated him; his diary is filled with new long entries insisting on Dreyfus's guilt, and when he was pardoned Strindberg noted (21 September): "The press does not believe in Dreyfus's innocence."

In the first week in October, Gernandt published The Saga of the Folkungs, Gustav Vasa and Erik the Fourteenth, to the usual mixed reception. Georg Nordensvan in Aftonbladet of 14 October thought that The Saga of the Folkungs read like a draft—"full of movement, action, variety, but . . . seems to have been written in haste and is often whimsical." The characters "scarcely seem people living individual lives, but rather give the impression of puppets which the author manipulates as he chooses . . . Too much happens off stage . . . it is a marionette play . . . a necklace of pearls, many glitter and some are genuinely beautiful,

---

*His housekeeper in Lund. He added a note: "aged 65, honest and considerate."

but they are held by an insufficiently strong thread." But, he concluded, all this may work on stage, and "that the play will grip its audience cannot be doubted." Karl Warburg in *Nordisk Tidskrift* admired Strindberg's idea of concentrating the destiny of the Folkungs into one figure, but thought the play too loosely constructed and not really thought through. Carl David af Wirsén in *Posttidningen* was predictably hostile. Admitting "great dramatic talent" in *Gustav Vasa*, he complained that the personalities were caricatured, the play full of coarse expressions, and the construction "naïve, puerile." "Concerning *Erik the Fourteenth*," continued Wirsén, "one would prefer to remain silent. . . The psychology is sadly superficial. The coarseness in this play exceeds all bounds." He especially objected to the child crying in the final scene, "I want to pee"—"a call of nature which one does not wish to hear in a theatre." Oscar Levertin in *Svenska Dagbladet* (12 December) had divided feelings about *The Saga of the Folkungs*, finding it "uneven, confused and muddled," yet admitting "many brilliant details, such as can never be absent from the work of such a genius and master as he." *Social-Demokraten* next day attacked Levertin for his "complete lack of understanding" of the play, saying that he was the head of the literary clique that now ruled in Sweden and that Strindberg's reappearance scared them (which was not far from the truth).

On 13 October, after less than eight weeks in Narvavägen, Strindberg moved into two furnished rooms a short distance away at Banérgatan 31. They contained both a portrait and a bust of Shakespeare, promising omens for his readopted career as a dramatist, and his landlady lent him a three-volume illustrated edition of the Bard's works.[12] Fredrik Wrangel, who had organised the appeal for him in Paris, visited him and was distressed to see how "plainly, even poorly" he lived; "but at least it could be regarded as an improvement on the little student room at the Hôtel Orfila." (Wrangel adds that "even in later years when he could afford to live more comfortably, he retained his simple bourgeois taste.")[13]

On 18 October, *Gustav Vasa* received its premiere at the Swedish Theatre and was a great success. The brilliant Harald Molander directed with his usual sensitivity and panache, and the critics, though in some cases bothered by historical inaccuracies, the modernity of the dialogue, and Strindberg's treatment of these historical giants as ordinary mortals, were full of praise. Alfred Lindkvist in *Stockholms-Tidningen* thought the final act "one of the most masterly . . . that exists in Swedish drama." Hjalmar Branting in *Social-Demokraten* wrote that Strindberg had "found himself again," and even Carl David af Wirsén in *Vårt Land*, while complaining that the play "lacks any unity and is dissipated into scattered scenes," had to admit that "these are often well and powerfully executed," and concluded: "One can only express amazement that an author who in other recent works has indulged in confused and horrifying hallucinations has here shown himself to have a powerful sense of reality." Tor Hedberg in *Svenska Dagbladet* wrote: "The audience greeted the play with the liveliest applause, which after the final curtain expanded into a unanimous and enthusiastic call for the author who, however, was not present to accept this tribute." As was his wont, Strindberg had attended the dress rehearsal but not the premiere; in a letter to Emil Schering on 11 November he described the scenic arrangements as "among the most beautiful I have seen." The production was to remain in the repertory, playing to full houses, for nearly two and a half years; Strindberg told Johan Mortensen that by the end of the year it had brought him 15,000 crowns. [14]

Gustav Vasa is one of Strindberg's best historical plays. When the action opens, Gustav has been king for ten years; the fiery young revolutionary portrayed in *Master Olof* has become the father of his people, a mixture, like most great kings, of benevolence and ruthlessness. He does not enter until the third act, but his presence dominates all that goes before. The fifth and final act shows him facing what seems to be irresistible revolution, ready to give everything up and flee the land, as in truth he once did consider doing; but he is saved by an army of Dalecarlians whom he supposes to be coming to the aid of the rebels but who have come to help him suppress them. Master Olof, meanwhile, has changed even more than his king and become a skilful politician, an obedient servant of his master and a devious spinner of webs. In a moving subplot, Olof sees his early self in his young son who wants to "tear down like Luther"; when he learns that Luther is dead, the son cries that he will tear down the universe, then himself. Olof tells him: "Begin with yourself; the universe will always be here . . . When I was your age I thought I knew and understood everything. Now I know nothing and understand nothing, so I limit myself to doing my duty and patiently enduring." The play is a tragedy of resignation; if it has a message, it is that even the greatest must see much of their labour wasted, endure ingratitude and the meanness of small men, and often be compelled to act against their consciences; and (as in *To Damascus* and *Easter*) that just punishment is a necessary condition of grace.

The following month, on 30 November, the Swedish Theatre presented the sequel to *Gustav Vasa*, *Erik the Fourteenth*. Harald Molander again directed, and Anders de Wahl, who had played Erik as a prince in the earlier play, naturally took the title role. But although *Erik the*

Fourteenth is a finer play than Gustav Vasa, it proved less of a success. Instead of a hero as its protagonist, it has an epileptic failure, and its more impressionist method, which makes it seem extraordinarily modern today, bothered the critics and audiences. Tor Hedberg in Svenska Dagbladet, while finding examples of genius in every act, regretted the play's "lack of unity and consequence" and felt that Strindberg "ruthlessly bares his own sad and embittered face." In fact, a notable strength of the play is that Erik, unlike Gustav Vasa, was a character with whom Strindberg could identify himself. Like Shakespeare, he knew that mediaeval kings were often hysterical weaklings. On the other hand, Edvin Alkman in Dagens Nyheter thought it even better than Gustav Vasa. Hjalmar Branting in Social-Demokraten found it confusing ("Erik vanishes from us into the mist"), as did Karl Warburg in Nordisk Tidskrift, who thought it untidy and subjective, too much of a personal sequel to Inferno and To Damascus, though he granted the fascination of Erik's "inner demon," which all the Vasas had, and admired the way Strindberg set this against the "outer demon" of his evil genius and adviser, Göran Persson. Warburg complained that "someone not responsible for his actions cannot easily be a tragic hero," praised Strindberg for not making Göran a conventional villain, and compared the play to the Tower of Pisa, saying that perhaps, like that builder, Strindberg "saw that it was leaning but continued, in order to show that such an unorthodox building could yet stand." Carl David af Wirsén, gleefully cataloguing the play's supposed faults in Vårt Land, concluded: "One would perhaps not have described the play's shortcomings in such detail had not the fanatical passion with which foolish admirers now apotheosise Herr Strindberg rendered it a duty to apply a small corrective."

Despite the mixed reaction, Erik the Fourteenth achieved 37 performances. Two weeks before it opened, Dramaten a hundred yards away had presented a sentimental drama on the same subject entitled Karin Månsdotter (the name of Erik's flower-girl mistress and later his wife), by Strindberg's Finnish friend, Adolf Paul, who had advertised his premiere by publicly attacking Gustav Vasa for its anachronisms. Tor Hedberg observed: "Times are changing. The historical play, which has for so long been virtually ostracised from our stage, has suddenly become the fashion . . . our kings and queens have never been so sought after . . . It is noteworthy that those who have praised it [Erik the Fourteenth] have been the ones who have condemned Adolf Paul's Karin Månsdotter, and vice versa." Paul's play has long been forgotten; Erik the Fourteenth is repeatedly revived in Scandinavia. The reason that it is so little known abroad is that Strindberg, as in all his Swedish historical plays, presupposes a basic knowledge of Swedish history which no foreign audience possesses. The play ends with Erik fleeing into the night; every Swedish schoolchild knows that he was subsequently imprisoned and murdered; it is as though an English play about Charles I were to end with him as Cromwell's prisoner but confident of ultimate success. It is a marvellous final curtain for anyone who knows the outcome, but would leave any non-Scandinavian audience bewildered. Yet a little ingenuity can overcome the problem; all that is needed is a couple of impersonal explanatory sentences spoken in a black-out after the play's conclusion.

1899 had been a good year for Strindberg, and the first volume of his *Collected Novels and Stories*, which Gernandt had published in October, had been well received. "Today I am sending you 500 marks," he wrote to the children in Helsinki on 19 December. ". . . This means that since last December you have received 8,375 marks. I have also repaid large debts this autumn. You should know that everything I owe my brother Oscar Sg., 2,300 crowns, has been repaid, also my debt to Eva Carlsson [their former servant], etc. . . . So it has been a good year; I doubt if next year will be as good, for writing cannot be driven like factories or workshops." But although 1900 was to begin with two inferior plays, it was to end with several of his best, and with a new relationship that was to change his life.

Chapter Twenty-Five

HARRIET

Thanks to the success of *Gustav Vasa* and *Erik the Fourteenth*, Strindberg greeted the new century in comparative affluence. "I haven't many expenses," he told the children on 9 January, "but am paying off big debts . . . I think you needn't worry, but you must be careful, as we have so often seen how transitory success can be." News came too that *Creditors* had been acclaimed in Vienna. "Life is more intense and rich here," he wrote to Axel Herrlin on 23 January. "Things have brightened for me, in my soul too, but the past is not forgotten." His diary records moments of depression, at seeing a flag at half-mast, hearing a pendulum stop, being awakened in the night by someone calling his name, drawing unlucky cards or seeing them lying in the street, hearing banging on walls, and the lack of a real home. "I . . . sit at the age of fifty [*sic*]," he wrote to Nils Andersson on 3 February, "like a traveller among other people's furniture in my own birthplace." On 16 February he found himself "gripped by a violent longing for Paris, especially the rue de la Grande Chaumière."[1]

On 26 February, *There Are Crimes and Crimes* had its premiere at Dramaten. All the reviews were favourable. Hjalmar Branting in *Social-Demokraten* described it as "a complete success . . . At the end of the play the applause was repeated again and again . . . the most effective modern drama that Strindberg has written since *The Father*." Georg Nordensvan in *Aftonbladet* liked it even better than *Gustav Vasa* and *Erik the Fourteenth*; Tor Hedberg in *Svenska Dagbladet* came nearer the truth in praising the first two acts but objecting that "the rest of the play is, apart from a few isolated scenes and lines, the work of a moralist and of a poor moralist." To the general amazement, the audience included King Oscar, whose disapproval of Strindberg was well known, but even he applauded heartily at the final curtain. "*Crimes and Crimes* seems to have been a great success," Strindberg noted gloomily in his diary (1 March), "but it brings me no joy . . . I am depressed, shy, have refused invitations to dinner and dare not go to a café." One can understand his disillusionment at the success of this pot-boiler when *To Damascus* had been rejected and *Miss Julie* remained unperformed in Sweden.

On 7 March he completed his play about Gustav Adolf, which he had been working on since September. It is an immense piece, some six hours long, the longest indeed that he wrote. Piqued by the accusations of inaccuracy which *The Saga of the Folkungs*, *Gustav Vasa* and *Erik the Fourteenth* had provoked, he researched *Gustav Adolf* minutely, clotting it with undramatic detail which blurs the many fine scenes it contains. Strindberg concentrated the action into the last two years of the King's life, when success in the Thirty Years' War has begun to turn sour and the political manoeuvring of both Catholics and Protestants has destroyed his vision; his old advisers urge one course, his young and idealistic commanders another; he dies bewildered, having accomplished nothing and impoverished his people. Strindberg hated warrior kings for the misery they caused in their search for glory, but his portrait of Gustav Adolf is subtle and sympathetic, and there are several finely drawn minor figures, such as the little drummer boy born during the long campaign who dreams of his native land which he knows only by description and will never live to see. The play contains almost as many characters as Hardy's *The Dynasts*, was never staged in Sweden in Strindberg's lifetime and has been performed there only twice since, the last time over fifty years ago; the political complexities are scarcely comprehensible, and too deeply interwoven with the plot to be easily cut. But *Gustav Adolf* should not be dismissed, as it usually has been; many of its scenes show Strindberg at or near his best.

Strindberg saw a fair amount of his sisters, Anna and Nora, that spring; during a "horrible" party at Anna's on 18 March, "I had the illusion that I saw all the guests naked and smelt each one's odour." He returned to chemistry and spent several weeks working on the synthesis of metals.[2] On 31 May a new name appeared in his diary; the entry, untypically squeezed into a narrow space, was evidently added at a later date. "Visit by Fröken Bosse, for the first time."

Harriet Bosse was a young Norwegian actress, just twenty-two, a sister of Alma Fahlström, whom Strindberg had met in Paris in October 1894. Small and dark, of Oriental appearance, the thirteenth of fourteen children, she had been brought up after her mother's early death by her elder sisters, who seem to have spoiled her. After starting on a theatrical career in her native Christiania, she left Norway suddenly in 1898, possibly as the result of an unhappy love affair, studied acting in Denmark and at the Conservatoire in Paris, came to live with a sister in Stockholm and in August 1899 was accepted into Dramaten, creating a considerable impression by the restraint and truthfulness of her approach. She represented the new school of acting, as exemplified by Stanislavsky and Eleonora Duse, in contrast to the declamatory method of Sarah Bernhardt and Henry Irving, which still held sway in Sweden, as in most of Europe. A few weeks after joining Dramaten, she attended the premiere of *Gustav Vasa* at the Swedish Theatre:

> I remember how the whole audience followed the play with tense interest, act by act. From that day I became obsessed with Strindberg's writings—read as much as I could, began to wonder what kind of person he was, felt great pity for him when I heard all that he had suffered. Came the New Year 1900. I celebrated New Year's Eve of 1899 on Skansen with my brother, a cadet in the Norwegian army. I remember I spoke much of Strindberg, said I had never seen him, and suddenly felt the impulse to wish him, without his seeing me, a happy new year. We went to Banérgatan, where Strindberg then lived. His apartment was on the ground floor. It was dark and silent—he had evidently gone to bed. With our noses against the glass, we stood there, my brother and I, and whispered "Happy New Year" through the window.[3]

That spring of 1900, Harriet played Puck in *A Midsummer Night's Dream*. Dramaten, impressed by the success of *Gustav Vasa, Erik the Fourteenth* and *There Are Crimes and Crimes*, now decided to take a chance with *To Damascus*; August Palme, who had been chosen to play the Stranger and was on friendly terms with Strindberg, suggested to him that Harriet might be suitable for the Lady and persuaded him to see *A Midsummer Night's Dream*, the cast of which also included other candidates for the role. It was the first time in years that Strindberg had visited a theatre, apart from rehearsals of his own plays. He chose Harriet—"mostly, he jestingly told me later, because I had such pretty legs"[4]—and sent her a message inviting her to call on him.

"Strindberg opened the door himself, with a bright sunny smile. No one could have such charm as Strindberg when the mood was on him, and I was completely bewitched." They talked of "everything between heaven and earth," though least about his writing; he showed her some pieces of paper stained with what he explained was gold of his own making. "I am sure that if he had shown me a dog and said it was a cat I would, in my blind worship of his knowledge, have said: 'Yes, of course it is a cat' . . . As I was about to leave, Strindberg asked if I would allow him to remove a feather which I had in my hat—he would keep it as a memento, put a steel nib in it and write his plays with it. He got the pen, I got myself a new and similar feather for my hat."[5]

Next day, 1 June, he went to stay with his sister Anna and her husband at Furusund. Since January, Hugo Philp had been seriously ill with diabetes; he and Strindberg had many conversations about death. But the happiness of the previous summer was not to be repeated. Strindberg quarrelled violently with Hugo, partly because the latter defended some writers whom Strindberg loathed, notably Heidenstam and Levertin, and partly because Hugo rebuked him for the way he had treated Siri.[6] In less than three weeks, on 20 June, he returned angrily to Stockholm. The city had begun to empty for the summer; he felt more than usually lonely. On 23 June, Midsummer's Eve, he noted in large letters in his diary a verse from Ecclesiastes: "This is what my soul seeketh but I find not; one man among a thousand have I found; but a woman among all those have I not found."

On 5 July, Harriet visited him briefly for the second time. "She accepted the role in To Damascus. Her sister waited outside, in a cab."* He was now working on a play which Albert Ranft had commissioned, a "religious comedy," as he curiously styled it in his diary,[7] but with little enthusiasm. "One would have expected that life would be somewhat brighter for me now," he wrote to Nils Andersson on 8 July, "but this is hardly so. Nor, sadly, does work now give me the joy it used to." His diary for these weeks contains copious chemistry notes intermingled with quotations from the Bible, as though to underline how much he had changed from the freethinker who had written The Father and Miss Julie: "Believe in the Lord your God, so shall ye be established . . . as long as he sought the Lord, God made him to prosper." "This," Strindberg added, "is the sum of all the wisdom that life has taught me." But the nightmares, whether he was sleeping or awake, did not cease. That same day, 15 July,

---

*Harriet, in her commentary to Strindberg's letters to her (Strindbergs brev till Harriet Bosse, Stockholm, 1932, p. 21), says that she did not hear from Strindberg after their first meeting until after the premiere of To Damascus on 19 November, but this is contradicted by Strindberg's diary entry for 5 July.

he noted: "In the evening I took a cab and drove around Djurgården. It was as though bewitched; I met only cripples of every possible kind; drunken, red, even children who resembled demons. A dog tried to jump up on the coachman's box; the coachman chatted to me on repulsive subjects; finally, I had to ride behind two whores, one of whom seemed to be in love with the other; one was dressed like a nun, black dress with high white collar; one was Frida [this word in Greek letters], the elder whore. In the grass at Rosendal lay groups, but always two men and one woman . . . It was horrible."

On 26 July he finished his "religious comedy," *Midsummer*, and Albert Bonnier died at the age of eighty, both of which facts he noted without comment in his diary. On 30 July he "dreamed Ibsen was dead. Have dreamed this before! in the daytime." Next day he received 6,000 crowns in royalties from Ranft, for *Gustav Vasa* and *Erik the Fourteenth*, and promptly "sent a cheque for four thousand [Austrian] crowns to Friedrich Uhl in Vienna. When I arrived at the bank a woman exactly like Frida Uhl but poor and shabbily dressed in black was standing outside the bank as though waiting. When I came, she went. . . Ibsen haunts me again."[8] On some days his diary contains the single word: "Calm." On 13 August, writing to Leopold Littmansson, he described Stockholm as "now big, beautiful and continental. Most of the old people are dead, the memories buried under new buildings and therefore not oppressive. Peace!" Johan Mortensen, now a docent at Uppsala, visited him and observed how he had changed in the two years since they had last met in Lund. "He seemed steadier and more self-assured. He was more elegant, dressed in a grey morning coat with black silk trimmings, a grey hat with a black ribbon and a black and white cravat . . . His hands were big and ungraceful and disfigured by the curious eruptions from which he sometimes suffered as a result of his alchemical experiments."[9]

His German disciple Emil Schering visited Stockholm that summer with his American wife, and Strindberg met him for the first time. On 19 August, *There Are Crimes and Crimes* received its German premiere in Breslau, directed by the young Alfred Halm, and got good reviews. "I haven't read any criticisms," Strindberg informed Schering on 27 August, "and don't intend to! I remain completely confident in you, who so 'providentially' appeared on my path and interest yourself in all aspects of my authorship and have not wearied despite such small pecuniary results." On 7 September a friend and enemy, Dr. Anders Eliasson, died in Ystad. That month Strindberg wrote a short puppet play, *Casper's Shrove Tuesday*; as the puppet-master goes off to find some paint to smarten his puppets up, they pop up out of their box and fight. The play reads slightly, but I have seen it done with puppets to make an enchanting half-hour.

Gustav Adolf was published in September, to mainly tepid reviews. Strindberg sought refuge in work, and in the space of an extraordinary three weeks completed two full-length plays, *Easter* and *The Dance of Death*, each of them in ten days.*

Easter is a very still play, a forerunner of those "chamber plays" which Strindberg was to write for his own Intimate Theatre seven years later. It takes place in a small provincial town, clearly Lund, between Maundy Thursday and Easter Eve, when nothing happens and nothing is heard from the street outside save the scraping of the creditor's stick and the squeaking of his galoshes. Mrs. Heyst lives with her son and daughter, the son's fiancée and a schoolboy lodger, under the shadow of her husband's imprisonment for embezzlement. The son, Elis, is suspicious and bitter; his sister, Eleonora, has run away from a mental hospital where she has been confined. They dread the coming of the creditor; but when he arrives in the final act, he turns out to be not the monster of their imagination, but a kindly man who feels in debt to them. It is a play of hope.

Elis is very much a self-portrait, of the arrogant, self-centred and intolerant man that Strindberg, in his better moments, knew himself to be. Eleonora was based on his sister Elisabeth. "She was like a twin to me," he was to write to Harriet after Elisabeth's death,[10] and he felt that by her suffering she had perhaps acted as a scapegoat for the sins and shortcomings of her whole family (just as he believed he might have done during his Inferno period). Eleonora was also, by Strindberg's own admission, partly based on the title-character in Balzac's *Séraphita* who, like Eleonora (and, he might have added, Prince Myshkin in Dostoevsky's *The Idiot*), was regarded as insane but was really a superior being, a visitor from another world.

Despite being one of Strindberg's more popular plays among theatre managers, *Easter* is one of the most difficult to make work. More even than *The Father* or *Miss Julie*, it depends on precise casting; if Eleonora is wrong, however good an actress she may be, the play not only fails but is liable to be an embarrassment. She must be innocent without being

---

*John Landquist, the editor of Strindberg's *Collected Works*, describes the extreme speed with which Strindberg wrote. "He generally made very few alterations . . . In later years he seldom corrected anything once it had been written down. He did not like to read through his works after completing them" (*Adam* [London], Strindberg centenary number, 1949, p. 15). There are even frequent inconsistencies between the cast lists, as written down by Strindberg, and the characters who actually appear in the various plays.

mawkish, a most elusive combination to attain; and she must be positive, not passive. She must have, as Charles Morgan wrote in his *Times* review of the 1928 London production, "the fire that gives light to the symbol." Elis, like all of Strindberg's self-portraits, is another problem, largely because Strindberg invested him with several of his own more tiresome characteristics, especially his self-pity. He must be positive and rebellious, like the Stranger in *To Damascus*; one has seen productions of *Easter* in which everyone behaved as though they were drugged. Yet with the right delicate casting, and the required sense of stillness, of people imprisoned in a house and waiting for release, *Easter* can work magically in a theatre. It is a play about prisoners; and, like (in their very different ways) *The Lady from the Sea* and *Antony and Cleopatra* and *Mary Rose*, a play for a very special kind of actress. If such an actress is not to hand, it is, like those plays, better left undone.

The contrast between *Easter* and *The Dance of Death* could hardly be more marked. *Easter* is a play of reconciliation and hope, *The Dance of Death* an expression of the blackest pessimism and hatred. The story of a couple locked in a hopeless marriage, it seems to have been influenced by Swedenborg's *De Coelo et Inferno*, which tells of "marriages of Hell" which "stand under the influence of evil." Partners in such a marriage, Swedenborg wrote, can talk to each other, and may even be drawn to each other through lust; "but inwardly, they burn with a mutual hatred which is so great that it cannot be described." The protagonists were cruelly and recognisably based on the Philps. Alice in the play is an actress who has given up her career for marriage, just as Anna had sacrificed her musical career; Edgar, like Hugo, is suddenly taken seriously ill; like the Philps, he and Alice have a silver wedding coming up; they even share the Philps's liking for a game of cards. There were other models too, but Hugo Philp certainly sensed the connection, for on reading the play he threw it into the fire. The resultant estrangement was to last for four years.

That Strindberg should have written this play in the same month as *Easter* is not as incongruous as some critics have supposed. It was characteristic of him to alternate with bewildering rapidity between opposing moods, and, taken together, the two plays portray him more accurately and fully than either play considered by itself. On the occasion of the 1928 London production of *The Dance of Death*, Charles Morgan wrote an anonymous review in the *Times* which reflects the bewilderment of even Strindberg's sympathisers during those early years. "Loose, tangled and contradictory though this play often is, it leaves an astonishing, an almost unaccountable, impression of genius. To the coldly regarding eye, it exhibits a crowd of faults—now of over-emphasis, now of forced movements towards a climax, now of rash inconsistency of structure; yet, as a beggar's cloak full of holes may have a kind of majestic beauty when the wind fills it, so this broken drama, having unmistakably the winds of vision in it, has beauty and dignity and power." One would answer that nowadays we do not expect or particularly like a play to be what the 1920s regarded as "well-made"; it is largely the jagged, uneven shape of Strindberg's dramas, with the characters veering sharply from mood to mood as people do under the stress of violent emotion, that makes him, more than Ibsen, the model for so many playwrights today.

Emil Grandinson and Nils Bonde, Dramaten's censor, both advised against accepting *The Dance of Death.* "It makes much too disagreeable an impression," Bonde reported to the board, ". . . is little suited to the stage."[11] Nor would any other theatre consider it. One of Strindberg's most frequently performed plays since his death, and now generally accepted as one of his masterpieces, it had to wait nine years before it was performed in Sweden, at Strindberg's own Intimate Theatre. *Easter,* however, was accepted by both Dramaten and the Schauspielhaus in Frankfurt-am-Main for production the following spring.

To Damascus was by now in rehearsal, but Strindberg was gloomy about its prospects. "The winds do not blow as favourably for me now as they did last season," he wrote to Emil Grandinson, its director, on 25 October. "So I am prepared for hostility." The summer break meant that he had been getting nothing from the theatres. "For the moment I can't send any money, since I have only debts," he told Karin on 28 October. Three days later, however, he managed to send them 300 marks. "If I get more in December, then you shall have more. Since May I haven't been performed and am borrowing money myself. My old age will, I suppose, be like my youth and middle years, with the difference that it is worse to have to go around borrowing when one is older! or to beg!" It embarrassed him that she had felt compelled to write to him on the subject. "He could not bear our asking him for help," Karin recalled. "It vexed him as much as it made him happy to be able to send us help voluntarily, when he decided, and as much as he decided."[12]

On 4 November he wrote his first letter in a year to Kerstin at her boarding-school (though he had sent her a dozen postcards). "I stayed the whole summer in Stockholm, and alone. Now I am tired and think of going to Switzerland to rest and catch up on my sleep. So tired I am." But his loneliness was soon to end, at least temporarily. His diary tells the story:

15 November 1900. First dress rehearsal of *To Damascus*. The inexplicable scene with [Bosse]. * It happened thus. After Act One I went up onto the stage and thanked [Bosse]. Made a remark about the final scene when the kiss has to be given with the veil lowered. As we stood there in the middle of the stage surrounded by many people, and I spoke earnestly about the kissing, [Bosse]'s little face was transformed, grew larger and took on a supernatural beauty, seemed to come close to mine, and her eyes enveloped me with black flashes of lightning. Then she ran away for no reason and I stood bewildered with the impression of a miracle and that I had been given a kiss which made me drunk. / Then B haunted me for three days, so that I sensed her in my room. / Then I dreamed of her, thus: [I lay in a bed. B. came in Puck's costume from the play; she was married to me. She said about me: "Behold the man who brewed me," gave me her foot to kiss. She had no breasts]. Absolutely none! / Gustaf Strindberg† who had seen *Damascus* said B was exactly like Aunt Philp (my sister Anna). Now, my second wife (The Lady in *Damascus*) was like my sister Anna. So B is like both.

Two days later he wrote to Nils Personne, the artistic director of Dramaten, concerning the production of *Easter* planned for the New Year. "Just a word about the girl (Eleonora)'s part. You know my weakness for Fröken Bosse. The fund of poetry and 'earnestness' which she possesses I do not find among her colleagues; and her childlike figure is appropriate to a girl with a pigtail down her back." On 19 November, the date of the premiere of *To Damascus*, he wrote his first letter to Harriet:

Dear Harriet Bosse,
    Since I shall not be at the theatre tonight, I wish now to thank you for what I saw at the dress rehearsal. It was great and beautiful (Damascus), although I had imagined the character as a little lighter, with hints of mischief and more outgoing. A little of Puck!—those were my first words to you—and they will be my last! A smile in the midst of misery suggests the existence of hope, and the situation does turn out not to be hopeless.
    Well; good luck on your journey through the thistles and stones. Such is the path. I merely strew a few flowers on it.
                                                    August Strindberg

Opinion as to the quality of this first production of *To Damascus* varies. Oscar Wieselgren, half a century later, recalled Grandinson's production as bold in intention but not good, and August Palme's performance in the

---

*Square brackets are used to indicate words spelt by Strindberg in Greek characters, a method he often employed in his diary when writing about something private or trying to conceal someone's name. This device is repeated in subsequent quotations.
†The son of Strindberg's brother Oscar.

lead as "sentimental and wholly unintellectual," the opposite of what Strindberg intended the character to be.[13] Tor Hedberg in *Svenska Dagbladet* praised the production as "an uncommonly bold and consistent effort to transcend ordinary theatre technique," but felt that the play read better than it acted. Pehr Staaff in *Dagens Nyheter* likewise praised the production but suggested that the play was of greater interest to Strindberg himself than to the public, and *Aftonbladet* thought "this oppressive fever-fantasy of a sick and tormented soul . . . is not suited to the stage." Hjalmar Söderberg in *Ord och Bild* declared that if anyone held the secret key to the play, he would be glad to know of it; "until such time, the whole thing bewilders me as it does the rest of the town." *Vårt Land* reported that the reaction of the audience was "somewhat muted." The only papers to praise the play were *Stockholms-Tidningen*, which summed up the evening as "a complete success," and *Social-Demokraten*, which regretted that the audience reacted with "a notable lack of understanding" to this "gripping" and "fascinating drama." On 25 November, Strindberg told Schering that "it is still playing to good houses and lively applause," and the production achieved the respectable run, for so demanding a play, of twenty performances.

That November, Strindberg's daughter Greta made her professional acting debut in Helsinki, in, by a strange coincidence, Frans Hedberg's *The Wedding at Ulfåsa*, the play in which her father had been offered his first stage part thirty-one years earlier. Schering wrote that he found *The Dance of Death* extraordinary, but feared theatre managers in Germany might find it too black. Strindberg reacted by writing a sequel, entitled simply *The Dance of Death, Part Two*, in which the children of the characters in Part One seek the happiness which escaped their parents. He completed this in a few weeks before the end of the year, but it did not help to get the play accepted; there are inconsistencies between the two parts which makes it difficult to stage them together (for example, the impoverished Captain of Part One has become unexplainedly affluent in Part Two). Part One works far better by itself, and lasts two and a half hours, which is enough for any evening in the theatre.

Full of hopes for *To Damascus*, and with *The Saga of the Folkungs* in rehearsal at the Swedish Theatre, Strindberg asked his brother Axel on 1 December to get him a new second-hand piano, "cost what it may," and to send 700 marks to the children in Helsinki. But Harald Molander, the director of the *Folkungs*, suddenly died at the age of forty-two, which, coupled with the illness of Anders de Wahl, who was cast in the lead, meant that the opening had to be postponed until the New Year. This and the withdrawal of *To Damascus* meant that Strindberg suddenly found himself short of money. He began yet another play in December, *The Virgin Bride,* and despite a recurrence of psoriasis, was to complete it in less than a month; four plays (plus a one-acter) in three months, including three of his best.

On 5 December, on the occasion of the final performance of *To Damascus,* he wrote his second letter to Harriet. "Miss Harriet Bosse. Reflecting that we finished our journey to Damascus today, I ordered some roses—with thorns, of course—there seem to be no others. And I send them with a simple thanks: now become our new century's actress." (Which, unlike Siri, to whom he had addressed the same words, Harriet did.)

"I live more alone here than in Lund," he wrote on 11 December to Axel Herrlin. "Find joy only in my work. The results do not give me joy even when they are good. And I seem to be in a state of disciplinary penitence. For I am isolated in such a way that when I seek company people wound me without wishing to, so that I withdraw. If I seek a pleasure, it turns out ill. If I have a friend, he is taken from me. The road to salvation is hard. When I think I have crept forward a little I fall back again . . . I now believe firmly that sin itself is the punishment. But the fact that one hates it and oneself must be good for the moment of death, which must always be the moment of liberation. Romans Chapter Seven seems to me to have solved the riddle: 'Who shall deliver me from the body of this death?' One's longing for purity and beauty manifests itself most strongly after sinning. It is strange. Is this the purpose of sin? . . . To remove our misery is to remove the punishment, but we are here to be punished. *Allons travailler* [let us work]. That surely is the sum of it all." Next day he noted in his diary: "Felt myself in telepathic communication with B."

The poor reception of *Gustav Adolf* and the rejection of *The Dance of Death* must have been especially depressing for Strindberg at a time when his writing was at its peak. As Karl Otto Bonnier observed, "all of his remarkable works from *Inferno* to *Gustav Adolf* had been greeted by the critics with wonderment rather than admiration, and hardly one of them had been a success in the bookshops."[14] By contrast, his editor at Gernandts, Gustaf af Geijerstam, was now enjoying considerable popular success both as a playwright and as a novelist (one of his books went into its thirteenth edition that December). Bonnier relates that Strindberg was, not without reason, "continually envious of his rivals on the Swedish Parnassus," and, less reasonably, complained to everyone at this time of the pressure that he felt Geijerstam was putting on him.[15]

Forgetful of how much Geijerstam had done for him in the past few years, Strindberg now cast him as the Enemy. On 27 December he wrote Geijerstam a deeply paranoiac letter:

> I sense something in your personality which oppresses me and threatens to make me sick. I also feel something menacing in your manner of behaviour, a desire, possibly with good intent, to interfere in my destiny. You have for example sought to rule my sympathies and antipathies, to determine the company I keep, force opinions on me, etc. I withdraw and beg you: do not seek me before I seek you . . . I wish you a good end to this old year and all good in the coming New Year.
>
> As before, amiably,
> August Strindberg

Geijerstam, who had lost his wife in May, took this in good part. But within a few years Strindberg was to libel him in a novel even more spitefully than he had libelled Siri in A *Madman's Defence*.

He told Gustaf Uddgren that he had a mind to start his own theatre, despite the failure of his attempt in Copenhagen twelve years earlier. "The theatre I seek is Maeterlinck's and not that of the past," he explained, referring to the intimate and symbolic chamber plays which the Belgian had written in the previous decade.[16] On 30 December he asked Richard Bergh to "enquire of the owner of the Blanch Theatre what he would want for me to hire the theatre; and if he is sure that one may perform plays there." (Theodor Blanch was a restaurateur who in 1879 had built a theatre next to his café, but he had recently used it as a shop and art gallery.) But Strindberg lacked the money and could not find backers, and it was to be nearly six years before this project would be fulfilled.

After the heady days of 1899, 1900 had been a bad year. His only success had been with a pot-boiler, *There Are Crimes and Crimes*. The death of Harald Molander was to prove a particular misfortune for Strindberg, since it meant that several of his more ambitious plays were to be inadequately staged, or not staged at all, until he founded his own theatre in 1907. 1901 was to be even worse. Although he was to have four Swedish premieres during the first four months of the new year, only one succeeded; the brilliant *Virgin Bride* was to be rejected, and he was to write four very modest plays. Towards the end of the year he was to write one of his finest, but that too was to be steadily rejected. Worst, his private life was to enter a period of chaos. The peace, or comparative peace, that he had found since his emergence from Inferno was to be shattered.

Although Strindberg had met Harriet only four times, she obsessed him. "Swedenborg haunts me," he noted in his diary on 2 January 1901. "But [Bosse] too. The smell of *Celery* has plagued me for several months; everything tastes and smells of *Celery*. When I take off my shirt at night it smells of *Celery*. What is this? My [chastity], my celibacy? . . . 13 Jan. [B] who read *Creditors* and *Simoom* on the 12th haunted me on the 12th. On the 13th this became more intense, and in the night she persecuted me. (First telepathic intercourse with [B].) I 'possessed' her when she appeared telepathically during the night. Incubus.* All this is repulsive to me, and I [prayed to God to deliver me from this passion] . . . 16 January. Possessed her!"

Professionally, the year started well enough. On 5 January he completed *The Virgin Bride*, a powerful drama, set in the countryside of Dalecarlia, about a peasant girl who gives her illegitimate baby to the old midwife to kill and bury, so that she may appear at her wedding wearing a virgin's crown. On 15 January *The Father* was staged in Nuremberg; *Dagens Nyheter* reported that "excellently acted, it achieved a great success, even if the third act proved too strong for the fragile nerves of some spectators." According to *Aftonbladet* (5 January), *The Father* was also to have been performed in Kiel that month, but was banned by the police. *There Are Crimes and Crimes* was produced in Turku, Finland, and on 25 January *The Saga of the Folkungs* had its belated premiere at the Swedish Theatre and was warmly received. Strindberg attended the dress rehearsals on the twenty-third and twenty-fourth, when he "saw G af G in the royal box staring at me with his owl eyes; one moustache was drooping and he had something black on his forehead. Of course it was not he, but for several minutes the illusion persisted." Harald Molander's place as director had been taken by Karl Hedberg, whose brother Tor wrote an enthusiastic review in *Svenska Dagbladet*, declaring this "the finest of all Strindberg's plays." Pehr Staaff in *Dagens Nyheter* said that Strindberg had written the play with the same "fiery inspiration and energy" as "the twenty [*sic*]- year-old who wrote *Master Olof* in the Stockholm archipelago," and that the final curtain was greeted with loud applause. *Vårt Land*, *Social-Demokraten* and *Stockholms-Tidningen* also deemed the evening a success. *Aftonbladet* and *Stockholms Dagblad* both found the play rather dull, and several critics had reservations about the performance; Anders de Wahl, a powerful and narcissistic actor, can

---

*An evil spirit supposed to descend on sleeping persons. Strindberg's original diary entry for 16 January and all but the first two sentences of that for 13 January are heavily and impenetrably deleted, and the entries quoted above are written in at the side, perhaps at a later date.

hardly have been good casting for the sensitive King Magnus. But in general the play was acclaimed as *Gustav Vasa* and *Erik the Fourteenth* had been.

The next night Strindberg "dreamed of [B]; she was acting on the stage. Then I saw her dressed as a boy, sitting hunched up, and I was surprised she was so small . . . Possessed her! x x x/x." He was to use these crosses frequently in his diary henceforth in this context, evidently as an indication of how many times he had "possessed" her. He began a new play, a third part of *To Damascus*, an uneven piece which concludes with the Stranger entering a monastery.

On 8 February, Harriet visited him to discuss *Easter*. "[I was ashamed . . . she was earnest, beautiful] and said '[God bless you] who wrote so beautifully in *Easter*.' I felt like an old Faust mourning his lost youth . . . She smiles with a mouth like that of an eight-year-old child." That evening he sent her *The Virgin Bride*, which no theatre would touch, explaining: "It is an attempt by me to enter Maeterlinck's wonderful world of beauty, forgetting analyses, questions and viewpoints and seeking only painting in beauty and mood.* I know I have only stopped in the gateway; I must burn the rubbish in my soul before I am worthy to enter." His diary continues:

> 11 February. In the evening a green ray of light from the lamp fell on my breast and followed me wherever I went. Will the light now come at last? Since [B's visit] I have entered a new phase of my life. I long for beauty, purity and harmony. Act 2 of *Damascus III* is influenced by [B] . . . Harriet and I have from time to time lived telepathically and "enjoyed" each other's presence from a distance, since she initiated me into the secret . . .
>
> 12 February. My telepathic relationship with [B] has intensified alarmingly. I live only with her in my thoughts. [Pray God to resolve this] which threatens catastrophe . . . What I am going through now is horrible and wonderful—I sit as though awaiting a death sentence. I sometimes think [she loves me] sometimes not. God's will be done! So far there have been as

*Strindberg was much excited by Maeterlinck at this time, for the same reason that *Séraphita*, *Zanoni* and Kipling had excited him. "How says Maeterlinck, 1896, *Le réveil de l'âme?*" he wrote to Richard Bergh on 31 January. " 'A time will come . . . when our souls shall see each other without the intervention of the senses.' " He translated part of Maeterlinck's collection of essays, *The Treasure of the Humble*, and asked Bergh: "Can you try to got hold of Maeterlinck's plays here in Stockholm? . . . I want to translate one and get it staged. Maeterlinck is not 'finished' as G[eijerstam] claimed when he wanted to block my new theatre." The previous autumn Strindberg had sent a copy of *To Damascus* in German to his doctor friend Gustaf Brand in Belgium asking him to forward it to Maeterlinck, but had received no answer. On 9 February he asked Brand to ask Maeterlinck if he, Strindberg, might "translate, publish and stage Maeterlinck in Sweden," but this too came to nothing.

many signs for as against. On her last visit I thought an angel was in the room, and I decided the sign was good, hoping for reconciliation with woman, through woman. For three days now I have had her in my room and have felt an uplifting, ennobling influence—which a demon surely cannot bring. If the High Powers are jesting with me I am ready to bear that too! . . . Shall love, the great and sublime, come again?

14th. All my thoughts centre on [B], but as if she were coming, good, loving, to give me back my faith in the good in woman and in mankind. [B] is like (1) my second wife (whom she played in *Damascus*) (2) my sister Anna (3) my mother (4) Mlle. Lecain the beautiful Englishwoman* who wanted to snare me in Paris; and who was like all of them; she often made a warm and motherly impression, so that at Mme. Charlotte's I often wished myself under her warm beautiful woollen cloak as in a mother's womb. But she was a demon said Goguin [*sic*] and she tempted men—and women. (5) She smiles like my son Hans when he was four years old, angelically . . . Is it an illusion? Demons can disguise themselves as angels . . . *She came!* Simple, gentle, good, not so dazzling . . . as the last time . . . At 4 o'clock I was overcome by an attack of weeping—wept in general at my own misery and that of mankind, without reason, an obscure feeling of happiness, of pain at not having happiness, in foreknowledge of a coming disaster.

He sent her *The Dance of Death* and a portrait of himself. "Thank you for the photograph," she wrote to him. "You made me so happy by this. I have only read part of *The Dance of Death*. I cannot bear to read much at a time; it affects me so powerfully. May I keep it for a few days longer?"[17] On receiving this, on 16 February, he noted: "The strange smell of incense came today more intensely than usual. The idea occurred to me that it was [B]. I smelled her letter and it smelled of incense. It is she, then. But the smell has become repulsive. At first it was good, uplifting; then it smelled of madness and witchcraft. In the end it became repulsive and frightening."

On 18 February he wrote to Richard Bergh: "As a result of my isolating myself from contact with the banalities of life, my sensitivity has become so magnified that soon I shall not even be able to endure people looking at me. I await a change in my destiny—a great crisis—a total break with the past. Perhaps the end of the road which now seems to me so dreamlike." That day Harriet visited him "kind, friendly, shy . . . When she went it became black again. She had a fur round her neck with two small claws, black, sharp . . . Night calm till 4. Said my morning prayers. x x x Possessed her. Who will deliver me from this sinful flesh?"

He temporarily abandoned Part III of *To Damascus* and started work on

---

*Strindberg met her at Mme. Charlotte's *crémerie* in the spring of 1895, and mentions her in Chapter 3 of *Inferno*. She has never been identified.

a new play, *Swanwhite*, a curious fairy tale about a princess who loves and
is loved by a young prince and, when he drowns, recalls him to life by the
purity of her love. It was influenced by Maeterlinck's early play *The
Princess Maleine*, which he had read earlier that month and which tells
how a wicked stepmother breaks up a love affair between a prince and a
princess so that the prince may marry the stepmother's daughter. In an
essay written in 1894, Strindberg had expressed his admiration of Maeterlinck's early plays with their naïve charm, as opposed to the archness of his
more recent work; *Swanwhite* was also influenced by Kipling's story "The
Brushwood Boy," in which two characters meet only in their dreams.
Strindberg wrote excitedly about this to Nils Andersson on 22 February;
the Swedish title of the story was "In the Land of Dreams," and it is in
such a country that Strindberg's prince and princess wander hand in hand.

   He sent Harriet *Easter*, asking her to play Eleonora. "Of course I
wanted to, but I was frightened of the demands it would make. I was well
aware that I had been unequal to the Lady in *To Damascus* and had only
half succeeded . . . and Eleonora in *Easter* was far more difficult."[18] He
"woke in the morning determined to free myself from [B]. Thought of her
hard, proud letter of yesterday; thought of the consequences of abandoning my power and my property, my freedom and my honour to a hard,
calculating woman from a hostile nation."[19] This mood, however, did
not last long. Next day, 27 February, he wrote to her: "It is improper that I
should invite you to visit me, and I dare not. But if I tell you that the
troublesome table is indeed laid at 2 but is cleared at 2.30, that leaves you
free to honour me with a visit as before. If this information too is
impertinent, then forgive me." That afternoon "she came around 3 p.m.;
dressed in black; vital, lovable, good. We talked intimately! intimately!"
Next day he "awoke with the feeling that my fate was now decided . . . So
strange; I feel I am as it were engaged and have today ordered furniture for
'my wife's' room from Bodafors's catalogue. I have bought new clothes
as though I were awaiting visits of congratulation. Suppose it is, and
remains, nothing but a fantasy? . . . This evening I felt as though all
contact with her was broken and it was all finished."

   On 2 March, "She came, beautiful, childlike, gentle, wise. But
immediately a banging started on all the walls . . . She had *To Damascus*
III with her and to my (as I thought) decisive question 'Should I let the
Stranger end in the monastery?' she replied: 'No, he has more to achieve
in life.' The hint was that I should burn my boats and ask her—but the
question remained unasked and she was gone." She wrote him a letter,
doubting her strength and fearing she would disappoint him but ending
with a clear acceptance of his as yet unstated offer: "I can well imagine the

little woman's joy if, despite her doubts, the Stranger quietly took her hand in his and led her towards the goal. And forgot the monastery."[20]*

On 5 March she visited him again. "He told me how harshly life had treated him, how he longed for a ray of light, a woman who could reconcile him with mankind and with woman. Then he placed his hands on my shoulders, looked deeply and intensely into my eyes and asked, 'Will you have a little child with me, Fröken Bosse?' I curtseyed and replied, quite hypnotised, 'Yes, thank you,' and so we were engaged."[21]

Harriet's forebodings about the marriage remained. "After the engagement with Strindberg I began to reflect on what I had done. I felt a great responsibility. How could I give this man anything worth while—wretched little me, how could I reconcile him with mankind and with woman? I was scared of the forthcoming marriage, and could not bring myself to tell him what I thought . . . As a fiancé, Strindberg was a great gallant—sent flowers, presents, thought of everything that could make me happy. He even forced himself to dine with me at the Hotel Rydberg—he hated to appear in public—but that dinner ended badly, for an unfortunate officer who sat at the next table gave me a few glances! I was beginning to become known as an actress. But he should not have, for the whiskers on Strindberg's upper lip began to rise, and with a hiss in the officer's direction he said to me, 'Let's go, I can't stand this.' That was our first and last [public] visit to a restaurant. We went to Bellmansro and Djurgårdsbrunn [two fashionable restaurants] but always in private rooms. He liked to ride in a carriage—sometimes all went well, but alas, how many times was the carriage ordered, I looking forward to it and ready to get in, when: 'No, I can't—we'll go back upstairs' came from his tight-bitten lips."[22]

Strindberg's new-found happiness seemed to blur his interest in his children by his previous marriages. On 11 March he wrote affectionately enough to Kerstin: "Do you think I can forget you, who led me through Inferno as my Beatrice . . .? Ah no! Such I am not and never will be!" but apart from a postcard the following month, this was to be his last communication to her for six and a half years; nor did he continue his hitherto regular correspondence with her grandmother. The same day he wrote an unpleasant, short letter to Greta, who had asked him for money: "Your attempts to blackmail me for cash by besmirching my name to the Finnish Women's League and my ex-relatives in Vienna show that you have lost all sense of decency." (The accusation was, of course, un-

---

*Her letter is dated 4 March; his diary entry, written in the margin of 2 March but evidently added later, states that she did not give him the letter until 25 April.

founded.) Furnishing his new bridal home, a five-room apartment in a new block round the corner, on Karlavägen, and acting the gallant to Harriet left him little money for anything else.

Easter received its premiere in Frankfurt-am-Main and proved a fiasco; it was withdrawn after a couple of performances, though this seemed not to trouble Strindberg, who wrote to Schering on 14 March that it "served me right, since it was a discourtesy to my country to let the premiere take place abroad"—the only occasion on record of his feeling that he ought to be courteous to Sweden. *Easter* stood for the past. "I am now writing my *Swanwhite* for Dramaten," he informed Emil Grandinson, the director there, on 23 March, "an idealistic play of pure beauty, the apotheosis of love." He finished it before the end of the month, but Dramaten rejected it, and it had to wait seven years for its premiere in Finland, with special music by Sibelius.

Love brought out the worst in Strindberg as a letter-writer, and he addressed several long and lamentable epistles to Harriet ("I embrace you, kiss your eyes and thank God for sending you, little dove with the olive branch, no more birches. The river of sin has passed, the old life is drowned, and the earth shall be green again"). [23] He sent her a terrible poem comparing her to a dove and himself to an eagle. On 1 April he broke his rule of never attending a public performance at a theatre by taking her to *Lady Windermere's Fan* at the Swedish Theatre, but they left early. "It is our way of visiting our friends the actors," he explained to one of them, Tore Svennberg, on 2 April. "We don't bother about the plays." It did not apparently occur to him that the actors might be offended by his not staying until the end.

On 4 April, Maundy Thursday, *Easter* had its Swedish premiere at Dramaten, to a mixed critical reception. Tor Hedberg in *Svenska Dagbladet* found it "flat and sentimental"; *Aftonbladet* complained that "the many beautiful lines are mingled with strange observations which seem absurd." But *Stockholms Dagblad*, *Dagens Nyheter*, *Vårt Land* and *Social-Demokraten* were all favourable; Oscar Gullicson in *Vårt Land*, noting that the play reminded one "with great dramatic power" that God is all-merciful and will take on Himself the burden of our sins and griefs, remarked how far the writer of *To Damascus* had progressed on his journey. The production and acting were generally praised, especially Harriet's, and the first-night audience greeted the final curtain with sustained applause. Yet the play failed with the general public, managing only six performances that spring, plus two more in the autumn. On 17 April his "religious comedy" *Midsummer* was staged at the Swedish Theatre, and fared even worse, being removed after five performances.

Tor Hedberg in *Svenska Dagbladet* summed it up as "empty and meaningless"; Pehr Staaff in *Dagens Nyheter* was astonished that a writer of Strindberg's perception could think it worth while to "preach this Sunday school sermon"; and *Vårt Land* wondered if "the celebrated author has now become puerile or senile."

Strindberg now quarrelled, as never before, with the children of his first marriage. Greta wrote to him, as Karin had earlier, that the money they had received lately from him—700 marks in December and 500 marks in February—was too little for them to live on, and that they needed at least 400 marks (280 crowns) a month. "I too have a right to live!" he replied on 25 April, "and more than people who deserve to die in the gutter there! And perhaps should end there! and end there! If you can beg, you can work, and get paid for your work, which I have not always been, and then you will know that there are workhouses and poorhouses, which some people seem not to know!" Karin comments: "None of us ever understood the reason for the sudden hatred which now trembled undisguisedly in his letters. He clearly thought we had been ungrateful, but we never managed to get any proper explanation from him of his grounds for these accusations . . . Our greatest grief was at being robbed of the warm image of the father we had come to love . . . He was suddenly transformed into this insane enemy . . . In my first passionate reaction I even wanted to change my name." She replied temperately that "our circumstances have been difficult in the extreme. Kind people have, however, helped us sufficiently for us to be able to have a roof over our heads, and our debts have also mostly been paid so as to give us a little breathing-space." In response to his assertion that their mother had brought them up badly, she enclosed a note from the school testifying that they were not so regarded. Strindberg returned this letter torn in pieces, and there was no further correspondence between him and the children for nearly two years. [24]

Strindberg's fortunes were, then, at a low ebb when, on 6 May 1901, aged fifty-two, he married Harriet Bosse, not yet twenty-three. Karl Otto Bonnier's son Tor recalled seventy years later, at the age of ninety, how Strindberg gave him 5 crowns and said, "We are marrying on Sunday and after the wedding we shall drive in an open carriage around Djurgården. Buy some bunches of violets, bring some friends to Djurgården and, when we pass, throw the violets into the carriage." [25] So the incongruous couple rode forth in style to inaugurate what was, even by Strindberg's standards, to prove an exceptionally disastrous union.

Chapter Twenty-Six

CRABBED AGE AND YOUTH

Strindberg's diary tells the story of that wedding night:

> 6 May. Married for the 3rd time. Our homecoming, the room full of flowers, and the whole apartment illuminated, was like a fairy tale. [Night. Harriet] has rupture (of the uterus). I wanted to comfort her by pretending it did not matter to me because I loved her. Then she became angry and wanted to blame me. I possessed her twice however. *

Three years later, on 2 June 1904, he wrote in his diary:

> On our first night H—t had a *prolapsus uteri.* I had heard before that she had uterine problems; I was sorry for her and wanted her and tried to comfort her, but then she became angry. Nevertheless I possessed her twice that night, though with distaste. Next day she pleaded menstruation. After some days we came together again, but I now thought I detected a preventative in her and became angry. I was badly torn and had to bandage myself; thought of going to a doctor but did not. She blamed me repeatedly that she had had no pleasure. I understood nothing, but possessed her twice each day, though without the expected pleasure. Often at the climax her uterus fell and pushed me out. It felt as though a hand from within slowly drove me back. In the end everything became all right and she was declared pregnant.

*These last lines, from "has rupture," are crossed out but legible.

Perhaps there must be strife! But how unlovely! (On the first night Harriet was so like my second wife that I became afraid.)*

Yet the diary for May 1901 continues:

7th. Harmony.
8th. She says I am the husband she wanted—in every respect! And I am certain she was destined for me. I call her my first "wife."
We walk around the apartment and wonder if it is true, if we may stay here or not. We do not think it "belongs" to us. This home was purchased with my *Collected Plays*, 30 years of toil . . .
An inexplicable longing seizes me to run away and lease an attic. I tell my wife this. She understands! . . .
The threads begin to wear. Harriet wants to go to a masked ball. I buy trunks and threaten to leave.

Harriet, thirty years later, recalled those first weeks:

Strindberg would not allow me to bring anything to the home he had furnished for me . . . Strindberg had not what one would call good taste concerning furniture. He had no eye for, or rather did not bother about, fashion. I neither dared nor wished to criticise his taste in surrounding himself with sofas from the eighteen-eighties, aspidistras on pedestals and dining-room furniture in terrible imitation German renaissance style, etc. He had done my little room in mahogany—imitation Empire. He had a green carpet laid down on the floor—he said it looked like a fresh field. Then he had bought a fire-red cover for the chaise-longue—but that was soon removed, as he thought it seemed disturbing. Nothing that might lead one's thoughts to anything earthly and sensual was permitted. It was Strindberg's religious period; he was done with the world and striving towards "the other side."
And in this home I now sat and tried to make myself at home. But I was by no means done with the world. I had just begun to catch a glimpse into it, and how many times did I not sit and look at the sun shining over Gärdet but never entering our northward-looking room. Then I wept and drew down the blind to avoid seeing how beautiful it was outside.[1]

---

*A note evidently added later to this paragraph in the diary reads: "Now on 5 August 1904 Harriet says that she has no [clitoris]. This after reading a book about sexual intercourse which she didn't know of before. But: 26 August this year, the day Harriet went to Finland, she slept at my apartment in the afternoon: her 'well' was closed as on our wedding night, that is to say [the rest of the sentence is so heavily deleted as to be illegible]." In an entry for 12 May 1908, Strindberg wrote: "She suffered from both *prolapsus uteri* and *inversio vagina* [slipping of the uterus and an inversion of the vagina]."

She adds: "Strindberg made me promise never to read A *Madman's Defence*, or to act *Miss Julie*, and I kept that promise."[2]

Strindberg's diary contains no entries between 8 and 29 May. Then:

30th. Explanations. [Sleeping apart.]
31st. [Reconciliation.]

A few days later he pasted into his diary a notice inserted by Przybyszewski in a Norwegian newspaper announcing Dagny Juel's death "by an accident," noting: "She was shot by a lover with whom she had run away to the Caucasus." This tragedy occurred in Tiflis; the lover had then killed himself.

Strindberg bought Harriet a grand piano, to replace the one he had hired. He would fantasise about what he believed to be Harriet's possible Asian ancestry. "'You are from Java,' he used to say to me."[3] He was working on a new play about the young eighteenth-century warrior king Charles XII, who, after a series of brilliant victories in northern Europe, leading his cavalry bare-headed into impossible situations from which he always emerged unscathed, attempted unsuccessfully to conquer Russia and was finally shot, probably by one of his own men, while besieging a fortress in Norway at the age of thirty-six.

On 22 June, Harriet went to celebrate midsummer at her sister's in the skerries. Next day Strindberg finished *Charles the Twelfth*. It may have been now (though it could have been earlier) that he began to draft a new play with a modern setting entitled *The Corridor Drama*, about a composer waiting in a theatre for his fiancée, who does not come. The summer passes, his bouquet of roses withers, and at last he hears that she has gone away; he dies, and the stage-door keeper scatters roses over him.

25 June. Harriet home . . . We are now convinced that our union will last for ever, for we are living in complete harmony. I am telegraphing to Kymmendö to lease a summer cottage. If none is available we shall go abroad. Harriet overjoyed to be at home in her "yellow room."

The reply came that the cottage was already let. Harriet takes up the story:

Strindberg came and told me—to my delight—that we were to travel to Germany and Switzerland. Plans were made, tickets ordered, trunks packed, and my anticipation cannot be described. The morning we were to depart—we were about to leave with our baggage—he groaned: "We must not go. The Powers do not wish it." I had to arrange for the tickets and the hotel rooms to be cancelled . . .

To cheer me up, Strindberg set the table with fruit and Rhenish wine, placed our chairs so that we looked over Gärdet and the sunshine, told me how much more beautiful it was to see the sun shine than to have it right in one's face, how much better it was to have people at a distance than to be in the midst of them, and then he gave me Baedeker so that I might read about a journey—thus one avoided all the troublesome realities of travel. But I, who loved both sun and people and travel . . . became impatient and nervous when, as a substitute for my summer journey, he gave me books to read in German, French and English. On top of everything, I would have to grind at foreign languages! Then I said through my tears that if he wasn't willing to come with me, I would go alone to Hornbaek in Denmark. And I did.[4]

He wrote her two melodramatic and self-pitying letters ("I am tormented by the thought of all the suffering I have unwillingly caused you; but at the height of my reproach I cry: 'But I could not act otherwise! I could not!' ").[5] He abandoned *The Corridor Drama*, the plot of which must have seemed uncomfortably close to his own situation, and on 2 July joined Harriet in Hornbaek, where they spent four weeks together. On 14 July a journalist from *Svenska Dagbladet* interviewed him. "His body is broader but as supple as of old . . . The chalk-white moustaches rise from his nervous lips like butterfly wings . . . [He said] 'I have become calm, I want to leave people in peace and I want them to leave me in peace . . .' Fru Strindberg is beautiful and bubbles with vitality and intelligence . . . Strangers might take her for a Greek . . . This wise and attractive lady will probably bring Strindberg closer to the theatre and so prolong the armistice between him and society." Strindberg's "calmness" expressed itself in a reconciliatory letter to Bengt Lidforss who, after their previous reconciliation in Lund in 1896 following two years of bitter hostility, had not unreasonably taken offence at some references to him in *Legends*. "When we meet again," Strindberg now wrote to him, "I beg you to regard me again as your friend."[6]

His peace was disturbed by a photographer who took a snapshot of Harriet bathing. Strindberg hit him on the head with his stick, which provoked a discussion in *Politiken* about the morality of taking photographs of people on the beach. On 1 August they left Hornbaek for Berlin. Harriet tells: "I was not allowed to stay in Berlin, but was taken to a boardinghouse in Grünewald—Strindberg's translator, Schering, lived in the neighbourhood. I was not at all happy there."[7] "Terrible day," Strindberg noted in his diary, "after scene with Harriet. She wanted to go to a whores' café, but I would not." Harriet fell ill. "The iller I became, the more Strindberg's eyes gleamed. Then he told me that I was probably pregnant . . . Strindberg regarded home, wife and children as the greatest happiness that life could offer."[8]

After only six days in Germany, they returned to Stockholm, where on 9 August Harriet's pregnancy was confirmed. Strindberg began a new play about Engelbrekt, the leader of a fifteenth-century peasant rebellion. What happened in the next two weeks we do not know. His diary tells only that on 20 August she told him that the child was to bear the surname Bosse, and that two days later she left him, sending a letter from her sister's to inform him that she had "gone for ever."

> 23 August. Alone. Sad. Wept much. Thought life a cruel joke . . . Life is a humbug.
> 25 August. . . . Read my diary and all my letters to Harriet. Everything that was great and beautiful rose before me: I blessed her memory and thanked her who had brought light and joy into my life (?)*

On 27 August he sent her a letter by hand begging her to return: ". . . you can shut your doors; open them and call to me when you wish; you need not explain yourself; and I shall be as little disagreeable as is possible for me." She replied the same day:

> Can you not understand why I left? To save at any rate the last remnant of feminine decency and self-respect.
> The words you spoke to me that day in Berlin which I can never forget have been forever ringing in my ears, the accusations you cast at me have so besmirched me that the warmest words from you could never wash them away or erase their memory.
> This sense of offended decency came over me so powerfully the other day that I felt I would be the most contemptible of women were I to remain with you after what has happened.
> I only blamed myself for being cowardly, *cowardly* in not leaving you in Berlin—my excuse is that I was sick.
> And were I to return to you now, you would naturally despise me even more, and next time you got angry about this or that you would again —worse—deluge me with the kind of words that I do not understand how a man could use to the filthiest prostitute—let alone to his wife . . .
> I assure you I have not been happy these last days, for you are, in spite of everything, my little child's father, but rather than look forward to a hateful

---

*The query and brackets are Strindberg's. In her detailed commentary on the letters which Strindberg wrote to her (*Strindbergs brev till Harriet Bosse*, Stockholm, 1932), Harriet does not mention this separation, nor include any of the letters he wrote to her during this period. The eight letters which she wrote to him between 27 August and 23 September were published by Torsten Eklund in his article "Strindbergs tredje äktenskap i ny belysning," in *Meddelanden från Strindbergssällskapet*, April 1956, pp. 4–8. Strindberg's letters to her are in Vol. XIV of his *Collected Letters*.

future full of unjust insults and torment for us both, I am leaving while I still remember affectionately all the beautiful things you have given me . . .

Strindberg replied next day with the usual accusations. ". . . you began to drop hints that the child was not mine . . . The day after our wedding you declared that I was not a man. A week later you let the world know that you were not yet Fru Strindberg and that your sisters regarded you as 'unmarried'. . . Then you glorified adultery, threatened that you would take a lover, boasted that you could get one any time . . . That was how you were to restore my belief in woman—and in mankind." He followed this the next day, 29 August, with an even wilder letter:

> In this ghost story which is our marriage I have sometimes sensed a crime. Does it surprise you that I sometimes thought you were playing with me and that like Emerentia Polhem [Swedenborg's fiancée, who appears in Strindberg's play *Charles the Twelfth*], you had sworn that you would see me at your feet. I mentioned this suspicion to Palme after the inexplicable incident at the dress rehearsal of *To Damascus*.* As early as your first visit to me that February, I thought you were playing with me, but I believed that your feelings gradually changed and that you had become really fond of me. It is true that your eyes were evil and that I never received a kind look. But I loved you and always hoped that in the end you would reciprocate. When after we married I witnessed your spiritual degeneration; how your malignance broke out, how cynically you treated what to me was sacred, how you hated me; how melancholy and despair seized you; then I believed you were tormented by a guilty conscience, for that is how that finds expression . . . This—our marriage—is the most inexplicable thing I have ever experienced, the most beautiful and the ugliest. Sometimes only the beautiful appears—then I weep. I weep myself to sleep so as to forget the ugly . . .
>
> Granted that our relationship is soiled by hatred and mistrust, everything gets soiled in the autumn, but the new spring which the child will bring will annihilate and remove into the background our selfish love . . .
>
> What will happen now? I don't know, but I long for an ending, even the worst.

Strindberg's diary, 1 September: "Horrible to live alone."
Harriet to Strindberg, 3 September:

> . . . It is best for us both that I do not come back. To go on with you suspecting my every word, every action, will kill me. And you would be martyred and tormented by these illusions, so that words which I am sure you would later regret would again pass your lips. Is it not better that you continue your life's calling, to <u>write</u>, without me, quite alone? And that I continue on the path I have begun to tread which to me is life, the most

*See page 410.

important thing after the little child I shall bear? Our goal was to work together; I think we shall do so best at a distance . . . You have given me so much that is beautiful, Gusten! Thank you for it!

On receipt of this letter, Strindberg wrote in his diary: "Rooms being torn to pieces . . . A big rainbow. A hawk and a crow." He replied around 4 September:

Did I not suppress my dislikes to please you? You got a grand piano, though I hate grand pianos; you got yellow and green in your room, though I hate yellow and green; I bought Grieg, though I found him old-fashioned . . . I followed you to Denmark, the worst land I know; sat at the *table d'hôte* which is torture to me; I bathed on the beach, something which occurs in my most horrible dreams. You got your freedom to hold court at the *pension* and be attended by cavaliers whom you yourself called coarse, but I was not allowed to appear equally cavalier among women who had been "engaged" eighteen times. Finally—and this was the last straw—you wanted to force me to admire that ungrateful, faithless disciple von Heidenstam . . . A volcano of suppressed feelings built up in me and had to explode—it did so in Berlin . . . You speak of my illusions. I have never had any, other than those which you gave me.

Strindberg's diary, 6 September:

This, to me, so great and extraordinarily beautiful love story has dissolved into a mockery, which has completely convinced me that life is an illusion, and that the most beautiful relationships dissolve like bubbles of dirty dish-water in order to make us loathe life. We do not belong here and we are too good for this wretched existence. My soul loved this woman and the brutality of marriage revolted me. Anyway, I have never properly understood what great love for a beautiful female soul has to do with the inelegant act of procreation. The organ of love is the same as one of the excremental organs. Isn't that typical? (Hegel has said the same thing, I found out four years ago.) But I cannot live in a spiritual marriage with a woman who is not my faithful wife, for if she is free and enters into a relationship with another man, she surrenders up my soul and transmits my love to a man—and thus makes me live in a forbidden relationship with a man's soul or body or both.

E. von Hartmann says that love is a farce invented by nature to fool men and women into propagating their species.

Life revolts me and has always done so. Everything is worthless. I have fulfilled my obligations and been tormented enough. I think I have the right to go my way. This time I took life with a holy seriousness, and life treated me cynically.

So it has always been; when I was a credulous young idealist, I was mocked for it; when I became a materialist, I was persecuted for that.

Life was as intractable as a woman; whatever I did was wrong, and I was abused for it.

When I was immoral I was abused, and when I became moral I was abused even more. *

People are not born evil, but life makes them evil. So life cannot be an education, nor a chastisement (which improves) but only an evil.

On 8 September, Harriet wrote to him: "One thing you must know, that I <u>cannot</u> come home again, cannot come, cannot." But that evening he met her (at her request, according to his diary), at her sister Dagmar's. "She behaved like an actress, false, scheming, wanting to gain something. She was so changed that after ten minutes I rose and said, 'I do not know you. This is a stranger.' Then I left without saying goodbye."[9]

Emil Schering told him that a new young German director had started a variety theatre in Berlin called Schall und Rauch (Sound and Smoke), and hoped that Strindberg might attend the forthcoming production of *There Are Crimes and Crimes* there. Strindberg replied on 9 September: "Not to mince words; to assist a movement such as Rauch and Schall [*sic*] imitating Chat Noir† from the last century, *fin de siècle*, now in the new century to which I have fought my way with so much endeavour, that I do not wish to do, I may not!" Had he but known, this new enterprise was to prove most important to him, for the young director was Max Reinhardt, who was to stage a series of notable and influential productions of Strindberg's plays.

Despite his contempt for Harriet, as expressed both in his letters to her and in his behaviour at her sister's, Strindberg informed her on 10 September: "I am writing *Christina* for you." (He had finished *Engelbrekt* the previous week.) But historical plays were not the best medium for expressing his confused emotions; a few days later he told her: "I am writing *The Rising Castle*, big, beautiful, like a dream—It is of course about you—Agnes—who is to free the Prisoner from the castle."[10] This was *The Corridor Drama*, which he now reworked in the manner of *To Damascus*, mingling reality with fantasy and, as in the trilogy, cutting swiftly and often apparently irrelevantly from one scene to another.

Strindberg's diary, 16 September:

> The woman who has gone has taken with her the best and the finest of my soul. From afar I feel how she goes around and besmirches my soul, which during my Inferno years I washed pretty clean. I feel as though through her I entered into a forbidden relationship with men and with other women. This alarms me, as I have always had a horror of contacts with my own sex. To the degree that I have broken off friendships when the friendship from the

*A reference to the mockery that had been levelled against Strindberg's return to religion, as expressed in *Inferno* and the books that had followed.

†See page 308n.

other party became like cloying love. (I have never been able to explain these breaches to people.)

Harriet to Strindberg, 21 September:

My dear!
Thank you for the beautiful flowers, which fill the whole room with the most glorious perfume!
Who do you think can miss more deeply than I our hours at the table? The joy of being with you in your work?
Your
Harriet[11]

On 22 September she visited him, and the same evening wrote him a confused letter:

I must not sit with you anymore, because if we come together again you will see it as ugly. Oh, that is what I fear! . . . The next time either of us expresses an opinion or a wish, the bomb will explode again. I with my inflexible views and you with yours . . . Imagine how it would be for me to hear again how I drag you down, I who want nothing more than to see you high above all! . . . Sometimes a crazy longing comes over me to laugh, to be joyful, to embrace everything and everyone out of sheer joy. If I deny myself this, I shall wither and die. And it would only make you unhappy to hear such things. So what is best for us, my dear? If you dare take me back knowing what I have just told you, accepting how I feel about this and promising to understand me just as I will try to understand you, then I shall come.[12]

On 28 September he wrote her a long and tender letter: "I am with you in my soul day and night, there is no distance between us. Life has no interest for me except through you. You were to me not a mortal, but a vision . . . When I saw your regal beauty on the seashore I trembled at my presumption in having dared to desire you, and I felt a fear that the world—the whole world—envied me. It was too much for me . . . I was ashamed—and became afraid. How could I be so foolish as to believe you loved me? That was my hubris—and it was punished; with the most dreadful illusions . . . My last words are: you gave and you took, blessings on you, my soul's beloved, my first bride and my last." They do not seem to have met again until 4 October; his diary contains no entries for that period. Then: "4 October. Out to Djurgårdsbrunn [restaurant] and dined with Harriet. Then home. x x x Then she went, promising to move in with me tomorrow." Next day she returned to him, four months pregnant. "Harriet came back! Light! P.b.t.g.! [Praise be to God!]"

Strindberg's diary contains few notes about Harriet during the months that followed, and such as they are, they suggest that the old pattern of happiness alternating with misery continued: "6 October. Peace! At the Opera. Heard *Aida* . . . 10 October. Peace! and light! But mixed with a certain uneasiness that it will not last. 11 October. Darkness!" He had finished *Christina*, a disappointing play which all the theatres rejected; it was not performed until 1908, at his own Intimate Theatre, though subsequently it has been staged fairly often in Scandinavia and Germany, because the title role offers opportunities for the kind of showy acting that attracts a certain kind of actress. He was now able to concentrate on *The Rising Castle*. Harriet remembered these days only with affection:

> The whole time I was expecting Anne-Marie, Strindberg was kind and considerate to me. Sometimes he could not avoid touching on the delicate question of women's rights. Strindberg's whiskers trembled, I wept—then he would go to a washstand he had in his room, wash his hands several times nervously and hastily—as he always did when he became upset about anything, and then the storm was over. One touching thing I remember especially from the time I was expecting Anne-Marie; I could not bear the smell of cigarette smoke, and as Strindberg smoked a lot I suffered from it. He noticed this and gave up smoking for several weeks, until I could endure it. He had a little cupboard in the hall into which he locked all his smoking things, and called it "the Poison Cupboard."
>
> Strindberg liked me to play the piano. He liked best Grieg's E minor sonata, Beethoven's sonatas, Schumann, Schubert and Peterson-Berger. He played little himself, but sometimes I heard him cautiously work his way through, among other things, Gounod's *Romeo and Juliet* and *Faust*, and some simple passages from some Beethoven sonata—his favourite composer.[13]

He encouraged her to model in clay, and painted energetically himself. Once, when she asked him what he was going to paint, he replied, "I don't know, I'll see what it becomes when I've finished." He urged her to read Balzac, Maeterlinck, Zola, Gorki, Emerson, Kipling and, surprisingly, Bjørnson. Ibsen he dismissed as "dry technique," and the champion of women.[14]

The Dance of Death was published in early October, to terrible reviews. Oscar Levertin, in *Svenska Dagbladet*, declared: "Never has Strindberg written a more unpleasant or, what is worse, a more boring play . . . One feels almost degraded merely by witnessing these scenes, this long monotonous quarrel . . . A coarse, slow and tedious clog-dance which cannot grip or interest us." *Aftonbladet* found it "infinitely depressing," and *Stockholms Dagblad* thought it "gives the impression of confusion and unreality." No theatre would touch it, in Sweden or abroad. *There Are Crimes and Crimes* received its Danish premiere at the Royal Theatre in Copenhagen, but was coolly received and was withdrawn after only six performances.

"You ask how things are with us," Strindberg wrote to Carl Larsson on 2 November. "Well, we have had sickness, and storms of course, ever since July, when a new little Bosse began to announce her entry into mortal life. Now for a month things have been joyously peaceful, and our hopes seem likely to be realised in March—a year? and what a year! since you surprised us at a table on Banérgatan. Life becomes ever more dreamlike and inexplicable to me—perhaps death really is the awakening."

On 18 November he finished *The Rising Castle*, renaming it, within a few days, *A Dream Play*. He had reduced his original theme, of the man waiting vainly at the theatre for his fiancée who never comes, to a sub-plot; his chief character now was Indra's Daughter, the child of a god who is sent by her father to live among mortals. She meets and marries a poor-man's lawyer, who spends his life vainly trying to right the wrongs of humanity; so she endures the agonies of human existence until, at last, she puts off mortal flesh and returns to her father. The play is over-long and needs cutting even more than most of Strindberg's works, by not far short of half its length; thus abridged, it makes a brilliantly exciting and disturbing ninety minutes in the theatre. It is bolder in its technique even than *To Damascus*; within a few years, Strindberg was to follow it with an equally bold and successful experiment in *The Ghost Sonata*. In a short preface to *A Dream Play*, he explained his intention:

> In this dream play, the author has, as in his former dream play, *To Damascus*, attempted to imitate the inconsequent yet transparently logical shape of a dream. Everything can happen, everything is possible and probable. Time and place do not exist; on an insignificant basis of reality, the imagination spins, weaving new patterns; a mixture of memories, experiences, free fancies, incongruities and improvisations. The characters split, double, multiply, evaporate, condense, disperse, assemble. But one consciousness rules over them all, that of the dreamer; for him there are no secrets, no illogicalities, no scruples, no laws. He neither acquits nor condemns, but merely relates; and, just as a dream is more often painful than happy, so an undertone of melancholy and of pity for all mortal beings accompanies this flickering tale.

His diary for 18 November, the day he finished *A Dream Play*, contains a revealing entry:

Am reading about the teachings of Indian religions. The whole world is but an illusion (= Humbug or relative meaninglessness). The divine Primary Force (Maham-Atna, Tad, Aum, Brahma) let itself be seduced by Maya or the impulse of procreation. In this the Divine Primary Element sinned against itself. (Love is sin; that is why pangs of love are the greatest hell that exists.) Thus the world exists only through sin, if it exists at all, for it is only a dream picture (hence my Dream Play is a picture of life), a phantom the destruction of which is the mission of the ascetic. But this mission conflicts with the instinct of love, and the sum of it all is a ceaseless wavering between sensuality and the pangs of remorse. This seems to me the answer to the riddle of life . . . All day I read Buddhism.

On 3 December *Engelbrekt* received its premiere at the Swedish Theatre and failed calamitously; it was removed after only three performances. Hjalmar Branting in *Social-Demokraten*, ignorant that he himself was the model for one of the principal characters (an aggressive democrat with the, to English ears, unfortunate name of Puke), deplored "the darkness of religion that has enveloped a once so intrepid spirit," and another old admirer, Pehr Staaff, wondered in *Dagens Nyheter* whether Strindberg was not now writing too many historical plays. The fifth and final volume of the *Collected Novels and Stories* appeared from Gernandt; and on 8 December, Strindberg was performed for the first time in Russia, when the twenty-nine-year-old Lydia Yavorskaia staged *There Are Crimes and Crimes* at her own New Theatre in St. Petersburg. She sent Strindberg a telegram saying that it was an "immense success," though in fact the reviews were largely hostile. Another three years were to pass before Strindberg had his first theatrical success in that country.

The first Nobel Prize for Literature was awarded at the end of 1901, and there was widespread speculation as to whom the Swedish Academy would choose. There was no shortage of worthy candidates; general opinion favoured Tolstoy, Ibsen and Zola. In the event, the Academy chose the now forgotten French poet Sully-Prudhomme, thereby setting the pattern for an extraordinary sequence of choices and omissions. The list of those honoured includes numberless writers now scarcely read even in their own countries. The slight to Tolstoy caused particular offence, and forty-two Swedish writers and artists, including Strindberg, signed a letter of protest and apology which they sent to Tolstoy. It is typical of the attitude of the Swedish establishment towards Strindberg at this time that several conservative newspapers suggested that he had signed only out of pique at not having been honoured by the Academy himself.

"Calm but sombre," he wrote in his diary on New Year's Day, 1902. "We play chess, play the piano; Harriet sculpts, reads, walks. Few visitors. Axel sometimes plays Beethoven. Harriet . . . happy about the child."

He had not much else to be happy about; his fortunes had changed drastically in the two years since *Gustav Vasa, Erik the Fourteenth* and *There Are Crimes and Crimes* had filled the Stockholm theatres. He now had nine plays lying unperformed on his desk: *Gustav Adolf,* both parts of *The Dance of Death, The Virgin Bride, Swanwhite,* Parts II and III of *To Damascus, Christina* and *A Dream Play. Easter, Midsummer* and *Engelbrekt* had all failed disastrously within the past year, and on 4 January, *Easter* failed again, in Munich, and closed after a couple of performances. *Miss Julie* still remained unperformed in Sweden after fourteen years. "What shall I write, what say, about *Engelbrekt* and *Easter* and the rest?" he wrote to Schering on 18 January.

> Adversity turns me dumb, for I can't blame anyone, and I cannot change my fate. Sometimes one has the wind in one's sails, now I have an adverse wind and can only wait. The worst thing is that I begin to lose interest in work when I get no encouragement. Anyway, it seems to me that I have said all I have to say just now; especially in a new Dream Play which is not yet copied. I am probably about to experience a change in my destiny, in which direction I know not . . . Schiller's [unfinished play] *Demetrius* which you sent me confirms my old belief that one must not plan in detail, for then one loses the joy of conception, so that the urge to write vanishes . . . I signed the address to Tolstoy. Now our miserable Academy says I was "envious." Seeing an injustice done does not make one envious. It makes one indignant. But the Academy understands nothing about logic or language. Besides, I cannot envy what I despise; and I despise the Swedish Academy, that illiterate clique, so much that I would *never* accept anything from them if they offered it to me.

On 13 February, *Charles the Twelfth* was premiered at Dramaten and, not surprisingly, for it is a poor piece, got a bad press. Tor Hedberg in *Svenska Dagbladet* praised Strindberg's conception of Charles's character, but summed up the play as "incomplete, whimsical, a hurried piece of work with brilliant moments"; he complained that the last act declined into trivialities, that the final scene was "tame and meaningless" and that the supporting characters were perfunctorily sketched. *Stockholms Dagblad* found it inconsistent and historically untrue. It is difficult to disagree with any of these criticisms. *Dagens Nyheter* and *Aftonbladet* were kind but unenthusiastic. Thanks to its subject matter, the play drew good houses for a few nights, but lasted only fourteen performances. Undeterred, Strindberg began a new historical play, about the eighteenth-century monarch Gustav III, a fascinating character who, though an autocrat, found much to admire in the French Revolution, wrote plays, founded the Swedish Academy and the Royal Theatre, and was murdered by a revolutionary at a masked ball, as portrayed by Verdi in *Un Ballo in Maschera*. This was someone with whom Strindberg could identify, and the result was one of his best plays. He finished it on 16 March, but it joined the other nine rejected manuscripts in his desk; Nils Bonde, the censor of Dramaten, reported to his board that "it cannot be right to slander on this stage the great patron and progenitor of the Royal Theatre."[15]

The decline in Strindberg's fortunes as a dramatist had now reached its lowest ebb. Apart from a brief production of *The People of Hemsö* (that play he so despised) the following March, he was virtually to disappear from the stages of Sweden for five and a half years until the opening of his own theatre in November 1907. Only in Germany, and to a small extent in other countries such as Russia and Finland, were his plays to be performed during that period, and even then the censors were sometimes to intervene; a projected production of *Miss Julie* in Berlin was banned because, *Dagens Nyheter* reported on 18 March, "the action too closely resembled certain events which recently occurred in a noble German household." A slight comfort was that on 11 March *The Bond* was at last performed, ten years after Strindberg had written it; Max Reinhardt staged it, with *The Stronger*, at his new Kleines Theater in Berlin, finely cast with Emmanuel Reicher and Rosa Bertens. *Berliner Tageblatt* declared it "an artistic triumph." Reinhardt was to direct two more Strindberg plays within the year.

On 25 March, Harriet gave birth to a daughter. "One of my sisters, who was with me, had read that Strindberg had written that it was only pleasure for a woman to give birth to a child. When my pains were worst, she went and opened the doors to the apartment where Strindberg was walking up and down. She wanted him to hear that it was not undiluted pleasure. Strindberg shut the door to my room, my sister opened it again. And so it continued for a good while. Agonised as I was, I could not help laughing through my tears."[16]

They called the child Anne-Marie.

That spring of 1902, Strindberg made a new literary discovery. "Through your review of Gorki's first book," he wrote to Tor Hedberg on 10 April, "I have discovered this author, with whom I feel a sort of kinship . . . In my opinion, Gorki is just the sort of man who should receive the Nobel Prize; the right mixture of beginner and master—and needy too. And it would be interesting to see if money gave him a different view of life (which I doubt! however!)." The book was *Sketches and Stories*, which, after having been rejected by numerous commercial houses in Russia, had been published by two idealistic radicals, a fact which, had

Strindberg known it, would additionally have endeared Gorki to him. It is ironic that these two fiercely independent spirits should each have been ignorant of the other's admiration; and they were to remain so until their deaths.

Bjørnson, despite his long estrangement from Strindberg, now publicly added his name to the list of giants who admired him. In an interview in *Aftonbladet* on 24 April, he deplored the lack of sympathy with which Strindberg's plays had been received in Sweden, and while regretting Strindberg's "feverish overproduction," declared him to be the most powerful genius among modern Swedish writers—a view markedly in contrast to that of the Swedish Academy which not only cold-shouldered him for the Nobel Prize but, to the end of his life, refused to admit him to its own ranks.

"I have given up writing and am back to chemistry," Strindberg informed Schering on 11 April. On 5 May, Max Reinhardt staged another Strindberg play in Berlin, a curious choice: *The Outlaw*, that old Viking piece which Strindberg had written as a student at Uppsala in 1871, and which had not been performed anywhere since its brief appearance at the Royal Theatre the same year. It was not enthusiastically received in Berlin, and achieved only nine performances. Schering sent Strindberg Gerhart Hauptmann's historical drama *Florian Geijer*, and Strindberg's reply (13 May) throws light on his own credo: "The spirit is lacking. It is so meticulously calculated that one wishes it were less so. A work of art should be a little careless, imperfect like any natural growth, where not a crystal is perfect, not a plant lacks its defective leaf. As with Shakespeare . . . I sit idle and feel written out—as I did in 1892."

A Dream Play was published at the beginning of June, together with *The Virgin Bride* and *Swanwhite*. Surprisingly, considering how far it was ahead of its time, *A Dream Play* got quite good reviews. Georg Nordensvan in *Dagens Nyheter* thought it "one of the most daring plays that Strindberg has produced of late," and Tor Hedberg in *Svenska Dagbladet* found it "one of Strindberg's most original works," adding that this kind of play was Strindberg's true element, since he could surrender himself to every impulse and not, as in the history plays, have to confine himself within imposed limits. Carl David af Wirsén in *Vårt Land* declared both *A Dream Play* and *The Virgin Bride* to be immature and over-hastily written, like all of Strindberg's recent work; *A Dream Play*, in particular, he thought confused and pretentious, but he quite liked *Swanwhite* because it left a "harmonious impression" (usually a sign that Strindberg was writing below his best). Strindberg made no money from this volume; his account with Gernandts was overdrawn by 1,500 crowns as a result

of the loan he had borrowed from them against the publication of his
Collected Plays.[17]

With the coming of summer, Harriet longed to get out of Stockholm
into the countryside, "away from this sitting quietly in Karlavägen."[18]
On 3 July they had a row. "<u>Absolutely frightful!</u>" Strindberg noted in
his diary. "But all ended well. Harriet went to the country, perfectly
friendly." She took Anne-Marie to Rävsnäs, near Mariefred, on Lake
Mälaren. He wrote long and desolate letters to her; on 18 July she returned to him for three days. But:

> Our marriage had begun to come apart. I felt imprisoned and sat in a
> cage; he thought it natural that I should stay at home. He may have been
> right, but since I was an artist, I thought it part of my work to get out and see
> new faces. We both had strongly individual personalities and, young as I
> was, I had, unfortunately, my own opinions. We were oil and water . . .
> Strindberg was kind and tender, never spiteful and frightening as he
> sometimes appears in his books. It was only when he took a pen in his hand
> that a demon entered into him—and when he was inspired, that demon
> released his genius . . . It was our great difference in age that separated us.
> Strindberg had lived his life, was finished with many things which I had not
> even begun to experience.[19]

She tells how they went to a party which Strindberg evidently enjoyed,
saying so when they got home. "How amazed I was when I read several
years later in his [novel] *Black Banners* with what a hellish intent this
dinner had been arranged—everybody malignant and the whole occasion
a failure." Sometimes he could fly into an irrational rage. Soon after the
birth of Anne-Marie, Harriet made herself a white coat. "He darkened,
and asked if I had bought the coat to 'walk the streets in.'" On another
occasion the writer Ellen Key was announced. Strindberg went to the
door; Harriet heard angry voices, then the door slam. "He returned in a
fury and said, 'I threw her out.' When I fearfully asked the reason, he said
that she had asked if I would take part in a reading to celebrate Bjørnson's
seventieth birthday. He would not permit it—he was afraid people would
take me from him."[20]

Harriet described Strindberg's daily routine:

> His daily walks from 7 to 9 a.m. were, strictly speaking, the only time he
> took fresh air. He rose at 6:30, made his own coffee in a Russian machine,
> then walked to Djurgården. He told me that during these walks he planned
> his day's work . . . Strindberg did not like reading newspapers. As regards
> reviews of his plays, he would say, "If eleven German papers say I have had a
> triumph in Berlin and a twelfth is critical, you can be sure the twelfth will be
> quoted in the Swedish press." . . . On returning home, he sat down
> immediately at his desk, charged with ideas. While he wrote, he chain-

smoked Finnish cigarettes. As is known, he usually had the shape of what he was to write, and the dialogue, ready in his head, so that there are few alterations in his manuscripts . . . He would read in the afternoon, preparing his next day's work, but never wrote then. In the evening he would wander up and down the apartment, mostly around the dining-room, forward and back. So as to be able to walk springily and lightly, he wore white rubber shoes indoors . . . He walked through the rooms with Anne-Marie on his arm, her little head rocking back and forth on his shoulder . . . I may mention that he was very moderate in his drinking. Strindberg was no gourmet. He liked best good home cooking . . . I never saw any evidence of madness in Strindberg . . . Strindberg was so afraid of women's power over him that he would refuse to admit a visitor if he knew she was a beautiful woman . . . I think Strindberg was afraid of being unfaithful to me even in thought—and in order not to risk that, he preferred not to expose himself to possible temptations. He was prouder of his chemical "discoveries" than of being a great writer . . . Strindberg always took an interest in my work. He comforted me if I had got bad reviews, shone like the sun when I had succeeded . . . On my return from Rävsnäs in the summer of 1902 we agreed to try to live together for one more year. Everything seemed promising, I had a lot to do at the theatre . . . so that I had no time to sit and think how unhappy I was. [21]

That July, Strindberg tried to work off his feelings about Harriet in a play, *The Dutchman*. His main character, the eternal wanderer, returns as always after seven years at sea, in his perpetual and ill-fated attempt to find "reconciliation through woman." He trots out Strindberg's old ideas on the subject in a tedious opening dialogue with his mother, then meets an ugly failed artist, Ukko, who becomes his Sancho Panza. The Dutchman meets and marries a young girl painter, Lilith, but they prove incompatible and she leaves him, as Harriet had left Strindberg. At this point he abandoned the play; no great loss, one feels, though somehow the work interested Ingmar Bergman enough for him to direct it twice on radio.

On 26 July: "Harriet came. Ate dinner . . . and left again, uncertain if we should have more children." On 6 August she returned to live with him. Neither his diary nor Harriet's memoirs give any hint of how things were between them that summer and autumn. *Aftonbladet* announced that he was planning to settle in Paris to write two plays about the French Revolution and Napoleon; but both projects lapsed, and he did not go. He worked at *Fairhaven and Foulstrand*, a miscellany of poems plus three moderate prose pieces, including *The Monastery*, a short novel about his marriage to Frida, which he had begun back in 1898 and now retitled *The Quarantine Master's Second Story*. He completed the book early in September; "The best is the verse," he told Schering (16 September).

On 13 October, Sarah Bernhardt performed in Stockholm; Harriet went to see her but Strindberg (again) did not. The same evening, Max Reinhardt presented his third Strindberg production within a year in Berlin to be lionised or 'appear' like Bjørnson! True, I feel I owe it to the Strindberg's realistic plays), with Emmanuel Reicher and Gertrud Eysoldt. It was a triumph, Strindberg's first big success in Germany since *Creditors* in 1893. Schering wrote that the production was to visit Vienna in December and suggested that Strindberg might come and see it. Strindberg replied on 22 October: "Thank you for the good hopes you daily send me, and I hope they may in time be realised. If I go to Berlin it will be to study and get new thoughts, for here the sleep of winter rules the whole year and I have now used up all the material I brought back from abroad last time. But surely you have never supposed that I would go to Berlin to be lionised or 'appear' like Bjørnson! True, I feel I owe it to the actors to watch a performance, from an invisible position, on an evening when no one in the theatre knows I am there, and although it is a torture to me to see my shadows and hear my words, I shall do my duty. On the other hand, I enjoy socialising in small groups, in informal dress and without ceremony . . . Everything public I hate, quite pathologically." But he did not go.

On 22 October, *Simoom*, the fifteen-minute melodrama which he had written for Siri in 1889, was revived, as a curtain-raiser at Dramaten with Harriet as the Arab maiden who hypnotises a French officer to death (a role to which she was much better suited than Siri). Several critics found the play "over-disturbing," but Harriet's performance was widely praised. It is a trivial little piece, but was to be seen quite frequently in various countries during the next decade (it was among the first of his plays to be staged in both Britain and the United States). At the end of October, *Fairhaven and Foulstrand* was published, to generally good reviews. *Dagens Nyheter*, *Aftonbladet* and *Stockholms Dagblad* all liked it, and even Carl David af Wirsén in *Vårt Land* was relieved to find in it "a gentler religious standpoint than hitherto," though he regretted Strindberg's "coarseness and cynicism." Bo Bergman, whom I used to see walking in Stockholm as a nonagenarian in the 1960s, complained in *Ord och Bild* that Strindberg "no longer always bothers to create an illusion —either because he no longer bothers about his craft or his audience, or because even he has become tired; perhaps a little of both."

The marriage proceeded on its uneasy course. Strindberg's diary that autumn contains frequent references to the smell of incense: "This smell throws me into ecstasy and makes me happy as soon as I sense it, but a happiness mixed with terror. (Witchcraft and madness.)"[22] He continued to paste in cuttings relating to the Dreyfus case, still obsessively convinced of Dreyfus's guilt, and ended the year by quarrelling irretrievably with Gustaf af Geijerstam. Strindberg was sitting one evening at the Grand Hotel with Daniel Fallström when Geijerstam came in and asked to join them. Strindberg refused and began to berate him, whereupon Geijerstam left, saying, "Now you are driving away your best friend." It was the last time they met; soon Strindberg was to take an exceptionally unpleasant revenge for the offences that he imagined Geijerstam had committed against him.

Erik the Fourteenth was staged in Schwerin on 17 November, but failed so badly that it was withdrawn after two performances, and when Reinhardt's production of *There Are Crimes and Crimes* visited Vienna in December it was received much less enthusiastically than it had been in Berlin. So 1902 ended on a low note. Financially, it had been an even worse year for Strindberg than 1901. A windfall of 3,000 crowns from the Bonnier Literary Foundation that December helped to keep the wolf from the door.[23] Only Schering's efforts enabled him to remain in the big apartment on Karlavägen; on 12 February 1903 he told Schering: "I have been living off Germany since the autumn."

Chapter Twenty-Seven

"NO END, NO NEW
BEGINNING"

On 23 January 1903, the Schiller Theatre in Berlin presented, for some reason, Strindberg's early play *The Secret of the Guild*, the first and last production which that clumsy piece was to receive in Germany. The critics found it old-fashioned, as indeed it was; they had expected something more from the author of *The Father* and *Miss Julie*. In February, Strindberg suffered a fearful blow. His publisher, Ernst Gernandt, was forced to call in a liquidator, and in due course was declared bankrupt with debts of 223,000 crowns.[1] This meant, amid much else, the cancellation of Strindberg's cherished project of the *Collected Plays*. On 17 March another bad early play, *The People of Hemsö*, was revived in Stockholm and managed only eleven performances. Next day, his diary recorded: "Harriet is telephoning a lawyer about a divorce," and two days later: "Gave Harriet back my wedding ring." It was a bad winter and spring.

Strindberg now offered his *Collected Plays* to Karl Otto Bonnier, who rejected them. "I knew from experience," Bonnier explains in his memoirs, "how small an interest the book-buying public had in Strindberg's plays."[2] On 29 March, Strindberg had to ask Vilhelm Carlhem-Gyllensköld to lend him "200 crowns for a week." The same day he offered the plays to Hugo Geber, who accepted them. Strindberg asked a lump payment of 15,000 crowns, but Geber would pay no more than

10,000. "Why do you bargain thus," Strindberg asked on 9 April, "when you know the works are worth this sum and you should guess that I am poor?" He added that if Geber agreed to 15,000 crowns, he would let him have the *Collected Novels and Stories* "for a price you may name." Geber stood firm; Strindberg offered the plays to Isidor Bonnier, who likewise thought Strindberg's price too high, so he accepted Geber's terms.[3] Karl Otto Bonnier's fears were proved right; when the *Plays* began to appear towards the end of the year, only 500 subscribers had been found for the edition of 3,200 sets, which eventually had to be remaindered.[4]

That March, Strindberg began a new volume of autobiography, entitled *Alone*. It tells of his first months after his return to Stockholm in 1899 and is one of his best books, exuding a mellowness and calm which are astonishing considering the circumstances in which he wrote it. On 4 April his name appeared for the first time in Bernard Shaw's letters. "Try something that will carry your weight," Shaw wrote to the actress Janet Achurch, who had been a memorable Nora in *A Doll's House* and an acclaimed Rita in *Little Eyolf*. "Strindberg, who is a great man, is still unexploited in this country."[5] Again one is struck by the contrast between Strindberg's acceptance by his peers, of which he was mainly unaware, and his denigration by the literary establishment in Sweden.

Albert Engström, the writer and artist who had first met Strindberg at Furusund in 1899 and had seen a good deal of him in Stockholm during the past two years, heard of his troubles and invited him to stay at Grisslehamn in the skerries. Strindberg arrived on 29 April and remained five days. Engström was the kind of hard-drinking extrovert, like Gauguin, with whom Strindberg found it easiest to relax. Expecting to find him at his most melancholy, Engström was agreeably surprised. "He arrived full of fun, healthy, lively . . . Strindberg later told Tore Svennberg that we had talked without interruption for seventy hours and that I had tried to flatten him with whisky—'but Albert did not succeed!' he added triumphantly . . . We certainly continued until we both fell asleep in our armchairs." Engström adds that Strindberg remained in an excellent humour throughout his stay. He noticed how little Strindberg was drinking, only very weak whisky and sodas at half-hour intervals; he had evidently moderated his habits since his time in Lund, for Engström says that Strindberg "never drank to excess" while he knew him. He adds that Strindberg hated big restaurants, flattery and servility, and seldom passed a mirror without looking to see if his mane of hair was tidy. He would shake it vehemently but then always comb it. He became angry when Engström said he thought *The People of Hemsö* (the novel, not the play) his best book, and exploded against "rustic realism," in both himself

and others. "Caricatures in words and pictures were repellent to him."
Engström noted the extreme smallness of Strindberg's head. "I think I
have never seen a smaller head than Strindberg's . . . That of course was
why he wore his lion's mane. Had he cut his hair short he would have
looked ludicrous." When he swam and ducked his head, he looked like "a
small seal," and always spent a long time afterwards in his bathing-hut to
dry it out before reappearing. During his stay at Grisslehamn, Strindberg
gave another example of that sixth sense that often impressed observers.
He suddenly said, "Today I shall get a telephone message that my
daughter is ill," and he did.[6]

His good humour did not long survive his return to Stockholm. On 20
March he had written his first letter to the children in Finland in nearly
two years, apart from one brief note to Greta in December 1901. The
main reason was probably embarrassment at not being able to send them
money. Now, on 5 May, he wrote unpleasantly to Karin, ending: "I owe
you nothing . . . Look after yourselves, since you will have it so." On 28
May he noted in his diary that Harriet had awakened him at 1:30 a.m. and
"exploded into the most frightful curses because she believed I was having
a criminal relationship with our cook Ellen, which is quite groundless, I
swear. Poor Harriet, who tried to poison me with jealousy. Now that
demon possesses her." On 9 June she left with Anne-Marie to stay with
her sister Inez at Blidö, near Furusund. Strindberg joined them on 22
June, but on 6 July "left Blidö after a ghastly scene."[7] Although he and
Harriet were to go on seeing each other, and even sleeping together, this
was the effective end of their marriage.

He had finished *Alone* some time in June, and quickly wrote a volume
called *Fairy Tales*, rather slight stories with moments of interest. To add
to his troubles, on 13 July *Svenska Dagbladet* published an announcement by a publisher named P. E. Nilsson that he was about to issue in
instalments *A Madman's Defence*, of which he had made a pirated
translation from Strindberg's original French. Next day *Svenska Dagbladet* printed a protest by Strindberg warning "booksellers, commission
agents, printers and advertisers" not to become "conspirators in this
roguery." But five instalments appeared before publication could be
stopped. At the end of July a new production of *Miss Julie* opened in
Hamburg, the first licensed performance of the play in Germany, and was
well received. His diary reveals little about this period; on 1 August it
contains the single sentence: "Cleansed the apartment of all the small
things that belonged to Harriet."

He brooded over the idea of a play about Martin Luther. On 8 and
again on 11 August he noted in his diary: "The Luther play persecutes

me," and on 16 August: "The Luther play came again; although I fought it off." On 21 August he reluctantly began to write it, under the title of *The Nightingale of Wittenberg*. Harriet had by now returned to Stockholm and moved with Anne-Marie into a furnished apartment on Biblioteks-gatan, a few yards from where Strindberg had first lived with Siri after their marriage a quarter of a century earlier. On 25 August he wrote Harriet a confused letter:

> What do you want of me? You are free now, and have peace and happiness, which you lacked when you were with me. Have you not seen that I was the cause of your unrest? Accept the happiness which I denied you, but let me keep my grief unsoiled. Follow your destiny, which you think you can control, but do not touch my destiny, which another controls. The One you do not know!

"Horrible night!" he noted in his diary on 1 September, and the next day: "The first half of today was almost the worst I have experienced. Around 5 p.m. things got better." He completed *The Nightingale of Wittenberg*, a full-length play, in two weeks. "It is better than *Gustav Vasa!*" he assured Schering on 5 September. "It is written for Germany." Schering replied, praising the play but saying that the portrait of Luther was over-bold and would shock German opinion, and advising that it should not be performed before *Gustav Adolf*, which was due to be premiered in Berlin that December.[8] *The Nightingale of Wittenberg* opens intriguingly with Luther, as a schoolboy, being visited in his parents' home by a scholar who turns out to be Dr. Faustus, but the rest of the play hardly lives up to this, and the character of Luther himself does not really develop. Strindberg now conceived the ambitious plan of writing what he called a "world-historical drama" about key figures of history; the Luther play would form part of this, and he would precede it with plays about Moses, Socrates and Christ, linking them by the figure of the Wandering Jew. He completed all three within about six weeks by 5 November, entitling them *Exodus*, *Hellas* and *The Lamb and the Beasts*, the beasts being the emperors Caligula, Claudius and Nero. Even Strindberg never wrote worse plays than these three, and he evidently realised this, for he does not seem even to have offered them to a publisher. They were not printed until after his death, and have been performed only very rarely, as curiosities. Written in many short scenes, their characterisation is rudimentary and their dialogue archaic; they are neither good drama nor good history.

Seemingly unexhausted by all this, Strindberg began, before the end of November, a novel, *The Gothic Rooms*, about the characters of *The Red*

Room twenty-five years on. Pathetically, he pinned great hopes on *The Nightingale of Wittenberg*. "It is the strongest and most youthful play I have written," he assured Schering on 15 November. "No doubts like Master Olof, no scruples, no women around his neck, no parents in the way, no compromises with friends. And such is the historical, traditional, Luther!" On 22 November: "The Luther play is my favourite . . . There is beauty, strength, courage, and a faith like mountains. With Luther I have rediscovered myself and my calling." Extra comfort came from the success of *Erik the Fourteenth* in Christiania, with Anders de Wahl in his old role as the King. *Verdens Gang* commented: "It is good that our National Theatre has realised that there is a great Swedish writer named August Strindberg, even if we had to have a Swedish actor to open our eyes to this." And the first two volumes of his *Collected Plays* now appeared from Gebers, cheaply priced at 60 öre apiece.

Towards the end of November, *Alone* was published by Bonnier and *Fairy Tales* by Gebers. Both were well received, especially the trivial *Fairy Tales*, which sold out its first edition of 2,500 copies within a week. Even Oscar Levertin praised it, in *Svenska Dagbladet*: "How admirable are the imagination and range and energy of this genius!" Levertin wondered that, in *Alone*, Strindberg could portray himself as lonely and hated. "Does he not see how he has become a classic, how the air around him is filled with sympathy, how his public has grown, and ordinary men and women rejoice in his plays? . . . Does he not see that he is now, with Fröding, the most popular writer in Sweden? No, the reason for Strindberg's loneliness is his ruthlessness and hypersensitivity." Yet, Levertin concluded, whatever one's objections to *Alone*, it had "a marvellous immediacy and freshness . . . Admiration must have the last word. What a man!" Although Levertin remained blind to the qualities of Strindberg's darker works, such as *The Dance of Death*, he retained his general admiration for the idol of his youth who had likewise admired him. But to Strindberg he irrevocably remained one of the Great Enemies.

Strindberg was still seeing Harriet. "He often visited us," she writes, "and it became the custom that Anne-Marie and I dined at his apartment every Sunday. This meant an end to our daily quarrels—we met only on these happy, festive occasions. Sometimes of course Strindberg became bitterly conscious of his loneliness."[9] An undated entry in his diary at this time reads: "Now she and I are experiencing the best time we have had. Harmony in all respects!"[10] They even continued to be lovers. On 2 December he noted: "Harriet to dinner. Then in the yellow room. Fear of a child. In the evening went to Harriet and Anne-Marie. Harriet was extremely nervous and I was afraid. Returning home I 'saw' a child's face on a card with roses propped against the calendar. Thought: now there will be another child." Three days later, after she had come to dinner, he noted again: "Fear of a child." Whether the fear was his, or hers, or shared, he does not say.

Although he seems to have known how bad his plays about Moses, Socrates and Christ were, for his letters contain none of his usual expressions of confidence in their quality, the idea of a series of "world-historical" dramas about major figures still appealed to him. He told Schering that he was planning to write plays about Frederick the Great ("His life is an Odyssey and an Iliad"),[11] and Peter the Great; mercifully, however, he abandoned this idea and instead wrote bad short stories about them for his collection *Historical Miniatures*, which appeared in 1905. On 4 December, *Gustav Adolf* was premiered in Berlin and failed calamitously; a Swedish observer reported that by the time it ended around midnight, every second stall was empty.[12] The production was removed after only six performances. It seems to have been hardly, if at all, cut, and was apparently ill staged. Strindberg had another failure in Germany towards the end of the month, when *The Bond*, which had succeeded under Reinhardt's direction the previous year in Berlin, was badly done in Munich.

His improved relationship with Harriet, however, seems to have made up for these disappointments. Albert Engström tells of a meeting with Strindberg shortly before Christmas, when a mid-afternoon dinner which lasted "all evening" was followed by supper with a good *smörgåsbord*. "We drank punch and chatted about literature, he told school stories and played Beethoven in his special way, slowly, as it were sucking the notes from the piano. With his spectacles on his nose he looked like an old mahatma. We spelled words in Hebrew and drank whisky, he sang French songs to an old guitar and soon it began to grow light behind the curtains. Then we went into the kitchen, got out bread, butter, chicken and aquavit, and had a *vickning* [feast] by the woodbin, just as in our youth." Engström gives an endearing example of Strindberg's impracticality about money. He told Engström that he had just received 25 crowns for three poems, and when Engström remarked that that seemed inadequate, Strindberg replied that it was all that he had asked. " 'I have thirty crowns and am now a happy man.' "[13]

For the past three years Strindberg had, at irregular intervals, held what he called "Beethoven evenings,"* at which a few friends would gather to

---

*The earliest invitation to these evenings in Strindberg's letters is dated 2 January 1901 (*Brev*, XIV, p. 6).

hear his brother Axel play the piano. Strindberg's musical preferences were predictably eccentric. He hated Beethoven's Ninth Symphony: ". . . joy was never my thing, so I find his Ode to Joy banal, which Beethoven can be when he tries to be happy. No, I see him in the Appassionata and the last movement of the Moonlight. That is for me the greatest (and I hate Mozart!)."[14] He often expressed his antipathy to Mozart, asserting that apart from two unspecified movements, Mozart's Requiem was "piano for one finger, or children's flute of Saxon porcelain. Of the whole of *Don Giovanni* I like only Leporello's aria and the Commendatore's chords. Beethoven's scherzos are Mozartian pipings and Axel always has to skip them. Haydn his teacher was deeper and more artistic. Well! That's what I think!"[15] Wagner had also found Mozart frivolous; but Strindberg, though (again with typical eccentricity) he admired Wagner's archaic librettos, especially *Tristan*, hated his music. In *The Gothic Rooms* he attacked Wagner violently, declaring: "He has only written unmusical and ugly music; 'written' is the word, for it is neither heard nor composed; it is written,"[16] and in his next novel, *Black Banners*, he was to dismiss Wagner as one of the three worst humbugs of the age, the other two being Ibsen and Pasteur.[17]*

His relationship with Harriet continued on its erratic course. "Rupture again for the thousandth time," he noted on 23 January 1904; but on 1 February: "Reunited with Harriet. Fear of a child. Believe we shall have a child." On 9 February: "We talked about getting divorced. Crash! She went; probably for the last time." On 23 February he finished his novel *The Gothic Rooms*. On 16 and 20 March she slept with him again in the yellow room: "In mood and manner Harriet was as she was when we were engaged . . . She became like a fourteen-year-old girl." They made love again on 27 March, but two days later she suffered a nervous breakdown and spent the next two weeks in bed in a rest home at Saltsjöbaden. † On 9 April she wrote to him asking for a divorce. "We could not go on, living apart thus," she recalled. "Either we had to live together again, or divorce . . . Being wrenched backwards and forwards in my marriage together with overstrain in my theatre work made me break down completely."[18] Strindberg agreed, and on 18 April: "To the lawyer and signed the divorce petition. I experienced a great and solemn calm." Next day: "I went up to

---

*Strindberg's sister Anna tells that he also loved Grieg's Sonata in E flat, Mendelssohn's Caprice in B minor and, among operas, Nicolai's *Merry Wives* and Weber's *Oberon* (Philp and Hartzell, p. 100).

†Harriet (*Strindbergs brev till Harriet Bosse*, p. 86) says "over three weeks," but Strindberg's diary records that she returned to Stockholm on 12 April and visited her lawyer the following day.

Hasselbacken and looked at the verandah and the bird-cherry where I sat at my wedding breakfast in the sun when I married Harriet. I felt almost no emotion; only a calm contentment at being free, and I did not regret what had happened; rather saw it as bright, almost beautiful, although it has been so ugly. NB! Three years ago today I published the banns." Yet that same day he wrote to her: "I long for you, but I fear a meeting, especially now with new matter for explosion; I know there must be conflict—for I am so distant from your theatre world, your Norway, your feminism—and I cannot keep silent longer, I must not! And above all, no shared home! No, it cannot be! And yet a divorce does not mean the end . . . It is horrible! No end, no new beginning." In place of a signature he ended the letter with a large question mark.

On 20 April, Geber published *The Gothic Rooms* in an edition of 4,000 copies, nearly twice that of *Fairy Tales*, but it met with a hostile reception. Strindberg's spiteful caricatures of old friends caused justifiable offence, and the long chapters of debate struck the critics, as they have struck most readers since, as irrelevant and boring. The novel opens brilliantly (like most things Strindberg wrote) with a reunion of the lively young men, now middle-aged, who had frequented the Red Room in Berns' restaurant a quarter of a century before. Vivid chapters about uneasy marriages then alternate with interminable discussions about sex, politics and economics, which an early champion of Strindberg sorrowfully summed up as "a rehash of what anyone could read for himself in the newspapers or Parliamentary records."[19] The last third of the book makes very tedious reading. It is difficult to disagree with Oscar Levertin's complaint in *Svenska Dagbladet*: "It may be unreasonable to expect from a novelist the orderly logic of a thinker, or a scientist's objectivity. But it is a fatal flaw to lack both those qualities if one spends as much time as Strindberg does discussing philosophical questions and scientific theories. At least half of *The Gothic Rooms* consists of arguments between learned minds about ideas and doctrines which interested the last two decades of the departed century." *Aftonbladet* regretted "the deeply depressing effect the novel makes through the bitterness it exudes against everything and everyone . . . We have heard all or anyway most of these outbursts repeated in so many previous books that we turn wearily from them." Several newspapers, including *Social-Demokraten* and *Dagens Nyheter*, both normally sympathetic to Strindberg, ignored it. Gustaf af Geijerstam, who was particularly spitefully portrayed in the book, commented sadly to Per Hallström: ". . . the man is clearly a pronounced paranoiac, not, as I had hoped until the end of 1900, a disturbed spirit who might one day fight his way to peace. The whole thing is tragic, tragic and horrible."[20] Strindberg obstinately retained his faith in the book. Gustaf Uddgren tells that "the year before his death, Strindberg reread *The Gothic Rooms* and repeatedly told his friends that he rated it highest among his novels."[21]

Strindberg was not quite alone in admiring this book. Max Brod has described how Franz Kafka, an addict of Strindberg's narrative fiction, "was highly delighted with the realistic and satirical power with which Strindberg depicts his age and setting. In this respect he considered Strindberg's novels *By the Open Sea* and *The Gothic Rooms* as master-pieces of a special order. He read them again and again and liked to read aloud from them. Other things—for example, *Inferno*—interested him more on account of their singularity. This does not mean that they had a lesser influence on him . . . Among the plays he loved, above all, *Easter*, because of the mild and benevolent spirit which, even in the face of the heaviest assaults, slowly and patiently gets the upper hand . . . Kafka had no special taste for the dramatic form. The autobiographical novels of Strindberg, however, had a powerful influence on him, and for a time he read nothing else."[22]

A few days after the publication of *The Gothic Rooms*, a new volume of Strindberg's *Collected Plays* appeared, containing *Christina* and Part III of *To Damascus*, both still unperformed. It is a mark of Strindberg's declining reputation in Sweden as a dramatist that few papers even bothered to review these plays, and of those that did even fewer had a good word to say for them. Sven Söderman in *Stockholms Dagblad* dismissed *Christina* as a fantasy cobbled together from "ludicrous errors, impudent assertions and plain distortions," and Per Hallström in *Dagens Nyheter* found it "dead, and worse than dead, for it is already decomposed and stinks."

But at least Strindberg was still admired in Germany, and on 10 May, Max Reinhardt staged *Miss Julie* at his Kleines Theater in Berlin, with Gertrud Eysoldt and Hans Wassmann. It was an immense success, the first really adequate performance that the play had received anywhere, and went on tour, visiting, among other cities, Budapest. But Strindberg had by now turned away from the theatre. In the six years from 1898 to 1903, he had written no fewer than twenty-six plays. Sixteen of these were still unperformed, including at least five of his best. He was to write no more plays for three years, between *The Lamb and the Beasts*, completed in November 1903, and *Storm*, in January 1907.

He was still trying to make gold that spring of 1904, but modern science did not interest him; he was to remain sceptical about both radium and X-rays until his death. He continued to exercise a hypnotic power over

Harriet. On 24 May she sent him "a loving, excited letter."[23] On 28 May he wrote to her: "We must live as man and wife, for I love your body as I do your soul . . . And we must risk having a child . . . Let us tempt Providence once more." On 30 May she dined with him at Karlavägen, and "we were 'reunited' (fear of a child!)." Two days later he left for Furusund with Anne-Marie. Harriet saw them off at the quayside. "I felt no emotion; only noted quite coolly that I had a young, beautiful wife, and felt grateful for it, and justifiably proud."[24] She travelled to Copenhagen, and thence with a woman friend via Germany to Paris. If she was to free herself from him, she needed to put distance between them. "Although I longed for Strindberg, I realised that we could never again share a common home. I could not be caged, my lively mind and my curiosity about life rebelled against this dead calm. I had to choose —was I to turn my eyes and ears from the outside world, and shut myself in with Strindberg? I was eternally torn, for I loved Strindberg but I loved my freedom."[25] Yet on 22 June she joined them at Furusund, and according to his diary, resumed their old relationship at once. "When she left my bed that night, she was not like herself, but had a long oval face (like her portrait as Miss Hopps*), and she exuded a fragrance so strong and delicious that I fell into ecstasy and almost lost consciousness. This is supernatural and I sometimes think she is from a sphere high above us and not an ordinary mortal."[26]

They spent seven weeks together at Furusund, in seemingly uninterrupted harmony. "My memory from this summer," Harriet tells, "is that it was the calmest period of our marriage."[27] Strindberg, too, was to evoke it affectionately, in his short novel *The Roofing Ceremony*. "Here I sit at Isola Bella," he wrote to Richard Bergh on 7 July, "with wife and child, sailing-boat, bathing-hut, fishing rods and lines, terrace and sunshine, just as in the best summer-joyful days I have known. *C'est la vie, quoi?* While it lasts! I don't know about tomorrow, much less the autumn." He even became reconciled with the Philps, after a four-year estrangement following his savage depiction of them in *The Dance of Death*. "Music, flowers, wine, ladies, speeches, youth, beauty," he wrote to Bergh on 8 August, his last day there. ". . . And then it was finished! But first we had several evenings together on the terrace with music from *Carmen*, a dinner and supper together at the Philps's, and an unforgettable bowling session which ended at night with a race (I set the record)." A photograph exists from one of these parties, with Strindberg looking unusually stout.

---

*The title role in a play by Jerome K. Jerome which she had performed at Dramaten in 1902–3.

Anne-Marie was now two, and able to walk and talk with him. One day she saw some puppies playing in a yard and asked Strindberg if she might have one. But his old fear of dogs of any size remained. "He stood with Anne-Marie on his arm, fighting with himself. 'I don't want to deny her anything—but I cannot give her a dog.' Then he turned away, to put the temptation behind him."[28]

On 9 August, Strindberg returned to Stockholm, where two weeks later he signed a contract with Karl Otto Bonnier for the publication of his *Collected Works*. The same day, 23 August, Bonnier paid him an advance of 5,000 crowns against a new edition of his autobiographical cycle, which appeared six months later in an edition of 3,000 copies.[29] Three days later Harriet left for a two-month engagement in Finland (including Part I of *To Damascus*), leaving Anne-Marie with him. He sent Harriet regular bulletins on her health for a few days ("She frightened us in the night with small stomach pains, was afraid of Mummy's bed because it was too big . . . I hear that fruit is dangerous to eat in the autumn . . . It is good to have the child in the house, and someone to fuss over").[30] But by 2 September his mood had changed. "To put an end to these eternal rendings, let us loose these bonds that mean nothing and only oppress us. Then let us see what happens!" Next day he noted in his diary:

> Life is so hideously ugly, we mortals so abysmally evil, that were an author to portray everything he had seen or heard, no one could endure to read it. There are things I remember having seen or heard done by good, respectable, well-liked people, which I have blotted out, never been able to bring myself to mention and refuse to remember. Breeding and education seem only to be masks for the beast in us, and virtue a dissimulation. The best we can hope for is to conceal our meanness.
>
> Life is so cynical that only a swine can be happy in it. And anyone who can see our ugly life as beautiful is a swine.
>
> Life must be a punishment! A hell; for some a purgatory, for none a paradise.
>
> We are forced to do evil and torment our fellow creatures. It is all sham and delusion, lies, infidelity, falsehood, farce. "My dear friend" is my worst enemy. "My beloved" should read "my hated."

His contract with Bonnier for the *Collected Works* apparently did not preclude his issuing some of them elsewhere, for that autumn another publisher, Fröléen, brought out the first three volumes of a cheap edition of his *Collected Novels and Stories*, containing *The People of Hemsö* and *Men of the Skerries*, "with about a hundred illustrations," as the advertisements proudly proclaimed, at only 25 öre each. (Each of the little paperback volumes contained around seventy pages.) The shortening days and Harriet's absence made Strindberg gloomy. "I wonder," he suggested to Bergh on 14 September, "if we shouldn't go out and be bohemian . . . I long for Montparnasse, Madame Charlotte, Ida Molard, absinthe, *merlan frit*, du Blanc, *Le Figaro* and [Café Closerie des] Lilas! But—but!!!"

On 27 September, Lydia Yavorskaia presented *The Father*, with herself as Laura, at her New Theatre in St. Petersburg, where three years earlier she had staged *There Are Crimes and Crimes*. It was preceded by *The Stronger*, though after a few performances this was replaced by a curtain-raiser by, of all playwrights, Strindberg's old enemy Przybyszewski. *Dagens Nyheter* reported that "at the final curtain the audience sat as if paralysed . . . the newspapers hold conflicting opinions about the play, but in general praise the performance." It ran for eighteen nights. Two weeks later, on 12 October, the fashionable Alexandra Theatre in St. Petersburg staged its own production of *The Father*, so that for a few nights the theatregoers of the city had two versions to choose from. Yavorskaia took her production to Moscow the following spring, and in September 1905 the New Theatre in Moscow presented its own production. The play created a powerful impression, and over the next few years it was seen all over Russia from Archangel to the Caucasus and as far east as Charbin. In Nizhni-Novgorod, four ladies had to be removed in hysterics by the police during the last act. It is told of the most famous Russian interpreter of the Captain's role, Mamont Dalski, that he played the last five minutes of the first act with his back to the audience in complete silence. "But he acted so powerfully with his head, hands, back and shoulders that the audience sat breathless."[31]

On the evening that Yavorskaia's production of *The Father* opened in St. Petersburg, an old childhood friend of Strindberg's turned up at Karlavägen: Gustaf Eisen, who had been his classmate at the Lyceum and in 1871 had supported him during his early days in Stockholm. For the past thirty years, Eisen had been living in San Francisco, where he had established a reputation as a zoologist and botanist. It proved a happy reunion. Strindberg took the opportunity to propound to this disting-uished scientist his own scientific theories, which Eisen found brilliant but impossibly unscientific. "For example, his idea that there were no fiery substances in the sun and that instead of warmth it produced electricity . . . He was more obstinate than ever." Strindberg showed Eisen two photographic inventions he had made which he was convinced would prove important. "One was that the simpler the lens, the better the picture. All his own photographs had been taken with a lens of his own invention, comprising only the unground glass . . . One result was a certain indefiniteness of line which I found almost attractive, since few if any people see objects as sharply as they appear in photographs. When I asked him why he bothered with photography, he replied that it was because all photographs that professionals took of him were so bad. 'I don't mind about my face,' he said. 'It's my soul I want people to see, and that comes out better in my photographs than in anyone else's.' "[32] Strindberg recorded in his diary: "We discussed among other things whether I might settle in San Francisco and learn English"; but he decided against it, and eighteen months later noted with some complacency that the city had been destroyed by an earthquake.

He had at length agreed to Harriet's demands for a divorce, and on 27 October this was made absolute. Two days later she returned from Finland and leased a new apartment, at Stureparken, ten minutes' walk from him. He now, irrationally, began to blame the Philps for the rift between himself and Harriet, just as twelve years earlier he had blamed Hugo Philp for the break with Siri. "I am <u>never</u> with my relatives," he wrote to Harriet around 27 November. "Those most responsible for separating me from my wife and child—them I do not know." He also, equally irrationally, became jealous of his nephew Henry Philp and of his niece Märta's fiancé Hugo Fröding. In this ugly mood he began a new novel, *Black Banners*, a venomous caricature of Gustaf af Geijerstam, his children and his dead wife, which in the blackness of its cynicism and pessimism anticipates *The Ghost Sonata*.

His sister Elisabeth fell ill with pneumonia in the mental home at Uppsala. Strindberg did not visit her, though he noted in his diary that she was dying and sent her a letter by one of his nieces inviting her to stay with him "in case she got better."[33] Four days after this diary entry, on 10 December, she died. He did not attend the funeral, merely recording, on the day of it: "At 1 p.m., when Elisabeth was to be buried, I read the funeral service in the prayer book."[34] Strindberg hated funerals and weddings; no doubt too, he was reluctant to meet the Philps.

The concluding volume of his *Collected Plays* appeared, containing such unperformed works as *Gustav the Third* and *The Nightingale of Wittenberg*. Their publication passed virtually unnoticed. The few reviews that appeared dismissed them with unconcealed condescension. On 19 December he wrote a long and bitter letter to Harriet about Anne-Marie: "I do not think she should bear my dishonoured and soiled, not to say hated, name. You know that no one believes her to be my child. And this was caused by your foolish utterances in August–September 1901, when you declared that I was not a man; also your unreflecting pretext for the divorce, namely, that I was too old . . . You cannot live without a man and you will remarry one way or another. Then it will be good that my name should not stand between the two of you in the child." But on Christmas Eve "the telephone rang. It was Harriet asking me to come and spend the evening there. I went. Everything was peaceful and pleasant."

On Christmas Day, inappropriately, he completed *Black Banners* (in only a month) and sent it to Geber, explaining: "I have had no pleasure in writing this book, but it hung over me like a duty of which I am now certain—I had to write it! I haven't read it through, so I beg you to keep a red pencil in your hand when you read it and delete immediately all inadvertencies." Geber replied two days later rejecting it as grossly libellous, as did four other publishers to whom Strindberg sent it. He did not offer it to Karl Otto Bonnier, a close friend of Geijerstam. It did not appear until 1907, when it was to damage Strindberg's reputation almost irretrievably.

Chapter Twenty-Eight

"MY DISHARMONIES REND ME"

The completion of divorce proceedings seems to have dissolved Harriet's inhibitions about sleeping with Strindberg; perhaps she enjoyed the sex and only disliked the marriage. "Am associating now with Harriet! As before!" he wrote in his diary on 3 January 1905; and on 20 January he asked her: "Would you like to have a door key and come straight into my rooms without ringing, any time you decide? Here it is as lonely as ever, a little more beautiful, for I have done things up for you. Your white nightdress is washed and hangs shining like snow, beside a pair of red shoes. Or may I visit you?" Yet on 10 February he noted: "Harriet at home tonight until 1:30 a.m. After midnight her face was transformed, became old and ugly. This means that she is another person at night, exteriorised. And she was always ugly when she slept; ugly and repellent!" Next day: "A feeling like a spider's web on my left ring finger."

He sent *Black Banners* to Schering, who expressed alarm lest Geijerstam, on reading so dreadful an account of himself and his family life, might kill himself, go insane or seek revenge. "A bounder does not shoot himself and cannot go mad," Strindberg replied. "Revenge? He has had that already, the vampire!"[1] He was working on a book of narrative sketches describing important events in world history, entitled *Historical Miniatures*, ranging in time from Moses to Napoleon and taking in Socrates, Nero, Attila, Luther, Peter the Great and Voltaire; one of the worst, a fanciful account of Henry VIII's dealings with Wolsey, he called, venturing rashly into English: "Old Merry England." Of all his books, this is perhaps the most unredeemably worthless; even the dreadful plays about Moses, Socrates and Christ contain a few lively pages, which is more than can be said for *Historical Miniatures*. Strindberg wrote the book in a month, and it reads like it. But he had to pay his bills, and he could not have done that by adding to his pile of unwanted plays.

Although he did not have a single production in Stockholm this year, at least he was still being staged abroad. On 9 March, Moscow saw its first Strindberg play when Lydia Yavorskaia brought her production of *The Father* from St. Petersburg; she followed it with *Simoom*, in harness with a Hauptmann play, but *Simoom* seems not to have succeeded, for she quickly removed it from the bill.[2] *Easter* was staged in Lübeck, and *Erik the Fourteenth* in Hamburg, where it was well received; *Hamburger Zeitung* wrote that it showed "a deep understanding of human nature, portraying the tragic destinies of ancient tragedy in a new dress. That a work of such compulsive genius can be virtually unknown in Germany is new and sad proof of the ruthless commercialism of German theatrical managers."[3] On 16 April a group of amateurs did *Simoom* in Warsaw, the first Strindberg play to be seen in Poland; it was also performed in Breslau, where it was not admired. He even enjoyed, if that is the word, his first two productions in America. Both took place in New York; Alla Nazimova played *Miss Julie* in Russian, and *Simoom* (yet again) was privately performed at the Vanderbilt mansion. It is fortunate that Strindberg was not present, for (according to an eyewitness report) "the men discussed business and the ladies their own and one another's dresses until at length the boring performance was finished. Then the host's trained chimpanzees cycled around the table, which, unlike the Strindberg play, was loudly applauded."[4]

None of these productions seems to have helped his financial position. On 26 March he wrote desperately to Nils Andersson in Lund: "My rent is due on Friday and I haven't got it . . . Lend me 200 crowns!" On 11 April he asked Vilhelm Carlhem-Gyllensköld for a loan of 500 crowns, and on 7 May requested Henrik Köppel to advance him the same amount on a forthcoming reprint of *Getting Married* in a cheap one-crown edition of 10,000 copies.*

His diary contains no entries about Harriet between February and May, in which month she twice came to supper with him. Since he does not record that they slept together, one must suppose that they had ceased to be lovers. On 22 May he sent the wretched *Historical Miniatures* to

---

*Köppel paid him 1,200 crowns, a fair enough royalty of 12 per cent.

Bonniers, and on 28 May: "Walked in the city, beautiful summer weather
. . . Thought of my youth and of going to the country, but I felt as though
this youth and delight in the countryside lay ahead of me, awaited me."
That June, at Schering's suggestion, he read Edward Gordon Craig's book
On the Art of the Theatre, which Craig had written in a week in Berlin and
which had appeared that year. "Craig is stupid sometimes, but there are a
few gold nuggets there," he told Schering (14 June); a fair assessment.

On 15 June, Harriet and Anne-Marie left for Denmark. The Curies
visited Stockholm, but Strindberg's hostility towards them persisted; on
22 June he noted in his diary: "The whole radium business strikes me as a
colossal fraud." On 30 June he went alone to Furusund, living not, as
before, at Isola Bella but on the other side of the island. Harriet writes:
"He begged me repeatedly to come with Anne-Marie and live with him
on Furusund, which however we did not do this summer. I suffered from
his inability to sever the bond between us . . . If he had been angry with
me or railed at me, it would have been infinitely easier for me to forget.
But he was always kind and helpful, which made me stay close to him."[5]
"If only I could grow old decently, quickly, and resign myself to it!" he
wrote to her on 23 July. "But I have become fat, red and brown." He
wrote to her ten times that month from Furusund, and fifty more letters
before the end of the year.

On 1 August he returned to Stockholm. Harriet joined the Grand
Theatre in Gothenburg, and Anne-Marie spent the whole autumn with
him. He was working on another book of historical sketches, *Sagas of the
Chieftains*, all mercifully set in Sweden from Viking times to the
sixteenth century; Swedish history sometimes brought out the best in
him, foreign history never.

On 23 September, uncharacteristically, Strindberg gave a party at
Karlavägen for several of the leading younger Swedish writers: Hjalmar
Söderberg, Henning Berger, Bo Bergman, Gustaf Jansson, Algot Ruhe
and Albert Engström. Bergman thought the apartment "furnished in the
most banal taste . . . My immediate reaction was: 'Someone must have
telephoned to NK [department store]: "Send up three- or four-thousand-
crowns' worth of drawing-room furniture, new, quick." ' " However, once
Strindberg had got over his first shyness, Bergman found the evening
"entirely agreeable . . . He became accessible, amiable, almost chum-
my, told stories and laughed at other people's . . . How sociable could
Strindberg, the brooder and anchorite, not be in his later years when the
mood took him!"[6] Bergman remembered how anxious Strindberg was
that no one should stain his ugly furniture and how he went around
shoving coasters beneath everyone's wineglass.[7] (Hjalmar Söderberg

believed that Strindberg "positively disliked 'beautiful' furniture; he felt disturbed by it").[8] The conversation revived Strindberg's thoughts of trying again to found his own theatre. "After a night with Young Sweden," he wrote to Harriet next day, "—we broke up at 6 a.m.—I . . . begin to think I must use the pound of talent I was granted as a theatre man, and that I must try to get my plays performed myself, since others don't wish to perform me. So . . . shall we create a theatre, and tour? But I need three players; if I have you and two others I shall borrow money, engage staff and have my small stage painted with screens . . . The night was interesting but a little tiring." The idea of the screens probably stemmed from his reading of Craig, who advocated their use and was to design a famously impossible set of them, most of which fell over, for Stanislavsky's *Hamlet*.

On 29 September, *The Dance of Death* was at last performed, in Cologne, five years after its completion; Part I that night, Part II the following night. Although *Stockholms-Tidningen* reported that "the ending jarred somewhat because of its improbability," the production was in general well received, and toured thirty cities in Germany and Austria.

"My disharmonies rend me," Strindberg wrote to Harriet on 4 October. "Loneliness forces me to seek company, but after each meeting, even the best, I withdraw wounded and find myself more and more turned in on myself; am ashamed without cause, suffer remorse without having done anything, am disgusted with myself without knowing why. I strive upwards, but go down; want to do so much good, but behave so badly; my old self strives against my new; I want to see life as beautiful, but it is not beautiful, only nature is beautiful; I pity people but I cannot respect them, cannot love them, I know them through myself. I find my only comfort now in Buddha who says plainly that life is a phantasma, an illusion, the truth of which we shall see in another life. My hope and my future lie on the other side, that is why life is so difficult for me to live . . . Wife, children and home were the best; a stern school, but the only protection against bad influences; without this protection I drift, fall into the hands of anyone; loneliness is not bad, but there I am faced by my stern chastising self, which scourges me."

He had relented somewhat towards theosophy, which he had so denounced when Torsten Hedlund had preached its merits to him. "Theosophy," he assured Harriet on 6 October, "is not dangerous; it is the beautiful teachings of Buddha which you read about in the Indian play,[*]

---

[*]Strindberg had sent Harriet an Indian play called *Sakuntala* in 1904. She played the title role in it at Dramaten in the spring of 1905.

but now reworked into a theology and with too many dogmas. Worth looking at; but more severe, narrow and vengeful than Christianity, which can forgive without revenge = without listing all the errors and follies one has committed (= the robber on the cross!)."

His letters to Harriet that autumn are full of love for Anne-Marie. The future novelist Gösta Gustaf Jansson, son of that Gustaf Jansson whom Strindberg had invited to the Young Sweden party, was the same age as Anne-Marie and lived in the flat below. Fifty years later he told me how he used to climb the stairs, ring the bell and ask the, as it seemed to him, infinitely aged man who opened the door if he could play with her. He remembered Strindberg as being very kind and gentle, as he always was with small children, and how one Christmas Strindberg gave him a paint-box. When I said, "Then you have a paint-box given you by Strindberg!" he replied sadly, "The next Christmas an aunt gave me a better one and I threw Strindberg's away."

On 16 October, Bonnier published *Historical Miniatures*, which was tepidly received, though, considering how very bad it was, less fiercely than might have been expected. *Aftonbladet* observed that all the characters talked like Strindberg characters and that, apart from the many factual errors, he had not really got to the heart of either the people or the events. Oscar Levertin in *Svenska Dagbladet* admitted that Strindberg's "passionate originality" occasionally peeped forth, but thought that as history the book was contemptible (which it is). As a former admirer who hated most of what Strindberg had written since 1900, Levertin continued: "A foreigner who knew nothing of August Strindberg but what he has written in the past five or six years, and heard him described as Sweden's greatest living writer, would surely shake his head in wonder. But even we who know his whole life's achievement, who have grown up with his work and can never lose our admiration for the boldness and genius of his writings, nor forget our grateful debt to the literary revolution which he started, perhaps the most far-reaching in our literature, even we must stand in wonder and bewilderment at his books of recent years." Levertin summed these up as "mechanical outpourings" and thought *Historical Miniatures* perhaps the saddest example. Yet, he concluded, "at least it is written in August Strindberg's prose, unique in our literature . . . which, even when thought and knowledge are conspicuous by their absence, still, continuously, by the brilliance of its impressionism, bears evidence of the great writer."

On 18 October, *Easter* was staged in Gothenburg, with Harriet in her old role of Eleonora, but although it got some good reviews, it failed, as it had in Stockholm. *Handelstidningen i Göteborg* deplored the audience's lack of interest, "if only for Fru Bosse's masterly interpretation of Eleonora." *Svenska Dagbladet* reported that "the house, which was not full, was clearly unsure what to think of it all." So that brought him little money. Five days later, Young Sweden returned his hospitality by inviting him to an evening of bowling and supper in a restaurant at Djurgården. Hjalmar Söderberg recalled that they had a *smörgåsbord* followed by goose, and that over the punch Strindberg made a charming speech of thanks, complimenting each of his hosts individually. "We had never before realised what geniuses we were."[9] Albert Engström, by contrast, remembered it as "a very painful occasion. All my contemporaries . . . were so meticulously correct that Strindberg suffered the agonies of the damned . . . They all stood up as soon as he stood and sat half-reluctantly when he sat. That was the kind of thing he least liked. It all seemed mechanical, without warmth, friendliness or understanding. When I dined with Strindberg the next day he told me he thought the whole evening had been frightful."[10]

On 23 October one of Strindberg's plays enjoyed a premiere even more belated than that of *The Dance of Death*. Josef Jarno staged *The Comrades* at the Lustspieltheater in Vienna, eighteen years after it was written. It was a tremendous success, thanks largely to Jarno's own performance in the role of Axel. For some reason, this moderate piece was to have an extraordinary appeal in Germany; over the next quarter of a century it was to be performed no less than 1,174 times there and in Austria, oftener than any other Strindberg play.[11]

Gustaf Uddgren saw a good deal of Strindberg around this time and recalled his insistence on punctuality:

> You had to arrive on the dot. If people were late, he became very nervous. So guests would assemble outside his door a few minutes early and then ring the bell when the nearby church clock struck the hour. He would greet us with a strong handshake, though he often avoided this because of the eczema in the palm of his right hand, which you could not but notice and about which he was very sensitive. When it was bad he would wear a black glove . . . He told me that he usually sensed when one of his plays was about to have a premiere in Europe. He would then smell smoke and the vapour of alcohol, which he interpreted as meaning that people were talking intensively about him in some theatre foyer. After he had retired around 10 p.m. and fallen asleep, he would start up in bed in alarm, wondering if he was in a theatre . . . After sensing applause in this manner, he would always receive news of some dramatic success . . . He would relive these experiences with such intensity that he would often become hot in the head. He would have to cool his forehead with cold water, and would dilute whatever he was drinking with water and lemon.[12]

Strindberg described to Uddgren his method of work: "When I return from my morning walk I am charged like an electric machine. After putting on a dry shirt, for I get very hot when walking, I sit down at this desk. As soon as I have pen and paper ready, it starts to flow. The words pour forth and my pen has to work at full pressure to get it all down. After a few minutes I have the sensation that I am hovering freely in space. It is as though a higher will than mine causes the pen to glide across the paper and write words that seem to come to me from without . . ." Uddgren continues: "He dreaded feeling empty, and so occupied himself for the rest of the day in every conceivable way. He had just acquired the big *Encyclopaedia Britannica* and read this eagerly. He also read languages and mathematics, and in the evening he studied the stars, as both astronomer and astrologer."[13]

Two artists executed portraits of Strindberg that autumn of 1905. The young sculptor Carl Eldh, seeing him passing under his window on his morning walks, had, unknown to him, made a statuette of him the previous spring. Strindberg now agreed to sit for him, and Eldh did a portrait head and a bronze bust. At the same time, Richard Bergh was painting him. "I have to do it fast," Bergh wrote to a friend on 8 November. "He won't sit for long and is terribly nervous . . . He is like an old, wounded but proud lion."[14] Another acquaintance points out that Bergh, who always painted very slowly, needed six weeks to finish the portrait, and that this was too much for Strindberg, who complained, "I can't stand people staring me in the eyes." To Bergh's great sorrow Strindberg broke off their friendship, and three years elapsed before he relented and Bergh was able to meet him again.[15]

Harriet's star was rising as Strindberg's waned. Albert Ranft offered her a three-year contract at the Swedish Theatre, at 10,000 crowns a year, and she left Dramaten after six years there.[16] She came from Gothenburg to Stockholm for two weeks in November before leaving on a short study trip to Berlin. Strindberg wrote to Schering asking if he could help to get her acting work in Germany, suggesting either *The Wild Duck* (surely the only instance of Strindberg recommending an Ibsen work) or Maeterlinck's *Pelléas and Mélisande*. "She has had enough of Sweden, as I have, this land where talent is hated and non-talents are rewarded with immortal honour."[17]* Schering gave her an introduction to Richard Vallentin, the director of the Deutsches Volkstheater in Vienna, who asked her to read *Simoom* and offered her a five-year contract at the

---

*A jibe at the Swedish Academy, the members of which were, and are, incongruously known as the "Immortals."

Hebbel Theater in Berlin, which he also ran. But Ranft refused to release her; which, Harriet remarks, was just as well, for Vallentin died a few months later.[18]

Bonniers published a collection of poems by Strindberg in November under the title *Word-Play and Minor Art*, containing those that had appeared in *Fairhaven and Foulstrand* and others more recent. It was sympathetically received, though several critics justifiably complained of uneven quality. No more than most of Strindberg's poems do they read well today. Like the poems of other distinguished writers who were not skilled poets, such as George Orwell, they sometimes say interesting things, or throw light on their author's mind and personality, without being very good poems.

Strindberg had by now come to accept that Harriet and he could no longer continue as hitherto. "I think," he wrote to her on 25 November, "we both stand on the threshold of a new era [in our relationship]. We noticed this last time we met. We can be friends but not lovers; for I found it dishonest to be your lover without obligations; anyway, another child would be our downfall. With love comes hatred, as you know, but affection without egoism lasts longer and is more edifying. We have both given each other back our freedom, why bind ourselves again? Neither of us can endure bonds. And when we hate the bond we transfer that hatred to each other, like all married persons and lovers." Her reply has not survived, but on 30 November he wrote to her: "Since you do not feel the bond between us is dissolved and no longer regard it as oppressive, what do you say to this suggestion, which is yours? I shall sell all our homes and come down with Anne-Marie and 3,000 marks, and we shall settle in Grünewald in a furnished apartment. I will look after the child while you work . . . But you must not consider yourself bound to me, by mutual word of honour, longer than you wish; but give me notice!"

She evidently refused (how could he have believed otherwise?), for on 2 December he wrote to her:

> It seems that our saga is finished, our joint destinies sealed—the Angel of Death flies over Karlavägen 40; the piano is gone, the Inferno painting too, on Monday the other paintings will go. But Anne-Marie too is moving away from me, is hard and alien—
>
> The worst thing is that the memories turn black and become ash.
>
> Swanwhite is dead—long ago—the Virgin Bride without her crown —Indra's Daughter begins to be happy among the garbage and to enjoy mortals' sufferings. The Easter girl [Eleonora] prefers revue to tragedy. Such is life!
>
> I no longer believe in our life together, because I do not believe in what

has been. You were perhaps the only one who understood me, at certain moments . . . however!

Whither I am now carried, I know not, but it leads outwards, but not downwards . . . Regard my last letter as unwritten and resolve to seek happiness elsewhere.

This was only deceit and illusion, and leaves no sense of loss, just nausea.

If I live much longer, this relationship of ours will become like smoke as the others did, and the child will be as alien to me as the others.

That will be a relative happiness! if only I achieve it.

On 8 December he wrote to her again: "Do you think we can be freed from each other, who have so entwined our lives? When you are anxious far away in a foreign land, my heart beats up here in my breast as though it were yours. Sometimes I feel your warm breath across my cheek, and then I believe that you are speaking my name kindly. Sometimes I have you within my coat, and I am you. How painful would not that operation be, to tear one of our lives out of the other's?" An art connoisseur, Ernest Thiel, bought three of his paintings for 1,000 crowns. A week before Christmas, Harriet returned to Stockholm, and Anne-Marie, who had been with her aunt Inez since the beginning of December, returned to live with her. Strindberg joined them as usual for dinner on Christmas Eve. On 29 December he noted in his diary that his brother-in-law Hugo Philp had had his leg amputated.

On New Year's Day 1906, Strindberg visited Harriet and Anne-Marie as usual, and they dined with him at Karlavägen. "Harriet calm and loving," he noted, and on 13 January: "At Harriet's this evening till nearly 10. She asked me to stay but I left." Next day: "Awoke after a restless night with an impression that I was now free from H—t, and made plans to flee. Around 10:30 a.m. a letter came from H—t; convinced that it was a 'final letter' I opened it with a certain emotion. It turned out to be a passionate love letter! . . . I went to H—t in the evening. She asked me to stay the night but I left." Is this a true picture of Harriet's feelings towards him, or was he already suffering from the hallucinations about her which were shortly to fill his diary? Her memoirs give no clue.

On 3 January, Lydia Yavorskaia appeared as Miss Julie in St. Petersburg, following a short tour in the first Russian production of the play. The censor had demanded certain cuts and alterations: for example, that Jean be raised to the rank of steward so as to reduce the social difference between him and his mistress. Like *The Father*, it was quickly taken up by touring companies; Vsevolod Meyerhold included it in his repertory when he toured southern Russia later in the year.[19] On 9 January,

Creditors was staged at Vasa Theatre in Stockholm and was well received, though some critics shrank from the theme. Sven Söderman in *Stockholms Dagblad* thought it the work of "a man suffering from monomania," but conceded that "the overall impression was extremely powerful" and that the audience was deeply stirred. *Aftonbladet* praised its "powerful, red-blooded energy . . . the spectator is as though ridden by a hideous nightmare while the curtain is up, and draws a sigh of relief when it descends," but concluded, somewhat illogically, that the play was "mainly of pathological interest." Anna Branting in *Stockholms-Tidningen* thought it horrible and its misogyny poisonous, though wittily and skilfully expressed; *Dagens Nyheter* found it "profound and powerful."

The Russian productions brought Strindberg nothing; nor, to his disappointment, did the German tour of *The Dance of Death*, which, the director informed him, although an artistic success, had lost 14,000 marks.[20] On 18 January, Strindberg gloomily informed Karl Otto Bonnier that he would have to give up writing. "I have a 400-page novel [*Black Banners*] which can find no publisher; I have worked hard for a whole year without reward. In Germany, whence relief should come, nothing has borne fruit. *The Dance of Death*, which has been performed sixty times, has not brought me a mark, nor have I seen a single kreutzer from Vienna, where *The Comrades* has been playing since autumn and is still in the repertory . . . Luckily I am used to this, and experience has shown me that once the graph reaches its nadir it begins to rise again." Bonnier responded by offering to issue a cheap edition of *The People of Hemsö* at one crown for a fee of 1,000 crowns.

The day Strindberg wrote to Bonnier, his brother-in-law Hugo Philp died at the age of sixty-one. Strindberg noted the fact in his diary with no comment except that it happened on "precisely the day . . . and the hour when he had his stroke six years ago," adding irrelevantly: "For six years Napoleon sat on St. Helena, for six years Bismarck sat in Sachsenwald, forgotten, mocked. For six years Heine lay in bed, Linnaeus for four years after his stroke." He did not attend the funeral.

Birger Mörner, back from diplomatic service in Australia, met Strindberg that February for the first time in seven years. He noted Strindberg's passion for having electric lights on everywhere, even in the cupboards, and records that Strindberg told him: "Writing plays is the most interesting thing. One sits like a little god, searching men's hearts and reins —judging them—punishing, acquitting or rewarding."[21] On 27 February, Strindberg "visited Harriet in the evening. Gloom: ill, decolleté, beautiful, evil, loving. She told me that last night she had intended to write me a final letter; this so upset me that I responded coldly to her addresses, which made her angry. I left quickly." Next day: "Harriet telephoned but I did not answer. Felt it was finished. Pitch dark." On 1 March: "Harriet telephoned and invited herself for the evening. She came; it became light again. Flowers, champagne and supper; she played. It was wonderful." On 5 March she went to act in Finland again; Anne-Marie stayed with Inez as before and, he reported to Harriet, "visits me daily."[22]

On 8 March he had another production in Stockholm, albeit a revival; Dramaten gave *There Are Crimes and Crimes*, first produced there six years earlier. *Aftonbladet* found the performance far less good than before, "flat, dull, lacking all fire," though the Crown Prince applauded warmly from his box. Before the end of the month, *The Comrades* was staged in Stuttgart, where (*Svenska Dagbladet* reported) it was received with "universal enthusiasm," and *The People of Hemsö* and *Pariah* in Altona, to "loud applause."[23] The latter play marked the first appearance in a Strindberg role of Paul Wegener, later to establish himself as one of his greatest interpreters. The Stockholm publishing house Ljus reissued *Swedish Destinies and Adventures* in forty tiny paperback volumes, each barely two-thirds the size of a modern paperback and averaging around fifty pages. It seemed that only his old works interested Swedish publishers and theatre managers; *The Dance of Death*, *A Dream Play* and *The Virgin Bride* gathered dust in his desk.

Eleonora Duse visited Stockholm that month, playing among other roles Rebecca West in *Rosmersholm*, but Strindberg did not go to see her even in her non-Ibsen plays, any more than he had bothered to see Bernhardt. Another distinguished visitor to Stockholm that March was Edward Gordon Craig, in whose *On the Art of the Theatre* Strindberg had found "nuggets" the previous year. Craig, born in 1872, son of the great actress Ellen Terry, had acted in Henry Irving's company but had failed to make much impression, and in 1897 had turned to stage direction and design; in 1903 he designed, and directed his mother in, Ibsen's *The Vikings at Helgeland*, and the same year went to Italy and founded a School for the Art of the Theatre in Florence. His mistress, the American dancer Isadora Duncan, got him a commission to design *Rosmersholm* for Duse, but she discarded the set after one performance. Craig had become disillusioned with actors, who he thought got in the way of the play, and cherished dreams of a theatre without them which would use "Super-Marionettes," somewhat in the manner of the Chat Noir in Paris. He wrote to Albert Engström asking to see "the play which Strindberg says he has written without words,"[24] though it is not known that Strindberg ever contemplated anything of the kind. According to Engström, Craig begged him to arrange a meeting with Strindberg, vowing that he and Isadora had come to Stockholm only for that purpose.

Strindberg had evidently heard of Isadora's reputation as a man-eater, for he rebuffed Engström's efforts to arrange an introduction, protesting: "I don't intend to expose myself to any attempts at seduction by that woman." He liked, however, some woodcuts which Craig had executed of designs for Shakespeare plays and had persuaded Engström to give him. "He was delighted and asked me to thank the donor. He could not thank him personally because he had seen him standing outside his apartment, 'and he had long hair and looked like a villain in a melodrama.' "[25] Craig persisted, and eventually gained entrance. Strindberg described the meeting in a letter to Harriet on 11 March:

> . . . Craig was here. We didn't understand each other; then I sent for [Henning] Berger to talk English and help him. Berger said we don't bother about ballet; *Svenska Dagbladet* attacked Duncan; Craig seems in love with her and like Schering has sworn that she must come and dance here. I frightened them off the enterprise . . . Craig was like Oskar [*sic*] Wilde; *der war mir zu schön* [he was too beautiful for me].

But he had not frightened them off. Two days later he reported to Harriet: "Duncan is coming to the Olympia from 1 to 7 May. Let her, I shan't go and don't want to meet her . . . New plays are beginning to grow in me again: big, weighty, mature, and I shall write them all." (He was in fact to write none until the following year.) On 19 March he proudly informed Harriet that Carl Eldh's bronze statue of him had been bought by the National Museum: "Eight votes out of nine by the board—the ninth was Wirsén!" On 22 March: "Next week Parliament votes on my pension and is expected to approve it." The previous November, Sweden had elected its first Liberal government under the premiership of Karl Staaff, an admirer and friend of Strindberg, like his brother Pehr; but even with his support, the measure failed, for although approved by the second chamber, it was rejected by the first, and a couple of months later Staaff's government fell. Strindberg was never to receive a pension. His letter of 22 March continued: "Isadora has had Craig write to Berger that she is willing to build a box for me on stage, since I *must* see her.* I told B. that I did not wish to see her . . . Schering writes that Craig is Isadora's lover and is ruining her, which is why he is less respected."

*I.e., concealed in the wings, to get around Strindberg's unwillingness to be seen in a theatre.

Fifty years later, in a radio talk broadcast in 1956, Craig, then eighty-four, recalled their encounter. Notoriously inaccurate on facts, even in his younger days, Craig misremembered the meeting as having taken place in 1907; he says that Schering, whom he had met in Berlin, where he saw Strindberg's name "everywhere, in bookshops and on theatre posters," had sent *On the Art of the Theatre* to Strindberg and told Craig to visit him in Stockholm. Craig found Strindberg "living in what seemed to be lodgings—furnished apartments," the furniture being "plentiful and ugly, especially his writing desk." Strindberg himself struck Craig as "a handsome baby, saint, lion—a queer mixture . . . I never heard him laugh and I do not recall a smile." Strindberg asked, "Have you any friends in Stockholm?" and on receiving a negative reply, added, "Neither have I." They talked in German. When Strindberg walked around the room showing Craig his paintings, Craig noted "the fine curve of his back, more like that of a young man of twenty than one of sixty, and which he emphasised by putting his hands in his jacket pockets." As Craig left, Strindberg invited him back that evening to join him and Engström, but Craig misunderstood Strindberg's German and did not come, thereby missing what sounds to have been a rewarding occasion, for Engström later told him that he and Strindberg had sat up talking and drinking until 3 a.m.[26]

In his *Open Letters to the Intimate Theatre* a couple of years later, Strindberg makes only a passing reference to Craig. "There is a good deal of literature about regenerating the theatre, and from this I would first single out Gordon Craig's handsome periodical *The Mask*. Craig has some curious ideas about the theatre. He wants everything to be visual; so that for him the text is dispensable. He paints the costumes and stylises them, works with lighting, colours, and even masks."[27] Strindberg was evidently intrigued by but distrustful of Craig's theories. He approved of creating atmosphere by imaginative lighting, but what was one to think of a man who wished to banish the spoken word from the theatre?

Strindberg worked that spring on two short novels, *The Roofing Ceremony* and *The Scapegoat*, the last novels that he was to write. *The Roofing Ceremony* takes place in the mind of a man as he lies dying after an operation. His reflections are troubled and paranoiac as pain and fever rack him, relaxed and nostalgic after injections of morphine, reflecting tender memories of the summer that Strindberg had spent with Harriet on Furusund the previous year. Reality and fantasy merge, as in *To Damascus* and *A Dream Play* (he had originally thought of writing it as a play, and one rather wishes he had). *The Scapegoat* is a straightforwardly realistic piece about small-town life; a failing restaurant owner who vainly tries to defy the Powers is contrasted with a lawyer who suffers for the sins of others and is finally cast out of the town. Both novels are among Strindberg's better non-dramatic works without being of outstanding quality.

Antibarbarus appeared at last in Swedish and was virtually ignored, but, as he noted in his diary, it stimulated him to return to his chemical experiments, "and my discoveries multiply. Metals are hydrocarbon where the carbon exists as graphite."[28] On 10 April, *Easter* opened in Helsinki, with Harriet as Eleonora.* On 14 April, Strindberg wrote her a strange, impressionistic letter:

> I want to move, but can't; feel as though I were walking out into the void, turn dizzy, lose my thoughts and memories, five years of them, stored in this apartment; come under the rod of strangers, their tastes, thoughts, am forced to pander to their weaknesses, mongrels, servant-maids. I feel I must either stay here, or really seek unknown voids, away from all this, over in the beyond.
>
> The play escaped me. Went its way! Empty! But I must try something else. The novel tempts me most. The theatre I loathe. Pose! Superficiality, calculation.
>
> Read Shakespeare's *Shrew*. It was awful. Circus; false, clumsy, untrue . . . Balzac's style of novel tempts me most now. As in *Alone*. There one can explain oneself, interpret people, study them deeply, thoroughly.

On 24 April, *The Virgin Bride* at last received its premiere, five years after Strindberg wrote it, at the Swedish Theatre in Helsinki, with Harriet in the title role. The part of Mats, her lover, was played by a young actor named Gunnar Wingård; he became her lover off the stage too, and in due course her husband before his short life reached its tragic end. The play was a success, so much so that Albert Ranft bought it for production at the Swedish Theatre in Stockholm the following year. Harriet did Strindberg a service during her stay in Helsinki; she persuaded Jean Sibelius to write music for *Swanwhite*.

"I fight with my upbringing," Strindberg wrote to her on 28 April, "but don't get far. But religion in the final analysis means to me: hope of a better existence, certainty of liberation, belief in God. Here there is not much to expect: 'For the good that I would, I do not; but the evil which I would not do, that I do. But it is no more I that do it, but sin that dwelleth in me. For I see another law in my members, warring against the law of my mind, and bringing me into captivity to the law of sin which is in my

---

*A legend has arisen that Siri acted as prompter for this production, but Gunnar Ollén tells me that Karin assured him that this rumour was unfounded.

members . . . O wretched man that I am, who shall deliver me from the body of this death?' "*

That spring of 1906, Strindberg's *Collected Novels and Stories* began to appear. They were cheaply priced, at one crown per volume, and Bonnier printed large editions: 35,000 copies of *The Red Room*, 30,000 of *The People of Hemsö*, 20,000 of *Men of the Skerries*, *The Son of a Servant* and *Utopias in Reality*, and 15,000 of *The New Kingdom*, *By the Open Sea* and *Spring Harvest*. Karl Otto Bonnier records that the series went well and brought in good money for Strindberg.[29] As though to balance this, Schering wrote that Strindberg's main German publisher, Seemann, had gone bankrupt. On 7 May, Ranft revived *The Secret of the Guild* at the Swedish Theatre, Strindberg's third production in Stockholm in four months. The production was generally criticised, but the play, moderate as it is, was praised, and Ranft, perhaps influenced by the success of the *Collected Novels and Stories*, announced that he was planning to present no less than seven more Strindberg plays during the next two years: *Sir Bengt's Wife*, *The Comrades*, *Pariah*, *The Dance of Death*, *The Virgin Bride*, *Swanwhite* and *Gustav the Third*.[30] In the event, he was to stage only one of these, *The Virgin Bride*, plus another, *A Dream Play*, not on his list.

On 23 May, Henrik Ibsen died, aged seventy-eight; he had been semi-paralysed for the past five years. Strindberg noted the fact in his diary without comment and, when Schering asked if he would write a brief tribute for the German press, curtly refused (28 May): "I do not wish to write about I—n, and I beg that you quote nothing from my writings or letters." On 15 June, while still working on *The Scapegoat*, he began to accumulate material for a new work, originally intended to provide a religious adage for each day of the year, with comments, based on an idea he had found in Goethe. Like Goethe's, Strindberg's book was to be non-denominational. Gradually it changed its nature and became a miscellany of random essays and reflections on a wide range of subjects, many of them less than a page in length; eventually he entitled it *A Blue Book*.

At the end of June, *The Comrades* enjoyed yet another German production, this time in Munich, where, again, it was a success. But some of these German productions were pirated; on 17 July, *Dagens Nyheter* carried an article stating that four of his plays had been performed there that year without authorisation, and that Schering had sued one

---

*Romans 7: 9–24. Strindberg slightly misquotes the passage.

such company to warn others off. That month in France, Alfred Dreyfus was at last declared innocent of all charges, readmitted to the army, promoted and given the Legion of Honour; Strindberg noted the fact furiously in his diary, denouncing the decision on the ground that Dreyfus's friends had falsified documents. He turned from chemistry ("It ruined my eyes, so that I had to give it up," he told Harriet, adding that he had had a recurrence of psoriasis) and returned to photography, proudly reporting: "I have made a camera of cardboard, which reproduces the face in its natural size, despite all the theories."[31] On 22 July he sent *The Roofing Ceremony* and *The Scapegoat* to Bonniers.

His daughter Greta came to Stockholm in July, to further her stage career. Strindberg's mood towards the children of his first marriage was still hostile, and on 11 September he wrote a wild and disagreeable letter to her at the boardinghouse where she was staying. "Be careful how you behave, for we do not have the same loose morals here as in Finland. Do not have men in your rooms after 9 p.m. . . . Do not interfere in other couples' lives . . . Do not go to the café each evening, and do not walk alone at night, for that arouses the attention of the police and can lead to incalculable consequences. Things have already gone so far that only a change in your conduct can salvage your name." He signed it, without any salutation: "August Strindberg." Greta replied that she had twice invited her cousin Henry Philp, Anna's son, to tea, and "as regards my interfering in any other couple's life, I swear I have never done any such thing . . . Where you have got these fantasies from is a complete mystery to me."[32] She was to become engaged to Henry Philp before the year was out.

In contrast to his attitude towards his children, Strindberg maintained a surprisingly cordial relationship with his siblings. His brother Axel visited him regularly to play Beethoven, and his sisters Nora and Anna kept in close touch; Strindberg's hostility towards Anna had vanished with her husband's death. His youngest brother Olle, a master gardener, came to see him that September; he found Strindberg working with a photographer, who happened in passing to mention that one did not need a diamond to cut glass but could do it under water with ordinary scissors. "Strindberg became hugely excited, sent his housekeeper to buy window-panes and brought a big basin of water into the room. Then he started his cutting. His delight at its success was great, the photographer was invited to stay to supper, and when it transpired that he was in financial straits, Strindberg gave him a couple of banknotes in gratitude for the new game he had taught him."[33]

On 18 September, *Miss Julie* was at last publicly performed in

Sweden.* A twenty-four-year-old actor-manager named August Falck, son of that August Falck who had been associated with the Swedish premiere of *The Father* in 1888, was running a touring company and asked Strindberg's permission to open the production in Malmö. Strindberg agreed, asking only that they open in nearby Lund; so, eighteen years after Strindberg had written it, it received its Swedish premiere, in a double bill with *Pariah* at the Academic Society in Lund. August Palme, who had created several Strindberg roles at Dramaten, including Charles the Twelfth and the Stranger in *To Damascus*, was granted a month off to play Jean opposite the Julie of a young actress, Manda Björling, whom *Arbetet* found "too weak, too tame, and showing no talent for seduction." But the play aroused much interest and even excitement as Falck toured it the length of the country, taking over the role of Jean when Palme had to return to Stockholm. Falck's entry into Strindberg's life was to have important consequences for them both.

•

*A semi-private performance had taken place at the Guildhall in Uppsala in the spring of 1905. (*Cf.* article by Gunnar Ollén in *Sydsvenska Dagbladet*, 21 November 1982.)

Chapter Twenty-Nine

THE CHAMBER PLAYS AND
BLACK BANNERS

On 21 September 1906, Strindberg's principal scourge among critics, Oscar Levertin, suffered a macabre fate. He was poisoned (or according to some reports, choked) while swallowing a gargle containing potassium chlorate during an attack of tonsillitis. Strindberg noted the event in his diary, adding: "Heard that L's body at once began to decompose, so that he had to be buried quickly because of the stench." But if he thought that was the end of Levertin's attacks on him, he was wrong, for nine days later *Svenska Dagbladet* published a review Levertin had written shortly before his death of Strindberg's *New Swedish Destinies*,* which had appeared in the now familiar form of a series of small paperbacks priced at 25 öre. "Several of the stories have neither head nor tail," Levertin complained, though admitting that a "genius" such as Strindberg was always worth listening to. *Nya Dagligt Allehanda* summed up the general reaction in stating that Strindberg's historical method was to say the opposite of what everyone else had said about anyone or anything; yet "however great one's distaste or boredom . . . it is with these stories as with everything Strindberg writes; one finds it difficult to put down the book until one has read the final page."

*Originally entitled *Sagas of the Chieftains* (see page 456). The publisher wanted to exploit the popularity of the earlier *Swedish Destinies*, which had been reprinted in a new cheap edition that spring.

On 9 October, Anna's daughter Märta, Strindberg's favourite niece, married Hugo Fröding, a cousin of the poet Gustaf Fröding who had edited the book of tributes to Strindberg in 1894 and was now insane in an Uppsala asylum. Strindberg did not attend, despite his reconciliation with her mother, but painted a fire-screen and sent it to her as a present. He had three more productions in Germany and Austria that autumn. *Miss Julie* was performed in Elberfeld and *Creditors* in Altona, and his old admirer Josef Jarno staged *The Dance of Death* in Vienna and subsequently toured it to several German cities. On 6 November his daughter Greta made her first appearance on the Swedish stage, at the Östermalm Theatre in Stockholm in a play called *The Prodigal Son. Dagens Nyheter* commented: "For many people in the stalls, the main <u>interest</u> undoubtedly centred on . . . August Strindberg's daughter," adding that "she seems to have possibilities worth noting." Strindberg did not go to see her, although the theatre was only a few minutes' walk from his apartment.

Now that he had finally separated from Harriet, he consigned her, at any rate temporarily, to the ranks of his enemies, as he had done with Siri and Frida. On 10 November he wrote in his diary: "NB: Since I freed myself from Harriet I have (1) regained a clear view of Christianity (2) in my mind reconciled myself with my worst enemies such as [G. af G., Adolf Paul, Philp, Sigurd, Wirsén], even [Levertin].* And I live as though I were preparing for death. The beautiful things I wrote during my life with Harriet seem to me now to have come about as a reaction against her evil; and by imagining her as beautiful, I sometimes managed to influence her towards good. She was the most evil creature born, by her own admission!" He noted on 28 November that he had not seen or spoken to her for seven weeks.

Strindberg was now working hard at histology, the science of animal and plant tissues, and on 24 November he sent Schering "a portfolio containing *Comparative Histology*, attempting to show that plants have arteries and veins, nerves, lymphatic vessels, tracheas, connective tissues, all fashioned like those of the most highly developed animals." *Historical Miniatures* appeared in Germany and was quite respectfully received, a measure of his greater reputation there. On 29 November he was performed in Britain for the first time when a company called the New Stage Club presented a triple bill containing *Simoom* and *The Stronger* for two performances at the Bloomsbury Hall in London.

---

*Strindberg wrote these names in Greek characters. Sigurd was the pen name of one Alfred Hedenstierna, a newspaper columnist who had frequently mocked Strindberg.

August Falck's touring production of *Miss Julie* and *Pariah* had proved so successful, especially in Gothenburg, that the young actor-manager sought Strindberg's permission to present it for a few performances in Stockholm. Strindberg asked Falck to visit him to discuss the plan. "It was the first time I had met him and I felt a little nervous," Falck recalled. "He stood for some moments leaning with one hand on the doorpost, gazing searchingly at me. I became even more confused . . . But then he held out his hand and said amiably, 'Your name is August! Your name is Falck! Welcome!' I did not immediately understand what this curious greeting meant . . . It was the 'Powers' at work. I had the same Christian name as he, and my surname was the same as that which he had given to his *alter ego* in *The Red Room*. In my young form he saw his own youth renewed."[1]

Falck told Strindberg how enthusiastically the two plays had been received in the provinces, and that the unfashionable though centrally situated People's Theatre in Stockholm was keen to have them for a couple of nights. Strindberg agreed to allow the production in. "We discussed also the possibilities of creating an intimate theatre in Stockholm where he could be played . . . The occasional productions of his plays abroad had often been far from adequate. He had long regarded himself as a great playwright, but an outsider, a pioneer whom people would not stage. This feeling oppressed him, although at the same time it acted as a spur . . . He revealed his passionate desire to be staged, to be staged, for he was not so bothered about the money. 'Were I rich, I would never accept payment,' he had written to me. But the many adventurous attempts that had been made to perform him, and the vain expectations that these had aroused, had made him distrustful. He both believed and did not believe that our new effort would succeed."[2]

So, on 13 December 1906, *Miss Julie* was at last seen in Stockholm. It fitted incongruously into the People's Theatre's repertory of farces and boulevard dramas (as, eighteen years earlier, *The Father* had at the Casino Theatre in Copenhagen), but despite the inexperience of the young cast, proved a triumphant success. For all its faults—the often melodramatic phrasing, the difficulty of making Julie herself sympathetic and her suicide convincing—it remains, even a century later, profoundly powerful and upsetting, and in those days it was doubly so. As in *A Doll's House*, the audience found itself hearing things said which they knew to be true but which had never been said in a theatre before. The critics acclaimed it. "*Miss Julie*," wrote Erik Nyblom in *Dagens Nyheter*, "is said to have been thought impossible to present on a Stockholm stage. August Strindberg's disturbing and deeply humane play was received with

warmth and understanding. Social boundary posts have been moved . . .
Where the directors of the Stockholm theatres dared not tread, a brave
little trio from the provinces has dared. And they have won a famous
victory." August Brunius in *Svenska Dagbladet* declared: "Our humble
expectations were far exceeded, another illustration of the fact that good
plays create good actors . . . The audience was gripped and applauded
loudly." *Aftonbladet* hailed it as "a decided success." Only the ultra-
conservative *Nya Dagligt Allehanda* found the theme repellent and the
play outdated, though Carl G. Laurin in *Ord och Bild*, while "grateful
that a play unique in Swedish drama and so typical of the author has at last
been performed, and performed so excellently," deplored its "coarseness
and sordidity." Public interest was such that five extra performances were
given before the company departed to fulfil its engagements in the north.

Aftonbladet carried a news item later that month to the effect that
"Eleonora Duse is said to be rehearsing the title role in Strindberg's
Miss Julie,"[3] but Duse never played the part, which would scarcely have
suited her and for which she would then have been somewhat old at
forty-seven.

Strindberg now heard a rumour, which turned out to be untrue, that
Harriet was engaged to a Finnish literary historian named Gunnar
Castrén, and at his request on 14 December "Harriet visited me for the
first time since 6 October; I visited her in the evening; everything as
before; no explanation! After over 2 months!" On Christmas Day: "H—t
and Anne-Marie to dinner . . . I associate with H—t and Anne-Marie,
but it is false: she is intimate with my enemies!" On 27 December, the
Swedish Theatre revived *Gustav Vasa*, bringing him money he badly
needed: Ranft's unfulfilled promise to buy seven of his plays had encouraged him to keep the big apartment at Karlavägen. Gustaf Uddgren says
that Strindberg earned barely 4,000 crowns (about £220) this year, and
that his annual rent took up one fifth of that.[4] On New Year's Eve:
"Row with Harriet. Because I would not go to her in the evening." So
1906 ended in a mixture of uncertainty and hope.

Strindberg spent the first weeks of 1907 brooding over plans for the new
theatre. Max Reinhardt's experiments in Berlin with a tiny auditorium
had shown how effectively plays such as Gorki's *The Lower Depths*,
Maeterlinck's *Pelléas and Mélisande*, and even *A Midsummer Night's
Dream* and Hofmannsthal's *Electra*, could be presented in a small space,
and in 1906 he had moved to the Deutsches Theater and set a new fashion
by adding a small studio theatre to the main house, the first time any

theatre had contained two auditoriums.* Reinhardt had been excited by Craig's articles in *The Mask*, suggesting the use of tall draperies instead of the usual quasi-realistic backcloths and borders and, above all, imaginative lighting to create atmosphere. Craig clarified what Reinhardt had already felt, that decor and lighting might be used as something positive instead of merely as background. "These wretched rags [i.e., backcloths and borders] still dangle in our theatres today from the time when they hung out the washing when the comedians entered," Reinhardt had complained as early as 1904, adding: "*Light* is the main thing. More light!"[5] He repeatedly invited Craig to design productions for him, without success. Reinhardt's own *Midsummer Night's Dream* in 1905 had been super-realistic, showing different parts of the Athenian forest on a revolving stage; but it was characteristic of him that he also recognised the virtues of suggestion (he was to persuade Edvard Munch to design *Ghosts* and *Hedda Gabler*).

Reinhardt's fame had enabled him to assemble a powerful company, including such players as Gertrud Eysoldt, Emmanuel Reicher, Agnes Sorma, Rosa Bertens and Alexander Moissi. But August Falck had no such reputation or skills, and his company was young and inexperienced; it would be foolhardy to expose them to the demands of such plays as *The Lower Depths* and *Pelléas and Mélisande* (which had been coolly received by the Swedish critics when Lugné-Poe brought it to Stockholm in 1894). Maeterlinck's chamber plays, such as *The Uninvited Guest* and *The Blind*, seemed a more promising model, with their avoidance of conventional plot and conflicts, elemental passions and big gestures, and their concentration on the inward dialogue which remains unspoken and which we sense behind and between the lines—what Maeterlinck called *la tragédie immobile* and *le théâtre statique*. Maeterlinck had written of this in *The Treasure of the Humble*, that collection of essays which had so fascinated Strindberg a few years earlier that he had given a copy to Harriet. That Strindberg had Maeterlinck's ideas in mind is evident from a letter he wrote to Adolf Paul on 6 January 1907, advising Paul on how to write his next play. "Seek the intimate, a small theme exhaustively treated, few characters, big viewpoints, free imagination, but built on observation, experience, closely studied; simple but not too simple; no elaborate apparatus, no superfluous minor characters, no conventional five-acters or 'old machines,' no drawn-out 'whole' evenings. *Miss Julie* (without an interval) has stood the test of fire here and shown itself to be

---

*Reinhardt's Kammerspielhaus in fact seated about three hundred people, nearly twice as many as the Intimate Theatre was to hold.

the form desired by this impatient age: searching but short!" This was an exact description of the plays he was about to write for his Intimate Theatre, and which, following Reinhardt, he called *Kammerspiele*, chamber plays.

Strindberg was still seeing Harriet occasionally, torn as usual between extremes of desire and loathing. "Stayed at home this evening, without going to Harriet," he wrote in his diary on 9 January. "There was light. I now believe that the darkness comes from her, and I want to be freed. At our last reunion I found her more stupid than before, as proud and as evil. Black and poisonous!" Next day he wrote to Madame Charlotte in Paris: "Life goes on, not badly, the theatres stage my plays, my children grow big and my daughter has just got engaged. You will know that the late Paul Goguin [*sic*], the friend of us all, has just been resurrected and that his fame as a great artist has reached its zenith in Paris. They say his paintings have reached a sale price of 60,000 francs each, which must delight you who own several of his masterpieces. That is life after death, one might say." On 13 January he advised Adolf Paul: "Write . . . about your own experiences and not about those of others, which you cannot know"; a fair summary of his own attitude and range, and fair advice, too, to the playwright of average talent, though it had not been heeded by the authors of *Agamemnon*, *Macbeth* or *A Doll's House*.

On 20 January he wrote in his diary: "Harriet and Anne-Marie came to dinner . . . Harriet stayed in the yellow room," adding in a note evidently appended later: "The last time." Thus this extraordinary sexual relationship at length ended, after nearly six years.

Meanwhile, August Falck was touring *Miss Julie* around the Swedish provinces, causing excitement everywhere. At Varberg, on the west coast, the local public prosecutor rushed up on to the stage in the middle of the performance, shouting, "Are you mad, woman, behaving like that?" Falck comments: "The play proceeded as though nothing had happened." Two weeks later at Halmstad, a member of the audience demanded, and got, three cheers for "Sweden's greatest living writer, August Strindberg," plus the sending to Strindberg of a telegram of congratulations and thanks.[6] The Swedish Theatre was rehearsing the world premiere of *A Dream Play*, and Strindberg wrote to Schering in Berlin begging him to urge Reinhardt to stage it and some of his early realistic work. "Why won't Reinhardt do *The Father*, which has never been performed in Berlin (virtually)?* Or *The Comrades*? Or *The Dream Play*, which is now to be staged at the Swedish Theatre with magic-

---

*The Freie Bühne had staged it briefly in 1890 (see page 229).

lantern pictures? Two magic lanterns, bought in Dresden as used at the theatre there. Or *Easter* (intimately)?" But Reinhardt was to direct no more plays by Strindberg until after the latter's death, though in the ensuing years he was to stage several memorable productions. (In all, he directed no less than seventeen Strindberg plays.)

Strindberg's short novel *The Scapegoat* began to appear that January, serialised in the Stockholm magazine *Idun*, and before the end of the month he began the first of his chamber plays, *Storm*. By 13 February he had completed it, a subtle and astringent ninety-minute study of resignation in old age, similar in mood to his autobiographical novel *Alone*, five years earlier. (The title, *Oväder*, really means *Stormy Weather*, for the storm which the old man awaits does not break, but that title has irresistibly incongruous associations in English.) The play contains a moving scene with the old man's young ex-wife: in a letter to Harriet on or around 7 May the following year, Strindberg described *Storm* as "a painful poem with which I wanted to write you and our child out of my heart."* Immediately after finishing it, he began work on a second play, *The Burned Site* (also known in English as *After the Fire*), about another old man who returns from America to find that his childhood home has burned down. Talking to neighbours, and seeing objects that have survived, he finds his rosy memories of childhood being replaced by uncomfortable truths, and returns, saddened and wiser, to the outside world. It is a less successful play than *Storm*, consisting of a lengthy monologue† interwoven with some rather melodramatic and unconvincing subplots (Strindberg was often curiously weak in his subplots, as with his subordinate characters). Even the great Alf Sjöberg's distinguished production with Max von Sydow at Dramaten in 1970 could not conceal the play's longueurs.

On finishing *The Burned Site*, Strindberg immediately began another play, which likewise took him only a couple of weeks, *The Ghost Sonata*. One of his most powerful and successful pieces, it explores, like *Storm* and *The Burned Site*, the relationship between illusion and reality, but where the two earlier plays are straightforwardly realistic (in so far as any of Strindberg's plays can be called straightforward), *The Ghost Sonata*, like *To Damascus* and *A Dream Play*, is set in that half-waking, half-sleeping

---

*Strindberg does not specifically identify the "painful poem" as *Storm*, but there seems little doubt that he meant it.

†"As you see from my Chamber Plays, I have returned to *long* speeches and monologues, as a result of reading Goethe's plays, *Clavigo*, *Stella*, etc. The French mode of dialogue has degenerated into catechistic questioning and has eliminated depth and searching treatment." (Letter to Emil Schering, 24 April 1907.)

world where reality and fantasy merge. A student, admiring a beautiful girl in the window of a rich house, meets a cripple in a wheel-chair who promises to introduce him to her. Inside, a macabre background is unveiled; the girl is the cripple's illegitimate daughter; her mother has sat for twenty years in a cupboard, "thinks she's a parrot" and is known as the Mummy; other grotesques gather. The cripple, Hummel, denounces them all, and is himself denounced as a murderer by the Mummy; he takes her place in the cupboard and hangs himself. In the final scene, the student finds that even the daughter has been tainted; "the source of life is poisoned in you." She dies, and the student's last words to her, which close the play, sum up Strindberg's view of life as his own approached its end. "Unhappy child, born into this world of delusion, guilt, suffering and death, this world that is for ever changing, for ever erring, for ever in pain. The Lord of Heaven be merciful to you upon your journey."

Meanwhile, the publishing house of Björck and Börjesson accepted his novel *Black Banners*, which had been rejected by every other publisher to whom it had been offered on its completion two years earlier. It was to prove a disastrous decision, not for the publishers but for Strindberg. Marie Uhl wrote to him that Kerstin, by now virtually abandoned by her mother, was longing for him, and suggested that he should visit her in Austria. Strindberg replied to Marie on 6 March, the first letter he had written to her for nearly six years apart from a solitary brief note on 22 February. It does not make attractive reading:

> For a long while I have been thinking about Kerstin's future. The child's destiny is of course bound to her mother's, and since I always believed that Kerstin would acquire a stepfather I did not wish to become involved in these disagreeable complications. Then I said to myself: Kerstin does not need me. In a few years she will be grown up and enter life as an individual in her own right. What need then of a titular father? Why rend the child and her feelings? She has a brother,* who does not belong to me, Kerstin knows that. No, I cannot creep back into this web. Through Kerstin I would enter into an indirect connection with her mother—I do not want that. I may not.
>
> I do not know if Frida is alive, whether she is married, etc. I could of course risk meeting her, and it is certain that Kerstin in childish simplicity would try to "reconcile" us. It would be no good. Why arrange tragedies? It is enough as it is.
>
> In three years Kerstin will be an adult, perhaps engaged, will have her own circle of friends, relatives . . . Then she will not need me at all. One knows how children are.

*Frida's son by Wedekind. He sometimes claimed to be Strindberg's son, became a Nazi and tried to get Arthur Koestler arrested in Spain. (*Cf.* Koestler's *Spanish Testament*, London 1937, pp. 38–40.)

Pontius Pilate could not have put it more clearly. Later in the year (27 November) he was to reject a pathetic appeal from Kerstin herself: "I live as alone as you. I am no company for a young girl—an old hermit who asks nothing more of life than to die."

The company to which his other daughter Greta was attached presented *Lucky Peter's Journey* at the Östermalm Theatre that spring, and although Strindberg had not bothered to see her earlier performance there, he decided that this was an excuse for Anne-Marie to see something of his work, and invited Harriet and her to the dress rehearsal on 8 March. Harriet tells how he "beamed contentedly with pride, both at his daughter's acting and at his own play."[7] *Lucky Peter* was a success, as indeed it usually was, and ran for forty-two performances. Five days later Harriet and Anne-Marie came to stay briefly with him, since they were moving house; an unwise experiment, one might have thought, and so it proved. "15 March. Everything as before, venomous, spiteful," he noted in his diary. "She blamed me, who am innocent, for all her troubles."

Strindberg was having domestic problems, with a series of bad cooks, and on 19 March his sister Anna came to look after him for a week. She remembered these days with affection:

The flat at Karlavägen 40 consisted of five rooms and a kitchen and was inconvenient, with long corridors. Beethoven's death mask hung on the green majolica stove . . . Some aspidistras could be glimpsed behind the closely drawn curtains . . . All the paintings in the various rooms were by him . . . He never painted from life, even his most realistic seascapes from the skerries were imagined . . . The best present one could give him was flowers. His day began at 7 . . . He could never lie in bed after that hour, for then "the walls began to throb and his bed to burn." With his hat on his head (so that his "thoughts should not fly away") he sat down to make his coffee alone; no one might watch him . . . Then quickly out for his long morning walk. "If people knew what they miss when they sleep in the morning," he used to say. His walk lasted for an hour or an hour and a half, usually around Djurgården. He seldom looked up at the people he met but walked like a somnambulist, staring fixedly ahead.

The first day I came to him, he warned me not to show myself when he returned from his morning walk. He would then immediately sit down, hot and tired, on a chair in the hall and change his boots. Once I forgot his warning and happened to enter the hall just as he entered. He simply looked at me and sweated with anxiety. I said nothing and shall never forget his eloquent eyes . . . I had disturbed his train of thought . . .

He seated himself at his desk and . . . smoking cigarettes vigorously . . . worked until about noon. Then he was exhausted and had to lie down on a sofa and rest, having first carefully locked away his manuscript in a portfolio. After a short rest he had relaxed and . . . received visits, talked, read or wrote letters . . . was friendly and talkative and smiling, a complete contrast to the man at his morning coffee. Then he would usually sit in one of the basket chairs under the big laurel tree in the dining room, the "laurel grove" as he called it, and decide the menu for dinner and whether guests should be invited to help pass the long afternoon. Dinner was at 3 p.m. sharp. There would be a small but good *smörgåsbord*, with dark beer, then "strong soup," as he called it, oxtail or consommé . . . The next dish would sometimes be game. His favourite was ptarmigan . . . His favourite wine was burgundy . . . We usually dispensed with dessert, as he did not like that . . . After dinner he would lie down and rest, a habit he had followed since he was twelve. By 6 p.m. he was sociable again, came in to me and discussed how we might best pass the evening. He lit the lamps throughout the apartment and opened the piano. "Play for me," he would often ask and, calm and happy, he would wander round the dining table, listening.

Sometimes he would invite Anna's children and their friends to join them.

They came gladly, for when "Uncle August" was in a good mood they could expect a merry evening with the best of hosts. Young people liked him, though he was often so shy and withdrawn as to be unapproachable . . . The young people would dance. "Uncle August" liked to see the latest dances and be *au fait* with the latest dance music . . . The children thought he could only be a woman-hater on paper . . . Over coffee . . . August would sit on an ordinary chair—he did not like to sit comfortably. He made the coffee himself, served the ladies with liqueurs and poured himself a whisky grog. . . . He told of his travels abroad, his mystical experiences or his making of gold. He seldom spoke of his writing . . . Once he pointed at the row of his books on a shelf in his study and said: "That is my monument, I need no other."[8]

Anna's departure led to another series of domestic upheavals.

26 March. *Anna left.* Alma [a new cook] came. Calm, clean and good. Clean food for dinner . . . Aversion to strong drink in evening . . . 29 March. Alma left because I remarked on the ruined food . . . 1 April. Sophie came to work here. Worse than ever. 2 April. Black meat for dinner, black soup because the enamel saucepan split . . . 3 April. Even more horrible. Indescribable . . . 5 April. Burned meat for dinner, and cold. Sophie left.

Loneliness and age were turning his mind more and more towards religion.* On 27 March, sending *The Ghost Sonata* to Schering, he

---

*On at any rate one occasion this year, Strindberg went to church. Axel B. Svensson, writing in *Dagens Nyheter* on 20 November 1948, recalled how when preaching one Sunday in 1907 in the Bethlehem Church in Stockholm, he was astonished to see Strindberg "standing straight as a candle behind the rest of the congregation. He was paying close attention."

wrote: "It is horrible like life, when the veil falls from our eyes and we see things as they are. It has shape and content, the wisdom that comes with age, as our knowledge increases and we learn to understand. This is how 'the Weaver' weaves men's destinies; secrets like these are to be found in every home. People are too proud to admit it; most of them boast of their imagined luck, and hide their misery. The Colonel acts out his private comedy to the end; illusion (Maya) has become reality to him—the Mummy awakens first, one cannot wake the others . . . I have suffered as though in Kama-Loka* (Scheol) during the writing of it and my hands have bled (literally). What has saved my soul from darkness during this work has been my religion (= union with the beyond). The hope of a better life to come; the firm conviction that we live in a world of madness and delusion (illusion) from which we must fight our way free. For me things have become brighter, and I have written with the feeling that this is my 'Last Sonata.'"

A week later he wrote again to Schering: "Now I am assuredly entering into something new. I long for the light, have always done so, but have not found it. Is it the end that is approaching? I don't know, but I feel that it is so. Life is, as it were, squeezing me out, or driving me out, and I have long since rested all my hopes on 'the beyond,' with which I am in contact (through Swedenborg). A feeling has also come over me that I have completed my work, that I have nothing more to say. My whole life seems to me to have been planned like a play, so that I might both suffer and depict suffering."

While Strindberg was writing *The Ghost Sonata*, the Swedish Theatre was rehearsing *A Dream Play*, which may have been one reason why, in *The Ghost Sonata*, he had returned to that world where, as he had stated in his introduction to the earlier work, "Everything can happen, everything is possible and probable." On 17 April he wrote to Schering: "It is 8 p.m. . . . and the curtain is now rising on the *Dream Play*, while I sit at home as is my custom at premieres. Last night I saw the dress rehearsal —and all my happy confidence in my most loved play, child of my greatest pain, vanished. I became gloomy, decided that it ought never to be performed—such things must not be said to people, and they must not murmur at their fate. I have been waiting for some catastrophe to intervene and prevent the performance. But now, as I say, it is 8 o'clock . . . 11 p.m. Telephone call from Bosse and Ranft that the *Dream Play* was a success."

---

*Kama-Loka—a kind of ghost or dream world through which mortals, or some mortals, have to wander before they enter the peace of death's kingdom.

Victor Castegren, the director of A Dream Play, had intended to meet the problem of the many scene changes by the use of magic-lantern slides projected from behind onto gauzes, as Emil Grandinson had tried to do with To Damascus in 1899; but, like Grandinson, he was forced to abandon his plans because of the technical difficulties involved. He had to resort to ordinary sets and backcloths, with predictable results. "The building that went on onstage," Strindberg later recalled, "disturbed the actors' mood and caused interminable intervals; and the whole perform-ance became a thing of materialisation, instead of the intended opposite (dematerialisation)."[9] He wanted Castegren to use light creatively, as Craig demanded, but was assured that this would remind the audience of cheap variety.[10]

A Dream Play, in its complete text, is full of longueurs and, even without "interminable intervals," runs for over three hours; more perhaps than any other of Strindberg's major plays, it needs ruthless cutting. (When thus reduced, it can work marvellously on stage, as Ingmar Bergman showed in his production in Stockholm in 1970, which he brought to London the following year.) The premiere in 1907 must have been taxing indeed for the audience, especially as, according to Tor Hedberg in Svenska Dagbladet, most of the cast tended towards "Maeter-linck recitation." Yet several critics perceived the quality of the play, and Harriet's performance in the leading role of Indra's Daughter/Agnes received particular praise. Forty years later Oscar Wieselgren wrote that the scenes between her and Tore Svennberg as the Advocate provided "probably the most powerful interpretation of Strindberg yet seen in our theatres,"[11] though he found the rest of the production weak. The first-night audience was enthusiastic, and at the close called repeatedly for the author until Ranft promised to telephone Strindberg to convey their acclaim. But subsequent audiences were bewildered, and the play was removed after twelve performances.

Strindberg had meanwhile begun a new "dream play" which he entitled Toten-Insel (The Island of the Dead), after his favourite painting by Böcklin of that name; but he quickly abandoned it. "The beginning was good (Kama-Loka),"* he explained to Schering on 26 April, "but I lost interest, as though I had lost interest in life and sense the end. For ten years I have prepared myself for death and have, as it were, lived 'on the other side.' Now I am reading the proofs of Black Banners, in which as you know I break with the 'Black Ones.' I suppose they will stone me, but I accept that as my calling and am used to it . . . I am wondering whether

*See p. 481n.

to take up my wanderer's staff again and venture out into the world of illusion. But I am sixty [*sic*] years old, tired, and hate the squalor of hotels, and squalid habits. Only one journey tempts me, the final one, and I want to die in my own country."

That month, he wrote a long preface to his chamber plays, which eventually appeared not as a preface to them (Geber refused the plays, and they were not published until 1909), but as a "Memorandum" in a volume entitled *Open Letters to the Intimate Theatre* towards the end of 1908. In this memorandum, Strindberg explained his reasoning behind his creation of an "intimate" theatre:

> When in the eighteen-sixties and seventies one offered a full evening's play to the Royal Theatre, the following requirements had to be met if it was to be performed. The play had to be of five acts, each act filling some twenty-four pages . . . Each act had to end in a tableau calling for applause . . . The play had to contain set pieces for the actors, known as "scenes," monologues were allowed and often provided the high points; a long outburst of emotion, or a punishment or unmasking, was considered virtually essential; and something had to be narrated, a dream, an anecdote or an event. And roles were demanded, rewarding roles for the theatre's stars . . . In the eighties, the new age extended its reforming zeal to the theatre. Zola rebelled against French comedy, with its Brussels carpet, lacquered shoes and lacquered plots, and its dialogue reminiscent of the questions and answers of the catechism.
>
> In 1887 Antoine opened the Théâtre Libre in Paris, and *Thérèse Raquin*, although only an adaptation of a novel, set a new example. A strong plot and a concentrated form . . . It was then that I wrote the trio of *The Father, Miss Julie* and *Creditors* . . . In 1889 the Freie Bühne opened in Berlin and by 1893 all my three plays had been performed [in Germany] . . . Then a certain silence descended, and the drama reverted to its old ways until in the new century Reinhardt opened his Kleines Theater. I was there in its early stages, represented by the long one-act play *The Bond, Miss Julie* and *There Are Crimes and Crimes*.
>
> Last year Reinhardt went a step further and opened his Kammerspiel-haus, which under his banner presents . . . the idea of chamber music translated into drama . . . Throughout Germany, theatres have sprung up called Intimate Theatres . . .
>
> We avoid all ostentation, all calculated effects, milking of applause, showy roles, solo numbers . . . When Director Falck decided to abandon long performances that end towards midnight, he also broke with the theatre of alcoholic refreshment. This was a bold step, since the retailing of spirits pays for at least half the rent of the big theatres. But this combination of scenic art and alcohol caused long intervals, the length of which was controlled by the licensee of the theatre restaurant . . . The disadvantages of allowing the audience to consume strong drink in the middle of a play are well known. Either the mood established is reasoned away, enthusiasm

cools . . . or people read the evening paper, chat with friends they meet at
the bar, are distracted, the threads of the play are snipped, the plot forgotten,
and the spectator returns to his seat in a completely alien state of mind to
seek in vain to recover his previous mood . . . Many people occupied their
tables before the play began and regarded the play as a series of distractions;
some even sat out an act if the velvet sofa was sufficiently soft and difficult to
rise from. The economy of the Intimate Theatre has suffered from this
breach with tradition, but in another respect the theatre has gained, in that
the attention of the audience is more concentrated on the stage and the
audience is able to leave at the end and discuss in peace over the supper table
what they have heard and seen.

   We sought a small space because we wanted the actors' voices to be heard
in the farthermost corners without anyone having to shout. There are some
theatres so large that actors have to force their voices, with the result that
every intonation sounds false and a declaration of love has to be shouted, a
confidence rapped out like a rifle shot, secrets of the heart bellowed, and
everyone on stage sounds either angry or in a hurry to get off . . .[12]

Strindberg went on to stress certain basic principles of acting: the
importance of a good spirit in the company, of speaking loud enough to be
heard at the back ("The prime necessity," he says surprisingly, "is to speak
slowly"), of actors making themselves familiar with the whole play and
not just their own lines, and of listening both before entering and when
fellow-actors are speaking ("There are listeners who drop their eyes and
look as though they were memorising their next line, which they are
already mouthing so as to have it ready . . . others who utilise this
opportunity to count the house, others again who flirt gently with the
audience, and with their eyes and shoulders or toes say: 'Hear how
stupidly he talks, wait till I speak' "). An actor must remember to sit down
and stand up gracefully; "one should be well shod onstage, for the eyes of
the audience are on a level with the actor's feet"; before entering, he
should pick up the tone of those on stage "and not rush in bringing a
completely alien atmosphere with him, as often happens." Nor must he
underline his words with gestures or "distract himself after leaving the
stage by reading or conversation." Above all, he must look at his
fellow-players and not the audience; "a declaration of love must always be
directed to the object of that declaration."[13]

Strindberg spent much of that spring and summer of 1907 working on
his *Blue Book*. Dedicated to the memory of Swedenborg and composed as
a series of dialogues between a teacher and his pupil, it ranges widely over
Strindberg's various interests: philosophy, religion, science, history, the
occult, mathematics (even Assyrian mathematics), linguistics (especially
Hebrew and Chinese), Shakespeare, Goethe, Oscar Wilde's *De Profundis*, cloud formations and wine. He rode all his old hobbyhorses as

tirelessly as ever, instancing even Cordelia as an example of the untrustworthiness of woman ("although as a daughter she loves her father, as a woman she hates him"), and attacking at length contemporary science, which he regarded as the main obstacle to his hoped-for religious renaissance. Radium and X-rays he denounces as hoaxes, and the evolution theory as "unscientific rubbish"; he doubts whether tuberculosis really exists, but asserts his belief in vampires and witchcraft. Even mountains, he declares, much more the human body, were shaped by the great master builder. The scientific investigation of religion is condemned; one must accept religion uncritically, the dogmas with the miracles. "All atheists are rogues and all rogues are atheists." The imperfections and injustices of life are explained by the theory that life is a hell through which we must pass to be purified; he even defends his own attacks on the living and the dead by claiming that this in some way purifies them. Many of the notes from his old green sack at last found their way into print. Inevitably, and not infrequently, nuggets can be glimpsed amidst the dross. Alf Sjöberg, one of Strindberg's most perceptive and vivid interpreters, has remarked that A *Blue Book* is, like so many of Strindberg's later plays, a collage, with fragments of reality, splinters of memory, the past and the present, all mingled.[14]

On 3 May *Playing with Fire*, the black comedy he had written in 1892, at last had its Swedish premiere. The occasion seemed humble enough at the time, for it was presented at a soirée in a Stockholm restaurant; but the leading role of the Friend was played by Mauritz Stiller, a gifted young Finn who was to become a pioneer in the field of silent films and is remembered as the discoverer of Greta Garbo.

On 12 May, Strindberg wrote to Harriet for the first time in five months: "When you suffer I am near you and suffer with you, but when you are happy I cannot always join you, since life has placed you among my enemies . . . I am resigning myself now to the great loneliness of summer, and hope no more from life, since everything has shown itself to be untenable, transitory, fugitive . . . I do not long to see you, for I see you when I wish and as I wish. People and life sought to part us, in a way, but I believe that we shall still meet, sometime, elsewhere, for we are kin and can never cease to be so." We do not know whether she replied, but his diary shows how briefly his "resignation" lasted:

> 18 May. Harriet "persecutes" me from morning till noon . . . She seeks me intimately and forces herself upon me . . .
> 19 May. When I married Harriet, we had a child at once. But she grudged me that great honour . . . alleged that I had deserted the bedchamber, but the fact was that she <u>asked me to change</u> bedrooms, since her

pregnancy had made her body unpleasing to her. She came back, the child was born. Then she did not want to have more children, yet continued to "live married." This resulted in distaste and repugnance. We separated, then divorced. Then we were reunited and I became her love and still am [*sic*]. Then one must ask: wherein have I offended? I was rehabilitated! yet am not! for her lies endure! despite all evidence to the contrary. I was no good as a husband of 50 but as a lover of 58 I was all right! It is sublime! Sublime! . . .

24 May. In the morning strong contact with H—t which continued all day, increasing towards evening. She is the most evil and vile person I have known, the stupidest and the ugliest, in a way, but sometimes the opposite, in all respects!

Schering sent him a play he had written, and Strindberg replied (18 May) with excellent practical advice, advising him that it contained too many short scenes. "This is how I wrote plays when I was 19! . . . The main fault is lack of build-up. Build-up is achieved by means of supporting characters. You have been in too much of a hurry! Impatience is the cardinal sin of playwriting, the sin I and all the others committed when young . . . Conflict and confrontation are drama. Here there is no confrontation. Don't lose courage now, for through failure one approaches success . . . Your play is now 42 pages. Reduce it to 25 and it will still fill an evening." This is not such a strange calculation as it sounds; assuming that each of Schering's manuscript pages was equivalent to two printed pages, twenty-five such would make it the same length as *The Father*.

On 19 May, *Black Banners* was published, in a limited edition carrying an announcement that "No new edition will be issued." A few weeks earlier, while reading the proofs, Strindberg had noted in his diary: "Wondered if the book was a crime and should be cancelled. Opened the Bible and found Job, where the prophet is compelled to prophesy even when he was in hiding. This comforted me. But it is a horrible book!"[15] *Black Banners* opens with a grotesque literary banquet, as formidable a chapter of narrative prose as Strindberg ever wrote. We then enter the home of the writer Zachris and his wife Jenny, a portrayal of married life as hideous as that in *The Dance of Death*. Zachris is one of Strindberg's vampires, a man who lives on the blood of others; he even tempts his wife to eat and drink so that she will grow fat and ugly and he will be the master. Another of his victims is a rival author, Falkenström, a disillusioned idealist with three broken marriages, an unconcealed self-portrait of Strindberg himself; Falkenström seeks comfort with two friends whose company provides him with the "monastery" he needs. This world of the monastery, a spiritual retreat for those who seek peace of mind, is contrasted with the atheistic world of writers and critics, the bearers of the "black banners." Finally Jenny, after leaving Zachris with their two sons to stay with a feminist friend, returns to him in despair, and as she lies dying, he writes a novel of revenge about her, occasionally sneaking upstairs to spy on her lest she should be writing similarly about him.

Black Banners contains scenes of power and brilliance, comparable to the best in Strindberg's plays. If only he had limited himself to Zachris and Jenny; for the "monastery" chapters, with their lengthy and often muddled discussions about religion and ethics, show Strindberg at his tedious and didactic worst, and occupy a large part of the book. Strindberg had originally intended to publish these religious reflections separately and did not decide to fuse them with the novel until he was halfway through it. But contemporary opinion was outraged by the undisguised way in which Strindberg had based Zachris on his former friend and publisher, Gustaf af Geijerstam. In every respect, not least physical appearance, the likeness was unmistakable. Geijerstam's recently deceased wife was equally grossly and recognisably caricatured as Jenny; Hanna Paj, Jenny's feminist friend, was patently based on Ellen Key; and several other leading literary figures, most of them liberals or radicals, were easily identifiable. The book was greeted with horror and disbelief. Bo Bergman in Dagens Nyheter summed up the general reaction: "A book which should never have been published . . . He rages like a poor madman . . . [but] not against the elements of society which formerly . . . abused him with every imaginable invective . . . Now . . . it is his old friends, who perhaps thought they were still that, who have become the new enemies." Several critics condemned Björck and Börjesson for publishing it, especially as Björck was a pastor. Carl Larsson wrote a letter of protest to Strindberg, who retorted by attacking him the following year in the third volume of A Blue Book, calling his wife "an evil demon" and accusing Larsson of murder.

The poet Per Hallström, a close friend of Geijerstam, who after his first meeting with Strindberg in 1900 had described him as "lovable,"[16] was convinced that the main reason for this virulent assault by him on an old friend and admirer was jealousy at the success which Geijerstam had achieved as a novelist and playwright, plus a suspicion that Geijerstam had taken Harriet's side over the divorce. Geijerstam "avoided reading Black Banners, but of course learned from others what it contained"; when it appeared, he was "already an exhausted and broken man [as a result of his wife's death], and this attack proved the death-blow."[17] Karl Otto Bonnier says Geijerstam was so shattered that the following year he refused to allow Bonnier to give a party to celebrate his fiftieth birthday because he knew that everyone present would have read the book; and when on that day Bonnier and his wife went to congratulate him in his home, "it was more than sad to see Geijerstam, once so exuberant and full of *joie de vivre*, a broken man at fifty and broken by the idol of his youth, the man he had loved and admired more than anyone."[18] He died barely a year later. Even then, Strindberg continued to attack him, including a revolting and easily recognisable reference to him in his last play, *The Great Highway*. Nothing that Strindberg wrote or did caused as much indignation as this extraordinary and sustained libel, and it made nonsense of the high religious ideals which he preached in the monastery chapters of *Black Banners* and had been advocating for the past decade.

Chapter Thirty

⚬⚬⚬⚬⚬⚬⚬⚬⚬⚬⚬⚬⚬⚬⚬⚬⚬⚬⚬⚬⚬⚬⚬⚬⚬

"CAN THE PIT SMELL OF ROSES?"

On 6 June 1907, Ola and Laura Hansson, who had organised Strindberg's departure to Berlin in 1892 and had not seen him since their quarrel later that year, visited him with their young son. Nineteen years later, Hansson painted a gruesome verbal picture of Strindberg a month after the publication of *Black Banners*. "His stomach was large and hung loosely; his back was rounded, his shoulders drooping. His lion mane was thinned and lay anyhow in long, sparse, unkempt tufts; and the once so proud Mongol face retained only the expression of a grimly bitter, fussy and splenetic old woman. His clothes were covered with grease stains, as though he was used to eating at the kitchen table; and on his feet he wore a pair of narrow, dirty women's shoes of white cloth, too small for him."[1] Hansson, like Adolf Paul when the latter wrote his reminiscences, remembered Strindberg as an enemy, and the testimony of enemies must be regarded with suspicion, but it is as essential a part of any biography as the evidence of friends.

On 13 June, Harriet wrote Strindberg a tender letter:

> My dear, beloved friend, yes, I still call you that, you must feel, you must know, that no one has taken your place in my affections.
>
> You do not want to see me, us, again; I understand you, and respect your wish.
>
> We are together none the less, and I am convinced <u>now</u> at least that even

were I at some time to link my future with another man's, you have so
coloured my life that I shall never forget you . . .

I am deeply fond of you—whatever may happen—I hold you dear,
perhaps because you have, through a great and boundless grief, filled my life
with meaning.

Goodbye, then.

Your Harriet

By 19 June, Strindberg had completed a fourth chamber play, *The
Pelican*, which he described the same day to Schering as "horrible but
good," adding: "Falck has extraordinary difficulties to contend with in
working for me." "*Black Banners*," Falck explains, "hung like a pall over
the theatre, and hatred of its author poured over us too."[2] On 23 June,
Greta Strindberg married her cousin Henry Philp. Strindberg noted the
fact in his diary without comment, and did not attend the ceremony,
presumably to avoid meeting Siri, but one of his nieces tells that "he
generously arranged a champagne dinner at Hasselbacken and even hired
a car to take us there and back. He also arranged for the band to play the
march from *The Wedding at Ulfåsa* as we went to table."[3] His generosity
did not stop there, for five days later he commanded Greta: "Send me the
bills for the wedding and I shall pay them at once."

On 26 June he inspected the building at Norra Bantorget which Falck
thought a possible venue for their theatre, and next day, according to his
diary, signed a contract for an annual rent of 15,000 crowns. They had
hoped to open as early as August or September, but had to make extensive
alterations to satisfy the health authorities which cost 45,000 crowns and
delayed the opening until mid-November. "Unexpected money from
Germany" on 30 May and "unexpectedly much money from Bonnier"
on 5 July helped to pay for this. Gustaf Uddgren says that Strindberg
earned 32,000 crowns during 1907, compared with barely 4,000 crowns
in 1906, and that he gave no less than 19,000 crowns before the end of the
year towards the founding of the Intimate Theatre. This included paying
the salaries of the twenty actors and actresses for the four months before
the theatre opened so that they should not take engagements elsewhere.[4]

Strindberg visited the theatre every day during the rebuilding, often
before taking his morning walk. He set out his views in a memorandum:

"1. No sale of intoxicants. 2. No Sunday matinees. 3. Short performances! 8–10 p.m. Short curtain-raisers, if any. 4. No curtain calls during
the performance. 5. No prompter. No orchestra, only music on stage. 6.
The text to be on sale at the box-office and in the foyer. 7. Summer
performances. Only 160 places in the auditorium. No danger of fire,
since smoking will be forbidden and the heating will be central and

electric." He insisted that there should be twenty dressing-rooms, so that each member of the company should have one instead of several having to share. He kept finding things on his walks which he thought could be useful and had them sent along; when Falck protested that they could not afford them, Strindberg told him not to bother: "In an extraordinary way, I get money from heaven." He regularly lent items of furniture from his own apartment. [5]

Falck rehearsed all four of Strindberg's new plays that summer and autumn. Strindberg attended none of these rehearsals but encouraged Falck to visit him for discussions; they often sat until three or four in the morning, always ending with a glass of cold milk from the ice-box. Falck noted how Strindberg "wrote at a rattling pace, throwing the finished pages unblotted onto the floor . . . would scatter notes around, on the table, in drawers, in his pockets," and was "the most coquettish man I have ever met. He always bothered about how he looked, for ever patting his moustache into place even when we sat alone. . . . When he had fastened the knot in his big cravat he would study it for a long time in the mirror before he was satisfied . . . In spring he wore suede gloves and, as he writes in *Storm*, 'a light summer cane, just to hold.' . . . His sense of beauty was upset by the smallest thing. Once he gave me a long lecture when I put my cigarette in the wrong place in a large ashtray. A military order prevailed there. Cigarette butts—Russian, with mouthpieces— had their ordained place, cigars and cigarillos theirs, with all the ash in the centre . . . He himself smoked intensely and regarded tobacco as a cure for many ailments." When Falck had an attack of pharyngitis, Strindberg sent him a note: "My lad! Smoke! Remember! The Hindus cure all illnesses with tobacco!"[6]

Strindberg had a life-size photograph of Harriet as Puck in his drawing-room, which he kept behind a curtain suspended by rings from a rod. "As we sat and talked, it often happened that Strindberg became restless, got up and went into the drawing-room. Suddenly I would hear the rattle of brass rings. There would be a moment's silence, then I would hear the rings rattle again, and he would return with his hand pressed tightly against his eyes as though he wished to shut out everything except the picture which had impressed itself on his retina. With difficulty, he would control his emotion and, to calm himself, would dip his hands in a saucer of iced water which always stood to the right of the stove."[7]*

*In *A Blue Book*, Strindberg writes: "In my lonely apartment, there was a room which I thought the most beautiful in the world. It had not been beautiful at first, but great and important things had happened there; a child had been born, a human being was dead there. In the end I furnished it as a temple to a memory, and I never showed it to anyone."

Strindberg was delighted with his new friend. Falck, he informed Schering, "is in every way the man for this enterprise; as manager, director and actor."[8] Sadly, the honeymoon did not last long.

On 13 July, August Lindberg came to see him. "Dare you visit me after *Black Banners?*" Strindberg asked. Then he told Lindberg to feel beneath his (Strindberg's) waistcoat. " 'Why should I do that?' 'To feel how empty my breast has become. Now I have nothing but the cancer left.' 'Nothing but—?' 'Yes, and I have known it for a long time.' "[9]

His domestic problems continued. "29 July. Harriet and Anne-Marie came, but Ellen had left so that there was no dinner. I laid out a cold meal myself at 5 p.m. Then Ruth came . . . 4 August. Ruth left. Miss Johansson came . . . 25 August. At noon I found the apartment full of the smell of roasting fowl. Went into the kitchen and asked the reason. The cook replied that a hazel-hen needed three hours. I looked up the cook-book and found it said three-quarters of an hour. So now the same misery is beginning as in the spring—that I must eat ruined food after some unknown person who eats before me. If I complain, the cook will leave and I shall have to fetch pig-swill for myself. Why must I suffer thus? What have I done? I have not treated my fellow-mortals thus . . . I do not wish to eat left-overs in my own house! and keep a vampire who sucks the strength from me!"

On 12 September the first volume of A *Blue Book* appeared, confirming, if any confirmation was needed, his conversion to a generalised religion. "He has now," Hjalmar Branting wrote in *Social-Demokraten*, "entered heart and soul into the service of the spiritual powers, against which in his youth and for many years afterwards he marshalled with such power the weapons of criticism and free thought." Branting found the book ill-reasoned, as it is. "Anyone who seeks a prime example of every imaginable sin against logic and respect for facts need not look beyond these pages. Here, for example, one may learn that apes stem from decadent humans; that the hairlessness of babies proves the illogicality of Darwinism . . . Need one add that the *Blue Book* contains the usual foolish and wearisome outpourings on woman, 'this uncompleted half-way-house between child and man'? . . . It would have embarrassed us had socialism alone among all his former ideals been spared, but fortunately it, too, receives a passing mortal thrust—'a purely Christian idea which in 1848 was taken over by the materialists.' " Sven Söderman in *Stockholms Dagblad* concluded: "The strongest things in the book are the conviction that a heaven exists, the need for faith, and the idea of faith as the highest form of intuition. The weakest are the author's monomania and narcissistic obsession that he is a martyr."

Gustaf Uddgren, who saw a good deal of Strindberg around this time, believed that Strindberg's main preoccupation during his last years was to find an explanation for the brute force and apparent meaninglessness of life, and that his religiousness was basically "a beautiful and gentle pose which he adopted to give himself the outward calm he needed . . . He felt that he needed to calm not just himself but the age he lived in. Each night he read the old Catholic prayer books to live himself into their peace, not to educate himself into Catholic beliefs . . . The fire which burned in him was so strong that he needed something to calm himself before he could find peace in sleep."[10]

Despite the critical reviews, *A Blue Book* sold well. The first printing of two thousand copies, priced cheaply at five crowns at Strindberg's request, sold out at once, and a third edition was in preparation by the end of October. But the demand fell off, partly because of disappointment with the second and third volumes; in November 1911 there were still 700 copies of this third edition of Volume One unsold, plus 500 of the first edition of both volumes Two and Three. But the *Blue Books* have their admirers. In 1949, Thomas Mann recalled: "The brilliant speculations of the *Blue Books* . . . left behind in me a ferment which has worked on me irrepressibly ever since. It is quite possible that in . . . my *Dr. Faustus*, this memory subconsciously played its part."[11]

On 14 September, *The Virgin Bride* received its Swedish premiere at the Swedish Theatre, with Harriet and Gunnar Wingård in the leading roles, as they had been in the earlier premiere in Helsinki. Strindberg did not attend even the dress rehearsal; even if he did not know about Wingård, how could he have endured to see Harriet act love scenes? She, if she did not quite suggest a peasant girl, finely caught Kersti's conflict of passion and guilt, and the play was generally admired, though Sven Söderman in *Stockholms Dagblad* made the usual complaint, as far as Strindberg's later work is concerned, that "one does not know what exists only in the girl's imagination and what is real" (one of the play's strengths), adding that it was "a painful reminder of the author's obsession about an earthly inferno."

But this production brought Strindberg nothing, since his account with Albert Ranft, the theatre's owner, was in the red. "My debts to you," he wrote to Ranft on 20 September, "have eaten up all my royalties since and including *The Saga of the Folkungs* in 1900," and he still owed Ranft 1,800 crowns. The cost of the alterations to the Intimate Theatre had left him with nothing to pay his own rent. Karl Otto Bonnier offered to publish something a year hence to celebrate his sixtieth birthday in 1909, but Strindberg could only suggest (24 September) his chemistry studies.

"They will come to about a thousand pages. I suggest either 100 copies at 100 crowns each for dilettantes, or a thousand copies at 10 crowns . . . I won't deny that the book will be unreadable for the general public, but it will be a quarry for chemists." Bonnier rejected this unpromising scheme. In October, Strindberg was threatened by the landlord of the Intimate Theatre with a writ if the rent was not paid. In desperation, he offered Bonnier (21 October) his *Occult Diary*, "My greatest *oeuvre posthume* . . . now in its eleventh year. It fills 548 octavo pages . . . As regards publication, well, that'll have to be after I'm dead, all the wonderful things I have experienced are there, intimate things, but with the names often spelt in Greek . . . I'm selling them because by noon tomorrow I must have 2,000 crowns or the bailiffs will be in." Bonnier accepted, and went to Karlavägen at once with the money.[12*]

Dramaten, whose old building in Kungsträdgården had long been too small and cramped, had by now almost completed its much larger new house at Nybroplan and announced that it would open with a new production of *Master Olof* in its third, verse version. Ranft decided to trump Dramaten by putting on the prose version of the play, which he did before the end of the year, following the success of *The Virgin Bride*. The production was strongly cast but, under the circumstances, rushed, and won few laurels.

On 26 November 1907, the Intimate Theatre at last opened with *The Pelican*. Much care and money had been expended to make the interior attractive. The auditorium was handsomely decorated in green and gold, with a pillar at each corner, and was illuminated from above through a ceiling of gold silk. It was much the smallest theatre that had yet been seen in Stockholm, holding only a hundred and sixty-one people, and the stage was tiny, six metres long and four metres deep. On either side of it, facing the audience, hung copies made by a local artist of the two Böcklin paintings which Strindberg so admired, *The Island of the Living* and *The Island of the Dead*. There was a small smoking-room, with gold leather wallpaper and sofas covered with buffalo hide, and an attractive ladies' room. In one corner of the foyer stood an enormous bust of Strindberg.[13]

Prince Eugen, a lover of the theatre and himself a talented painter, attended the premiere. But *The Pelican* is a heavily melodramatic piece, which even then needed considerable acting and directorial skill to avoid seeming ludicrous. The father of a family has died; his widow starves and

---

*Strindberg noted in his diary on 22 October that he had "pawned this diary . . . but with the right to redeem it," adding at the foot of the page: "Subsequently it was redeemed."

freezes her grown-up children and flirts with her son-in-law who, however, on finding that the dead man left nothing, loses interest in her. The son lights the stove to get some warmth and sets the apartment on fire; the mother throws herself from the balcony while the son and daughter die contentedly in the flames.

Max Reinhardt with his formidable company was to make something memorable of *The Pelican* after Strindberg's death, staging it as an expressionistic nightmare; but it does not bear realistic treatment, which was all that Falck's young company could give it. "It is regrettable," August Brunius wrote in *Svenska Dagbladet*, "that they should have chosen to open the theatre with this play, which demands enormous power to make it work. Herr Falck's company, with every respect to the young director's energy and courage, is inadequate to make a moderate play acceptable, even if it can, as with *Miss Julie*, carry a strong play to triumph." Bo Bergman in *Dagens Nyheter*, while praising the enterprise, also disliked the play; Sven Söderman in *Stockholms Dagblad* found it "pathological and, technically, unusually weak for Strindberg," and Anna Branting in *Social-Demokraten* thought it "immensely unsuitable for an opening production . . . pure parody." The houses were terrible; on the third evening they took only 39 crowns. Six days after the opening, Strindberg wrote to Falck that he thought they would have to close the theatre. Falck hastily revived *Miss Julie*, a measure he was to be forced to repeat when other productions failed.[14] As before, it got excellent reviews, though August Brunius noted the bewilderment of the audience at the end: "Most of them remained in their seats cheerfully waiting for a second act, in which they presumably hoped to see Fru Björling actually cut her throat."

On 5 December, Falck presented his second new production, *The Burned Site*. Another weak play, it was received as unfavourably as *The Pelican*. Brunius summed it up as "feeble-minded . . . there is no idea, no leading thread, not even the ruins of a plot . . . Is there no one who can protect a great genius against himself in his weak moments? It is infinitely painful to have to say this about Strindberg; but it must be said, before things get even worse." Bo Bergman dismissed it as "a whipped-up farrago of endless talk and cheap would-be profundities . . . one would have laughed at it all, were there not a genuine tragedy at the heart of it all, namely the author himself. So this is the nadir to which Strindberg has declined. One has said this time after time, and sees no glimmer of light." The play had to be withdrawn after seven performances. At Strindberg's suggestion, Falck tried to sell some of his paintings to raise money, but could find no buyers.[15]

On 8 December, King Oscar died and was succeeded by his son, Gustav V, who was to reign until 1950. On 30 December, Falck presented his third new production, *Storm*. It got better reviews than *The Pelican* and *The Burned Site*, though Bo Bergman was again hostile; Sven Söderman thought it the best of Strindberg's chamber plays yet seen (which it was) and wondered why it had not been shown earlier in the season. *Storm* was not really an appropriate play for a young company; it is a vehicle, and a splendid one, for an old actor approaching the end of his life like the character in the play, though for that very reason actors who would be ideal for the role tend to shrink from it. However, it managed the respectable number of twenty-three performances.

Nevertheless, Strindberg ended the year in gloomy spirits. "Now it's as it was in the autumn, but almost worse," he wrote to Karl Otto Bonnier on 30 December. "3,500 crowns for the theatre rent. But this time I've nothing to sell. I beg you to help me with an advance on forthcoming new work or the Collected Edition . . . I am owed 60,000 crowns—5 years' rent for the theatre, and yet they don't perform me." (What on earth can he have meant by that?) Bonnier generously sent the 3,500 crowns the same day.[16] "Falck now owes me 18,190 crowns," Strindberg noted in his diary on New Year's Eve. His income from Germany had suddenly declined; he had had only one production there in 1907, plus two in Vienna, *The Bond* and *The People of Hemsö*, and one (*Easter*) in Prague, and it seemed impossible that the Intimate Theatre, on which he had built such high hopes, could continue. "Help me with 2 or 100 crowns," he begged Karl Börjesson on 6 January. "I have only 10 and the New Year's bills are pouring in."

On 21 January 1908, *The Ghost Sonata* opened at the Intimate Theatre, to bewildered reviews. "To handle problems concerning servants and cooking in stylised language, and interrupt them with the entry of the Evil Spirit herself from the kitchen, rouged as though in farce, cannot but leave a final impression of parody," wrote Bo Bergman in *Dagens Nyheter*. Gunnar Bjurman in *Svenska Dagbladet* complained that "the eccentricities which characterise so much of Strindberg's later work have never flowered as profligately as they do here," and even Strindberg's old friend Anna Branting felt constrained to say in *Social-Demokraten* that she did not want to believe he was "pulling the Stockholm public's leg." Gunnar Ollén observes that the Maeterlinck method, with white phantoms sitting motionless in the half-dark intoning monotonously, ill suited the play.[17] It was removed after twelve performances, and was dismissed as unstageable until Reinhardt's famous production four years after Strindberg's death.

Strindberg, now busy on the second volume of his *Blue Book*, was so depressed by this sequence of failures that he considered moving back to Lund, at least for a while, and asked Nils Andersson to look for lodgings for him. "Those two rooms at the widow's attract me most," he wrote to Andersson on 26 January, "if she doesn't have friends who can literally be heard through the door. I'll pay more than she wants and eat once daily, preferably fish, but not thin gruels; i.e., cabbage or peas, strong soups. Small *smörgåsbord*, cheese, anchovies, reindeer, fried fish. In the evening a little milk—nothing else. (Coffee in the morning with an egg, of course) . . . Thank you for offering me your hospitality. But you know me. I must live alone—but have people to meet."

Playing with Fire was performed in Munich that month (it was frequently to be revived in Germany), and on 31 January the Intimate Theatre staged it, together with *The Bond*. Strindberg noted in his diary that they "went well," but the critics, though sympathetic to *The Bond*, disliked *Playing with Fire*. After thirteen performances, the latter play was replaced by *Pariah*, which was generally praised. It and *The Bond*, together or in other combinations, achieved over fifty performances.

The prospect of his diary being published in the lifetime of those named in it bothered Strindberg. "I feel," he wrote to Karl Otto Bonnier on 29 January, "as though I had sold my corpse to the anatomists! So let me make a deal. Three suggestions: you credit the money to my account; or you get all my poems; or my collected scientific works (= 2 cupboards full). What bothers me most is that the diary contains *inter alia* other people's secrets." Bonnier generously credited the amount of the loan against future works, whether new or reprinted, and the diary did not see the light until a much abridged version appeared in 1963, after Harriet's death, followed by a limited facsimile edition of the full text in 1977.

On 18 February, Dramaten, in its handsome new building seating nine hundred people, presented its revival of *Master Olof*. Anders de Wahl, who was to have played the title role as he had in Harald Molander's production of the prose version in 1897, fell ill during rehearsals and was replaced by Ivar Nilsson, who wrote to Strindberg for advice. Strindberg replied on 16 February with a letter full of the good sense which he so often manifested when talking about his own plays:

> He is no poetic Hamlet, but an angry man. It says so in the play. "The pale cleric," sharp in logic, thinks much, etc. "To fight with such a man requires Satan himself!" And M.O. says of himself: "I have lived on a war footing and slept on my sword. And I had the strength to defy a world." Brazen—very young! He is as proud as a king. He is snappish, vitriolic and sullen. The play was written 40 [*sic*] years ago; many have played your role,

mostly like Hamlet . . . Let us now in the new White House see my Master Olof, our Luther! for the first time! . . . Elsewhere when Brother Lars asks if Olof would be willing to make way for one stronger, M.O. replies: "There is no one" . . . So, a man of cast iron with an extraordinary self-assurance who is not sympathetic and does not bother to be.

Most actors have ended by playing him with warmth instead of with fire . . . His manner of speech is always arrogant whether he is addressing bishop, king or peasant . . . Even at his mother's death he is hard, but is "overwhelmed by sleep and weariness," as he himself says. If you act the part as it is written and get blamed for it, you may quote me (and the text) as authority . . .

I shall not come to see you! for I cannot expose myself in public; I am born that way. Tell your fellow actors this. I was invited to the dress rehearsal next Sunday evening, I supposed in private. Now I hear that the theatre will be full. So I cannot come. But I am with you from afar.

Unfortunately, this production, so eagerly awaited by Strindberg and the Stockholm public, proved disappointing, as that of the prose version at the Swedish Theatre had a few months earlier. Yet the play impressed, and when Dramaten revived it a few years later it remained in the repertory with a succession of distinguished actors in the lead. Apart from its intrinsic merits, it offers marvellous opportunities for a young actor.

Encouragement for the Intimate Theatre, after its disastrous start, came in the form of a public statement by Otto Borchsenius, a respected Danish writer and critic, and censor of the Royal Theatre in Copenhagen. He had come to Stockholm to attend the inaugural ceremonies of the new Dramaten, but he also took the opportunity to see Falck's production of *The Bond*. In an interview with a Swedish newspaper, he declared: "The best memory of Swedish theatre that I shall take back to Denmark is that of the Intimate Theatre. I know that the critics have found much to censure in its work, and it is easy to point to defects in their performance—they are all so young and lack training and perhaps adequate leadership. None the less, the evening I spent at the Intimate was exceptionally interesting . . . In the end I forgot about criticism and surrendered unconditionally to the wizardry of Strindberg's genius." He ended by expressing the hope that the company would visit Copenhagen, which, the following month, it did.[18]

On 25 February the Intimate revived another early Strindberg play, *Sir Bengt's Wife*. It was evidently not a good production (and is not a good play); yet, like *The Bond*, it drew the public and ran for forty-eight performances. But Strindberg was no longer able to subsidise the theatre. On 1 March he wrote to Falck: "1 April [quarter day] approaches, and then I shall file for bankruptcy and a receiver. I cannot raise any rent, and do not want to, for I no longer believe in the theatre's existence."

The echoes of *Black Banners* made it difficult for the theatre to borrow money; Falck tells how when two members of the company went to a banker with a letter from Strindberg asking for help, they were not even admitted and the letter was returned unopened. "Such was the feeling in all circles after *Black Banners*."[19] Fortunately, Prince Eugen came to the rescue and paid the rent in full. On 2 March, Strindberg began the third volume of his *Blue Book*. His loneliness oppressed him; on 5 March he begged his daughter Greta, "Come and talk to me a little more often."

On 20 March, Falck took his company to Copenhagen. They presented *Miss Julie*, the first time the play had been publicly performed in Denmark, and such was their success that a third performance had to be arranged in addition to the two planned. A week later, in Stockholm, on 27 March, they gave *Christina*, which had had to wait nearly seven years for its premiere. The play was savagely attacked. On publication four years earlier it had been dismissed by several critics as the worst of Strindberg's historical plays, and this judgement was repeated. "This ragbag of schoolboy howlers, insolent contentions and insane distortions has nothing whatever to do with Swedish history," Sven Söderman wrote in *Stockholms Dagblad*, "and the figures of history are represented by impertinent puppets . . . Even aside from its historical perversions, the play has no literary worth . . . and we are left with a vulgar, ignorant and unartistic work by a writer who is both intellectually and morally dead." Yet the play succeeded, as it usually has in Sweden; a monarch who abdicates exercises a peculiar hold on popular imagination, as any English man or woman who remembers 1936 can testify, and whatever the defects of the play, Christina is a rich role for an actress. (Harriet was to achieve one of her greatest triumphs in it fourteen years after Strindberg's death.) The Intimate Theatre's production drew the town, and ran for sixty-five performances, followed by a successful tour.

The critical attacks on Strindberg deepened his depression. "He withdrew into his shell," Falck remembered. ". . . His suspiciousness sometimes became very hurtful." The previous month (9 February) he had written to Karl Börjesson: "I must beg you never to lend Falck any more money or sign a guarantee."[20] The visits of his daughters brought him comfort. "Anne-Marie here," he recorded in his diary on 27 March. "I read fairy tales, played the nightingale pipe; we played blind man's buff in high style. She laughed as happily as I have not heard anyone laugh for a long time, a long time. Greta came." On 3 April, as he was walking with Anne-Marie: "At the corner of Karlaplan, Harriet in a cab. I did not recognise her; she was small, insignificant, ugly. I saluted her as a stranger. Scarcely saw her!"

Next day: "In the evening Anne-Marie came with a note from Harriet saying she is engaged [to Gunnar Wingård] . . . Yet in the afternoon H. had 'sought' me . . . The night that followed was wonderful! At 11:30 I sensed H—t but did not respond. Again at 3, and then . . .* In the morning again. On her engagement night!" His diary for the next seven weeks leading up to her marriage makes extraordinary reading:

> 5 April. A strange mood all day. I relive my engagement of seven years ago. In the evening I became happy and played [Gounod's] *Romeo*; sensed H—t, friendly, almost as if we had become engaged again.
>
> 7 April. Went out in the morning early; felt it was Sunday, so that I almost believed it. Remembered everything beautiful from my first days with Harriet. She is now as though dead, so that I can see her only as beautiful; mourn her and miss her as one dead; regret every hard word, reproach myself for everything, blame myself. Put aside the *Blue Book*! Did nothing; wept with pain at the dead illusions of love. Were they only illusions, that were so powerful?
>
> 8 April. In a light-hearted mood all day. Paid Harriet's book bill and had the receipt sent to her. Experienced a warm contact with H—t all day. She sought me. I thought she was unhappy. Her *Swanwhite* plays in Helsinki tonight. † Wrote a letter which I did not send.

But the following day he added to this letter, and sent it to her:

> When last Saturday you told me you were engaged, I almost knew it [already]. But I could not wish you happiness, for I do not believe in it, since it does not exist . . . But I would have liked to say goodbye, and now—thank you, in spite of everything, for everything, for those spring months seven years ago when after twenty years of misery I was allowed a glimpse of light . . . What was less beautiful vanished, only the beautiful remained . . . I wept, not from the pain of losing you, but from happiness that I had had these moments from you, with you . . .
>
> Shall I go away? I think I seem disturbing to you here, and from this apartment invisible wires stretch like inaudible sound waves which yet reach their destination . . . Our bond is not broken, but it must be cut . . . otherwise we shall be soiled . . . You remember our first days, when alien spirits radiated malice, which disturbed us, destroyed us, merely by thinking of us.
>
> You know I wanted to be free and to give you back your freedom; and every time you turned your feelings from me to someone else, I have been free, until you began to think of me again. Then things became muddied, and afterwards I reproached myself . . . So, now, when there is no

*The dots are Strindberg's.

†The Swedish Theatre in Stockholm had begun to rehearse *Swanwhite* with Harriet, but abandoned the project, so that the play received its premiere in Helsinki without her but with Sibelius's music. It was a considerable success.

returning, I beg you: do not think of me, neither evilly nor kindly; never speak of me, do not utter my name, and if others do so, stop them or stay silent. I do not wish to live this double life, ensnared in the eroticism of others. I would rather mourn you as one dead than remember you as another man's wife . . . I sometimes think it would be better and more fitting for us to part in hatred, real hatred (repulsion); then it would be ended . . .

I beg you: leave me in peace! In sleep I am defenceless like everyone else, not accountable; and afterwards I am ashamed . . .

His diary continues:

10 April. What I am now experiencing is so strange. I am friends with Harriet; she "seeks" me. I eat little, drink little; dress, for whom? I am as though engaged, live 1901 and see Harriet as young, seven years ago, great, glorious, ethereal . . .

11 April. During the night Harriet sought me twice violently, and I responded. But this after I had felt at about 10:30 p.m. that H—t had been in great anguish.

Strindberg to Harriet, 11 April:

I shall not survive your wedding night; no, not from jealousy, but simply from imagining what will happen . . . I must go before I, my immortal soul, am defiled. It does not help that I say to myself: Why should he touch my woman? She was not mine in the usual sense, and he had the right but still she was my creation! and in her there was something of me which he touches . . . it is me whom he caresses, and therefore I go! Why will you not let me go? What do you want with my old body? Take my soul if you will, but let me go! . . . Have you not noticed that so many who wanted to take you from me came to harm, died, lost wives and children? I did nothing, hardly dared to wish them harm, for I knew how dangerous that was. So I fear to disturb you, for then I shall suffer. Therefore let me go!

Next day he wrote and asked her, as he had when proposing to her seven years before: "Will you have a little child with me?"

13 April. In the night: from 11:30 I had Harriet in my arms; I "saw" her face, heard her breathe, kissed her little hand good night. And then we slept till morning, just as before when we were newly married.

What is this miracle which I have experienced for eight days? . . .

She becomes engaged to W.,* and at night she flies to me. We live like newly-weds, we correspond, I send her flowers in the mornings. I am as though newly married . . . I have begged her in a letter to let me go. I have prayed God to deliver me from this, to give me a thorn in my flesh, strike me

*Wingård.

in the face. But He does not move. I am happy when she seeks me and do not reproach myself. What is all this? . . .

Contact with H——t all evening. At 10:30 I had violent palpitations, so fierce that I had to put my hand on my heart and then I thought it was Harriet's heart; it quietened and stopped; I thought she died; but then it began again, but more calmly; I slept. At 11:30 the anxiety began again (I thought then that he was striking her: she wrote in her letter that "she had fought, been struck"). At 12 she lay on my arm, calm, friendly. Thrice in the night I was awakened and received her as my wife.

14th. . . . Now this evening Harriet is gone; I do not sense her, hostile or otherwise. NB! This W. resembles me, but looks like one dead; he was dying eighteen months ago but recovered. Is it possible that by acting me and through Harriet he has got me into himself? I assume too that the pair of them have been grubbing in me, rooting me out for a year, living through and on me and have become offshoots of me . . .

15th. H——t came again, but with no odour. Towards morning, however, it was otherwise. Ter. * 2 and 5 o'clock (on the stroke). After a glorious walk in Djurgården in only a jacket (so warm I am), home; now H——t came so intensely and exquisitely, as though she had just read my letter of yesterday. This continued until 2 when it vanished and for a moment [I] became uneasy. I ate dinner; cautiously and without aquavit. When I got up and opened the window a whole army of <u>White Flags</u> was waving to me (out on Gärdet). Then I understood, was moved so that I began to weep. Went to my desk and opened this diary. At that moment there came a scent of roses which threw me into ecstasy. But when I tried to rest, I was so oppressed that I had to get up; and then I stayed awake, without taking my afternoon nap, which has not happened for seven years. H——t sought me several times, but I resisted; for I have been "informed" that it is only permitted to happen at night . . . in the chaste darkness. Axel here in the evening; sombre, oppressive. H——t was absent the whole time. But then came night! And she came; I saw her! And she slept the whole night with me! 2 and 5 o'clock . . . †

16th. At 10:30 H——t began to seek me, but irresolutely, and so all night till 5 o'clock, when she found me, but without joy. There was hatred between us! And no soul. And without soul (love), no joy . . . I have not drunk for 14 days.

That same evening of 16 April, the Intimate Theatre staged its dress rehearsal of *Easter*, the twelfth and final play of the opening season, and Strindberg attended it. He made no comment in his diary, except: "[Anna] Flygare played Harriet's role." The occasion must have revived memories of Harriet's performance during the happy days of their engagement. *Easter* proved the Intimate Theatre's greatest success during its three-year existence, running for one hundred and eighty-two per-

*Three telepathic embraces.
†Strindberg's dots.

formances, thanks largely to Anna Flygare, who was universally praised. Even Sven Söderman, whom the company regarded as their severest critic, described her performance as "a poetic interpretation of reality, illuminated by a great poet's imagination." Next day Strindberg wrote savagely to Harriet: "Yesterday, Thursday morning, I woke with the impression that I was newly married again, begged you for a word; that word you know, which people want you to say to me but which I want only to hear from your mouth . . . In the evening came your reply. You sent your child with the Thrall's* bracelet! At that moment the child ceased to be mine. I renounced her, I renounce her! I do not wish to see her again, to protect her little soul from your evil. You are the most evil of created beings . . . Now you have sunk so low that only one, the Almighty, can lift you out of the abyss . . . You black Swanwhite! You took all my good thoughts with you, away! Now take everything, everything, the child too. And go!"

> Good Friday, 17th. . . . Experienced H—t, friendly, almost loving, until 2 o'clock. Then a storm began, first with palpitations, then explosions in the region of my stomach and a noise like grasshoppers in my ears. † (Falseness and sensuality according to Swedenborg.) From this I assume that she has only now opened my letter. Now came incense (= rosin), which must mean malice and hatred.
>
> 18 April, Easter Saturday. Night before: at 11:30 she sought me, kindly, lovingly; x x x. 3 o'clock ditto 11 o'clock. Six times! . . . Around 9 o'clock (she was at that moment playing opposite W. in *Elga* at the Swedish Theatre) she came like roses in my mouth. I sensed that she already longed to come home and rest. Around 11 she came, loving, with fire and roses . . .‡ Around 2 I experienced something most extraordinary. From the small of my back a sort of dragging began through my pelvis down to the opposite side, and I supposed from this that H—t was about to start her period. This was confirmed when later she sought me, shyly and without joy. We fought peaceably until morning, when I won.
>
> 19 April, Easter Day. H—t kind, loving, gives me roses in my mouth, the whole morning until 2 o'clock. H—t must have had her period from the 6th to the 12th when she was away, but sought me again on the night of the 12th with fire. Last night, when she felt her period approaching, she sought me with a taste or fragrance in her mouth like roses or fruit. Then I

*Wingård.

†Strindberg noted in the margin here, evidently at some later date: "the first symptoms of illness, which lasted into August." The stomach pains which Strindberg describes could, however, have been caused by peptic ulcers rather than by the cancer which was to kill him four years later. The fact that the pains occurred during a period of great mental and emotional stress and then ceased is consistent with ulcers.

‡Strindberg's dots.

asked myself: Can the pit smell of roses? No! Swedenborg says that when good spirits approach, there is a scent of flowers.

20th. In the evening she came again, full of love and longing. Night came, she slept on my arm, but did not desire me before morning, when x x x

22nd. Around 10:30 p.m. I was ill; an acute pain in the pit of the stomach, which I attributed to someone's hate, perhaps H—t's or W's. I lay the whole night twisting and wanting to vomit, without result.

24th. The morning glorious; I had H—t all morning, gentle, loving, like flowers in my mouth. Now I think that she is free and that we are united. No, she vanished in the evening when Axel came; and although I received a summons to go to bed at 10, she was not there to meet me. Slept and sensed infidelity; had bad dreams and was released towards morning when she sought me fiercely but without love. I responded x x x

28th. All day Harriet, loving, calm, unhappy, she seeks me. Drank wine in the evening, slept heavily; did not wake until 3, when she began to seek me—and around 5 we met x x x . . . I sensed that H—t had been set free.

Strindberg's conversion to a religious, if undenominational stand-point was such that on 18 April he wrote to Falck asking him to delete all anti-religious lines from his plays, notably *The Father*, in which both the Captain and the Doctor pour scorn on the Pastor's faith. Despite the drain which the theatre imposed on his pocket ("My economy is totally undermined by the Intimate Theatre," he complained to Karl Otto Bonnier on 27 April. "I must pay to be performed while others get paid"), he kept a close interest in its proceedings, and began that spring to address a series of letters to the company, stressing the basic principles which he had set out the previous spring in his as yet unpublished memorandum. *

His fantasies about Harriet continued. "1 May . . . In the night she sought me; eagerly imperious, but I said no! . . . Then she withdrew, angry. 2 May. H—t gone! I sensed her love today as pure deception. He must have rejected her yesterday, and thus abandoned she threw herself at me. To be out of all this and with my child would be best. She cannot change her nature! I cannot save her, who is made only of lies, treachery, evil and lust. Lust and hatred! 3 May . . . when I went to bed at 10, she was lying there waiting for me x x x Then at 5 x x x Finally at 6:30, but then she was sated." That same day he wrote her a long letter which Harriet did not choose to print in the collection she published in 1932:

> Now I have your soul in a little Japanese box on my desk. There lie all your letters; a ring with many small rings on it (one is missing); your bridal crown and veil . . . The most beautiful letters are from 1904 (when we divorced). . . My bride! of seven years ago! And now another's! And yet not!

*See pages 483–4.

Can you dissolve this bond? Can you? I cannot. I sometimes wonder if small creatures of a spiritual kind will result from our supernatural marriage. Surely something must come of such a union, in which extraordinary spiritual forces meet and merge. Sometimes I believe that you will have a child by me, though I do not know how. And it shall be born in love and become a power on earth, of small estate but powerful in word and deed. I fancy that some little soul is waiting to have us as parents and I believe I have seen her little face, one night in moonlight on a white sheet.

I take this opportunity to tell you so that you shall not be frightened if anything should happen. I have read in "a book" that false pregnancy can occur, with all the symptoms but without substance. I wonder if we may expect something of the kind. I have also read, but still doubt it, that a genuine immaculate conception can take place, i.e., telepathically. What should we believe, what would the world say? But anyway I shall know through my senses; for I have the spirit of your body in me . . . I sense everything you feel. When you are happy, when you are hurt (then I get a nail in my heart) and when He is angry with me, then I feel an explosion in my breast.

Harriet did not answer. "I cannot describe," she recalled twenty-four years later, "how I suffered during this time, when I knew that Strindberg thought of me every day and every hour. I wanted to cut off all contact with him, and begged him earnestly not to write to me, but to no avail."[21] Next day, 4 May, he wrote again. She replied:

No, I didn't answer you. I told you in my last letter that all contact between us <u>must</u> cease. I belong now to another man—shall marry him in June, put yourself in his position—how you would suffer—   You ask for *Swanwhite* back—one should never take back what one has given. However—here it is—for you to have staged at Dramaten or the Intimate Theatre. I relinquish it without bitterness—I can only rejoice that something so beautiful has been written—whoever will now speak your words from the stage.[22]

As the date of Harriet's marriage approached, Strindberg's diary became increasingly distraught:

5 May. Sent a new letter, equally sharp and ruthless . . . She storms me so that I am nearly suffocated! but she seeks me erotically too . . . At 11 p.m. I sensed that she was seeking me but could not reach me. Slept until 4, when she came x x x and at 6:30. But she came selfishly and left when she was satisfied; did not bother to wait for me. I thought she had her period towards morning.

6 May. I received my last letter back unopened. So much the better, for it was cruel. Then I burned the last three letters, which were evil; they swelled, formed figures and finally two hearts.

7 May. From morning to night H—t lived with me in love and eros. Under this influence I wrote a letter to <u>Falck</u> and asked him to find out if she is with child. If so, I offered to accompany her to Switzerland until the child is born; and she would not need to marry. Now at 5 p.m. she stormed me erotically; I was about to yield, but then there was a bang in the ceiling, sharp, purposeful. Then moving of furniture . . . Later she sought me, without joy or enthusiasm.

10 May, Rogation Sunday. Walked on Grev Magnigatan past the door of no. 12, where H—t lived when she was my fiancée. There was a glass pane through which we used to kiss good night; I wondered whether after seven years traces [of our kisses] could still be seen. Yes, they were there . . . This telepathic state of affairs (marriage which has also been real) began before our engagement, when H—t, in a to me inexplicable manner, sought me at night; I was awakened in my sleep and sensed in an illusory way that she lay beside me; I held her in my arms and possessed her, and had possessed her before I proposed . . . Since then it has happened every time we have been parted. And there is no distance. From Paris and Vienna she has sought me and we have found each other as man and wife. It can never cease!

11 May. . . . On 5 March 1901 I became engaged to Harriet; but before then I had possessed her <u>at night</u>, telepathically, from 13 January, 9 times, on 13 and 26 January, 12, 18, 20, 21, 22, 25 and 27 February. During that time she visited me in the day, looked as innocent as ever and pretended nothing had happened. It is strange. Does she not know of her nocturnal adventures and visits to me?

Harriet to Strindberg, 13 May: "I told you you must not write . . . My banns have already been published twice. Wish me all happiness—I believe—in happiness—Harriet." Undeterred, he wrote to her again next day:

Thrice have I written, and burned, these words, from the depth of my heart:

Wilt thou be my lawful wedded wife,
in the eyes of God, the law and the world,
for better and worse
in faithful love
for all eternity?

Must I burn this too?
Yes? or No?

But you must be free for marriage, so that you can receive in your womb a wanted and blessed child, in my embrace! which has never been offered to any other woman but you since I saw you, not even in thought.

Next day he wrote again, telling her that the apartment beneath him was vacant and "the rent need not be paid." He noted in his diary: "It would of course be ideal if she and Anne-Marie lived beneath me. I think it will happen!" She did not reply.

> 20 May. At dinner I drank, drank till 5, and rooted her out by <u>destroying</u> a <u>pile of photographs.</u> She rages at me. I burned all the photographs in a stove in the Green Room . . . At 9 I wanted to go to bed but was attacked so dangerously by—hatred = electric currents, that I did not dare to lie down. My chest was constricted, it is like a shower from above, from below . . . I fought and prayed to God for help, not daring to lie down. But I was driven whither I did not wish to go; and when she came into my arms I sensed no feeling of reproach, only a boundless happiness; and I felt as though she shared my feelings, in repeated embraces that threatened never to end.

The same day, he wrote to his photographer friend Herman Andersson that he had found a new way of making gold.

On 24 May, Harriet married Gunnar Wingård.

> 24 May. Heavy morning; wept mostly . . . Harriet came to me in love; and I gave her a sign that I had not abandoned her; she replied with roses in my mouth. Fell asleep. Was awakened at 12 and embraced her in endless love x x x (<u>When she was married</u>). Then she sought me at 5 and 6:30, but I did not respond.
>
> 25 May. . . . H—t called to me. I went into our yellow room. She welcomed me and we embraced six times . . . although she is married to W. . . . Prayed to God from the depths of my soul to be delivered from this adultery. Slept with my prayer book on my breast; even in my sleep prayed to God that He would take my soul . . . Read the Bible and prayed . . . Two o'clock came; then it came irresistibly and like a friendly summons; Harriet was in my arms and received me with joy. I felt no remorse, only joy and happiness. She sought me twice more later but we were not permitted to meet again. Then came the morning with remorse and despair . . .
>
> 27 May. Towards morning I seemed to be freed from Harriet; my body felt as though many small knotted bonds were being loosened; first in the nerves of my spine, then in my spleen, liver, lungs, heart, stomach and the small of my back. It felt like a blessed relief from tension . . . Got up and washed my whole body; put on clean linen and went out . . .

The same day, Strindberg wrote to Albert Ranft, who was planning to stage *Swanwhite* with Harriet. He enclosed a recent photo of her as Salome in Sudermann's *Johannes*, with arms folded imperiously across her bosom, and queried whether she was now right for the role. ". . . I have not seen Fru B. for nearly a year [*sic*]. Now that this portrait falls into my hands I am appalled and could weep. This <u>matron</u>, over 30 years old, must not be allowed to destroy my beautiful poem . . . It must be a little girl, 15 or 17; a drama student, inexperienced, even untrained, but not a matron! . . . I have someone from Falck's theatre, 17, a pearl, of good family . . . She has a weak voice but that can be trained during the summer."

The student in question was named Fanny Falkner.

Chapter Thirty-One

FANNY

Strindberg had first seen Fanny Falkner when she was a few months old, at her uncle's hotel at Skurup in southern Sweden in the spring of 1891. Her father was chronically unsuccessful. He had tried to make a career as a singer; he and his wife had been members of a choral quartet which toured Scandinavia, and Fanny, the eldest of their six children, remembered accompanying them on these journeys. But the quartet was dissolved in 1896. Her father got a job with a curtain manufacturer, tried to set up on his own, failed and went bankrupt. In 1907 he leased two apartments in a newly built house on Drottninggatan in Stockholm so that his Danish wife, Meta, an excellent cook, might run a boarding-house, as her sisters had successfully done in Copenhagen. [1]

When the Intimate Theatre opened in November of that year, Manda Björling, the company's leading actress, became a resident at the Falkners', and Fanny often accompanied her to the theatre. Fanny had been in Malmö when Manda played *Miss Julie* there in 1906, and had seen it four nights in succession. She had no desire to act, her talent being for painting, but she helped out at the Intimate on several occasions as a non-speaking extra. Strindberg first noticed her at the dress rehearsal of *Sir Bengt's Wife* on 24 February 1908, small, fair and dressed as a page, and remarked to Falck, "That is my *Easter* girl to the life. She must play Eleonora." Stella Falkner, in her moving account of her sister's relationship with Strindberg, comments: "She was more his *Easter* girl than Strindberg could have imagined. With her sensitivity and melancholy, overwhelmed by her family's griefs and debts, she was the incarnation of Strindberg's character, but she was not an actress who could interpret the role, and Strindberg's impulse to give it to her was to cause her much unhappiness."[2] Fanny, like Eleonora, lived in constant fear of the bailiff's rap on the door.

Strindberg did not meet her until after the dress rehearsal of *Christina* on 26 March. "I stood quite confused and overwhelmed, could only whisper 'Yes' to everything he said." Rehearsals for *Easter* began, but it quickly became apparent that she was inadequate for the role. She took speech lessons but found herself involved in conversations with Falck "aimed at making her lose enthusiasm for the role and for the theatre in general." Then one day the part was taken from her and given instead to Anna Flygare. At the dress rehearsal on 15 April, Fanny avoided Strindberg, supposing the decision to have been his. Afterwards he beckoned to her and asked, "Why didn't you want to act the role I gave you?" On learning the truth, he had a row with Falck, though Anna Flygare's triumph the following evening mollified him.[3]

Strindberg's agonies over Harriet's forthcoming marriage preoccupied him for the next six weeks. On 3 May, however, in a letter to Harriet partly quoted above,* he described Fanny as "a little child of 17, who is like you, can smile like you, but is melancholy. She is educated, of good family. Will you if need be adopt her as your pupil, spiritual child, etc., since you do not wish to have earthly children?" Harriet, with more important things on her mind, refused. Six days after Harriet's wedding, on 30 May, he wrote to Fanny asking her to come next day and read for him. "I have planned for you that you shall play Swanwhite at the Opera for Ranft . . . Say nothing to Falck or the others at the Intimate." Meanwhile he asked Alrik Kjellgren, an actor at the Intimate and also its stage manager, to come and read with Fanny a scene from *Easter*, and when Kjellgren protested that Fanny's voice was so weak that it could not be heard across the footlights, Strindberg replied, "That can be put right. I am taking the matter into my own hands." The reading moved Strindberg to tears, and after Fanny had left he said to Kjellgren, "She is a born actress, such eyes, such hair."[4]

A couple of days later he wrote to Fanny inviting her back. "He took me round his home to show it to me and dwelt especially on the little rococo room which was filled with various portraits of Fru Bosse. He stopped in

*See pp. 504–5.

front of one almost life-size photograph of her as Puck. It hung concealed behind a curtain, which he drew aside. He also showed me several photographs of his little daughter Anne-Marie and asked if he might pay for one to be taken of me." A few days later he asked her if she would like to play Swanwhite for Ranft. "I replied, 'Yes, but is not Fru Bosse to play it?' He sat down at his desk and pulled out a drawer and took out a photograph of Bosse as Salome, showed it to me and said, 'Can one play Swanwhite with arms like that?'"[5] In the event, Ranft was unwilling to risk the play with an untried actress in the lead, and Falck staged it instead, with Fanny and Kjellgren, at the Intimate that autumn.

Strindberg was continually afflicted that June with stomach pains, which he sometimes blamed on Harriet, sometimes suspected to be cancer. On 1 June: "Around dinner-time I was attacked by an extraordinary palpitation and explosion in my abdomen . . . I was in pain all afternoon . . . 6 June, Easter Sunday. H—t . . . stormed me so that my epigastrium almost burst . . . I have her in my mouth like a fragrance." He recorded similar pains every day until he closed his diary three weeks later.

> 13 June. My loathing for food so increases that I am losing weight incredibly. In 12 days I shall be dead! since only three-fifths of my body is left . . .
> At 5:30 the tension in my epigastrium begins, intolerably.
> After 60 years of torture I pray to God to be allowed to depart from life. The little joy there was was illusory or false. Work was the only thing! but that was largely wasted; or useless, or harmful. Wife, children, home, were all a mockery. The only thing that gave me an illusion of happiness was wine. So I drank! It also mollified the agony of existence. It made my torpid mind alert and intelligent; sometimes in youth, it stilled my hunger . . .
> Women gave me a great illusion of happiness which, however, immediately evaporated, and revealed its true nature. The first two left no memories behind them, only a keen loathing. In the last there was something from a higher sphere, but mixed with so much that was evil and ugly. Yet I remember her often very beautifully, though most of it was false. When my children were small they gave me the purest joy. But that soon vanished . . .
> 14 June. At 9 a.m. I was attacked so violently in my epigastrium that I had to go to bed . . . Around 1 p.m. the explosions began again . . . Is it she who stretches me? . . . I went to bed at 10. When Harriet began to attack me I embraced her to get peace. Found peace and fell asleep. But was awakened at midnight and was so tortured until 5 that I thought I would die. It came up from my stomach like two swords piercing my lungs. But I could not bring myself to abuse H—t; but then I sensed her hellish hatred with a repulsive smell as though of madness; as though she lay and murdered me by some arts. On the stroke of 5, when I am usually called to her arms, the tensions ceased.
> 16 June. She wants to keep me out of hatred and rob me of my strength, so

that I shall not be able to re-marry, which she fears I may. Or draw me into her hellish scheming! . . . Fröken Falkner came and played Mendelssohn for me.

17 June. Walked in Djurgården. At 9 I was <u>burst!</u> Arriving home I felt her in my mouth like <u>madness, primitive evil, hatred</u>, witchcraft, a taste from hell, of <u>brass and corpses.</u> At my desk she sought me erotically, but I did not respond. Slept. Around 1 I was burst and took wormwood. Now as I write this she seeks me erotically but is bursting me. So it is she! What does she want with me, when she has a husband? Terrible day and evening. Hatred! The night hard; was tormented by <u>pains</u> from 2 till 5:30 . . .

21st. Terrible day! And terrible night! Was tormented for five hours. Dreamed of H—t, chastely, beautifully; as when she once tied a cravat for me, and afterwards kissed me on the mouth as though I were her child.

22, 23 June, Midsummer Eve. 24th, Midsummer Day. Terrible days! So terrible that I shall cease to describe them. I pray only to God to let me die, and escape from these horrible physical and spiritual torments. A doctor has been called.

That same day, he wrote to Karl Otto Bonnier: "I am sure I have cancer of the stomach, with pains for twelve hours out of twenty-four, and am gradually ceasing to eat and sleep."[6]*

Despite this suffering, Strindberg continued to take a keen and even increasingly active interest in the Intimate Theatre. On 2 July, thanking a Member of Parliament, Hjalmar Wijk, for "help with the rent" of the theatre, he added: "Henceforth I shall be acting as stage director and shall devote all my time to the enterprise . . . I have nearly ruined myself and am working for nothing." Next day he wrote an offensive little note to Falck: "You didn't pay the rent yesterday, although Wijk gave the money expressly for that purpose. That was imprudent! To put it mildly!"

Strindberg nearly went to America that summer of 1908. Gustaf Eisen visited him again from San Francisco.

Strindberg had got the idea that he might accompany me back. What I had told him about the life, the landscape and the people out there on the West Coast had greatly fascinated him. "For a year," he said. "I'll only stay a year and write a new book there. I always settle down quickly in a new place and I'll get an advance from my publisher." All was decided; we would leave together. A few days before our departure I came up to his apartment and even before I had entered, he shouted at me in the doorway, "I'm not going! My destiny has warned me. It said, 'Don't go.'" He then told me that that morning during his usual walk he had happened on a torn piece of a poster on which he read the words: "Do not go . . ." Strangely enough, I had noticed this same poster, complete and pasted on a wall. It read: "Do not go to the country before buying your luggage at . . ." But he would not listen to this. He was now as opposed to going as he had been eager a few days before. "If that poster had been whole, of course I would never have been

*But see footnote on p. 503.

able to understand its significance. But now, by God, I am not going."
Swedenborg and Klemming had raised their heads again, and had strictly
forbidden him "ever to leave Stockholm." "For here, they told me, I must
fulfil my life's calling. Incidentally, I saw Klemming just before you arrived.
He was standing in the window behind the curtain and said, 'Don't go.'"[7]

Strindberg now decided to move from the big apartment at Karlavägen.
Falck says that the main reason was not financial, but the need to escape
memories of Harriet, and that for this reason he took virtually nothing
with him when he went, not even furniture.[8] He learned that Fanny's
father, whose boardinghouse was failing like all his other enterprises, was
looking for someone to take one of the two floors off his hands. Strindberg
turned up at 7:30 a.m. one day to discuss terms with Fanny's mother;
Fanny, watching them through a crack in the door, "hardly recognised
him, so curt and business-like; she suddenly found him horrid and
frightening." Nothing was decided then. "I am still reflecting about the
apartment," he wrote to Fanny's mother a week later, "but have been ill
and dulled by medicine, so that I have not been able to telephone a
decision." One morning, without warning, he appeared at the door "with
a cloak on his arm and a bag in his hand as though returning from a
journey and announced that he had come to stay. There followed only a
couple of cases containing books, photographs, clothes and his Beethoven death-mask.[9] He noted the fact of his departure briefly: "11 July.
Moved into Drottninggatan 85^{iv}."* Apart from one more terse entry,
"Wrote *The Last Knight*, 17–27 August," he closed his diary for ever.

The house at Drottninggatan was new and tall, with a green tower,†
only a few minutes' walk from the Intimate Theatre. Strindberg's apartment was on the fourth floor, comprising three poky rooms which he
quickly refurnished, conventionally and rather gloomily like the apartment at Karlavägen. But Fanny's mother, Meta Falkner, was an excellent
cook, so that hoary problem was solved. "Come and enjoy yourself with
me in my 'Green Tower' on the hill in Drottninggatan," he wrote to Nils
Andersson in Lund. "It . . . has a green roof, laurel wreaths and golden
horns of plenty, balconies, a shower-room, everything, and I have an
urge to write, good food, and Beethoven."

*Strindberg at first wrote "10 July" as the date of his move, then crossed this out and
wrote "11."

†The roof of the building is now blue, but was only painted that colour in the
1920s. Soon after moving in, Strindberg nicknamed his apartment the Blue Tower, after a
famous prison of that name in Copenhagen in which several celebrated Swedes had been
incarcerated, including Gustav Vasa's mother and sister. It pleased Strindberg to think of
his final home as a prison. (*Cf.* Torsten Måtte Schmidt, "Namnet 'Blå Tornet,'" in
Meddelanden från Strindbergssällskapet, May 1977, pp. 31–2.)

Within a week of his moving into the Tower, Strindberg had a distinguished visitor. George Bernard Shaw, seven years Strindberg's junior, had begun his career as a dramatist late, at the age of thirty-six, but in the fifteen years since, had written many of his best plays, including *Arms and the Man*, *Candida*, *Man and Superman* and *The Doctor's Dilemma*. He and his wife had come on a visit to Stockholm and, as he later put it, "I thought it my duty to pay my respects to a great man whom I considered one of the great dramatists of Europe." On the day of his arrival, Shaw sent Strindberg a note, and "got a letter in reply of enormous length, written, as well I remember, in several languages, French, German and English—any language but Swedish—and to some extent he seemed to be what people said he was. He said in his letter: 'I am dying of a mortal disease, I never see anybody. I never go into the streets except in the dead of night. I don't know your language. What is the use of a dumb man speaking to a dumb man?' He added that the interview would be useless. I thought that at any rate I had done my duty. The next morning a note came to say I was to go at once to see him."

They met at the Intimate Theatre. "He was quite a pleasant-looking person, with the most beautiful sapphire-blue eyes I have ever seen. He was beyond expression shy. My wife rose to the occasion and talked French to him, and after a time he came to himself, smiled, and we had an extremely pleasant talk." Shaw, whose French was uncertain, chose to speak in German. "Nothing could have been pleasanter or more charming, and no one could have imagined that he had been the intimate of one of those households he put on stage." Thus runs a report in the Baltimore *Sun* on 4 March 1928 of a speech Shaw made during a debate four days earlier following a special performance of *The Comrades* at the Everyman Theatre in London. Either the reporter or Shaw himself twenty years after the event seems to have fantasised, for in a postcard to William Archer on the day of his meeting with Strindberg, Shaw gave a much less cheerful account:

> . . . After some . . . conversation, consisting mainly of embarrassed silences and a pale smile or two by A.S. and floods of energetic eloquence in a fearful lingo, half French, half German, by G.B.S., A.S. took out his watch and said, in German: "At two o'clock I am going to be sick." The visitors accepted this delicate intimation and withdrew.[10]*

*It is unclear whether the meeting between Strindberg and Shaw took place on 15 or 16 July. Strindberg, in a letter to Manda Björling dated 16 July, refers to it as having taken place "yesterday," but so he does in a letter to Herman Andersson dated 17 July. Shaw's postcard to Archer is undated, postmarked 17 July and says the meeting took place "today"; it seems more likely to have been written on the 16th than the 15th.

Surprisingly—one can only assume that there was no room on the postcard—Shaw makes no mention of the fact that Strindberg had arranged a special performance that morning for him and his wife of *Miss Julie*. The company was on holiday, and Falck and Manda Björling were out in the skerries, but at Strindberg's request they took an early boat in, re-learning their lines as they went. Strindberg watched the play with the Shaws, the first time he had seen it unless (which we do not know) he had attended any rehearsals there or in Copenhagen in 1889. Falck relates that before the performance, Strindberg whispered to Manda Björling, "Take it a little easy, or I shall get upset." Afterwards, "Shaw thanked us with an engaging smile, but did not say much . . . Doubtless he had expected an experimental theatre with bold ideas of colour and form, and what did he see? A little naturalistic play."[11]

In one respect, the performance had the opposite effect to that which Strindberg intended. Six months later, in a letter to the *Daily Telegraph* published on 25 January 1909, Shaw wrote: "I am no believer in the 'théâtre intime.' When I was in Stockholm last year I attended the performance of one of the 'chamber plays' [*sic*] of that very remarkable genius who was left by Ibsen's death at the head of the Scandinavian drama, as far as European fame is concerned—I mean, of course, August Strindberg. There was a 'théâtre intime' for you if you like! It would hardly have made a refreshment-bar for the Criterion Theatre.* But the play, though this theatre was built expressly for its performance [*sic*], would have been much more effective in the Opera House." One can only surmise that the performance was unsuited to the tiny theatre, for, properly done, *Miss Julie* works more powerfully in a small than in a large space. In a letter to Falck that summer (24 July), Strindberg criticised his performance of Jean as being "monotonous, without nuances or pauses, and often in a tone of voice alien to the role and the situation . . . Shaw was more severe than I about your performance, but I won't repeat what he said."

Strindberg's new landlady, Meta Falkner, found him a demanding tenant. He issued her with a written list of rules. "1. If the door is bolted, give two short rings and it will be opened at once. 2. Do not disturb me with trivial matters, such as letters or parcels that require no answer, nor magazines, but wait until mealtimes. 3. Do not bring down cleaned glasses etc. except at mealtimes. 4. Do not admit strangers (workmen) without telling me, so that I shall not be disturbed by unknown persons in my rooms. 5. If the door is bolted, I am not 'angry,' I simply wish to be

*One of the smallest theatres in the West End of London.

undisturbed." He wrote out a list of people who were not to be permitted access to him if they called or telephoned; this list varied continuously. He sent a stream of peremptory notes to her and the two maids, Mina and Astri, rebuking the latter for not shutting the ice-box and not properly cleaning the glasses; ice had become something of an obsession with him, and a number of notes in his hand have survived, reading simply: "ICE! ICE!" He left buttons on the tops of cupboards and the top slat of the venetian blinds to check the dusting. Mina, if not Astri, passed all his tests and remained his devoted and trusted servant until his death, even after the Falkners had moved away.

At first he thought a Spartan regime would be good for his health, and lived largely on sandwiches, accompanied by milk or Vichy water. But his stomach pains must have eased ("I was ill, but am now well again," he wrote to Nils Andersson on 1 August), for we soon find him sending a note to Fru Falkner demanding "a French dinner, without *smörgåsbord*, for ten persons." Then he complained about the cost. "Director Falck has invited himself to dinner today. My first inclination was to say no, after the last dinner, when I was so shamelessly robbed that I thought of moving. Now I ask for an ordinary dinner, as previously, but if I glimpse the smallest evidence of malice I shall move, and you know what that means. [He was their only regular guest.] . . . So that you shall not mistake my kindness for naïvety, I shall not pay my board until the legal day, the 10th, if I decide to stay, depending on your behaviour." On another such occasion he complained that it would have been cheaper for him to have invited his friends to a restaurant. Meta Falkner "went down and explained why Russian caviar and oysters cost more than meat balls. She asked if he wanted a state of war to exist between them. Then he showed all his charm, stretched out both his hands and explained, 'Of course not, but someone has been here and poisoned my soul.' "[12]

These "poisoners" were not always private visitors. "If for example the caretaker had left a dustpan on the stairs, she had done it on purpose to annoy him and the dustpan would receive a kick. If the central heating was the wrong temperature, the caretaker had done this to make him uncomfortable. If he noticed that anyone on the street was looking at him, he got very annoyed—he interpreted this natural curiosity as an expression of public ill will." Once he thought a woman was following him, so he waited to let her pass and then trod on her heels. When, as occasionally happened, he did not like the food provided, he would leave a note on the tray: "When one expects mutton and gets pork which one does not like, it looks like malice"; "Are you trying to poison me?";

"Eskimo food"; "Keep your Danish pig-swill." Fanny recalled that "the size of the letters and the colour of the ink indicated the extent of his anger. Red ink was worst." Despite all this, the Falkners became fond of him. "Face to face, he was friendly and agreeable. He kept his bad temper for the little notes." He was charming to the children; if on his morning walk he saw Fanny's small sisters on their way to the French School round the corner, he would join them and buy them sweets. Falck remembered seeing him reading fairy tales to Stella, explaining difficulties to her patiently as she sat on his knee, and playing "shops" with her, weighing items, bargaining with her and handing over money "all very solemnly . . . I have hardly ever seen anyone as kind to children as Strindberg."[13] He was also generous to people who came asking for money, and would send Mina out with presents or used clothes. Once he wrote her an angry note, "My evening trousers and blue trousers are missing," and had to be reminded that he had parcelled them up himself and given them away; a messenger was sent to claim them back.

Although Strindberg was getting no royalties from the Intimate Theatre, 1908 was a good year for him in Germany. *Playing with Fire* was staged in Berlin, Munich and Mannheim, *Sir Bengt's Wife* in Cologne and Frankfurt-an-der-Oder, *Easter* in Düsseldorf, *The People of Hemsö* (which he so despised)* in Berlin, *Pariah* in Frankfurt-am-Main and *Miss Julie* in Konstanz. *The Pelican* was performed in Vienna and, farther afield, *The Father* in both Warsaw and Riga, and, in September, *The Dance of Death* (albeit unsuccessfully) in St. Petersburg. Moreover, that August he wrote, in eleven days, as the final entry in his diary records, a new historical drama, set in the sixteenth century, *The Last Knight*. Since, with its many characters and changes of scene, it was clearly beyond the resources of the Intimate Theatre, he sent this to Dramaten, which enthusiastically accepted it for production the following January.

Strindberg had wanted the Intimate to stage some at least of his historical plays, and had adapted several—*Gustav the Third*, *The Nightingale of Wittenberg*, *Charles the Twelfth*, *Engelbrekt* and even *The Saga of the Folkungs*—to meet its needs; for example, he removed six characters and the whole of the opening act from *The Nightingale of Wittenberg*, suggested doubling of roles and cut many lines in *Gustav the Third*, and

---

*Strindberg retained a particular hatred for his dramatisation of *The People of Hemsö*. Falck (p. 115) tells that when a theatre manager named Axel Engdahl met him in the street and enquired about the rights to it, "Strindberg stared at him, spat on the ground in front of him and walked on."

reduced the four acts of *Engelbrekt* to a single long act. His general recipe was to cut the first act and start the play in the heat of the action (not a bad recipe for playwriting). But despite such changes, Falck thought none of these plays suitable for the Intimate Theatre, with its declared aim to present, in a broad sense of the phrase, chamber plays; the stage and auditorium would have been too small for plays conceived on an epic scale. The three period plays which the Intimate did present—*Sir Bengt's Wife, Christina* and *The Outlaw*—are all intimately written.[14]

Strindberg had not hitherto attended rehearsals of any of his plays at the Intimate, apart from final dress rehearsals, but had been liberal with advice. Falck writes that he "regularly sent down copies of *The Studio* magazine, marking pictures of fittings, dresses, furniture and so forth which attracted him and which he thought might suit us; also *Art Journal*, with its reproductions of paintings and sculptures, and a book of Turner's paintings accompanied by a note: 'This kind of hazy painting should be followed at the Intimate, especially for the *Dream Play*.'" He also sent illustrated books about Japanese drama and poetry, and "often showed me Gordon Craig's magazine *The Mask*, and his book *On the Art of the Theatre* . . . He followed everything new that was happening in the European theatre."[15] Although Strindberg rejected Craig's belief that the spoken word was of little importance and could be dispensed with, he was excited by Craig's insistence on suggestive rather than realistically detailed decor, and his desire that the stage should not be cluttered with objects (in contrast to the realism which Strindberg had insisted on twenty years earlier in his preface to *Miss Julie*). "The Intimate Theatre," Falck explains, "was to be the home of the art of suggestion, to open up a perspective for the imagination, and so make the spectator himself participate in the dramatic process." Strindberg even urged Falck to use drapes rather than a realistic room for *The Father*, which they were preparing for the autumn, and to avoid windows and stoves unless the action demanded them. But "as time went on we leaned more and more to the view that the room in *The Father* ought to be a realistic stage room . . . the closed room, the suffocating milieu, the fight of the individual against the world that shuts him in,"[16] and Strindberg yielded.

Strindberg was not keen that they should revive this particular piece. "*The Father* is my worst play," he told Falck. "It's only that chap Levertin who ever thought it great . . . It's only a play for reading, and if you do it you must delete all repetitions, pettinesses and bickerings."[17] This resulted in their cutting half of the fine second act, and must have made it into a very short evening. We have seen how the anti-religious remarks made by some of the characters now offended Strindberg. *

Falck, himself fully occupied with the role of the Captain, felt that they needed someone else to direct the play, and to his amazement Strindberg expressed a willingness to do this. He insisted that the cast should be word-perfect for the first reading so that they could run straight through. "They will learn more from one performance than from thirty rehearsals."[18] His method of direction was unusual. He attended only four rehearsals, sitting silent in the darkened auditorium ("We saw only his white head and sensed his closeness"); then he left without saying anything, and sent the cast notes on small sheets of paper that evening or the next day.[19] Falck went frequently to his apartment, where they would discuss things over a bottle of whisky. Strindberg's advice, he says, was always clear and consistent, though Strindberg modestly dismissed his own contribution as director. "Soon after I started I found myself virtually superfluous. The players found their own way during rehearsals, adapted to one another under the eye of the manager [Falck] and achieved good results without my aid. If I add that I could not endure to hear my own words from a past age drummed into my ears day after day, and confess that my own writing bewitched me, I have stated the main reason why I gave up directing."[20]

Strindberg's relationship with Falck remained, nevertheless, uneasy and would have been more so had he known that Fanny was in love with her director. She did not hide this from anyone except Strindberg, although as yet she thought the latter's feelings towards her were only fatherly;[21] as, at that stage, they may have been. He wrote several obsessive letters about Falck that summer and autumn to Karl Börjesson ("That man will end in prison, and will put us there if we breathe a word of what he is doing"),[22] and to Falck himself, accusing him of not returning, and even of losing, manuscripts which Falck had never received. Often Falck wondered if all his work at the theatre was worth the trouble; but then a warm note would arrive, Strindberg would invite him to dinner, and he would be won over again.[23]

The Powers were still active. One evening Strindberg invited the company to a banquet at a restaurant. Before the meal he rose to make a speech and, as he began to speak of *Black Banners*, "a hellish noise was heard from the room above. Strindberg turned pale and changed the

*He also, around this time, had second thoughts about *Miss Julie*. On 17 July, in a letter to Manda Björling, he described Julie as "a poor creature, to whom I was perhaps too harsh in my younger days, when everyone's hand was raised against me, and mine against everyone."

subject, whereupon the noise at once ceased. A little later he approached this dangerous theme again, and there was more noise, this time as of chairs being pushed from a table across the floor. Strindberg's expression darkened and became stern, the party ended, and we had to go instead to his apartment in the Blue Tower, where we were offered coffee and wine. Some of those present had gone upstairs with the restaurant manager to ascertain the cause of the noise. In the room above were tables and chairs stacked in an orderly way, but no one had been up there, or could have got in. We could not explain what had happened . . . Another morning I was with Strindberg when the doorbell rang . . . It was August Lindberg. He was admitted and was asked to sit in a low leather chair with its back to the window . . . Lindberg explained his mission, which concerned the performing rights of certain plays. At that moment a large gull settled on the window-sill outside, just behind Lindberg's head, and rubbed its beak against the glass. Strindberg darkened, and with an alarmed expression offered his visitor his hand and showed him out. Afterwards he said to me: 'You see. I got a warning. He came to trap me.' "[24]

On 4 September, *The Father* opened at the Intimate Theatre, the first time it had been seen in Sweden since the original performance in 1888, apart from a brief revival at Vasa Theatre in 1893. The play was not well suited to so young a company; but, such is its power, it was generally acclaimed. Falck remembered it as "perhaps the biggest critical success that Strindberg ever had at the Intimate Theatre."[25] August Brunius in *Svenska Dagbladet* summed it up as "this brilliant, profoundly original and disturbing work," and Bo Bergman, one of the theatre's and Strindberg's harshest critics, wrote: "It is our greatest modern tragedy." After twenty performances Falck took it, together with *Miss Julie*, *Easter* and *Pariah*, to Copenhagen, where it was likewise acclaimed. It ran in Stockholm for seventy-seven performances.

The acceptance by Dramaten of *The Last Knight* had stimulated Strindberg to further dramatic writing, and by 7 September he had completed another play, albeit a very different one, for children, *Abu Casem's Slippers*. The idea for this came, according to Falck, from "a, to my eyes, horrible cloth which lay [on a table in Strindberg's apartment] with printed Oriental scenes; mosques and minarets, fairy-tale Arabs in turbans with camels, etc."[26] He borrowed the *Thousand and One Nights* from Fanny's young sisters to get the atmosphere, and wrote the play in verse. It is about a mean merchant in Baghdad who tries to get rid of a pair of old slippers which irritate him, but finds he cannot escape them as they keep coming back to him. It is a thin little piece, in humdrum verse; Falck refused it, as did Dramaten, but a touring manager named Karin

Swanström bought it and played it around the provinces that winter. By 23 September he had completed another historical play, *The Protector*, about the young Gustav Vasa shortly before he became king. A sequel to *The Last Knight*, it contains effective scenes, but does not add up to much. These three plays have rarely been revived, even in Sweden.

Fanny, meanwhile, was rehearsing *Swanwhite*, to the despair of Falck and the rest of the company. "To analyse a part for her, to get her to take direction," recalled one of her colleagues, "was hopeless. How we toiled with that girl."[27] Strindberg wrote her a series of letters giving the most elementary instructions ("Don't let your hands droop . . . keep your head high"), continually stressing the necessity of making herself audible (in that tiny space). Even he began to have doubts as the first night, 30 October, approached. But things turned out better than anyone could have hoped. Although unable to act, Fanny, with her unaffected innocence, was exactly right for the role. The critics were kind, and the houses excellent. On 12 November, Anna Flygare, Strindberg's original choice for the role, took it over on returning from an engagement in Denmark. "You must not be indignant," Strindberg wrote to Fanny. ". . . She had the part first, it was taken from her and given to you . . . When one has had the chance to live oneself, one must let others live too."[28] Some critics thought Anna, though incomparably the better actress, less effective in the part. But the play continued to draw good houses.

Strindberg now wrote a sequence of essays on ten of Shakespeare's plays, and Goethe's *Faust*. His admiration for Shakespeare had increased with the years; he hung a likeness of him on his wall and once remarked to a visitor, "Nobody beats that old boy."[29] His Shakespeare prefaces are, however, desperately unrewarding. A couple of essays he wrote at this time on historical drama contain a few items of interest, such as advice to budding dramatists to "begin with the last act," and the disclosure that when embarking on a historical play he always read Walter Scott to get the atmosphere and details of a past age. He confessed to a dislike of Molière and Kleist, astonishingly dismissing the latter as "a fossil-like Lessing,"[30] and adds some reflections on Maeterlinck. "Maeterlinck's . . . characters operate on another level from that in which we live, he is related to a higher world . . . When in Paris I came to read Maeterlinck, he was a closed book to me, so deeply immersed was I in materialism . . . Not until after my Inferno years did I read Maeterlinck again, and this time he struck me like a new country and a new age." He explains that Maeterlinck calls his best plays "marionette dramas" and thinks them unactable in a theatre: "By marionettes he does not mean what we call puppets, but lifesize figures worked by threads." (Craig was not alone in his desire to banish actors from the stage.) Strindberg concluded: "I think Maeterlinck is best unperformed."[31] These essays, together with the preface to the chamber plays which he had written eighteen months previously, appeared at the end of 1908 in a volume entitled *Open Letters to the Intimate Theatre*, a disappointing book which, apart from the remarks on Maeterlinck and some notes on the writing of historical plays, adds surprisingly little, from the man who had written *A Dream Play* and *The Ghost Sonata*, to the preface to *Miss Julie* which had appeared twenty years earlier. The advice to the actors, though sound enough, is unremarkable even for the time.

Before the end of the year, he also completed two further new plays, both uninspired. *The Earl of Bjälbo*, his twelfth and final play about Swedish history, concerns the thirteenth-century warrior Birger Jarl; it has little to offer, though Albert Ranft bought it for the Swedish Theatre, perhaps reckoning that any play about a Swedish hero might have public appeal. *The Black Glove* is a Christmas piece, a slight morality play about a shrewish young woman who loses a ring and accuses her servant of stealing it; for this, she is punished by having her small daughter stolen from her, regaining her only when she herself has been chastised and purified. Strindberg wrote it, as he did *Abu Casem*, in humdrum verse and, like *Abu Casem*, it was rejected by the Stockholm theatres but performed by a touring company in the provinces, with his daughter Greta in the lead. But unlike *Abu Casem*, which has a certain charm, *The Black Glove* was ill received. None of the five plays that Strindberg wrote this year enjoyed any theatrical life worth mentioning after their first productions.

Strindberg's interest in Fanny, though he seems as yet to have regarded it as no more than an affectionate friendship, stimulated gossip in the press that he had a fourth marriage in mind. He reacted strongly against this. "All the talk (in the papers) about my intending to remarry are unfounded," he wrote to Greta on 11 November. "The more so since I had decided never to remarry but only to live for the children I have. Tell people this."

On 26 November the Intimate Theatre celebrated its first anniversary. After the evening performance of *Swanwhite*, Falck held a party, which Strindberg attended. "He was in his most brilliant humour," Falck tells, "exuding all the unique charm of which he was capable when he so wished. After a small cold supper we were to dance on stage. To our surprise, Strindberg joined in." He remained with them until the small hours.[32] But although the theatre had recovered somewhat after its disastrous first few weeks, it was still draining Strindberg financially. He again had to ask Karl Otto Bonnier to advance him 2,000 crowns against all his unpublished scientific manuscripts, and Karl Börjesson to buy his library of three thousand books, "valued at 400 crowns," because he could not afford its rent at the pawnbroker's, where it had been since his move from Karlavägen. "Were you to take it over and auction it I might perhaps get back the few volumes I need."[33] Both publishers obliged. He still held his Beethoven evenings, with Richard Bergh, Carl Eldh, Vilhelm Carlhem-Gyllensköld and, when he could get up from Lund, Nils Andersson. He would light candles around the Beethoven death mask; sometimes the composer Tor Aulin and his quartet would perform, as well as Axel at the piano.

Easter reached its hundredth performance on 22 December, and in the New Year, Falck took his company to Norway where, as in Denmark, they aroused greater enthusiasm than in their own country. Strindberg was solicitous for Fanny's comfort. "When you told me how hungry and cold you were on the last tour (3rd class)," he wrote to her on 29 December, before she left, "I wanted to give you at any rate a fur coat for your next tour. But since you tell me that your parents would regard this as improper, I am sending you instead a gratuity of 120 crowns, to be used as you think best. It is possible that my innocent gift was ill-judged. Accordingly, and to avoid anything that might cause upset, I beg you not to visit me alone again in my room . . . If you have anything to say or ask, do it by open notes." Fanny, her sister explains, did not have a regular salary (she was the only member of the company who did not), but simply got paid for each performance; because of her mother's occupation, she was somewhat condescendingly regarded by her fellow-actors as "the little girl from the boardinghouse . . . It was thought not quite refined to cook for other people."[34]

When Fanny was not rehearsing, Strindberg employed her as a combination of informant and confidante. "Each morning at 10 she would come down and sit silently in front of his desk to receive a memorandum of what he planned to do during the day. First he wanted to hear about the theatre, how the performance had gone, how large the audience had been. He himself would speak about his morning walk. Sometimes he would go down to the new Dramaten . . . and check the bills [of the various theatres which were posted there] to see how many of his plays would be performed that evening. Fanny was expected to have read the newspaper thoroughly so that he could be kept informed of the most important events."[35] (He claimed he did not read the newspapers himself, "but [writes Falck] how many times did I not surprise him in this forbidden pursuit! He would then hastily shove the paper beneath his big leather chair and look innocent.")[36] He would note the newspaper posters during his walk and ask her about headlines that interested him. Once she told him that a botanist in China had named a flower after him. He said, "That pleases me more than if I had been elected to the Swedish Academy." Sometimes he would also telephone her later in the day asking her to come down. "He needed company after his long silence, and would sit for hours on end in the corner he called his laurel grove and speak of his life, his travels, art, science, religion, talked and talked so as to be able, after a long and lonely day, to hear his own voice, without considering how far beyond the horizon of his young listener these subjects lay."[37] He called Fanny his secretary and paid her 60 crowns a month for these services.

Strindberg's sixtieth birthday fell on 22 January 1909. The preceding evening, Fanny tells, "he was in high humour, had candles lit in all the rooms and played Beethoven with his brother Axel, preparing himself for the morrow's festivities."[38] On the day itself, Fanny and her sisters came down before it was light, dressed in white and carrying narcissi. There followed a steady stream of letters, telegrams and deputations. Carl Eldh arrived, with several of Strindberg's closest friends, to present him with Eldh's now completed bust, which won Strindberg's approval. (He had had gloomy forebodings about it, warning Falck five days earlier, "Do not accept Eldh's bust if it is—unpleasing.") "All day," Falck recalled, "the stairs were filled with boys carrying telegrams and flowers. Laurel wreaths and bouquets had to be forced through the door, which he would not open but left ajar on a chain."[39] Most of the newspapers printed tributes, some generous, some grudging; a number of liberals and socialists, including Hjalmar Branting, regretted that the burning social critic of earlier years had retreated, as they saw it, into religion and mysticism, and plenty of religiously minded conservatives dismissed his mysticism as superstition.

That evening, many theatres in Sweden gave performances of his plays in tribute. Dramaten presented the premiere of *The Last Knight* to a full house, including King Gustav, and record receipts.[40] The Intimate offered a new production of *There Are Crimes and Crimes*, the Swedish Theatre, *Gustav Vasa* and the Östermalm Theatre *Lucky Peter's Journey*. In the provinces, *Easter* was staged in Skara, *The Secret of the Guild* in Hälsingborg, *Abu Casem's Slippers* in Umeå, *Swanwhite* in Uppsala, and *Sir Bengt's Wife* in Sundsvall (all, ironically, minor works, except *Gustav Vasa* and perhaps *Easter*). Strindberg attended none of these performances, dining quietly at home with Falck and Nils Andersson, though he sent Fanny's small sisters to "represent" him (as he put it) at *Lucky Peter's*

Journey, where they sat in the author's box surrounded by laurel wreaths. Sixty years later, Stella remembered their excitement when the coachman whom Strindberg had ordered to collect them shouted "Strindberg!" at the entrance to the Blue Tower, and how "people gathered around the carriage and my sisters and I felt for a moment how it was to be famous."[41] The Social Democratic Youth Clubs held a celebration at Folkets Hus, so well attended that it filled four halls; then they marched in procession to the Blue Tower and sang the "Internationale" beneath his window. He had gone to bed but got up, dressed hastily and went out onto the balcony to acknowledge their acclaim. Next day he sent them a message: "My thanks for your greeting, spokesmen of the little people, among whom I shall always count myself, being the son of a servant."[42]

The Last Knight was, given the occasion, accorded a respectful reception, more so than it deserved. It tells the story of Sten Sture, the gentle and chivalrous ruler of Sweden during Gustav Vasa's youth, who was outmanoeuvred at every turn by his enemies, Archbishop Trolle and the latter's notorious ally, King Christian II of Denmark. As the title of the play suggests, Strindberg intended Sture as the hero, but he made him so gullible as to forfeit sympathy, like King Magnus in *The Saga of the Folkungs*. The main interest lies in Strindberg's portrayal of the young Gustav Vasa and the Archbishop; Strindberg was always good on villains, who are easier to make convincing than heroes. The play fades badly towards the end; despite its good critical and public reception, it ran for only nineteen performances and has never been revived in Stockholm. In a letter to Tor Aulin on 7 January, Strindberg had referred to it as "perhaps my most beautiful play," but he said that about many inferior works. (Later that year he was to claim it and the even worse *Earl of Bjälbo* as "my two best plays.")[43]

The day after his birthday, the Intimate Theatre set out on its tour of *Swanwhite*, with Fanny in the lead. Strindberg gave her a fountain-pen which he had not been able to come to terms with, and commanded her to write to him every day, which alarmed her. "I had never written to Strindberg before."[44] She sent him a series of ineloquent postcards, telling him of the success of the tour, to which he replied addressing her as "My dear protégée," or "Dear child." He still does not seem to have thought of her as anything else. "I have no illusions," he wrote to Nils Andersson on 10 March, "want no reconciliation with life. I think of it only as a great misfortune. But hush! I know nothing!"

Prince Eugen, who had rescued the theatre from bankruptcy in its early days and had sent Strindberg a handwritten letter of congratulations on his sixtieth birthday, now expressed the wish to meet him, and Falck arranged a private performance of *There Are Crimes and Crimes*, the other guests comprising half a dozen of Strindberg's close friends and their wives. But the evening was not a success. Falck had had the idea of hanging an exhibition of Strindberg's paintings (of which he owned a number) in the foyer, and the Prince offended Strindberg by saying of one of them in what the latter regarded as a patronising manner, "God, I think you've succeeded very well with this." Strindberg replied curtly and went off and sat alone in the auditorium in the fourth row, in front of the places reserved for the others. He remained there throughout the performance, and "the farewells which followed were . . . scarcely warm."[45]

On 26 March, *The Earl of Bjälbo* received its premiere at the Swedish Theatre, with Harriet's husband, Gunnar Wingård, in the cast, but the critics did not like it, reasonably enough, and it managed only sixteen performances. This, together with the failure of *The Last Knight* at Dramaten, was a bad blow to Strindberg (the other birthday performances of his plays had brought him little). He was still accepting no payments from the Intimate Theatre. Geber paid him 1,000 crowns for a new edition of *Fairy Tales*, not a generous payment considering that he had printed ten thousand copies, but a windfall arrived in the shape of royalties of 2,000 crowns from Karin Swanström's provincial tour of *Abu Casem's Slippers*. Falck tells that Strindberg at once "completely re-equipped the Blue Tower; furniture and curtains, tapestries and books."[46] It was a typical extravagance; a couple of months later (4 June) he had to ask Karl Börjesson to pay 775 crowns which he owed in tax, since "I possess nothing." Yet somehow, less than three weeks later, he was able to repay an old private loan of 2,000 crowns "at last—after twenty years. The first ten I was a beggar, since no one was willing to pay for my work, the other ten I spent repaying, the poor people first."[47]

Strindberg's extravagance sometimes proved an embarrassment to the theatre. Falck writes that he had a tendency to involve them in expensive purchases of "authentic" objects with which to dress the sets, such as genuine Indian vases and lamps for *Abu Casem*, and "every kind of thing" for the historical plays. A typical undated note to Falck reads: "Herewith the eagle, a portfolio and some beakers. Have the whisky bottle painted soap-green and it will look mediaeval. Polish the gold beaker." This stuffed eagle, Falck explains, "was in some way connected with the Powers . . . He would sometimes send this down to the theatre to help when things were particularly difficult; it was continually shuttled between the theatre and Strindberg's apartment."[48]

Chapter Thirty-Two

~~~~~~

THE LAST ENGAGEMENTS

Strindberg was lonely in Stockholm that summer of 1909, and more than ever dependent on Fanny's company with most of his friends out of town. "I don't find it easy to live," he wrote to Nils Andersson on 2 June. "But one has to. And one does, with a little religion, otherwise it would be impossible. Sometimes I sit like Elijah beneath the juniper tree and cry: 'Enough! Lord, take my soul!' Then I get up again and continue. And thus for sixty years!" "I sit alone in the Tower," he wrote to Richard Bergh on 28 June. "It is not fun, but I find great joy in my work (the languages)." He was deep into linguistics, especially the roots of languages, and on 6 July asked Karl Otto Bonnier, as a Jew, to help him find someone who could teach him "unpunctuated Torah (a year ago I learned a little Hebrew from a Russian Israelite). I imagine the young people at the synagogue read unpunctuated, since their psalter is unpunctuated."

Things in the Falkner household were going from bad to worse. "My father, if I can call him that," Fanny informed Strindberg, "beats me." Strindberg responded harshly: "I have so many sorrows myself, and worries (including economic ones), that I cannot carry those of others. I have opened the door for you. Now you must find your own way. But do something. Read, exercise your voice. Sg." She wrote a pathetic letter asking his forgiveness and assuring him that she had not given any of his money away, "but since my salary has been so small and I am nineteen I cannot ask that my parents should go on supporting me and I must help them." He replied: "I am no company for a young girl. Go out into the countryside and find young people . . . Tell me before you leave and you shall have money; but if you give away a single farthing I shall regard it as betrayal." He seems to have been afflicted with one of those moods when he could not bear company. "I too want the right to be alone," he informed Fanny, "and have the right to it." This withdrawal of his companionship greatly distressed Fanny. Her sister Stella observes: "She seemed totally hypnotised by his powerful personality, and completely disorientated when she was away from him."[1]

Despite his harshness towards Fanny, he arranged for her three small sisters, deprived of their usual summer holiday by the family's lack of money, to go and stay with his brother Olle, who was master gardener at a baron's country estate. "They will have their own room," he told their mother on 12 June, "a big garden with a greenhouse, a park with swan lakes, smithies and hammers, a castle and much else to look at and enjoy. Baron de Geer is a youngish man and a kindly soul. My brother is fifty, married, with a daughter of twenty; he is a sound and good person who likes children (himself an elderly child) . . . They can stay until 1 August . . . If the children cannot eat any particular food, we shall warn them and it can be changed." He gave them pocket money for the journey, and Stella remembered that when they left he presented each of them with "the prettiest little mother-of-pearl purse to keep our 25 öre in." He wrote them a series of charming letters during their stay.[2]

Falck sacked four members of the company that summer, including Fanny. Strindberg was furious, and wrote Falck an abusive letter on 27 June: "By dismissing distinguished artistes and engaging unknown talents you have sown discontent and the theatre is threatened with a split. It is essential that we two stand together. Otherwise the theatre is dead, although I can, if I so wish, give life to a new one. You must now begin by giving me a key to the second lock in the theatre door, otherwise I shall go to the landlord and demand, as lessee, to be given one. Further, you shall reply to my letters and keep your promises; not allow your domestic problems to push my rightful interests into the background." "There had been many disagreements this year," Falck explains. "He had often taken offence at my casting, since sometimes I could not follow his advice."[3] Strindberg's information about Falck's marital troubles did not extend to Fanny's infatuation with her director.

Since the spring, Strindberg had been working on a poetic drama, mainly in verse, *The Great Highway*, about a huntsman who has gone into the mountains to rediscover his soul, returns to humanity and is involved in various encounters culminating in a meeting with a blind woman in a dark forest. It made uneasy progress. "I have written a hundred pages of a play (in verse and prose)," he told Richard Bergh on 8 July, "but have thought for three months that it was bad and have scrapped it (but have not burned it)." He seems to have spent less time on the play than on the roots of languages, for three days later he sent his publisher Karl Börjesson a book forbiddingly entitled *Biblical Proper Names: Linguistic Studies*, explaining: "I herewith send you 'the most remarkable book ever written' (as Kipling's young man expressed himself). * I ask no payment for it. But to make its publication possible, we must look to Esperanto's colossal public. They acted my *Miss Julie* last year in Dresden. † And we must print it on the worst paper in the worst style at the worst printer's. I <u>know</u> how remarkable the book is, but we cannot count on the learned Sadducees, who hate the light. If you dare not take it on, I will turn to Koppel; then I shall bankrupt myself to publish it. For it must be published!" Börjesson refused it, but Bonnier, who paid him 7,000 crowns this year in various fees and royalties, accepted it for publication the following year.[4] Strindberg thereupon returned to *The Great Highway*, and on 19 August sent the completed manuscript to Börjesson: "Herewith my final symphony."

In mid-August, Fanny returned to Stockholm from her holiday in the skerries, for which Strindberg had paid. She found him in a more companionable mood than when she had left and began to visit him regularly as before; he bought a huge Japanese parasol, beneath which they sat on the balcony in the warm summer evenings. He had also acquired a telescope and made her look through it while he explained about the moon and the stars. Another of his purchases was a thick rope which, he explained, he would, in the event of fire in her parents' apartment, throw up to her balcony.[5] They can never have practised any fire drill, or he would have realised that it would have been more practical for her to keep it up there; but that would have eliminated his role as saviour.

Rumours had reached Strindberg that Harriet and Gunnar Wingård were separated and planning to divorce. On 2 September he asked his daughter Greta to find out if this was true, "since I can then again see Anne-Marie, whom I haven't seen for a year."‡ "I long to see my child again," he explained to Greta two days later, "but it cannot happen until

---

*A reference to Kipling's tale "The Finest Story Ever Told."

†At an Esperanto congress.

‡According to Falck (p. 257), Strindberg lunched alone with Anne-Marie at the Blue Tower on his sixtieth birthday, 22 January 1909.

the present home is dissolved or the separation has begun." The rumours proved true; before the end of the year, Harriet moved from the apartment at Strandvägen, enabling Strindberg to resume his walks to the park at Djurgården without fear of being scrutinised from her window.

An undated letter to Fanny in Strindberg's hand has survived from this year. "A week ago I learned for the first time that there is talk of my intent to enter into a new marriage, with a young girl. I found it preposterous and absurd that I, old and sick, should seek to bind a young person to my melancholy destiny, which nature will soon bring to its appointed close. I am not to blame for your name being involved . . . Do not reply to this, only trust in me as before and such talk will die."[6]

But by the autumn his feelings towards her had changed. On 5 September he lent her a novel by Axel Lundegård (who had translated *The Father* into Danish twenty-two years before) called *Mouche*, about the dying Heine's love for the young Camilla Sellden. In this book Heine says to Camilla, "I am the condemned prisoner, you are the fly in my cell," and so calls her Mouche, the fly. It is the story of a hopeless passion. Strindberg now began to address Fanny in letters as "Ma Mouche."[7] She takes up the tale:

> I began to sense that something was afoot, I did not really know what . . .
> One evening I came down at his bidding to look at Saturn. Strindberg stood
> behind me while I peered into the telescope. It was a cool evening, and he
> wrapped a shawl around me. He lifted me up a little so that I could have a
> better view. It was the first time he touched me. Then we went inside . . . I
> said I had a headache. He said, "Would you like me to hypnotise you?" I
> said I had no objection. Then he came and sat beside me, and put his hands
> on the arm-rest, and I expected he would stroke my forehead or perform
> some other hypnotic trick. But he did not. Instead he put his hand on mine
> and said, "Shall we become engaged, you and I?" "Yes," I replied,
> astonished . . . We smiled and were happy. After a while I got up and said
> good night, and he kissed me as I left. When the door had closed and I had
> come to my senses again, I collapsed in despair and tears.

Next day he gave her a "thick ring with a pearl in it," and another ring as thanks for *Swanwhite*.

> We stood a long while at the desk and he told me to keep what had
> happened secret for two weeks. Then he would dress in white tie and tails
> and ask my parents for my hand. "What do you think the old man will say?"
> he asked with a smile, of my father, who was younger than he. Then we
> would appear in public together, first at the premiere of *The Protector* at
> Dramaten. Immediately afterwards, we would marry . . .
> He warned me that I would receive many anonymous letters, which he
> asked me not to read; people would become very indignant about it all. He

said, "You must be prepared for it to be like entering a nunnery. You will not meet many people, only some of my old friends." I took this literally and became very frightened. Then he began to say how happy we both would be. He planned that we should live in some old country house . . . When he could not but notice that I was not happy, he at first asked if I thought I would miss my mother and sisters. We could take one twin with us and the five-year-old Stella. She would have a live pig to play with . . . He spoke of how many *beautiful* things he would write, and how lovely it would be for both of us to live in the country . . . I liked him awfully and wanted nothing more than to be able to give some happiness to this man—but I could not get rid of the thought that he was so much older than I. I liked to touch his hair and stroke his cheeks, but I could not love him as I wanted to. This was what made it so difficult—for I could not be without him. I would gladly live alone in the country with him, I would devote my whole life to him, I would never marry anyone else as long as he was alive—if only I could avoid being married to him . . . Once he asked me straight, "Perhaps you would rather I adopted you, so that you can call me uncle?" I replied, perhaps too quickly, "Oh, yes, please!" That made him sad. He had only said it to test me and was expecting me to say no.

Five days after I had accepted him, I summoned my courage. I went into his study, he kissed me as usual. Then I said simply, "I cannot." He understood immediately and said, "Why?" I merely replied, "I am so young." He became quite still and said, "Dear child, I can wait. I will not press you, you may come when you wish . . . and have thought it over." Then he asked, "Has anyone said anything . . . has anyone spoken ill of me?" I replied again, "I cannot." . . . We continued to meet as before. Sometimes with a forced nonchalance he would say, "Well, what shall we do now, shall we get married?"[8]

On 5 September, the day he lent Fanny Lundegård's *Mouche*, Strindberg wrote to his daughter Kerstin for the last time. Gently affectionate, his letter must have made bitter reading for the fifteen-year-old girl long since abandoned by her mother and now finally rejected by her father:

> My child,
> I have not had any letter from Dornach. And I have become so alien to everything that has anything to do with Austria—more than alien. It seems to me like an ancient saga, incredible, yet once it was true. Is your rich old great-grandmother alive? Wasn't she rich? Is Aunt Melanie alive? I know nothing, and am not eager to know anything, since everything has become alien to me.
> I am sixty years old and live in a boardinghouse . . . But I am a writer and life is to me simply material for plays, mostly tragedies . . .* Adieu! And think of me only as a memory.
>
> Your father

*The dots in both instances are Strindberg's.

Again, one is struck by his seeming indifference to her, in contrast to his intense affection, despite periods of irritation, for his four other children. Frida had wounded him no more than Siri; Kerstin lived abroad, but so did Karin and Hans, and at least he was not expected to pay towards Kerstin's upbringing. Admittedly, Kerstin had not grown up in his home as his four other children had, but this scarcely seems a sufficient reason. Did he perhaps, knowing of Frida's illegitimate child by Frank Wedekind, illogically suspect that Kerstin might not be his? In a letter to Marie Uhl on 20 December this year, the last he wrote to her, Strindberg suggested a more altruistic motive but hinted at possible doubts concerning paternity. "If I now claim my paternal rights, I shall be suspected of being an 'inheritance-seeker.' This cruel word was once spoken in Mondsee during my first visit there . . . But there is another side to the matter. If I renounce my paternal rights the child will lose her right to inherit anything from me. While I live I am poor, but when I am dead I shall probably become rich. Remember this! And tell Kerstin's mother to remember it too!" With that, all contact between Strindberg and the Uhls ended for ever.

Meanwhile, the Intimate Theatre was rehearsing *The Dance of Death*, about to enjoy its Swedish premiere nine years after its completion. Falck had decided to present the two parts separately on different evenings, though after some weeks of performance they staged them together. They held no less than eighty rehearsals, beginning in the spring; when they resumed in the autumn, Strindberg sat in on a few rehearsals as "director." As with *The Father*, he said little to the cast but sent them a series of notes, or "memoranda," as he liked to call them, giving often sound if sometimes unexciting advice. "First and last, the Captain must look old!" he commanded Falck. "His ugliness, age and whisky must be visible" —counsel which has not always been followed by Falck's successors in the role.

> "*The Dance of Death*, my boy! That's my best play!" Strindberg often repeated . . . "The Captain! What a part!" And he jumped up and acted it for me. "A refined demon! Evil shines out of his eyes, which sometimes flash with a glint of satanic humour. His face is bloated with liquor and corruption, and he so relishes saying evil things that he almost sucks them, tastes them, rolls them around his tongue before spitting them out. He thinks of course that he is cunning and superior, but like all stupid people he becomes at such moments a pitiful and petulant wretch."
>
> And with sweet-sour, fawning expressions, with gestures both jaunty and pathetic, he walked around or threw himself down in a chair. What he particularly liked to act was the powerful scene when Alice, with a bored expression, plays the march "The Dance of the Boyars," which incites and

hypnotises the Captain to dance—wildly and clumsily, terrifyingly. At such moments he was an excellent actor—a great dramatic talent. His vivid impersonation remains for ever in my mind's eye and echoes in my ears.[9]

Part I of *The Dance of Death*, on 8 September, had a mixed reception from the critics, as it had had on publication. August Brunius in *Svenska Dagbladet* mocked it as "a pathological study of various physical and spiritual illnesses; erotic hysteria and sclerosis of the heart and the like. A hospital theatre would be the most appropriate venue for *The Dance of Death*" (a comment which several critics had made a quarter of a century earlier about Ibsen's *Ghosts*). But other reviewers were more perceptive, and the play proved one of the Intimate Theatre's biggest successes, achieving eighty-five performances. Part II, first presented on 10 October, was, being less pessimistic, even more favourably received. *The Dance of Death* was also performed that autumn in Hamburg and Riga; other productions that year included *Creditors* at Strelitz, *Easter* at Weimar, *Miss Julie* at Essen, *The Pelican* at Elberfeld and *The Comrades* at Brünn and in Prague, while *Miss Julie* also received its Polish premiere at an experimental theatre in Lodz.

Three companies took his plays around the Swedish provinces that autumn. Helge Wahlgren, a former actor at the Intimate Theatre, toured *Creditors* and *Motherly Love*, Strindberg generously waiving his royalties,[10] and Erland Colliander did likewise with *The Virgin Bride*, with Greta in the title role, for five months to excellent reviews and good houses. Later in the tour, Colliander staged the first production of *The Black Glove*, but nobody seems to have liked it. Strindberg was delighted with the success of *The Virgin Bride*, and with Greta's good reviews. "This is the way to success," he wrote to her on 20 October, "to make people good and beautiful, and you, Greta, must never act my harsh plays from the past (*Miss Julie*, etc.) . . . Do not forget to thank the Giver! We have no share in these miracles." He had, indeed, changed from the free-thinker of the 1880s. A third company toured *Miss Julie*, with an eighteen-year-old youth named Karl Johnson as Jean; he was later to make his name as a revue artist of genius under the name of Karl Gerhard.

Open Letters to the Intimate Theatre was published in October, and *The Great Highway* in November, the latter to surprisingly good reviews. Sven Söderman, that stern critic of Strindberg's work, praised it in *Stockholms Dagblad* as "a poetic play often of the highest power," and the young poet Anders Österling in *Svenska Dagbladet* found it "a great work—one of the greatest to have appeared in recent years in Scandinavia . . . Its power is sometimes such that reading it becomes like a march through mountainous landscapes in a storm." Even the conservative *Nya Dagligt Allehanda* acclaimed it. Posterity has been less kind to the play; its verse is not much less humdrum than that of *The Black Glove*, and even Olof Molander's 1949 Stockholm production, to celebrate the centenary of Strindberg's birth, with a powerful cast led by Lars Hanson, could not totally rescue it from tedium. It is impossible not to be struck, as always, by the woolliness of Strindberg's dramatic verse in contrast to the sharpness of his prose; one must be grateful that he did not use verse, as he so easily might have, for *To Damascus* and *The Ghost Sonata*.

On 10 December, Strindberg was performed for the first time, albeit briefly, in the West End of London (*The Stronger* and *Simoom* in 1906 had been in unfashionable Bloomsbury). Lydia Yavorskaia, Strindberg's pioneer in Russia, had hired His Majesty's Theatre for a short season to present her St. Petersburg company in a selection of plays in Russian. An enterprise called the Afternoon Theatre (of which more anon) had been founded by Frederick Whelen to present plays of minority interest at matinées, and Yavorska (as she called herself in England) staged *The Stronger*, as a curtain-raiser to the final act of an Ostrovsky play, with herself in the silent but rewarding role of the mistress and Lady Tree as the wife. *The Era* reported that the audience was "thoroughly interested." Strindberg seems to have impressed Lady Tree favourably, for the following February she played Biskra in *Simoom* (a role for which she must have been grotesquely unsuited at the age of fifty-three) as part of a vaudeville programme at the Empire Theatre in Liverpool.

There was further English interest in Strindberg that winter, for on 21 January 1910, Ebba Nyström, the Stockholm representative of an international agent named Hugo Vallentin, wrote to Strindberg that His Majesty's Theatre wanted to see a script of *Lucky Peter's Journey*. Strindberg was, however, unwilling to be introduced to the general London public by a play which he despised, and on 10 February he wrote to Emil Schering asking him to send his German translations of *The Father* (despite his recent strictures on that play), *Easter*, *The Dance of Death* and *A Dream Play*. "England seems to be open," he wrote again to Schering next day. "Would it perhaps be worth while for your wife to go over with her [English] translations and German copies? But not the melodramas, *Sir Bengt's Wife*, etc., only the tragedies. No rubbish!"

On 16 February, *The Great Highway* was premiered at the Intimate Theatre, but the play proved too much for the young company. Sven Söderman, who had so praised it on publication, summed up the general reaction in *Stockholms Dagblad*: "The mere idea of presenting such a play at the primitive Intimate Theatre with its indescribably limited artistic resources was stillborn, and the result was as expected. For anyone who admires this work, it was painful to see it so botched in performance. The stage cannot offer the simplest decorative illusion, and the players lack the necessary vocal training." Several other critics found Falck, as the Wanderer, much too monotonous in his delivery, a complaint frequently levelled against his performances (and as director, he seems to have passed this fault on to his company). Hjalmar Söderberg, that gifted and imaginative novelist who so curiously disliked Strindberg's experimental work, rejected the play altogether, deploring, in the theatre magazine *Thalia,* "the same lack of technique . . . as in A *Dream Play.* And the same absence of comprehensible meaning." The production managed only sixteen performances. It was followed on 5 March by a double bill of Strindberg's early Viking play *The Outlaw,* revived for the first time in Sweden since its premiere in 1871, together with his feeble 1892 one-acter, *In the Face of Death;* an unpromising combination, and so it proved, for the bill was withdrawn after only nine performances.

Bernard Shaw now added his voice to those trying to persuade Strindberg to allow *Lucky Peter's Journey* to be staged in London. On 16 March he wrote to Strindberg explaining that Barrie's *Peter Pan* in 1904 had encouraged managers to look for other children's plays which could likewise be revived each Christmas. Maeterlinck's *Blue Bird* had proved a success at the Haymarket in December 1909, and Herbert Beerbohm Tree wanted something to match it at His Majesty's. "Your later pieces are quite impossible at his theatre; not because it is a very big one . . . but because his theatre is a favourite with the innocent bourgeoisie and their daughters, who would fly horror-stricken at the very first [moment] of Julie." The Afternoon Theatre, however, which operated at His Majesty's, might well do one of the later plays. "It would be thoroughly understood that *Lycko Per* was your *Midsummer Night's Dream* and not your *Hamlet;* and the mere discussion and reiteration of this fact would create a good deal of curiosity to see your Hamlet in London."[11]

Strindberg's answer has not survived, but he evidently summarised the plot of *Lucky Peter,* insisted that some other play of his should be presented in London first, and sent Shaw a copy of his Christmas piece, *The Black Glove,* in Swedish. Shaw replied that *Lucky Peter* sounded as though it would "suit Sir Herbert Tree exactly," and urged Strindberg to grant Tree the rights provided some other play of Strindberg's choice was first presented at the Afternoon Theatre. Strindberg's answer has, like his earlier one, disappeared, and in the event, nothing came of this project, which might so easily have opened the way for Strindberg in Britain (where, to date, *Lucky Peter* remains unperformed, at least professionally).[12]

Germany and Austria were bringing him more money this year. That winter and spring, *Miss Julie* was performed in Munich, *The Father* in Essen, and *Easter* in Berlin; and Josef Jarno staged a season of four of his plays in Vienna: *Creditors, Playing with Fire, Easter* and *Christina*. Jarno seems to have directed the plays more subtly than most of his contemporaries for the *Berliner Tageblatt* wrote of his production of *Creditors*: "Jarno stages Strindberg not as a cantankerous misogynist but as a deeply embittered worshipper of women who has changed sides . . . He does not allow Strindberg's women to appear as harridans but as very elegant, very placid, very coquettish cats. The most perfidious things are said in the most loving tones." In March, Strindberg was able to redeem his library from pawn. In April the Intimate Theatre visited Christiania. Strindberg was uncertain how his work would be received in Ibsen's home city, and the day before they left, tried to persuade Falck to cancel the trip. *Miss Julie* only half filled the house on the opening night, but next morning the critics were unanimous in their praise, and for the remaining eight nights of their engagement they were sold out, *The Father, Easter, Pariah* and *Swanwhite* being equally acclaimed.[13]

Strindberg's health seems to have been good that spring, as it had been throughout the two years since his move to the Blue Tower; his letters contain no reference to stomach pains. Gustaf Uddgren paints an affectionate portrait of Strindberg at this time:

> He had the feeling that he had at last found his Tusculum where he might live out the years of his old age in peace . . . He took different walks from those when he had lived at Karlavägen. He seldom now visited his beloved Djurgården, preferring to walk down Drottninggatan and Barnhusgatan to the Intimate Theatre at Norra Bantorget. He had his own keys to the theatre and would begin his day by inspecting it. He would study the posters advertising the repertory . . . [and] the progress being made with the new decor, especially that for his great Damascus cycle, though this project was never to be completed. After leaving the theatre he always stopped for a moment in the square to look back at it. If the sun was shining on the upper half of the façade he took this to be a good omen . . . In his last years he would walk up to Valhallavägen, at the end of which his youngest daughter lived . . . He often walked so far that he would completely exhaust himself. When he became tired he often had quite serious attacks of paralysis, all down one side, so that he had difficulty in moving. Then he would take a cab home. The paralysis soon passed. During the summer of the great strike [1909], he could not get cabs and was often compelled to go into a shop, where he would buy some small object and be allowed to rest for a quarter of an hour until the paralysis had passed and he could continue homewards.

The period of the strike deeply interested him. One of the few literary plans he dallied with in 1910–1911 was that of depicting a great strike in the manner of Victor Hugo, showing its crippling effect on individuals and society. When I asked him why he didn't go ahead with this, he replied: "I don't write anything which doesn't absolutely demand to be written.". . . He would sometimes cut loose and go with young people to play skittles at Lidingöbro Inn until the small hours and then drive around for the rest of the night, continuing after a couple of hours' sleep with an oyster breakfast at Fenix.[14]

With *The Great Highway*, Strindberg had said farewell not merely to the drama but to creative writing. There were to be no more plays, novels or stories. Linguistics still obsessed him, and his letters at this time contain many long questionnaires about Hebrew. He now turned, as feverishly as ever, to a different kind of writing which was to involve him in violent and protracted controversy.

Norway's repudiation in 1905 of the union with Sweden, forced on it after the Napoleonic Wars when the victorious allies had granted Sweden suzerainty over its neighbour, had been followed by a violent upsurge of nationalism in Sweden. The great warrior kings of the past had become objects of almost fanatical worship, and some extreme right-wing elements even demanded that Norway should be reconquered by force. The country was deeply split, with the liberals and the social democrats asserting that true patriotism ought to express itself in love not of dead kings, but of the oppressed majority of the Swedish people.

At the beginning of April 1910, a Carolingian Society was formed in Stockholm to honour the memory of Sweden's most famous warrior king, Charles XII, with Verner von Heidenstam and Sven Hedin among its leading figures. Charles XII had long been one of Strindberg's *bêtes noires*, the type of absolute, self-aggrandising monarch who, as Strindberg saw it, did nothing for his people, impoverished his country and encouraged the worst kind of jingoism, as well as causing the deaths of thousands. Strindberg despised Heidenstam and Hedin as typical jingoists; moreover, Heidenstam represented the aesthetic school of poetry which he hated, and Hedin's triumphant return from his Asian explorations in January 1909, when he was ennobled by King Gustav, had overshadowed Strindberg's own sixtieth-birthday celebrations.

A new liberal evening paper, *Afton-Tidningen*, had recently been founded, with offices next to Strindberg's home on Drottninggatan. Its editor, Valfrid Spångberg, tells how on 10 April, Strindberg dropped an article in without warning, asking if they would print it: "I write without

538 *The Homecoming (1898–1912)*

payment, but beg that you send me a proof and that I be excused editorial comment contradicting what I say." The article, entitled "Pharaoh Worship," appeared on 29 April. Strindberg did not mention Charles XII by name but left no doubt whose memory he was castigating. The conservative *Stockholms-Dagblad*, which had reported the founding of the Carolingian Society with enthusiasm, rallied next day to that society's defence. "Alas for the genius," it commented, "which thinks it knows everything from chemistry and physics to biblical names and history, and does not see that the glass through which it studies everything is flawed and distorted."

The liberals and social democrats were surprised to find Strindberg leaning towards their point of view and choosing one of their organs as his medium, for his utterances since *Inferno*, not least in the *Blue Books*, had been decidedly conservative. People in general (he seemed to feel) were malignant egoists, authority was ordained by God to keep them in check, and evil and suffering were sent to chastise them. He had shown no interest in social reform; socialists and the like were arrogant in setting themselves against the divine order of things. But now, over a period of five months until the end of September, he wrote some fifty articles for the left-wing press, *Social-Demokraten* as well as *Afton-Tidningen*, on subjects as varied as jingoism, atheism, aestheticism in literature, Bible criticism and linguistics, and the shortcomings of the Swedish Academy. Politically, he remained a maverick. The irreligiousness of the traditional left antagonised him; in *A Blue Book* he had declared that Christianity was "more radical than radicalism."[15] But he found to his surprise that the young adherents of the left were sympathetic to religion, and it was with the young social democrats that he in due course aligned himself, using their publishing house Fram [Forward] to issue his last collections of articles and essays.

On 15 June, Strindberg turned his guns against Heidenstam personally, mocking what he regarded as his former friend's shallow patriotism, and on 13 July he denounced Sven Hedin, asserting that some of the discoveries which Hedin claimed from his eastern travels had been made two centuries earlier by a survivor of Charles XII's Russian campaign. These personal attacks caused a far more violent controversy than his more generalised pieces. "Who will shoot Strindberg?" Ellen Key (another of his *bêtes noires*) wrote to Karl Otto Bonnier on 17 June, "for the criminal lunatic must be rendered harmless."[16] On 8 July, Fredrik Böök, Oscar Levertin's successor as chief literary critic of *Svenska Dagbladet*, asked in its pages: "Has Strindberg in his cultural criticism ever been inspired by anything but blind hatred, brutal malice and seething megalomania . . . has he ever really understood anything? Is not this astounding polymath one of the most ignorant writers who has existed . . . for in his pride and slovenliness of mind he has never got to the heart of anything? . . . Rodin's 'Thinker' presents a man who thinks with his muscles and fists; a sculptor who would portray the 'thinker' Strindberg, the disciple of Rousseau, the sex philosopher, the Swedenborgian, would need to show a man who thinks with his guts and twists, howling, in his agonies . . . One cannot believe that the Swedes will sink to worshipping a volcano, least of all a volcano that belches not fire but filth, dirt and stones . . . It cannot happen to a people that has loved Tegnér and Geijer and Viktor Rydberg [three traditional patriotic poets]." Hedin himself, in *Dagens Nyheter* on 22 July, dismissed Strindberg as "an astonishing mixture of titan, sphinx, vampire and parasite . . . Poor lonely and deserted pilgrim, living on the ruins of his own tragic life."

The liberals and social democrats rallied to Strindberg's defence. On 8 July, the same day that Böök's article appeared, the young John Landquist, who was later to edit the standard edition of Strindberg's works (and lived long enough to review a book by me in 1971 when he was over ninety), published an eloquent article in *Afton-Tidningen* entitled "Strindberg Is Right!" Dealing with Strindberg's attack on the "aesthetic" writers of the nineties and their denunciations of him, Landquist asserted that in romanticism no less than in naturalism Strindberg, not they, was the true pioneer. We are told, Landquist wrote, that "Heidenstam and Levertin and Selma Lagerlöf led us back to the promised land . . . I say that this whole picture is a lie. It was Strindberg who pioneered romanticism and great poetry with his romantic historical drama *Master Olof*. . . It was Strindberg who pioneered Swedish historical fiction and summoned those sleeping figures so powerfully that they reawoke to life . . . Beside his universal revolution—social, moral, literary—the acclaimed scribblers of the nineties are but a branch of revolt . . . While Strindberg, alone in a foreign land, confronted new destinies and crises and waged his hardest battle, the nineties writers marched safely at home under flying banners and with blaring trumpets, basking in the nation's adulation. That Strindberg should feel mortified on looking back at those years is surely human . . . Which writer is most read, most heard, today, whom do ordinary men and women name when they speak together? The answer is: no Swedish writer has ever been so widely read as Strindberg, no one has penetrated as deeply into the hearts and minds of the people as he."

A week earlier, on 1 July, a working man named Adolf Lundgrehn had added fuel to the flames. "It is a truism," he wrote in *Afton-Tidningen*, "that we Swedes offer nothing but wormwood and insults to our great men while they live, but canonise them once they are safely dead. If this is true of anyone, it is true of Strindberg. What has his country offered him, whose writing is more Swedish than almost any other man's? Even his outbursts of bitter hatred are typically Swedish . . . That the Swedish Academy has closed its doors to him is something that probably neither he nor anyone else regrets, now that it has become an ignominy to sit there . . . But that the Nobel Prize [which the previous December had been awarded to Selma Lagerlöf] was not given to him was an insult not only to him but to Swedish letters and to the broad mass of the people both in and outside our country." Lundgrehn ended by suggesting that if Parliament was not prepared to vote Strindberg a pension, a nation-wide appeal should be organised to which ordinary men and women could subscribe, however humbly. A correspondent named Ludvig Nordström, one of many supporting this idea, wrote that Strindberg "makes us all world citizens, while Heidenstam simply reminds us . . . that before all else we are Swedes . . . [Strindberg] has sensed that there is a desire in Sweden to cast off the rigid bonds of nationalism and make contact with other European spirits . . . It is obvious how merciless and ruthless this self-accounting must be, but it is necessary and inevitable."[17] The conservatives, led by Fredrik Böök and Per Hallström, opposed the idea of a national subscription, as, surprisingly, did some liberal organs such as *Handelstidningen i Göteborg, Karlstads-Tidningen* and even, at first, the usually enlightened *Dagens Nyheter,*[18] but the social democrats took it up and launched an appeal the following spring which was to meet with spectacular success.

Towards the end of July, the Falkners finally abandoned their ill-fated *pension* and moved to a smaller apartment on Valhallavägen—in the same house, by the kind of ghoulish coincidence that haunted Strindberg all his life, in which Harriet was living with Anne-Marie following her separation from Wingård. The Falkners' servant Mina, the only satisfactory one Strindberg had ever found in Stockholm, continued to attend to his needs, and he got his meals sent up by a Fröken Carlsson, who ran a café on the ground floor. Fanny continued to meet Strindberg at his apartment. "Strindberg's interest in her," Stella Falkner explains, "was the epitome of everything she could not find at home—calm and respect . . . She looked up to him as to God the Father. Fascinated by his personality, she warmed to his presence like a frozen child, and humbly served him in any way which could contribute to his comfort."[19]

His old friend from the Black Porker days, Dr. Carl Ludwig Schleich, visited him in Stockholm that summer and "was amazed to see how celebrated Strindberg was, and how wherever he went he was gravely and respectfully saluted. He was like a citizen king. Several times people stepped off the pavement and bowed, hat in hand, whispering as he passed: 'That is Strindberg!' " He surprised Schleich by the earnestness of his religious conviction. "It has," he told Schleich, "been as though I was a voyager who had set out to discover new lands in the world of the soul. Every time I thought I had found a new island, it turned out on closer inspection to be our old Bible and Testament. Nothing exists higher than the old wisdoms." Schleich adds that "he believed implicitly in immortality and in the higher development of the individual through death after the catharsis performed by earthly life." He invited Strindberg to visit him at the Grand Hotel; eventually Strindberg did, and as they sat down at the table which Schleich had booked in the restaurant, remarked, "This is the table where I and my wife [Harriet] sat for the last time. I knew you would choose it. That is why I didn't want to come."[20] On 23 July, he wrote to Nils Andersson: "Only the Bible and Swedenborg give me courage."

One day Fredrik Ström, the director of the Young Social Democrats' publishing house Fram, received a request from Strindberg to call on him.

> When I entered, he looked very serious, even solemn. He was not dressed as usual in a checked dressing-gown and slippers, but in a coat with frills and high-heeled shoes. Strindberg asked me to sit down.
>
> "I want to ask your opinion about something," he said. "What would the public say of a marriage in which the man was over sixty and the woman eighteen or nineteen? You must answer me honestly."
>
> I was at first perplexed, then thought, Strindberg is writing a new play about marriage. He wants to know how a theatre audience would react. I felt bound to answer honestly as he had requested, and said, "I think people would regard such a marriage as unnatural."
>
> "And you, personally?"
>
> "The same."
>
> I added some further, more pungent observations, since I found the idea quite repellent.
>
> When I had expressed my opinion, Strindberg's face became ashen, and he seemed to shrink. For some while he said nothing. I now realised that his question related not to a play but to some personal matter and that I had unwittingly wounded him. He remained silent; at last he stammered, "Thank you, I know your feelings. They are also mine. Go now. I need to be alone."
>
> He raised his hand slightly and looked at the door. I bowed and left. It was many years before I realised the truth, when Fanny Falkner's book about Strindberg appeared.[21]

Nevertheless, some time that July or August, soon after the Falkners had moved from the Blue Tower, Strindberg proposed to Fanny a second time and, albeit even more briefly than before, she again accepted him.

> I don't know why, but that day I felt less hostile to the idea than usual, listened attentively to his arguments and felt I might as well settle the matter. Suddenly it seemed to me quite an attractive prospect to be his wife . . . We would go to Brittany and spend a year or so away from Sweden until the talk had subsided. He no longer spoke of a marriage with him being like entering a nunnery. Again mesmerised, I said yes . . . But as soon as I was out of his bewitching presence, and had come to my senses, I felt hesitant and fearful. I felt I had no choice but to visit him again next day and tell him I had made a great mistake. As usual he listened with great patience and uttered no word of reproach.[22]

Strindberg's niece Anna-Lisa tells that after this second refusal by Fanny he lived "completely isolated from the world."[23] This is not quite true; he still had his Beethoven evenings, but he seems to have avoided everyone except his family and his closest friends. When Anna-Lisa got married, he did not attend the wedding but sent Mina to help with the arrangements and questioned her closely afterwards about how the bride was dressed and what food and wine were served,[24] and when his son Hans informed him that summer that he was to marry, Strindberg replied warmly, assuring him that he would do his best to help financially: "Tell me if you want a little at once, or monthly."[25] He remained as peppery as ever if his gifts and offers were not acknowledged immediately. "I sent Hans 500 marks over a week ago," he complained to Greta on 7 June. "No reply. Wired on Sunday and asked if he had got the money. No reply! It is disgraceful." He was still sending small sums to Hans and Karin that September.

A collection of Strindberg's newspaper articles from this summer, containing his political and social essays and his attacks on Hedin, Heidenstam, the nineties writers and the Swedish Academy, plus some swipes at French symbolism and contemporary fashions in Swedish art, appeared that autumn in a volume entitled *Speeches to the Swedish Nation*, published by Fram in three simultaneous editions: a normal one at one crown (10,000 copies), a cheap one at 50 öre (3,000 copies) and a de luxe one at 4 crowns (200 copies). The book's reception varied predictably according to political views. *Stockholms-Dagblad* grudgingly admitted that "one now and then meets a thought or an utterance that gives rise to serious reflection," but concluded: "The predominant mood is one of unhealthy mistrust and a curious desire to denigrate respectable persons." Hjalmar Söderberg in *Söndags-Nisse* dismissed it as "an un-broken jeremiad against the undeserved success of his antagonists."

Strindberg's hopes for the Intimate Theatre had faded. "I think it is doomed," he had written to Falck on 9 March, and in a later, undated letter, "I . . . feel it is undermined and threatened with closure. I also feel as though you were preparing to abandon me . . . Do not do that, for no blessing will follow."[26] Falck comments: "He had become tired of the Intimate Theatre, of me, of the business side of it all, yet did not want me to give up or 'prepare to abandon him.' . . . It was not always easy for a young man to work with a genius who had wild plans but very little idea of how they could be realised. Sometimes men would come from the electricity board and cut us off and I would have to rush around all day to find the money. When the staff arrived in the evening they would wonder if we had any lights."[27]

During the summer the Intimate had staged *The Comrades* to unusual-ly favourable reviews, and had revived *The Father, Christina* and *Easter*. On reopening in August after the July closure, Falck presented a new production of *Creditors*, convinced that, following the play's success in Germany and Austria, it would draw the town; but it managed only twenty-one performances. He had by now decided to stage, for the first time since the theatre had opened, a non-Strindberg play, Maeterlinck's *The Uninvited Guest*. Strindberg was furious. "If I am to continue to take an interest in the Intimate Theatre," he wrote to Falck on 14 September, "its programme must be fulfilled: i.e., first my unperformed plays! and not those of any foreigner! I cannot afford to make sacrifices for Maeter-linck, though I admire him. And my well-wishers and the friends of the theatre are prepared to make new sacrifices—for my sake, not that of foreigners or beginners (they have Dramaten!). A word of advice: beware of Uddgren! He has written a play, which he wants to get staged—if he doesn't, then he will destroy the theatre . . . Repel these attacks by staying loyal to me . . . I shall probably refuse the Anti-Nobel Prize and suggest a fund for the Intimate Theatre on the one simple condition: that I am performed!"

The Uninvited Guest was, nevertheless, staged on 23 September. It was a great success, "which Strindberg never forgave, and this was decisive for the fate of my theatre. Had I guessed that he would be so unreasonable as to destroy all my youthful efforts, I might have stopped in time."[28] In an attempt to mollify Strindberg, Falck prepared a production of Part I of *To Damascus*, but Strindberg would not be moved. "If Falck comes begging in my name," he wrote to Richard Bergh on 26 October, "treat him as a traitor. Please warn Bonnier and the Prince [Eugen]."

To Damascus, on 18 November, was coldly received, and Strindberg, in his most impossible mood, attacked Falck in *Afton-Tidningen* and applied to the public notary to investigate the theatre's affairs and ban Falck from staging any more of his plays. The Intimate was by now in such straits that on 6 December the landlord demanded sequestration of both Falck's and Strindberg's possessions to the amount of 9,700 crowns against unpaid rent, and this was granted.[29] Next day, Strindberg wrote a spiteful letter to the district judge advising him to padlock the theatre to stop Falck removing the furniture "under the pretext that it belongs to his brother-in-law or to his wife or children."

In these distressing circumstances, Falck's brave venture at the Intimate Theatre ended. On 11 December 1910 it staged its last three performances: *Christina* at 1:30 p.m., *The Father* at 4 and *Miss Julie* at 8, all to full houses. During the three years of its existence, Falck had staged twenty-four of Strindberg's plays. He blamed the theatre's failure on the "systematic hostility" of the critics, compared with the "endless good-will and warm satisfaction which they poured out over all the farces, operettas and insignificant new Swedish plays which frothed around us at the other Stockholm theatres."[30] These theatres, Falck complained, offered "expensive productions, self-indulgent solo performances and a style of direction which sought the maximum of elaboration . . . There was a serious public for whom this was not enough and whom in a humble way we tried to satisfy."[31]

This is not quite a true picture. A study of contemporary reviews of the Intimate Theatre's productions shows that the critics were by no means inimically inclined. The problem was twofold. Firstly, the new plays which Strindberg wrote for the Intimate were not good, apart from *Storm*, for which the youthful company was unsuited, and *The Ghost Sonata*, which was too far in advance of its time for the cast to encompass or the critics to understand. Secondly, the actors were too young and inexperienced to cope with Strindberg's earlier plays in which the protagonists are approaching, if they have not already reached, middle age, such as *The Father*, *The Dance of Death* and *To Damascus*. It is noteworthy that the Intimate's biggest successes, the only three which achieved a hundred performances, were plays in which the main characters are young: *Miss Julie*, *Easter* and *Swanwhite*. Oscar Wieselgren, a fair and perceptive judge, describes the company as little more than enthusiastic amateurs, adding that Strindberg, in his attempts to direct and give advice, was not always helpful because his view of acting, since he had seen hardly any theatrical performances in the past thirty years except dress rehearsals of his own plays, was old-fashioned.[32] Except for what he read of Craig, himself the most impractical of theatre men, Strindberg was untouched by new continental ideas, such as the production methods of Reinhardt, William Poel and Stanislavsky, the understatement of Duse and the colloquial naturalism of the Dublin Abbey. His good ideas were those he had held when he wrote the preface to *Miss Julie* in 1888. He was, Wieselgren concludes, "as far behind the times as a director as he was ahead of them as a playwright."[33] Yet the Intimate at least introduced an attempt at ensemble playing, seeking simplicity and truthfulness as opposed to showy theatrical declamation; and this was something not generally found in Sweden. The most eloquent tribute to Falck's company comes from Strindberg himself in one of his "open letters" to the Intimate Theatre: "When I see my play well performed and I do not notice the actors, then it has been well acted . . . honest, unaffected art, demonstrated by young, unspoiled people who have learned in a hard school . . . have not learned tricks, and do not show off, do not try to upstage each other." This could not have been found in any other Swedish theatre at that time.

Falck maintained his company for a further twenty years without a permanent home, touring the Swedish provinces as he had before and paying periodical visits to Denmark and Norway. As late as 1930 they played in Finland, Latvia, Lithuania and Estonia; they presented Carl Eldh's bust to the National Theatre in Riga. * As Falck and his company grew older, their ability to cope with Strindberg's middle-aged characters increased, so that on their visit to Copenhagen in 1926 an experienced critic, Louis Levy, was able to write in *Tilskueren*: "August Falck's production of *The Father* is the finest performance I have ever seen at the Royal Theatre . . . I regard Herr Falck's company, now regrettably homeless, as nevertheless the true Scandinavian Theatre."[34]

Abroad, *Creditors* was staged in Essen that autumn, *Playing with Fire* in Hamburg and *Christina* in Graz, followed in December by *The Comrades* in Cologne and *Playing with Fire* in Budapest. In November, Fram published a new book by Strindberg entitled *The People's State*, comprising fourteen essays which he had published in left-wing newspapers that autumn demanding the establishment of a socialist state in which the monarch would be no more than a ritual figurehead, and tracing the rise of such societies in the past through popular protests and revolutions. He still refused to identify with any single political party, insisting, as he was to do until his death, that he stood to the left of everyone.

*Now the Latvian Drama Theatre. The bust is still there, though it is no longer exhibited.

As though wearying of public controversy, he now returned to his latest substitute for alchemy, the roots of languages, tracing supposed relationships between Hebrew, which (following Swedenborg) he regarded as the source of all languages, and classical and modern tongues. His theories became increasingly fanciful, to the extent of asserting that the Greek *hyper*, Latin *super* and German *über*, all meaning "over," stem from Abarim, the Hebrew name for a mountain in Moab.

Chapter Thirty-Three

❧❧❧❧❧❧❧❧❧❧❧❧❧❧❧❧❧❧❧❧❧❧❧❧❧❧❧❧

"I NO LONGER EXIST"

Strindberg's correspondence in the last weeks of 1910 and the first months of 1911 give no indication that he was regarded at this time as the most explosive political writer in Sweden. His letters deal almost exclusively with word similarities in different languages, and business matters. On 31 January his play *The Protector*, about the young Gustav Vasa's acquisition of the Swedish crown in 1523—the middle play of the trilogy which begins with *The Last Knight* and ends with *Gustav Vasa*—was premiered at Dramaten. Although it contains powerful scenes and makes quite lively reading, it is a disjointed play and achieved only thirteen performances (and has seldom been revived). But enthusiasm for his plays in Germany was greater than ever. That winter and spring, *Christina* was staged in Munich, Altona and Mannheim, *Playing with Fire* in Karlsruhe and Baden-Baden, *The Comrades* in Aachen and *The Dance of Death* in Bremen.

Karl Otto Bonnier wrote to him offering to buy his collected works in exchange for an annuity during his lifetime, followed by an outright payment to his heirs after his death. Strindberg was dubious. "Your big proposal worries me," he replied on 21 February. "Like Tolstoy, I have become scared of money, and think it does not befit me as the end approaches. Nor have I any further ambitions in that area, no country cottage nor yacht, which I never had and do not want now as a gift. And these troublesome obligations which come with wealth—the bother of keeping it, the fear of losing it . . . This gives me more headaches than poverty—already!"*

On 1 March, Verner von Heidenstam, who had hitherto remained silent in the face of Strindberg's jibes, launched a violent and, for one who prided himself on being an aristocrat, surprisingly undignified assault on him in *Svenska Dagbladet.* "Strindberg," he declared, "is the full-blooded barbarian in our literature . . . He hates civilising powers with all his heart and soul . . . rumbling mist of confusion, suspicion, superstition and fear which is his world. He is a disintegrator, not a builder, and in his hands everything falls apart and becomes dust . . . He is a seeker, not a finder. He makes gold, but it is not gold . . . He is a carriage without shaft or traces, which lies one moment in the left ditch, the next moment in the right . . . He is not a sower. Nothing grows and blossoms around him . . . Strindberg has never been a fully mature person . . . His warlike rhetoric comprises exactly the kind of grotesque exaggerations which excite very young people . . . Mockery and accusation are the two feet on which Strindberg's philosophy dances and walks . . . Like all weak persons, he seeks truth in extremes . . . completely lacks true and noble objectivity." Next day Heidenstam continued his attack in the columns of *Aftonbladet,* turning his attention to Strindberg as a playwright. "We do not remember his characters as we do the creations of Ibsen and Holberg . . . No divine light shines over their heads. Heroism lies quite outside the range of his imagination. He writes for slaves. He is too small . . . His nature is wholly destructive . . . Those people who delight in whatever Strindberg writes . . . are of a special kind. There is nearly always something wrong with them. They . . . peer up at life through a rat-hole . . . cynical and coarse natures, broken minds . . . It is not they who should rule the world."

On 29 March, Strindberg's daughter Greta gave birth to a child; but it

---

*How modestly Strindberg was living at this time is shown by a letter he wrote to Bonnier on 11 January listing his annual outgoings:

Apartment with library and heating	1,790 crowns
Lighting	200
Food	840
Cleaning	360
Laundry	240
Hire of piano	120
	3,550 crowns

He can have spent little else, for he did not eat out, visit the theatre, travel or take a holiday, and entertained only occasionally.

died the same day. For two days her own life was in danger, but she recovered. She was not to have another child, and Strindberg never, in his lifetime, had the grandchildren he would so have cherished (though there were to be several after his death). It may have been around now (Karin does not give the date) that Strindberg and Siri spoke for the first and last time since their divorce nineteen years earlier; he telephoned Greta, Siri answered and, recognising his voice, asked him to wait a moment. "His voice dropped and trembled; some days later he asked Greta, 'Was that Mummy who answered the telephone?'" His attitude towards Siri had softened; three years earlier, on learning that she had injured a leg, he sent her two hundred crowns with a simple note, not writing her name ("Since I hear you are ill, I enclose 200 crowns"), and now, when she visited Greta in Stockholm, he chose wines that he knew she was fond of. "Today you shall have Beaune, Mummy likes that," he would murmur as he knelt to choose from his wine-racks. [1]

Meanwhile a committee had been formed to launch an appeal for the nation-wide subscription for Strindberg which Adolf Lundgrehn had suggested the previous July, and on 6 April this appeal was published, supported by over two hundred signatories, including many writers, artists, actors and politicians. The right-wing press, apart from *Stockholms-Dagblad* and a few provincial papers, printed it only as a letter and not in their news columns; *Nya Dagligt Allehanda* refused to mention it, and Fredrik Böök denounced it fiercely in *Svenska Dagbladet*. The left-wing press was divided, some social democrats feeling that the liberals should not be included in what they regarded as a socialist statement, and some liberals expressing scepticism concerning Strindberg's sudden abandonment of the conservatism which he had been preaching, in some areas at least, for a couple of decades. [2] Moreover, the memory of *Black Banners*, which had been reprinted in a large, cheap edition in July 1910 despite Strindberg's earlier promise that "no new edition will be published,"* still rankled across the whole political spectrum. All things considered, it is astonishing that the appeal met with the response it did.

Strindberg's health, which had been generally good since his move to the Blue Tower, now began to deteriorate. An eloquent pastel of him by Fanny this March shows an alarming change. [3] "Old, tired and sick," he wrote on 18 April to Birger Mörner, now consul in London. ". . . Have had two warnings—though no attacks! and have made myself ready for the last journey . . . no way out other than death." On 27 April he wrote to Nils Andersson:

*See page 486.

Old age has come . . . My "Last Will' is in the desk drawer; my papers are
in order—everything is ready. The Beethoven suppers are finished. Dinners very seldom. I live alone except for my daughter whom I have won back
and my son-in-law (a practising physician). I want nothing, hope for
nothing—on this side. One morning at 8 as the bell tolls for matins they will
carry out my dust—no one shall speak at my graveside, not even a priestly
ritual; it is so ordained in my "Last Will."

Now they have been playing the "Appassionata" in one of the apartments
below—I seldom hear it, for Axel is as tired as I, Aulin away, my friends
absent with their troubles. So one loosens the bonds of life—so it must be.
But should you come, there is still a bottle of "supernatural" Sauternes in
the hall, and then Axel will come along with a Nils Andersson symphony
and we shall have an illusion of something which, though only an illusion,
is yet a beautiful illusion.

On 1 May he wrote fondly to Karin: "Write on a sheet of paper and send
me: this year's expenses for Hans's terms, and (1) life insurance premiums
(2) mortgages. And I will take care of them. Tell him this. Greta is now
looking for two summer cottages so that she can have you to stay. She is
now recovered, and seems consoled, or to have forgotten her sorrow
—poor Greta! Henry and Greta came to dine with me yesterday. I have a
guest-room, too, if anyone should wish to come here." On 15 May he
wrote to Karin again: "That you may feel secure for the summer I am
arranging to send 100 marks to you both on 1 June for summer pleasures.
If you come to visit Greta, let me know and I will send you money for the
tickets." Six days later he wrote that he had heard Hans was having
problems on his small salary, and that if this was true, "I shall pay all his
debts and give him 100 crowns a month . . . And if you have debts, tell
me; *c'est mon métier* now to pay other people's debts since others are
paying mine."

That month, Bonnier published *The Roots of World Languages*, which
was dismissed in all but the social democratic newspapers as an eccentricity comparable to his efforts at gold-making. Strindberg had now turned
his attention from Hebrew back to Chinese, which he had begun to study
in his librarian days, and during the remainder of the year he wrote two
more short linguistic books, *The Origins of Our Mother Tongue* (about
similarities between Swedish words and those in other ancient and
modern languages), and *China and Japan*, plus *The Ancestry of Sweden*
(in which, among other theories, he denied the existence of a Bronze Age
in Sweden), and *Religious Renaissance*, in which he expanded the views
which he had set out in an article in *Social-Demokraten* on 19 July the
previous summer. "Since 1896, I have regarded myself as a Christian,"
he had begun there, adding that he was not a Catholic, although his

tolerance towards Catholicism had given rise to this rumour. "I am and shall remain a registered Protestant . . . I use Bible Christianity for internal private use to tame my somewhat vagabond nature, rendered such by the . . . Darwinism in which I was nurtured as a student; and I practise as well as I can the Christian teaching . . . For only through religion, or the hope of a better existence, and insight into the significance of life as a time of trial, a school, perhaps a place of correction, is it possible to endure the burden of life with the correct measure of resignation." But he stressed that this must be no passive resignation; the Christ he admired was the man who drove the money-changers out of the temple "in wrath and with a scourge." He expressed his admiration of Oliver Cromwell and George Washington as deeply religious men who did not hesitate to take up arms, and even Robespierre, "though his history has been so falsified that it is difficult to be sure of his true nature." He also declared his approval of the Japanese, whose "unshakable belief in a life after this, and conviction that this life is a journey through an alien country, gives them such joyous solace in the face of adversity that they meet death as an event not to be deplored." Darwinism and free thought he dismissed as the philosophy of the upper class; the common people, he concluded, know better.

On 29 May one of his major plays was at last performed in Britain, which had hitherto seen only *The Stronger* and *Simoom*. *The Father* was staged for three performances at the Pavilion Theatre, Whitechapel, in the East End of London, not in English but in Yiddish, with the celebrated American-Yiddish actor Maurice Moscovitch in the title role.* *Miss Julie*, too, might have been seen in London this year but for the English censor, who refused a request by Lydia Yavorskaia to perform it. (As well as playing it in Russian in St. Petersburg, she had acted it in German in Vienna.)[4] *Gustav Adolf* was to have had its Swedish premiere in Stockholm that spring with Anders de Wahl, and Greta Strindberg as the Queen, but this had to be postponed and the play was not performed there until shortly after Strindberg's death.

On 3 June he suggested to Greta that he might come and stay with her in her summer cottage while Karin and Hans were there, insisting that she must allow him to pay, and warning her: "I am not sick, but tired and ailing, am used to being alone and can't stand disturbance." But four days later he wrote: "I think we should arrange things thus this summer. You young ones should have each other to yourselves and I will sit in town and

---

*The London Yiddish Theatre was to present four more productions of *The Father* before its demise in the 1940s—all, apparently, of considerable power.

earn money for us all." Next day he sent Karin the money for the tickets from Finland.

On 11 June a Strindberg Exhibition was held in Stockholm, which lasted until 5 September. This was to publicise, and raise money for, the fund in his honour; it contained paintings and manuscripts, letters, examples of his work in various languages, portraits and busts of him, photographs of places where he had lived, and even material relating to his scientific work, including examples of his "gold." The hall was decorated with his favourite pelargoniums; seven hundred visitors came in the first week. Strindberg was especially pleased when one day two hundred working men came in a group at a reduced price of 50 öre.[5] Conservative newspapers such as *Svenska Dagbladet* and *Nya Dagligt Allehanda* used the occasion to denounce Strindberg afresh; to them, in his own fashion, he was now the ultimate and unforgivable enemy.

Despite his assurance to Greta, Strindberg wrote on 12 June to Nils Andersson that he had been "ill for the past two months; probably a latent internal complaint, which the doctor (my son-in-law) cannot identify. All my entrails in disorder, *bursting*; no room for them in my skin, although I am half starving myself and have given up my evening grog (my usual). It is as though a mad soul were seated in the wrong body—I have always felt this—that is why wine has been of help in keeping my spirit in the groove (fasting and temperance bring on depression, simply through cowardice). Self-examination, scruples of conscience which reproach one for everything, even for things one has never done. And when my last great interest ended—*The Roots of World Languages*—life went flat—to work on something so immense with no encouragement is not uplifting. Although I have proved conclusively that e.g. Chinese characters are monograms of Syrian, Hebrew, Arabian and Greek, composed like the Turkish symbols which we see on their tapestries—well, it doesn't help. People become dumb and confused, like an actor without a line."

He wrote often and tenderly to Anne-Marie that summer. "Dear Little One, [13 June] did your tennis go well? Next summer I shall get a little boat, a real one, to row in, and with a little sail; but first you must learn to swim, remember that! The easiest way is with an oar under each arm; or walk out from the shore and turn around, splash towards land, then there is no danger!" He sent her many presents: a hammock, cork bathing cushions, a gaff and fishing tackle, fireworks, toffee and fruit. He also posted regular small sums to Fanny, to help her in her new occupation as painter (she had failed to find any stage work since being dismissed from the Intimate Theatre and had abandoned her acting career, not without relief). Yet despite the warmth of his feelings towards these and his other children, he remained aloof from Kerstin, who needed him most.

Max Reinhardt visited Stockholm in June, but Strindberg refused to see him, pleading illness. Somehow he got it into his head that, as a result, his disciple had taken against him. "Reinhardt apparently won't play me any more," he wrote to Adolf Paul on 19 June, "because I was sick! in body and soul when he was here and so couldn't wait on or receive him. A good excuse!" Reinhardt's enthusiasm for Strindberg remained, however, unabated. He was to do even more for Strindberg's reputation after his death than he had during his lifetime.

Strindberg's negotiations with Karl Otto Bonnier for the outright sale of his *Collected Works* had at last been concluded. Bonnier had offered 150,000 crowns, which Strindberg thought too little; Bonnier now raised it to 200,000 crowns, to be paid in four instalments over the next four years, covering publication rights in perpetuity of all Strindberg's works printed to date plus the as yet unpublished *He and She*, but excluding performing and foreign rights. [6] "This arrangement," Strindberg explained to Greta on 26 June, "has the advantage that I cannot be regarded as rich now, and can accept the [national] subscription as though it were an ordinary Nobel Prize. Of the first 50,000, you three children shall each have 10,000 at once; your husband 6,000 = 36,000. We can discuss what to do with the rest." Kerstin and Anne-Marie he regarded as being adequately provided for (Harriet was earning a good salary). On 28 June, two days before he signed the agreement, he explained to Bonnier: "The reason I am doing this is so that the children, who have had no childhood, may now get a helping hand to start their life . . . I want to enjoy the final pleasure of seeing young people live . . . I regard it as the repayment of a debt to them." He remained, however, hesitant about one work. "The *Occult Diary*," he informed Bonnier on 30 June, "is so long and so intimate, so Swedenborgian, horrible and dangerous to other people's peace of mind that it must be burned or sealed." Bonnier and his descendants respected Strindberg's wishes to the extent of not publishing any of it until after Harriet's death, and then only bowdlerised extracts.

On Midsummer Eve a young theatrical company called Skådebanan which did open-air tours performed Strindberg's Viking play *The Outlaw* at Lidköping before, according to *Vecko-Journalen* (9 July), "a tensely interested audience of around ten thousand people." The director was a young man named Victor Sjöström, * shortly to make his name as one of the pioneers of the silent film. He staged it in repertory with Ibsen's *The*

---

*Known in America as Victor Seastrom. In his old age he played the leading role in Ingmar Bergman's film *Wild Strawberries*.

Vikings at Helgeland. Strindberg did not like the pairing, and in fact refused permission "because [he wrote to Sjöström on 25 May] it seemed sinful to stage this juvenilia (I was 20 when I wrote it) . . . the weakest of my forty [*sic*] plays—side by side with *The Vikings*. I offered you *The Virgin Bride*, but was told no, since you had no costumes." Sjöström begged Strindberg to relent, pointing out that they had chosen *The Outlaw* partly so that they could use the same costumes for both plays, and had not only rehearsed it but had actually opened, giving one-hour shows in Malmö during May. This, Sjöström explained nearly forty years later, was "to compete with the cinema, where performances then lasted one hour . . . we performed two one-act plays alternately each hour from 5 to 11 p.m. Among these was *The Outlaw*. The enterprise was very successful. In response to my appeal to Strindberg I received a negative reply but, young and bold (cheeky?) as I was, I did not give in, but wrote to him again and got a telegram: 'Go ahead then and leave me in peace.' "[7]

A few days after signing the agreement with Bonnier, Strindberg invited Karin, Greta and Hans to dinner in the Blue Tower:

> The dining table was covered with banknotes, which he had arranged in four piles, which gradually became mingled as he restlessly shifted around, shutting doors and ordering doors to be shut lest someone might come in and steal his riches. Then he took the money, one pile at a time, and handed it to each of his children with a little homily on thrift. We kissed him on the cheek and thanked him. Then he took the fourth pile. Clearly anxious to deal with the matter as quickly as possible, he glanced shyly at Karin and whispered, "This is for Mummy"; then added, even more softly, "It is an old debt."[8]

Karin tells that when she returned to Finland and handed her mother the money, Siri "listened motionless to what I had to say, then said with quiet pride, 'You must write and thank Daddy for me.' Then she added, in the same tone, 'I accept it as an old debt.' "[9]

Strindberg's letters of that summer of 1911 suggest that, although he does not say so, he sensed he had not long to live. On 1 July he told his brother Olle, the master gardener, that he had advertised for "a large garden with greenhouse and house attached, near Stockholm. My idea was that I should give it to you on a free lease and then be allowed to live with you; not interfering in the garden, just walking around and watching things grow." On 12 July he wrote to Nils Andersson in Lund of his wish "to play at creating a botanical garden and realise all my plans in that field from the 1870s (not 80s!). Not a new garden—old, gone to seed, but with a greenhouse! Perhaps one must make a pilgrimage backwards, make oneself aware of the contrast between past and present, reconcile oneself with the past—but also strike one's tents, grope backwards and go, living, into the grave . . . I long to get away from here. Not to the country, for I must have people, a bookshop and a wine store. So: a house in Lund with a large old garden, a greenhouse and sun." By 20 July he had changed his mind. "I believed then [he wrote to Andersson] that a change of scene might revive me; now I don't believe that, for I have been ill again and cannot move my limbs, much less move house . . . it was in foreknowledge of this that I put my worldly affairs in order for the children; which gives me peace, and gave me great joy. These last three years have drained my strength; in this 'tower' there was nothing beautiful; in the previous one, something—there was the child, and a couple of Christmas Eves." But three days later he asked Andersson again to look for a house and garden: "I must get away from here—to live again. This summer and the past three years have given me such a loathing for the whole society in which I live."

That same day, 23 July, *The Father* was staged in English for the first time, for two performances by the Adelphi Play Society, at the tiny Rehearsal Theatre in London's Maiden Lane, behind the Strand, a former synagogue described to me years later by an old gentleman who had attended Ibsen performances there as "a deathtrap at the top of a narrow flight of stairs." The press dismissed the play with contempt; *The Times* found Strindberg "extraordinarily naïve in some of his dramatic processes," while the *Academy* asked: "Why use the theatre for unrelieved depression and brutal aspects of human nature and relationships exploited in the name of art?" This attitude towards Strindberg was, sadly, to remain typical of the British press for half a century; yet the comments quoted give no indication, any more than the early press reaction to Ibsen, of how deeply his work impressed serious thinkers, especially his peers.

Sometime that July, Fanny visited Strindberg with a bouquet of wild flowers. She was now in love with a young man and says that although she did not tell Strindberg this, he sensed it, and did not ask her to return. "He accompanied me to the door as usual. We did not speak. At the door he nodded silently, and I remember that I curtseyed to him."[10] They did not meet again.

Karin wrote to him announcing her engagement to Vladimir Smirnoff, a Russian lecturer at Helsinki University. Strindberg was delighted. "Come and marry here," he wrote to her on 25 July, "and I shall host the wedding of my firstborn, who once gave me the first joy in my life. (Mummy will permit you that!) . . . I shall rejoice in your joy, for I have none and ask for none." On finding, however, that such a marriage would make her a Russian citizen, Karin considered instead living with Smirnoff in a free relationship. Strindberg urged her (11 September) to have at least a civil wedding for her children's sake, adding: "I shall welcome you both in my house, whichever you decide." She followed his advice, and on 19 September she and Vladimir had a civil wedding in Stockholm. Vladimir recalled:

> Despite his grey hair, he seemed fit, and by no means senile, even, at moments, youthful; one would never have guessed that he had only a few months to live . . . The "wedding" was celebrated the day after our arrival in Stockholm in Strindberg's apartment. He was in a brilliant humour. His brief, warm speech of good wishes at the dinner made up for the absence of any church ceremony. There were no other guests except his daughter Greta. When the cake was brought in, Strindberg told with an amused glint in his eyes how the pastry-shop owner who had baked it had supposed that Strindberg himself was getting married . . . During a week's stay in Stockholm I met August Strindberg daily, sometimes at his home, sometimes at the Philps'. The whole time he was friendly, gentle and thoughtful, with that trace of shyness which was characteristic of him even when in the company of those closest to him . . . He still had big plans. One day he asked me how I thought it would be for him to travel to China and Japan via Siberia, and whether he would be harassed by the Tsarist police. He was working on the origins of the Chinese language and was considering a possible trip to the Far East. [11]

Strindberg reported the occasion to Gustaf Uddgren on 22 September: "The wedding lasted several days, and several dinners were eaten, but the one with tail-coats and the cake took place in my apartment, prepared and served by Fröken Carlsson of number 85; it was excellent, and cost only 38 crowns, apart from the ice cream and the cake." A copy of the menu has survived: *smörgåsbord*, soup, crayfish, duck, artichokes, a sweet, cheese, coffee and liqueurs. [12]

A Scandinavian-American, Edwin Björkman, wrote to Strindberg from the United States asking leave to translate several of his plays into English. Terribly as these versions read today, they aroused widespread interest, exciting, among others, the young Eugene O'Neill and the young Sean O'Casey. A new medium, too, was about to adopt him; Gustaf Uddgren wrote to ask if his wife, Anna Hofman-Uddgren, who had already directed two films in Sweden, might film the Intimate Theatre productions of *"The Father* or *Miss Julie* or perhaps both?" Strindberg replied: "Please film as many of my plays as you wish." Anna did not limit herself to photographing the stage performance of *Miss Julie*, but took the action out of doors and, at the end, showed Julie's suicide, though the censor insisted on the removal of this scene. This film has not survived, but that of *The Father* has (the only one of her films to have done so); it was premiered in Stockholm shortly before Strindberg's death the following year, though he was too ill to see it. [13]

Work on the national subscription for Strindberg had been held up by a general election that summer, in which the social democrats had doubled their representation in the lower house and a new government had been formed under the premiership of Karl Staaff. Moreover, news of the Bonnier contract for the *Collected Works*, which plainly secured Strindberg's economic future, had lessened the committee's sense of urgency. On 24 September, to reawaken interest, a special matinee was held at the Swedish Theatre. Tor Aulin's music for *Master Olof* was performed; Anders de Wahl read a Strindberg poem; the opera singer John Forsell sang the Water Sprite's song from *The Virgin Bride* and other songs from the plays or based on the poems; August Lindberg read the opening scene of *The Keys of Heaven*; and several actors read the long poem *Trinity Night*. Finally, the Stockholm Workers' Association Choir sang another song from *The Virgin Bride*. Greta and Anne-Marie went onstage together to present a bouquet to Forsell. The performance was not outstandingly well attended, but Strindberg, according to his custom, was grateful. "Thank you," he wrote to Richard Bergh as representative of the subscription committee, ". . . for all the trouble you have taken to rehabilitate me as a man of letters." [14] It had been decided to name the award to Strindberg the Anti-Nobel Prize, a phrase that Strindberg himself had coined; Hjalmar Branting even suggested that it should be handed over on the day in December when the Nobel Prizes were presented, remarking that "if, as was likely, the Swedish Academy gave the prize again to some senile foreigner, our honouring Strindberg would have particular effect." [15] But since Strindberg wished especially to be honoured as a dramatist, and it would be difficult to arrange special performances of his plays in the Stockholm theatres on the evening of the Nobel ceremony, it was decided instead to make the presentation on his sixty-third birthday in January. It was noted with pleasure that Prince Eugen, despite the contretemps over the paintings, had sent 1,000 crowns, and even more that thousands of tiny donations were arriving from the working men at whom the appeal had been principally aimed.

Further evidence of Strindberg's standing abroad appeared in an interview with the Danish writer Herman Bang published in *Svenska Dagbladet* on 17 October. Bang, an experienced observer of the European literary and theatrical scene, declared: "One has to go abroad to learn what Strindberg really means in Europe. During these last years I have found that in Germany, Austria, Russia and fashionable circles in France, he is rated as comparable to Ibsen and is overshadowed only by Tolstoy." In another interview the same day with *Dagens Nyheter*, Bang confirmed this: "Wherever I went in Europe, his name was the same fire on the tongues of the young as Ibsen's once was. People in Sweden do not seem to know this."

Strindberg's health had deteriorated sharply since the summer. "I have been poorly all autumn," he wrote to Nils Andersson on 30 October, "have sometimes gone to bed at 7:30 because I couldn't bear being in my clothes. The doctor doesn't know what it is, but I recognise it: other people's hatred!" This, rather than any illness, he was convinced was the cause. "Almost the same symptoms as in 1896 (Inferno)," he told Andersson on 8 November. "I am sure it is the dreadful hatred of people. The presence of strangers seems to divert the current. I must have made some great discoveries, which some people have noticed. But they remain silent—and hate." Yet he felt well enough to hold his annual goose dinner when Andersson, as he did each November, sent a prime bird up from Lund. His new affluence resulting from the Bonnier contract caused him to write generously to Schering: "Since times are hard for you, keep all my fees until further notice as a loan, to be repaid when my German *Collected Works* can be sold *en bloc* for more than my fees amount to."[16] And he became so indulgent to Anne-Marie that Harriet had to beg him on 12 November: "Please don't send Anne-Marie these big sums each Saturday. It is so kind of you—but she cannot spend so much money on sweets and toys—give her some small amount when she visits you, or keep it till she is old enough to handle money."[17] Harriet wrote him several letters that autumn and winter, pleading with him not to give Anne-Marie unsuitable presents such as unneeded furniture for her room, signing herself never "Harriet" but always "Anne-Marie's mother." Strindberg did not reply to these letters, though he took note of the message.

He still felt antipathetic to his earlier realistic plays, which he regarded as godless. On 18 November he asked Adolf Paul, as a member of the board of the Neue Freie Volksbühne in Berlin, to "avoid the old played-out pieces (*The Father, Miss Julie*, etc.), and stage the chamber plays (*Ghost Sonata*) or *Erik XIV, The Virgin Bride*, etc." He read as profusely and as widely as ever. He had developed a passion for the English romantic novelist Marie Corelli, who this year, with *The Life Everlasting*, completed a cycle of seven novels dealing with what she called "spirit power and universal love," direr even than *Séraphita* or *Zanoni*; at his death, Strindberg's library contained twelve of her books in

Swedish translation. In his copy of her *Lilith* (1892), he underlined the words "Then this world is hell and you do not know it is."*

Maurice Maeterlinck was awarded the Nobel Prize that year, one of the less ridiculous recipients to that date, though his work has hardly worn well. Knowing Strindberg's respect for Maeterlinck, Birger Mörner suggested a meeting, but Strindberg replied (7 December): "I admire Maeterlinck's work, and have praised it in print—but one should never meet. One can't talk about what one has written . . . and the rest isn't worth talking about. Can you get this message to him—in case he thinks I am expecting a visit from him—without offending him?" One is re-minded of Arthur Koestler's dictum that to meet an author whose work you admire is like eating *foie gras* and then meeting the goose.

John Landquist, who had been so active in organising the Anti-Nobel Prize, visited him now for the first time. "The two rooms in which I saw him were unpretentiously furnished with smallish contemporary factory-built pieces. It was by no means tasteless but lacked any personal touch. I sensed a home that had been cobbled together quickly during a hasty journey through life." Landquist found him different from his busts and portraits—"more virile, more sensitive, and at the same time more authoritative . . . a *grand seigneur* . . . His bearing was noble and there was something regal in his expression. He moved with elegance and assurance like an actor . . . But my visit was not to end without my receiving the decided impression that there was also something sick about this charming man. I had left him and had taken a few steps down the stairs. Then I heard a metallic click behind me. I turned and saw through Strindberg's letter-box, the flap of which he had opened, his blue

---

*Strindberg's library at his death contained few English books, apart from a number of travel volumes relating to the Near and Far East and the American continent, Longfel-low's works, Charles Kingsley's novel *Old Margaret*, Hawthorne's *Wonder Book for Boys and Girls*, illustrated by Walter Crane, Upton Sinclair's *Love's Pilgrimage*, and numbers of *The Mask* and *The Studio* magazines. In Swedish or German translation he possessed nine novels by Scott, five by Marryat, Wilde's *De Profundis* (with caustic marginal comments), four plays by Shaw, much Dickens and Kipling, Whitman's *Leaves of Grass*, and a copy of Shakespeare's sonnets, on the title-page of which he at some stage wrote "Shit!," doubtless deploring the romantic view of woman expressed therein. His copy of Darwin's *Origin of Species* contains many such pencilled observations. He also had much of Balzac, Zola and Victor Hugo in French, and of Goethe and Schiller in German; Sophocles, Molière and Racine, twenty-four volumes of Baedeker, over three hundred books on linguistics and many on religion and mysticism. Even when he could least afford it, he bought rather than borrowed books. On his morning walks he would push orders for books under the locked doors of bookshops, or even write his orders on the margins of newspapers lying in the doorway. (*Cf.* Hans Lindström, *Strindberg och böckerna*, Uppsala, 1977, pp. 45 ff.)

eyes fixed searchingly on me. It made a powerfully disagreeable impression."[18]

The Dance of Death was performed in Munich that winter, both parts in a single bill. *Christina* was staged in Berlin shortly before Christmas, and *Simoom* in Chicago, perhaps the earliest recorded *public* performance of a Strindberg play in America. The early history of Strindberg productions there is ill documented; several were performed before immigrants in their native languages, Russian and Yiddish (at least) as well as Scandinavian. In Stockholm, a new Intimate Theatre had been built on Birger Jarlsgatan, near the Royal Library; August Falck, who had invested in it, had hoped to open it with two unperformed Strindberg plays, *Gustav the Third* and *The Nightingale of Wittenberg*, but was edged out and lost his money.[19] Instead, the theatre presented on Boxing Day the wretched *Black Glove*, which lasted only fifteen performances.

News of Strindberg's illness reached Frida in London, whence she sent him a telegram in French (from the Savoy Hotel): "Terribly anxious and sympathetic please send news."[20] He did not reply. He had by now started to prepare a new Swedish dictionary, and was corresponding assiduously with various linguists about etymology.

The New Year of 1912 brought a seeming improvement in Strindberg's health. "Thank you for your flowers and don't worry," he wrote to Anne-Marie on 5 January. "The illness seems to be over, but getting well is a slow business." On 12 January he told his American translator, Edwin Björkman, that he would probably soon be going to Switzerland.

The social democrats planned a torchlight procession to mark his sixty-third birthday. On 17 January he wrote to Richard Bergh: "Will you tell Branting that this being the case, I must greet them, and that I will come out onto the balcony; but they must not stop, talk or sing, for then I shall kill myself out of politeness. The truth is, I am still sick, though I imagined myself well. I have not been out. So that the procession may know my balcony from the others, I shall set out my most beautiful lamp shining a red eye towards Tegnér Square. If I am really ill I will have a message telephoned to the People's House, but shall signal in the windows my appreciation and gratitude; I may perhaps stand in my living-room window. I dare not invite anyone to dinner except my daughter, son-in-law and Axel, for fear of overtaxing my strength. Explain this to Branting."

The numbers taking part in the procession on the evening of 22 January 1912 exceeded the organisers' most optimistic hopes, for over fifteen thousand assembled. As they filled the streets in front of and around the

Blue Tower (a corner building), all the balconies within sight were filled with spectators, except one, on which a lamp burned. As Strindberg emerged, according to next day's *Dagens Nyheter*:

> A storm of cheering arose from the torch-illuminated street, the banners were lowered, the torches swung blazing in acclamation, hats and scarves were waved . . . "Long live August Strindberg!"; "Long live the poet king!"; "The People's Strindberg!"—as the van of the procession filed past and new throngs acclaimed him, the cries varied, followed always by cheers, applause and waving. Strindberg stood at the rail of his balcony acknowledging them, his top hat in his hand; his little daughter [Anne-Marie] had come out and threw flowers down onto the crowd, who bent eagerly to take up these souvenirs. Now and then the writer himself took a handful of long-stemmed roses, which were handed to him from within the room, and as though he, the acclaimed, wished himself to acclaim the torch-bearers, let them fall down upon these men and women who stood cheering up at him. On the pavement opposite, a workers' choir had gathered, surrounded by torch-bearers, and as the procession passed they sang the songs of freedom, workers' songs, the "Marseillaise." . . . It looked as though a broad river of fire filled Drottninggatan. Sometimes there was an interval of darkness, and it seemed as though the procession was ending, but then the tones of a new choir were heard and a blaze of fresh torches appeared. The writer still stood on his balcony. His son-in-law had taken a candelabrum and held it so that the light illuminated Strindberg's face. He had turned his coat collar up against the night cold, but at each new cheer he bared his head to greet the throngs.

The Swedish theatres did him proud that evening. Six in Stockholm presented various of his plays: *Erik the Fourteenth* at Dramaten, *Gustav Vasa* at the Swedish Theatre, *The Virgin Bride* with Greta at the People's House, *The Black Glove* at the New Intimate, *The People of Hemsö* (which he so hated) at the People's Theatre and *Playing with Fire* with *The Stronger* at the old Intimate (now renamed the Little Theatre, with Mauritz Stiller in charge). In the provinces, *The Last Knight* was performed in Gothenburg, *Creditors* and *Playing with Fire* in Hälsingborg, *Swanwhite* with an act of *The Great Highway* in Härnösand, *The Pelican* in Sala, *Creditors* again in Karlskoga, *The Father* in Linköping, *There Are Crimes and Crimes* in Uppsala, *To Damascus* in Ystad and *The Protector* in Örebro. A banquet was held in his honour at Berns', the restaurant he had made famous through *The Red Room*, and in Chicago, with its numerous Swedish immigrants (it contains more Swedes today than any Swedish city except Stockholm), the local Swedish Society assembled no less than four thousand members for a celebration, staging *Gustav Vasa* with Strindberg's early pioneer August Lindberg as the

King, and sending a telegram of good wishes to "the master and the man, the scholar and the explorer."[21]

There were many such telegrams and messages, gifts and flowers, and it is pleasant to record that Strindberg used the occasion to reconcile himself with a few old friends with whom he had quarrelled. He wired to August Falck: "The memory of the old Intimate Theatre's great days was revived by you yesterday. Your garland awoke in me feelings only of gratitude and perhaps of hope." And in an article published in the Danish newspaper *Politiken* on his birthday, he wrote warm words of those two early champions of his work from whom he had become estranged, Georg and Edvard Brandes.* The presentation to him of the Anti-Nobel Prize was delayed in order that further contributions resulting from the publicity surrounding his birthday might be included.

Strindberg became involved in a final political controversy that January. The previous year the conservative government had decided to build a cruiser to strengthen the country's defences; the liberals and social democrats had opposed the idea, saying that the money should be spent instead on social reforms, and this had been a key issue in the election which the left-wing parties had won. On 26 January a Swedish Cruiser Society was founded and issued an appeal to raise the money by public subscription; among the leading figures in this movement was Sven Hedin, who wrote a pamphlet entitled *A Warning* which by the end of the year had sold a million copies. Hedin warned that Russia needed ice-free ports and accordingly might well invade Sweden (though it is not easy to see what a single cruiser could have done about that). Strindberg replied with a series of articles in *Afton-Tidningen* and *Social-Demokraten*, asserting that the building of a warship was more likely to provoke than to deter Russia, and that the conservatives' main concern was with the internal enemy. Fram published these articles in early March as a pamphlet entitled *The Tsar's Courier*.[22]

Whether because of the birthday celebrations or for some other reason, Strindberg's health improved again. He was fit enough to hold a Beet-

---

*"Edvard was then, as he himself put it, 'the most hated man in Denmark,' being one of the opposition leaders in Parliament. Daily attacked and harassed, he was naturally bitter and always in a defensive mood, with his claws showing. I was too romantic for him and he smiled at my Utopias. He was too sceptical, even for me, so that no real confidence could exist between us, but his door always stood open to me, and his patience in listening to my complaints knew no limits." Strindberg says that he found Georg friendlier than Edvard. "But I never got really close to him, because he had a secret programme, poetry as servant not master, Pegasus yoked, etc., which sometimes rose like a wall between us." But he adds that Georg was intellectually flexible and receptive.

hoven evening on 9 February, and five days later told Aulin: "I am declared well, though not fully restored (pleurisy?), and have planned to go to Switzerland but lack the strength." He was still writing long letters about etymology, and even gardening, urging his brother Olle to grow unfamiliar things such as tea, coffee and magnolias. On 2 March, Branting presented him with the Anti-Nobel Prize of 45,000 crowns (the subscription had raised 50,000, of which 5,000 had been deducted for expenses). Now that he was financially secure as a result of the Bonnier contract, Strindberg gave most of this away. Albert Engström tells that on the day he received it, Strindberg read an appeal in a newspaper for a home for the handicapped, went that same day to the chairman of the appeal committee and handed him 5,000 crowns, insisting that the gift remain anonymous. "I have heard," Engström continues, "that he gave away the rest of this money, or anyway most of it. Once or twice I met long-haired and dirty young writers and artists on his staircase counting banknotes."[23] To one young journalist who wrote asking for a loan of 200 crowns, Strindberg replied that he did not lend money but enclosed a cheque for the amount. When the man called to thank him personally, Mina would not let him disturb Strindberg, who, however, sent him a note: "I now know that you have received it, and that is all; you need not thank me . . . This is only a pleasure, when one is in a position to do it, especially for me, who have troubled my fellow beings all my life."[24] He also sent 1,000 crowns to Nathan Söderblom, for the Paris Swedish community's fund for needy compatriots which had helped him in 1896.

The result of the national subscription provoked an astonishing outburst from Fredrik Böök, who had opposed the project from the beginning. In an article which appeared simultaneously in four Scandinavian magazines that March, Böök, later a notorious Nazi sympathiser, asserted that the idea of the subscription had not appealed outside a small coterie, that the result had been a great disappointment to its organisers, and that Strindberg was un-Swedish and his writing "alien to the Swedish people." John Landquist replied in Social-Demokraten that twenty thousand people had contributed and that the donations included eleven thousand of less than 50 öre, most of these being as small as 25 and even 10 öre. He added tellingly that the appeal had raised far more per head of the total population than the recent appeal in England for Charles Dickens's descendants.[25] The incident reflects the implacable loathing still felt for Strindberg by the Swedish literary and political establishment.

Among other gifts, Strindberg had sent Anne-Marie 10,000 crowns, and received a long and warm letter of thanks from Harriet, signed for once not "Anne-Marie's mother" but with her own name. "I don't understand business and so cannot offer any suggestion as to where to place Anne-Marie's money," she wrote. "Perhaps it would be best to invest the whole amount for her until she comes of age and can manage her money herself. I am so boundlessly happy at this gift—it is reassuring to know that if I die or became incapable of looking after her, she is economically secure. The older she grows, the more money she will need, and since I have taken on myself all the expenses of our home, it might in time become difficult for me to maintain Anne-Marie in a manner befitting her. So—warmest thanks on her behalf, and let the money stay put until she can handle it herself. Harriet Bosse."[26]

London saw another of his plays that March, when the Stage Society presented two performances of *Creditors* at the Prince's Theatre, with a distinguished cast: Guy Standing, Miriam Lewis and Harcourt Williams. *The Times* dismissed it as "an exhibition of epilepsy." Strindberg's illness had apparently still not been positively identified, for on 7 April he replied to a series of written questions from Professor Karl Petrén, who had been called in by Henry Philp: "Four years ago there was a periodicity which I don't have now. Now it hurts the whole day and night regardless of what I eat, sometimes it just aches a little, sometimes it gets worse, but I am never free of it. Whether I sit, walk or lie down. I go to bed to avoid wearing my clothes but this no longer helps. If I lie on my face, the pain ceases; on my left side is better than on my right, but on my back is worst. My desire for food is going. I now have an aversion to all food; and my distaste for life increases greatly. I can sleep for one or two hours, then the pain wakes me. The twelve-hour night (from 8 p.m. onwards) is endless." Cancer of the stomach was now diagnosed. He was tapped three times, on 16 and 26 April and 2 May; large quantities of fluid were removed from him, on the second occasion a half-bucketful. This eased his pains but sapped his strength. He had to be given morphine to sleep, and even this was not always effective. He had difficulty in speaking, attacks of breathlessness and violent vomiting, and could only eat liquid food, which he could not always keep down. Sometimes he would get up and walk to try to ease the pain.[27]

Yet on 10 April he sent Vilhelm Carlhem-Gyllensköld a detailed fourteen-page article on "The Origins of the Chinese Language," the last thing he was to write. He had considered doing a play about the recent British coal strike, and another about Robespierre, but when Karl Otto Bonnier wrote enquiring about the latter, Strindberg replied on 12 April: "The play is only an old fantasy of mine. I am ill and can do nothing, see no future." But he still corresponded with various people about a multitude of interests, including archaeology and photography. According to Gustaf Uddgren, he refused radium treatment because "he did not believe in radium."[28] His suffering did not make him insensitive to that of others. On learning that a poor woman in the same house was also suffering from cancer, he paid for her medical treatment; and on 15 April, hearing of the sinking of the *Titanic*, he dressed in black and played on his piano the hymn that the ship's band was said to have played in its last moments, "Nearer My God to Thee."[29] On 18 April he wrote to Professor Petrén: "In bed, excuse pencil . . . The pains are sometimes eased by morphine since the opium ceased to work (I vomit). No one wishes to operate but I want an end to these agonies." Next day he wrote to Anne-Marie: "My dear little daughter. Thank you for your red flowers. But you must not try to see me. There are so many medicine bottles, doctors and things here that it is no fun. Rejoice in your youth, among the young, and do not grieve for the old man who only wants to go away. Father." He likewise refused a request from Fanny to see him, in a last note thanking her for flowers.[30]

But although he did not want young girls whom he loved, or had loved, to see him thus, other visitors were allowed. His new young publisher Fredrik Ström came. "It was a beautiful spring day in the latter half of April. Strindberg was lying in bed and looked worn and harrowed . . . He said he might not be restored to health; his time was up, as ordained. 'I am the son of a servant-girl and I want to lie beside the poor in the churchyard, I want to be carried to my grave by working people, in the morning, not in the evening, and I ask that the People's House [the Social Democrat Party headquarters] shall arrange this and do me this last service. I have no more to say. Thank you for coming.' "[31]

On 22 April, Siri von Essen died in Helsinki at the age of sixty-two. The marriages of her three children had left her living alone, though Karin still visited her every morning. But, Karin tells:

> her strength declined, her will to live had gone, and she now earnestly wished to be allowed to die. One sunny spring day . . . death came calmly, as she had wished. She had been spared the experience she most dreaded, of having to see one of her children die. [Greta was to follow her within two months] . . . When Greta told Strindberg . . . that Karin had written of her mother's death, he asked to be allowed to hear the letter. Dreadfully emaciated, his mane of hair now thin, almost white . . . he sat in his old brown check dressing-gown and listened. The letter was factual, restrained, almost cold in its dry account, but he wept as she read and blew his nose unceasingly. When Greta had finished, he went into the next room and returned clad in an old black dressing-gown with a white tie as though he were in [mourning] tails. In his quiet fashion he wished to honour her,

whom he would soon follow into death . . . He sent a wreath of laurels and lilies without a card to be carried on her coffin. [32]

Over forty years later Karin paid tribute to Siri's "unending self-sacrifice, her vigilant and selfless solicitude, her ill-paid and untiring toil to keep privation at bay, her eternal willingness to submit to humiliation, to borrow for the children's sake during the Finland years . . . For as long as I can remember, Siri never, to the end of her life, had a corner to herself, far less a room, and was literally worn out before she reached her sixtieth year." [33]

Two days after Siri's death, Frida tried again to see Strindberg, wiring from London: "I beseech you from a bruised heart to allow me to come to nurse and serve you." [34] As before, he did not reply. She was the only one of his three wives whom he seems to have remembered with no affection. He had relented towards Harriet, as he had towards Siri. Harriet tells that "a week or so before he died his housekeeper [Mina] came up to me with an enormous bag. It contained only a letter to his daughter Anne-Marie and fifteen hundred crowns. Strindberg wrote to our daughter that he remembered that when we married he had given me a grand piano but later made me unhappy by changing it for an upright. 'Perhaps Mummy would now like to buy a grand piano with these fifteen hundred crowns?' . . . After Strindberg's death I was sent a Chinese chest containing all my letters to him, some small mementoes and my little, withered, myrtle bridal crown." [35]

Fanny tried once more to see him. Greta met her at the door. "She was kind, embraced me and wept, but thought I should not see him when he was suffering so, but should wait until he lay among flowers and was beautiful." On 11 May she tried again; she promised to be quiet and not disturb him, but Mina came back with the message: "He said that you must not be sad, for he has been thinking about you." "I replied that I did not mind whether he thought of me if only I could see him. Mina went back in and returned with an even stranger message: 'Herr Strindberg says that if you cry, he will smack you.' " [36]

His nurse, Hedvig Kistner, described his last hours:

> At 10 p.m., Dr. Philp wanted to give him his usual morphine injection, but Strindberg, who was not lucid, refused. The doctor and Mina went to bed, and I sat in a big armchair beside his bed. When he had lain for a while apparently sleeping, he woke, and when I saw that his mind was now clear I asked if he would like the morphine.
> "Yes, a big dose," and he rolled up his sleeve. He soon fell asleep, but woke now and then groaning and crying in great pain, though all the time

under the influence of the morphine. Around midnight I thought his condition so bad that I woke Mina and asked her to tell the doctor. As the doctor came in, Herr Strindberg woke, recognised him and said in a friendly, apologetic tone: "Have you been here all night?" and thanked him . . . Soon afterwards he fell asleep again and slept quite calmly till towards 2 . . . Then he woke again, by now completely lucid. His eyes, which had been so glazed during the day, were now brilliantly clear. Life flared up in him for the last time. He asked for some papers on which he had written notes. Mina went to look for them and at his request I put his spectacles on his nose. I think he wanted to make some last note, but it was some while before Mina found them and weariness overcame him and he fell asleep again.

We sat down as before, Mina reading and I dozing in the chair. He seemed to be asleep, he lay so calm and still, and a wonderful peace had settled on him, so I lay down on the floor, still wrapped in my coat, but all the time keeping my eyes on him. Scarcely had I lain down when he opened his eyes and, seeing that I was not in the chair, asked Mina, "Has she gone?" Before we could answer, he saw me on the floor, and never shall I forget the look he gave me. His eyes were more blue than ever and smiled so warmly at me. I half rose, but he said, "No, dear little child, lie still, I won't be angry with you." I got up to help him adjust his pillow, and sat in the chair again, but he said, "No, lie where you were before, don't bother about me, I no longer exist." . . . These were his last words and he fell into the sleep that comes before death . . . If the agonised cries which he uttered several times an hour were conscious, his suffering must have been terrible; the morphine no longer had any visible effect. When he drew his final breath of release, it was 4:30 a.m. on 14 May.

It had been a hard struggle, and Mina and I, the only ones present at his last moment, drew a sigh of relief when we saw the peace of death spread itself over his tormented face.[37]

He had expressed his wishes concerning his funeral in an affidavit dated 24 April 1912 and witnessed by his doctor and lawyer:

My dead body shall not be the subject of a post-mortem, nor placed on public show, merely seen by relatives. No death mask may be taken, and no photographs.

I wish to be carried to the grave at eight in the morning to avoid any gathering of the curious. There shall be no burial in any vault, far less in any church.

I wish to lie in the new cemetery, but not in the rich people's part, the market of vanity.

At the graveside there shall be no music, songs nor speeches, only the priest reading from the book of prayer . . .

Strindberg was buried on Sunday, 19 May. Despite the early hour, over ten thousand people followed his coffin to the cemetery, including representatives from the royal family (Prince Eugen), Parliament, the theatre, literature, the universities and, most numerous, the workers, marching under a hundred red banners. Despite Strindberg's request, some of his favourite hymns were sung, and banners were lowered in silence into the open grave. King Gustav had sent a wreath to lie on the republican's coffin, and tributes were paid in both chambers of Parliament. Only the Swedish Academy, as a contemporary bitterly noted, "gave no indication that it cared whether Strindberg was alive or dead."[38] Another who was present tells that "in pattern with the merciless fate which had persecuted him, Sunday holiday makers plundered his grave and tore apart the symbols of the people's respect which they had laid upon his mound."[39]

EPILOGUE

Two of Strindberg's five children died young. Greta was killed in a train crash on 16 June 1912, barely a month after her father's death, aged thirty-one, and Hans, who worked for an insurance company, died of a heart attack in 1917, aged thirty-three. Neither had children. Karin lived to be ninety-three; she died in 1973, leaving a daughter. Kerstin came from Austria to Stockholm at the age of twenty to learn to read her father's books in the original. She met and, in 1917 at the age of twenty-three, married a German lawyer and publisher, Ernst Sulzbach. They had a son, Christoph, born in 1919, but the marriage was unhappy and after eight years ended in divorce, whereupon she returned to Sweden for the remainder of her life. There, as Tor Bonnier (the son of Karl Otto) recalled, she led "a hermit-like existence which gradually became more markedly so, especially in her suspiciousness regarding her neighbours, who finally reported her to the authorities as being mentally un-balanced." She was removed to a mental home, where she remained for several years, occasionally being allowed home during her calmer periods. But her condition deteriorated and "eventually expressed itself in a total refusal of food, resulting, after many hard years, in her death, despite the efforts of the hospital staff to save her." She died in 1956, aged sixty-one. "How," Bonnier wrote, "can one speak of charm in a woman who often contorted her face and grimaced instead of uttering, or describe her as witty when her speech was continually broken by cries and

mumbles? . . . And yet Kerstin Strindberg was an uncommonly charming person, not merely original, but quick-witted and amusing."[1] Anne-
Marie was more fortunate. She married a Norwegian, Anders Wyller, a
year her junior, in 1926, and they had two sons. When the Nazis invaded
Norway in 1940, he became a leader of the resistance movement in
London, but died of cancer later that year. In 1974 Anne-Marie made a
second marriage with an old childhood friend, Gösta Hagelin, and
returned to Sweden, where she is alive as these words are written.
Strindberg's four grandchildren are all still alive, as well as seven of his
eight great-grandchildren. So, approaching ninety, is Friedrich Uhlsson,
Frida's son by Frank Wedekind.

Frida, after parting from Wedekind, continued to pursue men of
genius. In 1910, seeking the English painter and writer Wyndham Lewis
(who was fleeing from her) in Chelsea, she found instead, and ended up
in bed with, another painter, Augustus John. "I then dismissed the
incident from my mind," John characteristically wrote, "but it turned out
to be the prelude to a long and by no means idyllic tale of misdirected
energy, mad incomprehension, absurdity and even squalor." He came to
the conclusion that she possessed second-sight, for wherever he went, she
would appear, and "I admit that the sight of Madame Strindberg bearing
down on me in an open taxi-cab, a glad smile of greeting on her face,
shaded with a hat turned up behind and bearing a luxuriant outcrop of
sweet peas—this sight, I confess, unnerved me." She even arranged for
John to be shadowed by a private detective, and more than once sent her
maid to tell him that she had taken poison and would not last the night.
When John tried to flee to France, she met him at Charing Cross station,
"her only luggage a revolver," and staged another suicide pact at his hotel
in Paris.[2] She then opened a cabaret club in a basement in Soho, called
the Cave of the Golden Calf, with decor by, among others, Wyndham
Lewis and Jacob Epstein, where she planned to present some of Strindberg's plays. As the First World War approached, she left for the United
States, but soon returned to Europe and spent most of the rest of her life in
the old family home at Mondsee. She did not marry again, and died there
in 1943, aged seventy-one.

Harriet made a brilliant career, establishing herself as one of the
leading actresses in Sweden; her roles at Dramaten included Juliet, Viola
in *Twelfth Night*, Eliza Doolittle in *Pygmalion*, Hilde Wangel in *The
Master Builder*, Hofmannsthal's Electra, Kate Hardcastle in *She Stoops
to Conquer*, Anne Whitfield in *Man and Superman* and Shakespeare's
Cleopatra. Her second husband, Gunnar Wingård, committed suicide in
October 1912, nine months after Harriet divorced him; in 1927, she

married Edvin Adolphson, an actor fifteen years her junior, but their marriage ended in divorce in 1932. In his autobiography, published in 1972, Adolphson tells disappointingly little about Harriet except that the two of them met Bernard Shaw at a garden party in London in 1923 during the original run of *St. Joan*, that at forty she "seemed at least ten years younger," and that at their final parting she broke a mirror over his head.[3] She had the reputation of being difficult and temperamental professionally, and left Dramaten in 1925 after trying to insist on playing Ibsen's Nora in *A Doll's House* in an unsuitably short skirt, but returned in the next decade, appearing in, among other plays, Clare Boothe Luce's *The Women*. Oscar Wieselgren wrote that she could be charming, but that if she felt she had been slighted "it was not easy to deal with her," and that in her later years she became isolated and bitter.[4] But Mimi Pollak, who played Iras to Harriet's Cleopatra, remembered her only as friendly and helpful, and told me that when, in 1924, Birger Mörner published some of Strindberg's letters to him and the morality of this was debated, Harriet remarked forcefully, "Strindberg never wrote a word which he didn't intend to be published."[5]

Harriet in her later years spoke of Strindberg only with affection. Shortly before her death, she wrote to Sven Hedenberg: "I think he was the finest man I have known . . . We were associated for over seven years; I never saw anything but a good man, loyal, incorruptibly honourable." Hedenberg adds: "To my direct question, Fru Bosse replied that she 'never saw him do or say anything that suggested insanity . . . He never spoke of his "Inferno" period, never of electricity or hypnosis, but often of telepathy . . . I think he was more sensitive than other, more robust people.'"[6] She died in 1961, aged eighty-three.

Fanny Falkner was deeply upset by Strindberg's death; it affected her relationship with the young man with whom she was in love; he committed suicide, and she became seriously ill. "In those days," writes her sister Stella, "people did not speak of 'depression,' they said plainly that she was mad . . . Everything concerning Strindberg became a trauma which she could not think of without pain. Not until she settled in Denmark in the thirties could she find peace of mind to take up her painting seriously again. There she gradually gained a reputation as a respected miniaturist. The wounds from her time with Strindberg were never healed . . . She was one of those fragile persons for whom life in the end becomes a torment . . . People have made her out to be an insignificant girl, asserting that it was only her youth which attracted Strindberg. Nothing could be further from the truth. She had a considerable personality, and her charm lay in a combination of childlike weakness and artistic intuition. She had a great sense of humour, which made her great fun to be with—when she was in the humour. But at the heart of her personality lay a melancholy and a self-absorption which, as time passed, made her intensity exhausting to live with. Her oscillations between joy and melancholy became gradually sharper and split her personality. But in 1909 [when Strindberg knew her] she was a warm and vital person."[7] She died a spinster in 1963, aged seventy-three.

Stanislaw Przybyszewski, after four years in Norway, from 1894 to 1898, when he met Ibsen, Hamsun and Georg Brandes, returned to Poland, where he became a successful novelist and, especially, playwright, though he never wrote as well again after Dagny's death in 1901. Contrary to what has sometimes been suggested, he did not regard himself a disciple of Strindberg. A Polish critic states that during his time in Norway, which he devoted largely to popularising Scandinavian literature and art in Poland and Czechoslovakia (where he was admired), Przybyszewski "never said anything positive about Strindberg . . . nor made any attempt to launch him in those two countries," mentioning him only as a lunatic, not as a writer. In his memoirs, *Moi wspolczsni*, Przybyszewski was critical of Strindberg, granting only that some of the ideas expressed in the preface to *Miss Julie* represent "a break-through in the history of drama."[8] He died in 1927, aged fifty-nine; an illegitimate daughter of his, Stanislawa Przybyszewska, wrote a play before her early death on which Andrzej Wajda based his fine film *Danton*.

At the time of his death, Strindberg was immensely admired in many European countries by writers (especially dramatists) of his own stature, and in literary and theatrical elitist circles, but only in Germany, which then boasted over three hundred and fifty theatres, was he widely played. His popularity there increased steadily over the next decade, reaching its peak in the early 1920s. The year of his death saw 127 performances (not productions) of his plays there, the highest number yet. In 1912–13, this doubled to 281; in 1915–16 there were 789, in 1919–20, 888, and in 1922–23, 1,024, gradually declining to 363 in 1926–27. Between 1899 and 1927, his most frequently staged play in Germany was, surprisingly, *The Comrades*, with 1,174 performances, followed closely by *The Dance of Death*, and then, in order, *There Are Crimes and Crimes*, *The Father*, *Easter*, *Miss Julie* and *A Dream Play*.[9] Max Reinhardt continued to be his principal champion, with a succession of brilliant productions of both the realistic and the "dream" plays. Schering completed his monumental edition of the works soon after Strindberg's death, and it sold widely. The new generation of German expressionist playwrights, led by Ernst Toller and Georg Kaiser, acknowledged him as their master, and the realists admired him for his anti-establishment stance as well as for his realism about sex. "We felt him," Arnold Zweig wrote, "the very embodiment of defiant independence."[10] Brecht was little interested in him; his diaries and letters contain few references to Strindberg, and those mostly disparaging; he seems to have dismissed him (as he did Ibsen) as a poet of the middle class.

Stockholm saw only three productions of Strindberg plays in the two and a half years after his death: the premiere of *Gustav Adolf* (a memorial production in June 1912, which ran for only thirteen performances), *Swanwhite* at the Swedish Theatre and, more successfully, *Pariah* at the New Intimate, with the young Lars Hanson. 1915 saw a revival of interest, Dramaten presenting *The Father*, *Creditors* with *The Bond*, and *Motherly Love* with *Debit and Credit*, while Mauritz Stiller staged *Storm* at the New Intimate, and the Swedish Theatre *Lucky Peter*. But the public remained sceptical, and the literary establishment still dismissed him as a failed crank, or at best a failed genius. It was Max Reinhardt who radically changed this view. In November 1915 he brought his Berlin production of *The Dance of Death* to Stockholm, with Paul Wegener and Gertrud Eysoldt. The play had previously only been seen there in August Falck's production, with its youthful company and limited resources, and Reinhardt's staging created a sensation. It was, indeed, perhaps the first fully adequate production of a Strindberg play that the country had seen, and Swedish eyes were opened. The next two years saw productions in Stockholm and Gothenburg of *Gustav the Third*, *There Are Crimes and Crimes*, *The Comrades*, *A Dream Play*, *The Nightingale of Wittenberg*, *Miss Julie* and *The Virgin Bride*. In May 1917, Reinhardt brought to Stockholm his production of *The Ghost Sonata*, hitherto regarded as a theatrically impossible play; Reinhardt forced the Swedes to reconsider not merely it, but several other works. In 1920 he returned with *The Pelican* and *Storm*, directing the former powerfully as a nightmare, the latter as straight realism; and in 1921 he staged *A Dream Play* in Swedish at Dramaten. From 1920, August Lindberg's son Per, with a brilliant designer, Knut Ström, presented several imaginative Strindberg productions at the Lorensberg Theatre in Gothenburg, and early in the same decade another son of a famous father, Olof Molander, began a series of exciting productions in Stockholm which continued over thirty years. In the early 1930s he was joined at Dramaten by the equally gifted Alf Sjöberg, who remained active until his death in 1980. Ingmar Bergman, a passionate admirer of Strindberg, has directed several brilliant productions of his plays over the past four and a half decades.

In other countries Strindberg, however admired, was seldom staged in the thirty years after his death, and then usually on specialist occasions for a few performances only. France, where he had enjoyed a brief if heady success in 1893–94, was, unlike Germany, little open after 1918 to outside cultural influences. Georges Pitoëff, returning there after spending the war years in Switzerland, was shocked at the insularity of the French theatre and the general xenophobia. (Even Antoine, in 1921, advised against allowing performances of productions by Reinhardt at the Théâtre des Champs-Elysées.) Interest in Strindberg was limited to a small circle, and Paris saw only eight productions of his work between the wars, including one in Russian by an émigré group and Antonin Artaud's famously disastrous staging of A *Dream Play* in 1928, which caused riots in the theatre during the first of its two performances.[11] The other Mediterranean countries remained indifferent to Strindberg during these years, as they did to Ibsen.

In England his progress was equally slow. In 1914 the Birmingham Theatre presented, of all his plays, *The Outlaw*, directed by the poet John Drinkwater; the local *Evening Dispatch* dismissed it as "a wretched play by a wretched playwright." In 1921 Robert Atkins staged *Advent* briefly at the Old Vic Theatre in London, and between 1922 and 1927 an enthusiast named Pax Robertson performed ten of his plays in the cramped and humble surroundings of the "Pax Robertson Studio" at the Bedford Hall in Chelsea. The first person to stage Strindberg adequately in England was the Irishman J. B. Fagan who, between 1924 and 1927 at the Oxford Playhouse, with a gifted young company, directed *Creditors, There Are Crimes and Crimes, Easter* and *The Ghost Sonata*, the last-named transferring to the West End for two special performances in 1927. The same year, Robert Loraine's performance in *The Father* (and the following year in *The Dance of Death*) imprinted Strindberg's name in the annals of English theatrical history. The thirties saw no Strindberg productions in London except two brief revivals of *Miss Julie*, a production of *Pariah*, and four isolated performances of various plays by Sunday groups. The decline in German interest during the 1930s meant that at the outbreak of war in 1939 Strindberg was being staged very little outside Scandinavia.

In America he had scarcely been performed professionally at all, and then usually for a few performances only. The dreadfulness of the early translations, especially those by Edwin Björkman, proved an almost insurmountable obstacle. Much of Strindberg's quality depends on the jagged, broken-glass quality of his dialogue, and until recently none of his translators anywhere, including the admirably assiduous Schering, gave any hint of this. Yet, as in his lifetime, Strindberg continued to excite his peers. Eugene O'Neill, in a programme note to a production of *The Ghost Sonata* at the Provincetown Playhouse in 1924, declared: "Strindberg still remains among the most modern of moderns, the greatest interpreter in the theatre of the characteristic spiritual conflicts which constitute the drama—the blood—of our lives today." Twelve years later, in his speech of acceptance of the Nobel Prize, O'Neill acknowledged "the debt my work owes to that greatest genius of all modern dramatists, your August Strindberg. It was reading his plays when I first started to write . . . that, above all else, first gave me the vision of what modern drama could be, and first inspired me with the urge to write for the theatre myself. If there is anything of lasting worth in my work, it is due to that original impulse from him, which has continued as my inspiration down all the years since then."[12] O'Neill's second wife, Agnes Boulton, says that he read Strindberg's novels "even more frequently than the plays," and that he "considered Strindberg a greater and more profound playwright than Ibsen," and often read aloud to her from *Miss Julie*. Once, early in his career, O'Neill remarked that of all plays, he would most have liked to have written *The Dance of Death*. He also admired the expressionistic plays.[13]

Another passionate admirer of Strindberg was Sean O'Casey. In August 1927, after seeing Robert Loraine's performance in *The Father* in London, O'Casey wrote to Loraine: "Strindberg, Strindberg, Strindberg, the greatest of them all . . . Barrie sits mumbling as he silvers his little model stars and gilds his little model suns, while Strindberg shakes flame from the living planets and the fixed stars. Ibsen can sit serenely in his Doll's House, while Strindberg is battling with his heaven and his hell."[14] Maxim Gorki's admiration remained unabated. "Strindberg," he wrote, "has been the European writer who has been closest to me, the one who has most strongly inspired my thoughts and emotions. Every book he wrote spurred one to argue with him, to contradict him, every book deepened and strengthened one's love of and respect for him . . . To light the way for those who wandered in the perplexities of darkness, and show the path to understanding and freedom, he tore the heart from his breast, set it on fire and carried it as a torch to lead mankind."[15]

In Russia, only one new Strindberg production occurred between his death and the Revolution, when in July 1912 Vsevolod Meyerhold directed *There Are Crimes and Crimes* at Terijoki in Karelia to commemorate the writer's death. In March 1921 the Moscow Arts Theatre staged *Erik the Fourteenth*, after three hundred rehearsals covering several years, directed by Vachtangov, who died that year. This play had been banned by the Tsarist censor as being a disrespectful portrait of a monarch, and also because it ended in a successful revolution, but it now won official approval, not least for its contrast between the effete court and the vital masses. It was a great success, and over the next six years was performed a hundred and eighteen times; but this appears to have been the last production of a Strindberg play in that country.[16] In Poland the actor Karol Adwentowicz, who had achieved a personal triumph in *The Father* in 1908, continued to stage and perform in the play until 1946, when it was banned as inappropriate to the new social system. (He had also directed and appeared in *Miss Julie* and *The Dance of Death*.)

The 1939 war forms a watershed in the development of Strindberg's reputation and influence as a dramatist. When it began, he was admired by a small but discriminating minority, but was little performed anywhere outside Scandinavia. The average European or American playgoer, such as myself, had never seen a Strindberg play. After the war he began to be staged more and more in almost every Western country, including several that had ignored him for decades and others, such as Japan, Italy, Australasia and the South American continent, where his work had been virtually or completely unknown. Theatrical taste had changed; there was a new appetite for the kind of play that examined pessimism, cruelty and human suffering, the struggle of human beings driven by forces beyond their control. In France, Jean Vilar's Paris production of 1944 of *The Dance of Death* had seemed to mirror the ceaseless self-questioning of an occupied people, and a succession of Strindberg productions was staged after the Liberation. Eric Bentley observed in 1950: "One notes in France particularly a sort of re-enactment of the Strindberg revival which occurred in Germany a generation ago."[17] In Germany and Austria there was a new enthusiasm for his work matching that of the twenties, for the expressionistic as well as the naturalistic plays. In Russia he is still out of favour, but in Poland his plays have been much performed since the 1950s. This, ironically, brought about a revival of interest in Przybyszewski, whose plays were now republished and staged. "It is a curiosity of fate," a Polish critic writes, "that Przybyszewski should owe his successes to Strindberg, the man whose entry onto the Polish stage he had once obstructed."[18]

Britain saw few Strindberg productions until the end of the fifties, but many during the sixties and since, in both London and the provinces, and also on television and, especially, radio, in which medium several plays such as *The Virgin Bride, Erik the Fourteenth* and *Master Olof* have received their first British performance. In America there have been a number of productions of the realistic plays, notably *The Father, Miss Julie* and *The Dance of Death*, and, as in Britain, very many university and other amateur productions of both the realistic and the expressionistic plays.

The centenary of Strindberg's birth in 1949 led to many tributes. Thomas Mann wrote that his influence could be compared only to that of Tolstoy, perceptively adding: "One of the things they have in common is a kind of tremendous helplessness. In Strindberg this sometimes results in a half-voluntary and, to my mind, half-deliberate, demoniacal comic strain of incomparable power." Thornton Wilder praised "the unprecedented intensity and honesty he brought to the analysis of the relation of the sexes and of the artist in relation to society . . . In an explosion of courage, honesty and literary power, he created a drama for the generations that were to follow him . . . Strindberg is the fountain-head of all that is best in the theatre of our time." Bernard Shaw wrote: "He is among the greatest of the great." Sean O'Casey called him "one of the giants of drama . . . a prince among playwrights," and Arnold Zweig hailed him as "the very embodiment of defiant independence . . . Generations of our time will come away from stage and reading-lamp full of fire to take up arms against the warping of man by man."[19] Many post-war playwrights found in him a natural ancestor, whether for his realism regarding the sex war and his cult of the anti-hero, as with Tennessee Williams, John Osborne and Jean-Paul Sartre (a founder-member, with André Gide and Albert Camus, of the Société Strindberg and, like them, a confessed admirer), or for his exploitation of that border country where reality and fantasy merge, as with Camus, Arthur Adamov (who translated three of his plays, very badly), Harold Pinter and Edward Albee (though others whom one might have supposed his disciples, such as Samuel Beckett and Eugène Ionesco, have denied being influenced by him).[20]

Outside Sweden, Strindberg is today known almost entirely as a dramatist and as the author of *Inferno*. In Sweden, he is also, and rightly, revered as being the father both of modern Swedish prose and of the novel, *The Red Room* being the earliest book of Swedish narrative prose fiction which survives in its own right. A recent Swedish biographer, indeed, seems more interested in his novels and stories than in the dramas. To a non-Swede, these novels, while giving a vivid picture of Swedish society in his time, seem (always excepting *The People of Hemsö*) fatally flawed; *The Red Room*, *A Madman's Defence*, *By the Open Sea*, *Black Banners* and *The Gothic Rooms* are worth reading for their occasional fine scenes and descriptions of landscape, but are sloppily constructed and full of boring didacticism, which often amounts to a third or more of the whole. The same applies to his partly fictionalised autobiographical writings, *The Son of a Servant* and its successors, and to the *Blue Books*. These novels have been, and still are, admired in Germany, where even the best of that country's novelists have often shared Strindberg's faults. Franz Kafka's admiration of Strindberg's novels has already been quoted. * A wide gap exists between the German and Scandinavian idea, on the one hand, and the British, French and American idea on the other, of what a novel should be. One cannot say that either idea is wrong, only that the gap exists.

As a short-story writer, Strindberg possessed one of the virtues which made him such a fine playwright: the ability to encapsulate a drama in a short space. The art of the short story is much closer to that of the drama than is the art of the novel, and of the hundred and fifty-odd short stories which Strindberg wrote, perhaps twenty or thirty are of a high order. If this seems a small proportion, one should reflect that it is not much lower than the proportion of good to bad among his plays. As a poet, Strindberg seems to me much overrated in Sweden. He was ahead of his time in his use of free verse, and sometimes made sharp and perceptive statements in that medium; he wrote a few pleasing lyrics, such as the memory of his first meeting with Siri;† but he was not skilled at formal verse, liable, as in *Somnambulist Nights* and also in his various attempts at blank verse, to trundle along without much variation of rhythm. Nor, unlike Ibsen, was he a skilled dramatic poet, though he thought he was. From *In Rome* and the verse version of *Master Olof* to *The Great Highway*, there is hardly a speech, hardly indeed a line, that he would not have written better in prose. One senses this especially in plays which he wrote in a mixture of verse and prose, such as *A Dream Play*. The occasional eloquent phrase only throws into relief the general woolliness of the verse surrounding it.

As a dramatist, however, Strindberg was, as so many of his peers in that field have recognised, a giant. Tragic drama is the most difficult of all fields in which to achieve greatness. If one makes it a test of great tragedy that it should survive translation, there have been only seven indisputably great tragic dramatists since the theatre began: Aeschylus, Sophocles, Euripides, Shakespeare, Ibsen, Strindberg and Chekhov. Racine is not great in any language but French; and Ibsen was surely right when he said that Goethe and Schiller were very great poets but not really very good dramatists. [21] Has anyone ever made anything by these three work on stage in translation? Strindberg was wildly uneven as a dramatist, as in everything else, but at least nine of his plays—*The Father, Miss Julie,*

*See page 448.
†See page 58.

Creditors, The Dance of Death, Part I of *To Damascus, Erik the Fourteenth, The Virgin Bride, A Dream Play* and *The Ghost Sonata* —work as powerfully in the theatre today as when they were written; and there are others, such as *Master Olof, Gustav Vasa* and *Gustav the Third,* which remain splendidly valid to an audience with the basic background knowledge which Strindberg required of spectators of his historical plays. And others, too, such as *Easter* and *Storm,* which can be wonderfully moving with the right elusive personality in a particular part. What other tragic dramatist except Shakespeare and Ibsen has left as many?

In two distinct ways, Strindberg was greatly influential as a dramatist, though in both respects he was so far in advance of his time that it was years before this influence was felt. Firstly, he pioneered the depiction of men and women driven by love, hatred, jealousy or a mixture of all three to that nightmare border country where hysteria abuts on madness. All of his finest plays, from *The Father* to *The Ghost Sonata,* are set in this appalling landscape, which all of us, at some time in our lives, enter, though few of us, mercifully, are imprisoned in it as he was. He explored those dark corners of the human soul which most of us seal off like poisoned wells; he was unbalanced, but so were most explorers of that country—Swift, Melville, Dostoevsky, Kafka. Other dramatists had set foot there—Shakespeare in *Othello,* Ibsen in *The Lady from the Sea, The Master Builder* and *Little Eyolf,* Büchner in *Woyzeck*—but none had mapped it as ruthlessly and meticulously as Strindberg did. In Strindberg's time, and for decades afterwards, people, while content to explore that world in novels in the comfort and safety of their homes, did not in general want to be faced with it in a theatre as part of a crowd; but since 1945, in most countries, the theatre has become a place where people expect and even want to confront the human situation in all its ugliness. Similarly, Strindberg wrote about sex with a realism which none of his predecessors in the theatre, not even Ibsen, had matched. He knew, and said, that people can fuck each other and hate each other; he even suggested that that is what marriage often means. Before Strindberg, only married people or wicked people copulate; sexual realism in the theatre may be said to date from Strindberg.

Secondly, Strindberg pioneered the exploration in drama of another border country, that in which reality and fantasy merge. In those symbolic or expressionistic plays which he wrote after his Inferno crisis, such as the *To Damascus* trilogy, *A Dream Play* and *The Ghost Sonata,* he was, to quote again his own words, trying "to imitate the inconsequent yet transparently logical shape of a dream. Everything can happen . . . Time and place do not exist." Thirty years previously, Ibsen had attempted something of the kind in *Peer Gynt,* but not, as Strindberg did, overtly; Ibsen never makes clear that in the fifth act of that play he is showing us the inside of a dead or a dying man's mind, though we may infer that if we wish to. But Strindberg in his expressionistic plays openly dramatises the dreams, fears and daydreams of his characters so that we often do not know whether what we are seeing takes place inside or outside their heads. Many dramatists have done this since—Pirandello,* Toller, Kaiser, O'Neill, Pinter, Beckett, Ionesco—but Strindberg was the first.

As well as these innovations, he perfected a new shorthand of dialogue, terse, nervous and fragmentary. Anyone who has worked on a Strindberg play in the theatre knows how actors and actresses are often at first baffled by the seeming inconsequentiality of much of the dialogue, even in a realistic play such as *The Father* or *Miss Julie,* before they realise how precisely it charts the channels which they must follow between the reefs. His plays need the kind of acting that is not afraid to go close to those reefs; there is no room in them, when the crunch comes, for gentlemanly or ladylike understatement, any more than there is in Lear or Othello, Cleopatra, Clytemnestra, Oedipus, Woyzeck, Brand or Borkman. If these plays are not done big, they had better not be done at all. Strindberg achieved, too, an economy new in drama since the Greeks. Ibsen had reduced dialogue from poetic verbosity to a taut and spare colloquial prose, but Strindberg reduced it even further. Structurally, too, he achieved an economy beyond Ibsen's; as he proudly pointed out, the plots of *Miss Julie* and *Creditors* would each have sufficed for a five-act play but he had reduced both of them to a single act of less than ninety minutes, the length of Sophocles's *Oedipus Rex.*

Finally, a modern playwright, John Mortimer, observes that Strindberg was the first dramatist not to have presented himself as "the reasonable man of moderation, the sort of character of sterling common sense that his audience was flattered into believing it also represented," and relates this directly to Strindberg's relevance today: "The movement of modern drama has been, surely, a flight from reason into the terrifying abyss of Beckett, or the irrational fears of Pinter. John Osborne's . . . Jimmy Porter and Archie Rice are not reasonable men. They live in a different world from Shakespeare and Montaigne; their anger is at best an expression of the hopelessly absurd facts of existence, at worst a scream of paranoia. They are in Strindberg's world . . . He found the joy of life in its 'cruel and mighty conflicts,' and the exhilaration his best work brings is

*There is, I am assured, no evidence that Pirandello was interested in Strindberg's plays, or even that he had read them when he wrote his own plays between 1916 and 1932.

not that it is intelligent (like much of life, it is totally absurd); but that it is absolutely true. It is by facing the irrational truth of existence that the writer and his characters achieve such peace as they ever know. . . . [His] is not the voice of reason; but it is the true voice of experience hardly won, and it is the voice of modern drama."[22]

London–Stockholm
April 1979–June 1984

SELECT BIBLIOGRAPHY

ADAM (London), Strindberg centenary issue, 1949.

AHLENIUS, HOLGER. *Georg Brandes i svensk litteratur till och med 1890.* Stockholm, 1932.

AHLSTRÖM, STELLAN. *Strindbergs erövring av Paris.* Stockholm, 1956.

—— (ed.). *Ögonvittnen I. August Strindberg. Ungdom och mannaår.* Stockholm, 1959.

—— and EKLUND, TORSTEN (ed.). *Ögonvittnen II. August Strindberg. Mannaår och ålderdom.* Stockholm, 1961.

ANON. *Släkten Strindberg från Strinne.* No date nor place of publication given.

ANTOINE, ANDRÉ. *Mes souvenirs sur le Théâtre Libre.* Paris, 1921.

BÄVERSTEDT, BO, and CARLSSON, ERIK. *Strindberg, alkohol och absint,* in *Recipreflex* (Stockholm), February, 1975.

BAYERDÖRFER, HANS-PETER. *Strindberg auf der deutschen Bühne, 1890–1925.* Neumünster, 1983.

BERENDSOHN, WALTER. "Strindberg och Nietzsche," in *Samfundet Örebro stads- och länsbiblioteks vänner, Meddelande no. XVI.* Örebro, 1948.

—— *Strindbergs sista levnadsår.* Stockholm, 1948.

BERGMAN, GÖSTA M. *Den moderna teaterns genombrott, 1890–1925.* Stockholm, 1966.

BJØRNSON, BJØRNSTJERNE. *Brevveksling med danske, 1875–1910,* ed. Øyvind Anker, Francis Bull and Torben Nielsen, I–III. Copenhagen and Oslo, 1953.

—— *Brevveksling med svenske, 1858–1909,* ed. Øyvind Anker, Francis Bull and Örjan Lindberger, I–III. Oslo, 1960–1.

—— *Kamp-tid (brev fra aarene 1879–1884)*, ed. Halvdan Koht, I–II. Oslo, 1932.

BOETHIUS, ULF. *Strindberg och kvinnofrågan*. Halmstad, 1969.

BONNIER, KARL OTTO. *Bonniers: En bokhandlarefamilj*, III–V. Stockholm, 1931–56.

BONNIER, TOR. *Längesen*. Stockholm, 1972.

BRANDELL, GUNNAR. *Strindberg: ett författarliv*, III. Stockholm, 1983.

—— *Strindberg in Inferno*, trans. Barry Jacobs. Cambridge, Mass., 1974.

—— (ed.). *Strindberg i offentligheten*, I–IV. Uppsala, 1980–1.

BRANDES, EDVARD. *Om Teater*. Copenhagen, 1947.

—— *Litteræra Tendenser*. Copenhagen, 1968.

—— and BRANDES, GEORG. *Brevveksling med nordiske Forfattere og Videnskabsmænd*, ed. Morten Borup, Francis Bull and John Landquist, I–VII. Copenhagen, 1939–42.

BRANDES, GEORG. *Kritiker og Portraiter*. Copenhagen, 1870.

—— *Levned*, I–III. Copenhagen, 1905–8.

CARLSON, HARRY G. *Strindberg and the Poetry of Myth*. Berkeley, 1982.

DANIELSSON, BENGT. *Gauguins Söderhavsår*. Stockholm, 1964.

DELIUS, FREDERICK. "Recollections of Strindberg," in *The Sackbut* (London), December, 1920.

EDHOLM, ERIK AF. *Mot seklets slut*. Stockholm, 1948.

ENGSTRÖM, ALBERT. *Strindberg och jag*. Stockholm, 1923.

FALCK, AUGUST. *Fem år med Strindberg*. Stockholm, 1935.

FALKNER, FANNY. *August Strindberg i Blå Tornet*. Stockholm, 1921.

FALKNER-SÖDERBERG, STELLA. *Fanny Falkner och August Strindberg*. Stockholm, 1970.

FREY, TORSTEN. "Medicinska synpunkter på August Strindberg," in *Läkartidningen* (Stockholm), 1980.

FRÖDING, GUSTAF (ed.). *En bok om Strindberg*. Karlstad, 1894.

GEETE, ROBERT. *August Strindbergs ungdomshistoria. Personliga minnen upptecknade*. Stockholm, 1919.

GULLBERG, HELGE. "August Strindberg i Per Hallströms och Gustaf af Geijerstams brevväxling," in *Samlaren* (Stockholm), 1960.

HAGSTEN, ALLAN. *Den unge Strindberg*, I–II. Lund, 1951.

HAMSUN, KNUT. *Artikler*, ed. Francis Bull. Oslo, 1939.

HEDBERG, TOR. *Ett decennium*, I–II. Stockholm, 1912–13.

HEDÉN, ERIK. *Strindberg. En ledtråd vid studiet av hans verk*. Stockholm, 1926.

HEDENBERG, SVEN. *Strindberg i skärselden*. Gothenburg, 1961.

HELLSTRÖM, VICTOR. *Strindberg och musiken*. Stockholm, 1917.

HEMMINGSON, PER. *August Strindberg som fotograf*. Stockholm, 1963.

HERRLIN, AXEL. *Från sekelslutets Lund*. Lund, 1936.

JACOBSEN, HARRY. *Strindberg i Firsernes København*. Copenhagen, 1948.

—— *Strindberg och hans förste hustru*. Copenhagen, 1946.

JANNI, THÉRÈSE DUBOIS. *August Strindberg, en biografi i text och bild.* Milan, 1970; Swedish edition, Stockholm, 1972.

JÄRV, HARRY (ed.). *Strindbergsfejden*, I–II. Uddevalla, 1968.

JOHANNESSON, ERIC O. *The Novels of August Strindberg.* Berkeley, 1968.

JOHN, AUGUSTUS. *Chiaroscuro.* London, 1952.

JOHNSON, MELKER. *En Åttiotalist. Gustaf af Geijerstam 1858–95.* Gothenburg, 1934.

LAMM, MARTIN. *August Strindberg*, trans. and ed. Harry G. Carlson. New York, 1971.

—— *Strindbergs dramer*, I–II. Stockholm, 1924–6.

—— *Strindberg och makterna.* Uppsala, 1936.

LANDQUIST, JOHN. *Som jag minns dem.* Stockholm, 1949.

LARSSON, CARL. *Jag.* Stockholm, 1931.

LENGERTZ, W. *Strindberg i Lund.* Lund, 1940.

LIDFORSS, BENGT. *August Strindberg och den litterära nittiotalsreklamen.* Malmö, 1910.

—— "Strindberg som naturforskare," in *Nordisk Revy* (Stockholm), 1894.

LINDBERG, PER. *August Lindberg.* Stockholm, 1943.

LINDER, GURLI. *På den tiden.* Stockholm, 1924.

LINDSTRÖM, HANS. *Strindberg och böckerna.* Uppsala, 1977.

LUNDEGÅRD, AXEL. *Några Strindbergsminnen knutna till en handfull brev.* Stockholm, 1920.

LUTHANDER, LENNART. *Strindberg i Danmark.* Stockholm, 1977.

MEIDAL, BJÖRN. *Från profet till folktribun.* Stockholm, 1982.

MEYER, GUSTAV. *Studentliv i Uppsala för 60 år sedan.* Stockholm, 1930.

MEYER, MICHAEL. *Henrik Ibsen: a critical biography*, I–III. London, 1967–71.

—— Introd. and trans. *Strindberg: The Plays*, I–II. London, 1964, 1975.

MOLANDER, OLOF. *Harald Molander.* Stockholm, 1950.

—— *Harriet Bosse, en skiss.* Stockholm, 1920.

MORGAN, MARGERY M. "Strindberg and the English Theatre," in *Modern Drama* (London), September, 1964.

MÖRNER, BIRGER. *Den Strindberg jag känt.* Stockholm, 1924.

MORTENSEN, JOHAN. *Strindberg som jag minnes honom.* Stockholm, 1931.

MUNCH, EDVARD. *Brev.* Oslo, 1949.

NILSSON, NILS ÅKE. "Strindberg på rysk scen," in *Meddelanden från Strindbergssällskapet*, December, 1956.

NORRMAN, DAVID. *Strindbergs skilsmässa från Siri von Essen.* Stockholm, 1953.

OLLÉN, GUNNAR. *Strindbergs dramatik.* Stockholm, 1961; 4th revised edition, Stockholm, 1982.

PAUL, ADOLF. *Min Strindbergsbok.* Stockholm, 1930.

PERSONNE, JOHN. *Strindbergslitteraturen och osedligheten bland skolungdomen. Till föräldrar och uppfostrare samt till de styrande.* Stockholm, 1887.

PHILP, ANNA, and HARTZELL, NORA. *Strindbergs systrar berättar om barndomshemmet och om bror August Strindberg.* Stockholm, 1926.

PRZYBYSZEWSKI, STANISLAW. *Erinnerungen an das literarische Berlin,* trans. Klaus Staemmler. Munich, 1965.

SANDBACH, MARY, trans. and ed. *Inferno.* London, 1962, 1979.

—— Introduction to *From an Occult Diary.* London, 1965.

SCHLEICH, CARL LUDWIG. *Hågkomster om Strindberg.* Stockholm, 1917.

SCHMIDT, T. M. (ed.). *Strindbergs måleri.* Malmö, 1972.

SELANDER, EDVARD and NILS. *Carl XVs glada dagar.* Stockholm, 1927.

—— *Två gamla Stockholmares anteckningar.* Stockholm, 1920.

SHAW, BERNARD. *Collected Letters,* I–II, ed. Dan H. Laurence. London, 1965, 1972.

SMEDMARK, CARL REINHOLD, ed. and introd. *August Strindbergs dramer,* I–IV. Stockholm, 1962–4.

SMIRNOFF, KARIN. *Strindbergs första hustru.* Stockholm, 1926.

—— *Så var det i verkligheten.* Stockholm, 1956.

SÖDERSTRÖM, GÖRAN. *Strindberg och bildkonsten.* Stockholm, 1972.

SOMMAR, CARL OLOV. *Stockholmspromenad med Strindberg.* Stockholm, 1972.

SPRINCHORN, EVERT. *Strindberg as Dramatist.* Newhaven, 1982.

—— Introduction and notes to *The Son of a Servant.* New York, 1966.

STANG, RAGNA. *Edvard Munch,* transl. Geoffrey Culverwell and Anthony Martin. London, 1979.

STORR, ANTHONY. *The Dynamics of Creation.* London, 1972.

STRINDBERG, AUGUST. *Brev,* I–XV, ed. Torsten Eklund. Stockholm, 1948–76.

—— *Breven till Harriet Bosse.* Med kommentarer av Harriet Bosse. Stockholm, 1932.

—— *Före* Röda Rummet. *Strindbergs ungdomsjournalistik,* ed. Torsten Eklund. Stockholm, 1946.

—— *Ockulta dagboken.* Stockholm, 1977.

—— *Samlade skrifter,* I–LV, ed. John Landquist, Stockholm, 1912–19.

—— *Samlade otrycktya skrifter,* I–II, Stockholm, 1918–19.

—— *Ur ockulta dagboken,* ed. Torsten Eklund. (Extracts from *Ockulta dagboken,* with letters exchanged between Strindberg and Harriet Bosse, 1900–08), Stockholm, 1963.

STRINDBERG, FRIDA. *Marriage with Genius.* London, 1937.

STRÖM, FREDRIK. *Min ungdoms strider.* Stockholm, 1940.

SVEDFELT, TORSTEN. *Strindbergs ansikte.* Stockholm, 1948.

SWERLING, ANTHONY. *Strindberg's Impact in France, 1920–1960.* Cambridge, 1971.

THIIS, JENS. *Edvard Munch og hans samtid.* Oslo, 1933.

TOKSVIG, SIGNE. *Emmanuel Swedenborg, Scientist and Mystic.* London, 1949.

TORSSLOW, STIG. *Dramatenaktörernas republik.* Uppsala, 1975.
—— *Edvard Bäckström och hans dramatiska diktning.* Gothenburg, 1947.
UDDGREN, GUSTAF. *Boken om Strindberg. Början till en biografi.* Gothenburg, 1909.
—— *Andra boken om Strindberg.* Göteborg, 1912.
UGGLA, NILS ANDRZEJ. "Strindberg och Przybyszewski," in *Meddelanden från Strindbergssällskapet,* May, 1974.
—— *Strindberg och den polska teatern, 1890–1970.* Uppsala, 1977.
VENDELFELT, ERIK. *Då Strindberg gick i Jakobs skola.* Stockholm, 1943.
WIESELGREN, OSCAR. "Harriet Bosse," in *Meddelanden från Strindbergssällskapet,* December, 1961.
—— "Strindberg och den svenska kritiken," in *Svensk Tidskrift,* 1949.
WILLERS, UNO. *Från slottsflygeln till Humlegården. August Strindberg som biblioteksman.* Stockholm, 1962.
WRANGEL, F. U. *Minnen från konstnärskretsarna och författarvärlden.* Stockholm, 1925.

NOTES

The following abbreviations are used for sources repeatedly mentioned:

Brev—*August Strindbergs brev*, I–XV, ed. Torsten Eklund (Stockholm, 1948 ff.). No footnote references are given for dated letters, which will be found in their natural chronological position.

Br. br.—*Edvard og Georg Brandes Brevveksling med nordiske Forfattere og Videnskabsmænd*, I–VII, ed. Morten Borup, Francis Bull and John Landquist (Copenhagen, 1939–42).

SS—August Strindberg, *Samlade Skrifter*, I–LV, ed. John Landquist (Stockholm, 1912–19).

Ögonvittnen—*Ögonvittnen: August Strindberg*, I–II, ed. Stellan Ahlström (Stockholm, 1959, 1961).

SiO—*Strindberg i offentligheten*, I–IV, ed. Gunnar Brandell (Uppsala, 1980–1).

Bosse—*Strindbergs brev till Harriet Bosse*, med kommentarer av Harriet Bosse (Stockholm, 1932).

Where more than one source by the same author or editor is quoted, I have, after the first mention, used the initial letters of the title; thus, *Strindbergs första hustru* becomes *Sfh*.

Chapter One

1. Anna Philp and Nora Hartzell, *Strindbergs systrar berättar om barndomshemmet och om bror August* (Stockholm, 1926), pp. 7 ff.; *Släkten Strind-*

berg från Strinne, pp. 1 ff. The latter useful little pamphlet about Strindberg's ancestors and descendants bears no details of authorship, nor of its place or date of issue.

2. Philp and Hartzell, p. 9.
3. Allan Hagsten, *Den unge Strindberg* (Lund, 1951), I, pp. 45 ff.—an exhaustive investigation of Strindberg's early years to which this chapter is generally indebted.
4. Ibid., pp. 80 ff.; Heinrich Neuhaus, *Panorama över Stockholm på 1870-talet* (Stockholm, 1954), pp. 16 ff.; Nils and Edvard Selander, *Två gamla Stockholmares anteckningar* (Stockholm, 1920), p. 107 *et passim*; Oscar Heimer and Torsten Palmer, *Bilder från Stockholms malmar, 1894–1912* (Stockholm, 1972), *passim*.
5. Heimer and Palmer, p. 5.
6. Hagsten, p. 80.
7. Ibid., pp. 40–2.
8. Philp and Hartzell, facing p. 10.
9. SS, XVIII, p. 12.
10. Ibid., pp. 12–14.
11. Ibid. pp. 9–11.
12. Philp and Hartzell, pp. 15 ff.
13. SS, XVIII, p. 29.
14. Hagsten, I, pp. 94–8.
15. SS, XVIII, p. 19.
16. Ibid., p. 25.
17. Hagsten, I, pp. 87–8; Selander, p. 106.
18. SS, XVIII, p. 35; Philp and Hartzell, p. 11.
19. SS, XVIII, pp. 43–4.
20. Hagsten, I, p. 88.
21. SS, XVIII, pp. 38–9.
22. Robert Geete, *August Strindbergs ungdomshistoria* (Stockholm, 1919), p. 480.
23. Erik Hedén, *Strindberg* (Stockholm, 1926), p. 17.
24. SS, XVIII, p. 58.
25. Ibid., pp. 58–60.
26. Erik Vendelfelt, *Då Strindberg gick i Jakobs skola* (Stockholm, 1943), p. 7.
27. SS, XVIII, p. 96.
28. *Ögonvittnen*, I, pp. 18–19, 22.
29. Ibid., p. 19.
30. Ibid., pp. 19–20.
31. Philp and Hartzell, pp. 31–2.
32. Ibid., p. 15.
33. *Ögonvittnen*, I, p. 23.
34. Selander, pp. 75 ff.
35. SS, XVIII, p. 83.
36. Selander, p. 75.

37. SS, XVIII, p. 84.
38. Ibid., pp. 87–9.
39. Torsten Eklund, "Från Strindbergs barndomsmiljö," in *Strindbergssällskapets Meddelanden*, nr. 8, (Stockholm, 1950), p. 10.
40. SS, XVIII, p. 94.
41. Ibid., p. 46.
42. Martin Lamm, *August Strindberg*, ed. and trans. Harry G. Carlson (New York, 1971), p. 56.
43. SS, XVIII, p. 104.
44. Philp and Hartzell, pp. 30–2.
45. SS, XVIII, p. 138.
46. Philp and Hartzell, p. 40.
47. SS, XVIII, p. 152.
48. Ibid., pp. 151–3.
49. Ibid., pp. 184–5.
50. Ibid., pp. 173–4.
51. Selander, p. 31.
52. SS, XVIII, p. 193.
53. Ibid., p. 34.
54. Ibid., p. 202.
55. Ibid., pp. 208–10.
56. Ibid., p. 184.
57. Hagsten, I, p. 36.
58. SS, XVIII, p. 211.
59. Ibid., pp. 211–12.

Chapter Two

1. Lorentz Dietrichson, *Svundne tider* (Christiania, 1894–1917), II, p. 51.
2. SS, XVIII, p. 224.
3. Ibid., p. 228.
4. Ibid., p. 240.
5. Ibid., pp. 242–3.
6. Ibid., pp. 247–9.
7. Ibid., p. 250.
8. Ibid., pp. 265–6.
9. Ibid., pp. 275–8.
10. Ibid., p. 280.
11. Ibid., p. 285.
12. Ibid., pp. 292–3, 303.
13. Ibid., pp. 302–3.
14. Ibid., pp. 307–8.
15. Ibid., pp. 309–10.
16. Ibid., pp. 315–16.
17. Ibid., IV, pp. 169–70.

18. Ibid., XVIII, pp. 355–6.
19. Ibid., XVII, p. 208, and XVIII, p. 354.
20. Ibid., XVIII, p. 332.
21. Ibid., p. 332.
22. Ibid., p. 335.
23. Ibid., pp. 337–8.
24. Erik af Edholm, *På Carl XVs tid* (Stockholm, 1945), p. 261.
25. *SS*, XVIII, p. 339.
26. Ibid., pp. 341–2.
27. Carl Reinhold Smedmark (ed.), *August Strindbergs dramer* (Stockholm, 1962 ff.), I, p. 7.
28. *SS*, XVIII, p. 346.
29. Ibid., p. 344.
30. Ibid., p. 343.

Chapter Three

1. *SS*, XVIII, pp. 223–4.
2. Ibid., p. 359.
3. Ibid., p. 359.
4. Ibid., pp. 359 ff.
5. *Ögonvittnen*, I. p. 57.
6. Ibid., pp. 58–60.
7. Smedmark, I, p. 139.
8. *SS*, XVIII, pp. 379–80.
9. Ibid., pp. 281–2.
10. Ibid., pp. 386–9.
11. Ibid., p. 378.
12. Ibid., p. 141.
13. *Brev*, I, p. 33.
14. Ibid., p. 36.
15. Ibid., p. 36.
16. *SS*, XVIII, p. 391.
17. Ibid., p. 395.
18. Ibid., p. 396.
19. Ibid., p. 398.
20. *Ögonvittnen*, I, p. 61.
21. Ibid., p. 62.
22. *SS*, XVIII, p. 398.
23. *Brev*, II, p. 204.
24. *Brev*, I, pp. 63–4.
25. Hagsten, II, p. 39.
26. *Ögonvittnen* I, p. 44.
27. Ibid., pp. 44–5.
28. *Brev*, I, p. 66.

29. *SS*, XVIII, pp. 402–5.
30. Ibid., pp. 429–30.
31. Ibid., p. 431.
32. *Brev*, I, pp. 70–1.
33. Ibid., p. 74.
34. *SS*, XVIII, pp. 435–6.
35. *Brev*, I, pp. 86–7.
36. *Ögonvittnen*, I, p. 47.
37. Ibid., p. 47.
38. *Brev*, I, p. 25.
39. Smedmark, I, p. 181.
40. *SS*, XVIII, pp. 438–9.
41. Ibid., p. 448.

Chapter Four

1. *SS*, XIX, p. 8.
2. *Ögonvittnen*, I, p. 48.
3. *Brev*, I, p. 97.
4. *SS*, XIX, p. 8.
5. Ibid., pp. 8–9.
6. Ibid., p. 13.
7. Michael Meyer, *Henrik Ibsen* (London, 1967–71), II, p. 162.
8. *Brev*, I, p. 103.
9. *SS*, XVII, p. 240.
10. Martin Lamm, *Strindbergs dramer* (Stockholm, 1924–6), I, p. 90.
11. *SS*, XIX, p. 27.
12. Karl Otto Bonnier, *Bonniers: En bokhandlarefamilj* (Stockholm, 1931–56), III, p. 248.
13. *SS*, XIX, p. 56.
14. Ibid., p. 57.
15. Ibid., p. 72. Cf. also Torsten Eklund, "August Strindberg, Nordstjernan och Svensk Försäkringstidning," in *Lifförsäkrings-Aktiebolaget Nordstjernan 75 år* (Stockholm, 1946).
16. *SS*, XIX, p. 123.
17. *Brev*, I, p. 155.
18. Ibid., p. 155.
19. Uno Willers, *Från slottsflygeln till Humlegården* (Stockholm, 1962), p. 32.
20. Geete, p. 470.
21. Willers, pp. 115–16.
22. Johan Mortensen, *Strindberg som jag minnes honom* (Stockholm, 1931), pp. 46–7.
23. Willers, p. 41.
24. Göran Söderström, *Strindberg och bildkonsten* (Stockholm, 1972), pp. 51–2.

25. *Ögonvittnen*, I, pp. 83–6.
26. *Brev*, I, p. 166n.
27. Ibid., pp. 165–6.

Chapter Five

1. Karin Smirnoff, *Strindbergs första hustru* (Stockholm, 1926), p. 11.
2. Ibid., p. 74.
3. Ibid., pp. 57–8, 72–5.
4. SS, XXVI, p. 37.
5. Ibid., p. 44.
6. Smirnoff, *Sfh*, pp. 75–6.
7. *Brev*, I, pp. 227–8.
8. SS, XXVI, pp. 117–18.
9. Ibid., pp. 118 ff.
10. *Brev*, I, pp. 236–40.
11. *Ögonvittnen*, I, p. 90.
12. SS, XXVI, pp. 129–31.
13. Hagsten, I, p. 71.
14. SS, XXVI, pp. 161–2.
15. Ibid., pp. 163–4.
16. SS, LV, pp. 102–4.
17. SS, XXVI, p. 168.
18. Ibid., p. 169.
19. Ibid., p. 177.
20. SS, LV, pp. 133–4.
21. Smirnoff, *Sfh*, pp. 95–6.
22. Willers, pp. 54–5.
23. SS, LV, pp. 183–9.
24. Ibid., pp. 107 ff.
25. Ibid., XXVI, p. 224.
26. Bonnier, III, pp. 247–8.
27. Söderström, pp. 58–60.
28. SS, XXVI, p. 113.
29. *Brev*, I, p. 384.
30. Ibid., p. 384n.
31. Hagsten, I, p. 73.

Chapter Six

1. Anne-Charlotte Leffler, *En självbiografi* (Stockholm, 1922), pp. 64–5.
2. SS, XIX, p. 160.
3. *Ögonvittnen*, I, p. 88.
4. Ibid., p. 71.

5. Willers, p. 90; Geete, p. 474.
6. Geete, pp. 475–7.
7. Philp and Hartzell, p. 65.
8. Mortensen, p. 50.
9. *Brev*, VII, pp. 66–8.
10. *Brev*, II, pp. 52–3; Bonnier, III, pp. 250–1.
11. *Brev*, II, p. 76.
12. Ibid., p. 58n.
13. Bonnier, IV, p. 23.
14. *SS*, XIX, p. 109.
15. *Ögonvittnen*, I, p. 137.
16. Gunnar Brandell (ed.), *Strindberg i offentligheten* (Uppsala, 1980–1), I, pp. 1–2, 37, 98, 127.
17. *Br. br.*, IV, p. 290.
18. Ibid., II, p. 359.
19. Ibid., V, p. 150.
20. John Paulsen, *Samliv med Ibsen* (Christiana, 1906, 1913), II, p. 224.
21. *SS*, XIX, p. 174.
22. Lamm, pp. 123–4.
23. *Ögonvittnen*, I, pp. 100–1.
24. Ibid., pp. 99–100.
25. Geete, p. 474.
26. *Brev*, II, pp. 143–8.
27. M. Meyer, II, p. 135.
28. *Brev*, II, p. 184n.
29. Brandell, *SiO*, I, pp. 3, 24, 55, 183.
30. Geete, pp. 477–9; Gustav Meyer, *Studentliv i Uppsala för 60 år sedan* (Stockholm, 1930), p. 140.

Chapter Seven

1. Lamm, p. 96.
2. *Br. br.*, V, p. 169.
3. Per Lindberg, *August Lindberg* (Stockholm, 1943), pp. 26 ff.
4. *Brev*, II, p. 231n.
5. Ibid., p. 246; Bonnier, IV, pp. 31–3.
6. *Brev*, II, p. 247n.
7. *Ögonvittnen*, I, pp. 104–6.
8. Ibid., p. 106.
9. *Brev*, II, p. 268n.
10. Brandell, *SiO*, I, pp. 1, 4, 56, 102, 190.
11. M. Meyer, II, p. 144.
12. Ibid, III, p. 23.
13. *Brev*, II, pp. 275–6n.
14. *Ögonvittnen*, I, p. 119.

15. Brandell, *SiO*, I, pp. 6, 25, 56, 102, 133, 179, 183.
16. *Brev*, II, p. 337n.
17. Ibid., p. 325n.
18. Gunnar Ollén, *Strindbergs dramatik* (Stockholm, 1961), p. 65; Brandell, *SiO*, I, pp. 27, 57, 66, 103, 135.
19. Harry Jacobsen, *Strindberg i Firsernes København* (Copenhagen, 1948), pp. 11–12.
20. Willers, p. 127.

Chapter Eight

1. *Brev*, III, p. 18.
2. *Ögonvittnen*, I, pp. 111–15.
3. Ibid., p. 119.
4. Ibid., pp. 109–10.
5. *Br. br.*, VI, pp. 30–1.
6. Ibid., II, p. 135.
7. Ollén, p. 95.
8. Brandell, *SiO*, I, pp. 29, 58, 67, 104.
9. Øyvind Anker, Francis Bull, Örjan Lindberger (ed.), *Bjørnstjerne Bjørnsons brevveksling med svenske, 1858–1909* (Oslo, 1960–1), II, p. 124.
10. *Brev*, II, p. 120n.
11. *Br. br.*, VI, pp. 36–8.
12. *Brev*, III, p. 89.
13. Lamm, p. 110.
14. Ollén, p. 96.
15. *Brev*, III, pp. 168–9.
16. *Bjørnsons brevveksling med svenske*, p. 133.
17. Brandell, *SiO*, I, pp. 105, 186, 193.
18. Ollén, p. 98.
19. *Brev*, III, p. 166.
20. Ibid., p. 189.
21. Ibid., p. 189n.
22. Ibid., pp. 209–10.
23. Ibid., p. 241n.
24. Ibid., p. 252.
25. Ibid., p. 258n.
26. Kela Nyholm, "Henrik Ibsen på den franske scene," in *Ibsen-Årbok*, 1957–9 (Skien, 1959), pp. 149–50.
27. *Brev*, III, pp. 249–50.
28. Bonnier, IV, p. 38.
29. Ibid., pp. 40–1.
30. Ibid., p. 45.
31. *Ögonvittnen*, I, pp. 123 ff.

32. *Brev*, III, pp. 302–3.

Chapter Nine

1. *Brev*, III, p. 314n.
2. Ibid., p. 331.
3. SS, XIX, pp. 195–6.
4. *Brev*, III, p. 363.
5. Brandell, *SiO*, I, pp. 33, 62, 107, 108, 178, 187, 198; Bonnier, IV, p. 48.
6. *Brev*, III, pp. 351, 356.
7. Ibid., p. 365.
8. *Ögonvittnen*, I, pp. 130–2.
9. SS, XIX, pp. 197–202.
10. Halvdan Koht (ed.), *Bjørnstjerne Bjørnsons Kamp-tid (brev fra aarene 1879–1884)* (Oslo, 1932), II, pp. 178–9.
11. SS, XIX, p. 188.
12. *Brev*, IV, pp. 15, 19.
13. Ibid., pp. 26, 29.
14. Ibid., p. 32.
15. Brandell, *SiO*, I, pp. 138, 35, 63, 14, 144, 109.
16. SS, XVII, pp. 240–1.
17. *Bjørnsons brevveksling med svenske*, II, p. 174.
18. Bonnier, IV, p. 57.
19. Ibid., p. 58.
20. *Bjørnsons brevveksling med svenske*, II, p. 189.
21. Bonnier, IV, p. 58.
22. *Brev*, IV, p. 302.
23. *Ögonvittnen*, I, pp. 134–40.
24. SS, XVIII, p. 441.
25. *Ögonvittnen*, I, pp. 144, 154, 149.
26. Harry Jacobsen, *Strindberg och hans första hustru* (Swedish edition, Stockholm, 1946), pp. 39–40.
27. Smirnoff, *Sfh, passim*.
28. Jacobsen, *Sohfh*, pp. 39–40.
29. *Brev*, IV, p. 229.

Chapter Ten

1. Mary Sandbach (transl. and ed.), *Getting Married* (London, 1972), p. 31.
2. *Brev*, IV, p. 304n.
3. Sandbach, p. 38.
4. Ibid., pp. 38–9.
5. Ibid., pp. 42–7.
6. Ibid., p. 50.

7. *Brev*, IV, p. 302.
8. Smirnoff, *Sfh*, p. 199.
9. *Brev*, IV, p. 286n.
10. Ibid., p. 323.
11. Bonnier, IV, p. 63; Germund Michanek, *Skaldernas konung* (Stockholm, 1979), p. 326.
12. Sandbach, pp. 14–15.
13. *Ögonvittnen*, I, p. 177; Michanek, p. 318.
14. Brandell, *SiO*, II, pp. 204, 74.
15. Jacobsen, *SiFK*, pp. 10, 14.
16. Bonnier, IV, p. 63.
17. *Bjørnsons brevveksling med svenske*, II, pp. 196–7.
18. Bonnier, IV, p. 64.
19. *Bjørnsons brevveksling med svenske*, II, pp. 207–8.
20. *Bjørnsons Kamp-tid*, II, pp. 256–7.
21. Bonnier, IV, p. 68.
22. Ibid., p. 68.
23. *Ögonvittnen*, I, pp. 171–2.
24. *Brev*, IV, p. 379n.
25. Bonnier, IV, pp. 74n–5.
26. *Brev*, IV, p. 389.
27. Bonnier, p. 76.
28. *Ögonvittnen*, I, p. 179.
29. Bonnier, IV, pp. 76 ff.
30. Ibid., pp. 79–82.
31. *Brev*, IV, p. 410.
32. M. Meyer, II, p. 136.
33. Sandbach, p. 17.

Chapter Eleven

1. *Brev*, V, p. 15n.
2. Ibid., p. 38.
3. *Br. br.*, V, p. 250.
4. Ibid., VI, pp. 38–9.
5. *Brev*, V, p. 117.
6. Bonnier, IV, p. 82.
7. *Br. br.*, VII, p. 29.
8. Ibid., VI, p. 58.
9. Ibid., V, p. 257.
10. Ibid., VI, p. 64.
11. Smirnoff, *Sfh*, pp. 218–32; *Så var det i verkligheten* (Stockholm, 1956), p. 58.
12. *Ögonvittnen*, I, p. 184.
13. Smirnoff, *Svdiv*, p. 48.

14. Smirnoff, *Sfh*, p. 315.
15. Jacobsen, *Sohfh*, pp. 77–100.
16. *Ögonvittnen*, I, p. 185.
17. Söderström, p. 113.
18. Ibid., p. 113.
19. *Br. br.*, V, p. 258.
20. Bonnier, IV, p. 90n.
21. Ibid., p. 93.
22. Ibid., pp. 93–4.
23. *Brev*, V, p. 306.
24. *Ögonvittnen*, I, p. 192.
25. *Brev*, V, p. 355n.
26. Ibid., p. 368n.
27. *Br. br.*, VII, p. 37.
28. Bonnier, IV, p. 99.
29. *Brev*, V, p. 362n.
30. Bonnier, IV, p. 97.
31. *Ögonvittnen*, I, pp. 197–200.
32. Smirnoff, *Sfh*, pp. 235–6.
33. Ibid., p. 236.
34. Ibid., pp. 212–17.
35. *Br. br.*, VI, p. 69.
36. SS, XXVI, pp. 341–2.
37. Jacobsen, *Sohfh*, p. 88.
38. *Brev*, VI, p. 187.
39. Smirnoff, *Sfh*, pp. 313 ff.
40. Ibid., pp. 213–15.
41. Ibid., p. 217.
42. *Brev*, VI, p. 206.
43. Ibid., p. 121n.
44. *Br. br.*, VI, p. 93.
45. Ibid., p. 333.
46. Ibid., p. xv.

Chapter Twelve

1. *Brev*, VI, p. 141n.
2. Ibid., p. 155n.
3. *Br. br.*, VI, p. 98.
4. *Brev*, VI, p. 164n.
5. John Personne, *Strindbergslitteraturen och osedligheten bland skolungdomen. Till föräldrar och uppfostrare samt till de styrande* (Stockholm, 1887), pp. 1, 6, 16, 22, 33 ff.
6. Ibid., pp. 58–9.
7. Ibid., pp. 68–9.

8. Bonnier, IV, p. 99.
9. Ibid., p. 106.
10. Ibid., pp. 127–8.
11. Ibid., p. 161n.
12. Ibid., p. 155.
13. *Brev*, VI, p. 194.
14. *Br. br.*, VI, p. 102.
15. S. M. Waxman, *Antoine and the Théâtre-Libre* (Cambridge, Mass., 1926), pp. 128–30.
16. Smirnoff, *Sfh*, pp. 237 ff.
17. *Brev*, VI, pp. 238–9n.
18. Ibid., pp. 161–2.
19. Ibid., p. 262.
20. Ibid., pp. 251–2.
21. Ibid., p. 255.
22. Ibid., p. 257.
23. Ibid., pp. 265–6.
24. Ibid, pp. 269–71.
25. Brandell, *SiO*, III, pp. 77, 146, 162.
26. *Brev*, VI, p. 280.
27. Ibid., p. 275.
28. Bonnier, IV, pp. 164–5.
29. *Brev*, VI, p. 289.
30. Jacobsen, *SiFK*, pp. 42 ff.
31. David Norrman, *Strindbergs skilsmässa från Siri von Essen* (Stockholm, 1953), pp. 26–7.
32. Smirnoff, *Sfh*, p. 247.
33. Axel Lundegård, *Några Strindbergsminnen knutna till en handfull brev* (Stockholm, 1920), pp. 45–8.
34. Jacobsen, *SiFK*, pp. 51 ff.
35. Georg Brandes, *Levned* (Copenhagen, 1905–8), III, p. 225.
36. Jacobsen, *SiFK*, pp. 55–7; Lindberg, p. 219.
37. *Brev*, VI, p. 323.
38. Ibid., VII, p. 9.
39. Jacobsen, *SiFK*, pp. 66–74.
40. *Ögonvittnen*, I, pp. 218–20; Henrik Pontoppidan, *Familieliv* (Copenhagen, 1940), p. 46.
41. Jacobsen, *SiFK*, pp. 63–5.
42. Smedmark, III, p. 489.
43. Vilhelm Petersen, *Foran og bag Kulisserne* (Copenhagen, 1931), pp. 57–8.
44. M. Meyer, III, pp. 98–9.
45. *Ögonvittnen*, I, pp. 216–17.
46. *Brev*, VI, p. 335.
47. Bonnier, IV, p. 166n.
48. Brandell, *SiO*, III, pp. 7, 39, 48, 78, 128, 157, 161–2, 171, 173.

49. *Brev*, VI, p. 352n.
50. Ibid., p. 347.
51. Stellan Ahlström, *Strindbergs erövring av Paris* (Stockholm, 1956), pp. 102–3.
52. Brandell, *SiO*, III, pp. 8, 49, 68, 79, 97, 107, 127, 147, 157, 174, 177, 184–5.
53. Ollén, p. 113.

Chapter Thirteen

1. Lindberg, pp. 229–33.
2. Brandell, *SiO*, III, p. 10.
3. *Brev*, VII, p. 39.
4. Ibid., p. 76.
5. *Br. br.*, VI, p. 132.
6. Ibid., VII, p. 49.
7. Ibid., VI, p. 425.
8. Ibid., VI, p. 342.
9. *Brev*, VII, p. 95n.
10. Smirnoff, *Sfh*, pp. 252–61.
11. *Br. br.*, VII, p. 51.
12. *Brev*, VII, p. 101.
13. *Brev*, VII, p. 184.
14. Bonnier, IV, p. 188.
15. Ibid., p. 187.
16. Smirnoff, *Sfh*, p. 263.
17. *Brev*, VII, p. 147n.
18. Brandell, *SiO*, III, pp. 12, 50, 80–1, 99, 147, 158, 171, 174.
19. *Br. br.*, VI, p. 295.

Chapter Fourteen

1. *Brev*, VII, pp. 162, 177.
2. Brandell, *SiO*, III, pp. 13, 107, 128, 148; *Ny Illustrerad Tidning*, 22 December 1888.
3. Lindberg, p. 241.
4. Jacobsen, *SiFK*, pp. 130–4.
5. *Br. br.*, VI, p. 137.
6. Brandell, *SiO*, III, p. 13.
7. *Brev*, VII, p. 204n.
8. The correspondence between Strindberg and Nietzsche is published in Walter Berendsohn's "Strindberg och Nietzsche," in *Samfundet Orebro stads- och länsbiblioteks vänner, Meddelande no.* XVI (Örebro, 1948).
9. F. Nietzsche, *The Will to Power*, Aphorisms 957–8.
10. Smirnoff, *Sfh*, pp. 298–9.

11. *Brev*, VII, p. 212.
12. Julian Symons, *The Tell-Tale Heart* (paperback edition, London, 1981), pp. 93, 154, 202, 204, 211, 216, 240.
13. *Ögonvittnen*, I, p. 225.
14. *Brev*, VII, p. 224.
15. Ibid., p. 235.
16. Ibid., p. 240n.
17. Jacobsen, *SiFK*, pp. 125, 134–5.
18. Ibid., p. 136.
19. Ollén, p. 135.
20. Jacobsen, *SiFK*, pp. 153–4.
21. *Brev*, VII, p. 286n.
22. Smedmark, III, pp. 375.
23. *Br. br.*, VI, pp. 144–7.

Chapter Fifteen

1. *Ögonvittnen*, I, pp. 233–5.
2. *Brev*, VII, pp. 316–17.
3. Smirnoff, *Sfh*, pp. 287–8.
4. *Brev*, VII, p. 320.
5. Ibid., p. 323.
6. Brandell, *SiO*, III, pp. 53, 107–8, 130, 158.
7. Lindberg, p. 263.
8. Brandell, *SiO*, III, p. 20
9. Ibid., p. 116.
10. Ibid., pp. 131–2, 175, 158, 166.
11. Ibid., pp. 25, 58, 93, 141, 154, 202, 204, 211, 216, 240.
12. Birger Mörner, *Den Strindberg jag känt* (Stockholm, 1924), pp. 11–18.
13. *Br. br.*, VI, p. 299.
14. *Ögonvittnen*, I, pp. 230–1.
15. *Brev*, VIII, p. 58.
16. Ibid., p. 156.
17. Ibid., p. 81.
18. Ibid., p. 83.
19. Brandell, *SiO*, III, p. 119.
20. Quoted in *Handelstidningen i Göteborg*, 15 October 1890.
21. *Ögonvittnen*, II, pp. 19–21.
22. Norrman, pp. 40–1.
23. Brandell, *SiO*, III, pp. 30, 87, 103, 119–20, 152.
24. *Brev*, VIII, p. 139.
25. Ollén, p. 188.
26. Smirnoff, *Sfh*, pp. 306–8.
27. Smirnoff, *Svdiv*, p. 89.

Chapter Sixteen

1. Smirnoff, *Sfh*, pp. 309–13.
2. Norrman, p. 60.
3. *Brev*, VIII, p. 180.
4. Ibid., p. 182n.
5. Ibid., p. 184.
6. Ibid., pp. 206–7.
7. Mörner, pp. 59–60.
8. Ibid., p. 61.
9. *Ögonvittnen*, II, pp. 21–3.
10. Mörner, pp. 21–2.
11. Ibid., p. 36.
12. *Brev*, VIII, p. 249.
13. *Ögonvittnen*, II, p. 27; Stella Falkner-Söderberg, *Fanny Falkner och August Strindberg* (Stockholm, 1970), p. 13. Stella mistakenly states that her sister was a year old at the time.
14. Norrman, p. 75.
15. Ibid., pp. 75–6.
16. Ibid., pp. 98, 109.
17. Ibid., pp. 105 ff.
18. *Brev*, VIII, p. 333.
19. Ibid., p. 336.
20. Ibid., p. 340.
21. Ibid., p. 341n.
22. *Ögonvittnen*, II, pp. 31–3.
23. M. Meyer, II, pp. 293, 318; III, pp. 30, 50, 65–6, 81, 101, 111, 143–4, 163–4.
24. Norrman, pp. 114–18.
25. *Brev*, VIII, pp. 345–6.
26. *Ögonvittnen*, II, pp. 36–8.
27. Ibid., p. 40.
28. *Brev*, VIII, p. 365.
29. Ibid., p. 388.
30. Brandell, *SiO*, III, 31, 43; Ahlström, *SeaP*, pp. 142–4.
31. Ahlström, *SeaP*, p. 147.
32. *Brev*, IX, p. 16n.
33. *Ögonvittnen*, II, p. 50.
34. Ibid., p. 51.
35. Ahlström, *SeaP*, pp. 148, 150.
36. Norrman, pp. 197–8.
37. Ibid., p. 194.
38. Söderström, pp. 178 ff.; Brandell, *SiO*, III, pp. 65, 144, 105.
39. Smirnoff, *Svdiv*, pp. 210–11.
40. *Brev*, IX, pp. 62–4.

41. Smirnoff, *Sfh*, pp. 297–8.
42. Ibid., pp. 298–301.
43. Ibid., pp. 302–4.

Chapter Seventeen

1. *Ögonvittnen*, II, p. 54.
2. Stanislaw Przybyszewski, *Erinnerungen an das literarische Berlin* (trans. Klaus Staemmler; Munich, 1965), p. 181.
3. Ibid., p. 56.
4. Gustaf Uddgren, *Andra boken om Strindberg* (Gothenburg, 1912), pp. 49–50.
5. Ibid., p. 50.
6. Przybyszewski, p. 190.
7. Ragna Stang, *Edvard Munch* (trans. Geoffrey Culverwell and Anthony Martin; London, 1979), p. 90.
8. Ibid., p. 86.
9. *Samtiden* (Christiania), 1890, reprinted in Stang, p. 74.
10. *Ögonvittnen*, II, pp. 59–61.
11. *Brev*, X, p. 215.
12. *Aftenavis* (Oslo), 30 January 1929, reprinted in Stang, p. 98.
13. *Ögonvittnen*, II, pp. 62–3.
14. Adolf Paul, *Min Strindbergsbok* (Stockholm, 1930), pp. 41–4, 132–3.
15. Ibid., p. 46n.
16. *Ögonvittnen*, II, pp. 66–7.
17. Przybyszewski, p. 188.
18. Ibid., pp. 189–90.
19. Ibid., pp. 186, 194.
20. *Br. br.*, VII, p. 125.
21. Söderström, pp. 198–9.
22. Frida Strindberg, *Marriage with Genius* (London, 1937), pp. 24–6.
23. Full details of the Paris premiere of *Miss Julie* are given in Stellan Ahlström's *Strindbergs erövring av Paris* (Stockholm, 1956), pp. 158 ff.
24. Ibid., pp. 168–9.
25. Paul, p. 76.
26. Ibid., pp. 79–82.
27. Unpublished letter in the archives of the Swedish Academy.
28. Frida, p. 39.
29. Ibid., p. 43.
30. Ibid., p. 53.
31. Ibid., p. 53.
32. Ibid., p. 62.
33. *Br. br.*, VII, p. 126.
34. Frida, pp. 82–5.
35. M. Meyer, III, p. 253; Lindberg, p. 308.

36. Anonymous article in *Svenska Dagbladet*, 21 June 1901, quoted by Söderström, p. 213.
37. Stang, p. 292.
38. Frida, pp. 120 ff.
39. Ibid., p. 123.
40. *Brev*, IX, p. 187.
41. Stang, p. 84.
42. *Brev*, IX, pp. 158–9n.
43. Uddgren, pp. 55–6.
44. Paul, p. 86.
45. *Brev*, IX, pp. 168–9n.
46. Ibid., p. 176n.
47. Frida, p. 140.
48. Ibid., pp. 145–6.
49. Ibid., p. 150.
50. Ibid., pp. 117, 142, 154.
51. Ibid., p. 163.

Chapter Eighteen

1. Frida, pp. 185–6.
2. Ibid., pp. 169–70.
3. Ibid., pp. 174 ff. (covering the rest of Frida's account of the English visit).
4. Michael Orme (pseudonym of Alix Grein), *J. T. Grein* (London, 1936), pp. 127–31.
5. T. G. Rosenthal, "The Paintings of August Strindberg," in *Strindbergs måleri*, ed. T. M. Schmidt (Malmö, 1972), pp. 16–19.
6. Frida, p. 187.
7. Paul, p. 90; Andrzej Nils Uggla, "Strindberg och Przybyszewski," in *Meddelanden från Strindbergssällskapet*, May, 1974, p. 16.
8. Frida, p. 191.
9. *Brev*, IX, p. 231.
10. Paul, pp. 129–31.
11. *Brev*, IX, pp. 240–1.
12. Frida, pp. 194–200.
13. Ibid., pp. 205, 211.
14. Ibid., p. 228.
15. Ibid., pp. 231–2.
16. Ibid., pp. 239–40.
17. Söderström, pp. 221–2.
18. *Nordisk Revy* (Stockholm), 1894, p. 161.
19. Frida, pp. 236–7.
20. *Ögonvittnen*, II, p. 64.
21. Frida, p. 243.
22. Ibid., p. 244.

23. Ibid., pp. 246–9.
24. Bonnier, V, pp. 32–3.
25. Frida, p. 255.
26. Ibid., pp. 260–1.
27. Ibid., p. 255.
28. Ibid., p. 263.
29. *Brev*, IX, p. 348n.

Chapter Nineteen

1. Frida, pp. 267–8, 271.
2. *Ögonvittnen*, II, p. 77.
3. *Brev*, X, pp. 10–11.
4. Frida, p. 277.
5. *Br. br.*, VII, p. 15.
6. Frida, pp. 281–2.
7. *Nordisk Revy* (1895, nr. 1), pp. 157–61.
8. *Brev*, X, pp. 45n; Mary Sandbach (trans. and ed.), *Inferno* (London, 1979), p. 18.
9. *Brev*, X, pp. 49–50n.
10. Frida, pp. 287–8.
11. *Brev*, X, p. 94.
12. Ahlström, *SeaP*, pp. 185–6.
13. Ibid., pp. 210 ff.
14. *Brev*, X, p. 130.
15. Ibid., pp. 140–2.
16. Ibid., p. 208.
17. Frida, p. 335.
18. Söderström, pp. 249–51.
19. *Brev*, X, pp. 252–3.
20. Ibid., p. 258.
21. Ibid., p. 263; Frida, pp. 352, 364; Söderström, p. 254.
22. *Brev*, X, p. 265.
23. Frida, pp. 357–9.
24. Alexandra Thaulow, *Mens Fritz Thaulow malte* (Oslo, 1929), p. 76.
25. Frida, pp. 361–2.
26. Söderström, p. 259.
27. Ahlström, *SeaP*, p. 227.
28. Frida, p. 364.
29. Ibid., p. 367.
30. Ibid., p. 370.

Chapter Twenty

1. *Ögonvittnen*, II, p. 84.
2. Söderström, pp. 265–6.

3. *Inferno* (Sandbach trans.), pp. 101–2.
4. *Brev*, X, pp. 317–18n.
5. Ahlström, *SeaP*, pp. 248–56.
6. *Ögonvittnen*, II, p. 89.
7. Ibid., pp. 85–7.
8. Report in *Dagens Nyheter*, 10 November, 1897, of a talk given by Leclerq to the Academy of Science in Stockholm.
9. *Inferno* (Sandbach), p. 103.
10. Ahlström, *SeaP*, p. 282; Frida, p. 54.
11. Ahlström, *SeaP*, pp. 279 ff.
12. *Inferno* (Sandbach), pp. 106–7.
13. Brandell, *Strindberg: ett författarliv*, III (Stockholm, 1983), p. 109.
14. *Ögonvittnen*, II, p. 91; Ahlström, *SeaP*, pp. 272–3.
15. Söderström, pp. 281–2.
16. Ibid., pp. 288–9.
17. Mörner, p. 133.
18. Frederick Delius, "Recollections of Strindberg," in *The Sackbut*, London, December, 1920, p. 353.
19. *Inferno* (Sandbach), p. 114.
20. Delius, p. 353.
21. Sandbach, pp. 41–2.
22. Ahlström, *SeaP*, p. 287.
23. *Ögonvittnen*, II, pp. 92–3.
24. *Brev*, XI, p. 8n.; F. U. Wrangel, *Minnen från konstnärskretsarna och författarvärlden* (Stockholm, 1925), pp. 231–2.
25. *Brev*, X, pp. 392n, 394n, 396; Frida, p. 444.
26. *Brev*, X, p. 386.
27. *Inferno* (Sandbach), p. 120.
28. *Brev*, XI, pp. 5–6n.
29. Ibid., p. 24n.
30. *Inferno* (Sandbach), pp. 117–18.
31. *Ögonvittnen*, II, pp. 98–9.
32. Philp and Hartzell, pp. 80–3.
33. Smirnoff, *Sfh*, p. 345.
34. *Inferno* (Sandbach), p. 125.
35. *Brev*, XI, p. 79.
36. Ibid., p. 85.
37. Ibid., p. 91.
38. *The Letters of Oscar Wilde*, ed. Rupert Hart-Davis (London, 1962), p. 522.
39. *Inferno* (Sandbach), pp. 131–2.
40. *Brev*, XI, p. 132.

Chapter Twenty-One

1. *Inferno* (Sandbach), p. 133.

2. Uddgren, p. 68.
3. Delius, pp. 353–4.
4. *Inferno* (Sandbach), pp. 133–44.
5. Gunnar Brandell, *Strindberg in Inferno*, trans. Barry Jacobs (Harvard, 1974), pp. 110–11.
6. *La Paix*, 19 January 1883, quoted by Ahlström, *SeaP*, p. 277.
7. Anthony Storr (ed.) *The Essential Jung* (Princeton, 1983), pp. 284–7.
8. Ibid., p. 201n.
9. Delius, p. 354.
10. Jiri Mucha, *Alphonse Mucha* (London, 1971), p. 49.
11. Mörner, p. 134.
12. W. B. Yeats, *Autobiographies* (London, 1935), pp. 538–9.
13. *Inferno* (Sandbach), p. 145.
14. Philp and Hartzell, pp. 76 ff.
15. Edvard Munch, *Brev* (Oslo, 1949), p. 158.
16. *Inferno* (Sandbach), pp. 151–2.
17. Ibid., p. 155.
18. *Brev*, XI, p. 224n.
19. Ibid., pp. 222–4.
20. Delius, p. 354.
21. *Inferno* (Sandbach), pp. 174–6.
22. *Brev*, XI, pp. 273–6.
23. Ibid., p. 285.
24. *Ögonvittnen*, II, pp. 107–9.
25. Munch, *Brev*, p. 160.

Chapter Twenty-Two

1. *Inferno* (Sandbach), p. 188.
2. Ibid., pp. 189–90.
3. Ibid., pp. 190–2.
4. Ibid., pp. 193–9.
5. Sven Hedenberg, *Strindberg i skärselden* (Gothenburg, 1961), pp. 54–60.
6. Brandell, *S:ef*, III, p. 188.
7. *Inferno* (Sandbach), p. 201.
8. Brandell, *S:ef*, III, p. 200.
9. *Ockulta dagboken*, 9 and 13 September, 1896.
10. *Inferno* (Sandbach), p. 210.
11. Ibid., pp. 211–12.
12. Ibid., pp. 214–15.
13. *Brev*, XI, p. 319.
14. Ibid., p. 387.
15. *Inferno* (Sandbach), p. 234.
16. *Brev*, XI, p. 370.

17. *Ögonvittnen*, II, pp. 113–15.
18. *Inferno* (Sandbach), pp. 234–5.
19. Ibid., pp. 248–9.
20. *Br. br.*, VI, p. 181.
21. *Ögonvittnen*, II, pp. 115–18.
22. Erik Lie, *Erindringer fra et dikterhjem* (Oslo, 1928), pp. 102–3.
23. Hedenberg, pp. 69 ff.
24. *Ögonvittnen*, II, p. 138.
25. A. W. Anderson, "Strindberg's Illness," in *Psychological Medicine*, I (London, 1971), pp. 104–17.
26. Torsten Frey, "Medicinska synpunkter på August Strindberg," in *Läkartidningen* (Stockholm, 1980), pp. 231–6.
27. Hedenberg, pp. 64–5.
28. Ibid., pp. 65–6.
29. Frey, p. 236.
30. Brandell/Jacobs, p. 95.

Chapter Twenty-Three

1. *Brev*, XII, p. 13n.
2. Ibid., p. 6n.
3. Ibid., p. 13.
4. Ibid., p. 22.
5. *Inferno* (Sandbach), pp. 250–1.
6. Ibid., p. 251.
7. Sir Oliver Lodge's introduction to Swedenborg's *Divine Love and Wisdom* (London, 1912), p. xii.
8. Signe Toksvig, *Emmanuel Swedenborg* (London, 1949), pp. 235, 248.
9. *Inferno* (Sandbach), p. 256.
10. Toksvig, pp. 136–7, 161, 181.
11. Johan Mortensen, *Strindberg som jag minnes honom* (Stockholm, 1931), p. 33.
12. Ibid., pp. 8, 15, 18–19.
13. *Ögonvittnen*, II, pp. 126–7.
14. Mortensen, p. 33.
15. SS, XXVIII, p. 215.
16. *Ögonvittnen*, II, p. 130.
17. SS, XXVIII, p. 233.
18. *Brev*, XII, p. 99n.
19. Ollén, p. 122.
20. Söderström, p. 320.
21. Mortensen, p. 22.
22. Ibid., pp. 23–7.
23. Ibid., pp. 41–2, 51, 52.
24. *Ockulta dagboken*, 22 April 1897.

25. *Brev*, XII, p. 107.
26. *Inferno* (Sandbach), pp. 263–4, 266.
27. Ibid., p. 261.
28. Brandell/Jacobs, p. 130.
29. Ibid., p. 140.
30. *Social-Demokraten*, 12 May 1914, reprinted in Söderström, p. 322.
31. *Brev*, XII, p. 193n.
32. *Aftonbladet*, 13 April 1898.
33. Smirnoff, *Sfh*, pp. 251–2.
34. Smirnoff, *Svdiv*, p. 12.
35. *Inferno* (Sandbach), pp. 125, 181.
36. Letter to Gustaf af Geijerstam, 17 March 1898.

Chapter Twenty-Four

1. *Ögonvittnen*, II, p. 129.
2. Mortensen, p. 21.
3. Ibid., pp. 53–4.
4. *Br. br.*, VII, pp. 235–7.
5. *Brev*, XIII, p. 62.
6. Uddgren, pp. 80–3.
7. Ibid., p. 84.
8. Bonnier, V, p. 49.
9. *Svenska Dagbladet*, 19 May 1912. It is stated there that Brøchner sent Strindberg the questionnaire in May 1897, but this is probably a misprint. For various reasons, 1899 seems the more likely date. Strindberg is known to have been in touch with Brøchner then; he did not discover Kipling until 1899; and it is very unlikely that in May 1897 he would have named his favourite occupation as writing dramas, when he had not written any for five years. (*Cf.* Walter Berendsohn, *Svensk Litteraturtidskrift*, 16/1953, pp. 175–7.) I have followed the text of Strindberg's manuscript in English (in the Royal Library in Stockholm), which differs in some details from that printed in *Svenska Dagbladet*.
10. Nils Åke Nilsson, "Strindberg på rysk scen," in *Meddelanden från Strindbergssällskapet*, December, 1956, p. 7.
11. *Ockulta dagboken*, 15 August 1899.
12. Ibid., undated marginal note, p. 102.
13. Wrangel, pp. 272–3.
14. Mortensen, p. 95.

Chapter Twenty-Five

1. *Ockulta dagboken*, 16 February 1900.
2. Ibid., 15 May 1900.
3. *Strindbergs brev till Harriet Bosse, med kommentarer av Harriet Bosse* (Stockholm, 1932), pp. 17–18.

4. Ibid., p. 19.
5. Ibid., pp. 20–1.
6. Ollén, p. 355, quoting a conversation with Anna's daughter, Märta.
7. *Ockulta dagboken*, 8 April 1900.
8. Ibid., 2 August 1900.
9. Mortensen, p. 95.
10. Bosse, p. 131.
11. Stig Torsslow, *Dramatenaktörernasrepublik* (Uppsala, 1975), p. 289.
12. Smirnoff, *Sfh*, pp. 389–90.
13. Oscar Wieselgren, "Strindberg och den svenska kritiken," in *Svensk Tidskrift*, 1949, p. 54.
14. Bonnier, V, p. 53.
15. Ibid., pp. 50, 53.
16. Uddgren, p. 109; Letter to Gustaf Uddgren, 12 December 1900.
17. Strindberg, *Ur ockulta dagboken*, ed. Torsten Eklund (Stockholm, 1963), p. 26.
18. Bosse, p. 27.
19. *Ockulta dagboken*, 26 February 1901.
20. *Ur ockulta dagboken*, p. 34.
21. Bosse, p. 30.
22. Ibid., p. 30, 52.
23. *Brev*, XIV, p. 57.
24. Ibid., pp. 85–6n; Smirnoff, *Sfh*, pp. 392–7.
25. Tor Bonnier, *Längesen* (Stockholm, 1972), p. 33.

Chapter Twenty-Six

1. Bosse, pp. 53–5.
2. Ibid., p. 217.
3. Ibid., p. 54.
4. Ibid., pp. 55–6.
5. *Brev*, XIV, p. 95.
6. Ibid., pp. 104–5.
7. Bosse, p. 61.
8. Ibid., p. 61.
9. *Ockulta dagboken*, 8 September 1901.
10. *Brev*, XIV, p. 131.
11. *Ur ockulta dagboken*, p. 55.
12. Ibid., p. 56.
13. Bosse, p. 64.
14. Ibid., pp. 62–3.
15. Nilsson, p. 7.
16. Bosse, p. 65.
17. *Brev*, XIV, p. 188.
18. Bosse, p. 65.

19. Ibid., pp. 75–6.
20. Ibid., pp. 76–7.
21. Ibid., pp. 78–83.
22. *Ockulta dagboken*, 14 October 1902.
23. *Aftonbladet*, 18 December 1902.

Chapter Twenty-Seven

1. Bonnier, V, p. 55.
2. Ibid., pp. 61–2.
3. *Brev*, XIV, p. 264n.
4. Bonnier, V, p. 65.
5. Bernard Shaw, *Collected Letters*, ed. Dan. H. Laurence, II (London, 1972), p. 320.
6. *Ögonvittnen*, II, pp. 176–80; Albert Engström, *August Strindberg och jag* (Stockholm, 1923), pp. 11–26.
7. *Ockulta dagboken*, 6 July 1903.
8. *Brev*, XIX, p. 288n.
9. Bosse, p. 84.
10. *Ockulta dagboken*, undated entry, p. 196.
11. *Brev*, XIV, p. 322.
12. *Svenska Dagbladet*, 7 December 1903.
13. Engström, pp. 28–32.
14. *Brev*, XIV, p. 271.
15. Ibid., p. 276.
16. Victor Hellström, *Strindberg och musiken* (Stockholm, 1917), pp. 64–6, 71–2.
17. SS, LXI, p. 32.
18. Bosse, p. 86.
19. Lamm/Carlsson, p. 441.
20. Helge Gullberg, "August Strindberg i Per Hallströms och Gustaf af Geijerstams brevväxling," in *Samlaren* (Stockholm), 1960, p. 95.
21. Uddgren, p. 101.
22. *Adam* (London), Strindberg centenary issue, 1949, p. 12.
23. *Ockulta dagboken*, 24 May 1904.
24. Ibid., 1 June 1904.
25. Bosse, p. 99.
26. *Ockulta dagboken*, 22 June 1904.
27. Bosse, p. 112.
28. Ibid., p. 112.
29. Bonnier, V, p. 68.
30. *Brev*, XV, pp. 60–1.
31. Nilsson, pp. 8, 10–11; Ollén, 4th edn. (1982), p. 112.
32. *Ögonvittnen*, II, pp. 181–2.

33. Anna-Lisa Werth, "Ensling i Blå Tornet," in *Stockholms-Tidningen*, 11 April 1954.
34. *Ockulta dagboken*, 17 December 1904.

Chapter Twenty-Eight

1. *Brev*, XV, p. 107.
2. Nilsson, p. 11.
3. *SiO*, IV, p. 116.
4. Ollén, 4th edn., p. 192.
5. Bosse, p. 155.
6. *Ögonvittnen*, II, pp. 186–8.
7. Told by Bo Bergman in old age to the novelist Pär Westberg, who told me.
8. *Ögonvittnen*, II, p. 192.
9. Ibid., p. 193.
10. Ibid., p. 185.
11. Ollén, 4th edn., p. 379.
12. Uddgren, pp. 124–5, 129.
13. Ibid., p. 136.
14. *Ögonvittnen*, II, p. 195.
15. Ibid., p. 196.
16. *Brev*, XV, p. 198n.
17. Ibid., p. 204.
18. Bosse, pp. 202–3.
19. Nilsson, p. 11.
20. *Brev*, XV, p. 266n.
21. Mörner, p. 140.
22. *Brev*, XV, p. 231.
23. *SiO*, IV, pp. 332, 121.
24. Engström, p. 38.
25. Ibid., p. 38.
26. Recording in the BBC sound archives, London.
27. *SS*, L, p. 290.
28. *Ockulta dagboken*, 25 April 1906.
29. Bonnier, V, p. 71n.
30. *Dagens Nyheter*, 9 May 1906.
31. *Brev*, XV, pp. 280, 288.
32. Ibid., pp. 303–4n.
33. *Ögonvittnen*, II, pp. 202–3.

Chapter Twenty-Nine

1. Falck, pp. 19–20.
2. Ibid., pp. 20–1.
3. *Aftonbladet*, 19 December 1906.

4. Uddgren, p. 128.
5. Gösta M. Bergman, *Den moderna teaterns genombrott, 1890–1925* (Stockholm, 1966), p. 248.
6. Falck, pp. 36–7.
7. Bosse, p. 82.
8. Philp and Hartzell, pp. 90 ff.
9. SS, p. 289.
10. Ibid, p. 289.
11. Wieselgren, p. 54.
12. SS, pp. 9–13.
13. Ibid., pp. 17–30.
14. A programme note in *Dramaten* (Stockholm, 1970–1), p. 22.
15. *Ockulta dagboken*, 16 April 1907.
16. Gullberg, p. 89.
17. Ibid., pp. 97–9.
18. Bonnier, V, p. 58

Chapter Thirty

1. *Ögonvittnen*, II, p. 224.
2. Falck, p. 40.
3. Werth, *op. cit.*
4. Uddgren, p. 128; Falck, pp. 57–8.
5. Falck, pp. 54–8, 64, 79.
6. Ibid., pp. 59, 74–83.
7. Ibid., pp. 74–5.
8. Letter to Emil Schering, 25 August 1907.
9. *Ögonvittnen*, II, pp. 224–6.
10. Uddgren, pp. 115–18.
11. *Adam*, p. 1.
12. Bonnier, V, p. 72.
13. Falck, pp. 54–7; Bergman, pp. 285–6.
14. Falck, p. 68.
15. Ibid., p. 94.
16. Bonnier, V, pp. 72–3.
17. Ollén, 4th edn., p. 531.
18. Falck, pp. 126–7.
19. Ibid., p. 155.
20. Ibid., p. 151.
21. Bosse, p. 280.
22. *Ur ockulta dagboken*, pp. 137–8.

Chapter Thirty-One

1. Stella Falkner-Söderberg, *Fanny Falkner och August Strindberg* (Stock-

holm, 1970), pp. 5, 13, 15–16, based on Fanny's memoirs as recorded by Algot Ruhe (*cf.* p. 456) in *Strindberg i Blå Tornet* (Stockholm, 1921). The latter book contains considerable gaps, partly out of consideration by Fanny for her family and partly because Strindberg's executors withheld permission for her to publish his letters. When his letters entered the public domain in 1962, Fanny thought of writing a fuller record, but became depressed on being reminded of her family troubles, her unhappiness as an actress and her relationship with Strindberg. It was not until 1970, after Fanny's death, that her sister Stella used Fanny's memoirs and Strindberg's letters to her to compile a moving book.

2. Ibid., pp. 13–14.
3. Ibid., pp. 17–18.
4. Ibid., pp. 21–2.
5. Ibid., pp. 24–5.
6. Bonnier, V, p. 75.
7. *Ögonvittnen*, II, pp. 182–5.
8. Falck, p. 182.
9. *Ögonvittnen*, II, p. 237; Philp and Hartzell, p. 104; Falkner-Söderberg, p. 27.
10. Charles Archer, *William Archer* (London, 1931), p. 303.
11. Falck, p. 173.
12. For this and the following paragraph, cf. Falkner-Söderberg, pp. 31–2, 35–7, 56; *Ögonvittnen*, II, pp. 238–46.
13. Falck, pp. 152–3.
14. Ibid., pp. 159–62.
15. Ibid., pp. 190–3.
16. Ibid., pp. 207–8.
17. Ibid., p. 211.
18. SS, L, p. 139.
19. Falck, pp. 197, 199, 209–11.
20. SS, L, p. 140.
21. Falkner-Söderberg, p. 48.
22. Letter to Karl Börjesson, 15 August 1908.
23. Falck, pp. 153, 181.
24. Ibid., pp. 113–16.
25. Ibid., p. 212.
26. Ibid., p. 183.
27. Falkner-Söderberg, pp. 41–2.
28. Ibid., pp. 47–8.
29. Fredrik Ström, *Min ungdoms strider* (Stockholm, 1940), p. 350.
30. SS, L, pp. 271, 40.
31. Ibid., pp. 294–5.
32. Falck, pp. 237–8.
33. Letters of 15 and 29 November 1908.
34. Falkner-Söderberg, pp. 60–1.

35. Ibid., pp. 63–4.
36. Falck, p. 306.
37. Falkner-Söderberg, pp. 63–5; *Ögonvittnen*, II, p. 244.
38. Falkner-Söderberg, p. 66.
39. Falck, pp. 255–6.
40. Ollén, 4th edn., p. 563.
41. Falkner-Söderberg, p. 67.
42. Falck, p. 258.
43. Undated letter to Fanny Falkner (Falkner-Söderberg, p. 75).
44. Ibid., p. 68.
45. Falck, pp. 260–1.
46. Ibid., p. 187.
47. Letter to Klaes Fahraeus, 22 June 1909.
48. Falck, pp. 293–4, 313–14.

Chapter Thirty-Two

1. Falkner-Söderberg, pp. 77–87.
2. Ibid., pp. 88–91.
3. Falck, p. 264.
4. Bonnier, V, p. 73n.
5. Falkner-Söderberg, p. 107.
6. Ibid., p. 109.
7. Ibid., p. 111.
8. Ibid., pp. 116–24.
9. Falck, pp. 282–3.
10. Letter to Helge Wahlgren, 9 September 1909.
11. Shaw, II, pp. 906–9.
12. Ibid., II, pp. 917–18.
13. Falck, p. 268.
14. Uddgren, pp. 142–6.
15. SS, p. 617.
16. Bonnier, V, p. 116.
17. *Afton-Tidningen*, 3 August 1910.
18. Cf. John Landquist's introduction to *Strindbergsfejden*, ed. Harry Järv (Uddevalla, 1968), I, p. 6.
19. Falkner-Söderberg, p. 106.
20. C. L. Schleich, *Hågkomster om Strindberg* (Stockholm, 1917), pp. 57–9.
21. *Ögonvittnen*, II, pp. 269–70.
22. Falkner-Söderberg, pp. 143–4.
23. Werth, *op. cit.*
24. Ibid.
25. Letter to Hans Strindberg, 23 May 1910.
26. Falck, p. 311.
27. Ibid., pp. 181, 293–4, 313–14.

28. Ibid., p. 317.
29. Ibid., p. 325.
30. Ibid., pp. 336–7.
31. Ibid., p. 333.
32. Wieselgren, p. 55.
33. Ibid., p. 55.
34. Falck, p. 346.

Chapter Thirty-Three

1. Smirnoff, *Sfh*, pp. 413–14.
2. Björn Meidal, *Från profet till folktribun* (Stockholm, 1982), pp. 206–8.
3. Torsten Svedfelt, *Strindbergs ansikte* (Stockholm, 1948), illustration 105.
4. Letter from Birger Mörner in Kungliga Biblioteket, Stockholm.
5. Walter Berendsohn, *Strindbergs sista levnadsår* (Stockholm, 1948), p. 152.
6. Bonnier, V, pp. 76–7.
7. Letter from Victor Sjöström to Torsten Eklund, 18 June 1948, in Kungliga Biblioteket, Stockholm.
8. Smirnoff, *Sfh*, p. 415.
9. Ibid., p. 415.
10. Falkner-Söderberg, pp. 158, 163.
11. *Ögonvittnen*, II, pp. 275–7.
12. In the Strindberg collection at Kungliga Biblioteket, Stockholm.
13. Ollén, 4th edn., pp. 120, 152.
14. Meidal, pp. 219–20.
15. Ibid., pp. 198–9.
16. Berendsohn, p. 128.
17. Strindberg collection at Kungliga Biblioteket, Stockholm.
18. *Ögonvittnen*, II, pp. 281–2.
19. Falck, pp. 328–9.
20. Söderström, p. 406.
21. Berendsohn, p. 166.
22. Meidal, pp. 277 ff.
23. Engström, pp. 73–4.
24. *Vecko-Journalen* (Stockholm), 11 July 1915.
25. Meidal, pp. 224–7.
26. Strindberg collection at Kungliga Biblioteket, Stockholm.
27. Hedén, p. 470.
28. Uddgren, p. 160.
29. Hedén, pp. 470–1.
30. Falkner-Söderberg, p. 160.
31. Ström, p. 353.
32. Smirnoff, *Sfh*, pp. 418–19.
33. Smirnoff, *Svdiv*, p. 92.
34. Söderström, p. 406.

35. Bosse, p. 311.
36. Falkner-Söderberg, p. 162.
37. Ögonvittnen, II, pp. 293–5.
38. Hedén, p. 472.
39. Uddgren, p. 163.

Epilogue

1. *Cf.* Tor Bonnier's and Åke Thulstrup's introduction to Strindberg's *Brev till min dotter Kerstin* (Stockholm, 1961), pp. 5–6; Tor Bonnier, *Längesen* (Stockholm, 1972), pp. 234–5.
2. *Horizon* (London), November, 1942, p. 127; Augustus John, *Chiaroscuro* (London, 1952), p. 116.
3. *Edvin Adolphson berättar om sitt liv med Fru Thalia, Fru Filmia och andra fruar* (Stockholm, 1972), pp. 84, 116, 165.
4. Oscar Wieselgren, "Harriet Bosse," in *Meddelanden från Strindbergssällskapet*, December, 1961, p. 3.
5. Told to me by Fru Mimi Pollak on 3 October 1983.
6. Hedenberg, pp. 158–9.
7. Falkner-Söderberg, pp. 106–7, 166.
8. Nils Andrzej Uggla, "Strindberg och Przybyszewski," in *Meddelanden från Strindbergssällskapet*, May, 1974, p. 16.
9. Hans-Peter Bayerdörfer, *Strindberg auf der deutschen Bühne, 1890–1925* (Neumünster, 1983), quoted by Ollén, 4th edn., p. 379.
10. *Adam*, p. 5.
11. Anthony Swerling, *Strindberg's Impact in France, 1920–1960* (Cambridge, 1971), pp. 39–43.
12. Louis Shaeffer, *O'Neill, Son and Artist* (London, 1974), pp. 124, 463.
13. Agnes Boulton, *Part of a Long Story* (London, 1958), p. 71; Shaeffer, p. 558.
14. *The Letters of Sean O'Casey, 1910–1954*, ed. David Kranse (New York, 1975, 1980), I, p. 217; II, pp. 568–9.
15. Berendsohn, p. 171. He does not name his source.
16. Nilsson, pp. 10, 14.
17. *Theatre Arts* (New York), February, 1950, quoted by Swerling, p. 75.
18. Uggla, p. 29.
19. *Adam*, pp. 1 ff.; *The Letters of Sean O'Casey*, II, pp. 568–9.
20. Swerling, pp. 74, 111, 143.
21. M. Meyer, II, p. 247.
22. John Mortimer, "The New Drama?" in the *Spectator* (London), 3 January 1976.

INDEX

Since most readers of this book will be unfamiliar with Swedish usage, whereby å, ä and ö are listed after z, these letters are here treated as a and o.

ABOUT THE AUTHOR

MICHAEL MEYER, author of *Ibsen: A Biography*, which won the Whitbread Award for the best biography of the year, has translated sixteen of Ibsen's plays and eighteen of Strindberg's into English. For the latter achievement he was awarded the Gold Medal of the Swedish Academy. From 1947 to 1950 he was lecturer in English literature at Uppsala University in Sweden, and in 1978 he was visiting professor of drama at Dartmouth College. He has written a play about Strindberg, *Lunatic and Lover*, which was successfully produced in England, and a number of television and radio plays for the BBC. He is a fellow of the Royal Society of Literature and lives in London.